# Sports, Media, and Society

Kevin Hull, PhD

University of South Carolina

# Sports, Media, and Society

Kevin Hull, PhD

University of South Carolina

HUMAN KINETICS

**Library of Congress Cataloging-in-Publication Data**

Names: Hull, Kevin, 1978– author.
Title: Sports, media, and society / Kevin Hull.
Description: Champaign, IL : Human Kinetics, [2025] | Includes bibliographical references.
Identifiers: LCCN 2023045552 (print) | LCCN 2023045553 (ebook) | ISBN 9781718217591 (paperback) | ISBN 9781718217607 (epub) | ISBN 9781718217614 (pdf)
Subjects: LCSH: Mass media and sports—Social aspects—United States—Textbooks. | Mass media and sports—Social aspects—United States—Case studies. | BISAC: SPORTS & RECREATION / Cultural & Social Aspects | SPORTS & RECREATION / General
Classification: LCC GV742 .H85 2025   (print) | LCC GV742   (ebook) | DDC 306.4/83—dc23/eng20240202
LC record available at https://lccn.loc.gov/2023045552
LC ebook record available at https://lccn.loc.gov/2023045553

ISBN: 978-1-7182-1759-1 (print)

The web addresses cited in this text were current as of November 2023, unless otherwise noted.

**Acquisitions Editor:** Andrew L. Tyler
**Developmental Editor:** Jacqueline Eaton Blakley
**Indexer:** Katy Balcer
**Permissions Manager:** Laurel Mitchell
**Graphic Designer:** Dawn Sills
**Cover Designer:** Keri Evans
**Cover Design Specialist:** Susan Rothermel Allen
**Photograph (cover):** Brad Smith/ISI Photos/USSF/Getty Images for USSF
**Photo Asset Manager:** Laura Fitch
**Photo Production Manager:** Jason Allen
**Senior Art Manager:** Kelly Hendren
**Illustrations:** © Human Kinetics
**Production:** Westchester Publishing Services
**Printer:** Color House Graphics, Inc.

Printed in the United States of America    10  9  8  7  6  5  4  3  2  1

The paper in this book is certified under a sustainable forestry program.

**Human Kinetics**
1607 N. Market Street
Champaign, IL 61820
USA

*United States and International*
Website: **US.HumanKinetics.com**
Email: info@hkusa.com
Phone: 1-800-747-4457

*Canada*
Website: **Canada.HumanKinetics.com**
Email: info@hkcanada.com

E8918

# CONTENTS

Preface ix • Acknowledgments x

## PART I  SPORTS MEDIA BASICS

1 **Theoretical Foundation: Gatekeeping**                                        2

The sports media has the opportunity to report on thousands of different stories and games each day, but only a select few will reach the audience. Through gatekeeping, the media has more power than many might realize.

2 **History and Evolution of the Sports Media**                                  8

Fans used to have to wait until the morning newspaper to get the latest sports news, but now everything is instantly at their fingertips thanks to the Internet.

3 **Business of the Sports Media**                                               17

The sports media is more than just broadcasting and reporting about the games. It is ultimately a big business involving multibillion-dollar deals between the media, leagues, teams, and players.

4 **Case Study: NBC and the Olympics**                                          25

In the United States, we don't really watch the Olympics; we watch NBC's version of the Olympics. How does NBC's coverage influence how we feel about the biggest sporting event in the world?

5 **Case Study: *Sports Illustrated***                                          36

Once one of the biggest entities in sports journalism, *Sports Illustrated* has gone through ups and downs that reflect the changing world of sports media.

6 **Social Media in Sports**                                                    45

The innovations that came with social media are likely known by most. However, the changes in the various professions in the sports media have led to new jobs, changed job descriptions, and required a new set of skills for those working in the field.

## PART II  THE IMPACT OF TELEVISION

7 **Theoretical Foundation: Agenda Setting**                                    54

The stories on the front page of the newspaper or the lead highlight on *SportsCenter* are often recognized as the most important of the day. But who makes those decisions? And what is the impact of those decisions on the audience?

**8  ABC Sports**                                                              **60**

Sports television had been on for decades, but ABC and the program *Wide World of Sports* turned televised sports into something that viewers couldn't miss.

**9  ESPN**                                                                    **67**

ESPN's debut in 1979 created a sports media powerhouse. It is nearly impossible to be a sports fan and not consume at least some of ESPN's content, but issues loom for the television sports leader.

**10 Fox Sports**                                                              **76**

When Fox Sports acquired the television rights to NFL games in late 1993, the broadcasting of sports on television was about to change dramatically. Fox's technological innovations and financial investment changed how people expected to watch sports.

**11 Case Study: *League of Denial***                                          **82**

ESPN and PBS agreed to jointly investigate concussions in the NFL, but ESPN pulled out just before the documentary was set to air. The question, even years later, is why.

**12 Case Study: ESPN and the SEC Bias**                                       **90**

Media outlets often get "obsessed" with stories, seemingly talking about the same teams, people, or events nonstop. For college football fans, watching ESPN has them wondering if the network favors one conference over the others.

## PART III  SOCIAL ISSUES

**13 Theoretical Foundation: Social Identity Theory**                          **97**

For some, being a fan of their favorite team is as much a part of their identity as their family background. The better the team, the better its fans might feel about themselves.

**14 Theoretical Foundation: Framing**                                         **102**

If a journalist repeatedly says that a specific game is important, does that automatically make it important? The way something is presented in the media can influence the opinions of the audience regarding that topic.

**15 Media Coverage of Race in Sports**                                        **106**

The American sports media has reflected American society at large in its treatment of ethnic minorities. In both realms, progress has been made, but more is needed.

**16 Case Study: Colin Kaepernick**                                            **115**

In 2016, San Francisco 49ers quarterback Colin Kaepernick began protesting during the national anthem. The media and societal reaction caused a nationwide conversation about the intersection of sports, race, and politics.

**17 Stick to Sports**                                                         **123**

Following the election of Donald Trump as U.S. president in 2016, media members and athletes began to discuss political issues more openly on social media. The response from fans was often "stick to sports."

## 18 Media Coverage of Women's Sports 130

Fans of women's sports have often struggled to find the latest information about their favorite teams. For decades, the sports media focused almost exclusively on men's sports, seemingly ignoring the accomplishments of women athletes.

## 19 Case Study: U.S. Women's Soccer Team 140

Even while women's sports were generally ignored, one women's team started to gain traction nationally. The U.S. Women's Soccer Team brought in record viewership, world championships, and compelling stars—seemingly forcing the sports media to pay attention.

## 20 Women in the Sports Media 148

Sports journalists typically face long hours, challenging job circumstances, and early days of low pay. For women in the field, those struggles are often compounded by additional harassment, questions about their knowledge, and an increased scrutiny of their appearance.

## 21 Media Coverage of LGBTQ+ in Sports 157

Athletes in the LGBTQ+ community have begun making headlines in the sports world after many years of LGBTQ+ issues being considered taboo. While their success has made an impact on the field, the media's coverage of those topics hasn't always been accurate.

## 22 Case Study: Michael Sam 166

Michael Sam was once on track to be the first openly gay player to suit up in a regular-season NFL game. However, that never happened—and the media might be the main reason why.

# PART IV    CRISIS COMMUNICATION

## 23 Theoretical Foundation: Crisis Communication 173

Sometimes things go wrong. How people and organizations defend themselves during a threat to their reputation can be an important factor in how they publicly recover.

## 24 Case Study: Tiger Woods 179

For years, Tiger Woods was nearly unstoppable on the golf course. However, incidents off the course ultimately threatened to derail his promising career.

## 25 Case Study: Lance Armstrong 188

For a period in the 2000s, Lance Armstrong was one of the biggest stars in sports. However, as he was winning races there were whispers that his victories were boosted by performance-enhancing drugs.

## 26 Case Study: LeBron James and *The Decision* 196

In 2010, LeBron James announced on ESPN that he was "taking my talents to South Beach." What should have been a celebratory day for James turned into a public relations nightmare for the basketball star and the television network.

## 27 Case Study: Death of Kobe Bryant 205

When Kobe Bryant died in a helicopter accident in 2020, media outlets rushed to be the first to report the story. However, in their rush to be first, many got the details wrong.

**28 Case Study: Houston Astros Cheating Scandal**                    **214**

In 2019, it was revealed that the Houston Astros had been engaged in an elaborate cheating plot when they won the World Series a few seasons earlier. The team's crisis communication during this time was a textbook case of what *not* to do.


## PART V   EMERGING TRENDS IN SPORTS, MEDIA, AND SOCIETY

**29 Theoretical Foundation: Two-Step Flow and Weak Ties**           **223**

For years, information was passed from influential people to an audience through personal connections. This process has evolved due to social media, meaning that now anyone can be an influencer.

**30 Team and Player Media**                                          **228**

Fans used to rely on newspapers and television to get their news, but now teams and players are creating their own content that can be delivered directly to the fans. This begs the question: If teams can give this news themselves, why do we need the traditional media?

**31 Lasting Impact of COVID-19**                                     **236**

The COVID-19 pandemic caused many to reassess their traditional routines in an attempt to stay healthy. The sports world was no different—and several years later, much to the dismay of some journalists, many of those changes are still in place.

**32 Mental Health**                                                  **246**

While a broken bone can be easy to diagnose, athletes battling mental health struggles have been harder to recognize. A new generation of athletes have brought the mental health conversation to the forefront.

**33 Esports**                                                        **253**

While millions of people will watch the Super Bowl, even more watch the League of Legends World Championships. Perhaps the fastest-growing area of sports is competitive video gaming, and the sports media is attempting to figure out where and how to report on these gamers.

**34 Sports Betting**                                                 **261**

For hundreds of years, sports leagues did their best to distance themselves from gambling. However, as laws throughout the United States have changed, sports betting has become almost impossible for fans to ignore.

References 271   •   Index 312   •   About the Author 325

# PREFACE

For years, the sports media and sports fans primarily cared about what happened in the games, and anything happening outside the stadium or arena was considered unimportant to the result. However, in recent years off-field content has become almost as relevant as the final scores. Fans might have a hard time remembering Colin Kaepernick's record as a quarterback during the 2016 season, but most of them vividly remember his decision to kneel during the playing of the national anthem before those games. Social issues have become part of the sporting world narrative, and the sports media is there to document those stories. However, *how* the sports media discusses those topics is an important aspect in how they are relayed to the public.

Therefore, the purpose of this textbook is to investigate the growing impact of societal issues in sports and consider how the sports media reports those stories. Many students receive lessons in *how* to create sports media content, but there is a growing interest in understanding the *why* behind this content. Essentially: Why does the sports media operate in the manner that it does, and what is the impact of its decisions on the audience? An important goal of this book is to create sports fans who, when seeing sports stories involving societal issues, are thoughtful sports media consumers.

This book is a resource for students and instructors in sports media classes and can also be of interest to those looking to learn more about the history of the sports media. It will be particularly useful in courses that address the intersection of sports, media, and society, but also in courses in sport management, sociology, and history, as well as social issue–based classes. In addition, this textbook is accompanied by an instructor guide, test questions, and PowerPoint presentations that can be accessed through HK*Propel*. The instructor guide includes a sample syllabus, chapter outlines, lecture notes, recommended responses to the textbook's review questions, and an assignment for each chapter. The test questions can be used for classroom exams at the end of each section of the book, while the PowerPoint presentations can be used for in-class lectures.

The book is organized into five parts that enable readers to learn about how sports, media, and society intersect beyond the action in the games. Each section contains a theoretical base, major topics to be addressed, and relevant case studies.

Part I includes the book's first six chapters, which introduce some of the **sports media basics**. This section gives a background and brief history of the sports media and its gatekeeping practices, introduces the business aspects of the sports media, and discusses the tremendous impact that social media has had on the world of sports. In addition, to demonstrate the evolution of the sports media, both *Sports Illustrated* and NBC Sports' coverage of the Olympics get a closer look.

Part II of the book discusses the **impact of television**. In chapters 7 to 12, the agenda-setting power of the media is introduced before deep dives on ABC Sports, ESPN, and Fox Sports—three legendary television sports entities that have had a lasting impact on how people watch sports on television. Part II concludes with a look at the controversy surrounding the *League of Denial* documentary and what happens when television networks are perceived to be biased toward one group.

Part III tackles many of the **social issues** that have become a more prevalent part of sporting fandom. Sports media coverage of race, gender, ethnicity, and LGBTQ+ topics is discussed, along with case studies for each topic. These 10 chapters provide a foundation for readers looking to understand how sports and the sports media have evolved in their treatment of those who were, at one point, considered "outsiders" in the sports world.

Part IV discusses **crisis communication** and how athletes, teams, and the media respond when there are issues that could potentially damage their reputation. Following a chapter that explains crisis communication and how organizations can respond in these situations, the five case studies examine how famous athletes such at LeBron James and Tiger Woods used crisis communication in an effort to repair their images following public missteps.

Finally, Part V looks at **emerging trends in sports, media, and society**. As of the writing of this book, these topics are still in their infancy, but are ones that could have a major impact on the future of the sporting world. These six chapters address growing topics such as mental health in sports, esports, and sports betting.

# ACKNOWLEDGMENTS

I appreciate everyone at Human Kinetics for trusting me to contribute a second book to their impressive library. This opportunity would not have come about without Drew Tyler, who guided me through my first book and was a pleasure to work with on this book as well. Jackie Blakley made the editing process a breeze and I appreciate all her assistance throughout.

I owe a special thank-you to Ted Spiker at the University of Florida. In the first semester of my PhD program, I was invited to sit in on his Sports, Media, and Society class and it is no exaggeration to say that my life changed that day. I was in complete awe of his lecture and realized that teaching a class about the sports media was exactly what I wanted to do when I became a professor. Having the opportunity to write this textbook is yet another surreal moment for me that can be traced back to that day in Professor Spiker's classroom.

Thank you to my family for their encouragement throughout the writing process. Danielle has been my biggest cheerleader for many years now and that support has kept me going when I needed it the most. My parents fed my love of sports and the sports media by letting a younger me watch games on television, read the latest sports stories in the newspaper, and dream of working in sports broadcasting. This book is a culmination of all those topics that I developed a passion for thanks to the opportunities they provided me. And, of course, thanks to Grandpa for just being the best.

# SPORTS MEDIA BASICS

One of the goals of this book is to create better sports media consumers by helping people understand why journalists report on topics in the manner that they do. Therefore, it is appropriate to begin with a look at the basics of the sports media by providing a foundation that can be referenced throughout the book.

Chapter 1 introduces the concept of gatekeeping, one of the most relevant theories that will be revisited in many chapters. The media has the power to decide what stories are reported on and what stories are ignored, and their selection process plays a major role in how the audience gets their sports news.

Chapter 2 covers the history and evolution of the sports media, starting with early reports from the 1700s all the way up to the modern era of sports journalism. Chapter 3 reminds our readers that the sports media is ultimately a business, and while the fans are watching a competition on the television screen, there is also a competition going on between the television networks.

Chapters 4 and 5 are case studies looking at gatekeeping and the business aspect of the sports media in action. NBC spends billions of dollars to broadcast the Olympics, but their gatekeeping practices mean that fans are not always able to watch everything on their televisions. Meanwhile, *Sports Illustrated* was the dominant name in the sports media for decades, but changes in how fans get their sports news have forced the magazine to adapt. Chapter 6 wraps up this section with a look at social media, which is one of those ways in which fans' access to sports has changed.

# 1

# Gatekeeping

## CHAPTER OBJECTIVES

After completing the chapter, the reader should be able to do the following:

- Understand what gatekeeping is and the history behind it
- Identify how gatekeeping is used in the sports media
- Recognize how social media and team and player media are changing the role of the gatekeeper
- Examine the role of the gatekeeper in the media's coverage of social issues

There is little debate that the sports media plays a major role in how fans consume sports. What teams, games, and stories are shown on television, written about in the newspaper, or shared online are often determined by a very small group of people in leadership roles at each individual media outlet. The concept of *gatekeeping* demonstrates how the media has that power and how they can use that influence in determining what stories reach the public.

In a hypothetical situation, a local college's athletic department might send a press release to the media informing them about three events happening on campus tomorrow: a women's soccer game, a track and field event, and a blood drive sponsored by the men's tennis team. The newspaper elects to print only a story previewing the women's soccer game and ignores both the track and field event and the blood drive. Therefore, readers who use that newspaper as their only source of local information might have no idea that either the track and field event or the blood drive is happening. There

are multiple events happening at the college, and it was not the readers who decided what was important—the newspaper's editors decided for them. Situations like this one occur all the time in newsrooms across the world and perfectly demonstrate the concept of gatekeeping.

## Definition of Gatekeeping

In terms of communication and the sports media, **gatekeeping** is the process through which information is filtered for the public's consumption. The process works as follows: There are many different news items that media members are presented with each day. The media then screens these potential stories and decides which ones to present to the public. This process has given journalists the label of "gatekeepers" because they are the ones who decide which news items get past them and reach the audience. News consumers rely on the media to not only examine the numerous stories going on in the world each day and present the most relevant ones to the public but also to frame them in a way in which the most important aspects of those stories are presented. Figure 1.1 demonstrates how gatekeeping would work in a sports department newsroom using our example of the three local college events.

- The athletic department is on the left side of the figure, sending three stories to the media.
- The media, in the middle of the graphic, chooses to allow only one of the stories to pass through the "gate" to the public, while the other stories are rejected and do not reach the audience.
- The audience, on the right side of the image, will hear about only the one story because that is the only one presented to them.

Newspaper editors serve as the gatekeepers because they determine which stories will make it into the newspaper and which will not.

## Origin of Gatekeeping

While gatekeeping is known primarily as a media-related theory, that is not how it got its start. One might be surprised to learn that gatekeeping originated as a theory explaining how food ended up on a family's dinner table. A manuscript written by Kurt Lewin in 1947 is widely recognized as the first formal appearance of gatekeeping in research. In it, he states that not all the stages of meal planning are equal and that certain people, perhaps unknowingly, play an important role in an evening's dinner. He labeled those people as gatekeepers of the process (Lewin, 1947).

For example, in the grocery store, the manager determines what products that store will carry, making them an early gatekeeper in the consumer's food-buying process. If the manager decides that the store will carry just chicken and turkey that week, then shoppers at that store will be able to purchase only those items

and will be out of luck if they wanted hamburgers. The person doing the shopping is also a gatekeeper. If they buy the chicken instead of the turkey, then that family will be having a chicken dinner. What type of chicken will be decided by another gatekeeper, as the person doing the cooking will decide whether it will be baked, fried, or grilled. However, the home chef might not be cooking anything if the person in charge of putting away the groceries forgets to place the chicken in the refrigerator and accidentally leaves it out to spoil (yet another gatekeeper). As demonstrated here, a family's fried chicken dinner might seem like a simple meal, but it is actually influenced by multiple gatekeepers along the way before it reaches the table.

## Gatekeeping in Communications and the Media

While the concept of gatekeeping was introduced by Lewin, it was a journalism professor who ultimately adapted it to the communications field, in which it is more commonly known. In an article published in 1950, David Manning White examined how a newspaper editor determined which stories appeared in the newspaper and which were left out. For one week, an editor of an unnamed newspaper in the Midwest agreed to keep a record of all the stories that came into the newsroom from the various national and international news services. From that list, the editor would determine which stories would be published. At the end of each day, the editor (cleverly referred to as Mr. Gates in this gatekeeping study) would make a note of why the rejected stories did not make the cut (White, 1950).

Following the full week, White found that 90 percent of the stories that came into the newsroom from these services were rejected by Gates. As for why, White noted

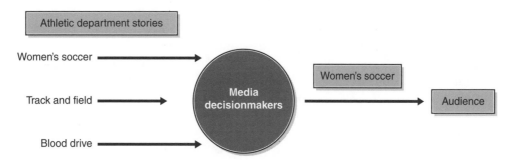

**FIGURE 1.1**　A visual representation of gatekeeping.

that almost every decision was "highly subjective" and "based on the 'gatekeeper's' own set of experiences, attitudes and expectations" (1950, p. 386). Gates rejected articles that he considered propaganda, trivial, or in poor taste. While some stories were rejected based on Gates's values, others were discarded simply because he had either already selected a similar story or did not have room in the newspaper to include it. Ultimately, White came to the conclusion that an entire community of newspaper readers will only know about stories that the individual editor considered to merit the space, thus demonstrating the incredible influence of these gatekeepers (White, 1950). The study was replicated in 1967 with the same editor and the results were similar, with the author noting that "Mr. Gates still picks the stories he likes and believes his readers want" (Snider, 1967, p. 427). While the type of story that was the most popular choice of Mr. Gates had changed—hard news stories were now more prominent than the human interest stories that had dominated 17 years earlier—the study further demonstrated the influence of the gatekeeper in the newsroom process (Snider, 1967).

## What Makes It News?

It is worth examining biases and addressing what aspects of a story make it worthy of being considered for broadcast or publication. To put it more simply: What makes something news? Shoemaker and Vos determined that "a primary characteristic of newsworthy events is whether the event, the people, or the issues are deviant" (2009, p. 25). Therefore, if the event is out of the ordinary, then that makes it more newsworthy. For example, NBA superstar Steph Curry making a three-point basket in the first quarter of a basketball game is not necessarily newsworthy because players (especially Curry) make three-pointers all the time, and a basket in the first quarter is likely long forgotten by the finish. However, since that same basket made Curry the NBA's all-time leader in three-pointers made, the seemingly insignificant event is suddenly very newsworthy (Jackson, 2021). Setting a record is out of the ordinary, so the basket is now more interesting to reporters and the public.

Other elements that make a story newsworthy include audience interest, proximity, and timeliness (Badii & Ward, 1980; Berkowitz et al., 1996; Shoemaker & Vos, 2009; Stempel, 1962).

- **Audience interest** stories come about through news organizations surveying their consumers and determining what stories they would like to hear more about.
- **Proximity** refers to where the story takes place, which can be an important determinant when it comes to local news. For example, the Los Angeles media will likely focus a great deal of attention on the Los Angeles Dodgers baseball team, while practically ignoring the New York Yankees.
- When the event takes place (**timeliness**) is also a key factor when determining the newsworthiness of an event. An evening sports broadcast will have highlights of games that happened that day, while events that happened two weeks ago will not make it into that broadcast.

While sometimes the newsworthiness of a story is obvious, in other cases, individuals make judgments regarding importance of events. The gatekeeping studies from White and Snider both revealed that the editor's personal opinions and experiences had a significant impact on which stories made the newspaper and which were omitted. In the example that was used in the introduction to this chapter, the blood drive was deemed by the newspaper's editors to not be a newsworthy event. However, if one of those editors had a family member who had a life-saving procedure thanks to blood donations, they might consider that story something the public needs to hear about. In that case, the editor's personal history would play a role in the inclusion of the blood drive story. The story is the exact same, but the person judging it is different, and that causes it to suddenly become more newsworthy to a gatekeeper.

## Evolution of Gatekeeping

As will be discussed further in chapters 6 and 30, the increased use of social media by teams and players has created a scenario in which the traditional sports media's role as gatekeeper is under attack. In the past, if a team wanted to get the latest information out to the public, they would send a press release to the media and hope that the local newspaper or broadcast outlet would report that news. Similarly, if an athlete had a story they wanted to tell, they would need to be interviewed by the media and then have that story told by the reporter. However, thanks to social media, teams and players can now reach their audience directly.

As shown in figure 1.2, the team simply bypasses the gatekeeper with the latest news and sends it directly to the audience. Once again using the example from the

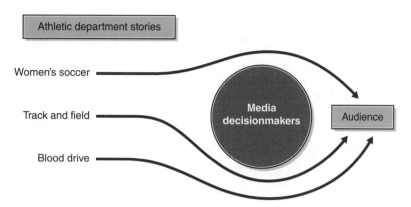

Athletic department stories

Women's soccer

Track and field

Blood drive

Media decisionmakers

Audience

**FIGURE 1.2**   When teams and players use social media, they are able to avoid the gatekeeper and reach the audience directly.

introduction to this chapter, the college has the three stories it would like the public to know about. With the media gatekeeper present, only the women's soccer story made the newspaper, while the track and field event and the blood drive were ignored. However, if the school's athletic department uses social media to preview all three events, they can reach their followers directly. They essentially go around the gatekeeper by putting the information on social media where followers can get the information sent directly to their feed. Instead of needing the local newspaper, radio station, or television station to deliver the information, fans can follow their favorite teams and players and hear directly from them. As will be discussed in chapter 30, teams and players not necessarily needing the traditional media to report news stories is a major concern for sports media departments.

Social media has also created a scenario in which the audience can play the gatekeeper role themselves. If a Twitter user retweets a story to their followers, then, in a way, that individual has become the news deliverer. Therefore, as pointed out by gatekeeping researchers, the audience now controls the flow of information as well: "We must conceptualize readers as having their own gate, and they send news items to others in the audience when the interaction between newsworthiness and personal relevance is strong enough" (Shoemaker & Vos, 2009, p. 124). And again, personal relevance and influence also can add importance to a story. A news item shared online by a reporter might not necessarily catch the audience's attention, but if an individual user's close friend shares the story online with a caption of "you HAVE to read this!" written above or below the post, then that article might get a second look. Due to this newfound influence, scholars are recognizing that audiences now have direct and indirect impact on news construction and consumption (Groshek & Tandoc, 2017).

# An Example of Gatekeeping in Sports Media

As will be discussed in chapter 9, ESPN is often the first media entity that sports fans will turn to when they want the latest sports news. For decades, that meant watching the flagship news and highlights show SportsCenter. Before instant access to highlights became the norm on websites and social media, fans would wait until the latest airing of SportsCenter to see highlights from what the show's producers labeled the biggest game of the day.

That ability to label a game or a sport as "important" illustrated the gatekeeping power that *SportsCenter* had. A demonstration of this influence can be seen during a college basketball season. At the conclusion of the 2022-2023 season, there were more than 350 NCAA Division I men's basketball programs. Almost all of them will play games on Saturdays, meaning that ESPN has more than 150 games to choose from when selecting which highlights to broadcast during those busy weekends. However, with *SportsCenter* traditionally being just about an hour long, they cannot showcase every game. Therefore, the producers of the show use their gatekeeping practices to decide which teams will make the show and which will be cut. It is likely that teams in the top 25 will be shown, with additional highlights featuring teams from big conferences or with loyal followings. Along with those games, some broadcasts might feature a dramatic buzzer-beater or a remarkable individual performance. That might bring the grand total to about 30 games featured during that show. Fans of the other teams and games are simply out of luck and will have to find another way to see their teams play.

When Steph Curry broke the NBA's three-point record in 2021, it was newsworthy because it was out of the ordinary.

This example considered only Division I men's basketball; there are Division II and Division III teams that will almost never see their highlights on ESPN; and women's college basketball, despite its increasing popularity, still lags well behind the men's game when it comes to coverage on highlight shows. There are hundreds of college basketball games happening every weekend during the season, but ESPN uses its power as a gatekeeper to determine which will get the most attention.

## Gatekeeping of Social Issues

As will be discussed in several chapters throughout this book, the media plays a key role as the gatekeeper in their coverage of social issues. For topics in sports such as equal pay for women athletes and racial justice protests, the gatekeeping media determines how many of those stories will reach the audience. In some cases, the race, ethnicity, and sex of the media members might strongly influence how those stories are told. Most sports editors throughout the United States are White men (Lapchick, 2020, 2021), meaning they might not have the same interest or personal experience to tell the stories of people identifying with other demographics. Without that background, it is worth examining how the media chooses which stories to publish when the topic involves social issues. This issue will be explored throughout this book, including in chapters 15, 18, and 21.

## Summary

There are millions of potential stories happening each day in the world, and it is up to the media to determine which of those are worthy of inclusion in their product. With sports, there are games and events that sports journalists must evaluate to determine which are most important to their audience. Without the media to narrow down those potential news items, the audience would likely be overwhelmed with stories. Therefore, the media's role as gatekeeper is perhaps one of its most important functions.

This gatekeeping role is not without controversy, however. While there are many accepted reasons for why a story would be considered newsworthy, those decisions are often ultimately very personal ones made by a select few people within a newsroom. An individual bias could lead to some stories not reaching the audience based on nothing more than that one person's preference. In addition, a lack of time or space can also lead to a story not appearing on a broadcast or in the newspaper. That is why many teams and players have turned to social media to deliver their news directly to the audience and bypass the gatekeeper. This direct-to-fan communication has created a situation in which the gatekeeping role of the media is perhaps not as prevalent as it once was.

## KEY TERMS

**audience interest**—Stories that a news organization believes their audience wants to hear.

**gatekeeping**—The process through which information is filtered for the public's consumption.

**proximity**—Where a story takes place. News departments tend to prefer stories that are close to their home location.

**timeliness**—When a story takes place. News departments tend to prefer stories that happen more recently.

## REVIEW QUESTIONS

1. Based on the information provided in this chapter, is the media being a gatekeeper a good thing?
2. What potential issues are there with the media being a gatekeeper?
3. How has the role of the gatekeeper changed over time?
4. How should a gatekeeper decide which information should reach the public?

# 2

# History and Evolution of the Sports Media

## CHAPTER OBJECTIVES

After completing the chapter, the reader should be able to identify key moments and people in the following disciplines:

- Newspaper journalism
- Radio journalism
- Television journalism
- Internet streaming
- Social media

The history of the sports media could be an entire book on its own, so this singular chapter should not be taken as a replacement for a detailed look at this history. However, some of the important years, people, and moments will be introduced to help the reader better understand and appreciate some of the evolutions that will be discussed throughout this book.

There is little doubt that, in the United States, the Super Bowl is the biggest sporting event of the year. It has the most viewers, the highest interest level, and fosters the greatest anticipation among fans and journalists. For the 2022 game, NBC used 122 cameras, with 40 of them focused solely on the action on the field (Reedy, 2022). Not only were there dozens of cameras there to capture the action, but it took more than 700 employees, 50 miles of camera and microphone cables,

and 130 microphones to make sure everything made it on the air looking and sounding great (NBC Sports Group, 2022). That is certainly a far cry from the 11 cameras NBC used for Super Bowl I in 1967 (Reedy, 2022). From newspapers to radio to television to the Internet, the sports media has come a long way from its humble beginnings and has turned into a multibillion-dollar industry.

## Early Sports Coverage in the Newspaper

In 1733, the *Boston Gazette* published one of the first recognized sports articles in the Americas when a reporter very briefly described a boxing match that had occurred in England several months earlier. In the years immediately following, newspaper stories in the American colonies addressed horse racing, cricket, and participatory sports such as hunting and fishing. However, as the American attention turned to the Revolutionary War, sporting coverage in the newspaper was overshadowed by reports about the quest for independence (Washburn & Lamb, 2020).

As the 1800s began, and the United States of America was in its infancy, sports stories began to slowly reappear in print, with boxing being the focus for several decades. The fights captivated the public and the newspapers were there to recap the biggest battles in the ring. The other main sport of interest at the time was horse racing, with some minor attention being given to a newly emerging sport known as baseball (Washburn & Lamb, 2020). However, those reading the newspaper were almost exclusively upper class, as they were the few who could afford the expensive daily editions. A technological advance would soon change that, transforming not only who read the newspaper, but what types of articles were in it.

## The Impact of the Penny Press

In the 1830s, technology evolved that allowed for newspapers to be printed on machine-made paper instead of handmade paper. This less-expensive production method allowed the daily editions to be sold at a lower rate, meaning that reading the newspaper was no longer just a hobby of the rich. The **penny press**, so named because many newspapers that came out of this invention cost just one cent, created a new audience for newspapers, and those readers were looking for different types of articles (Campbell, Martin, & Fabos, 2019).

The newspapers of the penny press era began covering more sensational and scandalous stories, while also looking for topics that were of interest to a wide range of people. Sports stories were identified as being able to fill that role, and many readers were captivated by the latest stories from boxing, horse racing, and baseball. The *New York Herald* not only reported on sports but would often put those stories on the front page, further demonstrating the increase of interest in the games and events (Washburn & Lamb, 2020).

## Henry Chadwick

While sports stories were popping up more often in newspapers, it was often overworked journalists who were covering a variety of different topics that were doing the writing. That trend began to change in 1857 when the *New York Clipper* hired Henry Chadwick to become what many believe to be the first full-time sportswriter in the United States (Washburn & Lamb, 2020). Chadwick's expertise was baseball, and his contributions to the sport are still on display today. It was he who created the first modern box score, informing his readers of statistics from the game. Chadwick would then take those statistics to develop two more long-standing parts of the game: batting average and earned run average. The mark he left on the game was so prominent that in 1938 Chadwick was inducted into the National Baseball Hall of Fame (Henry Chadwick, n.d.).

## Sports Departments Begin to Form

Chadwick's hire as a full-time sportswriter was just one way in which the importance of sports stories was being demonstrated. In 1880, newspapers in the United States devoted less than 1 percent of their space to sports, but that number had risen to nearly 20 percent by 1920 (McChesney, 1989). Along the way was the creation of the first sports department at a newspaper in 1883 (*The New York World*) and the first distinct sports section in 1895 (*The New York Journal*) (Washburn & Lamb, 2020). In addition to newspapers, magazines such as *The Sporting News* were also helping to increase the awareness and popularity of sports among the American public (Bryant & Holt, 2009). By the 1930s, 80 percent of all male newspaper readers said they read at least some portion of the sports section, while a decade later, newspaper management estimated that 25 percent of daily newspapers were being purchased strictly because of the sports coverage (McChesney, 1989).

## Early Prominent Writers

As newspapers continued to rise in readership and popularity, the sportswriters themselves gained prominence as well. Readers would pick up that day's edition looking for articles written by their favorite journalists who were, in some cases, becoming just as well known as the athletes on which they were reporting. While there are many who stand out during this time, three who left a lasting mark on the industry were Grantland Rice, Dick Young, and Sam Lacy.

## Grantland Rice

After starting his sportswriting career in 1901, Grantland Rice soon became one of the most respected and well-known journalists of his time. His syndicated column, *The Spotlight*, appeared in newspapers throughout the country, with a poetic writing style that had not been seen before in sports articles. While Rice wrote hundreds of pieces in his career, the one he is almost certainly most remembered for is his recap of a 1924 football game between Notre Dame and Army (Berkow, 2000). The opening paragraph paints the picture of the game, while also demonstrating how Rice's writing was different from modern sportswriters:

> *Outlined against a blue-gray October sky, the Four Horsemen rode again. In dramatic lore they are known as Famine, Pestilence, Destruction and Death. These are only aliases. Their real names are Stuhldreher, Miller, Crowley and Layden. They formed the crest of the South Bend cyclone before which another fighting Army football team was swept over the precipice at the Polo Grounds yesterday afternoon as 55,000 spectators peered down on the bewildering panorama spread on the green plain below. (Rice, 1924, para. 1)*

Further highlighting how sportswriting has changed in the years since is the fact that Rice's opening paragraph gives many details of the game except perhaps the most important: the final score. In the modern era of the inverted pyramid writing style, in which the most important information should be placed at the beginning of a sports article, Rice's opener would almost certainly be questioned by his editors if submitted today.

## Dick Young

While Rice was recognized for his poetic writing style, Dick Young was perhaps best known as being a thorn in the side of many professional athletes. His combative nature put him on the opposite sides of arguments with athletes, owners, and sometimes even his fellow sportswriters. Perhaps his most famous battle was his run-in with baseball pitcher Tom Seaver. When Seaver was in a contract dispute with the New York Mets in 1977, Young's column took the side of team ownership, and in one instance, mentioned Seaver's wife and how the money might affect her relationship with another player's wife. Once Seaver read that column, he informed the Mets that he wanted to be traded, and 30 years later, Seaver cited Young's piece as the final straw that made him want to leave New York (Madden, 2007).

While Mets fans may never forgive Young for his role in the departure of a franchise legend, his primary contribution to sportswriting goes well beyond aggravating athletes. Before Young, sportswriters would watch games from the press box and then write only about what they saw. Young was one of the first to go into the locker room after the game to interview the players and coaches to get their opinion about what happened (Berkow, 2000). Locker room interviews are now a staple of nearly every sports league, with most requiring teams to open their clubhouse to inquisitive journalists almost immediately after a game concludes.

## Sam Lacy

While Sam Lacy might not have had the same-size audience as many of his contemporaries, his impact on sports might be greater than all. Lacy was one of the first prominent minority sports reporters but, because of his race, he worked primarily for African American newspapers. He was assigned to cover Jesse Owens, Joe Louis, and other prominent Black athletes of the time, but it was his work with baseball's Jackie Robinson that stood out. Major League Baseball had banned Black players from participating, but Lacy contacted several team owners and the league's commissioner to try to change that. His calls went essentially ignored until Brooklyn Dodgers owner Branch Rickey met with Lacy and agreed that the time was right for a change.

The Dodgers signed Robinson, making him the first Black player in league history, and Lacy was there to document those first seasons. However, he found that, just like Robinson, he was not welcome everywhere. Lacy was banned from many press areas due to his race, and he and Robinson often found themselves having to eat dinner with just each other at Black-only restaurants when the team traveled. However, just as Robinson would go on to a legendary career, Lacy's impact on the sport and his role in the Dodgers signing of Robinson would not go unnoticed. Lacy was inducted into the writers and broadcasters wing of the National Baseball Hall of Fame and is considered an important part of the sport's desegregation (Litsky, 2003; Vascellaro, 2013).

# The Impact of Newsreels on Newspapers

Before televisions were in nearly every home in the United States, people had to go to the movie theater to see video footage of prominent news stories. These

Afro American Newspapers/Gado/Getty Images

**Sam Lacy was one of the first prominent minority sports journalists.**

short films, known as **newsreels**, were often shown before a feature movie. Instead of just reading stories in the newspapers, the audience could now watch the action unfold on the big screen. While news stories were often the focus, sports highlights would soon find their way into the reels, with boxing, football, and baseball represented (Washburn & Lamb, 2020). While these newsreels helped increase the popularity of sports, they were also a direct threat to newspapers. People now had a new way of getting information on their favorite sporting events. However, even as newsreels began to infringe on newspapers, an emerging technology known as radio was about to change the sports media industry even more significantly.

# Sports Broadcasting on Radio

Radio station KDKA in Pittsburgh, Pennsylvania, is not only recognized as one of the earliest commercial radio stations in the United States, but also as a pioneer

when it comes to the broadcasting of sports (KDKA, 2010). KDKA was home to the first-ever sporting event that was broadcast live on radio: a 1921 boxing match between Johnny Ray and Johnny Dundee (Romano, 2017). Less than five months later, the first-ever radio play-by-play of a professional baseball game was also on KDKA, followed soon after by the first live broadcast of a college football game, that of the University of Pittsburgh's win over West Virginia University (KDKA, 2010; NCAA, 2020).

While these early sports broadcasts were providing content to the audience, they were primarily a tool to sell more radios. The logic was simple enough: If a fan wanted to hear each pitch of the World Series, they would need to buy a radio to do so. Broadcasters needed to give the public a reason to purchase this new technology, and sports was doing the trick. In the weeks leading up to a highly anticipated 1927 boxing match, one New York department store estimated selling over $90,000 worth of radios to fans who were wanting to hear the fight (Betts, 1952).

## Recreating the Action

While these early radio broadcasts were great for fans who could not be at the game, many did not realize that the announcers giving the play-by-play were not actually there, either. Someone at the stadium or arena would send the results for each play back to the radio station via a telegraph wire. The announcer at the station would then read the telegraphed action and describe what happened in his own words. This sports broadcasting method became known as a **recreation**, and it was more than just the game description. The announcers would add elements to make the action sound more exciting, including hitting a wooden ruler against a desk to mimic the sound of a bat hitting a baseball (Catsis, 1996).

For radio stations, these recreations were primarily a way to save money. By not sending an announcer directly to the game, management did not have to pay for the cost of travel, or, more importantly, the telephone lines, which were expensive at the time. Instead, they subscribed to a budget-friendly service from Western Union to deliver the telegrams, or they paid a newspaper reporter to call in the results to the station every couple of innings (Catsis, 1996; Nufer, 1991).

## Graham McNamee

Graham McNamee was never supposed to be the star of early radio broadcasts. Instead, he was scheduled to only talk in between innings of baseball games, while legendary newspaper reporter Grantland Rice was going to be the centerpiece of the program and discuss the action on the field. Instead, Rice quit after just a few games, McNamee slid into his seat, and one of the most decorated radio careers in broadcast history was underway (Catsis, 1996; McCurty, n.d.; Smith, 2001).

McNamee was not the first sports announcer on the radio, but by the 1920s, he was the most recognizable. NBC selected him to be its lead radio announcer for championship boxing fights, baseball's World Series, and top football matchups. In addition, he broadcast the first Rose Bowl carried by NBC, and the first three Major League Baseball All-Star Games (Schneider, 2019). His 1925 radio call of the World Series resulted in listeners sending in 50,000 letters of appreciation to radio station WEAF (National Baseball Hall of Fame, n.d.). His legacy has lasted for decades and will continue to do so, as McNamee is widely considered to be the man who invented play-by-play broadcasting (McCurdy, n.d.).

## Concerns About Radio

McNamee and other announcers like him had audiences captivated, but for the teams and leagues, those broadcasts might have been *too* good. Team owners feared that if fans could listen to the games at home, they would have no reason to come to the games, meaning those teams were losing out on valuable ticket revenue. Instead of being considered a boost to the team's popularity, the radio broadcasts were viewed as the enemy.

Therefore, many teams decided to ban live broadcasts of games, and would not even allow announcers to enter the stadium. That did not stop some of the more industrious broadcasters, however, as they would climb trees beyond the outfield walls of baseball stadiums so they could see inside and still report on the action (Catsis, 1996). It was not until businesses offered to become advertisers during these broadcasts that the teams began to relent. Owners soon realized that money they might lose on ticket sales from the broadcasts could possibly be made up through advertising revenue (Covil, n.d.).

# Early Days of Television Sports Broadcasting

While radio was slowly being accepted by teams and leagues as a viable way to grow the popularity of sports, the invention of television was about to change things dramatically. Sports fans would now be able to both hear *and* see live broadcasts involving their favorite teams and athletes. Early broadcasts were very basic, using just a camera or two to get all the action, but it was still enough to forever change how fans consumed sports content.

## Sports on Television Firsts

The first televised sporting event was the 1936 Berlin Olympics. At the time, Adolf Hitler wanted all of Germany to see the events, so he arranged for viewing stations to be set up in cities throughout the country. He had hoped to show off both the athletic successes of German athletes and also technological advances of the television camera that had occurred under his leadership (Given, 2016). While the German team did win the most medals that year, the broadcasts were equally as impressive (Olympics, n.d.). The success of the limited showings throughout the country helped pave the way for other broadcasts to soon follow throughout the world.

In the United States, the first televised sporting event was a college baseball game in 1939 between Columbia and Princeton. While current baseball broadcasts have multiple cameras stationed all over the stadium to capture different angles, this first game had just one camera that was stationed high above the field to the left of home plate (Columbia Athletics, 2009). While the game is recognized as the first televised sporting event in the United States, it was not seen by many people. Fewer than 400 television sets were in use at the time in that viewing area (Koppett, 1999).

Just a few months after that college baseball game, the same channel in New York televised a professional game between the Brooklyn Dodgers and the Cincinnati Reds. This time the game featured two cameras, one on the third base line and another high above home plate. As a sign of how new the technology was, an article in *The New York Times* expressed amazement that the broadcast could be seen up to 50 miles away and, as the reporter wrote, "at times it was possible to catch a fleeting glimpse of the ball" (History.com Editors, 2020; McGowen, 1939, para. 2).

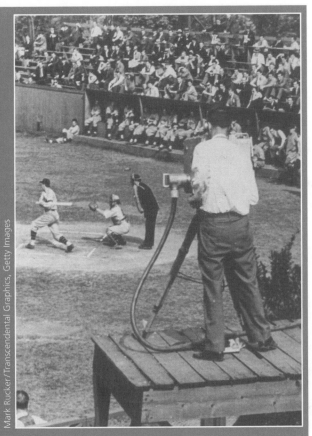

Mark Rucker/Transcendental Graphics, Getty Images

**NBC showed the first televised sporting event in the U.S. on May 17, 1939, in New York, a baseball game between Columbia University and Princeton in Manhattan.**

Just over a month later, the first football game was televised when Fordham University and Waynesburg College faced off. The game was played in the New York City area and only available on television locally, and so fans of Waynesburg, located in Pennsylvania, could not watch (Caldwell, 2014). In September 1939, Duke University faced off with the University of Pittsburgh in a college football matchup on NBC that was the first sporting event broadcast throughout the country (Cramer, 2016; Halberstam, 2019). On that same day, CBS broadcast the first college football game in color, despite only a few cities carrying the broadcast (Halberstam, 2019).

Also in 1939, newspaper reports about a matchup between football's Brooklyn Dodgers and the Philadelphia Eagles gave the impression that the game was nothing historic. *The New York Times* reported on the Dodgers' 23–14 win but neglected to mention what ultimately made the game remarkable: It was the first professional football game ever broadcast on television. There were two cameras and one microphone capturing the action for NBC, with an estimated 500 people watching on television (Fitzpatrick, 2016; Pro Football Hall of Fame, n.d.).

## Cable TV and the "Thrilla in Manila"

For sports broadcasting, one of the most important developments was the creation of cable television. Instead of just receiving channels through antennas attached to the TV set, cable promised a clear signal that could pick up programming from all over the world. When the technology was still in its infancy, not everyone was convinced it would be a success. Ultimately, it was a sporting event that demonstrated the power of cable and had companies lining up to get a satellite.

In 1972, cable's first pay-TV network, Home Box Office (HBO), debuted and, perhaps surprising to current viewers of the channel, had just as much of an emphasis on live sports as it did movies. In fact, the first program on HBO was not a movie, but a hockey game between the NHL's New York Rangers and the Vancouver Canucks (Kissel, 1992; Leverete, Ott, & Buckley, 2008) However, only those within a few hundred miles of New York City were able to get the channel, so its impact was limited (Koplovitz, 2015). Within a few years, though, new satellite technology allowed for nationwide broadcasts. Not everyone was convinced it was the wave of the future, but those early concerns were quickly dispelled following one of the biggest boxing matches in sports history (Leddy, 2015).

In 1975, Muhammad Ali and Joe Frazier were set to face off in what would be the third and final bout between the two. This matchup, billed as the "Thrilla in Manila," was scheduled to take place in the Philippines, and HBO arranged for a live satellite feed to broadcast the video back to the United States. The head of programming for HBO was gambling that a successful fight broadcast would prove the value of cable television (Anderson, 1975; Koplovitz, 2015).

When the fight began, it was clear that satellites and cable television were a good investment. One cable company president said, "The fighters looked like they were in the next room, the picture quality was that extraordinary. We knew we had a winner. We knew this was a big day" (Leddy, 2015, para. 18). Following the successful broadcast of Ali's victory, cable companies all across the United States raced to install their own satellite dishes (Koplovitz, 2015).

## ESPN

Cable television opened the door for many new specialized channels, and for sports, none have had a greater impact than ESPN. While the network went through some growing pains following its 1979 debut, the chan-

nel evolved into the broadcast home for major sporting events and must-see highlights shows. *SportsCenter* revolutionized how fans got sports results, as they were previously limited to the highlights of their local teams on the local evening news. At one point, ESPN was the home to all four major sports leagues in North America and also broadcast major college sports. Chapter 9 has more on the history and significance of ESPN.

## The Internet

While cable channels were able to provide nonstop coverage of sports, the Internet provided an additional layer of information for sports fans. With websites and social media, fans could get the latest statistics, scores, and highlights immediately, with no need to wait until the morning newspaper or the next edition of *SportsCenter*. In addition, streaming platforms meant that fans could watch games from anywhere with a smartphone, tablet, or computer.

## Websites

For years, if a fan wanted to know who won that day's big matchup, they would either need to be watching it live or would have to read about it the next day. When websites started popping up on the Internet, a key draw for fans were the up-to-the-minute score updates

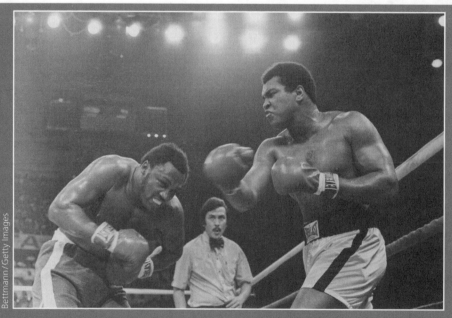

Bettmann/Getty Images

The successful satellite broadcast of the Thrilla in Manila showed that cable television had a future.

and game recaps. A fan could log on to ESPN's website and find out the score during the game, with statistics, without needing to wait. Soon after, websites that had nearly everything a sports fan could possibly want were continuing to pop up—no matter how obscure. For example, someone wanting to know the batting average of the starting second baseman for the Boston Red Sox in only the month of August 1986 could visit baseball-reference.com, and within a few clicks find out that Marty Barrett hit .313 that month (Baseball Reference, n.d.). From there, a search of "Red Sox August 1986" on YouTube, a video hosting platform, would reveal that a full game from August 10 of that year was available to watch, including Barrett's fifth-inning single (This Is Where You Find Baseball, 2022). Websites allowed fans to get the latest information, while also reliving great moments of the past. In addition, as will be discussed in chapter 30, teams and leagues created their own websites to deliver information straight to the fans without needing traditional journalists to relay the news.

## Blogs

Among the many websites being created emerged a subset of pages known as blogs. These were pages that provided constant updates on a topic or event through posts that are usually displayed with the newest content at the top of the page. Blogs became increasingly popular in the early 2000s due to the availability of free, easy-to-use blogging websites (Blood, 2000). Many of these pages were fan-driven, as those outside the traditional media created blogs about their favorite teams and leagues. While they may not have had the same access as journalists, bloggers were still able to provide updates by simply watching the games and giving their own opinions on the action. Blogs such as *Deadspin* and *Barstool Sports* soon became some of the most popular sports blogs on the Internet, capturing younger audiences with edgier content that was not traditionally seen in the sports media.

Seeing the growing popularity, media members began creating their own blogs, which led to several innovations that would later become staples of social media (de Zúñiga et al., 2011). For example, reporters would "live blog" sporting events by providing live updates through multiple blog posts throughout the event. During the 2007 Masters golf tournament, ESPN's Jason Sobel would update his blog every three to five minutes with the latest news from the course (Gisondi, 2018). Additionally, blog comment sections allowed readers to directly contact the author or interact with other users. This was a dramatic change from when media outlets would simply deliver the news and the audience was a passive receiver of information. These elements that made blogging unique—the ability to provide instant updates and interactivity among readers and journalists—would soon be incorporated into social media.

## Social Media

Websites created a dream situation for sports fans with instant information, and blogs allowed fans to become content creators and interact with other users, but social media took those elements to another level. Social media accounts allow users to have information, including sports news and scores, delivered instantly to their news feed. In addition, sports fans can interact with others from all over the world in real time through social media posts.

While immediacy and interactivity have made social media especially appealing to sports fans, they are not the only ones benefiting. Athletes are able to connect directly with some of their most loyal supporters and, in some cases, have online conversations with those fans. For teams, social media has allowed messages to directly reach the audience without needing the traditional media to report the news. Finally, journalists send their latest updates through social media directly to a captive and engaged audience. Chapter 6 has more on social media in sports.

## Live Streaming

The days of needing to sit in front of a television to watch sporting events have also become a thing of the past due to the Internet. Live streaming has allowed people to watch games over the Internet on a variety of portable media devices. In 2001, Major League Baseball became one of the earliest to use this technology when they announced they were offering a package in which fans could pay to live stream every game (Hu, 2001). This was the beginning of MLB.TV, an Internet service run by the league itself in which fans can stream games directly to their computer, phone, tablet, or television through a streaming device. Previously, fans would be limited to just watching the teams in their local area, but now a Colorado Rockies fan in Philadelphia could see his team through the subscription service. Other leagues soon followed with their own streaming options, while ESPN introduced ESPN+ to stream games from all over the world.

Streaming also provided broadcast options beyond the big leagues. Many high school sports programs use the Internet to live stream audio and/or video from their games. Depending on how elaborate of a production the school wishes to create, a few cameras and additional technology can be purchased, and with a few clicks on the computer, games can be streamed live across the world.

# Summary

When newspapers made their way to the United States, articles about sports soon became some of the most popular in each edition. Newspaper leadership, noting the interest among readers, began investing more in sports coverage, including hiring sportswriters and creating departments devoted solely to covering the teams and games in that area.

Soon after, radio stations used sports as a way to drum up interest in the sale of radio receivers. If the audience wanted to hear the blow-by-blow coverage of the big boxing match, they would have to purchase the new technology. Radio coverage would be overtaken by television broadcasts, as the opportunity to both hear and see the games gave the TV stations an advantage. Televised sports continued to grow after the creation of cable's ESPN, a channel devoted entirely to sports 24 hours a day, 7 days a week, and 365 days a year. From there, the Internet allowed sports fans to get the latest news and scores instantaneously, while social media provided an interactive element that had been missing from the traditional media platforms that came before it.

The history of the sports media can perhaps best be marked through the technological advances. The sports media was quick to embrace new information delivery methods, which meant there were new ways to follow the world of sports. Ultimately, that almost always resulted in the fans being the ones who were to benefit the most.

## KEY TERMS

**newsreels**—Short films of news and current events that were shown in movie theaters.

**penny press**—Technology developed in the 1930s that allowed for newspapers to be printed inexpensively. The newly created editions were often sold for one penny.

**recreation**—During early radio broadcasts, the announcer was often not at the game. He would read the description of the game that was sent via telegraph and then "re-create" the action on the radio.

## REVIEW QUESTIONS

1. Why was the penny press important in the rise of the amount of sports coverage in early American newspapers?
2. Radio broadcasts were a key element in the growth of the popularity of sports, but why were teams and leagues skeptical of these early live programs?
3. Sports have been an important part of the advancement of technology throughout the years. Why might that be?
4. How did the Internet change how fans get their sports news?

# Business of the Sports Media

## CHAPTER OBJECTIVES

After completing the chapter, the reader should be able to do the following:

- Understand how the business of print journalism has evolved
- Identify how the Internet has influenced both print and broadcast journalism
- Examine the value of rights fees for major television broadcasters
- Analyze how cord cutting is affecting cable television

While winning or losing might feel like life or death to many fans and players, it is easy to forget that sporting events are ultimately a game. However, the sporting world as a whole is also a business. Teams are trying to sell tickets, players are looking to perform at their best in order to sign big contracts, and leagues want the most lucrative sponsorship deals. Highly involved in the business of sports is the media, both as a payer and recipient of big-money deals. Throughout this book, the impact of the sports media on teams, leagues, and players will be discussed repeatedly, but all those interactions return to a similar concept: The sports media is driven by money and nearly every decision revolves around getting the biggest return on investment.

## Return on Investment

A key element of nearly every business, sports or otherwise, is having a high **return on investment (ROI)**. To put it simply, ROI shows how much money has been

made or lost during a project after factoring in the initial cost. This is calculated by dividing the net profit or loss by the initial investment. Net profit is determined by subtracting the initial investment from the current value.

$$\text{Return on Investment} = \frac{\text{Current Value} - \text{Initial Investment}}{\text{Initial Investment}}$$

A high ROI indicates that the investment was a good one, and that the money spent could result in a profit for the organization. While there are other factors to consider, such as how long it took to reach that point, ROI is a basic measurement that can tell a company a great deal about its financial investment.

A simple example would be if someone was trying to make money selling baseball cards. If they bought an Aaron Judge rookie card for $50 and then sold it for $75, the ROI would be 50 percent.

$$\frac{75 - 50}{50} = 50\%$$

However, if that same fan sold the card at $35, the ROI would be –30 percent.

$$\frac{35-50}{50}=-30\%$$

The first situation demonstrates that the investment was a success and should be repeated, while the second example should result in the seller determining what should be avoided in the future.

For media companies, this ROI is an important factor in determining how and where to spend money. When television networks spend billions on live sports, the leadership needs to determine if that is a good investment. As will be explained later in this chapter, the NFL earns the most money from television networks because executives at those channels believe investing in the league's television broadcast rights will have a high ROI. The numbers demonstrate that might be true. In 2020, NFL games were 71 of the 100 most-watched broadcasts throughout the year, and advertising revenue for the games was $3.7 billion (The Daily Upside, 2021).

# The Business of Newspaper Journalism

As discussed in chapter 2, newspapers were the dominant means of getting information about current events for many years. Whether it was news, sports, business, or weather, people would read the newspaper every morning in order to be knowledgeable about what was going on in the world. For sports fans, those newspaper articles recapped games, gave the latest team news, and previewed upcoming events. For businesses, newspapers were a way to reach a dedicated audience who would see their advertisements in each edition. However, as the newspaper industry changed, the business of print journalism was altered dramatically.

## Newspaper Sales and Advertising

For the majority of its history, the newspaper industry primarily made money through subscriptions, newsstand sales, and advertising. Those numbers all work in harmony with each other, as the more newspapers that are sold and read each day, the more the publisher can charge companies to advertise. As the printing of newspapers became less expensive and large corporations took over ownership of papers throughout the country, the number of readers began to skyrocket. Circulation, defined as the number of newspapers available each day for purchase or through subscriptions, increased from just over 41 million in 1940 to over 62 million in 1970. Even when radio and television became major competition for the newspaper, it was still an industry on the financial rise. Between 1965 and 1975, newspaper advertising rates rose 67 percent. The rates would go even higher, with advertising prices rising 253 percent from 1975 to 1990 (FCC, 2011).

Another important revenue stream for newspapers was classified advertisements. These are different from traditional advertisements, as they were often brief, text-only, and placed by individuals instead of companies. The newspaper would charge by the word or line of text, with people advertising used cars for sale, job openings, and other opportunities. Before 1995, classified advertisements made up 40 percent of newspaper revenue and were often the primary reason that some people bought the newspaper (AdPerfect, n.d.).

# The Impact of the Internet

The business model of newspapers was relatively unchanged until around 2005. By that time, the Internet had started to influence all aspects of the industry. Subscriptions to physical newspapers were declining, companies were moving their advertising to cheaper options online, and classified ads were being placed on specialty websites. The main revenue streams had moved elsewhere, and newspapers were beginning to suffer.

A deep dive into the numbers demonstrates just how dire the situation has become. Circulation was at 62 million in 1970 but had fallen to an estimated 24 million by 2020. While the number of daily visitors to newspaper websites was just below 14 million in 2020, that nowhere near made up the difference in the number of readers lost from print. In 2005, total estimated advertising revenue for the newspaper industry was over $49 billion, but that had dropped to an estimated $9 billion by 2020 (Pew Research Center, 2021). While online advertising grew by about $1 billion from 2005 to 2010, that still represented a deficit when factoring in the loss of print advertisements. A report from the U.S. Federal Communications Commission summarized the problems the money loss was creating:

*This led to the saying in the newspaper world that "print dollars were being replaced by digital dimes."*

*That turns out to be a rather cheerful way of phrasing it. More accurately: each print dollar was being replaced by four digital pennies. (FCC, 2011, p. 39)*

In addition to the advertising revenue from companies disappearing, the classifieds were also moving online. However, those were not moving to newspaper websites, but instead to alternative pages such as Craigslist and Facebook Marketplace. *The Washington Post* noted that the number of classified advertisements in major newspapers dropped between 14 and 20 percent from 2005 to 2006, while visits to online classified websites grew about 23 percent at the same time (Diaz, 2007).

In response to news readers moving online, many newspapers embraced digital subscriptions and an "online first" mentality. Sportswriter Manie Robinson recalled that during his time at *The Greenville News* in South Carolina, newspaper management decided to focus almost exclusively on the website: "It was well known that we were now a digital organization that happens to print a newspaper" (Hull, 2022, p. 87). In 2020, *The New York Times* reported that, for the first time in its history, it had earned more revenue from digital sources than from print. In addition, the newspaper had 6.5 million total subscriptions, with 5.7 million of them being digital-only (Tracy, 2020).

## Loss of Newspapers

The pivot to a digital focus has slowed some of the negative trends surrounding the finances of newspapers, but it has not stopped them. For some, the changes came too late, or the deficit was too much to overcome. From 2005 to 2022, a quarter of all newspapers in the United States, about 2,500, went out of business (Simonetti, 2022). Those that remained had made cuts to staffing, with fewer reporters covering fewer topics. In sports departments, the combination of these financial woes was compounded by the COVID-19 pandemic in 2020. Sports editors throughout the country were forced to institute furloughs or layoffs of sportswriters, with some wondering if they would ever return to previous levels (Strauss, 2020). This loss of journalists ultimately meant that fans were not getting the same level of coverage of their favorite teams and sports that they once had. Travel budgets were cut, sports departments were minimized, and the ability of journalists to be at every game and practice became more challenging. As will be discussed in chapter 30, this drop in the number of sports reporters employed at newspapers has led to the rise of team media, in which teams hire their own journalists to essentially report on themselves. This creates a situation in which decreasing media coverage can be compensated for by the team itself, but the unbiased journalist has been replaced by a team employee.

Jaap Arriens/NurPhoto via Getty Images

**With the advent of the Internet, many newspapers embraced digital subscriptions as a way to survive.**

# The Business of Broadcasting

Print and online journalism primarily involves reporters attending the games and practices in order to update the audience on the latest developments. While broadcasting outlets have a similar goal in many aspects, there is the added element of networks showing live games. While highlight shows such as ESPN's *SportsCenter* are still a staple of the daily schedule, it is the live sports that are the jewel of the calendar. Within the business of sports broadcasting, there are several elements worth addressing:

- Importance of viewership ratings
- Broadcasting live sports
- Cable television fees
- Cord cutting
- Streaming

## Importance of Viewership Ratings

The **rating** of a television program is best described as the approximate number of people who are watching. For decades, the Nielsen Media Research company would send written diaries to television viewers, who would simply write down what they watched throughout the day. Over the years, the process became automated, and Nielsen is now able to obtain viewership information electronically.

Ratings are often reported in numbers and shares. For example, the 2022 Super Bowl between the Los Angeles Rams and the Cincinnati Bengals drew a 36.9 rating and a 72 share (Rowan & Hurst, 2022). That rating means that of all the television households in the United States, 36.9 percent of them were estimated to have tuned into the game. Additionally, of all the television households *that had a television on* during that time, 72 percent of them were estimated to have been watching the game. Approximate viewership is also reported; NBC's broadcast of the 2022 Super Bowl averaged 99 million viewers throughout the game (Rowan & Hurst, 2022).

However, the truth is that Nielsen does not know *exactly* how many people are watching a program. Not every television set in the United States is monitored, so instead the company uses a small sample of viewers and extrapolates those numbers to the entire population. In 2022, the company used just over 42,000 homes

in the United States to determine what everyone was watching (Casey, 2022). It is entirely possible that all the Nielsen-monitored homes are viewing something completely different from the rest of the country, causing results that are wildly inaccurate. However, that is unlikely: Nielsen takes special care to ensure that they have a diverse audience that would not sway the results incorrectly (Nielsen, n.d.).

While networks want to have the highest ratings and viewership possible, those numbers are for a lot more than just bragging rights. Ratings are used by the television networks to determine how much to charge companies for advertising during a program. If ESPN can demonstrate through previous ratings that millions of people will be watching the college bowl games on their channel, they can essentially promise advertisers that number will likely be watching that company's commercials during those games. The more viewers who are expected to watch, the more money a network can charge.

## Broadcasting Live Sports

While studio shows such as ESPN's *SportsCenter* provide the latest information on the games, players, and leagues, those programs are not the main draw for networks. Instead, it is the broadcasting of live sports that has become the most valuable content. While there are many factors, one of the main reasons why sporting events are appealing for networks is that the games are "DVR-proof."

In 1980, 83 million people tuned in to CBS on a Friday night in November to find out "who shot J.R." It was a highly anticipated episode of the television program *Dallas*; the main villain on the show had been shot at the end of the previous season, and fans wanted to know who pulled the trigger (Darwish, 2020). Those who wanted to find out had no choice but to watch it live, as home video recording technology was still in its infancy. Television programs had large audiences during their initial showings because in many cases it would be the only time they could be viewed.

However, as technology that enabled viewers to record and play back content advanced, the need to watch shows "live" decreased, and viewers are now just as willing to watch these shows at their own convenience. People record episodes through a digital video recorder (DVR) or stream shows through a variety of online options, giving viewers the option to watch the programs when they are ready. In 2019, the finale of the show *The Big Bang Theory* brought in 23.4 million viewers, but over 5 million of them watched the episode in the three days following the live airing through either a recording or streaming (de Moraes, 2019). While the program had millions of loyal viewers, many of them did not feel it necessary to watch the finale live. This could be because there are two main perks to watching recorded shows: People can watch when it is convenient for them, and it allows for fast-forwarding through the commercials.

While there may not be a need to watch a sitcom live, that is not usually the case for sporting events. It is highly unlikely that a football fan would record the Super Bowl and wait several days to watch it. By the time that fan sat down to enjoy the game, he or she would already know the final score and all the key plays. That is why sports is given that label of being "DVR-proof." Sports fans want to watch games live so they can talk about them with friends, follow along on social media, and see the biggest plays as they are happening. Since those fans are watching live, that means they are also watching commercials. This makes live sports especially appealing to advertisers, who know their product pitches will not be fast-forwarded through.

## Cost of Broadcasting Rights

Television networks have discovered that showing live sports is a great way to bring in a large audience and receive advertising dollars, so the competition is high to show those games and events. That battle has translated to millions, and sometimes billions, of dollars for the leagues and conferences in exchange for the exclusive rights to the broadcast. From 1980 to 2023, the five largest professional sports leagues in the United States earned more than $210 billion from just broadcast media rights. Based on the history of those payments, that number may continue to rise. For example, in 1998, television networks paid the NFL, NBA, MLB, NHL, and MLS a combined $3.4 billion to show their games. However, that number skyrocketed in the ensuing years; with streaming platforms getting in on the action, those same five leagues earned $15.4 billion in 2023 (Smith, Ingold, & Pogkas, 2022). The most desirable league for media rights is the NFL, which has the highest television ratings and viewership. That translates to billions for the league: In 2021, CBS, NBC, Fox, ESPN, and Amazon agreed to pay the league a total of $110 billion over 11 years to show games throughout the season (Belson & Draper, 2021).

## ESPN's Investment in Live Sports

ESPN's history will be discussed in depth in chapter 9, but it is nearly impossible to discuss the investment in live sports without including the network in the discussion. ESPN's executives made a decision that showing sporting events would be the primary element of the primetime schedule. Before ESPN went on the air in 1979, it reached an agreement with the NCAA to show a variety of sports, with the network paying the participating schools $3,500 for each basketball game broadcast, and $1,000 per game for other sports (Miller, 1979). From there, the network would increase their investment in live sports by spending millions to broadcast games from the NBA and NHL. A few years later, as will be discussed in greater depth in chapter 9, the network made its biggest payout yet by agreeing to a $153 million deal to show select NFL regular-season games (Pierson, 1987). That deal changed the national perception of ESPN from a minor league cable channel into a true player in the world of live sports broadcasting.

That NFL deal was only the beginning. ESPN would spend billions of dollars from 2002 to 2004 to be the broadcast home for the four main sports in North America, as the NBA, NHL, MLB, and NFL were all on the network. ESPN also invested heavily in college football, bidding $125 million for the television, radio, and digital rights for the BCS National Championship games from 2011 to 2014 (Zinser, 2008). That move signified more than just a financial investment; for one of the first times ever, a major sporting event was now only going to be shown on cable. ESPN certainly had no regrets and proved so a few years later when it agreed to pay an additional $5.64 billion over 12 years to continue being the home of the college football championship game (Bachman, 2012). From 2023 to 2027, ESPN was expected to pay at least $44.9 billion in rights fees to a variety of professional and college leagues to show games and highlights from those entities (Crupi, 2022).

# Cable Fees

While ESPN and other cable channels are shelling out millions of dollars to show sports on their networks, there needs to be a way to pay for that. While advertising revenue does contribute, it is not be enough to be the lone financial stream for the networks. Instead, cable networks put the cost back on the cable companies and the viewers.

When cable television debuted, channels would pay the providers to get a spot on the channel listings. However, in 1983 ESPN executives created a plan to take advantage of the fact that the network was the top-rated

David J. Griffin/Icon Sportswire via Getty Images

**ESPN spends billions of dollars to broadcast live sports.**

channel on cable. Instead of paying the cable companies, ESPN told the cable companies that they would now have to pay ESPN for the rights to carry the channel. It was a bold declaration, and one that was unprecedented at the time. It was just a few cents a month, but for ESPN that was now income instead of an expense (Alfano, 1983). The gamble was that ESPN had become so popular among sports fans that cable companies would have no choice but to pay. Those companies quickly figured out that they did not have to pay that fee out of their own pockets and could instead pass the cost onto subscribers. Cable television customers now pay about $9 each month to have ESPN as part of the channel selection, whether they watch it or not. Viewers pay similar monthly fees for the Fox Sports channels, NFL Network, and other sports-specific channels (Gaines, 2017).

With this arrangement, ESPN has created a dual-revenue model. The cable companies pay the network a rights fee, while ESPN is also able to charge for advertising. Therefore, when a game is shown on ESPN, the network is essentially getting paid twice—once from the network and once from the advertisers. In 2011, it was estimated that the dual-revenue model at ESPN made the network more valuable than the NBA, NHL, and MLB combined (Bennett, 2011).

However, not all stories involving cable fees have been a success. In 2014, Time Warner Cable launched the channel SportsNet LA, primarily focusing on showing Los Angeles Dodgers games. Time Warner wanted cable and satellite companies to pay $4.90 per month to broadcast the channel. However, the rising cost of sports channels was beginning to become a concern, and DirecTV was among those that balked at paying the fee and refused to carry SportsNet LA. Neither side would budge, so 70 percent of the Los Angeles area could not see Dodgers games for several years before the dispute was finally settled in 2020 (Castillo & Shaikin, 2020).

## Cord Cutting

ESPN and other cable sports networks turned those rights fees into a major element of their yearly balance sheet, but that began to change when millions of consumers canceled their cable television and turned to streaming services to get their entertainment. From 2018 to 2022, the number of cable TV subscribers dropped from 87 million to 63 million (Smith et al., 2022). This trend, known as **cord cutting**, means that channels such as ESPN are losing out on the rights fees they had been depending on. It is not just sports channels, as networks such as the Weather Channel, USA Network, and CNN all have reported a drop in viewership as people leave their cable subscriptions behind (Andreeva & Johnson, 2019). However, as will be discussed in chapter 9, ESPN is perhaps the cable channel that has been most affected by cord cutting. The network had factored in those rights fees when negotiating the billions of dollars' worth of deals they struck with various sports leagues. In addition, with fewer viewers, cable companies will have a hard time charging businesses the same rates for advertising.

## Streaming

Cord cutting is a major concern for television networks, and some have turned to Internet streaming to make up for the revenue lost due to fewer subscribers and decreased advertising revenue. Streaming platforms, sometimes referred to as **over-the-top media services**, are a way for people to watch video content over the Internet. These files are played back in real time, as opposed to needing to be downloaded completely before being played. ESPN's attempt to jump into the streaming market is through ESPN+, discussed in chapter 9. Fans who pay about $10 a month have access to live sports, ESPN documentaries, and other programs that are not available on television. While not an exact swap for the cable package, it could still satisfy those sports fans who are looking for games after dropping cable (Brown, 2019).

Other streaming platforms have also turned to live sports in an effort to increase subscriber numbers. Amazon reached a $1 billion deal with the NFL to show Thursday night football games on that company's streaming platform, Prime Video (Battaglio, 2022). For Amazon, the investment makes their service a must for NFL fans who want to see every game. Apple TV's *Ted Lasso* is a fictional tale of an American soccer coach in England, but the platform was counting on the real thing to increase subscribers. Both MLB and MLS reached deals with Apple TV, with an exclusive baseball game each week and nearly every game of the MLS season (Rueter, 2022; Shaikin, 2022). Peacock, the streaming service run by NBC, broadcasts events from the Olym-pics, Sunday night games in the NFL, college football, and Premier League soccer (SVG Staff, 2022).

While these streaming services have been touted as the way to counteract cord cutting, early returns have indicated that this is not necessarily the case. In 2022, Disney (which owns the streaming platforms Disney+, Hulu, and ESPN+) lost almost $1.5 billion on its streaming division in just three months; it placed most of the blame on Disney+ and Hulu, not on ESPN+ (Fischer, 2022). Executives with Peacock estimated the company would lose over $2 billion in 2022, even as subscriber rates reached new highs (Fletcher, 2022). As with cord cutting, the issues are not sports-specific. AMC+, a streaming platform that focuses on movies and television shows, reported not having enough subscriptions to make up for the loss of cable viewers, forcing layoffs and a reevaluation of the platform's future (Mullin, 2022).

## Summary

The sports media has changed dramatically since the first sports articles appeared in the newspaper, and those changes are perfectly demonstrated in the business aspects of the industry. Newspapers made millions on advertisements and subscriptions, but the Internet would change how people got their news and sports information. Due to that shift, many newspapers throughout the country shifted to a digital model, while others could not survive and went out of business. In television, networks demonstrated that they would spend billions of dollars for the opportunity to broadcast live sporting events. While those games brought in viewers, the cable television industry was changing. Customers were getting rid of their cable package, resulting in a decrease of revenue for networks such as ESPN. As the sports media continues to evolve, the future may lie in Internet streaming video.

### KEY TERMS

**cord cutting**—People getting rid of their cable television subscriptions.

**over-the-top media services**—A way for people to watch video content over the Internet.

**rating**—The approximate number of people who are watching a program on television.

**return on investment**—How much money has been made or lost during a project after factoring in the initial cost.

## REVIEW QUESTIONS

1. Why is "return on investment" important for a business?
2. Could the newspaper industry have done anything to avoid the impact the Internet had on their industry? If so, what could they have done?
3. Why are live sports appealing to advertisers?
4. How can cable companies combat the loss of subscribers that is happening through cord cutting?

# NBC and the Olympics

## CHAPTER OBJECTIVES

After completing the chapter, the reader should be able to do the following:

- Identify the history of the Olympics in the media
- Recognize the historical importance of NBC winning the rights to show the Olympics
- Analyze and evaluate the criticisms faced by NBC due to their coverage of the Olympics
- Examine NBC's changing role as the gatekeeper of the Olympics on television in the United States

The Olympics are one of the biggest sporting events in the world, drawing athletes from countries all over the globe. It is also a major media event, as journalists report and broadcast the results back to the athletes' home countries. In the United States, a fan of the Games has no choice but to watch NBC's coverage, as the network has spent billions of dollars to be the exclusive home of the Olympics on television and online. However, while that decision has brought in millions of viewers and billions of dollars in advertising revenue, it has also come with criticism from frustrated viewers.

## History of the Olympics and the Media

Although there are some who argue the Olympics started years earlier, most believe the first edition took place in 776 BC to honor Zeus, the father of the Greek gods and goddesses. Taking place in Olympia, Greece (hence the name "Olympics"), it was not the event-filled two-week extravaganza that we are used to today. In fact, that first year there was only one event—a 192-meter race called a "stade." The legacy of that race lives on many years later, as this is where the word *stadium* originated.

As has been traditionally the case since, the summer version of the Olympics would take place every four years in August and September. Other events were eventually added, including longer footraces, boxing, and even chariot racing. The events were not for everyone, however, as women were not allowed to participate, and married women were not even allowed to attend as spectators. In AD 393, Emperor Theodosius I banned the Olympics for religious reasons, putting a halt to the Games for 1,500 years (History.com Editors, 2010). However, when the Games returned, the media was there to document the event.

## Coverage from Newspapers, Newsreels, and Radio

In the 1890s, Pierre de Coubertin, a French baron, was inspired to bring back the Olympics with a goal of promoting physical fitness and education. He would later create the International Olympic Committee (IOC), and in 1896 the first "modern" Olympics were held. When the Games began, newspaper writers were there to cover the action, although the stories certainly varied between the different media outlets. The *Los Angeles Herald* gave overall results, Boston newspaper writers focused on the local athletes participating, and London's *The Guardian* gave detailed directions on how to travel from London to Athens to watch the Games, warning readers that the railway journey was "objectionable" due to its poor service and speed (Shedden, 2015; The Guardian, 1896, para. 1; The Herald, 1896).

In the early 1900s, coverage evolved from the written word to moving pictures. The public could now see the Olympic athletes in action through recorded video pieces that were later shown in movie theaters. These films, known as **newsreels**, contained short videos of events that had happened weeks earlier (Larrosa, 2016; The Olympic Museum, n.d.). Although only available in black and white and without sound, these short videos captured the public's attention and led to increased exposure and excitement for the events (Billings et al., 2018; Larrosa, 2016). As technology improved, these newsreels eventually added color and sound before the medium was phased out in the 1960s (Larrosa, 2016).

By 1924, the Olympics were becoming a worldwide event that was drawing increased attention thanks to the media members who were converging on the host city. The 1924 Games in Paris, France, were covered by more than 1,000 journalists, making it one of the biggest sporting media events in the world at the time (Olympics.com, n.d.). Another technological marvel debuted that year with the addition of partially live radio coverage. Broadcasters could report live from the events, giving the play-by-play of the results and interviewing the athletes afterward. This was highly controversial at the time, as organizers were worried that the live radio broadcast would have a negative impact on ticket sales. Their fear was that if people knew they could follow along with the events directly from their homes, they would be less likely to purchase tickets. Ultimately the opposite happened, and the radio coverage actually increased interest. Some 625,000 spectators attended the events, much more than the disappointing attendance from four years earlier in Belgium (Larrosa, 2016; Rosenberg, 2018).

## Olympics on Television

The Olympics first came to television in 1936, but the broadcasts were limited to a small audience. Germany's leader, Adolf Hitler, wanted to use the Berlin-hosted games as a propaganda device for his Nazi government. German-made video cameras captured the action, and 25 television viewing rooms were set up in Berlin, allowing those in the area to watch the events for free (The Olympic Museum, n.d.). The technology was perhaps not quite completely ready for this showcase, as *The New York Times* reported at the time that "all that you can see are some men dressed like athletes but only faintly distinguishable, like humans floating in a milk bath" (The New York Times, 1936, para. 2). In addition to the viewing issues, Hitler also did not plan on an African American, Jesse Owens, becoming the biggest star of "his" Olympics, winning four gold medals and the adoration of the German audiences and even the Nazi broadcasters (Given, 2016).

While the Olympics were starting to be broadcast throughout the world, the United States was slightly behind the times. Instead of showing the events live, American broadcasting companies would show only short highlight programs a few days after the events had been completed. Those who wanted to watch the events as they happened were out of luck. The decision to not broadcast the events live in the United States was both a financial and technological determination by the networks. Not only would it have cost too much to show the events in real time, but it was also an acknowledgment that television was still in its infancy and had not been widely adopted by the public (Billings et al., 2018).

However, by the time the 1960 Winter Olympics came to Squaw Valley, California, most homes in the United States had a television and were ready for live sports. Therefore, with the technology more accepted, and the Olympics taking place in the United States, the stage was set for the first live broadcast of the events in America. CBS paid $50,000 to be the exclusive home of the Olympics that year in the United States, an amount that is almost laughable when compared to how much is spent in modern times (Ellerbee, n.d.). While CBS did not dedicate its entire **primetime** schedule to the Olympics (as is done currently), the first live broadcast in the United States was ultimately a success.

That 1960 broadcast might best be remembered not for action itself, but instead for the now ubiquitous sports television staple that was first employed during those Olympics. During a slalom event, Olympic officials were unsure if a skier had missed a gate during his turn on the mountain. In order to make a ruling, the officials asked CBS if they could watch a videotape of that run to review exactly what had happened. While other networks, such as Canada's CBC, had systems that could replay game action several minutes later on the broadcast, this request from Olympic officials gave CBS the idea of having a system where viewers could *instantly* see what just happened during a sporting event. Thus, the Olympics of 1960 are often cited as the birthplace of television's instant replay (Ellerbee, n.d.).

## ABC Sports and the Olympics

ABC would take over Olympic coverage in 1964 and begin a 20-year run of being the primary television home for the Games in the United States. Chapter 8 has more on the impact that ABC Sports had on the world of sports broadcasting, and the network's showing of the Olympics is a big part of that history. ABC was credited with increasing Americans' interest level in the Games by

- showing events during primetime,
- focusing on human interest stories, and
- devoting more hours to the events throughout the years (Billings et al., 2018).

Between 1964 and 1988, ABC exclusively aired 10 of the 14 Olympics that took place. Throughout those years, the network's coverage was aided by advances in technology. For example, in 1964 ABC would record the events in Austria and then put the black-and-white film on a plane back to New York where it would be broadcast on tape throughout the United States (Adams, 1964). However, just four years later, those plane trips were no longer necessary as the now-color broadcasts were able to be shown live due to the network's use of satellites (Billings et al., 2018). As the years progressed, ABC found itself broadcasting some of the most historic moments in American Olympics history.

## *1968 Mexico City Protests*

In 1968, Americans Tommie Smith and John Carlos stood atop the medal podium following their first- and third-place finishes in the 200-meter sprint at the Mexico City Olympics. As the *Star-Spangled Banner* played to signify the American gold medal win, Smith and Carlos each raised one fist while wearing a black glove. The pair said it was done as a human rights salute, but the International Olympic Committee was not pleased. Both Smith and Carlos were immediately banned from the remaining days of the Olympics (Maraniss, 2018).

Americans Tommie Smith and John Carlos raise a fist in the air during the 1968 Olympics.

Bettmann/Getty Images

On ABC, the runners' protest was not shown live, but instead replayed the next night on *ABC Evening News*. The entire anthem—with a camera focused on Smith and Carlos—was rebroadcast during the segment. Immediately afterward, an interview between Smith and ABC's Howard Cosell was aired. Cosell asked Smith several pointed questions about the events on the podium, to which Smith was given ample time to respond. The next night, after Smith and Carlos were kicked out of the Olympic Village, Cosell gave a commentary in which he blasted Olympic officials and expressed sympathy for Black athletes (Maraniss, 2018). It was, at the time, a remarkable scene: a White man on a major broadcast network showing complete and total support for Black athletes while criticizing the Olympic programming that was on his network.

## Munich in 1972

During the 1972 Summer Olympics in Munich, West Germany, a group of Palestinian terrorists stormed the Olympic Village apartment of the Israeli athletes, killing two and taking nine others hostage. The sporting events stopped during this time but ABC's coverage continued, with Jim McKay reporting live on the network for 14 hours straight about the latest developments. Since ABC was the broadcast home of the Olympics, most Americans watched its coverage (Billings et al., 2018). Following a standoff at the airport between the terrorists and police, many in the media reported that the hostages were rescued, and the attackers had been killed. However, at 3:24 a.m., McKay reported the truth in a chilling statement that has, unfortunately, become one of the most memorable in Olympic broadcasting history:

> We just got the final word . . . you know, when I was a kid, my father used to say, "Our greatest hopes and our worst fears are seldom realized." Our worst fears have been realized tonight. They've now said that there were eleven hostages. Two were killed in their rooms yesterday morning, nine were killed at the airport tonight. They're all gone. (McKay, 2002)

## "Miracle on Ice"

Eight years later, one of the saddest moments in the history of American Olympic broadcasting was countered with one of the most jubilant. In 1980, the Soviet Union's men's hockey team was perhaps the most dominant team in all of sport, having won four Olympic gold medals in a row. They were the heavy favorites to win again, and a semifinal matchup with a seemingly overmatched United States team did not figure to slow them down. However, that game is known as the "Miracle on Ice" for a reason: With the United States leading 4–3 and the seconds winding down, ABC broadcaster Al Michaels uttered perhaps the most famous words in the history of American sports broadcasting: "Do you believe in miracles? Yes!"

The game has been called "the top sports moment in the 20th century" (Goldberg, 1999), and Michaels' words at the finish have been labeled the best sports call ever (Vaccaro, 2015). Amazingly, Michaels being a part of that game was as much a stroke of luck as it was a credit to his broadcasting skill. In 1980, he was the only person on the ABC Sports staff who had ever done play-by-play for a hockey game, so, almost by default, he was chosen to broadcast the games. Thirty years later, Michaels would say: "You talk about getting fortunate. As I tell people to this day, there were not a lot of miracles on the biathlon course" (Reedy, 2020, para. 17).

## 1984 in Los Angeles

With the 1984 Olympics slated to take place in Los Angeles, ABC took a calculated gamble that interest would be higher than ever in the United States. As part of that gamble, the network bid $225 million to be the host network, which was three times more than NBC had paid for the 1980 Summer Olympics and nine times more than they paid to show the 1976 Summer Olympics (Lindsey, 1979). Once the events began, ABC devoted 180 hours of coverage, more than the network had ever set aside for a broadcast of the Olympics. One reason for this all-in strategy was that since the Games were in the United States, executives did not have to worry about start times that were from dramatically different time zones on the other side of the world. That meant many of the events could be shown live (Mifflin, 1984). ABC's strategy paid off. More than 180 million Americans watched the 1984 Olympics on ABC, making it the most watched event in television history at the time (Wertheim, 2021).

# ABC Loses the Olympics

While the Olympics did appear on NBC and CBS a few times from 1964 to 1988, the Games were mostly broadcast on ABC. However, that would soon change. After losing hundreds of millions of dollars in 1988 on live sports broadcasts that fell well short of their advertising goal (including the Olympics), ABC's new ownership, Capital Cities Communications, chose to be conservative with its bids on future sporting events (Chad & Reid, 1989). While ABC put forth restrained financial offers in its bids for the Olympics, other networks did not, and the Games were soon to be no longer broadcast on ABC.

CBS would co-broadcast the Winter Olympics in 1992, 1994, and 1998 with cable channel TNT. At the time, putting the Olympics on pay television was a novel concept because it had always been available through free, over-the-air channels. However, this was not some landmark move designed to change the future of television as much as it was a decision CBS made to save money. In an effort to offset the costs of broadcasting the Games, CBS elected to simply resell some of the rights it had acquired to TNT; the cable channel broadcast events during the day, while CBS's coverage would take place at night (Dempsey, 1996).

The most-watched moment of the CBS years took place during the 1994 Olympics. Less than two months before those games were to begin, American figure skater Nancy Kerrigan was attacked by a man trying to break her leg and force her out of the competition. That attacker, who was unsuccessful, was hired by the ex-husband of Tonya Harding, another American figure skater. Harding denied knowledge of the plan to attack her biggest rival, and so both were allowed to skate at the Olympics. The night of the preliminary round of the figure skating competition was one of the most drama-filled moments in sports history, as "Nancy versus Tonya" took center stage. CBS might have been the biggest winner, though, as the broadcast that night was, at the time, the third-highest-rated sports event in television history (Nidetz, 1994).

# NBC Takes Over the Olympics

While CBS and TNT had a short run of broadcasting the Winter Olympics following ABC's departure, the Olympics were about to become the exclusive property of NBC. In 1989, Dick Ebersol was named the new head of NBC Sports, and he decided to make the Olympics the centerpiece of the network's sports portfolio. Under Ebersol's leadership, NBC has been the broadcast home of the Summer Olympics in the United States since 1988, has been the home of the Winter Olympics since 2002, and, as of this writing, will continue to be the network of both until (at least) 2032. This decision has not come cheaply. Over the years, NBC has paid nearly $20 billion to be the exclusive

broadcaster of the Games for every Summer and Winter Olympics since 2000 (Isidore, 2014).

## Why Broadcast the Olympics?

With NBC spending billions of dollars on the Olympics, it is important to address why a television network would want to broadcast the Games. First, there is a prestige that is associated with the Olympics, and having the events can boost the reputation of that network. NBC proudly touts that it is America's home for the Olympics and begins promoting their coverage months in advance of the Opening Ceremonies.

In addition, the Olympics take place during summer and winter months that are traditionally slow at television stations. Most programming is on reruns during this point and the sporting calendar is filled with regular-season games that will likely not draw the sports media's attention away from the Olympic coverage. Therefore, the Olympics gives a network live, brand-new programming when most other stations are broadcasting shows or events that will be of less interest. This makes the Olympics especially appealing to viewers and advertisers. Even in 2022, when Olympic viewership was among the lowest ever, NBC was still expected to be the most-watched channel during all 17 nights of the Games (Reedy, 2022).

## Many Viewing Options

While NBC spends billions of dollars to broadcast the Olympics, not all the events end up on the main channel. This practice first started in 1992 when the network debuted the TripleCast, a pay-per-view system in which customers could order a specific channel (Red, White, or Blue) that would show events beyond what was on the main network. With the Games in Spain that year, NBC assumed that fans who did not want to wait until the tape-delayed showing of the events that night would pay between $95 and $170 to watch live during the day (Sandomir, 1992). However, very few people signed up, and media experts estimated that NBC lost somewhere around $100 million on the TripleCast (Mulligan, 1992).

Despite that financial loss, NBC had hit on an idea that would stick for many years to come: putting the events on multiple networks. During 2021's Tokyo Olympics, 250 hours of coverage aired on NBC, while over 1,300 hours were on various cable channels under the NBCUniversal (NBC's parent company) umbrella. Those cable channels included USA, CNBC, The Golf

Mike Stobe / Getty Images

**NBC seeks to leverage the prestige of televising the Olympics by promoting it well in advance of the Games. Here Paralympic athlete Jimmy Joseph attends the 100 Days to Sochi Winter Olympics Event at NBC's Today Show.**

Channel, NBC Sports Network, and The Olympic Channel, a 365-day-a-year channel devoted solely to Olympic sports. In addition, there were another 5,500 hours available on the Internet through NBC's streaming platforms (NBC Sports Group Press Box, 2021).

## Coverage of Women on NBC's Olympics

As will be discussed in great detail in chapter 18, coverage of women's sports in the United States by the media has been lacking for decades. Women's professional sports leagues and college championships get fractions of the amount of time and space when compared to men's sports on broadcasts, in print, and online. However, NBC's Olympic broadcasts have become an outlier to this decades-long trend. Not only is the coverage equitable, but the women actually receive *more* time during the primetime broadcasts than the men. During the Tokyo Olympics in 2021, excluding mixed-sex sports, women's sports were shown 57.95 percent of the time, while men's sports were shown 42.05 percent of the time.

This was the largest difference between the two sexes in NBC's Summer Olympic history (Billings et al., 2021). This trend continued the next year during the 2022 Beijing Winter Olympics, with women's sports receiving 60.05 percent of primetime coverage and men getting 39.95 percent when mixed-sex sports were not counted. This was the largest coverage gap in favor of the women's sports coverage since a team of researchers began examining the breakdown in 1994 (Billings et al., 2022).

## Criticisms of NBC's Broadcast

While NBC has been lauded for its increased focus on women's athletes during the Olympics, the overall coverage has not come without criticism. In fact, during the Olympics, the hashtag #NBCFail is often trending on social media due to the many complaints from viewers. Those upset with the coverage often focus on three main factors: a pro-American bias, primarily showing certain sports and athletes, and broadcasting events on tape delay instead of live.

## Pro-American Bias

If a casual viewer watches the Olympics on NBC, they will likely see many Americans participating, even if those athletes are not the top competitors. A headline from *The New York Times* proclaimed that "Little is medal-worthy about NBC's coverage of foreign athletes," with the accompanying article pointing out several incidents from the 2016 Olympics in which NBC announcers seemingly ignored all the non-American competitors (Sandomir, 2016). In an examination of all the NBC-broadcast Olympics from 1996 to 2016, researchers found that at least seven of the top ten most-mentioned athletes in each year's primetime coverage were Americans (Billings et al., 2018). Not only were they being featured, but in some cases, the announcers were openly rooting for the United States medalists. When an American swimmer won the 100-meter freestyle race in 2016, NBC's swimming analyst, Rowdy Gaines, shouted, "I am one happy camper!" during the broadcast (Sandomir, 2016, para. 6).

A counter to the argument that the pro-American bias is negative for viewers is that NBC is the American home for the Olympics, so showcasing more American athletes does make sense considering the audience. In addition, NBC could also rightly point out that it is simply showing the best athletes. The U.S. team is traditionally among the top two or three overall medal winners at the Olympics, so this pro-American bias could be more a reflection of the success of the U.S. team and less of a conscious programming decision. NBC is also not alone in their displays of patriotism. On China's CCTV telecast, announcers will use personal pronouns such as "us" to describe Chinese athletes and "them" when referring to the—creating an "us versus them" scenario (Billings et al., 2011).

## Primarily Showing Certain Sports and Athletes

Instead of NBC showcasing a little bit of every Olympic event, the network tends to devote the vast majority of its primetime coverage to a select few sports. For example, if a viewer is a fan of archery, taekwondo, or rowing, then they are likely going to be out of luck when it comes to seeing their favorite sport on NBC's nighttime coverage. However, fans of swimming will be able to see just about every race during the Games.

When the Tokyo Olympics took place in 2021, NBC showed just over 43.5 hours of competition during primetime. Of that time, NBC spent 32 hours showing only 6 of the 74 sports: women's gymnastics, women's beach volleyball, both men's and women's swimming, and both men's and women's track and field (see figure 4.1). That means, of all the sports to choose from to broadcast, NBC spent almost 75 percent of the primetime schedule on just those six. Thirty-five sports had less than a minute's worth of airtime during

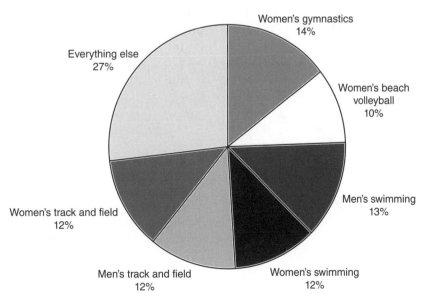

**FIGURE 4.1**  Primetime coverage of sports by NBC in the 2021 Olympics.
Data from Billings et al. (2021).

primetime, with some not getting a single second on the broadcast (Billings et al., 2021).

In some cases, the divide is striking among the sex of the athletes. Fans of gymnastics could have watched nearly six and a half hours of women's action, but less than two hours of men's. That divide is even larger in beach volleyball, where the men's games were on in primetime for just five minutes while the women's games were broadcast for four hours and 20 minutes (Billings et al., 2021).

## Tape-Delayed Events

While an American bias and primarily focusing on certain events have upset viewers, there is seemingly nothing that gets audiences riled up more than NBC's decision to show events on **tape delay**. In this scenario, NBC records an event as it is happening and, instead of showing it live, broadcasts that recorded version in the evening. For many years, this meant that fans of specific sports would have to wait hours before seeing the event. NBC's television hosts would admit that what they were about to show had happened earlier in the day but would not reveal the results beforehand. Executives with the network labeled this practice as showing events "plausibly live" (Sandomir, 2012, para. 1).

Before the Internet gave fans immediate access to scores and results, tape delaying event coverage did not lead to nearly the same amount of frustration that occurs now. However, thanks to instant access of scores and results online, fans now know exactly what happened as soon as the event is over. The idea of making viewers wait several hours to see something that is already completed has many fans frustrated. In some very publicized missteps, NBC has demonstrated it has not perfected the practice of tape delay. Just minutes before airing swimmer Missy Franklin's prerecorded 100-meter backstroke race in the 2012 Olympics, a commercial promoted Franklin's appearance on the next day's episode of *Today* and spoiled the fact that she was just about to win the gold medal in that race (Strecker, 2012).

While NBC attracts the most attention for their "plausibly live" tactics, the network is hardly the first to show the Games in this manner. Both ABC and CBS used the practice of tape delay when they were the broadcast home of the Olympics. In fact, two of the most recognizable events in Olympics history were both tape delayed: the Miracle on Ice in 1980 by ABC and the Nancy Kerrigan versus Tonya Harding figure skating session in 1994 by CBS (Sandomir, 2010). For the U.S.A. versus U.S.S.R. hockey game, the action began at 5 p.m., but the game was over by the time it began during the primetime coverage at 8 p.m. (Allen, 2015). Not only was it delayed, but the most famous hockey game in American history was also not even shown in its entirety, as ABC edited out several portions of the game to save time. Executives later admitted they expected the Soviet Union to win in a blowout, so they had plans to show other sports during the action when the U.S. deficit became too great (Sandomir, 2000).

## NBC's Reasoning for These Decisions

While the pro-American bias, focus on certain sports, and tape delaying events are decisions made by NBC that are often criticized, the reasoning behind them often comes down to money. With the network spending billions of dollars to broadcast the Games, they need to maximize their viewership numbers to recoup some of that money with advertising sales. NBC's Olympic leadership team has determined that showing more Americans, especially in sports in which American athletes excel, during a time when most people can watch, will lead to the highest number of viewers. While this determination might upset many, the numbers back up NBC's decision to show the Games in this manner. For the 2012 Olympics in London, NBC elected to tape delay nearly everything so that it all could be aired in primetime in the United States. That decision resulted in what was, at the time, the most watched television event in history. That allowed NBC to charge prime rates for advertising, which earned them $1.25 billion from ad sales (McNear, 2016). While many seemingly disliked these tape delay tactics, it did not stop viewers from watching.

In some cases, NBC has little choice but to tape delay events due to where the Olympics are taking place. When the Games are on the other side of the world, the start and finish times are often the exact opposite of when most people would be watching in the United States. Tokyo, Japan, is 13 hours ahead of America's East Coast, meaning Tokyo Olympics events started at sunrise on New York's time. During the 2021 Tokyo Olympics, when American gymnast Suni Lee won the gold medal, it was just after 9 a.m. in New York (ESPN, 2021). Showing her event during that time period would not result in the best viewership numbers. During the 2000 Olympics in Australia, NBC broadcaster Bob Costas said the time difference forced the network to sometimes show events the next day. "I was presenting events that in some cases I had attended and that I then read about in the Sydney newspaper while being driven to the broadcast center," Costas said (Sandomir, 2012, para. 6). While NBC does have some influence on what time the events begin, such as the year they convinced Olympic officials to start the swimming finals at 10 a.m. local time in Beijing so Michael Phelps's races would be live in primetime in the United States (Crouse, 2008), they are often at the mercy of the local and Olympic officials.

While time zones play a key role in the decision to tape delay some of the competition, NBC executives have also stated that Olympic viewers are different from the traditional sports fan. Specifically, NBC's chief marketing officer John Miller stated:

> The people who watch the Olympics are not particularly sports fans. More women watch the Games than men, and for the women, they're less interested in the result and more interested in the journey. It's sort of like the ultimate reality show and mini-series wrapped into one. (Tannenwald, 2016, para. 23)

By tape delaying the events, NBC can focus more on the personalities and the story. Instead of waiting for a competitor to start, the network will showcase athletes by talking about their upbringing, training, or obstacles that they have overcome. Once the audience has devel-

oped a reason to cheer for the athletes and is emotionally invested in how they do, NBC can immediately begin playing the recorded action from earlier.

## Streaming to Curb Complaints

Despite the criticisms, NBC has continued to broadcast its primetime coverage in the same manner. However, the network has also taken steps to appease those who want live coverage. One way in which it has been able to show more events is through the use of cable channels affiliated with NBC. However, the biggest change is in viewers' ability to watch more events through online streaming. Starting in 2008, NBC began showing live online coverage for the first time, with over 2,000 hours available online (NBC New York, 2008). By 2021, the network was streaming over 5,500 hours of live coverage, including every sport and every medal event (NBC Sports Group Press Box, 2021). Fans could now watch the sports and athletes they wanted, live, instead of just getting what NBC was showing on a tape-delayed format. While television viewership was down tremendously for the 2022 Winter Olympics, some argued that those numbers were not telling the whole story.

Jamie Squire/Getty Images

When Suni Lee won the gold medal in the 2021 Tokyo Olympics, NBC broadcast it on tape delay.

One journalist argued that "the 2022 Olympics will be one of the most-watched events in U.S. history. It's just that we're watching on our phones and in our browsers" (Socolow, 2022, para. 3). The author cited the fact that some YouTube videos of Olympic highlights were getting over ten million views and were not counted as part of television viewership (Socolow, 2022). After the 2022 Olympics concluded, NBC announced that viewers had streamed 4.3 billion minutes of content during the event, up 78 percent from four years earlier (Battaglio, 2022).

# NBC's Gatekeeping of the Olympics

As discussed in chapter 1, the concept of gatekeeping plays a key role in how people consume sports. With their exclusive contract to broadcast the Olympics in the United States, NBC is the gatekeeper to how most Americans will watch the events. The network determines which sports are shown on the broadcast and which athletes are given a spotlight. In the 2021 Tokyo Olympics, there were 339 different events in 33 sports, with around 11,000 athletes competing (Ansari, 2022). While NBC has paid billions of dollars for the rights to show every single sport and athlete on its network, only a select few of each have traditionally been shown on television.

NBC was acting as the gatekeeper by deciding which events and athletes would be shown to the television audience. The network's executives, much like the newspaper editors discussed in chapter 1, decided which sports would be of the most interest to the largest audience and chose to focus most of NBC's primetime coverage on those sports. While this resulted in high viewership, it also created many complaints from those looking to see some of the less popular sports. By emphasizing specific sports and athletes, the network was creating a situation in which viewers were not getting the full picture of what was happening during the Olympics. Instead, they were only getting the option to watch the specific events that NBC was allowing them to see. Therefore, while it might seem strange, viewers were not really watching the full Olympic Games; they were actually watching NBC's version of the Olympics.

However, just as streaming has helped to reduce some of the complaints about NBC's Olympic coverage, it has also redefined the network's role as the gatekeeper. Fans are no longer at NBC's mercy when it comes to what events they can watch. With streaming available seemingly all day online, fans can pick and choose what events they want to watch and at what time. A fan of a less publicized sport can now log onto one of the network's streaming options and see nearly every minute of the action from that event. Even NBC's Dick Ebersol noted this change, saying back in 2008: "For the first time, the average American will be able to create their own unique Olympic experience whether at home, at the office or on-the-go" (NBC New York, 2008, para. 4).

# Summary

In the United States, the Olympics and NBC are nearly synonymous. After decades of rotating between broadcast partners ABC, CBS, and NBC, the Games ultimately became the exclusive property of NBC thanks to billion-dollar agreements with the network. Since 2000, an American cannot watch the events without watching at least one of the channels in the NBCUniversal family. While NBC devotes hours of primetime coverage to the Olympics during the two weeks of the Games, those broadcasts are not without controversy. The network is often criticized for its focus on specific events, athletes, and the desire to show only the most popular events during primetime—even if that means tape delaying the broadcast. However, NBC's pivot to online streaming has created a scenario in which viewers can watch nearly every minute of every event, allowing them to bypass NBC's role as the gatekeeper of the Olympics.

## KEY TERMS

**newsreels**—Short films of news and current events that were shown in movie theaters.
**primetime**—The hours between 8 p.m. and 11 p.m. in which television viewership is traditionally the largest.
**tape delay**—The process of recording an event and showing it at a later time.

## REVIEW QUESTIONS

1. Now that you have read about how NBC shows the Olympics, what do you think? Does NBC show the Olympic in the proper way? If not, what would you do differently?
2. The NBC chief marketing officer said that more women watch the Olympics than men, and women are less interested in the results

and more interested in the journey. What do you think about that statement?

3. Television networks seem to believe that streaming is the future of watching television, not just for sports content. For an event like the Olympics, what are the pros and cons of streaming for the viewer?

4. The Olympics are considered one of the most desirable television programs that a network can broadcast. Will that still be the case in 20 years? If you were running a network, would you bid on the Olympics?

# 5

# Sports Illustrated

## CHAPTER OBJECTIVES

After completing the chapter, the reader should be able to do the following:

- Identify the key moments in the history of *Sports Illustrated*
- Understand why media outlets would be motivated to do a brand extension
- Analyze the ethical and moral issues involved with the yearly swimsuit issue
- Evaluate the future of the magazine industry as a whole

For decades, the most trusted name in the sports media was *Sports Illustrated* (commonly abbreviated to *SI*). Sports fans would read it cover-to-cover, writers considered it a dream job, photographers wanted their photos to be featured, and athletes who were the subjects of stories were some of the most recognizable in the world, even when those same athletes did not necessarily want to be on the cover of the magazine. In addition to articles about the latest sports news, one issue a year quickly became one of the most controversial in the entire magazine industry. However, as the media landscape has changed, *SI* has seen a decrease in readership and has struggled to remain relevant among a younger audience.

## The Early Years of *Sports Illustrated*

In the early 1950s, Time Inc. founder Henry Luce was leading a publishing empire. With several top-selling magazines already in his company's portfolio, Luce decided that sports would be the subject of his next weekly initiative. However, not everyone in the company shared his excitement. Several of his top advisers argued against developing a sports magazine, saying that it would be expensive to produce and, perhaps more importantly, that there was not a demand for sports content among readers or advertisers. Despite the opposition, Luce pushed forward with his goal to create a sports-only magazine (MacCambridge, 1997).

The first issue of *Sports Illustrated* hit newsstands in August 1954. Baseball player Eddie Mathews graced the cover of the 144-page debut edition, with an action photo of him mid-swing in front of a stadium full of fans. However, the cover of the first issue was not indicative of what the early days of the magazine turned out to be. Instead of being targeted exclusively at sports spectators with recaps and previews of the biggest games, the magazine's management focused equally on sporting participants. They hoped to attract an audience that was more upscale, and those watching sports were considered anything but. One Time Inc. executive said that the people who might read a magazine about sports were "either juveniles or ne'er-do-wells and the advertising agencies know it" (MacCambridge, 1997, p. 22), implying that no company would spend money advertising in a magazine with that type of readership. This led to covers that depicted fishing, yachting, and horseback riding. However, this also created some covers that today would be looked upon as curious for a sports magazine. For example, a May 1955 cover touted the issue as the "Bird Watchers' Guide," with a cartoon of several birds in a tree, while another cover from that year featured two dachshunds named Jewell and Adele with an accompanying article inside about that breed of dog and how "more people are wanting to pet it all the time" (Wells, 1955, p. 36). As an *SI* writer noted in the magazine's 35th anniversary issue, it was not normal sports fare: "In our first four years we devoted 15 covers to horses, eight to dogs, five to birds—counting one that was dead and in the mouth of one of the dogs— four to fish and one each to a seal, a monkey and a lion" (Wulf, 1989, p. 12). This early strategy to focus more on participatory sports and less on professional sports proved to be a misstep. In a survey of those who had canceled their subscriptions, the number one reason given for opting out was the minimal amount of coverage that was being devoted to major sporting events (MacCambridge, 1997).

In the early years, those who cautioned against starting a sports magazine appeared to be correct. It took more than 12 years before *SI* became profitable, with the magazine losing $6 million in just the first five months it was in print in 1954 (MacCambridge, 1997). Advertisers were still not convinced that the average sports fan was worth targeting, so the magazine struggled to attract sponsors that could help offset the early sales struggles. The first issue had 74 pages of advertisements, but the remaining 19 issues in 1954 had only 244 ad pages total for an average of less than 13 per issue (MacCambridge, 1997).

In order to stand out from the competition, *SI* did something that many magazines at the time were avoiding: printing photos in color. Many magazines in the 1950s and 1960s were entirely in black and white; however, *SI*'s leaders correctly determined that they could not compete with daily newspapers when it came to delivering timely information, and so color photographs were seen as a way to set the magazine apart. The technology would not allow for the color photos to be current (from the big boxing match of the previous week, for example), but the editors could plan weeks ahead with photos that they believed would be of interest when the issue was ready to print.

*Sports Illustrated* ultimately became the most successful sports magazine of all time, and that climb to the

The first issue of *Sports Illustrated* was published August 16, 1954.

Susan Wood/Getty Images

pinnacle came in harmony with the growth of television. Thanks to the newfound prominence of television in the 1960s, more people could watch sports at home, thus increasing the public's interest in the games and athletes. *Sports Illustrated* quickly pivoted, and the focus on participatory sports was replaced with an eye on the biggest and most popular sporting events. New editor André Laguerre helped guide the magazine to become more of a preview and recap of sports news, with less emphasis on the participatory sports that had dominated the first years of its history.

# The Cover

For nearly every magazine, the cover image is perhaps the most important element of each issue. The cover is what draws people to pick it up at a newsstand and then, the editors hope, purchase that issue and then subscribe. While the articles provide the information, experts say it is the cover that "sets a mood" for the entire issue (McManus, 1976, p. 195) and gives prominence to the subject that is portrayed (Spiker, 2003). Once *SI*'s leaders made the editorial decision to focus more on spectator sports, being on the cover of the magazine meant that, for that one week, that athlete was one of the most important people in the sporting world. At the time of this writing, basketball superstar Michael Jordan has appeared on the cover the most times, but that has not been something with which he has always been entirely happy.

In 1993, Jordan retired from basketball to play professional baseball. He signed with the Chicago White Sox to play for one of their minor league affiliates. However, the transition from basketball to baseball was not a smooth one, and the NBA champion struggled mightily in his early games. In response to his start, *SI* put a Jordan at-bat on the cover with a photo of him swinging at and missing a pitch; the words "Bag it, Michael!" ran in large, bold yellow letters. The small text below that read, "Jordan and The White Sox Are Embarrassing Baseball." While the statistics might have backed up *SI*'s claim, it was criticism that Jordan never forgot or forgave. Since that cover was printed in 1994, Jordan has refused to speak to *SI* or pose for any future covers. Instead, any subsequent interviews with Jordan in the magazine came from press conferences, and the cover photos were action shots from games (Bulls Insider, 2020).

Despite the accolades that one would assume would go along with being on the cover of *SI*, there are some athletes who do not want to be on it. In fact, the cover is associated more with a jinx than it is with success. One research study found that over 37 percent of those who have been on the cover have had something bad happen to them in the following weeks (Smith, 2002). This could be anything from significant losses to winning streaks being snapped to an injury. For example, in 2010 four members of the New York Yankees posed for a cover photo; within a week, three of those four were injured (Marchand, 2010). In 1998, boxer Michael Spinks posed for a cover photo with "Don't count me out" as the caption before his championship fight with Mike Tyson. Just days after that issue hit newsstands, Spinks was knocked out in 91 seconds by Tyson and never boxed again (Parco, 2016). *SI* even acknowledged the curse itself with a 2002 cover that had a photo of a black cat with the words "The cover that no one would pose for. Is the *SI* jinx for real?" (Smith, 2002).

# Readership

There were 350,000 subscribers when the magazine started, and almost 90 percent of the issues available on the newsstand were purchased, giving SI the largest circulation number for a new magazine in history (MacCambridge, 1997). **Circulation** refers to the number of issues that have been distributed through both subscription and newsstand sales, so a high circulation number traditionally represents that a magazine is successful. By 1960, the magazine had a circulation of nearly one million readers each week; it reached two million readers by the mid-1970s and three million by the mid-1980s (Bevis, n.d.; MacCambridge, 1997). By 1989, SI had reached a peak circulation of 3.5 million (Wulf, 1989). However, for reasons that will be discussed later in this chapter, the circulation totals for SI dropped dramatically in the years since. In 2018, the number of issues sold through subscription or newsstand sales was down to 2.75 million before falling to less than 2 million by 2020 (Lee, 2020; MacCambridge, 2018).

# Special Issues

While the editors and writers at *Sports Illustrated* are best known for the latest news and feature stories, there are special issues each year that are designed to go beyond the traditional weekly previews and recaps. These special issues are often dedicated to one specific topic and are created to boost readership. Examples of special issues include season previews with regional covers, the Sportsperson of the Year issue, and perhaps the most famous single issue in the entire magazine industry—the yearly swimsuit issue.

## Season Previews and Regional Covers

Some of the most anticipated issues each year are the season preview issues for both professional and college sports. For example, the Major League Baseball preview issue in 2021 contained a brief preview of all 30 teams, feature stories about key players and executives, and a World Series winner prediction (the Atlanta Braves, which proved correct). These special issues provide a detailed synopsis for everything that happened in the offseason and outline what needs to happen in the upcoming season for each team to be successful.

While the magazine employed some of the top sportswriters in the business for decades, that does not mean every prediction was as spot-on as the 2021 World Series winner. In fact, one of the magazine's most memorable predictions was also in baseball: In 1987, two players from the Cleveland Indians were on the MLB season preview cover, and the writers predicted the team would be the best in the American League. Instead, Cleveland finished with the worst record in all of baseball (Posnanski, 2017). Perhaps this was, yet again, an example of the cover jinx in action.

Another added twist to these season previews is that for some issues, not everyone in the United States receives the same cover photo. Instead, the cover image that subscribers and newsstand readers receive is based on where they live. For example, the 2019 college football issue had a headline of "Year of the QB" no matter which issue a reader received. However, the player featured on that cover varied depending on where the issue was being sold or sent to subscribers. Quarterbacks Trevor Lawrence (Clemson University), Jake Fromm (University of Georgia), Sam Ehlinger (University of Texas), and Justin Herbert (University of Oregon) were on four different covers and were featured in the area where there was predicted to be the most interest in that player (Lombardi, 2019). Newsstands on the West Coast would sell the version with the Oregon player, while subscribers in the Southeast would likely get the quarterback from the University of Georgia on the cover. *SI* uses these regional covers to increase excitement about the issue in various regions, which they hope will translate to higher sales.

## Sportsperson of the Year

One of the last issues of each year is the Sportsperson of the Year edition. Unlike the Most Valuable Player awards given out in the different leagues, *SI*'s year-end honor does not necessarily go to the best player in all of sports. Instead, the award is given to the "athlete or team whose performance that year most embodies the spirit of sportsmanship and achievement" (Chavez, 2017, para. 1). The concept debuted during the magazine's first year and was given to Roger Bannister after he was the first person to run a sub-four-minute mile (Holland, 1955). Originally, the award was named the Sportsman of the Year, and that title was appropriate based on who was being chosen for the award. It was not until 1972 that the first woman would win (Billie Jean King), and only 7 of the first 50 years of the award (1954-2003) featured a woman honoree. In those years only, it was renamed the Sportswoman of the Year before permanently changing to Sportsperson of the Year in 2015 when tennis player Serena Williams was named the winner (Price, 2015).

## Swimsuit Issue

While season previews with regional covers and the Sportsperson of the Year award are both designed to bring in new readers, there is no more anticipated edition each year—both positively and negatively—than the swimsuit issue. In January 1964, the magazine ran a story titled "Swimsuits that are made to get wet" with five accompanying pictures of women in bathing suits and a photo of a woman in a bikini on the cover (Smith, 1964, p. 7). While not officially labeled a swimsuit issue by the editors at the time, it is widely recognized as the first in the series.

The creation of the swimsuit issue came about due to a void in the sports calendar. Editors were looking for content during the slow winter months between college football bowl games and baseball's spring training (Deford, 1989). With no major sporting events on the calendar, editors wanted to create a reason for people to purchase the magazine during that time. The plan worked brilliantly, as the swimsuit issue quickly became the signature edition in the magazine's yearly portfolio. For decades, it was part of a regular weekly issue of the magazine, with photos of the swimsuit models followed by articles about traditional sports. In 1997, *SI* began treating it as its own special edition and sent out two issues to subscribers and newsstands that

Stephen Lovekin / Getty Images

In 2012, LeBron James was chosen as SI's Sportsman of the Year. James would be honored again in 2016 and 2020, making him the only three-time honoree.

week—one regular with the latest sports news and one that focused solely on the swimsuits and the models in them (Isidore, 2005).

## Popularity

The editors' goal of creating a special issue that would help fill the downtime during the slow winter months was realized above and beyond what they likely could have imagined. A 2011 article estimated that *SI* had sold one million copies of the swimsuit issue on the newsstand, which is ten times more than most regular issues of the magazine (Kelly, 2011). *SI* believed that 34 million adults read the 1987 edition (Deford, 1989), while the 1989 edition, which was the 25th anniversary edition of the swimsuit issue, is the best-selling issue—swimsuit or otherwise—in the magazine's long history (Fleder, 2005).

With millions of people reading each yearly edition, the models in the issue—especially those on the cover—have become celebrities themselves. The women have turned their cover appearances into acting jobs, endorsement deals, and even more lucrative modeling opportunities. Kathy Ireland, who appeared in 13 editions of the swimsuit issue, including three covers, started a career as a successful entrepreneur. She said, "Nothing had a greater impact on launching my career than Jule [Campbell, the swimsuit issue's longtime editor] and 13 years of appearing in *SI*" (Lippe-McGraw, 2022, para. 3).

## Criticism

The most obvious criticism lobbed at *Sports Illustrated* when it comes to the swimsuit issue is: What do bikini-clad models have to do with sports? The magazine's editors attempted to bring some focus back to the sporting world by having some women athletes pose in swimsuits, but that has not slowed the calls of sexism from many detractors of the issue. Some say the issue promotes **hegemonic masculinity**, defined as the idea that men are dominant in society over women. Essentially, the argument states, the magazine, with a mostly male readership, puts women on display in sexual poses for men to gaze at (Davis, 1997).

While millions of readers pay for *SI* to be delivered to their home, that does not mean they are all happy about the inclusion of the swimsuit issue. Dating all the way back to the very first edition in 1954, readers have sent in letters to the editor complaining about its contents. The first published letter expressing outrage at the photos stated, "I most certainly do not want such pictures coming into my home for my young teen-age son to ogle, much less myself" (Curtis, 2010, para 8).

The outrage hit a new high in 1978 when a photo of model Cheryl Tiegs in a fishnet bathing suit with her nipples exposed caused more than 340 people to cancel their subscriptions (MacCambridge, 1997). The magazine would eventually give subscribers the option of not having the swimsuit issue be delivered.

An additional criticism of the swimsuit issue was that the models were almost exclusively White. To combat that claim, and in an attempt to be more representative of the entire population, *SI* expanded the portfolio of model demographics throughout the years. In 1996, Tyra Banks became the first African American to appear on the cover of the swimsuit issue, the first of her three appearances in that spot (Trebay, 2019). In 2021, the magazine proclaimed that year's issue to be the most diverse ever, with a transgender person on the cover and pages filled with models representing a variety of body types, sizes, colors, and ages (Cohen, 2021).

### A Moneymaker

Love it or hate it, it is impossible to ignore that the swimsuit issue has been big business for *Sports Illustrated* and its longtime publisher, Time Inc. The issue became one of the strongest revenue drivers for the company, bringing in more than $1 billion since its debut. In 2005 alone, the issue generated $35 million in sales of advertisements; this single issue represents 7 percent of the advertising revenue for the entire year (Madden, 2013; Spector, 2013). It is not just a moneymaker for the magazine and its publishers. The 2004 issue featured a photoshoot in Chile that resulted in a 34 percent increase in visitors to the country according to Chile's Board of Tourism. A boost in sales can also be seen by the manufacturers of the swimsuit and jewelry worn by the models (CNBC, 2010).

With the amount of money involved in the swimsuit issue, it should come as no surprise that *SI* looked to capitalize further on that popularity. The magazine introduced the swimsuit edition calendar and a behind-the-scenes video about the making of the issue. Later investments included reality television shows, Internet exclusives, and even trading cards. By 2005, these additional swimsuit issue offerings had brought in an extra $10 million in revenue for the magazine (Isidore, 2005). In 2017, Time Inc. announced the creation of Sports Illustrated Swimsuit Enterprises to partner with models for business opportunities and, perhaps not surprisingly, market Sports Illustrated Swimsuit Issue swimsuits (Grant, 2017).

# Brand Extension

While the magazine itself was traditionally the focus of the *SI* team, they have also used the concept of a brand extension in order to bring in new readers. A **brand extension** is when a company uses its established brand name on a new product to give that product extra credibility at launch. Three ways in which *SI* created new brands under its umbrella was through new magazines, television, and the Internet.

## New Magazines

As can probably be expected, the *Sports Illustrated* brand was deemed to be especially important when the company launched new sports magazines aimed at narrowly targeted audiences. *SI*'s median reader is a 38-year-old White male that has a higher-than-average household income (Bredholt, 2012). While that type of reader is reflected in the content in the various issues, it also gives the magazine an opportunity to reach other readers through alternative means.

The first attempt at a spinoff debuted in 1989 with the introduction of *Sports Illustrated for Kids*. The concept was a monthly youth sports magazine that targeted both boys and girls from the ages of 8 to 13 (MacCambridge, 1997). In a pitch to advertisers, executives stated that *SI Kids* "presents sports the way kids want to read about them, providing the ultimate destination for great action photos, easy-to-read stories about athletes, helpful tips from the pros, humor, comics, and a host of fun activities" (SI Kids Media Kit, 2021, para. 3). Issues contain articles that are written at the reading level for that age group, trading cards that can be torn out of each issue, and a poster. At the magazine's debut, the editors had a goal of breaking even financially by year five, but they exceeded that expectation by becoming profitable by the third year (MacCambridge, 1997).

While *SI for Kids* became a successful spinoff for Time Inc., that was the exception to the company's efforts. For example, *Sports Illustrated for Women* (later shortened to *SI Women*) debuted in March 2000. The magazine's goal was to focus strictly on women's sports by being "aimed at women ages 18-34 who have a passion for sports as participants and fans and who strive to lead active and healthy lifestyles" (Affinito, 2000, para. 3). In November 2002, after just 20 issues, Time Inc. ceased publication of *SI Women*, citing a need for a bigger financial investment that was not going to be possible at the time due to a downturn in the economy (Media Life, 2002).

Lisa Lake/Getty Images for Sports Illustrated

**Reece Whitley poses with his 2015 Sportskid of the Year cover.**

In 2005, Time Inc. launched *SI Latino*, a Spanish-language magazine that was published six times a year and sent free to *SI* subscribers who identified as Latino. Original articles were created, not translations of already published articles, and each issue was smaller than the traditional issue of *SI* (Liebeskind, 2005). However, just like *SI Women*, the magazine only lasted a few years, and *SI Latino*'s run ended in 2008 (Kelly, 2008). Other titles such as *Sports Illustrated Australia* and *Sports Illustrated on Campus* met similar fates within a few years after each magazine's debut.

## Television

In addition to expanding into other magazines, the *SI* brand also attempted to take on ESPN's television empire through a partnership with CNN. The channel CNN/SI debuted in 1996 as a 24-hour sports cable network that focused on news, not live games, so the content was almost exclusively highlights and reports from *SI*'s writers. Those involved with this channel quickly realized that ESPN's head start as the cable television home for sports would be too much to overcome. While the ESPN family of networks was available in nearly 90 million homes, CNN/SI was only in 20 million (Associated Press, 2002). That made it much harder to get advertisers to pay top dollar, as companies would much rather pitch their products on the channel with more viewers.

After less than six years of running a financial deficit, the network went off the air in 2002 (Associated Press, 2002). Perhaps most aggravating for those at *SI* who were hoping to expand into television is that instead of competing with ESPN, they could have been colleagues. Back in 1984, Time Inc. was presented with an opportunity to purchase ESPN from its then-owners but ultimately passed, allowing ABC to buy the network instead (MacCambridge, 2018).

## Internet

*SI*'s website debuted in the late 1990s and contained the latest news and opinions from the world of sports. In addition, many of the magazine's top writers produced online-only content to help drive traffic to what would eventually become SI.com. Perhaps the best example of this was the wildly popular Monday Morning Quarterback column written by *SI*'s Peter King. The column was longer than most articles that appeared in the magazine thanks to the lack of space limitations on the Internet. Monday Morning Quarterback was the most popular column on SI.com, reaching more than ten million readers a month, until King's departure from the company in 2018 (MacCambridge, 2018; Wagner, 2017). In 2021, *SI*'s co-editor-in-chief announced that the company's website would move to a subscription model for certain premium content. Several sections that were previously free to access on SI.com would now cost about $5 a month, including access to the digital archives of every article that had appeared in the print version of the magazine (McCarthy, 2021).

## A Changing Media Landscape

While the Internet has given people greater access to results and stories, it has also shifted the media landscape. Sports fans no longer want to wait hours, let alone several days, to get the latest information. Therefore, news sources that do not give immediate updates—such as weekly magazines—have suffered. Fans do not want to sit around until Thursday's issue of *SI* arrives in their mailbox to get the recap of Sunday's Super Bowl.

Magazine sales have also been hurt by the new ways in which people buy books. For years, large bookstores were where people would buy the latest best-sellers and browse an expansive magazine section. However, many of these major book retailers are either out of business or have closed many of their stores due to people doing more book-buying online. With fewer places to buy magazines, circulation has dropped for many. In 2007, magazine industry newsstand sales were $4.9 billion, but that number dropped to $2 billion by 2017. In addition, by 2018, 6 percent of a magazine's circulation came directly from single-issue sales, down from 20 percent just 10 years earlier (Silber, 2018). As stated previously, *SI* has not been immune from this changing landscape, as circulation had been cut nearly in half by 2020 from its peak in 1989.

## New Ownership

For decades, Time Inc. was one of the most prominent companies in the magazine industry. It published some of the top-selling brands, including *Time*, *People*, and *Sports Illustrated*. However, financial challenges for the company forced management to look for new ownership, and in late 2017 Time Inc. was purchased by the Meredith Corporation for nearly $3 billion (Stelter & Gold, 2018). While a boon for many of those in the Time Inc. family, *Sports Illustrated* was the odd one out. Meredith Corporation focused lifestyle magazines marketed to a female audience, such as *Better Homes and Gardens*, and a sports magazine aimed at a male audience did not appear to fit in their portfolio. Perhaps not surprisingly, Meredith sold *SI* to Authentic Brands less than two years later (Kelly, 2019).

However, this also appeared to be an odd fit. Authentic Brands is a marketing company, not a publisher. Therefore, Authentic Brands was less interested in the physical magazine than in the intellectual property of the brand name. A month after that sale, another company, Maven, took over the publishing of the magazine and the SI.com website (Kelly, 2019).

## Fewer Issues

As *Sports Illustrated* was cycling through ownership groups, it was also undergoing changes to the magazine. Perhaps most prominently, the weekly issues were becoming a thing of the past. Starting in 2018, the magazine's editor announced that *SI* would now be published every other week. As a tradeoff for fewer issues, the editor said that these new editions would be larger with more long-form stories and photos (Edmonds, 2018).

In 2020, the number of issues decreased even further. The magazine began sending just one issue a month, plus four special issues and the swimsuit issue—totaling just 17 issues in an entire year. Additionally, each magazine had to be sent to the printer at least three weeks before the publishing date, meaning every issue was now even more dated than before (Roberts, 2019). Instead of being able to do a Super Bowl preview issue, *SI*'s writers would now have to write generic feature articles because they would not even know what teams were in the game. Timeliness has long been an issue with the magazine, but the move to monthly issues made that problem even more noticeable.

## Summary

Before the days of immediate access to the latest sporting news through cable channels, websites, and social media, *Sports Illustrated* was considered by many to be the crown jewel of the sports media. While local newspapers had stories about athletes from that city, *SI* exposed fans to a national sporting world. With full-color photographs and award-winning writing, the magazine quickly became a must-read for many. Along the way, *SI* branched out from sports to create the swimsuit issue, a yearly staple that attracted both criticism for detractors and millions of dollars from advertisers. As the media landscape shifted, the magazine attempted several spinoffs with varying levels of success. In the late 2010s, what was once an industry leader was now cutting issues and content, trying to maintain its place in a crowded sports media market.

### KEY TERMS

**brand extension**—When a company uses its established brand name on a new product to give that product extra credibility at launch.

**circulation**—The number of issues that have been distributed through both subscription and newsstand sales.

**hegemonic masculinity**—The idea that men are dominant in society over women.

## REVIEW QUESTIONS

1. *SI* was a money loser for the first decade of its existence. What were the key factors that helped turn it around and make it one of the most prominent sports media entities in history?

2. The "Sportsperson of the Year" award does not necessarily go to the best athlete each year, but instead has a focus on sportsmanship. How does this influence who wins the award?

3. Should the swimsuit edition still exist? There are many who are in favor of it and many who are critical, but should it still be around in modern times?

4. *SI* was once one of the most prominent ways in which sports fans received news about their favorite teams and leagues. However, technology might ultimately be one of its biggest downfalls. What are some examples of how technology affected *SI* negatively?

# 6

# Social Media in Sports

## CHAPTER OBJECTIVES

After completing the chapter, the reader should be able to do the following:

- Understand what social media is
- Define the seven key elements of social media
- Identify how social media has influenced the ways teams, fans, and players communicate with each other
- Understand how the professions within mass communications have changed due to the use of social media

*Chapter note: Shortly before this book was published, the social media platform Twitter was rebranded to X. Due to the timing of the announcement, it will be still be referred to as Twitter in this chapter and in others.*

There would likely be a spirited debate about what developments have led to the biggest changes in how sports are consumed and promoted among fans, teams, and leagues. Some might suggest the increased availability of cable television created a scenario in which more games than ever could be televised. On-demand media with video and podcasts allowed fans to consume content at their convenience. That is just a start, as there are numerous other answers that might qualify as the most impactful in the world of sports. However, one answer that might come up repeatedly is *social media*. Fans and teams are now able to communicate with each other in ways that were previously unavailable.

## Social Media Definition

Before getting into the influence that social media has had, it is worth examining what exactly social media is. As Hull and Abeza (2021) noted, the phrase **social media** is made up of two very distinct words that influence the definition. *Social* addresses how people are connected with others, while *media* is the mode of information delivery. Therefore, based on those two words, a possible definition for social media could be: Online resources open to the public that people use primarily to share content and engage in two-way conversation on Internet applications (Hull & Abeza, 2021).

## Characteristics of Social Media

While there have been numerous technological advances throughout the years that have influenced communication, there are a few aspects of social media that make it different from other platforms. Researchers have identified seven elements as defining characteristics of social media (Hennig-Thurau et al., 2010; Hull & Abeza, 2021):

- *Community Driven*: Users can create content that can be commented on or reacted to, which cultivates an online community.
- *Content Availability*: Social media activities are visible to other users and can be seen instantly after being produced as well as long afterward.
- *Dynamism*: Social media platforms are constantly evolving in terms of features and tools.
- *Multipurpose*: Social media platforms can be used for a wide range of purposes.
- *No gatekeeper*: Users create and post content without needing approval from another person or administrative body. Chapter 1 of this book has more information on gatekeeping.
- *Omnipresence*: Users can reach others at any time, with few limitations on location or boundaries. Social media is "always on."
- *User-Generated Content*: Users produce the content that is posted on social media. In previous mediums, the writers/editors/publishers of the site would create the content and the audience could only consume it.

Figure 6.1 illustrates these characteristics.

# Social Media in Sports Leagues and Teams

While social media has a place in nearly every industry, it has perhaps made one of its biggest impacts as an important communication device in sports. For sports leagues and teams, social media provides an opportunity to directly reach a large audience. For example, the Twitter account for the NBA's Sacramento Kings can send scores, news, highlights, behind-the-scenes stories, shopping opportunities, and game reminders to the more than one million fans that follow that account. An examination of the Instagram activity of Major League Baseball teams found that posts fell into one of four categories: business objectives (such as selling tickets or merchandise), sporting objectives (such as game action), charitable organization (such as visits to hospitals), or non-baseball-related posts (Kim & Hull, 2017). It can be assumed that most teams use social media for three main reasons:

- Growing the brand
- Engaging fans
- Generating money

*Growing the brand* involves attempting to make the team more relevant and popular. This is especially helpful for smaller organizations or those without decades of history. In Major League Baseball, the New York Yankees

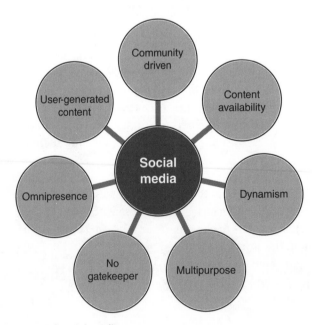

**FIGURE 6.1**  Defining characteristics of social media.

have existed since 1903 and have multiple generations of fans who live and die with every pitch. While the Yankees are very active on social media, they are likely not doing so with the main goal of attracting new fans. For them, it is a way to stay connected with the millions they already have. However, a team like the Miami Marlins has only existed since 1993 and has a smaller fanbase than the Yankees. Therefore, the Marlins are using social media to increase fan excitement and make the team more relevant to those living in Miami and the rest of the world.

*Engaging fans* is a way to keep the audience interested. Social media can strengthen the relationship between fans and the teams, which should make the fans more invested in the team's success. Dan LaTorraca, who has run social media accounts for both the Carolina Panthers and the Carolina Hurricanes, said that fan engagement is the most important part of any social media campaign. These more invested fans may want to watch additional games on television, buy tickets, or purchase merchandise such as a hat or sweatshirt.

Engagement leads to the final, and perhaps most important, reason why teams use social media: *generating revenue*. While every team hopes to win games, an additional goal for nearly every owner of a team is to make money. Sports, as noted in many chapters throughout this book, is ultimately a business, so while teams want to win, the management does not want to do so at a financial loss. There are three main ways in which teams use social media to make money:

- *Ticket sales*—Ticket sales make up more than half of the revenue for many teams, so social media can be used to help sell tickets.
- *Merchandise sales*—Social media can help support e-commerce revenue by linking directly to online shops that sell team souvenirs.
- *Corporate partnerships*—Because sports teams generate a great deal of engagement online, major brands want to be a part of the action. Therefore, companies will pay a premium to be associated with teams through social media advertising plans.

# Social Media and Athletes

While it is nearly a necessity for every team to have its own social media account, the appeal for athletes was apparent from the start. In the early days of Twitter, a *Sports Illustrated* journalist wrote that it "peels back the curtain on an athlete's existence, showcasing personality layers never seen at press conferences. When athletes share details of their most mundane tasks, joys and frustrations, fans are fascinated" (Gregory, 2009, para. 5). However, that same author wondered if fans were already getting "Twittered-out" and if the platform would soon be a relic of the past (Gregory, 2009). That, of course, proved incorrect, as the social network continues to be an important part of athlete communication more than a decade later.

In the early days of Twitter, sports stars used the social network to create positive exposure for themselves, engage fans, and increase their own visibility (Pegoraro, 2010). A study of golfers during The Masters tournament found that many of the participants spent their time away from the course sending out tweets to their followers about everything from what they bought in the gift shop to on-course strategy (Hull, 2014). Many athletes use social media as a way to give fans a glimpse into their personal lives. They will show photos of their families, give opinions on entertainment or sports, or discuss their hobbies. For example, during the 2018 Winter Olympics, many athletes posted "behind the scenes" photos from the Olympic Village that gave fans an unusual glimpse of what it was like to be an athlete off the course (Robertson, 2018).

# Sedona Prince and Athletes Doing Good on Social Media

Athletes are on social media for a variety of reasons, but some have used the platform to draw attention to important causes. For example, basketball's LeBron James uses his Instagram account to raise awareness about various social causes, while football player J.J. Watt asked for donations on his Twitter page to help those affected by Tropical Storm Harvey (Barshop, 2017; Heifetz, 2018). However, in 2021, one athlete's social media post created a change in the NCAA that was likely decades overdue.

Due to the COVID-19 pandemic, the NCAA centered the 2021 men's and women's basketball tournaments in one city each to eliminate travel in hope of keeping the virus at bay. The men's tournament took place in and around Indianapolis, Indiana, while the women's was in San Antonio, Texas. While both were sponsored and organized by the NCAA, the differences between the two were stark. Those differences were known only by the players themselves until a social media post from University of Oregon women's player Sedona Prince informed the rest of the world. In a 38-second video posted to TikTok and Twitter, Prince compared the weight room setups, showing that the men's weight room was a large, state-of-the-art facility while the women's tournament had only 12 hand weights and some yoga mats (Witz, 2022).

Prince's video went viral almost immediately, resulting in over 13 million views in just a few days. Many expressed outrage at the discrepancies, and that led to an examination of gender equity in sports, specifically regarding the NCAA's treatment of its women's athletes compared to its men's (Brassil, 2021). Within a year, the NCAA expanded the number of teams in the women's tournament to equal the men's (68), branded the women's tournament as "March Madness" (previously reserved for the men's tournament), and made sure the gifts given to both the men and women were the same (Witz, 2022). While it is possible that the NCAA might have made these changes eventually, it was Prince's social media post that was the catalyst for the immediate decisions.

# Athletes Behaving Badly

While many athletes have used social media for personal, professional, or societal gain, there are also instances in which athletes have gotten themselves in trouble for their social media use. In some cases, the posts have led to simple misunderstandings or minor issues. However, in other instances, an athlete's misdeeds have led to personal financial loss or issues for their teams.

## Marvin Austin

In 2010, University of North Carolina (UNC) football player Marvin Austin tweeted, "I live in Club LIV so I get the tenant rate . . . bottles comin' like it's a giveaway." Austin's tweet was a reference to a song, but it got the attention of the NCAA. Without knowing the background of the social media content, officials wondered if Austin was getting preferential treatment by getting free champagne at a popular nightclub in Miami. While there are conflicting reports about whether Austin was actually receiving benefits from an agent that night—he said he was not—the NCAA found enough other evidence that the player and several teammates had received improper benefits (Associated Press, 2010; Barbour, 2015). However, Austin's social media activity was about to create an even bigger problem for the North Carolina athletic department.

After reviewing Austin's other social media posts, the NCAA felt they had enough evidence to investigate the football team for academic fraud. It was soon discovered that an academic tutor had given inappropriate help to players on class assignments. Austin was kicked off the football team and two teammates were declared "permanently ineligible" by the NCAA. The damage did not stop there, as the team's head coach was fired, the athletic director resigned, and the football team was given a one-year postseason ban and forced to reduce its scholarship number by 15 (Beard, 2012). In addition, the school was cited for failing to monitor the social media activity of its student-athletes (NCAA, 2012). While UNC was guilty of several infractions, it was Austin's social media activity that alerted the NCAA to those various issues.

## Cardale Jones

In 2012, Ohio State football player Cardale Jones went on Twitter to discuss his frustrations with having to attend class. He tweeted: "Why should we have to go to class if we came here to play FOOTBALL, we ain't come to play SCHOOL, classes are POINTLESS" (SI Wire, 2017). While Jones is certainly not the only student who has expressed frustration about school or classes, he was, at the time, a freshman quarterback for one of the most prominent teams in college football. His tweets brought unnecessary negative to attention to himself and, in turn, the Ohio State football team. Jones was suspended for one game and the university was forced to send out a statement reminding players to "not post or tweet anything that could embarrass themselves, their team, teammates, the university, their family or other groups, organizations or people" (ESPN .com News Services, 2012, para. 5).

While this was certainly an embarrassing situation for Jones, the story does have a happy ending. During his NFL playing career, Jones continued his education and graduated from Ohio State in 2017. At the graduation ceremony, Jones poked fun at his past as he wrote a message on his graduation cap that read, "Sum 1 once said 'We ain't come here to play school'" (SI Wire, 2017).

## Rashard Mendenhall

In 2011, much of the world, especially people in the United States, was reacting positively to the news that a well-known person had died. Pittsburgh Steelers running back Rashard Mendenhall tweeted a conflicting point of view when he wrote, "What kind of person celebrates death? It's amazing how people can HATE a man they have never even heard speak. We've only heard one side . . ." (ESPN.com News Service, 2011). While in theory that is a noble and admirable stance from Mendenhall, this social media message might

Matthew Visinsky/Icon Sportswire/Corbis/Icon Sportswire via Getty Images

**Ohio State quarterback Cardale Jones speaks at a press event.**

have been a bit misguided. The person who had died that day was Osama bin Laden, the man who is widely considered the mastermind behind the attacks on the United States in 2001. By coming to the defense of bin Laden, Mendenhall had alienated himself from fans and teammates, and he lost an endorsement deal with Champion (Bryant, 2011).

## Fans

While teams and athletes have found multiple reasons to use social media, it is likely the fan involvement that has influenced that interest more than any other factor. If fans were not gravitating to social media, then teams would have little reason to follow. For some, using social media during a game has become an important part of the experience. Nearly 80 percent of sports fans aged 13 to 37 responded that they are using multiple screens when watching live sports (Zilles, 2022). For example, a fan might watch the game on the television (screen 1) while monitoring a social media feed on their phone

(screen 2). This younger generation of fans using multiple screens to enjoy games has created what researchers have labeled "the connected fan." These fans use social networks as both an information source and as a way to connect with others online (Hull & Lewis, 2014), so it is the *interactivity* and *immediacy* of social media that are key drawing points for those logging on.

## Interactivity

Instead of simply reading about or watching the games, fans can now be interactive with the teams, players, and other fans from around the world. Therefore, these fans are not just a passive audience, but an active member of the action. For example, Twitter users can directly connect with others using the @ symbol and find topics they wish to follow by using a hashtag. For many, talking about the games is just as enjoyable as watching them, so this interactive element of social media creates a scenario in which people can discuss teams, games, and players with people from all over the world. Instead of simply talking with friends, a conversation about the WNBA's Las Vegas Aces could go global as fans debate the team's latest signing, trade, or game result. That is one reason why Twitter has been labeled "a virtual sports bar" where fans of the game can discuss the day's sports news with each other (McCarthy, 2019).

## Immediacy

The immediacy aspect of social media aligns perfectly with how fans follow sporting events. One would have to have a very pressing conflict to decide to record the Super Bowl on Sunday, avoid all results and conversations for several days, and then watch it on Wednesday. People want to watch sports as they are happening, and social media can deliver game updates, commentary, and fan discussion in real time during the game. The up-to-the-second element of social media means that fans do not have to wait until the next day's newspaper to get a breakdown of the game, as they can instead have that information instantly. Social media users are able to get scores, statistics, photos, videos, and interviews all in their newsfeed.

# Sports, Social Media, and Mass Communications

Social media has affected sports teams and leagues as a whole, but several of the individual professions within sports have seen their workflow and duties change with the implementation of Facebook, Twitter, and other platforms. This has been especially true for jobs that fall under the umbrella of mass communications, including professions in journalism, advertising, public relations, and visual communications.

## Journalism

For many years, newspaper journalists could only tell their stories in the morning newspaper and television journalists could deliver information on the evening newscast. If a major story occurred at 3 p.m., the audience would likely not find out about it until later that night on television or the next morning in the newspaper. The Internet, and specifically social media, has created a situation in which journalists can now, and are expected to, update the audience as soon as an event occurs. If that 3 p.m. story happened now, the journalist would be expected to have updates on Twitter, Facebook, and other platforms within minutes.

For fans, these instant updates address their need for immediacy. However, for the journalists, it means that the job has become one that is now 24 hours a day, 7 days a week. If a story happens, no matter the day or time, the sports journalist is expected to write about it on social media. Regarding this "always on" mentality that now exists, a local sports broadcaster said, "So many stories and story updates first come to light on Twitter, we can't afford to ignore it" (Hull, 2016). An ESPN executive stated that Twitter has created a "second-by-second news cycle" (Fry, 2012).

## Advertising

Much like the issues addressed in the previous section on journalism, companies wanting to advertise their product or service had limited options for many years. They could either spend money promoting their product on television or in the newspaper. Those advertisements would go to everyone, so the companies simply had to hope that their intended audience would see their product and become interested. Social media and the Internet allowed for digital advertisements that could be targeted to and reach a specific group of people. Advertisers are able to pay to have their ads show up on specific websites and in the social media feeds of people who they believe will want to buy their product. While companies pay a premium for these targeted ads, this investment might be worth it in the long run.

On social media, there are often two different types of advertising and promotion that occur: overt and covert. **Overt promotions** are explicitly stating exactly what you are trying to get the audience to do. For example, an advertisement for a new sweatshirt in the team store would be an overt promotion. **Covert promotions** are getting people excited about your product without openly telling them to buy something. In this example, a player would be wearing the new sweatshirt, with an Instagram caption that comments about how good he looks. That could cause fans to go to the team store to find that specific sweatshirt. While the team did not overtly promote the buying of the sweatshirt, it did still result in fans wanting to know more about it.

Social media also provides an alternative way to reach the audience. A 30-second Super Bowl commercial in 2022 cost $6.5 million, and while the Super Bowl is the most-watched television event of the year, that money might go farther on social media. That amount of money could instead be spent on Facebook, where that same $6.5 million could result in an ad being seen 650 million times. That's more than six times the number of people who watched the 2022 Super Bowl, so companies might be wise to take a second look at social media advertising before investing in television ads (McCoy, 2022).

## Public Relations

In sports, public relations refers to promoting teams, players, and organizations through various media channels. Previously, when a team had a news item they wanted the public to know about, they would contact the local newspapers and television stations with the hope that the outlets would report on it. However, the reliance on newspaper and television to deliver news is no longer necessary, because on social media, these teams have essentially become their own media content producers. If an organization has a major announcement to make, they can simply do it themselves on the various social media platforms, with a link to their own website. Fans likely follow the accounts of their favorite teams, so they are now able to get these details directly from the teams themselves.

By delivering their own content to the audience, teams can also control the message that is being sent out. On social media, teams can focus on positive news, ignore or "spin" negative news, and present their organization in the most positive way possible. This can blur the lines between public relations (promoting the team) and propaganda (providing information meant to influence the audience). This rise in "team media" using social media is discussed in greater detail in chapter 30.

## Visual Communications

Visual communications is the concept of using visual elements, such as graphics, photos, or videos, to communicate an idea or a topic to the audience. When it comes to sports and social media, it is impossible to ignore the impact visual communications has had on the industry. Research has demonstrated that people are more likely to stop scrolling through their social media feeds if they see something that catches their attention, and visual elements are often the method by which this is accomplished. For example, LinkedIn posts with images have a 98 percent higher comment rate than average, Twitter posts with a visual element are three times more likely to get engagement, and Facebook posts with photos get more likes and comments (Sehl, 2019).

On a Saturday afternoon, a college football team might use visual communication throughout the game to get fans more excited on social media. Before the opening kickoff, photos of the team's jersey that day will let fans know what uniform combination the team is wearing. Immediately following the first touchdown, a premade graphic will showcase the player who just scored, while a video of the touchdown will be posted within a few minutes. Another graphic could show the halftime and final scores, and a video of the coach's postgame speech from inside the winning locker room will make the fans feel like they are part of the action. The team could very easily send out simple text-only messages throughout the game on social media, but these visual elements can create additional excitement for fans following along on social media.

## Summary

Social media has influenced almost every aspect of the sports world. Teams are able to use these platforms as a way to connect with and attempt to make money from fans. In turn, those fans can connect with others around the world and get scores, highlights, and news delivered immediately and directly to their news feed. Athletes have found social media to be a platform in which they can deliver messages to and connect directly with fans. However, while there are advantages for athletes in using social media, some have found themselves in trouble after a regretful post. In the areas of mass communications, social media has changed how journalists, advertisers, public relations professionals, and visual communication artists do their jobs. For those professions, along with teams, leagues, and athletes, social media has provided an opportunity to rethink the connection with fans, and it is the audience that often benefits the most.

## KEY TERMS

**overt promotions**—Explicitly stating exactly what you are trying to get the audience to do or buy.

**covert promotions**—Getting people excited about your product without openly telling them to buy something.

**social media**—Online resources open to the public that people use primarily to share content and engage in two-way conversation via Internet applications.

## REVIEW QUESTIONS

1. What is it about social media that makes it different from traditional media such as newspapers and television?

2. How should teams and leagues be using social media?

3. How should athletes be using social media?

4. How has social media changed how journalists do their jobs? Is this a good thing?

# PART

# II

# THE IMPACT OF TELEVISION

Part II contains six chapters that explore how television has changed the way people follow sports. Once TVs became common in American homes and satellite technology allowed the broadcasting of sports from all over the world, fans no longer had to be in attendance to see their favorite athletes perform, and they were exposed to many more sports than had been possible before. The rise of television led to an increased popularity of sports as a whole, while also creating an "arms race" of sorts among the television stations themselves as networks spent billions of dollars to be the exclusive home of various sporting events.

Part II begins with chapter 7's look at agenda-setting theory. The news media can influence the perceived importance of an issue by discussing it more than others. This can be seen in television coverage of sports, with highlight shows and game coverage focusing on a select few teams, giving the impression that those are more important than other teams.

Chapters 8, 9, and 10 focus on three influential entities in sports television broadcasting and the lasting impact they have had on how fans watch games on TV. ABC Sports (chapter 8) and their program *Wide World of Sports* became appoint-

ment viewing for many, showing some of the biggest American sporting events and bringing sports from all over the world to U.S. television. Meanwhile, in 1979, ESPN (chapter 9) debuted on cable and, after a rough start, became a channel that sports fans could seemingly not ignore if they wanted to see the biggest games and hear from the most prominent athletes. However, television was not full of much innovation throughout that time, with games being broadcast essentially the same way they had for decades. That all changed when Fox Sports (chapter 10) took over part of the broadcasting rights for the NFL in a stunning media rights deal. Fox introduced several technological advances that are still in use today.

Part II concludes with two case studies that demonstrate the importance of the financial bottom line in television sports broadcasting. Chapter 11 discusses ESPN's dilemma regarding the *League of Denial* documentary and having to essentially choose between their journalistic side and their business side in relation to the network's partnership with the NFL. ESPN is again the focus in chapter 12, as we will take a closer look at the claims of an "SEC bias" that some believe the network has during college football season.

# 7

*THEORETICAL FOUNDATION*

# Agenda Setting

## CHAPTER OBJECTIVES

After completing the chapter, the reader should be able to do the following:

- Understand the history of agenda setting
- Identify how agenda setting is used in the media
- Recognize how priming is an offshoot of agenda setting
- Evaluate the media's coverage of Tim Tebow and how agenda setting might have been a factor in his popularity

The media can, with or without intention, cause the public to believe that certain issues, events, or people are more important than others. For example, sports fans living in the central and western parts of the United States often complain about a perceived East Coast bias from the sports media. The argument states that journalists are geographically biased and give more attention and credit to teams that play their games on the East Coast compared to those that play elsewhere. For example, these fans will cite the high percentage of Boston Red Sox versus New York Yankees games that appear on ESPN, while other matchups involving non-eastern teams are seen at not nearly at the same frequency (Cespedes Family, 2015). This creates a situation in which fans, without explicitly being told so by the media, are trained to believe that eastern teams are more important than western teams based on the constant attention that these eastern teams are receiving. The idea that the media can create this perception simply through the amount of attention given to a topic is known as agenda setting.

As discussed in chapter 1, there are millions of stories occurring in the world daily, and the media must choose which to report on and which to ignore. That process, known as gatekeeping, means that the media has a powerful role in determining what information reaches the public through their newspapers, broadcasts, or online sources. However, what stories are chosen also plays a role in how the public will perceive world events. Walter Lippmann was one of the first to establish a connection between the media, world events, and the public's perception of those events (1922), while in 1963, researcher Bernard Cohen wrote:

> *The press is significantly more than a purveyor of information and opinion. It may not be successful much of the time in telling people what to think, but it is stunningly successful in telling its readers what to think about. (p. 13)*

This is the basis for the theoretical foundation known as agenda setting. Millions of people trust the media to deliver unbiased and factual accounts of what is happening in the world. The average consumer does not have the time or resources to sift through all the events and decide which ones are worth reporting on; therefore, they trust the media to do it for them. Thus, one may assume that if the media is talking about a specific topic, then that topic must be important. This means the media sets the world's agenda by selecting the topics that it covers as opposed to the topics it ignores. Therefore, **agenda setting** is defined as the ability of the media to influence the importance placed on specific topics (Baran & Davis, 2012).

## Origin of Agenda Setting

While Cohen is generally credited with developing the concept of agenda setting (Baran & Davis, 2012), it was two University of North Carolina researchers who confirmed the theory was valid. Maxwell McCombs and Donald Shaw examined how news reports influenced the public's perception of issues in the 1968 presidential election. The two interviewed 100 registered voters and asked the participants what they thought were the key issues in the upcoming election. McCombs and Shaw then compared those answers with the amount of time on television and space in the newspaper that was devoted to the various issues (McCombs & Shaw, 1972).

The two found that the news media played a major role in what voters believed were the key issues of the campaign. Results demonstrated that there was a direct correlation between media attention and public perception, as the more time and space that a news organization spent on a topic, and how prominently in the broadcast and newspaper the issue was discussed, the more important that voters believed that topic to be. Issues that were on the front page of the newspaper were deemed more important by the audience than those that were in the middle of the newspaper or not featured at all. They wrote: "Readers learn not only about a given issue, but how much importance to attach to that issue from the amount of information in a news story and its position" (McCombs & Shaw, 1972, p. 176).

## Priming

McCombs and Shaw's study was published in 1972 and has remained relevant in the years since. Meanwhile, another group of researchers connected agenda setting to the idea of **priming**, or the idea that news consumers quickly link news stories to concepts with which they are already familiar. While agenda setting tells the audience what to think about, priming creates a situation in which the public can create an opinion about a topic (Iyengar et al., 1982). For example, if the sports media is talking about a football game that they deem to be important, the audience will soon also think that it is a big game because they have been primed by the media to believe so.

## Ethical Implications of Agenda Setting

While the media wields a great deal of power through agenda setting, there are ethical and moral implications involved in this influence. As discussed in chapter 3, the sports media is ultimately a business, so editorial decisions made by newsroom leaders will, at times, focus more on the financial benefit for the company rather than what might be "best" for the audience. For example, women's sports were essentially ignored for decades by sports journalists who believed the public cared more about men's sports. The implication of that decision was essentially "we will sell more newspapers if we talk about men's sports instead of women's sports."

However, this raises moral and ethical questions regarding the treatment of women athletes by sports journalists. One could argue that sports journalists, who are mostly male, are responsible for women's sports not being seen as equal to men's sports. The ethical and moral implications involving this gender-based decision have had a decades-long impact on women's college sports, the WNBA, the LPGA, and other women's leagues. This topic will be addressed further in chapter 18, and can also be seen regarding coverage of both minority athletes and sports that may not be as mainstream as football, baseball, and basketball.

## Tim Tebow and Agenda Setting

While previous research on agenda setting has primarily focused on news stories, especially those involving elections, it is a theory that is also applicable in the world of sports. In this chapter, we will take a deep dive into an example of agenda setting involving a football player. For about a decade, Tim Tebow was one of the most prominent athletes in the United States, and while his accomplishments as a college quarterback make him worthy of attention, it was the agenda-setting practices of the media, intentionally or not, that turned Tebow into a sensation. Even as a high school senior, the quarterback was the top story in print, broadcast, and online. That attention only grew as he moved to college and then to the professional ranks, with ESPN making Tebow the centerpiece of their programming focus. Therefore, the media's interest surrounding the quarterback can be traced to three different times in his life:

- High school star
- Florida Gator
- Professional athlete

## High School Star

In 2006, Tebow was the top-ranked high school senior quarterback in the country by popular recruiting website Rivals.com (Rivals.com, 2016). At the time, fan interest in college football recruiting was starting to rise, and major media companies were taking advantage. Instead of the top players making a verbal commitment to a school in front of just friends and family, as had been done for decades, these announcements were now being broadcast live on national television. With Tebow being one of the top players in the country, it was no surprise

that his declaration that he was heading to the University of Florida was shown live on ESPNEWS, a sister station of ESPN (Dirocco, n.d.).

However, Tebow's time on the ESPN family of networks did not stop with his commitment announcement. Later that week, ESPN aired a one-hour documentary about Tebow that focused on his life, his devotion to his religion, his high school career, and the college decision he had been facing when choosing between Florida and the University of Alabama. The documentary was titled *The Chosen One*, a not-so-subtle nod to his religious background, and what would later become a nickname that would stick with him for most of his career (Dirocco, 2008; MacKay, 2013). This documentary was the beginning of the agenda setting that was soon to surround his career. Just like readers of those North Carolina newspapers in 1968 when it came to political issues, ESPN viewers were being trained to think that Tebow was the most important recruit in the United States. That attention would continue once he suited up in college.

## Florida Gator

Once the 18-year-old landed on the University of Florida campus in the fall of 2006, the hype and publicity surrounding him grew. The freshman was the backup

Stephen M. Dowell/Orlando Sentinel/Tribune News Service via Getty Images

**While Tim Tebow accomplished a great deal as an athlete, it was the agenda-setting practices of the media that turned him into a sensation.**

quarterback at Florida but played more snaps than a typical substitute. Announcers hyped up every Tebow appearance, marveling at his throwing and running ability that went along with his infectious personality. As Florida marched to the national championship, one journalist wrote, "fans and the media immediately took to Tebow" (Kahn, 2021, para. 3), and the backup player was undeniably more popular than many of the starters on the team.

In his sophomore season, Tebow set the Southeastern Conference (SEC) record for total touchdowns and became the first sophomore in college football history to win the Heisman Trophy, awarded annually to the sport's best player. It was during this season that "Tebow-Mania" reached a fever pitch. Florida officials received 1,000 speaking requests for him from December 2007 to May 2008 after he won the Heisman (Dirocco, 2008). The media could not get enough of him either, as Tebow was on the cover of magazines and it was said that "ESPN talking heads drool in his presence" (Frenette, 2009, para. 7).

Before his junior year, Tebow was named a preseason All-American by nearly every media outlet. However, the quarterback refused the honor from *Playboy* magazine because it conflicted with his religious beliefs as a devout Christian (Powell, 2008). This demonstrated how Tebow's religious beliefs had become a key part of the media's narrative surrounding him, as many outlets reported on how he did not want to be a part of the *Playboy* team. During games, the quarterback would wear references to Bible verses written on the black tape below his eyes, which meant that every time there was a close-up shot of Tebow's face during a game, a practice that happened quite frequently based on the increased attention, the viewer would see that verse (AL .com, 2009). In that case, Tebow was using the agenda-setting practices of the media to his advantage by using their focus on him to spread his religious messages to a wider audience.

Following a midseason loss to the University of Mississippi, Tebow gave a passionate speech during a postgame press conference in which he promised:

> *You have never seen any player in the entire country play as hard as I will play the rest of this season, and you'll never see someone push the rest of the team as hard as I will push everybody the rest of this season. You will never see a team play harder than we will play the rest of the season. God bless. (Whitley, 2018, para. 3)*

In an era before social media, this sound bite essentially went "viral" as it was played on nearly every sports news show repeatedly. Once again, by showing Tebow repeatedly, even in his lowest moment, the sports media was insinuating that he was the most important player in college football. The public seemed to be buying in as well, as demonstrated when millions of people tuned in to watch Florida play Oklahoma in the national championship game. It was the Fox network's most watched Bowl Championship Series (BCS) title game, with viewership up 16 percent from the year before (Paulsen, 2010). During the game, announcers were gushing about the popular quarterback, with play-by-play broadcaster Thom Brennaman saying, "If you're fortunate enough to spend five minutes or 20 minutes around Tim Tebow, your life is better for it" (Butterworth, 2013, para. 7). His championship eye black had "John 3:16" written on it, and for the next 24 hours that Bible verse was the highest-ranked Google search term with 90 million searches (Tenety, 2012).

Florida finished Tebow's senior season ranked no. 3. The final numbers for his collegiate career were impressive both on the field and when it came to the media's interest in his play. Throughout his four years in Gainesville, Florida, Tebow was on the cover of magazines, was featured in thousands of highlights, and was part of many high-profile games. At the time, CBS Sports had a deal with the SEC that allowed the network to show a premier SEC game each week to a national audience at 3:30 p.m. ET. In order to get the most viewers, CBS would pick the teams and players that would have the most interest nationally, so that naturally meant a lot of the University of Florida and Tebow. Between regular-season and postseason games, Florida's games were featured 23 times in Tebow's four seasons, for an average of about six games a season. By constantly showing that team and player, CBS essentially told the audience "this is the most important player and team in the conference." This attitude perfectly sums up the ideas behind agenda setting, as viewership and interest in Tebow demonstrated that the public could not get enough of the quarterback.

## Professional Athlete

Following his college career, Tebow entered the world of professional football, and the interest from both the media and public did not waver. The 2010 NFL Draft in which Tebow was a first-round pick was, at the time, the most-viewed draft in ESPN history (Paulsen, 2010).

Now that he was a professional with the Denver Broncos, ESPN made Tebow a focus of their NFL coverage, ramping up the attention beyond what was seen during his college days.

One former ESPN Radio host said that during his time at the network, "I was told specifically, 'You can't talk enough Tebow'" (Koblin, 2012a, para. 2). There is certainly evidence that what the host said was true. On the day of Tebow's 25th birthday, ESPN conducted an entire party on *SportsCenter*, with the hosts wearing birthday hats, giving out presents, and standing in front of a birthday cake—all without Tebow present (Koblin, 2012b). ESPN's coverage made the attention he received during his college years seem tame. When he won the Heisman Trophy in 2007, ESPN.com mentioned Tebow 87 times that year, but that number grew to 3,520 times in just 2012 alone (Duffy, 2013). Making this even more surprising was the fact that Tebow was not one of the more successful quarterbacks in the NFL. In fact, after just three seasons, Tebow was out of the NFL following the 2012 season after not being able to secure a job with a team.

Through agenda setting, ESPN had made Tebow one of the most important people in the NFL, and the public responded accordingly. The former ESPN Radio host who was told he could not talk enough about Tebow admitted, "For whatever reason people can't get enough of that story" (Kobin, 2012b, para. 4), while another ESPN personality said, "I agree with our bosses who say, 'OK, it's the business. Look at the ratings'" (Kobin, 2012b, para. 17). Shows on ESPN that spent time debating and discussing Tebow had more viewers than those that did not (Kobin, 2012b). A fan poll from 2016 demonstrated that, despite having not played a regular-season game in the NFL in four years, Tebow was still the fifth-most popular quarterback in the league (Reimer, 2016). After his professional football career faded out, Tebow tried a career in professional baseball before returning for one last shot at the NFL. Not surprisingly, both stories were big news in the sports media. Some might say that the public interest in Tebow's minor league baseball career was almost exclusively due to the previous agenda-setting practices of journalists during his time in football.

## Regrets from ESPN

There is little argument that Tebow is one of the greatest college football players of all time. He won two national championships and the Heisman Trophy, making him more than worthy of many of the accolades that came his way throughout his career. However, it is also safe to say the media may have taken their focus a bit too far. Even ESPN would later admit as much, with the network's president acknowledging that they had gone overboard in their coverage of Tebow. While viewership certainly improved when the network discussed Tebow, the president said that they should have done a better job of thinking long term instead of just getting the quick ratings boost (Gaines, 2012).

By constantly talking about Tebow, the media made him out to be the most important player in football. Due to this attention, fans had been primed by the media to believe that games with Tebow were more important than any other college football matchup. Essentially fans had been trained through priming to think: "Since Tim Tebow is playing in this game, it must be the biggest game of the weekend because he is the player that everyone is always talking about." The attention given to those games by the public proved that the agenda setting and priming by the media was effective. High television ratings of games in which Tebow played showed that fans considered him to be more important than other players, and they tuned in by the millions to watch all his college matchups.

## Summary

Agenda-setting theory states that the media does not tell people what to think, but instead what to think about. Reporters do this by discussing some issues more than others and giving more prominence to specific stories. Research has demonstrated that the public will likely conclude that news items that are reported on more by the media are of greater importance than those that are not. In addition, through priming, the audience not only concludes that something is more important, but also develops opinions on that topic based on previous information provided by the media. In Tim Tebow's case, the media focusing an inordinate amount of attention on the quarterback made him one of the biggest stars in all of sports. Games that he was playing in had more viewers and ESPN responded by making him the centerpiece of its NFL coverage. Through agenda setting, the sports media had given additional prominence to Tebow and made it appear as if he was the most important player in all of football.

## KEY TERMS

**agenda setting**—The ability of the media to influence the importance placed on specific topics.

**priming**—News consumers quickly link news stories to concepts with which they are already familiar. Priming creates a situation in which the public forms an opinion about a topic.

## REVIEW QUESTIONS

1. How is agenda setting used by the media?
2. How was agenda setting first studied during the 1968 presidential election?
3. How is priming related to agenda setting?
4. How was the rise of Tim Tebow's popularity an example of agenda setting?

# 8

# ABC Sports

## CHAPTER OBJECTIVES

After completing the chapter, the reader should be able to do the following:

- Identify how and why ABC Sports was created
- Recognize the lasting impact of Roone Arledge
- Describe key moments in ABC Sports history
- Evaluate the impact that ABC Sports had on sports broadcasting

The rise in the popularity of sports can be almost directly tied to the invention of television. Fans no longer had to buy a ticket to see the top athletes, but instead could follow them from the comfort of their own homes. Television stations soon learned that sports could also be profitable for them, as advertisers wanted to be a part of the action and showcase their products during the games. Networks were turning to sports as a way to increase viewership and the bottom line. However, for ABC, broadcasting sporting events was instead thought of as a way to simply stay in business. Not only did sports such as college football help save the network, but they would soon turn ABC into a major power among the early television stations. ABC Sports would lead the way in technological innovations and the broadcasting of everything from professional football to the Olympics to a stuntman flying over buses. It is not overstating to say that ABC Sports defined how entities create and broadcast sports media and also how the audience consumes it.

## Birth of ABC Sports

In the 1940s and 1950s, the three main commercial television stations in the United States were ABC, CBS, and NBC. However, ABC was the newest of the three networks and struggled to keep up with the competition. There were only a handful of ABC affiliates throughout the United States, while the competing networks had stronger signals and were available in more homes. Most media experts agreed that it was just a matter of time before ABC went out of business (Vogan, 2018).

As a way to differentiate itself from CBS and NBC, and perhaps as a last-ditch effort to save the network, ABC's leadership decided to devote much of the network's programming time to sports. In the 1950s, ABC agreed to deals to broadcast Sunday NFL games, MLB's *Game of the Week*, boxing, and college football. Over that decade, the amount of sports content on the network increased 600 percent. As the 1960s began, ABC created the first division devoted solely to sports at a major network with the development of ABC Sports (Vogan,

2018). That decision to focus on sports turned out to be a wise one, as by the mid-1970s, ABC had gone from third place to the most-watched network among the main commercial stations (McChesney, 1989).

# Roone Arledge

Any discussion about the history of ABC Sports would be incomplete without mentioning the influence of Roone Arledge. Arledge started his career working for the (now defunct) DuMont Television Network and NBC before moving over to ABC shortly after the network acquired the rights to broadcast college football. In 1960, Arledge wrote his bosses a memo in which he described how, if in charge, he would change the ways in which the sport would be shown on television. The memo was a bold declaration from a non-executive, but it got the attention of those in charge. Instead of focusing solely on the game, as had been done since the first broadcast, Arledge proposed showing more than just the action on the field. He wanted to see the cheerleaders, fans, bands, coaches, and everything else that made college football a spectacle when one was attending a game. His goal was to make the viewer feel like they were there at the stadium (Washburn & Lamb, 2020). Decades later, many of Arledge's ideas are still being used in the broadcasting of sports.

From there, he created *Wide World of Sports*, was instrumental in the network's Olympic coverage, and helped kick-start *Monday Night Football*. Arledge was cited as the man responsible for the turnaround at ABC and was later moved from ABC Sports to become the president of ABC News (Rushin, 1994). In *Sports Illustrated*'s 40th anniversary issue, the magazine ranked the 40 people who "significantly altered or elevated the world of sports in the last four decades" (Smith, 1994, p. 46). Numbers one and two on the list were sports legends Muhammad Ali and Michael Jordan. Ranked third was Arledge: "Roone Arledge is largely responsible for having made sports on television look and sound and *succeed* the way it does," declared the magazine (Rushin, 1994, p. 55).

## *Wide World of Sports*

While ABC's decision to show more athletic events brought the eyes of the sporting world to its channel, Arledge's creation of *Wide World of Sports* in 1961 is often seen as the turning point for the network. The premise for the show was simple: Showcase sports that did not neces-sarily get mainstream coverage. That meant the program was primarily designed not to show baseball and football, but events from around the world with which many Americans may not have been familiar. Obscure track meets, international car racing, and cliff diving were early staples of the program, which aired on Saturdays on ABC affiliates throughout the United States (Vogan, 2018). It was hosted by legendary sportscaster Jim McKay, who opened each episode with the same iconic lines:

> *Spanning the globe to bring you the constant variety of sport. The thrill of victory . . . the agony of defeat . . . the human drama of athletic competition. This is ABC's* Wide World of Sports.

As the years progressed, the program became increasingly popular, but the sports that were broadcast remained obscure; rodeo, jai-alai, and demolition derby made regular appearances on the show (ESPN Press Room, 2011). However, also appearing on the program was boxing, which would soon become a staple of the ABC Sports lineup. While CBS and NBC also showed sporting events on the weekend, both were upstaged each week by *Wide World of Sports*, as the program became one of the most popular sports shows on television (Vogan, 2018). While the lineup of events may have looked different from what most sports fans were used to, in retrospect it was quite revolutionary. *Wide World of Sports* was the first American program to broadcast Wimbledon, the Indianapolis 500, the NCAA Men's Basketball Championship, the Little League World Series, and horse racing's Triple Crown (ESPN Press Room, 2011). In addition, the globetrotting program helped set the stage for ABC Sports' most elaborate early broadcasts: the Olympics.

## The Olympics

As discussed in chapter 4, the Olympics were a key part of the growth of the ABC Sports brand. Between 1964 and 1988, ABC exclusively aired 10 of the 14 Olympics, and the network's broadcast was credited with growing the popularity of the event in the United States. While the Olympics had been shown on television previously, ABC Sports treated the Games as a major global television event by showing events during primetime and devoting more hours than networks previously had to the broadcast (Billings et al., 2018).

The ABC Sports broadcast of the major news events during the 1968 Mexico City Olympics and the 1972 Munich Olympics demonstrated that the content was

Focus on Sport/Getty Images

**Iconic sportscaster Jim McKay covers the 1988 Preakness Stakes for ABC's *Wide World of Sports*.**

more than just final scores and highlights, as the sports department led the way on coverage of two international news stories. When Tommie Smith and John Carlos were banned from the Olympics following their protest on the medal stand in 1968, it was ABC Sports' Howard Cosell who had the exclusive interview with the pair and then defended them in a commentary following their dismissal (Maraniss, 2018). During the 14-hour standoff between Palestinian terrorists and Munich police in 1972, it was not a traditional news journalist leading ABC's coverage, but sportscaster Jim McKay who relayed the latest developments, including his final statement of "they're all gone" to announce the deaths of the hostages (Billings et al., 2018).

ABC Sports had demonstrated an ability to do outstanding reporting during those newsworthy moments, but it was also up to the challenge when the sports dictated. The 1980 U.S. hockey team's upset win over the Soviet Union is regarded as one of most memorable Olympic moments of all time, and it was ABC Sports that had the broadcast (Vaccaro, 2015). Four years later, as the summer edition of the Games came to the United States in Los Angeles, ABC devoted the most hours it had ever committed to show the Olympics. With ABC Sports announcers relaying all the action to the Ameri-

can public, the 1984 Olympics became, at the time, the most watched event in television history (Wertheim, 2021). More information on ABC's role in the historic moments of the 1968, 1972, 1980, and 1984 Olympic broadcasts can be found in chapter 4.

## Other Major Events on ABC Sports

In addition to the Olympics, ABC Sports was becoming the channel that was broadcasting the most in-demand sports programming. Whether it was for one-time events or weekly games, sports fans were tuning in to ABC, raising the profile of the entire network beyond just the sports coverage. The most attention-grabbing sports broadcasting moments on ABC Sports included:

- "The Battle of the Sexes"
- Evel Knievel's jumps

## "The Battle of the Sexes"

As will be discussed in chapter 18, one of the most monumental moments in sports history occurred in 1973 during a tennis match between women's star Billie Jean King and men's star Bobby Riggs. Broadcasting King's straight-set victory was ABC Sports, and the network was responsible for much of the hype around the big match. However, it would cost them, as the network paid $825,000 to broadcast it on television and another $300,000 to air it on radio (Vogan, 2018). ABC's executives felt the investment was worth it, as they recognized the match had the potential to be a major statement for equal rights for women.

On the night of the broadcast, the program played up the "man versus woman" angle with their selection of music, graphics, interview subjects, and the commentary from the announcers. As King methodically took down Riggs, the announcers marveled at her ability and noted the impact of the match on gender equality. Additionally, the network's hunch that the public would be interested was proven true. Over 90 million people tuned in worldwide to watch, including more than 50 million in the United States (Sun, 2018; Vogan, 2018).

## Evel Knievel's Jumps

While ABC Sports was bringing in the traditional sports fans, one of the biggest stars of *Wide World of Sports* was a not a traditional athlete but instead a motorcycle daredevil. In 1967, the show broadcast Robert Knievel, better known by his stage name of Evel Knievel, jumping over 15 cars aboard his motorcycle (Vogan, 2018). With that leap, the daredevil had begun capturing the interest of the American public.

Soon after, Knievel was a staple of the weekly program, wearing his patriotic red, white, and blue jumpsuit while jumping motorcycles over cars, trucks, and buses. One of his more famous jumps occurred in 1974 when he attempted to pilot a "sky cycle," basically a rocket-type contraption, over the Snake River Canyon in Idaho. As he launched into the air, the rocket's parachute opened earlier than expected and Knievel crashed into the canyon. Those in attendance would later admit that Knievel was lucky to be alive; had he landed directly in the water, the parachute mishap might have proved deadly. Despite the failure, ABC Sports still broadcasted the attempt to millions of viewers the following week (Ross, n.d.; Vogan, 2018).

By the end of his career, Knievel had appeared on *Wide World of Sports* 17 times, and his appearances ranked as the most-watched and third-most-watched episodes in the program's history. The most watched, his 1975 jump over 14 Greyhound buses, earned a 52 share,

meaning 52 percent of the people watching television at the time were tuned into his attempt (Ross, n.d.).

# Howard Cosell

While Roone Arledge is considered the innovator behind many of ABC Sports' biggest successes, Howard Cosell was perhaps the public face of the network. Cosell was synonymous with some of the biggest events and athletes in the world of sports, all while working at ABC Sports. Starting out as a radio host, Cosell eventually made the transition to television in the early 1960s. While most broadcasters at the time were either ex-athletes or announcers with soothing voices, Cosell was neither. His brash and combative style made him one of the most polarizing broadcasters in the United States.

## Relationship with Muhammad Ali

In 1964, boxer Cassius Clay upset heavyweight champion Sonny Liston to become the new star of boxing. The next day, Clay announced he was changing his name to Muhammad Ali and converting to Islam. The decision by Ali was not received well by many in the public, but Cosell stood by his side, becoming the first, and at the time only, person in the media to refer to him as Ali (Vogan, 2018). Cosell also supported Ali when the boxer refused to fight in the Vietnam War, which led to the champion being stripped of his boxing titles (Sandomir, 2016). The partnership between the two became key for ABC Sports, as Ali had become one of the most famous athletes in the world but was not trusting of most media members. Despite that mistrust, nearly every time Ali was on the screen on *Wide World of Sports*, Cosell was there with him. The two would debate politics, race, and religion, sometimes ignoring boxing completely. The two had forged a friendship of sorts that was being broadcast on ABC. Additionally, Cosell was ringside for some of Ali's biggest fights, providing analysis for the television broadcast.

However, instead of broadcasting the fights live, *Wide World of Sports* would show the full-length replays several weeks after they occurred. For example, Ali's 1975 defeat of Joe Frazier in the "Thrilla in Manila" was not aired on ABC Sports until nearly four months later. On that broadcast, Cosell discussed the boxers' pre-fight training and reviewed the first two fights between the rivals before the full 15-round fight was shown. After the replay ended, Cosell interviewed Ali on the *Wide*

Bettmann/Getty Images

**The partnership between Howard Cosell and Muhammad Ali became key for ABC Sports because Cosell was one of the few media members Ali trusted.**

*World of Sports* to get his firsthand account on what happened in the ring (Paley Center for Media, n.d.). That broadcast was the second-most-watched episode in the show's history (Vogel, 2018).

## The Face of ABC Sports

As his star grew at ABC, Cosell became involved in other projects, including being a part of the network's Olympics coverage, World Series baseball, and hosting his own sports investigative show, *SportsBeat* (Shapiro, 1995). *SportsBeat* allowed Cosell to show off more of his journalistic side and less of the showman persona that was on display elsewhere. The program was a critical success, winning multiple awards for its work, but few people watched. Despite low ratings, it was a program he was incredibly proud of, saying, "If I had to choose one show that I'd like to stand as my legacy in this business, *SportsBeat* would be it" (Cosell, 1973, p. 189).

However, it is more likely that Cosell's on-air style is his most enduring legacy. While most sportscasters at the time were complimentary of athletes and sports, Cosell was one of the first to be overly critical. He would challenge athletes in interviews, speak his mind when he did not agree with something, and even go against

his own network's wishes. His distinct voice was often imitated, and he was labeled as arrogant by coworkers. Viewers either loved him or hated him, as proven by the fact that he was once voted both the most popular and the most disliked sportscaster in America (Shapiro, 1995; Thomas, 1995).

## Cosell's Departure

Cosell's most prominent role at ABC Sports was his position as the lead announcer for the NFL's *Monday Night Football*. However, it was an incident during that broadcast that also led to the end of his television career. In 1983, after receiver Alvin Gentry caught a pass for Washington, Cosell said, "That little monkey gets loose, doesn't he?" To many, Cosell's comments about Garrett, who was Black, appeared to be racist. ABC was inundated with complaints from viewers and religious groups who called for a boycott. While Cosell had a long history of supporting Black athletes, with many convinced he was in no way racist, the damage was done. He was removed from the broadcasts for three weeks; at the end of the season, he resigned from *Monday Night Football* and instead chose to focus on *SportsBeat*. However, after Cosell insulted Arledge and other ABC coworkers in his 1985 autobiography, his days at the network were numbered. A month after an excerpt of the book was published in *TV Guide*, *SportsBeat* was canceled, and Cosell decided to quit ABC (Vogan, 2018).

# Monday Night Football

In the 1960s, the NFL was *the* sport to watch on Sundays, but Pete Rozelle, the commissioner of the league, was looking to expand the broadcasting options. Rozelle envisioned a game played other than on Sunday afternoon—a weekly primetime game that had the potential to reach an even bigger audience. After vetoing Friday or Saturday nights to avoid conflicts with high school and college football games, the NFL zeroed in on Mondays. Trial games were played each year from 1966 to 1969, with a more complete schedule planned for 1970 (*The New York Times*, 1968).

At the time, NFL games were televised on either CBS or NBC, but when the Monday night games were proposed, neither channel was interested because they did not want to disrupt their existing primetime programming. ABC, which was still the least-watched network of the three, took a chance and agreed to air *Monday Night Football* (Sandomir, 2005). However, with Arledge in charge, these would not be traditional football broadcasts. The ABC Sports team determined that games airing on Monday nights needed to be entertainment. With that in mind, the announcing team consisted of a traditional broadcaster (Keith Jackson), a controversial lightning rod full of opinions (Cosell), and the charming ex-athlete who the audience loved (former quarterback Don Meredith). There were more cameras and newer technology than was traditionally seen at pro football games, all with the goal of making the audience feel like they were closer to the action. With a great deal of fanfare, and 60 million people watching, *Monday Night Football* debuted in September 1970 with a game between the New York Jets and the Cleveland Browns (Sandomir, 2005; Vogan, 2018).

## Memorable Games and Moments

From then on, *Monday Night Football* became appointment viewing for football fans, and while not every game was a classic, some of the most memorable in football history were played on Monday night. Perhaps none was more significant than a 1985 matchup between the Chicago Bears and the Miami Dolphins. The Bears were undefeated at 12-0 and looking like they could finish the season with a perfect record. However, on ABC's premier program, the Dolphins pulled the major upset, shocking Chicago for the team's only loss of the season. That night, 46 percent of all televisions that were on in the United States were watching the game, making it the most-watched game in *Monday Night Football* history (Casey, 2016; Florio, 2015).

Another memorable moment in *Monday Night Football* history had nothing to do with the game. On a Monday night in 1980, singer John Lennon was shot and killed outside his home. As *Monday Night Football* was showing the Dolphins and the New England Patriots, Cosell stopped describing the action and said

*An unspeakable tragedy confirmed to us by ABC News in New York City. John Lennon, outside of his apartment building on the west side of New York City, the most famous, perhaps, of all of The Beatles—shot twice in the back. Rushed to Roosevelt Hospital— dead on arrival. Hard to go back to game after that news flash. (Chase, 2015; TLPFAS, 2010, :43)*

## Monday Night Football leaves ABC

In 2005, ABC Sports elected not to renew its contract with the NFL, and the *Monday Night Football* package went to ESPN, which, like ABC, was owned by the Walt Disney Company. The move was framed as a financial one, as ABC was losing more than $150 million per year on the broadcasts (Sandomir, 2005, Vogan, 2018). However, media experts recognized that the decision was another sign that the future of ABC Sports was looking bleak. Disney management was ready to move the company's sports properties almost exclusively to ESPN.

# The End of ABC Sports

One year after losing the *Monday Night Football* package, ABC Sports was essentially retired by Disney. The decision was made to merge ABC Sports and ESPN, with ESPN becoming the dominant partner. The ABC Sports graphics, music, and name were all replaced by ESPN branding, and soon after, all sporting events shown on ABC were labeled as *ESPN on ABC* (Sandomir, 2006). As will be discussed in the next chapter, ESPN had become *the* major power in the sports media, and ABC Sports, despite its decades of innovation and history, had become a casualty of that rise.

# Summary

When discussing the evolution of sports on television, a major part of that past involves ABC Sports. Some of the biggest events in history have aired on the network, including the 1980 U.S. hockey team's upset win over the U.S.S.R. in the Olympics, the "Battle of the Sexes," and many of Muhammad Ali's most famous boxing matches. In addition, the network's executives created innovative coverage, from *Wide World of Sports* to *Monday Night Football*. ABC Sports' broadcast changed how people watched sports on television, and many of the initiatives created for those broadcasts are still being used today. However, as the years progressed and ESPN began its rise in prominence, the company that owned both channels made the decision to focus on the all-sports cable channel. ABC Sports was quietly phased out and ESPN became the home for all things sports in the Walt Disney Company. While ABC Sports may no longer exist as it did for decades, it is impossible to ignore the lasting impact the organization had on televised sports.

## REVIEW QUESTIONS

1. What made ABC decide to get into the business of showing sports on television?
2. What made *Wild World of Sports* such a revolutionary program?
3. How did *Monday Night Football* demonstrate the popularity of the NFL?
4. Why did Disney eliminate ABC Sports?

# 9

# ESPN

## CHAPTER OBJECTIVES

After completing the chapter, the reader should be able to do the following:

- Understand what caused the early struggles at the network
- Identify the key moments throughout ESPN's history
- Debate the successes and failures of ESPN's brand extensions
- Discuss the future of ESPN and the impact of cord cutting

When it comes to sports media, perhaps no outlet has had a greater impact than ESPN. While it barely survived its first few years, it eventually grew into a channel that, like it or not, every fan had to watch to stay up to date on the latest sports news and events. Today ESPN is home to some of the biggest sporting events in the world, from championship games in college sports to professional playoff games to major golf and tennis tournaments. With that modern lineup it might seem impossible to believe that a sailing competition was one of the first "must-see" events on the network.

In 1986, ESPN broadcast 79 hours of the America's Cup, the oldest international competition in the world. ESPN treated the event like it was the only sport that mattered, with live cameras on the boats, expert analysis, and, perhaps surprising to nearly everyone involved, over a million viewers glued to their televisions to watch every second. The coverage would prove to be one of the most important moments in the network's history. Soon after, the NFL agreed to a deal that would allow regular-season games on ESPN, and it was the America's

Cup broadcast that convinced the NFL that ESPN could handle the responsibility (Couch, 2017). ESPN was off and running as "The Worldwide Leader in Sports," a label the network has used from the beginning and which remains valid decades later.

## Creation of Cable Television

In the early days of television, many Americans were able to get a broadcast signal through antennas located on their television sets. Millions watched their favorite shows by moving what were playfully known as the "rabbit ears" on top of the set back and forth in an attempt to get the best reception. However, there were large parts of the country that, no matter how much they tried, could not get a workable signal. For example, those living in mountainous areas or those surrounded by tall buildings had difficulty in getting a clear signal through their antennas. In order to ensure that everyone could watch television, cable systems were created in several locations in the United States in 1948 so that homes could connect to a community antenna tower and not have to worry about their individual home reception (CCTA, n.d.).

Just a few years later, cable television executives began recognizing that their technology could have a more far-reaching impact. Instead of simply providing a clear signal for local stations, cable companies could pick up television stations from hundreds of miles away, opening the door for a variety of different programming options. This revolutionary discovery allowed for new 24-hour channels, including the first pay-TV network (HBO) and a local television station in Atlanta that went nationwide (TBS) (CCTA, n.d.). Other networks would soon follow, including a channel that, if approved, would be the home of Connecticut sports and not much else.

## ESP(N) Development

In 1978, Connecticut residents Bill and Scott Rasmussen, a father and son, conceived the idea to create a cable television channel that was devoted entirely to Connecticut-area sports. The ESP Network, or Entertainment and Sports Programming Network, would focus on University of Connecticut sports, the NHL's Hartford Whalers, minor league baseball's Bristol Red Sox, and other area teams. Despite the local focus, there was skepticism from New England–based cable companies, and the majority stated they were not interested. Despite that, the Rasmussens pushed forward.

The plan of a Connecticut-only focus on ESP would soon change. The owners were informed that if they bought a satellite feed, they could reach the entire country, and, perhaps surprisingly to the father and son, it would actually be cheaper than just sending the channel to a regional audience without using a satellite. With money already tight, the two picked the cost-effective, nationwide option. Being broadcast in the entire country meant that the Connecticut-centric plan no longer made sense, and ESP was now going to show sports from all over the world (Miller & Shales, 2011; Vogan, 2015).

ESP fashioned itself as a major television network, but it was an oil company, not a media entity, that was the first to buy in. Getty Oil agreed to become the first majority owners of the network, purchasing 85 percent of the company from Bill Rasmussen. Shortly after, Anheuser-Busch became one of the first sponsors, agreeing to a deal that was, at the time, the largest advertising contract in cable television history. With a major corporate sponsor and new money from the Getty Oil purchase, ESP was able to work out a deal with the NCAA to broadcast 18 different college sports (Miller & Shales, 2011).

## September 7, 1979

As the opening day of the network inched closer, ESP got a little lucky. In early 1979 NBC televised the NCAA men's basketball national championship game, which featured Earvin "Magic" Johnson's Michigan State team against Larry Bird's undefeated Indiana State team. Over 40 million people tuned into NBC to watch the game, a record that, as of this writing, still stands as the most-watched title game in men's basketball history (Mehler & Paikert, 2018). For ESP management, which had only two weeks earlier secured rights to broadcast future NCAA basketball games, this was incredible and fortunate timing. Suddenly, there were millions of people who were hooked on college basketball, and, thanks to the deal with the NCAA, fans now needed ESP to watch.

Starting fresh with the new name ESPN, the network debuted on September 7, 1979. In the opening seconds of ESPN's history, anchor Lee Leonard told the audience: "If you're a fan, *if you're a fan*, what you'll see in the next minutes, hours, and days to follow may convince you that you've gone to sports heaven" (ESPN Front Row, 2018, 0:03). After a brief explanation of how the satellite technology worked, and the first edition of *SportsCenter*, the network was off and running. However, the first live game on the network was not from the NFL, NBA, or MLB. Instead, as perhaps an unintentional demonstration of just how far the network had to go to reach the mainstream, the first-ever sporting event broadcast on ESPN was a men's professional slow-pitch softball game between the Milwaukee Schlitz and the Kentucky Bourbons (Malinowski, 2019).

## Early Struggles

As evidenced by the matchup between the Schlitz and the Bourbons, the early days of ESPN were not exactly appointment viewing for sports fans. Without deals with major professional sports leagues, the network's schedule was filled with nontraditional sports such as Australian rules football, tractor pulls, skeet shooting, and karate (Rosenthal, 2019). The situation quickly became dire, and ESPN was very close to going out of business. Viewership was low, which meant advertisers were not willing to pay top dollar for commercials, so ESPN was losing over a million dollars a month in its early years (Vogan, 2015). However, Anheuser-Busch remained confident, re-upping its sponsorship and then giving the network an additional $5 million to keep it afloat (Kohler, 2013). For the popular beer company, the investment was not charity. It was one that, according to an Anheuser-Busch executive, they hoped would pay off in the long run:

> We gave them $1 million that first year. And if we hadn't, they'd have gone under . . . I believed the beer drinker was a sports lover . . . The next year we gave them $5 million. I think it turned out to be the best investment we've ever made. (Kohler, 2013, para. 8, 9)

## SportsCenter

The sporting events being broadcast early in the history of ESPN might not have appealed to most fans, but the program *SportsCenter* was enough to keep many tuned in. The show aired on the network's very first day in 1979 and has been a constant ever since. The concept of *SportsCenter* is rather unremarkable in modern days, as they showed highlights from all sports while also delivering the latest news. Being able to see every team at any time is what all fans expect now, but at the time the show was groundbreaking.

Before ESPN, most sports fans were limited to getting video highlights from local broadcasters on the evening news. A fan in Los Angeles could tune in to a local television station and see the best plays from baseball's Dodgers, basketball's Lakers, and other teams from that area. However, the odds of seeing a highlight from the Dallas Mavericks, Denver Broncos, or Boston Red Sox were slim, as fans in Los Angeles could basically only see Los Angeles sports. *SportsCenter*, on the other hand, brought national sports to a local audience. It no longer mattered where someone lived. If a sports fan wanted to see a highlight of the Milwaukee Brewers baseball game, they did not have to move to Wisconsin. Instead, they could just turn on *SportsCenter*. While the Internet would eventually make watching national and global sports even easier, the legacy of *SportsCenter* lies in how it changed the ability of fans to see more action than ever before.

Chuck Solomon /Sports Illustrated via Getty Images

**Dan Patrick and Keith Olbermann anchor a 1992 episode of *SportsCenter*.**

# Prominent Sports Broadcasters

For many journalists, being able to host *SportsCenter* meant that they had finally made it in broadcasting. Kevin Negandhi had worked at ESPN for 15 years, reporting live from some of the biggest events in sports, and said his proudest moment at the network was still the first time he had appeared on *SportsCenter*: "I realized a dream come true since I was a 14-year-old kid" (Derscheid, 2020, para. 3). Negandhi is one of many who have sat in the anchor chairs, with three of the most prominent being Chris Berman, Stuart Scott, and Linda Cohn.

## Chris Berman

In 1979, just one month after the network's debut, ESPN hired 24-year-old Chris Berman to host the overnight edition of *SportsCenter*. Berman's style of choosing to have fun and hoping to entertain, not strictly inform, was different from most sports broadcasters at the time. He soon became perhaps the most famous person on the network, hosting a variety of shows beyond just *SportsCenter*. The standout was *NFL Primetime*, a Sunday night program that aired during football season with the scores, news, and highlights from that day's games. Peppered into those highlights were Berman's signature nicknames such as Andre "Bad Moon" Rison, Curtis "My Favorite" Martin, and Tim Couch "Potato." Millions would tune in on Sunday night to get "Boomer's" (Berman's nickname) take on the games. ESPN's vice president of production said that Berman was the network's "most important person" and that "he is the face of ESPN" (Eaton-Robb, 2008, para. 13).

## Stuart Scott

When Stuart Scott was anchoring *SportsCenter*, an outstanding play would be emphasized with his signature phrase, "Booyah!" It was one of many expressions ("cool as the other side of the pillow") that made Scott stand out from the others on the show. Scott was the most prominent Black sportscaster for ESPN and used his love of hip-hop music as a way to connect with his audience. His high-energy and unique style made him one of the most popular and influential people in the history of the network. As Scott's career at ESPN evolved, he would branch out beyond *SportsCenter*, hosting NFL and NBA programming, two of the network's most high-profile assignments. Sadly, Scott's career and life was cut short when he tragically passed away due to cancer at age 49 (Sandomir, 2015).

## Linda Cohn

In 1992, shortly after being hired at ESPN, Linda Cohn anchored her first *SportsCenter*. At the time, it might have seemed like just another edition of the show, but years later, that night would prove to be the start of something big. There have been more than 60,000 episodes of *SportsCenter*, and Cohn has anchored more of them than anyone else. In 2016, she was on the anchor desk for her record 5,000th edition of the show and, after celebrating 30 years at ESPN, did not appear to be slowing down, signing a contract extension in 2022 to continue on *SportsCenter* (Hall, 2016, 2022).

Perhaps making it more remarkable is that, as will be discussed in chapter 20, Cohn is a woman in a male-dominated field. Cohn would later say that changing the perception that male viewers had of her was one of the most rewarding parts of the job:

> As soon as I started hosting SportsCenter regularly, there were calls made to the ESPN switchboard wondering, "Why is this woman on the air?" Later, guys would come up to me and they would say, "Hey, Linda, don't take this the wrong way." And I'm like, "OK," bracing myself. They would say, "You know, I never took sports from a woman before you. And you know what? You're good. It's OK. I like you." And I was like, "That's the greatest thing I've ever heard. Thank you for that compliment." (Front Row Staff, 2019b, para. 10)

# Partnerships with Pro Sports Leagues

While *SportsCenter* was a major draw for sports fans, the network was going to need more than a popular highlights show and hours of Australian rules football to be successful. Ultimately, without professional sports, there would be little reason to tune into ESPN. Therefore, management's goal became to work out a deal with at least one professional league with the hope that it would motivate others to sign on as well. It was ESPN's desperation for literally any programming that helped it work out an early deal with the NFL.

## The NFL Draft

The NFL Draft has become one of the signature yearly programs on ESPN. Millions tune in to watch teams select the best college players in what has become a made-for-TV event that is spread over multiple nights. However, in 1980, when ESPN approached the NFL about broadcasting the draft, the NFL commissioner Pete Rozelle's response was that of confusion: "Who's going to want to watch the NFL draft?" (Front Row Staff, 2019a, para. 21). At the time, the draft was just a room full of people on the phone, getting the picks from their team, and then hand delivering those selections to the commissioner. It was not exactly thrilling television, so most NFL officials thought it was a terrible idea to broadcast it, and the team owners overwhelmingly rejected ESPN's proposal. Despite that vote, Rozelle saw the value of television, went against the wishes of the owners, and allowed for the draft to be broadcast (Ellenport, 2020). For those at ESPN, it was not necessarily the program itself that was monumental, but what it signified. ESPN was, at the time, a minor league network, but they were now showing a major league event. Chet Simmons, one of the first broadcasters

hired at the network, would later say, "The draft put us in business with the NFL, and that was huge" (Miller & Shales, 2011, p. 65). From its humble beginnings, the NFL Draft has turned into one of the most-watched non-game sporting events each year on the channel. The 2022 version was shown on two Disney-owned networks, with 4.446 million watching on ESPN and another 3.803 million tuning in on ABC (City News Service, 2022).

## More Leagues Join and Financial Changes

The success of the NFL Draft on ESPN showed other leagues that there might be a viable spot for them to broadcast games on cable. Soon after, the NBA, NHL, and the professional football league the USFL all reached deals to broadcast games on the network. While viewership was increasing, not everyone was thrilled. In 1982, a woman in Texas named ESPN a codefendant in her divorce case, saying that it was the network's fault her marriage was ruined because her

From its humble beginnings, the NFL Draft has turned into one of the most-watched non-game sporting events each year on ESPN.

husband was watching too much sports on television (Freeman, 2001).

Around this time, ESPN executives hatched a plan that would take advantage of the growing demand. For years, cable channels paid the cable companies for distribution and hoped to make up the cost of that fee through advertising. ESPN elected to flip that model and instead began charging cable companies to carry them (Front Row Staff, 2019a). The gamble was that sports fans would demand ESPN from their local cable companies and so those companies, despite now having to pay, would have no choice but to carry ESPN. Chapter 3 has more on how this plan works, but it turned out to be a lifesaver for the network. Despite its growing popularity, ESPN was still not making enough money from advertisers; in 1984, Getty Oil lost interest in supporting the struggling network and sold it to ABC. By 1985, with new owners, a new subscription fee plan for cable companies, and increased demand from consumers, ESPN had turned a profit for the first time (Vogan, 2015).

## 1987: The NFL Comes Aboard

Years after that first broadcast of the NFL Draft, ESPN's decision to show the event would pay off in one of the most monumental moments in the network's history. In 1987, the NFL, which had some of television's highest viewership numbers each week during the season, was debating creating a package of games that could be shown on cable. This would be a historic moment for the league, as up to that point NFL contests were only on local over-the-air channels such as ABC, CBS, and NBC. Thanks to its NFL Draft coverage, ESPN was well positioned to be a part of the new deal (Ellenport, 2020).

Ultimately, ESPN agreed to pay the NFL $153 million to show eight Sunday night regular-season games, four preseason exhibition games, and the Pro Bowl all-star game for the 1987, 1988, and 1989 seasons (Fabrikant, 1987). ESPN's president at the time called it "the most significant sports agreement in cable television history" (Pierson, 1987, para. 20). The impact of the agreement paid off almost instantly for ESPN, as the preseason games a few months later earned the biggest sports ratings in cable history (Chad, 1987). Additionally, the network's decision to have cable companies pay them proved to be a good one, as demand for ESPN rose higher than ever. The NFL package was credited as the reason for ESPN's 700,000 new subscribers, making

it the most widely available cable network (Miller & Shales, 2011).

## Future Deals

In the ensuing years, ESPN added deals with MLB, MLS, NASCAR, and a host of other professional sports leagues. At one point in the early 2000s, all four major professional sports leagues in North America had a broadcasting deal with ESPN, which meant that sports fans had almost no choice but to watch the network if they wanted to see the latest games. As Lee Leonard had promised on ESPN's first day, the network had become "sports heaven." However, acquiring the programming was not cheap. By 2020, ESPN had agreed to pay about $7.5 billion in rights fees just to show all these major sporting events (Crupi, 2020).

## Brand Expansion

With more programming and partnerships, ESPN was running out of available time slots to show everything. The solution was to create a new channel. The company debuted ESPN2 in 1993 with a goal of attracting younger viewers by showing sports such as hockey, arena football, and BMX racing (Frager, 1993). Eventually, it simply became an extension of ESPN, even dropping the ESPN2 name in all on-air references and only using the brand in programming guides (Leitch, 2007).

The network's expansion would soon be ramped up even further. In 1996, the Walt Disney Company purchased ABC and with it the ownership of ESPN. Christine Driessen, the former chief financial officer at ESPN, said that move changed the trajectory of the channel. Before Disney's ownership, ESPN was content as a television network, but Driessen said that the new owners challenged them to expand their brand to try to capture other consumers (Front Row Staff, 2019b). Soon after, *ESPN The Magazine*, ESPN-branded video games, and even ESPN Zone restaurants debuted as a way to increase the reach of the network (IGN Staff, 1999; Mulligan, 1997; Strauss, 2019).

## More Television Channels

While selling hamburgers at its restaurants was designed to increase revenue, the primary focus of ESPN was still on television. ESPNEWS debuted in 1996 as a 24-hour sports news channel, ESPN Classic was launched in 1997 to show legendary games from years earlier, and ESPNU started in 2005 with a focus on college sports (Cotey, 2005; Hofmeister, 1997; Sandomir, 1996). College sports became a continued focus: ESPN created the Longhorn Network, which had an almost exclusive focus on University of Texas sports (Fang, 2015), and launched both the ACC Network and SEC Network as partnerships with those college sports conferences (Morton, 2019; Sandomir, 2013). As of 2022, ESPN had eight cable networks on which people could watch games and get the latest news (ESPN Press Room, n.d.).

## ESPN Digital

In April 1995, in association with the men's college basketball Final Four, ESPN debuted its first website. The page, ESPNET Sports Zone, gave fans access to the network's writers, player statistics, and online discussion areas (Cozart, 2014). In the years since its debut, the title of the website has gotten shorter (ESPN.com), but the options have gotten larger. ESPN's website now features video, fantasy sports, and separate subpages devoted to specialty topics such as women's sports (ESPNW). It is perhaps no surprise that ESPN.com is one of the most visited sports websites each month (ebiz, n.d.).

The same could be said for ESPN's social media properties. ESPN's Snapchat page debuted a *SportsCenter* edition in 2017 that was geared specifically for the fast-paced environment of that social network. Instead of an hour of highlights, the Snapchat version was about seven minutes, had brief highlights, and focused on the lighter side of sports. Less than two months after its debut, it was getting more than two million unique visitors a day, with 75 percent of them between the ages of 13 and 24 (Brady, 2018). On the social media platform TikTok, ESPN was the third brand in the world to reach 25 million followers and would eventually become the most-followed brand of any on the service (Panitz, 2023; Soltys, 2022).

## ESPN+

In 2018, ESPN created its own video streaming platform known as ESPN+. Early proposals stated that there would be more than 10,000 games available to stream, along with sports documentaries and new programming designed specifically for the service (Draper, 2018). Some fans hoped that the streaming service could replace the need for cable television, as many had been looking for alternatives to the traditional (and expensive) cable package. That, however, would not be the case. While ESPN+ would show a variety of sports, it would be only events that were not available on television (Brown, 2019). So while viewers could now watch sports on a streaming device, it would not include the main draws of ESPN, including the NFL, major college football games, and daily network programming such as *SportsCenter*. The response from critics was disappointment, as one popular website labeled the initial offering "underwhelming" and "a missed opportunity" (McAtee, 2018). However, sports fans had a different opinion. ESPN+ had more than one million paid subscribers within five months of launching (Melvin, 2018) and more than 22 million subscribers by the end of 2022 (Dixon, 2022).

# Business Failures and Challenges

While ESPN has evolved into the premier sports television network, that ascension has not come without some criticisms along the way. Some of those are discussed elsewhere in this book, including debate about its political leanings (chapter 17), the multibillion-dollar partnerships with the leagues it is supposed to be unbiasedly covering (chapter 11), racial and gender discrimination in hiring (chapter 23), and charges of bias and favoritism toward certain athletes, teams, or leagues (chapter 12). With those criticisms covered elsewhere, this section will focus on two of the business failures and challenges that ESPN has endured and will continue to face in the future.

## Mobile ESPN

In the mid-2000s, as cellular telephones were becoming commonplace, ESPN attempted to get in on the action by creating Mobile ESPN. The primary feature was that fans could get scores, news, and highlights delivered directly to their phone. At the time, this was an unheard-of idea, but the cost proved to be a major sticking point for many. The required phone retailed for around $400 and the monthly plan was four times as much as the competition. Disney had invested $150 million in the initiative, including an expensive Super Bowl commercial, but fans were seemingly not interested.

About one year after the phone's debut, Disney pulled the plug on the project (Belson, 2006). There had been warning signs that the phone project might not be a success. During a Disney board meeting, Steve Jobs, who would later prove to know a thing or two about cellphones with the success of the iPhone, told the ESPN president, "Your phone is the dumbest [expletive] idea I have ever heard" (Miller & Shales, 2011, p. 623).

While Mobile ESPN might fall in the "failure" column of ESPN's history, perhaps the concept was simply ahead of its time. Seemingly every cell phone now can access scores and highlights, fans can stream live video of games while on the go, and the ESPN app is the top sports app in the United States based on both visitors and downloads by a wide margin (Adler, 2021). When phones started to become more technologically advanced, ESPN was ready to pounce based on their experience with the failed mobile plan. Some have gone as far as to state that Mobile ESPN set the foundation for the network's ability to dominate this digital space (Gordon, 2015).

## Cord Cutting

While people getting rid of their cable subscriptions was discussed briefly in chapter 3, it is worth revisiting here, because perhaps no sports entity has more concerns about "cord cutting" than ESPN. Millions of consumers have elected to drop their cable plan, which has severely damaged ESPN's financials. The company's plan decades earlier to charge cable companies per customer helped turn it into one of the most successful media companies, but now its reliance on that income has become an issue. About $9 of everyone's monthly cable bill goes toward ESPN, no matter how much a viewer watches sports (Koo, 2020). Therefore, for years ESPN got $9 per customer, per month. However, thanks to cord cutting, the total number of those customers dropped dramatically, meaning that by 2015, ESPN had lost over a billion dollars in expected revenue (Yoder, 2015).

While losing out on that amount of money would be challenging enough, ESPN is also saddled with billions of dollars in rights fees that allow the network to show the NFL, NBA, MLB, and other top sports. Without that money from the cable companies, ESPN needs to find ways to make up the missing money. This is one of the reasons that the streaming service ESPN+ has become an important part of the network's future plans. While it might not make up for the total number of people leaving cable, it can perhaps help to offset the dollars that are being lost to cord cutting.

## The Future of ESPN

Based on how quickly the sports media changes, it can be difficult to guess what the future of ESPN might look like. In the network's early days, a priority was placed on journalism, with interviews and in-depth reporting being a key drawing point for viewers. However, as the years progressed, a theme of "embrace debate" started to overrun the network. Hard-hitting journalism was replaced with shows in which two hosts debate the day's news, although that debate could often best be summarized as "two guys yelling at each other." Decades earlier, the thought of such a program being on ESPN for several hours a day, five days a week, would have seemed out of place from the rest of the content.

Ten years from now, the programming on ESPN could be very different from what is available now. However, the network's commitment to live sporting events figures to still be a centerpiece of the schedule. Additionally, the network's commitment to digital properties such as its website, phone apps, and streaming platform will likely continue to be a focus as long as that technology remains at the forefront of how people communicate and consume content.

## Summary

When sports fans want to know the latest about their favorite teams, it is almost impossible to ignore ESPN. The network has news updates, more live games than any other network, and websites and apps that can deliver scores and statistics. It's hard to believe now that ESPN almost did not make it past its first few years; a lack of compelling sports, no interest from advertisers, and cable companies that questioned the interest in a sports-only channel nearly halted the network before it could get off the ground. However, partnerships with the NFL and other major professional leagues would make ESPN a channel that fans demanded, even if it meant more money on their cable bill. The nightly highlights show *SportsCenter* transformed how fans got the latest sports news, showing athletes and teams from all over the country—not just those in the vicinity—to the viewer. As technology evolved, ESPN invested heavily in websites and social media accounts that quickly became the most popular in the sports genre. With consumer interests changing, ESPN debuted the streaming service ESPN+ in an effort to counteract the impact of the cord cutters that were getting rid of their cable package.

## REVIEW QUESTIONS

1. How did cable television change how people would watch television?
2. Why did ESPN struggle financially initially?
3. Why was broadcasting the NFL Draft seen as a major milestone in the history of ESPN?
4. Why is cord cutting a major concern for ESPN?

# 10

# Fox Sports

## CHAPTER OBJECTIVES

After completing the chapter, the reader should be able to do the following:

- Understand the creation of the Fox television network
- Discuss how the addition of the NFL legitimized the channel
- Recognize the innovations, both successful and not, that Fox Sports brought to television
- Debate the lasting impact of Fox Sports on broadcast television

In 1992, the animated television show *The Simpsons* was one of the few hits on the new Fox television network. While other shows came and went, the family from Springfield was in the beginning years of a lifespan that would see the show become the longest-running American sitcom in history. In an episode from that third season, Homer Simpson begins spending more time with his daughter Lisa after realizing that she could correctly pick the winner of the football games on which he was, up until she started helping, unsuccessfully betting. After a heated argument in which Lisa realizes that Homer was only spending time with her because she was picking games correctly, she lays out her biggest prediction of the season: If Washington beat Buffalo in the Super Bowl, it meant she still loved him, while a Buffalo win meant she did not. Homer agonizingly watches the game, rejoicing after the Washington win—a feat that would be repeated in "real life" in the actual Super Bowl just a few days later (Kogan et al., 1992).

In the episode, the NFL was just a side element to tell the main story about the relationship between a father and daughter, as the true stars of the episode were Homer and Lisa. For the next few years, the NFL remained the main draw on other television channels, and the antics of the Simpsons family remained one of the few programs worth watching on the struggling Fox network. However, that would change in 1994. In a stunning (and expensive) reversal, the Simpsons would become the second banana at the network, and the NFL would go from plot reference to the unquestioned star of the newly created Fox Sports division—the first step toward legitimizing the Fox channel.

## The Creation of Fox

For decades, American television had three main commercial stations: ABC, CBS, and NBC. In 1986, a fourth broadcast station quietly debuted, with the Fox Broadcasting Company entering the competition in an attempt to turn the "Big Three" into a "Big Four." The network signed affiliation deals with 79 television stations throughout the country and broadcast just one program, a live late-night talk show hosted by Joan Rivers (Associated Press, 1986). A year later, the number of shows had increased, but the outlook was already bleak for the future of the network. Rivers' show was a ratings dud, new primetime programming such as *Married . . . With Children* was labeled "crude" by television critics, and viewers were not tuning in to watch (Hale, 2012). Additionally, while Fox was supposed to be a national network, it technically was not, as only 91 percent of the country had a local Fox station (Lippman, 1990). Primetime shows were coming and going quickly, some affiliates were looking to get out of their deals, and Fox, despite its best efforts, was not considered serious competition for ABC, CBS, or NBC.

## The Super Bowl Halftime Show

In 1990, Fox debuted the primetime sketch comedy show *In Living Color*. It featured primarily Black actors and comedians, which was a rarity on national television at the time (O'Connor, 1990). It was an instant commercial and critical success. More than 22 million people tuned in for the first episode, and it won an Emmy Award for outstanding variety, music, or comedy series after its first season (In Living Color, n.d.; Morgan, 2021). However, the show's lasting impact on the network—and sports media as a whole—happened during the 1992 Super Bowl.

For years, the Super Bowl halftime show was an afterthought when compared to the game. There was entertainment such as marching bands and the feel-good singing group Up With People, but nothing that remotely resembles the modern halftime extravaganzas (Williams, 2013). The 1992 Super Bowl was in Minnesota, and the Winter Olympics were just weeks away, so the halftime performance was set to have a theme of "Winter Magic." The show featured figure skaters, ballroom dancers in winter coats, and, for just a fraction of the time, singer Gloria Estefan belting out her hits (Goodman-Hughley, 2020). Halftime was, as one television historian described it, the most "disposable part of the broadcast" (Williams, 2013, para. 30).

It was almost an expectation that people would tune out of the halftime show, and an advertising executive saw an opening. The idea was to put an alternative halftime show on a different network opposite the official one. After much discussion, Frito-Lay agreed to sponsor a live *In Living Color* halftime show that would air on Fox

at the same time as "Winter Magic." The edgy program started just as the game went to halftime on CBS and displayed a countdown clock in the corner of the screen so fans would not miss the start of the second half. As costumed snowflakes danced on the screen during the Super Bowl's official show, the *In Living Color Super Halftime Party* on Fox showcased some of the show's most popular characters and their risqué humor. It was estimated that 28.9 million people watched the alternative halftime show, a number that included both fans who had turned the channel from CBS and those who were not watching the Super Bowl to begin with (Goodman-Hughley, 2020).

The *In Living Color* halftime show has a legacy that endures years later for two main reasons. First, the show was a wakeup call to the NFL that their idea of a halftime show was no longer going to cut it. For the next year's game, the league increased the budget, turned the show into a spectacle, and hired superstar Michael Jackson to be the musical act (Goodman-Hughley, 2020). Without *In Living Color* disrupting the status quo, the modern-day halftime shows featuring the biggest musical acts in the world might not exist. Even the NFL would later acknowledge the impact of the show, naming the *In Living Color* halftime program one of the "100 Greatest Game Changers" in league history (NFL, n.d.). Additionally, the halftime show gave Fox a taste, albeit from a distance, of the NFL and how big events could lead to high viewership. The network was on the outside during the 1992 halftime show but would not be for much longer.

## The NFL on Fox

Despite small victories such as the halftime show, Fox was still considered a distant fourth in the early 1990s behind the "Big Three" networks and not a threat to change that status any time soon. However, in 1993, the network probably still best known for *The Simpsons* suddenly became a major media player thanks to an investment in sports. The most popular sport in the United States was professional football and the NFL, and Fox wanted a piece of the action.

### Legacy of CBS

Since 1956 the NFL had been a part of the programming at CBS, with the network airing games throughout the afternoon on Sundays and broadcasting several Super Bowls. Not only did the network have a historical legacy with the sport, but CBS had the rights to the National Football Conference (NFC), which, in the late 1980s and early 1990s, was the league's premier conference, having won nine straight Super Bowls. In addition, the NFC had teams in major American cities such as New York, Dallas, and Chicago, meaning the millions of fans in those large metropolitan areas needed to watch CBS to see their local team play (Curtis, 2018). For those reasons, the NFC package was especially appealing to any broadcasting outlet.

## Fox Enters the Negotiation

In 1993 the NFL's deal with CBS was set to expire, but there was little expectation that anything would change. Fox had attempted to get an NFL broadcasting package twice previously, but the league did not seem interested in doing anything beyond using the Fox bid as a way to drive up the cost for the existing partners. However, this time the offer would be different. Before talking money, Fox promised to have more cameras and microphones at every game, and to promote the league all year long and not just during football season (Curtis, 2018).

When it came time to make an offer, CBS bid $250 million a year to renew their deal. Fox blew that out of the water, as the upstart network outbid CBS by more than $100 million a year, part of a total offer of four years and $1.6 billion (Wulf, 1993; Sandomir, 1993). The money was staggering, and the NFL had no choice but to accept. The head of Fox, Rupert Murdoch, said at the time, "We're a network now. Like no other sport will do, the NFL will make us into a real network" (Wulf, 1993, para. 4). Fox might have been a newcomer to football, but it leaned on some legends to help establish instant credibility. With CBS no longer broadcasting NFL games, Fox raided their announcers, hiring the well-respected Terry Bradshaw, Pat Summerall, and John Madden to show the public that they were serious about the games (Curtis, 2018).

## The Impact of the NFL

By paying to show NFL games, Fox was signaling that they were now a major player in the world of broadcast television. Before the deal, the local Fox affiliates in some cities had a weaker signal than the ABC, CBS, or NBC stations, meaning that it was harder to receive on television antennas. However, once the NFL was going to be broadcast on Fox, the network became much more appealing. Less than a year after agreeing to the

pact with the league, Fox signed a deal with a broadcast ownership company that resulted in eight CBS stations switching to Fox affiliation. Demonstrating the power of the football broadcasts, six of those eight stations were in cities that had a team in the NFC (Carter, 1994). In 1997, the first Super Bowl on Fox resulted in 128.9 million viewers, the most in the history of the network (Jackson, 1997). While many in the media had questioned the logic behind Fox's enormous bid in 1993, it turned out to be the moment that turned the "Big Three" into the "Big Four."

## NHL on Fox

With a hole in its programming following the loss of the NFL, CBS focused on gaining the rights to professional hockey with the NHL. However, a familiar foe put that plan on ice. Fox outbid CBS by about $5 million a year, meaning that the new Fox Sports division now had its second property. As part of the deal, Fox had the rights to the All-Star Game, regular-season games, and select playoff contests (Sandomir, 1994). Fox had made it clear that the network viewed sports as a way to legitimize itself and was willing to spend millions of dollars to prove it.

## Innovations

Another aspect of Fox's sports coverage that soon became apparent was that the channel was willing to take some risks. For decades, sports broadcasts had been essentially identical, with the same camera angles, announcers, and music. Almost immediately, Fox demonstrated that they were going to do things differently. They hired younger announcers, placed a focus on audio before and during the games, expanded the pregame show, and had a mandate of "make it fun" from the new leadership at the newly created Fox Sports (Curtis, 2018). While some initiatives were a success and remain today, others are perhaps best left in the past. Two innovations that demonstrate the wide range between the good and the bad were the "Fox Box" and the glowing hockey puck.

## The "Fox Box"

David Hill was an executive with the British television network Sky Sports when he found himself watching a soccer match on a different channel and wondering who was winning. According to Hill, the announcers went about 20 minutes without saying the score, and there were no graphics were on the screen updating the goals. In 1992, Sky Sports won the rights to show Premier League matches, and one of Hill's early initiatives was to put a small graphic in the corner that would constantly run the score and time (Sandomir, 2014).

When Fox Sports won the NFL rights, Hill, who admittedly knew little about the sport, was hired by Murdoch and put in charge of the coverage. One of his first initiatives was to bring his "always on" scoreboard to Fox's coverage. Hill's logic was that because the score and time remaining were the most important aspects of the game, those statistics should be on the screen at all times (Curtis, 2018). The "Fox Box," as it came to be known, made its debut during the first preseason game and was different from anything NFL viewers had seen before. For some fans, it was perhaps *too* different, as Hill recalled receiving five death threats from people who were angry about how the small scoreboard was ruining their enjoyment of the game (Sandomir, 2014).

However, those viewers were in the minority, as the "Fox Box" went from a curiosity to a mainstay on nearly every sports broadcast moving forward. In addition, the scoreboards have become even more elaborate, now showing down and distance remaining for a first down, balls and strikes in baseball, and, for some events, room for a sponsor to place an advertisement. Fans watching replays of old games might be shocked to see that it was not always possible to know the details of the game at all times. It was Fox that had the innovative idea to put the score on the screen, an idea that now seems so obvious that a former ESPN executive would later say, "Why didn't someone think of it before?" (Sandomir, 2014, para. 24).

## The Glowing Puck

Shortly after winning the rights to show NHL games, David Hill had another idea he was ready to install. However, this one garnered the opposite reaction from viewers. Hill wanted to develop a way in which fans could follow the hockey puck better when watching a game on television. His idea developed into FoxTrax, which is perhaps better known by its description: a glowing puck. Fox created a technology that was embedded inside the puck that, when shot on a modified camera, would create a blueish glow around the puck. If a player took a shot that was over 70 miles per hour, a red comet-like tail would appear behind the puck (Wyshynski, 2017).

While the idea was certainly innovative, as no one had seen anything like it before, it was also highly ridiculed. A fan poll on ESPN rated it one of the worst ideas in sports history, and it was especially panned by Canadian fans who grew up loving the sport (ESPN, 2002; SBJ, 2017).

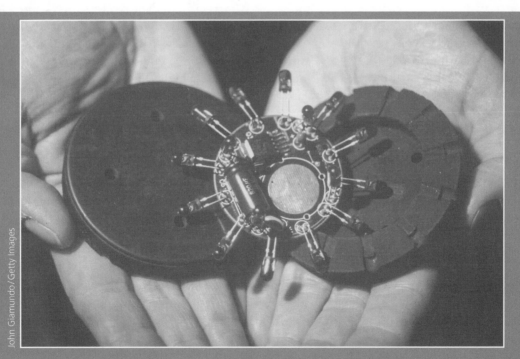

John Giamundo/Getty Images

**Electronic technology embedded in the puck allowed for the creation of a glowing puck effect in NHL games.**

Some viewers found the glowing puck to be distracting, while others wondered why a black puck on a white sheet of ice needed more attention drawn to it in the first place. The glowing puck was out of hockey after just two seasons; however, it was not due to enraged fans. Instead, the NHL signed a new broadcast deal with ESPN and the glowing puck stayed with Fox. While it was long ridiculed, the legacy of that glow now lies elsewhere. The technology was repurposed years later by the company that developed FoxTrax and can be seen in the digitally added yellow first down line that appears on the screen during football games (Wyshynski, 2017).

## Fox Sports Grows

The NFL and NHL were only the beginning of what eventually became a full portfolio of events in the Fox Sports family. The next league package acquired was Major League Baseball in 1996; the network split the coverage with NBC before taking over the coverage exclusively in 2000 (Sandomir, 2000). In the years following, Fox acquired NASCAR and college football's Bowl Championship Series, which included the national championship game. By 2022, Fox Sports had broadcasting deals with major conferences in college basketball and football, MLB, soccer's World Cup, NASCAR, NFL, and MLS (Presspass, n.d.). Those major sports have resulted in high viewership totals, including the 17.7 million who watched the 2022 men's World Cup soccer championship, which was a new record for the men's final in the United States (McCarthy, 2022). In all of 2022, fans watched 265.3 billion minutes of live sports on Fox, more than any other channel (Mulvihill, 2023).

## Fox Sports 1

As Fox acquired more sports to broadcast, it made sense for the company to expand its offerings on cable. In 2013, Fox announced they were converting two existing channels that the company owned into Fox Sports 1 and Fox Sports 2. However, the new emphasis on cable would not be just a simple rebrand—Fox management was trying to take on ESPN for cable sports dominance. An aggressive marketing plan was created to tell fans that Fox Sports 1 (later shortened to FS1) would be an alternative to ESPN for those who wanted something different. Management hired former ESPN employees,

created studio shows, and developed *Fox Sports Live* as a direct competitor to *SportsCenter* (Baysinger, 2013). After a strong first day, the viewership totals cratered after just a week, with fewer than 100,000 homes watching what were supposed to be the signature programs on the network. Less than five months later, one episode of *Fox Sports Live* drew just 7,000 viewers. Shows were coming and going quickly and FS1 was proving to be little competition for ESPN (Fang, 2017).

In the years following, FS1 went in several different directions, including an "embrace debate" mandate in which daytime shows featured less reporting and more arguments between sports media members. This model had proven successful at ESPN years earlier, but did not have the same result at FS1 (Reedy, 2019). However, elements of that style remained for the next few years until the network attempted to reinvent itself again. A focus on live sporting events and programming that executives called "smart, entertaining, and interesting" helped FS1 to start to live up to some of its early promises (Reedy, 2019, para. 2). The network had become an alternative to ESPN by creating an additional channel for sports fans to get the latest news, scores, and game action.

## Summary

It appeared as if the Fox television channel might not make it past its first few years. Viewership was low and there was not much on the programming guide that was going to change that. However, the over-the-top bid to acquire the NFL demonstrated the value of live sports, while also making Fox a legitimate channel in the eyes of many. Fans tuned in to the professional football games by the millions, so having the NFL meant that Fox suddenly had a new batch of viewers it did not have access to previously.

The investment was the first of many for the new Fox Sports division of the network, as professional hockey and baseball soon followed, with college sports, World Cup soccer, and auto racing not far behind. Leadership at Fox Sports did not stop with just showing the games; they wanted to show them *differently*. Innovations ranged from the wildly successful "Fox Box" to the nearly universally panned glowing puck. However, what it demonstrated was that Fox Sports was willing to take chances in an effort to make the games more enjoyable for fans to watch.

## REVIEW QUESTIONS

1. Why was the 1992 Super Bowl halftime show something that Fox felt it could compete with?

2. How did getting the NFL games affect Fox?

3. What made the "Fox Box" such a unique innovation?

4. What is one way in which Fox Sports attempted to compete with ESPN?

# League of Denial

## CHAPTER OBJECTIVES

After completing the chapter, the reader should be able to do the following:

- Summarize the issues surrounding the NFL and head injuries
- Recognize the importance of the *League of Denial* book and film
- Evaluate the issues surrounding ESPN's withdrawal from the *League of Denial* film
- Analyze how media companies report on entities with which they are in a business partnership

The NFL's Super Bowl is regularly the most-watched television event of the year in the United States, and every regular season game draws in millions of viewers. There is little debate that football, especially professional football, is the most popular sport in America. For many, one of the most appealing aspects of the action is the bone-crunching hits delivered by these world-class athletes. While players are routinely battling easily diagnosable physical injuries such as broken bones and torn ligaments, brain injuries can be harder to detect. As former NFL quarterback Steve Young puts it, "If my knee is hurt, I know it and everyone knows it, and we can go deal with it. There is only one place in your body that you really don't understand. People always say, 'the brain is the last frontier'" (Kirk, 2003, 0:29:41).

As awareness regarding the dangers of head injuries in sports has increased, so has the realization that those big hits could be causing long-term damage to the players' brains. In 2013, two versions of *League of Denial* were produced: a book and a documentary film. The two projects shined a light on the dangers of concussions in football

and the role the NFL may have played in the downplaying of those injuries. While the project was enjoying critical success in print and on the screen, a media-based controversy was happening behind the scenes.

## Concussions, CTE, and the NFL

There are two main brain injuries that are the focus of the *League of Denial* story: **concussions** and **chronic traumatic encephalopathy** (more commonly abbreviated to CTE). The Centers for Disease Control and Prevention (2019) describes concussion as a traumatic brain injury that is caused by a hit to the head or body that causes the head and brain to move rapidly back and forth. This movement causes chemical changes in the brain and can sometimes damage brain cells. While concussions had long been assumed to be a part of professional football, two high-profile injuries in 1994 brought the injury to the forefront. Dallas Cowboys quarterback Troy Aikman and Chicago Bears fullback Merrill Hoge both suffered concussions in a game, with Aikman saying later he did not remember even playing in the game, while Hoge said he could not recognize his wife or brother after the game in which he suffered his injury (Ezell, 2013).

CTE is a degenerative brain disease that is commonly associated with repeated hits to the head. Its impact on boxers had been known for decades but it gained increasing attention in the NFL in the early 2000s. CTE can only be discovered through an autopsy, so it is impossible to determine if a former or current player has been afflicted with the disease while they are still alive. A 2021 article stated that CTE had been found in the brains of more than 315 former NFL players, including two dozen who had died in their 20s and 30s (Shpigel, 2021).

# *League of Denial* Project

After reporting a story on former NFL linebacker Fred McNeil in 2011, ESPN investigative reporter Mark Fainaru-Wada approached his brother Steve Fainaru about writing a book about the dangers of head injuries among football players. The two determined that the story was not just a potentially controversial health topic involving the multibillion-dollar professional sports league, but also could be seen as them conducting a public service by providing information about this crisis (Lelinwalla, 2015). For the next 18 months, the two worked on what ultimately became titled *League of Denial: The NFL, Concussions, and the Battle for Truth*. Their work included a book and a documentary film that was based on the reporting in the book.

# Book and Documentary Summary

There are many similarities between the book and the documentary, so a brief description of the issues that are discussed in both follows here. This section should not be perceived as a replacement for consuming the *League of Denial* media but should instead be seen as a summary of three of the key topics within each to give the reader of this book an idea of the contents. Those topics are

- the NFL's reluctance to acknowledge head injuries,
- Mike Webster and Bennet Omalu, and
- what did the NFL know and when did it know it?

In order to minimize the number of in-text citations, note that the information in this section is gathered from the book (Fainaru-Wada & Fainaru, 2013) or the film (Kirk, 2013) unless otherwise noted.

## The NFL's Reluctance to Acknowledge Head Injuries

While concussions had been considered a dangerous part of football dating back to the early days of the game, the NFL did not fully acknowledge brain injuries until 1994. In that year, the league created the Mild Traumatic Brain Injury (MTBI) Committee to study the effects of concussions on football players. While the league was addressing this topic for the first time, they remained dismissive. One representative said, "Concussions are part of the profession, an occupational risk" (Farber, 1994, p. 40). Additionally, the league named a rheumatologist the chair of the committee, which was a curious choice considering that rheumatology is focused on joints and tissues, not brain injuries. That chair filled the committee with other NFL team doctors who were loyal to the league.

By 2000, the MTBI committee had several years of data, and they determined that concussions were not a serious threat to player safety. According to the organization, brain injuries were both minor and uncommon. The committee also stated that if a player did suffer a concussion, getting back on the field either during that same game or a later one did not lead to an increased risk of getting a second head injury. Simply put, the NFL, through their official head trauma committee, stated that concussions were not a serious injury.

The NFL's official stance on head injuries was in great contrast to what independent doctors were saying at the time. Researchers were discovering links between former players who had suffered concussions and long-term injuries. One study found a connection between depression and players who had suffered concussions. Alzheimer's disease was found in NFL players who had a history of concussions. The stage was being set for a conflict between the NFL and the medical community when it came to head injuries among players.

## Mike Webster and Bennet Omalu

The dangers of head injuries were brought to light in both the book and the documentary through two key people: Mike Webster and Bennet Omalu. Webster had a storied career as the center for the Pittsburgh Steelers in the 1970s and 1980s. He won four Super Bowls, played in nine Pro Bowls (the NFL's all-star game), and was

George Gojkovich/Getty Images

**Pittsburgh Steelers center Mike Webster was the first professional football player diagnosed with CTE.**

inducted into the Pro Football Hall of Fame in 1997. He is widely considered one of the best centers in NFL history. However, his lasting legacy may ultimately be what happened in his post-playing life.

Following retirement, Webster struggled with physical and mental illness, bouncing between bouts of homelessness and living with family members. He had amnesia, dementia, and depression, and was in severe pain from the pounding his body went through as a professional football player. The center position might be one of the most physical positions in football, requiring hiking the ball to the quarterback and then immediately driving head-first into the opponent in front of him on nearly every single play. In 2002, at just 50 years old, Webster suffered a fatal heart attack.

Following Webster's death, forensic neuropathologist Bennet Omalu conducted the autopsy. Omalu, an immigrant from Nigeria, knew nothing about football or Webster's career when examining the body. While the autopsy determined that Webster's body was riddled with physical injuries, there was something else about the case that immediately stood out to Omalu. Webster's body was broken down, but his brain appeared to be completely fine. This seemed odd to

the experienced doctor, who expected the brain to be just as damaged as the rest of the body, and he immediately asked for the brain to be preserved so it could be examined further.

This decision proved to be the key first step in the research involving brain injuries in professional football players. Omalu's additional analysis showed that there were spots on Webster's brain that suggested the former football star was suffering from CTE, making him the first professional football player diagnosed with the injury. Omalu would publish his findings in a medical journal, hoping that the NFL would be interested and want to do something to help curb what could be a major injury. Instead, the opposite happened, and the NFL's MBTI committee sent a letter to the journal demanding a retraction due to what they said was an incorrect diagnosis by Omalu. The journal's editors refused, and Omalu would soon publish a follow-up confirming his diagnosis after examining the brain of another former NFL player who had recently passed away. Eventually, Omalu elected to step away from this line of research, saying, "I wish I never met Mike Webster. CTE has dragged me into the politics of science and the politics of the NFL" (Kirk, 2013, 0:55:45). However, another doctor, Ann McKee, would soon take over as the most prominent examiner in this field, and she would continue the battles with the NFL.

## What Did the NFL Know and When Did It Know It?

While Webster's CTE diagnosis was the first of its kind among football players, it was not the NFL's first exposure to the severity of his injuries. Before his death, Webster filed a lawsuit against the league, looking for financial restitution for the injuries that he sustained while playing the game. A group of independent doctors determined that Webster should be eligible for disability benefits from the league because his playing had caused his dementia. The NFL hired their own doctor to examine Webster, who came to the same conclusion. In 2000, the retirement board gave Webster monthly payments and acknowledged in their settlement statement that the sport can result in head injuries. It was the league's first admission that playing football could be the cause of these brain traumas, although this was kept from the public. The NFL's words were not discovered until many years later when authors Fainaru-Wada and Fainaru were doing their research.

In the following years, the NFL heard directly from Omalu, McKee, and other doctors about the dangers of head injuries. However, each time, the league's leaders, including the NFL commissioner, shifted the focus elsewhere. They would either deny the science entirely or place more of a concern on what this information could mean for the future of the league. The NFL's own science was starting to demonstrate that they might be incorrect to ignore the topic. An article from *The New York Times* revealed that a study commissioned by the league itself had shown that Alzheimer's disease was diagnosed in former players at a much greater rate than the rest of the population (Schwarz, 2009a). Less than three months later, for the first time publicly, the NFL acknowledged the long-term effects of concussions. The league's spokesman was quoted in *The New York Times* as saying, "It's quite obvious from the medical research that's been done that concussions can lead to long-term problems" (Schwartz, 2009b, para. 2). The NFL pledged to be more proactive with head injuries by donating money to research centers and forcing players to be cleared by an independent doctor before reentering the game following signs of a concussion.

The *League of Denial* documentary concludes with information about the settlement of a lawsuit between former players and the league. More than 4,500 players joined together to sue the NFL, claiming that the league knew about the dangers of head injuries but neglected to tell the players. The settlement meant that the case would not go to court, with the NFL agreeing to pay $765 million to victims, pay for medical exams, and support additional research on the dangers of head injuries in the sport. However, despite the league paying more than three-quarters of a billion dollars, one of the terms of the settlement was that this financial payout did not serve as an admission of liability by the league. Therefore, while the NFL was paying this money, it did not mean that they were saying that playing in the league was the cause of long-term brain injuries among its former players. Instead, the league continued to adamantly deny that there was a link between playing football and major head injuries.

## Critical and Public Response

Both the documentary and the book were received positively by critics. The book won the PEN/ESPN Award for Literary Sports Writing, with judges calling it "a compelling and important book" (Pen America, 2014, para. 2). Meanwhile, the documentary won a Peabody Award, which is given for excellence in storytelling and public service by a media organization (Taddonio, 2014).

There were mixed results for *League of Denial* when it came to the public response. The documentary averaged more than 2 million viewers on PBS, more than the usual 1.5 million viewers who traditionally watch a *Frontline* episode. Additionally, the day the documentary aired was one of the busiest days on the *Frontline* website (Sandomir, 2013). However, while the book debuted as the no. 1 best-seller in the sports and recreation category in its initial week, sales soon stalled. Nielsen BookScan revealed that fewer than 10,000 print copies were sold in the first two months it was available, a number that was much lower than experts had anticipated. However, the book's publishing company pushed back on that assessment, saying those numbers did not include the popular e-book versions (Kaplan, 2013).

## Concussion

Just over two years after the *League of Denial* documentary was finished, another film about the NFL and concussions debuted. This movie was a drama, with actors portraying several of the key people from the nonfiction version. The movie, titled *Concussion*, focused less on the NFL's response to concussions and more on Bennet Omalu as the hero of the story. In addition to actor Will Smith's portrayal of Omalu, other actors recreated the roles of Mike Webster and NFL commissioner Roger Goodell, among others (Landesman, 2015). Shortly before the film's release, *The New York Times* reported that Sony Pictures Entertainment had changed part of the script to avoid upsetting the NFL. The article stated that moments that were "unflattering" to the NFL were removed or changed (Belson, 2015, para. 6). When it came to concussions, the NFL, and the media, this was not the first time that some had suspected a major media corporation had changed plans to appease the NFL.

## ESPN and *League of Denial*

As stated earlier in this chapter, the documentary film was originally a partnership between ESPN and PBS. The investigative units of both networks would work together to create a two-part special in which reporters would examine issues surrounding concussions in the NFL. The partnership was greeted with great fanfare but never made it to the finish line. Many speculate that pressure applied behind the scenes by the NFL caused ESPN to remove itself from the project before the documentary was completed.

## The Initial Partnership Develops

In November 2012, ESPN and PBS announced that the two networks would work together to investigate concussions in the NFL. ESPN touted the partnership as a "year-long effort [that] will examine the latest research on brain injuries and football, the impact on players and the NFL's effort to deal with a crisis that threatens the long-term health and popularity of the sport" (Scott, 2012, para. 3). PBS executives stated that "ESPN is a terrific partner for this investigation" (Scott, 2012, para. 4). As part of that year-long partnership, the networks' two investigative shows, *Outside the Lines* (ESPN) and *Frontline* (PBS), would co-create a podcast, launch a *Concussion Watch* website on PBS.com, and broadcast the full-length documentary film in concert with the release of the *League of Denial* book (Hebert-Farrell & Scott, 2012).

## ESPN's Withdrawal

In August 2013, less than two months before the documentary was supposed to air, ESPN announced that they were no longer going to be involved in the project. This was a somewhat surprising announcement, as the two networks had already paired up to create nine joint television and online stories that appeared on both networks' television shows and websites (Sandomir, 2013). However, ESPN executives said the decision to leave the project was based on a lack of editorial control over the documentary that was set to air on *Frontline*. Essentially, they were saying that because PBS had final say over the documentary, ESPN did not want its name or logo to be associated with the piece (Associated Press, 2013). In a statement from PBS, *Frontline*'s executive producer stated that "we regret ESPN's decision to end a collaboration" but that the show would continue as scheduled (Moughty, 2013, para. 2). PBS executives also revealed

NFL Hall of Famer Harry Carson, Mark Fainaru-Wada, Steve Fainaru, senior coordinating producer at ESPN Dwayne Bray, and filmmaker Michael Kirk speak onstage during the "League of Denial: The NFL's Concussion Crisis" panel at the PBS portion of the 2013 Summer Television Critics Association tour at the Beverly Hilton Hotel on August 6, 2013, in Beverly Hills, California.

that had ESPN not left the project, they would have had the opportunity to screen a nearly final edit of the film and give suggestions for possible changes (Moughty, 2013). Without ESPN's involvement or input, the two-hour show aired on PBS in October 2013.

## The Mystery of ESPN's Departure

When ESPN executives announced they were pulling out of the partnership with PBS, many immediately speculated that the NFL had something to do with this decision. After all, ESPN was in the middle of an eight-year, $15.2 billion deal with the NFL to show *Monday Night Football* games and highlights throughout the day with no limitations on time (Richwine & Baker, 2013). ESPN was quick to challenge those claims and stated that the decision was theirs alone, saying "The decision to remove our branding was not a result of concerns about our separate business relationship with the NFL" (Associated Press, 2013, para. 10). *Frontline* deputy executive producer Raney Aronson said they were not told why ESPN dropped out: "It's anybody's guess right now about what actually happened" (Associated Press, 2013, para. 13).

However, there are some well-sourced media reporters who believe they do know what actually happened, and they dispute ESPN's claims that the NFL partnership was not a factor. James Andrew Miller, who cowrote a book about ESPN, and Ken Belson, an NFL writer for *The New York Times*, coauthored an article headlined "N.F.L. pressure said to lead ESPN to quit film project." The story recounts a combative lunch between NFL and ESPN executives, in which the NFL commissioner was among those expressing his dissatisfaction with the documentary and ESPN's involvement with it. One week after that meeting, ESPN announced they were pulling out of the project (Miller & Belson, 2013).

However, the seeds of doubt had already been planted among some at ESPN even before that fateful lunch. At a press event just over a week earlier, a two-minute trailer for the documentary aired to preview the contents and tone of the film. The trailer ends with neuropathologist Ann McKee, a main source of information throughout the film, stating that she wonders if "every single player" does not have some sort of brain injury due to playing football (Waldron, 2013, para. 1). ESPN's then-president John Skipper had not seen the trailer before the showing and later said he found that comment from McKee to be "over the top" (Lipsyte,

2013, para. 11). According to Skipper, this trailer was the moment at which he began to consider removing ESPN's affiliation from the project. He would admit to the ESPN ombudsman that his lunch with the NFL did occur eight days later, and that the documentary was the primary topic of that meeting. However, he stated that it was his decision to pull out of the project and that no one at the NFL demanded he do so (Lipsyte, 2013).

While Skipper was steadfast that the decision was his alone, there were some within ESPN who were skeptical. Several news articles were published in which employees stated their doubts about ESPN's reasoning that there were simply concerns over co-branding. An article on *Sports Illustrated*'s website stated that some at ESPN had feared the network would pull out of the project as much as a month earlier, and directly stated that pressure was being put on ESPN by the NFL (Deitsch, 2013). Other journalists said they could not find anyone at ESPN who believed the NFL had nothing to do with the decision (Sherman, 2013).

## ESPN and the NFL

With so many doubting that the NFL did not pressure ESPN to drop its involvement in the documentary, it is worth examining the partnership between the professional football league and the sports network. At the time of the documentary, ESPN was in an agreement to pay the NFL billions of dollars to be the exclusive home of *Monday Night Football*. That investment means ESPN is essentially a business partner with the league. Therefore, both the NFL and ESPN are motivated to have a large audience for those Monday night games. For ESPN, that high viewership is especially important because the network needs to find a way to make up some of that investment through advertising. The more viewers that ESPN can show are watching, the more they can charge companies to advertise during the games.

The documentary caused some to reassess their football fandom. Knowing that concussions have been proven to result in serious health injuries for the players resulted in fans having to reconcile their own personal entertainment with the health of those in the game. One journalist wrote after the documentary aired:

> To deny the implications of the show and not, at the very least, take that potential hypocrisy very seriously, would be delusional. If I keep watching, it is at my own ethical risk. And I honestly don't know what I'm going to do. (Humphrey, 2013, para. 10)

Quotes such as this one could be a potential disaster for ESPN. If millions of people agreed with this journalist and decided not to watch NFL games any longer, then the network could face a severe financial hardship. This documentary about concussions was ultimately a journalistic piece, but that might not always mesh with the goals of the executives at the company. As one unnamed ESPN journalist said, "ESPN's business interests will always be at odds with its journalism. It is not a journalism company. It's an entertainment company" (Zirin, 2013, para. 6).

Ultimately, ESPN's lack of involvement in the piece might have backfired. Millions of people tuned in to watch the documentary when it aired on PBS, and the YouTube video of the entire episode has resulted in hundreds of thousands more views. A few media experts cited ESPN's withdrawal from the project as a reason why viewership was so high. ESPN's decision to leave the project was certainly controversial and resulted in articles in many major newspapers and websites discussing the change in plans. This ultimately gave *League of Denial* a tremendous amount of free publicity, putting the film, PBS, and the contents of the documentary in articles throughout the United States (Flint, 2013; Sandomir, 2013).

Perhaps most troublesome to ESPN was the potential blow to its reputation. When ESPN dropped out of the partnership, no matter what the reason, the network was giving the impression that it did not want to discuss concussions. Its business partnership with the NFL was immediately a topic of conversation, which can cause some to wonder about how ESPN might report on the league in the future.

## *Playmakers*

The *League of Denial* documentary is not the first time that ESPN and the NFL have had a disagreement about content with which the network was involved. However, in 2003, it was not an investigative report that caused the issue, but a scripted television show. *Playmakers* was ESPN's first attempt at an original drama series. The show focused on a fictional football team that, in addition to their time on the field, faced many controversial off-field topics. Episodes addressed drug use, sex, and domestic violence by the players. The 11-episode first season had some of the highest ratings on the network outside of live sports, but the NFL was not happy.

Early in the season, the NFL commissioner complained directly to the chief executive of the Walt Disney Company (ESPN's parent company) about the show. Ultimately, that first season of *Playmakers* proved to be the only season of the show. Unlike the *League of Denial* departure, ESPN explicitly stated that the NFL's objection to the show was the reason for the cancellation. The executive vice president of ESPN said at the time, "We're not in the business of antagonizing our partner, even though we've done it, and continued to carry it over the N.F.L.'s objections. To bring it back would be rubbing it in our partner's face" (Sandomir, 2004, para. 5).

## ESPN Promotes the Book

While ESPN did not want to be associated with the *League of Denial* film, it did heavily promote the book of the same title. A week before the book's release, ESPN aired interviews with the two authors on *SportsCenter* and *Outside the Lines*, posted an excerpt from the book on ESPN.com, booked the authors on an ESPN radio show, and had them participate in an ESPN.com chat (Scott, 2013). However, in this case, the network might have been attempting to appease two of their most decorated employees. The authors, brothers Mark Fainaru-Wada and Steve Fainaru, were ESPN employees at the time, serving as investigative reporters. While the two are also featured prominently in the documentary, they are the only authors of the book.

However, even on ESPN's website, the two expressed frustration with how their employer handled its exit from the film. In the ESPN.com chat, they wrote: "We've said repeatedly that this was a disappointing episode, especially since the partnership worked so well" (Fainaru-Wada & Fainaru, 2013, para. 28). The two also acknowledged the conflict between the journalism side and the business side of ESPN's empire: "In the book, we note that ESPN pays the NFL nearly $2 billion a year to air *Monday Night Football*, which is like staging a $120 million Harry Potter [movie] every week. So it's not surprising that there's tension there" (Fainaru-Wada & Fainaru, 2013, para. 28).

## Summary

The *League of Denial* book and documentary put a spotlight on concussions in the NFL. For decades, the league and its fans celebrated the big hits that occur during the game action, but these investigative pieces caused society to rethink those collisions. The hit may take just a second, but the impact could last for the rest of a player's life.

While the documentary was released to critical acclaim, it debuted without the previously agreed upon partnership involving ESPN. The network stated it left because it was not part of the film's development, but others wonder if the NFL put pressure on ESPN to drop out of its arrangement with PBS. As one writer put it, what actually happened might ultimately simply come down to money:

> We'll probably never know the full circumstances of ESPN's departure from League of Denial, but when a network shells out more than a billion dollars for broadcast rights and when broadcast rights become a major driver of profits, quality journalism can be the element of that balance that is unfortunately easy to sacrifice. (Waldron, 2013, para. 7)

The *League of Denial* saga should remind sports fans both about the health risks involved with full-contact sports and the issues relating to media-league partnerships. Fans should examine who is delivering their sports news and what impact business relationships might have on that reporting.

## KEY TERMS

**chronic traumatic encephalopathy**—A brain disorder often found in people who have suffered repeated head injuries.

**concussion**—A traumatic injury that impacts a person's brain.

## REVIEW QUESTIONS

1. Why might people be skeptical of the NFL's own examination of head injuries in the sport of football?
2. Why did ESPN state that they were dropping out of the partnership with PBS for the *League of Denial* documentary?
3. Why might the NFL have been able to pressure ESPN to drop out of the *League of Denial* documentary?
4. Why was ESPN's departure from *Playmakers* different from its departure from *League of Denial*?

# 12

# ESPN and the SEC Bias

## CHAPTER OBJECTIVES

After completing the chapter, the reader should be able to do the following:

- Understand why ESPN is accused of having an SEC bias
- Recognize what Fox Sports is doing to counterprogram that supposed bias
- Debate what a possible SEC bias might mean for fans watching
- Identify why being accused of being biased should be a concern for any journalist

In 2014, the University of Alabama football team shut out Texas A&M 59–0 in a matchup of two Southeastern Conference (SEC) squads, leading many to speculate that Alabama was one of the best teams in the country. However, not everyone was sold. Former UCLA head coach Rick Neuheisel said, "I know how to become a top five team . . . just play Texas A&M" (Duffey, 2014, para. 2). The implication of his tongue-in-cheek comment was clear: The former coach believed that simply beating an SEC school gave opponents more credibility than might be deserved.

That argument had been gaining steam for several years and came to a head during the 2021 season. The University of Georgia, an SEC school, won the national championship, but the conference's postseason record that year was six wins and eight losses (Wittry, 2022). So while Georgia had proved to be the best team in the country, the conference's other schools were struggling in these showcase games. A quiet frustration among supporters of other conferences was starting to get louder,

with some critics arguing that if the SEC is top-heavy, then beating lesser teams in the conference is not worth as much. On Fox Sports, announcer Joel Klatt said that the entire conference was simply riding "the coattails of two or three great programs" (Speak, 2021, 1:47).

However, for many college football fans, the issues surrounding the SEC are not solely focused on the quality of teams. Instead, some believe the sports media is to blame for the conference getting more attention than perhaps it deserves. That has led to talk that there is a pro-SEC bias among many in journalism, meaning the media is showing favoritism to the league, with extra vitriol focused on one media outlet in particular.

## Early Media Hype

The media hype surrounding the SEC might have become a national conversation point in the early 2020s, but the conference was being promoted well before that. Through revolutionary television deals and winning football programs, the league found itself getting attention outside just its regional footprint. While that was good for the SEC, this growth was the beginning of the frustration felt by other fans.

## National Television Deals

In 1984, the SEC made a deal with TBS to show one nationally televised game from the conference each Saturday. While fans in the Southeast certainly knew about SEC football, the conference was about to get exposure throughout the entire country, a move that would raise the profile of the league. The commissioner of the SEC at the time said, "Regardless of what the network and ESPN were doing, you could turn on the television in any city in the country and see SEC football, and that set us apart" (Dunnavant, 2004, p. 179).

After that deal expired, the SEC was back on regional television and the advantages gained from that TBS deal were gone. The leaders of the conference soon embarked on a plan to get back on a network that would give them that national exposure. After being outbid by Fox for the NFL package (see chapter 10 for more), CBS was looking for new sports programming to replace what was lost. The network stuck with football but moved to the college ranks, agreeing to a five-year, $85 million deal to show select SEC games starting in 1996 (Sandomir, 1994).

While the money was certainly appealing, the major draw for the conference was the commitment to show an SEC game each week during the college football season at 3:30 p.m. ET. Media members and fans could watch the SEC each week no matter where they lived, and for the conference the timing could not have been better. Schools from the SEC won the national championship in both 1996 and 1998, had a Heisman Trophy winner in 1996, and were the home of arguably the biggest star in the sport, Tennessee's Peyton Manning (Myers, 2022; NCAA, n.d.). Just as the conference was starting to enter the upper echelon in college football, its television deal gave it a tremendous advantage over the rest of the country, which might have been the start of the SEC bias among the media.

## *Sports Illustrated*

As stated in chapter 5, *Sports Illustrated* (*SI*) was perhaps the most influential sports media outlet for decades, and if the magazine published an article about a player,

team, or sport, that gave that entity extra credibility. Therefore, when *SI* published one of its first articles on the rising profile of the SEC in 1995, that meant people nationally were about to take notice of the league. The article called the SEC "the toughest conference in the land" while running down what made the games worth watching (Stone, 1995). Just over a decade later, as the SEC was starting to emerge as a national powerhouse, *SI* proclaimed it to be "the best, toughest, wildest conference in the land" (Taylor, 2006). It did not stop there, as three years later *SI* had one more cover story, with a 2009 piece proclaiming, "SEC Football—Nobody does it better" with the SEC's Tim Tebow in the accompanying image. Players and coaches were quoted throughout the article emphasizing how much better their conference was than any other in the country. The head coach of the University of Mississippi at the time said, "I watch [teams in] other conferences all the time and think, Boy, I'd like to play them" (Bradley, 2009, para. 17).

## Associated Press Top 25 Poll

Each week during college football season, a collection of more than 60 sports broadcasters and writers throughout the county vote for who they believe are the best 25 teams in the country. Each media member ranks the teams from 1 to 25, with the most points awarded to the best team. For example, the no. 1 team in a vote get 25 points, while the no. 25 team gets 1 point on each voter's ballot. The rankings of all the voters are combined into one master list by the Associated Press (AP), resulting in the weekly AP Top 25 poll (Parks, 2022). The voters are scattered throughout the country, primarily to avoid any sort of regional favoritism. However, that did not stop fans of other conferences from accusing the voters of having an SEC bias in 2014.

For the first time in the history of the poll, which dates to 1934, one conference had four of the top five spots in the voting results in a midseason poll. That conference was the SEC, and the trending hashtag on social media afterward was #SECBias. However, a closer look at the voters revealed that the Ohio voters from Big Ten country and California voters in the heart of the Pac-12 footprint all had at least three SEC teams in the top five of their ballots (Russo, 2014). That information was of little interest to fans, some of whom wondered if their schools had a chance to compete with the media's (alleged) favorite conference.

## ESPN's Business Deals

While several different media outlets have been accused of perpetrating an SEC bias, most will quickly point to ESPN as the main culprit. Almost since its debut in 1979, ESPN has developed media rights deals with professional leagues or the entire NCAA. While that has sometimes raised concerns of bias when examining ESPN's reporting (see the previous chapter), the coverage is traditionally focused on an entire sport, so the individual teams have little about which to complain. Therefore, when ESPN elected to enter into an expensive partnership with the SEC, schools outside of that conference took notice.

## SEC Network

In 2013, the SEC and ESPN announced a 20-year partnership to create the SEC Network, a television channel and digital platform that would be devoted to all things SEC sports. ESPN stated that events from all 21 sports sponsored by the conference would be shown, including

45 football games each year (Siegal, 2013). For the SEC, it meant more money for each school, expanding the 15-year, $2.25 billion deal the conference had signed with ESPN in 2008 (Sandomir, 2013).

Shortly after the announcement, some affiliated with other conferences began to express concern. Bo Pelini, the head coach at the Big Ten's University of Nebraska at the time, said, "I don't think that kind of relationship is good for college football. Any time you have a relationship with somebody, you have a partnership, you are supposed to be neutral. It's pretty hard to stay neutral in that situation" (Goodbread, 2014, para. 2). Questions about ESPN's ability to stay impartial were starting to be raised, and a further investment in the league a few years later would only amplify those concerns.

## Exclusive Starting in 2024

The conference's deal with CBS to show a featured football game each week was slated to expire after the 2023 season, and the SEC wanted to lock up a new package before that one lapsed. At the time, CBS was

ESPN held a media open house in August 2014 to celebrate the beginning of the new SEC Network.

Jeff Siner/Charlotte Observer/Tribune News Service via Getty Images paying $55 million a year for the 3:30 p.m. weekly game, but the rights for the new deal were expected to be multiples of that price. In 2019, CBS bid close to $300 million annually, but ultimately recognized that ESPN was going to trump their offer and backed out of the negotiation (Ourand, 2019). Disney, which owned ABC and ESPN, agreed to pay the SEC $3 billion over ten years for the rights to the best Saturday afternoon game and select primetime football games. Most significant was the fact that all the league's games would appear on either ESPN or ABC starting in 2024 (Draper & Blinder, 2020).

## SEC Promotion

With ESPN spending billions of dollars to show SEC games, it has to hope that fans will watch in order to make up some of that money through advertising. To do that, the network has been accused of overly promoting SEC games and players. This attention is another factor in why some claim the network has an SEC bias.

However, for the teams in the league, it is hard to ignore the advantages that come with being partnered with ESPN in a media deal. In 2012, Texas A&M had recently moved from the Big 12 conference to the SEC. Freshman quarterback Johnny Manziel was having a historic season, and ESPN chronicled his outstanding play on *SportsCenter* and *College Football Live*. ESPN replayed some of the most exciting plays of his season repeatedly and began hyping up Manziel as the possible first-ever freshman to win the Heisman Trophy, given each year to the best player in college football. After Manziel did win the prestigious award, the Texas A&M athletic director was overt in his praise for ESPN's role in promoting SEC players: "If we were in the Big 12, I don't know that Johnny Manziel would have won the Heisman" (Miller et al., 2013, para. 19).

## Fox Sports Fights Back

With some believing that ESPN is promoting the SEC more than they should, it is possible that fans from other conferences might start looking for alternative programming. For example, sitting through ESPN's Saturday pregame show *College GameDay* might not be appealing for fans of the Big Ten who do not want to hear the latest information about SEC schools. To fill that void, Fox Sports embarked on a programming strategy that would present itself as an alternative to the SEC favoritism that many saw on ESPN.

## Big Ten Coverage

Much like ESPN's broadcast agreement with the SEC, Fox had a deal with the Big Ten to create the Big Ten Network starting in 2007 (Sandomir, 2006). That partnership would expand in the years following, with Fox paying for the rights to show games on Fox's main channel, while also moving the most prominent Big Ten game each week to a noon ET kickoff (Crawford, 2019; Ourand & Smith, 2016). In addition, Fox aired *Big Noon Kickoff*, their version of ESPN's *College GameDay* preview show, and reported live from the most important Big Ten game of the weekend. Fox Sports was leaning into the cries of #SECBias among Big Ten fans and was presenting itself as a place to turn for those fans looking to boycott ESPN. One sports media analyst noted in 2019 how Fox embracing those anti-ESPN viewers could pay dividends:

> The past few weeks I've talked to fans of Big 12 and Pac-12 schools who all pointed to ESPN's close ties to the SEC as a growing annoyance. To many, the current system feels rigged against them, and they believe ESPN is in the middle of it helping facilitate the status quo. What Fox has done the past few months in cozying up to Ohio State and Michigan is something they can continue to employ in future years in an effort to flip more fanbases to preferring Fox over ESPN. (Koo, 2019, para. 30)

Early on in that strategy, it did appear that Fox's Big Ten emphasis was working. In both 2021 and 2022, more people watched the Big Ten matchup between Michigan and Ohio State on Fox than any SEC game. In 2021, three of the five most-watched college non-bowl games were Big Ten contests on Fox (McVeigh, 2022; Shepkowski, 2021).

## ESPN Gets Defensive

With more viewers tuning in to Fox, and the narrative surrounding a possible SEC bias gaining steam, ESPN found themselves on the defensive. In 2014, Chris Fowler, the then-host of ESPN's *College GameDay*, took time out of the program to defend his employer and push back against the people who think ESPN wants only the SEC to be successful:

> They think that . . . we love the idea that all these teams from one little region control the balance of power at the moment in college football. That's great for the SEC, it's great for the SEC Network. It's great

*for CBS. It's not great for anyone who televises a bracket. What's good for the sport overall, what's good for interest in a playoff and ratings is to have teams from all over the country represented. (Schwartz, 2014, para. 2)*

Paul Finebaum, a radio host whose show was simulcast on the SEC Network, said he did not believe his network played favorites, and questioned why Fox was not getting the same criticism about a Big Ten bias (Sprung, 2018).

## Battle Not Ending Any Time Soon

Starting in the 2023 season, Big Ten games moved entirely off ESPN after the conference agreed to a deal with Fox, CBS, and NBC to show games on those channels and their streaming options (Auerbach, 2022). With ESPN not carrying Big Ten games at all, the link between the conferences their television networks had become stronger. The battle for supremacy was just as much ESPN versus Fox as it was SEC versus Big Ten. The battle between the networks could also be seen during conference realignment. When Texas and Oklahoma joined the SEC, followed by Southern Cal and UCLA joining the Big Ten, many believed that ESPN and Fox were behind those decisions (Bucholtz, 2022).

Once again, how ESPN would handle this public division became a popular talking point among fans and media observers. After the Big Ten deal was announced, *College GameDay* was live at Ohio State University, a Big Ten school. ESPN's Rece Davis told the fans in attendance that just because their school was now going to be exclusively on Fox, that was not going to stop the show from coming to and promoting Ohio State: "If you think some television contract is gonna keep us from coming to [Ohio State], Hell no!" (Gulick, 2022).

However, not everyone was convinced. One media analyst questioned why ESPN would even bother promoting the Big Ten at all after the conference took all their games from the network. He asked, "Why would ESPN spend extra time on the air, on their social platforms, on their digital side, to promote something they don't have access to?" and suggested that the time allotted to Big Ten highlights and discussion would get shorter as the years progressed (Shea, 2022, para. 10). If that happened, it certainly would not do much to temper the SEC bias calls from non-SEC fans.

## Counterargument

While many believe there is an SEC bias that is perpetuated by the media, there is also one indisputable fact that serves as a counterargument: The SEC has produced some of the best teams in recent memory. From when the Bowl Championship Series debuted in 1998, through the implementation of the playoff system in 2014, and up to and including the national championship game in 2023, there were 24 college football champions. Of those 24, 14 were from the SEC, including seven years in a row from 2006 to 2012 (NCAA, n.d.). It is not just the teams who are successful, as the SEC had the most players picked in the NFL draft for 16 years straight from 2007 to 2022 (SEC Staff, 2022). While not denying the favoritism charges against ESPN, former SEC Network announcer Brent Musburger pointed out the conference's success in the debate: "Somebody said we've got SEC bias. Deal with it. They're the best" (Sherman, 2014, para. 2). Musburger's words raise an interesting question: Can a network be biased based on the amount of coverage if that conference has earned that coverage by being the best?

## Why This Matters

This might appear to be a somewhat trivial problem facing ESPN, but it ultimately raises a question of trust. Viewers want to know that what they are watching is the complete and unbiased account of what is happening in their favorite sport. If fans have even a small concern that the accounts are biased, then that might make them wonder about other information they are getting from the network. If fans cannot trust ESPN's reporting on the SEC, they might look elsewhere for the rest of their news as well.

For ESPN, this is not the first time they have faced concerns regarding their business practices with sports leagues. As was discussed in the previous chapter, ESPN's multibillion-dollar relationship with the NFL was blamed for the network dropping out of the *League of Denial* documentary. Having to separate the business interests from the news delivery can be a struggle for major media organizations such as ESPN.

## Summary

In 2014, ESPN agreed to a 20-year business partnership with the SEC, and then expanded that relationship even further with a $3 billion deal in 2020. For fans of the

SEC, the deal meant their favorite schools now had a network devoted solely to their conference and was the focus of attention on the most-watched sports network. However, fans of other conferences began to wonder what that partnership might mean for their favorite teams. Cries of ESPN having an SEC bias began to come from those schools outside of the SEC, worried that the network's influence on the sport might negatively affect their program's chances of getting equal coverage.

The outcry from some fans reveals the difficult position that ESPN put itself in through their deal with the SEC. While they were now in business with the dominant conference in college football, they also were giving off a perception of not treating all schools equally. The partnership had the potential to be a financial boon for the network, which pleased ownership, but those involved on the news side of the network had to constantly defend themselves from the charges of bias. The potential for an SEC bias demonstrates the struggle between what is best for the media's business side and what is best for a news department that is hoping to appear impartial.

## REVIEW QUESTIONS

1. What made the SEC deal with TBS in 1984 one of the early developments in which people perceived an SEC bias?
2. What were some concerns about the SEC Network from non-SEC-affiliated people?
3. How has Fox Sports countered ESPN's supposed SEC Bias?
4. Why does it matter if there is an SEC bias?

# PART
# III
# SOCIAL ISSUES

Sports and social issues often intersect, blurring distinctions between what happens on the field and in the world outside the games. Part III addresses many of those social issues by providing a breakdown of each topic, followed by a case study that takes a closer look at a particular person or event that best summarizes that social issue. Part III begins with an examination of two key concepts: social identity theory (chapter 13) and framing (chapter 14). Both are relevant in explaining how people identify with specific groups and how the media can influence people's opinions of a topic.

Chapter 15 explores the history of media coverage involving athletes from ethnic minority groups. For decades, sports journalism was a field dominated by White men, which directly influenced how non-Whites were depicted. In 2016, Colin Kaepernick began kneeling during the national anthem, sparking a renewed debate over how the media portrayed Black athletes (chapter 16). Also around this time, athletes and media members began to increasingly use their platforms to discuss their own opinions on political issues. However, some members of the audience were not

interested in these conversations and asked those weighing in on social issues to "stick to sports" (chapter 17).

Women's sports coverage has long been lacking when compared to men's sports. The media has traditionally devoted the majority of its coverage to events involving male athletes, while seemingly ignoring anything involving women (chapter 18). However, as chapter 19 reveals, the United States women's soccer team may be a team that can change the narrative; they have earned front-page coverage, high television viewership, and equal pay with the men's team. It is not just the women athletes who have struggled, as chapter 20 discusses the obstacles that many women in the sports media face while trying to do their jobs.

Part III concludes with a look at media coverage of LGBTQ+ in sports (chapter 21). The chapter examines some of the key moments in the media's history of covering that population of athletes, while chapter 22 looks closely at Michael Sam as a case study. Sam was on pace to become the first openly gay player in a regular-season NFL game, but some believe the media might be the reason why his dream was not fulfilled.

*THEORETICAL FOUNDATION*

# Social Identity Theory

## CHAPTER OBJECTIVES

After completing the chapter, the reader should be able to do the following:

- Understand the elements of social identity theory
- Explain why social identity theory is important in sports and the sports media
- Identify examples of how social identity is used in sports
- Understand how Major League Baseball used social identity to recruit new fans

There are many different aspects of a person's personality, interests, and background that factor into creating a complete social identity. These traits could be everything from gender to ethnicity to being a fan of a sports team. The individual importance of these aspects will vary from person to person, as people may choose to weigh them differently. For example, one may be passionate about their ethnicity, while others may not consider that to be more important than their gender.

Some social identities are not created at birth; a Dallas Cowboys fan may consider that fandom to be the most important part of their public life. Membership in these groups becomes a key part of how people identify as individuals.

In the world of sports, these group memberships can help explain fandom and how the media reports on different types of people.

## Social Identity Theory Definition

**Social identity theory** states that people classify themselves into social categories and associate with the groups in which they feel most comfortable (Tajfel & Turner, 1985). These chosen groups provide a personal social identity to the individual that creates a feeling of self-belonging (Tajfel, 1978). This social identification can create a situation in which the individual perceives the fate of the group as their own fate (Ashforth & Mael, 1989). For many, this group identity can be very important (Jenkins, 2014).

A group dynamic assumes that there are some commonalities between people involved and that this membership helps to mold an individual's social identity, fill an individual's need for belonging, and create positive self-esteem (Abrams & Hogg, 2006; Fiol, 2002; Wang et al., 2009; Zhang et al., 2007). The group membership can also lead to favoritism toward those with similar characteristics (Tajfel & Turner, 1985). This is especially true in minority groups, as research has demonstrated that minorities tend to have a higher sense of group identity when compared to non-minorities (Korzenny & Korzenny 2005).

## Social Identity, Hispanic Ethnicity, and Family

To demonstrate how social identity can define individuals in a group, this section will focus on the relationships between people with Hispanic ethnicity and family. Research has found that people of Hispanic ethnicity state that being with family is an important part of their daily activities (Skogrand et al., 2005); time spent with family is greater among Hispanic people than those of other ethnic groups studied (Padilla et al., 1976). However, this connection consists of more than just those who are related, as friends, neighbors, and organizations are all considered "family" in a Hispanic household (Madsen, 1964; Santiago-Rivera et al., 2002; Skogrand et al., 2005). This is not just for elder Hispanics, as those aged 18 to 34 also emphasized the importance of family within their culture (Lopez, 2013). This demonstrates that, for Hispanics, being a part of a family, whether a nuclear family or not, is a key part of developing their own personal social identity.

## Social Identity in Sports

While social identity theory is most commonly used to examine commonalities among people through demographics such as age, gender, race, and ethnicity, it is often used in the world of sports when discussing fandom (Brown et al., 2013). A fan believes that his team is better than the other (Swan & Wyer, 1997), even when that team might not be playing well (Wann & Branscombe, 1990). Fandom also creates an "us versus them" situation, in which fans are so loyal that they believe themselves to be part of the team.. This means that team success can often be equated with individual success, with declarations of "we won!" after big victories (Underwood et al., 2001). For sports organizations, getting fans to the level at which they consider a team to be an important part of their social identity can be financially rewarding. An examination of sports fandom found that fans that were highly identified, involved, and invested with a team had a greater likelihood of attendance and willingness to spend money on the team (Wann & Branscombe, 1993).

## Importance in Media Coverage

Social identity theory will be the foundation for several of the upcoming chapters in this book. A quick preview here demonstrates how being an in-group or out-group can influence media coverage. For decades, the sports media has consisted of primarily straight White men. Therefore, when it comes to topics involving ethnicity, gender, and LGBTQ+, the social identity of the media can make it challenging for them to report properly on the story. For example, chapter 18 will focus primarily on the coverage of women's sports and women athletes. There is a perception, probably correct, that male sports reporters did not cover women's sports because they believed the women were lesser athletes. The men instead focused on the athletes who were part of their own gender social identity. This created a scenario in which, for the entire history of the sports media, women's sports have received a fraction of the coverage given to men's sports.

## Example of Social Identity in Sports

While fandom is often cited as the most obvious example of social identity in sports, many sports teams are taking advantage of other aspects of a person's identity in order to establish a connection between fan and team. As discussed previously, people of Hispanic background have a strong connection to both their ethnicity and family. There is also a storied history among Hispanics when it comes to baseball. The game was introduced in Latin America in 1864 with the creation of the Havana Baseball Club in Cuba before spreading throughout other Latin American countries (Echevarria, n.d.). It quickly became one of the most popular sports in the region and maintained that interest for more than 100 years. Hispanic people living in the United States are 27 percent more likely to be avid baseball fans than the average member of the population and attend more Major League Baseball (MLB) games than they do NBA, NFL, NASCAR, and NHL events combined (Kulik, 2009). MLB's smartphone app allowed fans to watch games in Spanish, a decision that helped it become one of the highest-grossing apps in Mexico (Newman, 2015).

In 2016, two MLB teams created separate Instagram accounts in Spanish in addition to their English-language Instagram pages. The New York Yankees (@yankees_beisbol) and the Arizona Diamondbacks (@losdbacks) were the only two teams that, at the time, had these Spanish-language accounts. The popularity of the posts demonstrated that social identity was a strong indicator of how the audience responded to the photos and videos (Hull et al., 2019).

## Showcasing Hispanic Players

Perhaps not surprisingly, the Spanish-language accounts showed many Hispanic players in their posts. In the videos and photos that contained a player, 49 percent of those were of Hispanic ethnicity. Considering that, at the time, less than 30 percent of MLB players were Hispanic (Lapchick, 2016), these accounts were showcasing players of Hispanic descent at a rate higher than perhaps expected. These players were not always top stars either, as Dominican Republic native Rubby De La Rosa appeared in more posts (nine) on the Diamondbacks account than games he won as a starting pitcher (four).

While fandom has been proved to be an important part of the social identity of sports fans, this example also demonstrated that the ethnicity of the players was important to followers of this account. On the Diamondback account, a joint "Happy Birthday" post to both Hall of Fame pitcher Randy Johnson and All-Star first basemen Paul Goldschmidt (both White Americans) earned fewer likes (150) than a "Happy Birthday" post a month earlier for a part-time player, Venezuela native David Peralta (225). Similarly, for the New York Yankees, a midseason post featuring a statistically inferior player from the Dominican Republic earned more likes than a post showcasing the Japanese starting pitcher on Opening Day. This demonstrates how a sports fan's social identity can consist of a variety of factors, including both team fandom and ethnicity.

## Showcasing Hispanic Culture

In addition to spotlighting Hispanic players, both accounts created posts that showcased Hispanic culture. The Diamondbacks posted a picture of their special-edition jerseys that had "Los DBacks" written on them instead of "Diamondbacks," while specifically saying they were wearing the uniforms to celebrate Hispanic heritage. Other posts focused on authentic

Norm Hall/Getty Images

**The special-edition Los DBacks jerseys celebrated the heritage of the MLB team's Hispanic players.**

Hispanic food and entertainment that were available at the ballpark. Like the posts with players, these posts highlighting Hispanic culture averaged more likes than those that did not. Therefore, once again, while fans were likely following these accounts to get the latest information on their favorite teams, it was the cultural aspects of their social identity that were an important part of why these fans liked certain posts and chose not to like others.

## Showcasing Family

As stated previously, the concept of family is an important part of the social identity of Hispanic people. This has also been proven in social media, where Hispanic people said they prefer websites that show pictures of grandparents (Singh et al., 2008). For both Spanish-language accounts, the most liked post of the entire 2016 season was one that depicted family. After the Yankees' Alex Rodriguez (an American-born player of Dominican ethnicity) played in the final game of his 22-year career in August, the @yankees_beisbol account posted several images of Rodriguez during the game. However, it was a photo of Rodriguez hugging his two daughters after the game that earned nearly 2,000 likes, which was the most of every picture examined during the season. Once again, this showcases how a person's social identity is made up of several different elements.

## Social Identity Implications

While the demographics of the followers of these accounts was not examined, one can safely assume that the majority of users who chose to get updates from a Spanish-language Instagram account were of Hispanic ethnicity. While sports fans have long demonstrated that fandom is an important part of social identity (Brown et al., 2013), the followers of these Spanish-language accounts revealed that their ethnicity might be even more important. While the followers are likely fans of these two teams, it was not always the best players and big victories that garnered the most likes and engagement on Instagram. Instead, it was the posts that showcased the Hispanic players, no matter how high-profile they were, and Hispanic cultural events that were the most popular. This demonstrates that in the hierarchy of an individual's social identity, a Hispanic person's ethnicity appears to be of great importance.

Golden Pixels LLC/age fotostock

The concept of family is an important part of the social identity of Hispanic people.

# Summary

Social identity theory examines how people classify themselves and the importance that being part of a group plays in that classification. In the world of sports, social identity theory is commonly examined in the realm of fandom. For many, their diehard support of a specific team or player can become an important part of that person's identity. This support can lead to financial gain for clubs, as these highly identified fans are more likely to spend money on tickets, merchandise, and other items to show their individual support. However, fandom is often just a small part of a social identity, as demonstrated when Hispanic baseball fans routinely showed a preference to Hispanic players on Spanish-language Instagram accounts.

## KEY TERM

**social identity theory**—People classify themselves into social categories and associate with the groups in which they feel most comfortable.

## REVIEW QUESTIONS

1. How does social identify influence how a person interacts with others?
2. How is social identity relevant in the world of sports?
3. Why would sports teams be interested in fans developing a strong social identity that is connected with the team?
4. How is social identity theory important in media coverage of sports?

# 14

# Framing

## CHAPTER OBJECTIVES

After completing the chapter, the reader should be able to do the following:

- Understand what framing is
- Differentiate between framing and agenda setting
- Apply how framing might be used by sports journalists
- Recognize how framing has been used regarding coverage of women's sports in the sports media

Following the 2020 NFL season, a journalist reporting on the Cincinnati Bengals might have written a story noting that the team had doubled their win total from the previous season. At the same time, a different journalist might have focused their story on the team's dismal eleven losses. Both statements are correct: The Bengals did improve from two wins in 2019 to four in 2020, and the team's final record in 2020 was 4 wins, 11 losses, and 1 tie. The Bengals' record is indisputable, but how it is discussed can be greatly disputed. One journalist described the season in a positive way, implying that the improvement from the previous season is a sign they are on the rise. The other focused on the negative, disappointed in another double-digit loss season resulting in a second straight last-place finish. Depending on which article a Bengals fan reads, they might walk away with very different opinions of their favorite team. These two hypothetical articles about the exact same team demonstrate the influence journalists can have on their audiences through the use of framing.

## Framing Theory

Sociologist Erving Goffman (1974) developed framing theory with the belief that people use their own personal "frameworks" to understand and interpret events happening in their lives. In the years since Goffman's research, the theory has been adapted by communication scholars who have used framing to explain how the media discusses current events and politics. Therefore, in the context of mass communications, **framing** refers to how the media presents information to the audience. Journalists can focus on specific events and then discuss them within a certain context to encourage the audience to think in a specific way (Entman, 1993).

As implied by the name of the theory, framing can best be visualized through the idea of a picture in a picture frame. For example, a photo of a family at the beach might show smiling faces and a group that appears to have had a wonderful vacation. The image in that frame has been chosen to portray a very specific memory. What the audience does not see is everything outside of that frame—the baby having a tantrum at the hotel, the rainy weather, and the car breaking down on the drive. Through framing, the photo tells the audience what they are supposed to think about this family's vacation.

One of the first communications scholars to research framing was Robert Entman (1993). He wrote that four key elements in the framing process were the communicators, the text, the receiver, and the culture:

- "*Communicators* make conscious or unconscious framing judgements in deciding what to say, guided by frames that organize their beliefs" (p. 52)

- "The *text* contains frames, which are manifested by the presence or absence of certain keywords, stock phrases, stereotyped images, sources of information, and sentences that provide thematically reinforcing clusters of facts or judgements" (p. 52)

- "The frames that guide the *receiver's* thinking and conclusion may or may not reflect the frames in the text and the framing intention of the communicator" (pp. 52-53)

- "The *culture* is the stock of commonly invoked frames" (p. 53)

When those are all used together, the audience receiving the message can interpret the information based on the four elements.

In this chapter's opening example about the Bengals, the two journalists use framing to discuss the team in very different contexts. One put a positive spin on the season, while the other focused on the negative. The concept of framing is important because, as one researcher noted, "it can have subtle but powerful effects on the audience" (Tankard, 2001, p. 96). A Bengals fan who read the positive article might feel a lot better about the team's future, while a fan who read the negative article might be ready to fire the head coach. The way the team is framed by each journalist has an impact on the audience's opinion.

## Importance of Language in Framing

Framing demonstrates how highlighting or omitting aspects of the story can influence how a person understands the event. For example, if a casual fan of an MLB team was asked if they would rather their team won 81 games or lost 81 games, they would likely rather have the wins. However, what that fan might not realize is that an MLB season is 162 games, so 81 wins would also be 81 losses. By omitting the fact that there are 162 games in a season, the question asker has forced the fan to use only the frames provided (81 wins or 81 losses) to make their decision. Therefore, it is not surprising that without that key piece of information, 81 wins sounds much better than 81 losses. As Entman wrote, "Most frames are defined by what they omit as well as include, and the omissions of potential problem definitions, explanations, evaluations, and recommendations may be as critical as the inclusions in guiding the audience" (1993, p. 54).

## Framing or Agenda Setting

Chapter 7 discussed agenda setting, which is considered a very similar mass communications theory to framing. In fact, framing is sometimes referred to as *second-level agenda setting*. As a reminder of the information from the previous chapter, agenda setting is defined as the ability of the media to influence the importance placed on specific topics (Baran & Davis, 2012). They do this through mentioning some topics more than others, giving the audience the impression that the more mentioned topics must be more important.

Framing has similar traits but takes it a step further. Several researchers have noted that agenda setting tells people "what" to think about. Framing goes beyond that, hence the label of second-level agenda setting, by also telling people "how" to think about those specific topics (Baran & Davis, 2012). If a newspaper runs many articles about the local minor league hockey team, then the audience may think that team is important (agenda setting). However, if those articles are not about the play of the team, but instead how the tickets are too expensive, then the audience may be less likely to attend a game because of the focus on the pricey tickets (framing).

## Framing and Objectivity

One of the main tenets of journalism is that reporters should be objective when it comes to reporting on stories. It is sometimes stated that "there is no cheering in the press box," meaning that reporters should not be rooting for a specific team but should instead be impartial observers of the action. However, framing challenges that motto, and instead implies that journalists should present specific sides to a story.

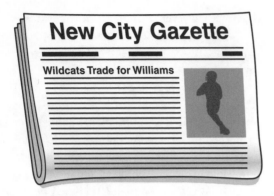 

The decision to place this story on the front page (*left*) represents agenda setting; the placement tells readers it is an important story. The second headline (*right*) represents framing; it suggests an opinion about the story (that the player is old and possibly not worth trading for).

The framing versus objectivity debate might ultimately come down to who is writing the story. In a newspaper's sports department, there are often two different types of writers: beat writers and columnists. **Beat writers** are traditionally tasked with covering a specific team or sport. That person goes to a team's practices, games, and press conferences, all with the goal of writing impartial articles, and they are tasked with being neutral observers of the team. **Columnists**, however, are writers who have the freedom to give their personal opinion on a topic. The newspaper will often clearly label them as columnists so that readers know that this is the opinion of one person and not necessarily the opinion of the newspaper staff as a whole.

For example, the *Miami Herald* has a beat writer who job is to solely cover the NFL's Miami Dolphins. That person may write an article about a quarterback controversy on the Dolphins, with statistics, quotes from the two quarterbacks, and a quote from the head coach. From that article, fans get the information about what is happening at the quarterback position directly from those involved. A columnist from the same paper might write an article stating who exactly the columnist thinks should be the starter and why. The beat writer impartially gave the facts and information, while the columnist stated an opinion.

## Framing of Gender in Sports

Chapter 18 will discuss the issues surrounding media coverage of women's sports, but it is appropriate to introduce some of the concepts now that framing has been used to better understand the media's role in that coverage. There is not only less coverage of women's sports when compared to men's, but the athletes themselves are depicted differently. For example, during the 2012 Summer Olympics, broadcasters often framed female athletes "as 'girls' rather than 'women'" and "gave them secondary status compared to male athletes" (Kian, Bernstein, & McGuire, 2013, p. 143). When the announcers use those terms, the audience may have the impression that women athletes are less worthy of attention.

Additionally, while men athletes are portrayed as athletic, the media will often portray women athletes in more feminine roles, focusing on their looks. Athletes in women's sports are often portrayed in a passive pose as opposed to the active action shots that display men's action (Godoy-Pressland & Griggs, 2014). An analysis of photos on sports blogs (Clavio & Eagleman, 2011) and in *ESPN The Magazine* (Cranmer, Brann, & Bowman, 2014; Hull, Smith, & Schmittel, 2015) found that the women were more likely to be posed in sexually suggestive manners, something that was not happening for the men. In addition, an examination of the televised Olympics coverage in the 1990s revealed that commentators were more likely to discuss the attractiveness of the women participating than they did the men (Eastman & Billings, 1999).

The portrayals of men and women in the sports media are often dramatically different, but that assumes that women are portrayed at all. An examination of the magazine *SI for Kids* demonstrated that men were in more than 75 percent of all photos. Of those pictures, the men were shown being active in 58 percent, compared to an only 15 percent active rate for women (Hardin et al., 2002). The covers of *Sports Illustrated*, a magazine dedicated to showing the best in the world of sports, feature almost exclusively men (Martin & McDonald, 2012; Weber & Carini, 2013).

Through this framing of women's sports and women athletes, the media has given the audience a perception of women's sports being less important. Men's sports are discussed more often, and when women's sports are discussed, it is on a smaller scale and often with a focus not on the athletes' athletic ability. This gives the impression to the audience that women should be admired for their looks and not their sporting ability.

# Summary

The impact the media has on how fans consume sports content is discussed throughout this text. One of the most prevalent examples is the use of framing. Journalists can not only tell fans *what* to think about, but also *how* to think about certain topics. If a reporter chooses to focus a story on the negative aspect of a team, then the audience may have a lesser opinion of the team because of that article. Throughout the history of the sports media, the impact of framing has been especially seen in the coverage of women's sports. Women athletes are often given less attention, and the attention that they do get is often outside of athletic competition. Therefore, the audience should be aware of framing tactics that reporters use when getting information about their favorite teams and players.

## KEY TERMS

**beat writers**—Newspaper writers who are tasked with covering a specific team or sport.

**columnists**—Newspaper writers who have the freedom to give their personal opinion on a topic.

**framing**—How the media presents information to the audience. Journalists can focus on specific events and then discuss them within a certain context to encourage the audience to think in a specific way.

## REVIEW QUESTIONS

1. What is framing?
2. How is framing different from agenda setting?
3. What is the difference between a beat writer and a columnist?
4. How has framing been used in the media coverage of women's sports?

# 15

# Media Coverage of Race in Sports

## CHAPTER OBJECTIVES

After completing the chapter, the reader should be able to do the following:

- Examine the demographic makeup of the sports media in terms of ethnicity
- Identify issues involving the sports media's coverage of Black athletes
- Debate how the sports media should report on athletes whose first language is not English
- Recognize how Native American mascots became a troubling part of the world of sports

In 2016, swimmer Simone Manuel became the first African American to win an individual swimming Olympic medal, taking home the gold in the 100-meter freestyle. It was a historic moment for all that it represented for United States swimming, and, for Manuel, it demonstrated that a Black person could succeed in the pool. At the time, USA Swimming estimated that 70 percent of Black Americans did not know how to swim and that African Americans ages 5 to 19 drown in pools at a rate of 5.5 times that of White people (Whitten, 2017). In the press conference after the win, a tearful Manuel said, "I just want to be an inspiration to others that you can do it" (Gibbs, 2016, para. 6).

However, that same media session also demonstrated some of the racial issues that are the focus of this chapter. ESPN's Jesse Washington was in attendance and tweeted that he was the only Black journalist at Manuel's press conference (Washington, 2016). For this groundbreaking moment in African American sports history, there was just one African American journalist who might be able to use their own experiences to help put this victory into a greater cultural context.

In addition, nearly every question during the media session was about race, which, while obviously a big part of the story, seemed to wear on the new champion. She would eventually say, "I would like there to be a day when it is not 'Simone the Black swimmer'" (Gibbs, 2016, para 13). Nearly five years later, Manuel would look back on that time and again note that while she understood why much of the focus remained on her race, she was hoping to be recognized as a great swimmer, not just a great Black swimmer (Azzi, 2021).

When journalists discuss race and ethnicity there are numerous challenges involved, including the ethnic identity of the media, regretful comments from prominent media members regarding ethnicity, and, at times, a language barrier. In some cases, the teams and leagues themselves make it difficult for journalists to avoid negative racial and ethnic stereotypes because of the use of objectionable team names and mascots.

## Race and Ethnicity

Before examining the issues involving the coverage of race and ethnicity in the sports media, it is important to understand what those terms refer to. The American Psychological Association (APA) defines **race** as a socially defined concept used to designate a portion of the population with common physical characteristics, ancestry, or language. Meanwhile, **ethnicity** is based on a person's membership in a cultural or ethnic group (APA, n.d.).

## Demographics of Sports Journalists

Before examining some of the issues involved with coverage of race and ethnicity in sports, it is relevant to examine the racial makeup of those working in the sports media. In 2020, more than 77 percent of sports editors, columnists, and reporters at major newspapers and websites in the United States and Canada were White (Lapchick, 2020; see figure 15.1). While this trend applied throughout both countries, some individual areas saw even starker differences. For example, that same year in Boston, Massachusetts, just 10 percent of the 126 full-time sports media members in the city were Black, a statistic one journalist called "pathetic" (Silverman, 2020, para. 2). An examination of ESPN

announcers during high school football's National Signing Day found that 98 percent were White, while the field of play-by-play broadcasting is dominated almost entirely by White men (Curtis, 2020; Lewis et al., 2019).

The low number of non-White sports media members caused some to question journalism industry's commitment to diversity. In one research study, Black sports broadcasters reported that if a local television station already had one Black sportscaster, they believed that would be the limit. One wrote, "If another Black sports journalist is at the station, some of us don't even bother in applying to that job" (Hull et al., 2022, p. 11). ESPN has been lauded for its commitment to diversity, being labeled an industry leader for hiring people of color as sports editors and columnists (Lapchick, 2020). However, some who work there told a different story. Behind-the-scenes employees at ESPN claimed that racism was still prevalent at the television station, and that the company limited career paths for Black personnel (Draper, 2020).

Several incidents involving the sports media's coverage of topics involving race and ethnicity will be discussed in this chapter. One cannot help but wonder if the racial makeup of the sports journalism industry plays a part in how these stories are told. Instead of having a sports department in the newsroom staffed by a diverse group of journalists, the lack of representation can lead to minority athletes receiving media attention that can be considered less than flattering at best, and racist at worst.

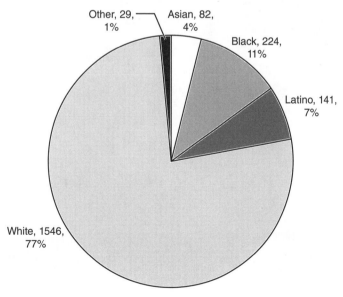

**FIGURE 15.1** Breakdown of ethnic makeup of sports editors, columnists, and reporters at major newspapers and websites in the United States and Canada as of 2020.
Data from Lapchick (2020).

# Early Media Coverage of Black Athletes

From the early days of sports journalism, Black athletes were often battling both opponents in their sport and biased coverage from the media. Boxer Jack Johnson found himself in the middle of some of those attacks in the early 1900s. Johnson was the first Black heavyweight champion of the world, a fact that upset large portions of White America. Several journalists took up the cause in their newspapers, rallying against Johnson and hoping for a "Great White Hope" who could defeat the Black champion. However, Johnson beat nearly all comers, and many newspapers treated his wins as somber events for their mostly White staff and readership (Washburn & Lamb, 2020). The *Los Angeles Times* even warned its Black readers "do not point your nose too high" and "No man will think a bit higher of you because your complexion is the same as that of the victor in Reno" (*Los Angeles Times*, 1910, para. 7).

As the years progressed, other top Black athletes faced similar treatment in the daily newspapers of the time. Track star Jesse Owens was called a "noble savage" by famed sportswriter Grantland Rice, while Brooklyn Dodgers star Jackie Robinson was consistently referred to as "The Dodgers' Negro Star" in recaps of his games (Washburn & Lamb, 2020, pp. 101; 109). This was common at the time, but even as the years progressed, those controversial and in some cases outright racist, statements would continue.

## Controversial Statements

Chapter 34 will discuss the impact that prominent Las Vegas bookmaker Jimmy "the Greek" Snyder had on the rise of the acceptance of sports betting in the media, but his racially insensitive comments led to his downfall. During an interview in 1988, Snyder was asked about civil rights advancements during a breakfast celebrating Dr. Martin Luther King Jr. Instead of addressing the question asked to him, he went on a tangent about Black people being "bred" to be better athletes than Whites. He said:

> *This all goes back to the Civil War, when, during the slave trading, the slave owner would breed his big Black to his big woman so that he would have a big Black kid. That's where it all started.* (Solomon, 1988, para. 16)

While Snyder expressed remorse for his comments, CBS, his employer at the time, fired him within days, ending a dozen-year run at the network (Solomon, 1988).

In 2007, New York City–based radio host Don Imus was discussing the Rutgers University women's basketball

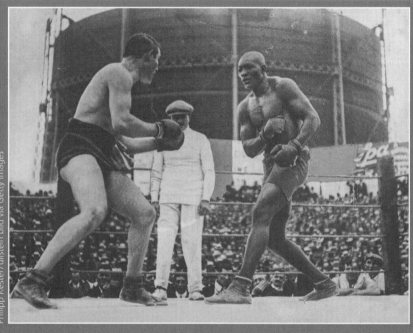

Philipp Kester/ullstein bild via Getty Images

**Jack Johnson defeated reigning heavyweight champion Tommy Burns in this 1908 fight to become the first Black heavyweight champion of the world.**

team, which had made a run to the national championship game. The team, which featured nine Black players, was described by Imus as a team of "nappy-headed ho's" (Carter, 2007, para. 8). Imus, who was one of the most popular radio hosts in the country with millions of listeners each day, was instantly vilified for his comments. NBC News, which simulcast the video of his show on MSNBC, and CBS Radio, which carried the audio version, both suspended Imus for two weeks (Carter, 2007). However, the anger toward the comments did not die down after the punishment. Black leaders, other journalists, and the Rutgers players all expressed disappointment with Imus's words, and some advertisers threatened to pull their commercials and funding from his program (Carter & Story, 2007; Strauss, 2007). Three days after the suspensions were announced and as pressure continued to mount, both NBC and CBS canceled Imus' show immediately (Carter & Steinberg, 2007).

## Framing of Race in Sports

As discussed in the previous chapter, framing refers to how the media presents information to the audience. The way in which journalists discuss certain topics will lead to people thinking in a specific way about those subjects (Entman, 1993). When discussing the media coverage surrounding topics of race, framing is often the theory that is used to note the differences in racial descriptors. For decades, there have been numerous research studies that have addressed these disparities:

- A study from 1977 revealed White professional football players were more likely to be praised by the announcers, while Black players were more likely to be criticized for a bad play (Rainville & McCormick, 1977).
- College basketball announcers stereotyped Black players as naturally athletic and powerful, while the White players were praised for their hard work, effort, and smarts on the court (Eastman & Billings, 2001).
- An analysis of 162 hours of college and professional football coverage revealed that quarterbacks were described differently based on race. The Black quarterbacks were succeeding because of their athletic skill, while, when the White quarterbacks failed, it was because they lacked that athleticism (Billings, 2004).
- A look at 41 NFL Draft previews demonstrated White players were discussed in terms of mental traits, while non-White players were described based on their physical traits (Schmidt & Coe, 2014).
- Newspaper articles regarding Heisman Trophy finalists framed Black finalists in terms of "brawn" while White finalists were framed in terms of "brains" (Cranmer et al., 2014).
- Major League Baseball announcers framed White players as succeeding because of their intelligence, while non-White players failed because of a lack of intelligence (Arth & Billings, 2018).

One of the implications of these comments was summed up in a research paper from 1997. While that may feel dated now, the sentiment remains the same: If a Black athlete is consistently being called gifted and succeeding based on only natural ability, that could imply that the athlete is lazy and does not have to work hard in order to be successful (McCarthy & Jones, 1997). In addition, if White players are constantly being praised for being "smart," while Black players are praised for being "athletic," that would imply that all White athletes are smarter than Black ones.

## A Call for Equitable Reporting

In addition to how Black athletes are discussed, another issue is the amount of coverage they receive. This is especially notable in sports where Black and White athletes often compete together at high levels. By her ability and success on the court, tennis star Serena Williams became one of the biggest stars in all of sports, but not before being overshadowed for years in the media by White players who had achieved less (Whiteside, 2022). In women's basketball, stars in both the college and professional ranks have noted that White players often get more attention than Black ones (Barnes, 2022). When Paige Bueckers, a White women's basketball player from the University of Connecticut, won the "Best Female College Athlete" award at the 2021 ESPY Awards, she devoted much of her acceptance speech to praising Black women:

> With the light that I have now as a White woman who leads a Black-led sport and celebrated here, I want to shed a light on Black women. They don't get the media coverage that they deserve. They've given so much to the sport, the community and society as a whole and their value is undeniable.

*I think it's time for change. Sports media holds the key to storylines. Sports media and sponsors tell us who is valuable, and you have told the world that I mattered today, and everyone who voted, thank you. But I think we should use this power together to also celebrate Black women. (Sterling, 2021, para. 2, 4)*

# Coverage of Hispanic and Latino Athletes

In 2022, the Institute for Diversity and Ethics in Sport tabulated that 28.5 percent of all the players on MLB opening day rosters were Hispanic or Latino (Lapchick, 2022). With many of those 278 players born outside of the United States, where English is not the primary spoken language, there exists a language barrier when speaking with sports journalists. These Hispanic and Latino players are often some of the most successful and popular, but fans often do not hear directly from them because of that language gap.

For example, during the 2022 season Boston Red Sox star third baseman Rafael Devers admitted he was hesitant to answer reporters' questions in English since it was not his first language. Instead, he would have a Spanish language translator present during interviews to translate the question to him and then his answer back to the journalists. However, despite his concerns, Devers' teammates and coaches kept encouraging him to speak English to the media, believing that it would open him up for more endorsement opportunities and raise his profile among fans (Jennings, 2022). While those sentiments may be true, the situation also demonstrates the burden that is placed on the players and not the media. There was not a push for Boston journalists to speak more Spanish to ease Devers' concerns, but instead it was expected for the player to speak more English. For those players, an incident from the previous decade might have made them hesitant to speak in a language that is not their native tongue.

During the 2016 season, the Houston Astros were struggling on the field and much of the blame was being placed on one of their top hitters, Dominican Republic–born Carlos Gomez. In an article published in the *Houston Chronicle*, Gomez was quoted by the author as saying: "For the last year and this year, I not really do much for this team. The fans be angry. They be disappointed" (Smith, 2016, para. 9). While that might have been exactly what Gomez said, the journalist's use of the broken English quote was not received favorably by the player or the public. Critics complained that the quote was used to make Gomez sound unintelligent instead of being a situation in which someone was dealing with a language barrier.

Other journalists revealed that the common practice in a situation such as that one is to paraphrase the athlete or use partial quotes. The *Houston Chronicle* chose not to do either; following the blowback, the editor of the newspaper issued an apology to the player (Prince, 2016). In a Spanish-language interview he conducted with ESPN soon after, Gomez said that he felt ridiculed by the article's writer, especially after he himself had made the effort to learn English to help make a connection with local journalists (ESPN.com, 2016).

# Native Americans in Sport

In 1950, the Associated Press named Jim Thorpe the greatest athlete of the first 50 years of the 20th century, and his resume more than confirms that honor. Thorpe was a professional baseball player, football player, and an Olympic gold medalist. Beyond his profile as a world-class athlete, Thorpe was Native American, making him one of the most famous members of a tribal nation. However, in the years since his career ended, Native Americans in sports went from starring on the field to having their heritage become a sideshow during the games themselves.

## Representation as Mascots

While there are Native American athletes, the representation most seen among that group in sports comes in the form of mascots. Those mascot names, logos, and associated team actions are almost always considered offensive. However, for decades, teams tried to pass off the names as a way to honor Native Americans, but monikers such as Indians and Braves did anything but. The National Congress of American Indians, an organization created to protect the legal rights of tribal governments, stated that "sports mascots are symbols of disrespect that degrade, mock, and harm Native people, particularly Native youth" (NCAI, n.d., para. 3).

Not only are the team names troublesome, but the logos associated with those organizations often depict offensive imagery. For example, the Cleveland Indians baseball team used "Chief Wahoo" as its mascot and logo starting in 1948. For years, the logo, described in *The*

# Washington, DC, Football Team's Name

The numerous examples of Native American imagery in sports were often met with protest from groups recognizing the harm these mascots were causing. While some college programs were willing to change their athletic team names to avoid hurting Native American groups, many in the professional ranks refused. For decades, there was no greater example of an organization being unwilling to budge on their team name and logo than the Washington, DC, NFL team.

## History of Name

In 1932, the NFL awarded a franchise to Boston to begin play later that season. The team would share Braves stadium with baseball's Boston Braves, so the football team elected to keep the continuity and also chose Boston Braves as its name. However, after just one season, the franchise moved to Fenway Park, home of the Boston Red Sox, and made a change (Commanders, n.d.). The Boston Redskins were born—a name chosen, many suspected, to honor the team's Native American coach (Pollin, 2013). However, history tells a different tale, as the team's owner would later admit that, while he changed the name to avoid confusion with baseball's Braves, this also allowed the team to save money by keeping the same Native American logo they were already using (McCartney, 2014). In 1937, the team moved from Boston to Washington, DC, and the Washington Redskins were born (Commanders, n.d.).

## Early Opposition to the Name

Before diving into the debate surrounding the team's name, it should be noted that the word *redskin* is considered offensive and a slur against Native Americans. The history of the word dates back to the 1700s and 1800s, when it was negatively used to describe Native Americans (Barry, 2016; Gandhi, 2013; Shapira, 2016). However, even as the NFL team played for decades with the name and an offensive Native American logo on their helmets, there was little vocal opposition.

However, the tide slowly began to turn in the early 1970s due to newspaper coverage in the DC area. In 1971, the *Washington Daily News* published an article questioning the use of Native American team names. The following year, the *Washington Star* asked if the name was defaming Native Americans, but the *Washington Evening Star* quoted the team's president saying the

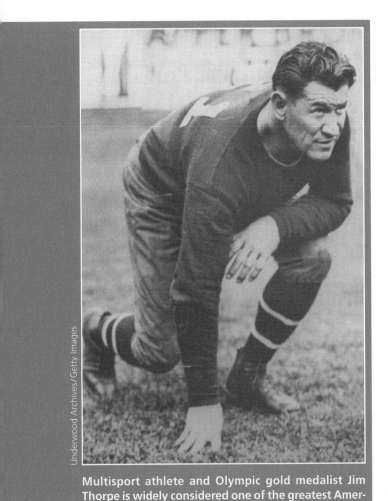

Multisport athlete and Olympic gold medalist Jim Thorpe is widely considered one of the greatest American athletes of the 20th century.

*New York Times* as a "cartoonish caricature of a Native American," was prominently featured on the team's jerseys, hats, stadium, and merchandise (Waldstein, 2018, para. 3). In 2018, after much pushback from the organization and its fans, ownership announced that they would stop using the Chief Wahoo logo beginning with the next season (Waldstein, 2018).

Additional stereotypes are often used during home games of teams that have a Native American name. Baseball's Atlanta Braves used the "tomahawk chop" starting in the 1990s. A drumbeat would play over the speaker system, and fans would "chop" their arms up and down, often while holding a foam tomahawk that was available in the team gift shop (Anderson, 1991). A similar scene could be found at Florida State University's athletic events, as their teams are known as the Seminoles (Billings & Black, 2018).

debate was "silly." By 1972, the organization did agree to make a small concession by changing the offensive lyrics in the team's fight song (Steinberg, 2014). However, beyond that lyric alteration, no other major changes were made or, seemingly, were even being considered.

## The Media's Role

Due to the name being what it was, journalists had almost no choice but to use the offensive word constantly. In February 1988, despite the emerging concerns surrounding its usage, the front page of *The New York Times* proclaimed, "Redskins rout Broncos, 42–10, in Super Bowl" (Berkow, 1988). Stories about the team's trades, signings, injuries, coach hirings, coach firings, and anything and everything else about the organization would have to use the slur. Other media outlets not only used the team's name, but also other stereotypical offensive references, such as a July 1969 *Sports Illustrated* cover that read "The scalping party begins," with the team's quarterback and coach pictured (SI Staff, n.d.).

However, after decades of opposition that was seemingly falling on deaf ears, journalists began to take up the cause. Prominent sports writers and newspapers, including the local *Washington City Paper*, announced that they would no longer use the team's name in print and would

instead refer to them as the "Pigskins" (Madden, 2012; Plotz, 2013). *The Washington Post* was a mixed bag: The editorial board announced it would stop using the team name, but the sports reporters would continue to write it (Shin, 2014).

While the Washington journalists avoiding the team's name may have caused some embarrassment locally, the issue went national in 2013 when one of the most prominent football writers in the country announced he was going to stop using the moniker. Peter King wrote for *Sports Illustrated*, and his offshoot website, *MMQB*, which stood for "Monday Morning Quarterback," was one of the most popular football pages online, reaching more than 10 million readers a month (Wagner, 2017). Just before the 2013 season was to begin, King announced in his column: "I've decided to stop using the Washington team nickname. It's a name you won't see me use anymore" (King, para. 15). He wrote that because the nickname offended too many people, and he felt he could successfully do his job without using it, that it was not necessary to continue. King wrote:

> *I have no idea if this is the right thing to do for the public, or the politically correct thing to do, and I'm not going to sit here and try to preach about it and tell you if*

**As public opposition to the use of Native American team names and symbols grew, sports teams and their corporate sponsors felt increasing pressure to change.**

John McDonnell/The Washington Post via Getty Images

*you like the name you're wrong or if you hate the name you're wrong. I can just tell you how I feel: I've been increasingly bothered by using the word, and I don't want to be a part of using a name that a cross-section of our society feels is insulting. (King, 2013, para. 16)*

## Changes Elsewhere, But Not in DC

As the public perception regarding Native American mascots was beginning to change, some began reassessing their usage. Considering a team name change was not a new concept; some had occurred years earlier, such as when St. John's University moved from the Redmen to the Red Storm in 1994 (*New York Times*, 1994). By 2015, more schools were following suit. The University of North Dakota changed its sports teams from the Fighting Sioux to the Fighting Hawks, although fans were slow to accept the change (Borzi, 2016).

In the professional ranks, dropping the offensive nicknames was being met with a great deal of pushback. While Cleveland's baseball team eliminated the Chief Wahoo logo in 2018 following pressure from the MLB commissioner, a team name change was not considered (Waldstein, 2018). Meanwhile, it did not seem as if changes were coming in Washington, DC. Team owner Dan Snyder told the *USA Today* in 2013: "We'll never change the name. It's that simple. NEVER—you can use all caps" (Brady, 2013, para. 4).

## Pressure from Sponsors

On July 2, 2020, several major team sponsors announced they would no longer give money to Washington, DC's football team if the name was not changed. Most notable of those was delivery service FedEx. That company was not just another business giving some money to the organization. Instead, they were the major sponsor. The team played at FedEx Field after the company paid the team $205 million for the stadium naming rights (Neuman, 2020). That same day, Nike removed all Washington gear from its website, meaning that fans of the team could not order new shirts or hats with the offensive team name and logo on it (McDonald, 2020). The pressure was mounting, and the organization was left with little choice. The next day, it released a statement that they were "undergoing a thorough review of the team's name" (NFL.com, 2020, para. 2). Ten days after that examination was initiated, a team statement revealed that the long-awaited change was coming: "Today, we are announcing we will be retiring the Redskins name and logo" (Commanders, 2020, para. 2).

Ultimately, while some fans and Native American organizations had protested the name for decades, it was the loss of money that may have been the turning point. Once sponsors threatened to withhold funds from the team, the ownership group began to seriously reconsider the impact the name was having. It is perhaps not a coincidence that the name review came the day after FedEx announced it was pulling its money from the team. Without the sponsor boycott, one might wonder if the name change would have happened.

## The Commanders

Because the name retirement happened rather abruptly, the organization was not fully prepared for what would come next, including not having a new team name ready to replace the old one. Therefore, for both the 2020 and 2021 seasons, the team was known simply as the Washington Football Team. In 2022, the new, permanent name was revealed as the Washington Commanders, a tribute to the military due to the team being located in the capital of the United States (Keim, 2022). While it took them perhaps longer than many would have liked, the team's name change was quickly followed by another. The Cleveland Indians announced that they too were retiring their team's name, and they became the Cleveland Guardians starting in 2022 (Bell, 2021; Waldstein & Schmidt, 2020).

# Summary

This chapter describes the various challenges that many journalists face when discussing race and ethnicity. However, in many cases, those challenges are brought on by the journalists themselves with ignorant opinions that are broadcast to the world. In an effort to change the narrative surrounding athletes of various races and ethnicities, it is important that people of many backgrounds are telling the athletes' stories. To put it more simply: The media cannot consist of only White men if these topics are to be reported on in a respectful way. While one would hope that most journalists are attempting to do the right thing and tell these stories in an equitable way, that may not always be possible due to differing life experiences. Therefore, it is up to sports media outlets such as ESPN, Sports Illustrated, and local television stations and newspapers to think about diversity when hiring because race and ethnicity has become a key part of the conversation surrounding sports.

## KEY TERMS

**ethnicity**—A person's membership in a cultural or ethnic group.

**race**—A socially defined concept used to designate a portion of the population with common physical characteristics, ancestry, or language.

## REVIEW QUESTIONS

1. Why are the demographics of sports journalists an important aspect of the media's coverage of race and ethnicity?

2. What has traditionally been the difference in how White athletes are portrayed compared to how Black athletes are portrayed in the sports media?

3. What are some of the concerns from athletes who do not speak English as their first language when they are doing interviews with the American media?

4. What is the issue with how Native Americans are portrayed in sports?

*CASE STUDY*

# Colin Kaepernick

## CHAPTER OBJECTIVES

After completing the chapter, the reader should be able to do the following:

- Understand the history of the national anthem at sporting events
- Identify why Kaepernick elected to not stand for the anthem
- Recognize the media's role in the dissemination of this story to the public
- Analyze how the anthem protests, and the public's reaction, have evolved in the years since Kaepernick's initial stance

In 1862, before the start of a baseball game, a live band played *The Star-Spangled Banner*, more commonly referred to today as simply the national anthem of the United States. The song was played traditionally only on opening day after that, but in 1918, it made a return during the World Series. However, it was not played before the game, but instead during the seventh-inning stretch. The song was received so well by the players and the fans in attendance that the practice was repeated the next game before being moved to the pregame ceremony (Cyphers & Trex, 2020; Goldman, 2018).

It was not until 1931 that the song officially became the national anthem, but by then it was already a key part of live sporting events. While the practice of playing it before games abated in some places in the years following, it became a permanent pregame staple during the Vietnam War in the late 1960s. The NFL commissioner required players to stand at attention while the anthem was being played, and that is how most athletes in all

sports have acted since (Brady, 2021). However, in 2016, an NFL player chose not to stand, and his protest made headlines throughout the country.

## Kaepernick's Early Career

Colin Kaepernick was born in 1987, a biracial baby who was adopted by White parents shortly after his birth. A star athlete in high school, Kaepernick accepted a scholarship to play quarterback at the University of Nevada, where he set several NCAA records and led the team to some of its best finishes in school history (Branch, 2017). Following his senior season, the San Francisco 49ers traded up in the second round to select Kaepernick with the 36th overall pick in the NFL Draft (Associated Press, 2011). In his second season in the league, Kaepernick took over the starting quarterback job midway through the campaign and led his team all the way to the Super Bowl, a game they lost by just three points (Associated Press, 2013; Klemko, 2012). After two more strong seasons, Kaepernick's career took a surprising turn; he began to struggle with his play, ultimately costing him his starting position (Wesseling, 2015). As the 2016 season approached, Kaepernick was expected to remain the backup quarterback and likely out of the headlines. However, a preseason event was about to make him one of the most recognizable people in all sports.

## Kaepernick's Protest Begins

During the third preseason game in 2016, 49ers beat reporter Jennifer Lee Chan sent what she assumed was just a funny tweet that included a picture of the team on the sideline and a caption about how they were standing in a very unorganized way during the national anthem. However, a closer look at the photo revealed that Kaepernick appeared to be sitting alone on the bench at the time of the anthem (Chan, 2016). Later that night, the team confirmed that he was the player in question, and further reporting revealed that he had actually sat on the bench during the anthem for the first two preseason games also. However, few noticed because he was not wearing his uniform at the time due to an arm and shoulder injury (Florio, 2016; Garafolo, 2016). The first signs of Kaepernick's protest had been discovered.

## Mahmoud Abdul-Rauf

While the protest caught many by surprise, there was a precedent for this act. About 20 years earlier, basketball player Mahmoud Abdul-Rauf, a guard for the NBA's Denver Nuggets, remained in the locker room during the national anthem before each of his team's games. His absence was not a major story until a Denver newspaper writer asked him why he was not standing with his teammates before the game. Abdul-Rauf's response was that it was an act of protest as part of his Muslim beliefs, and he called the American flag "a symbol of oppression, of tyranny" (Diamos, 1996, para. 11).

Once NBA officials became aware of Abdul-Rauf's protest, he was suspended indefinitely without pay. However, the league's stance was that he was not punished because of his beliefs, but instead because he was violating a league rule that stated: "Players, coaches and trainers are to stand and line up in a dignified posture along the sidelines or the foul line during the playing of the national anthem" (Diamos, 1996, para. 5).

Ultimately, the player missed just one game, as the league compromised and agreed to let Abdul-Rauf pray silently during the anthem as long as he was standing up and in line with his teammates. However, the damage was done. Abdul-Rauf was booed soundly at most arenas each time he entered the game and touched the ball. The Nuggets traded him that offseason, and within two years Abdul-Rauf was out of the league (Washington, 2016).

Lou Capozzola/NBAE via Getty Images

**Mahmoud Abdul-Rauf of the Denver Nuggets prays during the national anthem prior to the game against the Philadelphia 76ers in December 1995.**

In an interview in 2017, Abdul-Rauf was explicit that he believed his anthem protest led to the end of his career:

> I don't have any doubt. Initially, I was hesitant in saying it. But as I look back and I'm thinking about the pattern, how things went, I'm thinking, oh definitely. There's no question.... The year that that happened, I was at the height, in my prime.... But then all of a sudden this happened. Come on. I mean, really. (Fainaru-Wada, 2017, para. 40)

# Media Coverage of Kaepernick

Abdul-Rauf might have slipped under the radar initially, but Kaepernick had no chance of that happening in the era of social media and 24-hour news cycles. Immediately after the game, Kaepernick was approached by NFL.com reporter Steve Wyche and asked why he was not standing for the national anthem:

> I am not going to stand up to show pride in a flag for a country that oppresses black people and people of color. To me, this is bigger than football and it would be selfish on my part to look the other way. There are bodies in the street and people getting paid leave and getting away with murder. (Wyche, 2016, para. 3)

Following a conversation with a former Green Beret, Kaepernick altered his protest moving forward from sitting on the bench to kneeling. While his initial anthem protests were discovered almost by accident thanks to a photo of the entire sideline, journalists were ready for the next game. Photographers were trained on Kaepernick during the national anthem of the team's fourth preseason game, and pictures of him kneeling were splashed all over newspaper front pages, social media, and evening television newscasts (Boren, 2020).

An examination of the media framing of Kaepernick's protests in the *San Francisco Chronicle*, *The New York Times*, and *The Washington Post* found that four common themes emerged:

- **The action, not the issue:** Articles discussed the kneeling itself and did not focus on *why* he was kneeling.
- **The military:** The media took Kaepernick's kneeling as connoting disrespect toward the military because he was kneeling during the national anthem when the American flag was being displayed.

- **Patriotism versus freedom of speech:** There was a conflict between those who believed in Kaepernick's right to freedom of speech and those who believed his actions were anti-American.
- **Moral outrage due to a discrete action:** Kaepernick was framed as a rogue individual conducting these protests rather than part of a greater social movement (Doehler, 2023).

A different research study found that the discussion of patriotism was the focus, while topics involving race were pushed to the side. Those researchers also noted how media members, especially those who are paid to give their opinions in columns, were coming down on both sides of the argument (Graber et al., 2020).

## "Through Our Prism"

NFL.com reporter Steve Wyche was the first to talk with Kaepernick about the anthem protests, and while Wyche acknowledged that his reporting skills got him the story, he also said that it was not the only factor. Wyche said that being Black helped him have a nuanced conversation with Kaepernick:

> I can't tell you how many locker rooms I go into or how many press boxes I sit in and I'm the only Black person, or one of two or three. And when I go into locker rooms, players will sometimes say, "Man, there are some things we want to say. But we don't know if we can say them honestly to people who might not be able to tell the story through our prism." (O'Neal, 2016, para. 8)

Wyche said that reporters of other races might have gotten the story, but that Kaepernick perhaps felt more comfortable talking to him because of a shared background. The media's lack of diversity, as discussed in the previous chapter, was soon a key element of the Kaepernick story (Warren, 2016).

## The Message Is Lost

Research demonstrated that one of the key media narratives following Kaepernick's protest was his supposed disrespect toward the military (Doehler, 2023). However, the player would later emphasize that the military had nothing to do with his kneeling. Following a matchup against the Chargers, Kaepernick said:

> The media painted this as I'm anti-American, anti-men-and-women of the military and that's not the

Michael Zagaris/San Francisco 49ers/Getty Images

**Colin Kaepernick, center, kneels with teammates Eli Harold (left) and Eric Reid (right) during the national anthem before an October 2016 game against the Buffalo Bills.**

*case at all. I realize that men and women of the military go out and sacrifice their lives and put themselves in harm's way for my freedom of speech and my freedoms in this country and my freedom to take a seat or take a knee, so I have the utmost respect for them. I think what I did was taken out of context and spun a different way. (Peter, 2016, para. 3, 4)*

This incorrect information became part of the narrative surrounding the protests, with some falsities coming from the media and some coming directly from the NFL. League commissioner Roger Goodell said he personally did not agree with Kaepernick's pregame kneeling, adding: "We believe very strongly in patriotism in the NFL" (Boren, 2016, para. 3). That comment implied that Goodell believed Kaepernick's stance was not patriotic, perhaps contributing to the public's confusion regarding the protest.

## More Protests

Following the 2016 season, Kaepernick opted out of his contract with the 49ers and elected to become a free agent. However, no team signed him to a deal, so the 2017 campaign began without him. Despite his absence from the league, Kaepernick still loomed large as a polarizing figure, with millions who supported him and millions who opposed him. One of those in

opposition was the president of the United States, and comments from him pushed the anthem debate back into the headlines.

## President Trump Takes Aim

In 2017, President Donald Trump was speaking at a campaign rally for Alabama politician Luther Strange when the focus of his comments went away from the candidate and instead to the NFL. Specifically, Trump, without mentioning him by name, seemed to take aim at Kaepernick. To his supportive crowd, Trump proposed: "Wouldn't you love to see one of these NFL owners, when somebody disrespects our flag, to say, 'Get that son of a bitch off the field right now, out. He's fired. He's fired!'" (Gottlieb & Maske, 2017, para. 3).

While public reaction to the president's comments predictably fell along political party lines, the players themselves were nearly unified in their disapproval. Several used social media to speak out, while the executive director of the NFL Players Association said the union would not back down (Gottlieb & Maske, 2017). That weekend, every game featured at least one player kneeling or sitting on the bench during the national anthem, with some coaches and team owners joining their protests (Boren, 2017a). One Dallas Cowboys player remarked, "Trump can't divide this" (Bieler et al., 2017, para. 4).

# National Anthem on Television

As might be expected when there is a conflict between the president of the United States and the athletes in the most popular sport in the United States, the anthem protests became one of the biggest stories in the country. How players would react during the anthem following the president's comments became of interest to many, and the television networks showing the games took notice. Traditionally, the national anthem is only shown on television during major sporting events, such as before the Super Bowl. In most regular-season weeks, only those fans in attendance will see and hear the anthem being played or sung.

On the weekend following President Trump's remarks, the two networks that air Sunday afternoon NFL games, CBS and Fox, elected to show the national anthem at every game. In addition, the issue was discussed at length during the pregame shows on both channels (Yoder, 2017). For many observers, what the players did before the game was more interesting to them than the actual game itself, so the networks leaned into that by showing the pregame festivities.

However, at Fox, the move lasted just one week. Even though the story was still dominating national conversation on sports and news programming, the Fox Sports president announced that the anthem coverage would not continue. He cited a commitment to airing commercials as the reason, but the decision was considered a curious one. Some speculated that the backlash that the NFL was facing from some corners of the country may have led to the anthem airings coming to an end. The reasoning was that if fans are being turned off by the players kneeling, then they might not want to watch the games (Yoder, 2017). By not showing the protests, the network might perhaps eliminate a reason for those fans to want to change the channel or not watch at all. While the networks may want to deliver the news, they also must consider their viewership numbers.

# A Standing Player Stands Out

With all the attention on the players kneeling, those who did not do so began to get attention as well. In their game following President Trump's comments, the Pittsburgh Steelers elected to stay in the locker room area and not be on the sidelines while the anthem was being played. However, as the team stood in the tunnel between their locker room and the field, away from the view of the fans, one player emerged from his teammates. Offensive lineman Alejandro Villanueva, a former Army Ranger who served three tours in Afghanistan, stood alone with his hand over his heart during the national anthem in view of the fans and the media. Pictures of Villanueva soon went viral on social media, making the

Joe Robbins/Getty Images

**Alejandro Villanueva of the Pittsburgh Steelers stands by himself in the tunnel for the national anthem prior to the game against the Chicago Bears in September 2017.**

player a hero to many who were against the protestors. Amazingly, in the 24 hours after the kickoff of that game, Villanueva, a relative unknown to most fans, had the top-selling jersey of any player in the league on both NFL.com and popular sports clothing retailer Fanatics .com (Perez, 2017).

While it might have looked like Villanueva was trying to draw attention to himself, he would later reveal that him standing alone at that moment was actually a misunderstanding. Following a pregame team meeting, he believed the team captains would be standing behind him during the anthem. Instead, the plan hit a snag when they arrived at the entrance to the field too late and security would not allow the captains to move behind him once the music for the anthem had started. In a meeting with the media several days later, Villanueva expressed regret for how the situation transpired and apologized to his teammates, coaches, and the Steelers organization (ESPN.com staff, 2017). By the end of the season, his no. 78 jersey remained one of the top sellers in the league, and Villanueva donated some of his unexpected royalties to charities in Pittsburgh and the cities of the Steelers' three divisional rivals, Baltimore, Cincinnati, and Cleveland (Jones, 2018).

## Kaepernick Returns to the Spotlight

While the national anthem protests were making headlines, the man who started the trend was still away from the game. Kaepernick had not signed with a new team, with some organizations saying that his protests were the reason they had decided not to sign him. Both the Baltimore Ravens and New York Giants were reportedly considering bringing in the quarterback, but negative reaction from fans forced them to reassess and decline to offer Kaepernick a contract (Boren, 2017b). Kaepernick felt he was the victim of collusion, and he filed a grievance against the league stating that the teams were working together to keep him unemployed. In early 2019 the sides reached a confidential settlement, signifying that a return to the league might be possible (Maske, 2019a).

## Nike Campaign

Even before his settlement with the league, one of the NFL's biggest partners was already gearing up for Kaepernick's possible return. Just before the start of the

**A 2018 Nike ad featuring Colin Kaepernick is displayed in Times Square.**

ANGELA WEISS/AFP via Getty Images

2018 season, and one year before that agreement with the NFL, Nike announced that it was continuing its endorsement deal with the still unemployed quarterback, promoting him as the face of their newest advertising campaign. Despite not playing in the league at the time, Nike produced a Kaepernick sneaker, T-shirt, and other merchandise. The slogan superimposed across his face in advertisements read "Believe in something. Even if it means sacrificing everything" (Draper & Belson, 2018).

The move was a gamble from Nike, as it is a major sponsor of the NFL and one could assume that the league would not want the anthem protests brought back into the public consciousness. The company did face criticism from some consumers, as the hashtag #BoycottNike was used more than 100,000 times after the debut of the ad, with people posting images of themselves cutting the Nike logo off their socks or setting their old Nike sneakers on fire. The positive seemed to outweigh the negative, however, as Nike announced the ad campaign had resulted in record online engagement and an all-time high for the company's stock price (Creswell et al., 2018; Draper & Belson, 2018). However, even with Nike's support, no teams signed Kaepernick to a new contract.

## Team Tryout

In 2019, the quarterback received an offer from a surprising ally in his efforts to get back onto a roster. The NFL organized a tryout on Kaepernick's behalf to take place at the Atlanta Falcons' facility in mid-November. All 32 teams were invited to see him throw and conduct interviews to gauge his interest in signing with their squad (Schefter, 2019).

In the leadup to the event, Kaepernick stated that he had been waiting three years for an opportunity such as this one, but as the day inched closer, the plan began to fall apart. The quarterback and his representatives asked for the event to be moved to a different day, for the event be open to the media, and that he not sign a league-mandated liability waiver; the NFL refused all three requests. On the day of tryout, less than 30 minutes before it was set to begin and with 25 teams expected to show up, Kaepernick abruptly canceled the NFL-organized session and instead announced that a new one organized by him would take place an hour later at a local high school. Only eight teams made the drive from the Falcons' facility to the new tryout (Jones, 2019; Maske, 2019b). Kaepernick threw at the high school, but ultimately did not sign with any team.

Following the tryout, ESPN's Stephen A. Smith, one of the network's most recognizable and promoted broadcasters, went on social media bashing Kaepernick. In a three-minute video posted to his Twitter account and viewed more than five million times, Smith was openly critical of the quarterback's decision to move the event and avoid the help that the NFL was giving him. Smith believed that Kaepernick never had any intention of signing with a team. Smith remarked, "He don't want to play. He wants to be a martyr" (Smith, 2019, 2:05).

# Athlete Protests of 2020

While Kaepernick's chances of returning to the NFL may have ended during that tryout, the public would be reminded of his legacy the following year. In 2020, Jacob Blake, a 29-year-old Black man, was shot seven times by a White police officer in Wisconsin. A video of the shooting was captured by a bystander and posted to social media. Response to the video led to protests throughout the United States, and the sports world was not immune to the outrage (Morales, 2021).

With playoff games taking place in the COVID-19 bubble in Orlando at the time (see chapter 31 for more), the NBA was in the midst of the culmination of its season. However, the Milwaukee Bucks announced they would not play their playoff game that night, instead wanting to draw attention to what was happening back in their home state of Wisconsin. The NBA then made the unprecedented move to postpone all the games that evening, a move that was shortly followed by the WNBA and several games in MLB (Martin et al., 2020).

Attention to social justice causes was already being seen during the 2020 season. When the NBA resumed following the postponement due to COVID-19, the words "Black Lives Matter" had been painted onto all the courts. In addition, in nearly every professional sports league, players were kneeling during the national anthem.

- NHL's Matt Dumba knelt during the national anthem during the Stanley Cup qualifying games (Douglas, 2020).
- Players from both the Chicago Fire and New York City F.C., along with the referees, took a knee just before kickoff of the final game of the regular season in MLS (Murungi, 2020).
- At MLB's opening day, several players expressed their support for the Black Lives Matter movement by kneeling during the national anthem (Wagner, 2020).

- The WNBA, also in a COVID-19–related bubble, had players not standing as a sign of protest as the national anthem played (Abrams & Weiner, 2020).

These athlete protests brought to mind Kaepernick's earlier stances, but there was one major difference. In 2020, those kneeling and calling for a boycott were almost universally supported by team and league management, something that had eluded Kaepernick. Perhaps most telling was an interview conducted with NFL commissioner Roger Goodell in which he was asked what, in 2020, he wished he had said to Kaepernick in 2016: "The first thing I'd say is I wish we had listened earlier, Kaep, to what you were kneeling about and what you were trying to bring attention to" (Acho, 2020, 5:08).

# Summary

In 2016, a photo of the San Francisco 49ers sideline during a preseason game led to one of the biggest stories in both news and sports. Colin Kaepernick, the team's backup quarterback, was sitting on the bench as the national anthem was playing, an act that was out of the norm for most in the sporting world. Kaepernick was vilified by some and labeled a hero by others. His protest's purpose was to draw attention to racial injustices, but his message got lost along the way due to several competing narratives that emerged, including an incorrect belief that he was anti-military.

Following the 2016 season, Kaepernick would leave the NFL but remain a key part of the league. He accused the league's owners of conspiring to keep him unsigned, was a part of a major advertising campaign from Nike, and had a failed tryout attempt after disagreements with league officials. Kaepernick's cause would be somewhat validated in 2020 when players in nearly every professional sport took a knee to protest racial inequality. While Kaepernick was no longer a professional athlete himself, it was impossible to ignore the impact his previous protests had on the current players at the time.

## REVIEW QUESTIONS

1. How was Colin Kaepernick's anthem protest first discovered?
2. What happened to Mahmoud Abdul-Rauf after his anthem protests?
3. What was one reason that NFL.com reporter Steve Wyche believed Kaepernick felt comfortable talking with him during the anthem protests?
4. NFL broadcasters showed the anthem protests in 2017 after President Donald Trump made comments that upset many players. However, on Fox, those protests were shown for only one week. What is the speculation as to why?

# Stick to Sports

## CHAPTER OBJECTIVES

After completing the chapter, the reader should be able to do the following:

- Understand the background of the phrase "stick to sports"
- Identify key moments in history when athletes did not "stick to sports"
- Understand how the Internet led to the rise of sports journalists giving political opinions
- Recognize how "sticking to sports" might not be possible for athletes and journalists

After winning the Super Bowl in 2017, several New England Patriots players elected not to take the traditional trip to the White House to be honored by the president. One of those players, Martellus Bennett, said he was opposed to Donald Trump and the president's politics. The response from some was that of outrage, as they believed Bennett should be honored to be invited to the White House and that it was not a political event. They saw the player as an athlete only and did not want him to weigh in on social issues. Many Twitter users responded to Bennett's account with the same three words: "Stick to sports" (King, 2017).

## "Stick to Sports" Definition

When an athlete or a sports journalist discusses a topic other than sports, especially a topic that is political or a social issue, the response from the audience is sometimes "stick to sports." For many, sports are an escape from those often-divisive topics, so hearing about them from someone who they feel should be focused on the games might not be welcome. The "stick to sports" response can be loosely translated to: "This is not why I choose to pay attention to you or what you do. I only want you to talk about sports."

## Athletes and Political Statements

One of the most prominent sports stars of all time went out of his way to avoid making political statements. In 1990, the United States Senate race in North Carolina was down to Republican Jesse Helms and Democrat Harvey Gantt. The election was divided along both political and racial lines as Gantt, a Black man, was challenging the incumbent Helms, who opposed making Dr. Martin Luther King Jr.'s birthday a national holiday. Gantt's campaign approached basketball superstar and North Carolina legend Michael Jordan about appearing in an advertisement to support their candidate. Jordan declined, later telling his teammates "Republicans buy sneakers too" (Granderson, 2012, para. 8). Years later, Jordan would say that he did not want to be an activist, and was solely focused on playing basketball, making it his own decision to "stick to sports" (Washington, 2020).

## The Impartial Media

For many years, journalists not only avoided giving their opinions on issues outside of sports, but they were also quiet about their feelings regarding the games too. The phrase "no cheering in the press box" was created to illustrate that media members were not there to root for teams or players but to be impartial observers. These journalists are to be objective and simply document what happens, so, in theory, they do not care who wins or loses. For many, this impartiality moved from not just covering sports, but to topics outside the playing field as well.

## Exceptions

While Jordan was among the majority of athletes who elected to focus on the games, there were exceptions. As discussed in chapter 4, Tommie Smith and John Carlos held one of the most famous political protests in sports history when they each raised a fist on the Olympic medal podium in a human rights salute (Maraniss, 2018). Tennis star Billie Jean King was an outspoken advocate for gender equality, basketball player Kareem Abdul-Jabbar wrote about racial and religious issues, and Muhammad Ali refused to fight in the Vietnam War (Chang, 2021; Hess, 2021; Rhoden, 2013). Among journalists, Howard Cosell, the longtime broadcaster for ABC Sports, was one of the few who openly supported Black athletes, including Ali, which was a rarity for the mostly White media at the time (Sandomir, 2016). However, Cosell was perhaps the most famous sports media member at the time, giving him the freedom and power to make political statements without fearing for his job.

## Athletes Speaking Out

Starting in the 2010s, societal and political issues became harder for athletes to ignore. As was discussed in the previous chapter, Colin Kaepernick's kneeling during the U.S. national anthem was one of the more visible examples of athletes speaking out on social issues, but it was far from the only example. Following the death of Trayvon Martin in 2012, LeBron James and his Miami Heat teammates posed in hooded sweatshirts, a reference to what the 17-year-old was wearing when he was fatally shot by a neighborhood crime-watch volunteer (ESPN.com News Services, 2012). In 2014, members of the St. Louis Rams walked on the field using the "hands up, don't shoot" gesture that protestors in Ferguson, Missouri, had been using after Michael Brown was shot by police in that city, while several NBA players wore "I can't breathe" T-shirts, memorializing the last words of Eric Garner as he was put in a fatal chokehold by a police officer (Sanchez, 2014). U.S. President Barack Obama noted the change, singling out LeBron James as someone who in his mind was doing the right thing by changing how athletes talk about issues outside of sports:

> We went through a long stretch there where [with] well-paid athletes the notion was: just be quiet and get your endorsements and don't make waves. LeBron is an example of a young man who has, in his own way and in a respectful way, tried to say, "I'm part of this society, too" and focus attention. I'd like to see more athletes do that. (Westfall, 2014).

Athletes began appearing at election campaign rallies to speak out on racial issues, despite the fact that in many cases these political mentions had negative implications on the athletes' public image (Mudrick et al., 2019; Redford, 2017; SI Wire, 2016).

## ESPN and Caitlyn Jenner

One of the events that is often cited as the beginning of the "politicization of the sports media" happened in 2015. At its awards show that year, ESPN presented the Arthur Ashe Award for Courage to Caitlyn Jenner. The honor traditionally goes to individuals whose contributions transcend sports, with previous winners including Muhammad Ali, Billie Jean King, and Nelson Mandela (Moyer, 2015). Jenner, who was known as Bruce Jenner when she was the men's Olympic decathlon champion in 1976, had transitioned to a woman earlier that year. While Jenner was greeted with multiple ovations on the night of the ceremony, there was not universal praise for the selection (ESPN.com News Services, 2015). Longtime NBC sportscaster Bob Costas called the decision to honor Jenner "a crass exploitation play—it's a tabloid play," while NPR's Frank Deford said, "I don't think it rises to the level of courage" (Moyer, 2015, para. 6, 10). For many, the anger was not directed at Jenner, but at ESPN. There was a sense that the network has crossed an imaginary line from just a sports channel to one with a political, liberal-leaning agenda. For those not on that side of the political spectrum, the move was unforgivable (Putterman, 2017a).

# Internet Influence

While ESPN may have been making political decisions that affected the entire company, the Internet had created an opportunity for individual reporters to speak for themselves. In a traditional newsroom, anything that appears in the newspaper or on a broadcast will often go through several layers of approval. For example, a newspaper editor will likely look over any story before it reaches the public. The Internet, and specifically social media, has allowed journalists to send their thoughts immediately to the public through a carefully (or not so carefully) worded tweet. Sportswriter Greg Bedard likely would never have been able to comment about politics in the pages of *Sports Illustrated* when he was a writer there, but in January 2017, in between tweets about football, he wrote: "Go nuts banning Muslims from countries that haven't harmed us . . . as soon as you end the 33,000 annual gun deaths in this country" (Bedard, 2017). Twitter gave journalists a 24/7 opportunity to write about whatever they wanted with no one to approve or disapprove of the material.

# Sports Journalists' Political Interests

The 2016 presidential election in the United States was one of the most bitter political races in decades, as Republican Donald Trump faced off with Democrat Hillary Clinton. The debates, mudslinging, and accusations from both sides became almost all that anyone could talk about, and that included sports journalists. The public was almost evenly split regarding the candidates, as demonstrated by the close results of the final vote, but what became apparent was that there was not an even split among journalists. ESPN's public editor, a position comparable to an ombudsman, wrote that he believed there was a strong liberal leaning among ESPN employees (Brady, 2016).

It was apparent that ESPN's journalists were not the only ones whose political views were more Democratic than Republican. In an article titled "Sportswriting has become a liberal profession," *The Ringer*'s Bryan Curtis wrote, "In sportswriting, there was once a social and professional price to pay for being a noisy liberal. Now,

there's at least a social price to pay for being a conservative" (Curtis, 2019, para. 18). Curtis would quote baseball writer Rob Neyer:

> *How many sportswriters have you seen on Twitter defending Donald Trump? I haven't seen one. I'm sure there must have been a few writers out there who did vote for him, but there's a lot of pressure not to be public about it.* (Curtis, 2019, para. 16)

For the few openly conservative sportswriters, ESPN became a popular target. One writer sold MSESPN shirts on his website, a reference to his opinion that ESPN was appearing more and more like MSNBC, a liberal-leaning cable network (Strauss, 2017). However, those opinions were in the minority, as sports journalists were almost exclusively liberal.

# Jemele Hill

As the media became more willing to not simply "stick to sports," it was ESPN's Jemele Hill who garnered many of the headlines. Hill, who began her career in local newspapers, started a meteoric rise at ESPN in 2006. She hosted podcasts, was part of her own show on ESPN2, and was eventually promoted to be the cohost of *SportsCenter*, the flagship program at the network (Crawford, 2017). Even with that high-profile job, Hill said she had no plans to avoid political talk or debates about societal issues. Demonstrating her unwillingness to bend, Hill soon found herself in hot water.

# "White Supremacist"

In 2017, in a Twitter exchange discussing President Donald Trump, Hill tweeted that the president was "a white supremacist who has largely surrounded himself w/ other white supremacists" (Manzullo, 2017, para. 1). The tweet became major news, as this was a prominent figure at a major television network expressing her political views in a very explicit manner. The White House press secretary called for Hill to be fired because of her comments. ESPN did not take that route, but the network did issue a statement that her comments "do not represent the position of ESPN," while Hill would later tweet: "My comments on Twitter expressed my personal beliefs. My regret is that my comments and the public way I made them painted ESPN in an unfair light" (Draper, 2017, para. 5, para. 7). As many noted, Hill did not back down from her comments, only regretting the impact they had on her employer.

ESPN's Michael Smith and Jemele Hill host a pregame show during the 2017 NBA Finals.

## NFL Protests

About a month later, Hill was back in the news. Following several NFL players' decision to kneel during the playing of the national anthem, Dallas Cowboys team owner Jerry Jones said that he would bench any of his players who disrespected the flag. On Twitter, Hill suggested that fans who opposed Jones' statement should boycott the sponsors of the Cowboys. It was, once again, a political and societal commentary from an ESPN employee. In this case, Hill was suspended by the network for two weeks for what executives labeled a violation of ESPN's social media guidelines (Draper & Belson, 2017). Reaction from some of her then-current and former ESPN colleagues was almost universally negative regarding the decision to suspend her (Putterman, 2017b).

## The Fallout

For many, the decision to not suspend Hill for her "white supremacist" comments, but then to suspend her for criticizing an NFL team, seemed curious. ESPN, which at the time was in a multibillion-dollar partnership with the NFL to show *Monday Night Football*, appeared to be more interested in making sure the league was not shown in a negative light as compared to the president of the United States. Bill Simmons, the former ESPN

columnist who was suspended in 2014 for his comments about NFL commissioner Roger Goodell, wrote after Hill's suspension, "I was advised a few weeks later by someone very, very, very, very, very high at ESPN that I should lay off Goodell" (Simmons, 2017, para. 37). While "stick to sports" was being given as the reason while Hill had violated the network's social media policy, others questioned if it was the target, not the content, of the second tweet that led to the suspension. Hill would later say that she understood the decision and deserved the suspension due to her comments, but her time at ESPN would come to an end in September 2018 when she announced she was leaving the network (Bogage, 2018; Bonesteel, 2017).

## Social Media Policies

As politics and social issues began appearing more frequently in the tweets of sports journalists, some major media outlets began revisiting their social media policies. Most notably, both *The New York Times* and ESPN publicly revealed changes that were made in 2017, perhaps as a way to be more transparent and accountable. Most notably, both were very explicit that political opinions were no longer to be shared online.

*The New York Times* is home to hundreds of employees, some of whom do cover politics and have to report on political issues, so the language in the new social media policy had to be universal for all. The new company mandate stated that journalists must not express partisan opinions, promote political views, or endorse political candidates on social media. In addition, the newspaper was very explicit that these rules were for everyone, including sports journalists:

> These guidelines apply to everyone in every department of the newsroom, including those not involved in coverage of government and politics. (New York Times, 2017, para. 22)

At ESPN, the directive was similar: No politics. News reporters were instructed to not have any partisan political opinions on social media or take any position on social issues when online. For the ESPN personalities who had the authority to give a commentary beyond reporting just the facts, any political topics and coverage had to first be discussed with leadership to "ensure a fair and effective presentation" (ESPN, 2017, para. 21).

For both ESPN and *The New York Times*, one of the major concerns was that the audience often does not separate the employee from the employer. When Jemele Hill tweeted that President Trump was a white supremacist, many did not solely associate the comments with her, and instead believed that all of ESPN thought that President Trump was a white supremacist. For media outlets looking to stay impartial, this can be a problem. A reporter from *The New York Times* acknowledged that, even though his account has his name on it, it is nearly impossible to remove his connection from the newsroom:

> The reality is that my Twitter account is a Times account. The Times does not control it, but the Times is held accountable for what appears on my feed. Indeed, the casual reader interprets my social accounts as an extension of our digital platforms, for good and ill. I think all of us at the Times need to embrace this as the price of our employment by a major media institution. (And in fairness, to the extent my Twitter account is influential or widely read, it is largely because I am employed by The Times.) (New York Times, 2017, para. 25)

## ESPN and "Stick to Sports"

The new social media policy might have been a start, but ESPN was committed to avoiding political talk as much as possible. Shortly after Hill's tweets about President Trump, ESPN's president John Skipper sent a memo to all his employees, reminding them that the network's goal was to cover sports and not to be a political organization. He wrote, "We need to remind ourselves that we are a journalistic organization and that we should not do anything that undermines that position" (Stelter, 2017, para. 16). After Skipper was replaced as ESPN president by Jimmy Pitaro, the new leader attempted to distance the network even further from the perception about ESPN's political leanings:

> If you ask me is there a false narrative out there, I will tell you ESPN being a political organization is false. I will tell you I have been very, very clear with employees here that it is not our jobs to cover politics, purely. (Phillips, 2018, para. 3)

While Skipper and Pitaro may have been relaying their own vision for how the network should be run, research would soon demonstrate that the public was on their side.

In 2019, ESPN's own research found that 74 percent of sports fans preferred not to hear about politics when reading about or watching sports. Perhaps most eye-opening for leadership was that 85 percent of what the network labeled "avid fans" said they did not want politics on ESPN. Therefore, by talking about these issues, ESPN was alienating their most loyal viewers. In open-ended responses, sports fans were telling executives that they can watch politics anywhere, but sports fandom is an escape from that. By having politics in sports, fans could no longer escape (*Sports Business Journal*, 2019). Pitaro would say, "Without question our data tells us our fans do not want us to cover politics" (Battaglio, 2019, para. 23).

## Work Mandates versus Personal Rights

The "Stick to Sports" debate can also create a tension for the athletes and media members who find themselves trying to balance their personal beliefs against the expectations of their employers. For example, ESPN was concerned about turning off their audience with too many political conversations, so limiting that topic was likely determined to be best for their financial bottom line. However, this means that reporters at the network might have had to stay silent about topics that are personally important to them. In one very public case, that proved to be exactly what happened.

Clemson University football players attend a protest at Bowman Field in 2020.

In 2023, ESPN *SportsCenter* anchor Sage Steele announced she was leaving the network so that she could "exercise my first amendment rights more freely" (Battaglio, 2023, para. 2). Steele had previously criticized the network's mandate that all workers get the COVID-19 vaccine and had even taken ESPN to court after her criticisms of the policy resulted in a suspension (Battaglio, 2023). Away from ESPN, Steele believed she would be able to talk about issues that were personally important to her, without having to worry about the opinions of her employer. Steele did not want to "stick to sports," but her employment at ESPN made that nearly impossible at the time.

## Is "Stick to Sports" Realistic?

While many fans have indicated that they would prefer athletes and the media to "stick to sports," that might not be realistic in the current political environment. In 2020, following the high-profile deaths of George Floyd and Breonna Taylor at the hands of police officers, athletes began speaking out more loudly about social justice than they had in years. Prominent players supported the Black Lives Matter movement, mentioning the two cases in interviews and on social media (Brunt, 2020). Following the police shooting of Jacob Blake in Wisconsin, NBA, WNBA, and MLB players refused to participate in games that night, forcing the league to postpone those events (Martin et al., 2020). Throughout the year, athletes would march in protests, organize voting drives, and publicly support political candidates (Brunt, 2020). The days of sports stars thinking they should not speak out because "Republicans buy sneakers too" appeared to be in the past.

As these athletes were making their voices heard, sports journalists were there documenting every move. When the NBA postponed playoff games following the player boycott after the shooting of Blake, it was instantly one of the biggest sports stories in years. ESPN had multiple writers, broadcasters, and commentators reporting on the postponements and, more importantly, the reasoning behind the protests (Bontemps & Andrews, 2020). It has become increasingly impossible for sports journalists to focus only on final scores when societal issues are a large aspect of the players' lives off the court. Even ESPN backed off its previous "stick to sports" stance, with a spokesman saying that, while they will not cover politics exclusively, they will when it intersects with sports (Flynn, 2020). When politics and social issues have become so intertwined with the daily lives of many, it may be almost impossible for sports to be insulated from those discussions. If that is the case, then the sports media cannot ignore these conversations, no matter what the audience prefers from networks such as ESPN. While "stick to sports" was long the mantra of athletes and the sports media, it would appear those days may soon be in the past.

# Summary

For decades, with few exceptions, athletes and media members elected to "stick to sports" and avoid addressing political and societal issues. However, starting in the mid-2010s, athletes began speaking out on topics, mostly involving race, that affected them. During the 2016 presidential election in the United States, sports journalists became more likely to share their (mostly liberal) opinions. The rise of social media helped to kick-start this trend, as journalists no longer needed approval of editors or management before sending a message to the audience. This led to media outlets having to revisit their social media policies, explicitly telling reporters not to engage in partisan conversation. However, even as fans report that they overwhelmingly do not want to see political conversations from athletes or journalists, it is becoming nearly impossible to avoid those topics. Even though "stick to sports" might be the response to non-sports comments, it is becoming harder for those in the world of sports to ignore societal issues.

## REVIEW QUESTIONS

1. What might someone mean when they say "stick to sports"?
2. Why was ESPN's awarding of the Arthur Ashe Award for Courage to Caitlyn Jenner considered controversial to some?
3. How has the Internet led to a rise in sports journalists not "sticking to sports"?
4. When *The New York Times* and ESPN both revised their social media policies in 2017, what was one of the primary purposes?

# 18

# Media Coverage of Women's Sports

## CHAPTER OBJECTIVES

After completing the chapter, the reader should be able to do the following:

- Understand the importance of Title IX in the evolution of women's sports
- Recognize major moments in women's sports
- Understand the "chicken or the egg" dilemma facing women's sports
- Identify some of the obstacles female athletes face trying to get media coverage

In the 1960s, Joan Weston was one of the highest-paid female athletes in the world (Deford, 2010). However, representative of the respect surrounding women's sports at the time, Weston was not participating in what many would consider a traditional game. She was not playing on center court at Wimbledon, sinking a long putt to win a golf major tournament, or capitalizing on her success at the Olympics. Instead, Weston was making her money as the star of *roller derby*.

It was not as if Weston was not a superior athlete in other sports, as she famously hit eight home runs in one game for her college softball team. But after graduation from college, there were limited opportunities for women who wanted to play sports professionally. As roller derby grew in popularity on television in the 1950s, Weston became the main attraction due to both her skills and her movie star looks (Thomas, 1997).

While Weston's story is certainly a remarkable one, it also speaks directly to the place of women in the world of sports for decades. The modern Olympics debuted in 1896 with no women's sports, professional leagues were essentially nonexistent for years, and television and newspapers wanted little to do with women playing sports. While the opportunities for women who wanted to play sports would change almost instantly in 1972, the media's interest in them would still lag behind men's sports, with many struggling to gain any amount of attention.

## Title IX

In 1972, U.S. President Richard Nixon signed an education bill aimed at prohibiting sex discrimination at institutions that receive federal funding. The bill affected schools at all levels, including primary, secondary, and higher education institutions, meaning that as of 2022 it applied to more than 17,000 school districts and more than 5,000 colleges and universities (Tumin, 2022a). The passage, known as Title IX, was just 37 words long:

*No person in the United States shall, on the basis of sex, be excluded from participation in, be denied the benefits of, or be subjected to discrimination under any education program or activity receiving Federal financial assistance. (Tumin, 2022a, para. 3)*

To put it simply: Schools receiving federal funding must provide the same opportunities for men and women. Title IX was intended to equalize admissions into college, but perhaps the most visible result was the impact the legislation had on sports (Tumin, 2022b). Men's sports had dominated school athletics since the beginning days of those events, but now women were to have the same opportunities that the men had when it came to athletics at schools. Essentially whatever was offered to male athletes, whether that be equipment, scholarships, locker rooms, ideal practice times, or any other benefits that come with being a student-athlete, would now have to equally be offered to women. On the 50th anniversary of the passing of Title IX, a study from the Women's Sports Foundation demonstrated just how effective it had been:

### Number of High School Girls Participating in Sports:

- 1972: 294,015
- 2019: 3,402,733

### Number of College Women Participating in Sports:

- 1972: 29,977
- 2021: 215,486 (Staurowsky et al., 2022)

Specific examples included North Carolina State multiplying its budget for women's sports by 15 in the four years after Title IX was passed and the University of Michigan going from zero women's sports to 10 from 1973 to 1978 (Rothman, 2017). Additionally, the amount of money invested in women's sports on the collegiate level went from practically nothing in 1971 to more than $100 million by 1982 (Uhlir, 1982).

# Major Moments in Women's Sports

As Title IX was increasing opportunities, some memorable events involving women in athletics were also raising their profile. Three such events were

- the "Battle of the Sexes"
- Mary Lou Retton at the 1984 Olympics
- equality at the Olympics

## "Battle of the Sexes"

In 1973, former Wimbledon champion Bobby Riggs had retired from professional tennis but was looking for a way to return to the spotlight. Riggs brashly stated that women's tennis was inferior to men's and that he, even at his advanced age for an athlete at 55, could beat any top women's player of the time. Margaret Court, the winner of all four major tennis tournaments in 1970, accepted the challenge. On Mother's Day of that year, Riggs made quick work of Court, beating her easily in straight sets. The 6–2, 6–1 victory would later be known as "The Mother's Day Massacre."

However, Riggs's preferred opponent that day was not Court; the player he really wanted to face was Billie Jean King, who was widely regarded as the best in women's tennis. King initially rejected the idea, believing it was more of a stunt than a legitimate match. However, after Court's defeat, and Riggs's boasting afterward, King recognized that she had no choice but to accept the challenge, setting up the "Battle of the Sexes" (Drucker, 2021).

Four months later, King and Riggs were set to face off in the Astrodome in Houston. More than 30,000 people packed into the stadium, making it the largest audience ever to watch a tennis match in the United States. The "man versus woman" element was played up heavily by the organizers, as Riggs gave King a "Sugar Daddy" lollipop before the match began, while King gave Riggs a pig to represent his attitude toward women. While the winner of the match would receive $100,000, in King's mind there was much more on the line. She would later say, "I thought it would set us back 50 years if I didn't win that match. It would ruin the women's tour and affect all women's self-esteem" (Greenspan, 2013, para. 8).

Almost immediately after the start, it was clear that this would not be another "Mother's Day Massacre." King ran Riggs all over the court, watching as the aging former men's star tired trying to chase down her perfectly placed shots. The match was a rout, with King winning 6–4, 6–3, 6–3. For many, a woman beating a man in sports was a shock, and the recap in *Sports Illustrated* conveyed that feeling:

*What in the world kind of occasion was this in which the woman not only defeated the man but swamped him; outplayed, outclassed, outpsyched, outnerved and beat the living bejeezus out of him as well. (Kirkpatrick, 1973, para. 5)*

The victory was a turning point in not just women's sports, but the entire women's equality movement. By

Billie Jean King and Bobby Riggs shake hands following King's victory in the Battle of the Sexes tennis match.

beating a man, Billie Jean King had proven that women did not need to be considered second-class citizens, and that they should be considered for the same opportunities as men.

## Mary Lou Retton in 1984

In 1984, the Summer Olympics came to Los Angeles and an American gymnast soon captured the heart of the country. Sixteen-year-old Mary Lou Retton capped off the all-around competition with a perfect 10 score on the vault. That result gave her the gold and made her the first American woman to ever win the gold medal in the all-around gymnastics competition in the Olympics. The four-foot-nine-inch Retton was a tiny powerhouse on the mat, but had just become larger than life to many watching at home (Mifflin, 1984a).

When it comes to the topic of women in sports, perhaps the most remarkable part of Retton's victory happened after the Olympics were over. Companies were lining up to have the gold medalist endorse their products, and she signed deals with haircare product manufacturer Vidal Sassoon, fast-food restaurant McDonald's, and cereal company General Mills. The deal with General Mills made her the first woman to be an official spokesperson for Wheaties, a cereal that had previously only been marketed to men (Mifflin, 1984b).

Her role endorsing "the breakfast of champions" led to some small changes for Wheaties, which had an official slogan of "What the big boys eat." In a television commercial following the Olympics, Retton is shown with a bowl of the cereal in her hands as she says, "Watch out big boys," signifying that this breakfast was now for all athletes (TheOlympicsHistory, 2013, :27). This was a sign that women in sports were now being accepted among advertisers for more than just products aimed specifically at women. While the Wheaties commercial might just look like another ad, it was a significant moment in the history of women's athletics.

## Equality at the Olympics

While Retton's 1984 performance created a women's sport star, the Olympics soon became one of the most gender-equal competitions in all of athletics. The first Olympics did not allow women to compete at all, but by the 2012 Summer Olympics, there was a women's sport for every men's competition, and every nation had at least one female athlete on the team (Donnelly & Donnelly, 2013; Minsberg, 2021).

In the 1972 Summer Olympics, the year Title IX was passed, U.S. women won 23 medals, while the men won 71. By 2016, it was apparent how much the women had benefited from the opportunities provided by that landmark legislation. During that year's Olympics, the American woman won 61 medals to the men's 55, including 27 of the country's 46 golds (Myre, 2016). American women were not only competing at the Olympics at an equal rate with men, they were outperforming them once they got there.

## A Lack of Media Coverage of Women's Sports

With professional women's sports leagues in golf, tennis, basketball, and soccer, there are numerous opportunities for women to make money as professional athletes. In addition, women athletes are being

**Mary Lou Retton celebrates with coach Bela Karolyi after scoring a perfect 10 on vault.**

hired by major companies to endorse products, a sign that these organizations feel that they can help them sell merchandise. With all the opportunities that are now available, one could argue that this is the golden era of women's sports. There are more scholarships, more youth leagues, more professional opportunities, and more money for women who want to play sports. However, people might not realize that if they watched or read sports media coverage.

## Revealing Statistics

The lack of attention given to women's sports by journalists is not an anecdotal observation. Instead, decades' worth of statistics reveal that men's sports dominate the national media conversation. A team of researchers conducted a longitudinal study that examined the amount of attention given to women's sports on television from 1989 to 2019. Their results demonstrated that women's sports lag far behind in coverage when compared to men's sports. Their 2009 edition of the research found that just 1.3 percent of ESPN's *SportsCenter* program was related to women's sports. That number had climbed to 5.7 percent by 2019, but that still put it well behind the attention given to the men (Cooky et al., 2021). Other researchers demonstrated that *SportsCenter*'s former competition *Fox Sports Live* had a similar ratio (Billings & Young, 2015), and it took the Olympics decades before

it had an equal representation between men and women on the broadcasts (Billings & Angelini, 2019). Results such as those prompted a team to title one of their studies "Women play sport, but not on TV" (Cooky et al., 2013).

This phenomenon is not exclusive to broadcast television. An examination of the top newspapers in the United States found that stories focusing exclusively on men's sports outnumbered those that focused on women's sports by a ratio of 23 to 1. That same study revealed that 92.3 percent of all photographs in the sports section were of men, while fewer than 5 percent of all the stories were devoted to women only (Duncan et al., 1991). From 2000 to 2011, *Sports Illustrated* featured women on only 4.9 percent of the 716 cover images. Perhaps surprisingly, that number was actually worse than the percentage from 1954 to 1965 following the magazine's debut (12.6 percent) (Weber & Carini, 2013). On social media, journalists do not have the time and space constrictions that exist on television and in the newspaper, which should mean there is an opportunity to devote more attention to women's sports. However, that has not happened, as an examination of nearly 20,000 Twitter posts from local television sports broadcasters revealed that just over 4 percent of the tweets were solely about women's sports, while 77 percent were about men's (Hull, 2017).

As will be discussed in chapter 20, the majority of the producers of sports media content are men. A 2014 study found that 90 percent of sports editors at newspaper were men, a percentage that has not significantly changed in the years since (Morrison, 2014). It is worth wondering if the amount of media coverage devoted to women's sports would be higher if more sports reporters and editors were women.

## Chicken or the Egg?

When asked why women's sports do not get the same amount of attention as men's sports, the traditional response is something along the lines of the fact that television ratings and attendance are lower for women's sports, and the media only reports on what the fans are most interested in. Dan Shaughnessy, a longtime columnist for *The Boston Globe*, once said that his job is to focus on what his audience wants to read about. "I know what people are interested in," he said, explaining why he did not write more about women's sports (Ottaway, 2016, para. 23).

When looking at the numbers, one can see that there is some truth to the perception when examining the popularity of comparable sports. In 2022, the WNBA Finals averaged 534,000 viewers per game on television, while the NBA Finals averaged 12.4 million per game. In the college ranks, the NCAA women's basketball championship game had 4.85 million viewers, while the men's final had 18.1 million viewers (Brooks, 2022; Rajan, 2022; Shea, 2022a, 2022b).

However, those viewership totals fail to tell the complete story. It is similar to the chicken-or-the-egg debate: "Which came first, the chicken or the egg?" For women's sports, the question is, "Which will come first, media coverage or viewership?" In this case, the following two statements are accepted as fact by many:

- "Women's sports don't get media coverage because they aren't popular."
- "How can women's sports get more popular? More media coverage."

Therein lies the "chicken-or-the-egg" problem with women's sports. They cannot get media coverage without being more popular, but they are not going to get more popular without getting more media coverage. Journalist Kate Fagan once said: "Comparing TV ratings of men's and women's sports is like comparing the speed of two cars, but on one you left flat tires & never filled the tank" (Fagan, 2015).

## Media's Focus on Looks

When women do get attention in sports, it is often not about their athletic achievements. A simple web search of a term such as "women golfers" demonstrates the battle that these athletes face. While some results show the player rankings and tournament scores, many of the top returned options include something along the lines of "20 hottest female golfers" or "most beautiful women in golf." These athletes are not getting attention for their play, but instead the focus is on their looks.

## "Sex Sells"

In 2013, an ESPN article summed up the plight facing many women in sports: "If a female athlete wants to succeed in the endorsement game, she should be willing to trade on her body and her looks first, her athletic talent second" (Fagan, 2013, para. 2). The implication was that companies and media outlets are only interested in women sport stars who look a certain way, and are not as interested in these women's actual athletic ability. The athletes certainly appear aware of this, as a study of women trying to make the Rio Olympics in 2016 found that the athletes felt pressure to post suggestive pictures of themselves on social media in order to increase their online popularity (Geurin, 2017).

Major media outlets are also guilty of this focus away from sports. Before it ceased publication, *ESPN The Magazine* created a yearly "Body Issue" in which athletes, both men and women, would pose naked. While all the athletes were without clothes, and there were more men than women in the issues, the manner in which they were posed was different. Female athletes were photographed in more non-athletic poses than the men, seemingly downplaying their sporting accomplishments (Martin et al., 2018).

This emphasis on looks creates a challenging scenario for women in sports. Most would prefer that they are taken seriously as an athlete, but also recognize that athletic prowess alone might not result in a front-page article or a prominent position on ESPN programming. What is perhaps most troubling for many involved in women's sports is that there are signs of this trend not going away. As college athletes began capitalizing on the opportunities to make money with the 2021 passing of the name, image, and likeness (NIL) rules, the same "sex sells" debate was pushed back into the spotlight. While many women athletes began working with com-

*ESPN The Magazine's* annual Body Issue pictured male and female athletes without clothing, although female athletes were more likely to be shown in non-athletic poses than male athletes.

panies based primarily on their outstanding athletic performances, that was not the only reason some were getting endorsement deals. Shortly after the new rules were enacted, *The New York Times* profiled Louisiana State University gymnast Olivia Dunne. Dunne had quickly become one of the most in-demand athletes for companies to work with, and the article implied that it was her appearance that played a big role in making that possible:

> *But the new flood of money—and the way many female athletes are attaining it—troubles some who have fought for equitable treatment in women's sports and say that it rewards traditional feminine desirability over athletic excellence. (Streeter, 2022, para. 12)*

In that same article, legendary Stanford women's basketball coach Tara VanDerveer lamented how the NIL rules were leading to female college athletes posing provocatively in photos, an extension of the disappointing trend that was previously only seen in the professional ranks. "This is a step back," she remarked (Streeter, 2022, para. 18).

## Lolo Jones

In the mid- to late 2000s, Lolo Jones was one of the best hurdlers in the world, winning world champion-

ships and setting American records. However, much like most track and field stars, Jones had a hard time getting national attention beyond the years in which the Olympics took place. In order to increase her profile more consistently rather than just every four years, Jones began posing more suggestively on magazine covers and telling intimate details of her life story. Her plan worked, as she became more recognizable and endorsement deals soon came her way (Bazelon, 2012).

Two days before her race in the 2012 Olympics, *The New York Times* published a piece titled "For Lolo Jones, Everything Is Image." In the piece, the author discounted Jones's ability on the track and instead stated that the amount of media attention that she was getting was not based on any achievements that she had earned. The author wrote that Jones had little chance of winning a medal, but that had not stopped her from being one of the most publicized athletes:

> *Jones has received far greater publicity than any other American track and field athlete competing in the London Games. This was based not on achievement but on her exotic beauty and on a sad and cynical marketing campaign. Essentially, Jones has decided she will be whatever anyone wants her to be—vixen, virgin, victim—to draw attention to herself and the many products she endorses. (Longman, 2012, para. 2)*

Jones would finish fourth in the 100-meter hurdles that year and appeared on NBC's *Today* to address her performance. When host Savannah Guthrie asked her about the article, Jones became tearful in her response: "The fact that they just tore me apart it was heartbreaking" (Macht, 2012, para. 7). Many others came to Jones' defense, with one reporter calling the piece "one of the nastiest profiles I've ever seen" (Rosenberg, 2012, para. 1). Even the public editor of *The New York Times*, the newspaper that published the original article, wrote "in this particular case, I think the writer was particularly harsh, even unnecessarily so" (Brisbane, 2012, para. 3).

The events surrounding the critical article demonstrated the struggles that many women in sports face. Jones was not getting much media attention, so she tried a different tactic to get journalists to write about her. She told her life story and posed for magazines in attention-getting outfits, a plan that successfully made her one of the most recognizable track stars in the United States. However, even before she had run a race in that year's Olympics, she was overly criticized for the method by which she got that attention. Some women athletes feel as if they are in a no-win situation. They cannot get attention without acting in a certain sexualized way, but are then admonished for acting in that manner.

## Times Are Changing

While stories like Lolo Jones's may be disheartening for women in sports, there are signs that the trends of sexualized coverage, or the complete lack of coverage, have begun to change. For the first time since 1983, *Sports Illustrated* named a woman the sole winner of their "Sportsman of the Year" honor in 2015. The honoring of tennis player Serena Williams also forced the magazine to reassess the title given to the winner, as Williams was instead named the "Sports*person* of the Year" (Price, 2015).

In 2010, ESPN created ESPNW, a separate section of its website that is devoted solely to women's sports (Thomas, 2010). The page has top headlines from a variety of women's sports, with accompanying videos and photos. While one can certainly argue if having a separate website for just women is actually helping or hurting the perception of women's sports, it does create a location in which these articles can exist, when before there were almost none.

As stated in chapter 4, coverage of women's sports on NBC during the Olympics outpaces that of the men. Both the Summer Olympics in 2021 and the Winter Olympics in 2022 had record amounts of women's sports shown when compared to men's sports (Billings et al., 2021; Billings et al., 2022). In an event where men and women both participate, it was the women that were deemed a bigger draw by executives at NBC.

*Slam* magazine, geared at diehard basketball fans, featured a woman on the cover for the first time in more than 20 years when the WNBA's Maya Moore graced the front of an issue in 2018. The overwhelmingly positive response was instantaneous, as it took just two hours for Moore's cover image to get more likes on the official *Slam* Instagram account than the previous issue's cover that featured men (Dool, 2018). It also spoke to the growing popularity of women's basketball, and specifically the profile of the WNBA.

## WNBA

With the backing of the NBA, the WNBA debuted in 1997 with the hope of becoming the first women's professional sports league to gain mainstream attention for an extended period. The phrase "We got next" was the league's slogan, and eight teams debuted in cities all over the United States. As its start, the WNBA agreed to deals with NBC, ESPN, and the Lifetime Network, meaning that the games would be televised to a national audience. However, those broadcasting deals were a mixed bag. All three networks agreed to show games, but instead of paying rights fees to do so, the league and the channels agreed to share profits (Fastis, 1996). In most traditional media rights deals, the media outlets pay an upfront fee to the leagues for the ability to show the games, so the partnership revealed that the networks had some concerns about the potential interest. In the years following, after becoming more established and demonstrating that people were watching on television, the league was able to secure traditional rights deals, including bringing in $27 million in 2021 (Associated Press, 2007; Megdal, 2022).

However, just because the league has survived for more than 25 years, longer than most professional sports leagues, does not mean it has avoided some of the same issues that plague other sports. In 2016, star player Elena Delle Donne noted how, even despite her play, many still focused on her appearance:

> I just can't wait for the day where people want to talk about your skills on the court and not your looks. I wonder how many times a Tom Brady is asked about how handsome he is, or a J.J. Watt. It's something that us female athletes have to deal with all the time. (Gavilanes, 2016, para. 4)

Alex Slitz/Getty Images

**Elena Delle Donne of the Washington Mystics plays in a June 2023 game against the Atlanta Dream.**

While media attention for the WNBA still lagged behind most men's sports, the league made some advancements that demonstrated its growing profile. The popular video game series *NBA 2K* featured WNBA players for the first time in 2019, meaning that gamers could now control some of the best women's athletes in the world (Barnes, 2019). In addition, and perhaps most significantly, television viewership in 2022 was at a 14-year high for the regular season, demonstrating a rising interest in the league as a whole (WNBA, 2022).

## College Sports

Among college sports, the number of sports television networks has led to more opportunities for women's games to be broadcast. Networks such as the SEC Network and CBS College Sports are devoted solely to college sports, and women's contests have become a key part of the programming. As women's sports have continued to rise in popularity, two sports that have seen their coverage grow have been basketball and softball.

### Basketball

The first women's sport in which colleges played against each other was basketball in 1896. However, the sport, as with many others involving women, remained an afterthought and was actually actively discouraged from being played at most institutions (Stanford, n.d.). Following Title IX, women's basketball became one of the fastest-growing sports, but the media coverage was still lacking. From 1982 to 1990, CBS showed only the championship game of the entire women's basketball tournament.

Even the NCAA's own media treated the women's tournament as lesser when compared to the men's. The men's tournament had "The Final Four," while the women's tournament final teams were part of the "The Women's Final Four." In addition, the @FinalFour social media account was only about the men's tournament (VanTryon, 2022). The implication was clear from these decisions: The men's was the "real" tournament while the women's tournament needed an identifying mark to show that it was not the "actual" tournament. As was discussed in chapter 5 regarding social media, in 2021 Oregon's Sedona Prince used her social media accounts to draw attention to the differences between the tournament's weight rooms, which led to changes at the sites of the events (Witz, 2022). It also led to a bigger conversation, as the next year the @FinalFour social media handle, which was reserved for the men's event previously, was replaced by @MFinalFour and @WFinalFour handles to demonstrate a more equal social media presence between the two tournaments (Clarke, 2022).

ESPN now shows every game in the women's NCAA basketball tournament, but they are not doing that solely because they feel it is the right thing to do. The network had 77 sponsors who advertised during the tournament in 2021 and every available ad space was sold during the 2022 tournament (Lefton, 2022). Therefore, not only is ESPN showing these women's tournament games, but they are making money doing so. In addition, viewership is at peak levels, as the 2022 tournament had some of the most-watched games and rounds in more than a decade (Brooks, 2022).

The network further demonstrated its commitment to the sport by giving the 2022 championship game between the University of South Carolina and University of Connecticut a production worthy of a national title contest. ESPN showed practices, interviews, extended pregame shows, and had over 45 cameras for the Final Four games. In addition, during the games, the network had multiple video feeds available to fans (Dachman, 2022). That plan paid off, as the game averaged 4.85 million viewers, which made it the most-watched college basketball game, men's or women's, to air on ESPN in nearly 15 years (Brooks, 2022). That viewership number was shattered just one year later as a record 9.9 million watched the 2023 women's basketball championship game (Tumin, 2023). From only showing the championship game to having multiple feeds of one game with millions of viewers, women's college basketball had overcome the lack of early coverage to become one of the most-watched college sports on television.

### Softball

In the early 2000s, ESPN executives noticed that softball coverage was getting more viewers than they had expected. To determine if that was just a temporary blip or if it was the start of a consistent trend, the network made a commitment to air every game of the Women's College World Series (Baldwin, 2005). Soon after, ESPN was setting viewership records year after year during the championship rounds and additional regular-season games were being added to the schedule. In 2021, the college softball World Series (1.2 million) averaged more viewers per game than the college baseball World Series (755,000) (Brennan, 2021). For the 2023 season, ESPN planned to broadcast nearly 200 softball games on its various television channels, with more than 2,000 available on streaming platforms, demonstrating a dedication to growing the sport and showcasing top college women's sports (Elchlepp, 2023).

# The Next Generation

While media coverage of women's sports has slowly increased, there are signs that an even greater commitment could be coming. The NWSL, a women's professional soccer league, signed a seven-figure broadcasting deal in 2022, and women's college basketball was estimated to be worth $100 million a year in media rights (Schad, 2022). Athletic apparel companies Adidas and Nike have created marketing campaigns aimed at attracting women to play sports, specifically younger girls (Dutch, 2022; Palmieri, 2022).

In addition, NIL deals for college athletes have given women opportunities to make money that were not previously available. While, as noted, some of those NIL endorsement deals might be influenced by an athlete's appearance, women college athletes have been able to work around the lack of media attention facing women's sports and take advantage of their social media presence. Women college athletes often have more followers than their male counterparts, making them an appealing group for advertisers to work with. Six of the top ten college sports for NIL compensation are women's sports, demonstrating that the next generation of women athletes have opportunities to make money that were previously not available (Balasaygun, 2022). While media coverage of women's sports still has a long way to go to achieve equality with the men, there is one team of women that has grabbed the country's attention and kick-started the equality conversation. As will be discussed in the next chapter, the U.S. women's soccer club is one of the most recognizable teams, men's or women's, in the country, with millions of girls watching games on television, reading articles about the team online, and following every move on social media. As media coverage increases, it might be the U.S. women's soccer team that can have the largest impact moving forward.

# Summary

The passage of Title IX gave women equal access to sports opportunities at the college and high school levels and created generations of women athletes who previously may not have been able to play sports. In the decades since, women have starred in college sports, at the Olympics, and in the professional ranks. However, the attention of the sports media remained almost solely focused on men's sports. Women's events were essentially ignored, with only some athletes finding an opportunity to break through into the mainstream. For others, the only way to get journalists to write stories about them was if the focus was on their looks instead of their sport.

While the media coverage remains skewed toward the men, strides have been made to close the gap. Women's college basketball and softball are bringing in record numbers of viewers, the WNBA's popularity is rising, and NBC's primetime broadcasts of the Olympics are dominated by women. The audience has demonstrated that they are interested in women's sports, which should only increase the number of games available on television and the number of stories written about women's sports.

## REVIEW QUESTIONS

1. What is Title IX and why is it important in the history of women's sports?
2. How has media coverage of women's sports traditionally compared to media coverage of men's sports?
3. Why is NBC's coverage of the Olympics an outlier when compared to traditional coverage of sports?
4. How has media coverage of women's sports changed on the college level?

*CASE STUDY*

# U.S. Women's Soccer Team

## CHAPTER OBJECTIVES

After completing the chapter, the reader should be able to do the following:

- Recognize the history of the U.S. women's soccer team
- Identify why the 1999 and 2019 teams helped change the conversation regarding women's sports
- Relate the women's soccer team's impact to other societal issues
- Discuss the impact Title IX had on the women's soccer team

In 2015, as the United States women's soccer team was marching through the World Cup tournament, *Sports Illustrated*'s Andy Benoit tweeted that women's sports were not worth watching. In previous years, Benoit's musing might have gotten quiet nods and agreement from some, along with very little pushback from other media members. However, the response this time was anything but quiet. Benoit was soundly criticized, his boss at *Sports Illustrated* openly expressed his disagreement, he was mocked on national television, and he was forced to delete the tweet and apologize (Bonesteel, 2015).

While women's sports had become more mainstream at the time, it was also the American soccer team's play that caused the outrage from the public. The women were on national television, winning convincingly, and doing so in an entertaining way. Suddenly, decades of mocking and disinterest in women's sports were no longer allowed. These women were strong, powerful, successful athletes, and they were in the process of becoming one of the most important teams in American history.

## Title IX and Women's Soccer

As discussed in the previous chapter, Title IX was a revolutionary moment in the history of women's sports. The law passed in 1972 prohibited discrimination based on sex at any school or organization receiving federal funding. Prior to the ruling, women's sports had been essentially ignored for decades at both colleges and high schools, with most not feeling any need to offer competitive athletics for women. However, under Title IX, if those schools wanted to continue receiving federal funding, they were going to have to make a change (Tumin, 2022).

With women's sports now essentially required, schools had to make quick decisions on how to become compliant with the law. For many, adding a women's soccer team was a relatively inexpensive way to make progress. Schools already had soccer fields, balls, and goals, and the teams normally had at least 15 players, which was a quick way to begin equalizing the male-to-female ratio of athletes. In 1974, there were 6,446 girls playing high school soccer, but by 2018 that number had exploded to over 394,000. Prior to the NCAA making women's soccer an officially sponsored sport in 1982, there were less than 2,000 women playing college soccer. By the 2020-2021 season, almost 28,000 women played NCAA soccer (Petri, 2022). Title IX affected all women's sports, but one of the lasting legacies of that law might be the fact that it helped kick-start the amazing run of the U.S. women's soccer team.

# Humble Beginnings of the U.S. Women's Team

While the U.S. team has become one of the most recognizable and dominant organizations in the world, it did not always appear to be headed in that direction. When the team was preparing for its first organized match in 1985, there was little interest in the sport or the team. The women wore hand-me-down jerseys from the men's team, received $10 a day, and then went winless in their first four games while on a playing tour of Italy (Wahl, 2019). A few years later, the international soccer governing committee (FIFA) organized a women's tournament to determine if there would be an international audience for women's soccer. The U.S. team participated, traveling to China in 1988, but lost in the quarterfinals (Wahl, 2019). It was not the start that many would imagine for the future world powerhouse, but better days were ahead.

## 1991 M&M's Cup

After the experience with the 1988 tournament, FIFA elected to move forward with a women's World Cup—although they did not want to call it that. Worried that the tournament would not be a success, FIFA was hesitant to use the phrase *World Cup* out of fear that the title might be tarnished with a bad tournament. Instead, the 1st FIFA World Championship for Women's Football for the M&M's Cup was to take place in 1991. That mouthful of a name was not the only difference from the men's game, as the matches were 80 minutes instead of 90 and there were fewer days off in between matches in order to save time and money. Surprisingly, organizers also wanted to use a smaller soccer ball for the women, but officials changed their mind before the event began (Wahl, 2019).

The United States marched through the tournament with little resistance and little fanfare. Despite winning games by large margins, including outscoring its three opponents 11–2 in the group stage, the American media basically ignored it, with only a few outlets providing any coverage. However, as the team reached the semifinals, more journalists began to pay attention. *The New York Times*, *The Washington Post*, and *Sports Illustrated* all sent reporters to China; they were in attendance when the American team won the championship, beating Norway in the finals (Lisi, 2010). While FIFA did not want to use the title at the time, the organization would later officially recognize the 1991 event as the first Women's World Cup (Wahl, 2019).

Nearly 30 years after that win, hundreds of thousands of fans would line the streets of New York City for a ticker tape parade to celebrate the 2019 U.S. Women's World Cup champions (Honan & Christovich, 2019). There was not the same fanfare back in 1991. When the triumphant winners of the M&M's Cup returned home to a New York airport, there were only a few people there to greet them, including just three journalists. As one author would later write about the team's return: "There were no parades. No celebrations. No anything" (Lisi, 2010, p. 20).

## Champions Ignored

Not only was there was no party in 1991, there was not much of anything for the women's team in the ensuing years. The United States was set to host the men's World Cup in 1994, so nearly the full attention of the U.S. Soccer Federation was given to that event. Money was funneled to the men's team, which was heavily promoted, and the women became an afterthought (Lisi, 2010). In 1992, the women's team played just two games all year, losing twice in three days to Norway (S.A.S.H., n.d.). With scant resources and attention, the players on the team had to step away from the sport and return to their lives outside of soccer. In 1995 their attempt to defend their World Cup title came up short, with the United States losing in the semifinals (Associated Press, 1995).

## 1996 Olympics

The 1996 Olympics in Atlanta, Georgia, marked a significant moment in women's soccer because it was the debut of the sport as a medal event. The U.S. team took home gold, defeating China in the championship in front of 76,481 fans (Vecsey, 1996). However, there were *zero* fans watching the entire game on television in the United States. NBC, the broadcasting network of the Olympics, elected to show none of the 15 women's soccer games that were played before the final, and only televised the last 20 minutes of the gold medal game (Linehan, 2021). An Olympic historian told *The New York Times* that NBC's decision was "scandalous to ignore such a powerful historic moment" (Sandomir, 1996, para. 5). While the team was successful on the field, there still appeared to be skepticism about the popularity of the sport among the media. That would change dramatically a few years later.

## The 1999 World Cup

While the women's team might have been ignored in the lead-up to the 1994 men's World Cup, the success of that event in the United States convinced the U.S. Soccer Federation to bid to host the women's version of the World Cup. In 1996, just before the team won Olympic gold, FIFA awarded the 1999 tournament to the United States. However, FIFA was still not convinced that women's soccer would be a draw and requested that the United States put all the games in smaller football stadiums based only in the eastern time zone (Jones, 1996). A few months later, those 76,000 fans who packed into a Georgia stadium to watch the gold medal game convinced organizers to aim higher. Instead of every match in small stadiums, six of the eight venues were stadiums that sat more than 50,000 fans, with only two "smaller" facilities that sat around 26,000 each (Linehan, 2021; Longman, 1997). Not everyone was confident that decision was a wise one, as even the players had concerns according to American star player Kristine Lilly: "We were worried. We didn't want to play that World Cup before empty stands in big stadiums" (FIFA, 2019, para. 4). Considering the women's tournament in Sweden just four years earlier had an average attendance of 4,316 per game, those fears were certainly valid (FIFA, 2019).

Ticket sales might have been a concern, but media coverage was not. After NBC dropped the ball covering women's soccer in the Olympics, ABC was determined not to repeat that mistake. All 32 matches of the tournament would be shown on either ABC, ESPN, or ESPN2, with 27 of them airing live (Linehan, 2021). In addition, almost 2,000 media members were given credentials to cover the games, including about 950 journalists and 410 photographers (FIFA, 1999).

From the opening kick, the tournament could not have gone much better for the American organizers, media, or the team itself. The United States' first game was played in a sold-out Giants Stadium in New Jersey, with over 77,000 fans filing in to see the women play Denmark (Longman, 1999a). As the players were riding the team bus to the game that afternoon, they were wondering why there was so much traffic—"What the heck is going on?" Brandi Chastain recalled thinking. They would then realize that all those cars were headed to see them play (Leyden, 2013). That was not the only game with massive attendance, as the tournament averaged 37,319 fans per game (FIFA, 2019).

The American team would go undefeated on their way to facing off with China in the championship game. In front of more than 90,000 fans in the Rose Bowl in Los Angeles, Chastain kicked the game winner during the penalty kick session, ripped off her shirt, twirled it over her head, and celebrated in her sports bra as her teammates surrounded her (Longman, 1999b). On television, ABC estimated that about 40 million people watched that championship game, more than had watched the NBA Finals (New York Times, 1999).

ROBERTO SCHMIDT / AFP via Getty Images

**Brandi Chastain celebrates after kicking the winning penalty kick to seal a victory for the U.S. women's soccer team in the 1999 World Cup.**

# Media Coverage Changing

The next American World Cup teams had trouble matching the success of the 1999 squad. The United States finished in third in both 2003 and 2007 and was the runner-up in 2011. However, the team was becoming a major draw. The championship game loss to Japan in 2011 set a record at the time for most tweets per second in the history of Twitter (Banks, 2011). When the U.S. team did win back the World Cup trophy in 2015, they did so in front of the largest television audience ever to watch a soccer match in the United States. Over 26 million people watched on either Fox or Telemundo, beating the previous record of a men's game by more than 8 million (Associated Press, 2015).

With an enormous number of fans talking about the team on social media and watching on television, the media had almost no choice but to reevaluate its coverage. Following the win in 2015, *Sports Illustrated* did not just put the team on the cover of its next issue; instead, it released 25 different covers—one traditional team picture, along 23 covers for each individual player on the team and one for the head coach (SI Staff, 2015). Journalists were no longer writing pieces that focused on the players' personal lives or sex appeal, but instead about the team's strategy and tactical formations (Keh, 2015). The difference from previous years was apparent. Former national team member Julie Foudy told a journalist how she and her teammates had noticed the change:

> I was just having a conversation with Abby [Wambach] a couple of days ago, actually, and she was saying, "I think it's great. It shows that people care and that people pay attention. They're covering us like athletes." And I couldn't agree more. We begged for it back in the day. (Schaerlaeckens, 2015, para. 11)

The statement "they're covering us like athletes" is telling. For decades, the women's soccer team was treated as an afterthought and not worthy of media attention. When they did get coverage, as stated in the previous chapter, the stories about women in sports often focused on their lives off the field, their bodies, or their sex appeal. The attention had changed. The soccer players were no longer simply residents of "Babe City," as talk show host David Letterman had labeled them in 1999 (Goodman, 1999). Instead, they were athletes.

# The Perfect Storm: The 2019 Women's World Cup

By the time the 2019 Women's World Cup arrived, the U.S. women's soccer team had become one of the most recognizable and successful teams in the world. They were winning on the field, support was there from media and fans, and the women on the team represented the future of the sport. As the 2019 event kicked off, it became clear that this team personified several of the different societal and media-related topics that are discussed throughout the book. Essentially, this team was the perfect storm of Sports, Media, and Society.

## Media Support

Fox Sports is the broadcast home in the United States of some of the most prominent sporting events in the world (see chapter 10 for more), and its coverage of the 2019 World Cup was right up there with some of those headline events. The network of the Super Bowl and the World Series treated women's soccer as a marquee sport, something that decades earlier would have been unthinkable. Every game was broadcast live on a Fox television channel, pregame and postgame shows aired from a Fox set located directly across from the Eiffel Tower, and every goal was posted to the Fox Sports Twitter account. Not only were they spotlighting the women on the field, but there were women in the broadcast booth as well. More than half of the on-air reporters for Fox were women, which, as discussed in chapter 20, is not traditionally seen in the sports media (Deitsch, 2019).

## Strong Women

Many young girls interested in athletics had grown up without role models, as women's sports were rarely on television or given any sort of national attention. The U.S. soccer team was changing that narrative, with women athletes playing at the highest level and having their games broadcast to millions. Instead of watching men's sports on television, these girls could now turn on their television and see women. This leads to empowerment of women that might not have existed previously; girls could now see these role models and say, "I could do that too." In addition, these women are providing *different* role model types from the Barbie dolls and Hollywood stars that are often presented as aspirational goals. An article about this phenomenon in *The Atlantic* summarized what these changing role models can mean:

> What that says to a girl or young woman who's watching, [political science professor Kelly] Dittmar added, is "that her role doesn't have to be a more traditionally feminine, stereotypical role—that in fact, this is a model of the type of woman [she] could become." She can be valued by the public, in other words, by being assertive, outspoken, and physically strong. (Fetters, 2019, para. 8)

Following her goal against England in the semifinals, Alex Morgan gave a "sipping the tea" hand gesture. While Morgan said the celebration was a nod to one of her favorite television shows, others, especially the British media, deemed it to be a direct taunt to the British team based on the Revolutionary War history of the two countries. Morgan's celebration was deemed to be "over the top" by many, and she was soundly criticized for the gesture. The American star was quick to point out that, just because she was a woman, that did not mean she should be held to different standards:

> I feel that there is some sort of double standard for females in sports. To feel like we have to be humble in our successes and have to celebrate, but not too much or in a limited fashion. You see men celebrating all over the world in big tournaments, grabbing their sacks or whatever it is. And when I look at sipping a cup of tea, I am a little taken aback by the criticism. (Hays, 2019, para. 5)

The message was clear: Women can, and should, celebrate however they like and that a generation of strong and powerful women were not going to demur to how some in the public think they "should" act.

## LGBTQ+ Representation

As will be discussed in chapter 21, many LGBTQ+ athletes struggle with coming out. They worry about being accepted by teammates, fans, and even family, so many hide their sexuality from others as a way to cope with the pressures. Former U.S. women's soccer star Abby Wambach wrote in her book that she once thought, "If I play well, my mother might forgive me for being who I am," a reference to her own sexuality as a lesbian (Quinn, 2016, para. 1). The 2019 team was anything but shy about their sexual orientation. The team's head coach and five of its players were openly gay, including two of the players who were engaged to each other (Compton, 2019). After the team's quarterfinal win over France, American star Megan Rapinoe said "Go gays! You can't win a championship without gays on your team—it's never been done before, ever. That's science, right there!" (Wrack, 2019, para. 2). After the team won the World Cup, the official Twitter account of the U.S. women's soccer team tweeted "Told ya" with a photo of Rapinoe and two other openly gay players on the team kissing the trophy and their winning medals (USWNT, 2019).

## Nationalism

Any time an event pits country against country, the concept of nationalism becomes one that fans can hardly ignore. Fans in the United States may or may not be followers of women's soccer, but they are likely fans of America, so they will root for any team with "USA" on its jersey. In that aspect, rooting for the women's team is something that most in the country can agree on, even those who cannot agree on much of anything. Following the championship win, Barack Obama and Donald Trump, the former and then-current president of the United States (who are on opposite sides of most issues), both tweeted congratulations to the team (Allen, 2019).

## Success All Around

After the United States beat the Netherlands 2–0 in the final, it was obvious that the American team winning the championship was one of big successes from the 2019 World Cup. However, the victories went even beyond that. Viewership of the championship game in the United States was 22 percent higher than the men's World Cup final just one year earlier (Hess, 2019), further demonstrating the public support and interest. Nike announced that the women's national team jersey was the top selling soccer jersey, men's or women's, ever sold on Nike.com, while another online retailer said the jersey sold 500 percent better than the women's one four years earlier (VanHaaren, 2019). Once again, women's sports were in the headlines, as millions were watching, the media was covering it, and advertisers were starting to line up to feature women's soccer players.

**Fans celebrate at a parade for the World Cup champion 2019 U.S. women's soccer team.**

# Professional Soccer Leagues

Despite the popularity of women's soccer in global tournaments, the demand for a professional version of sport in the United States was not there. Hoping to build on the success of the 1999 World Cup, the Women's United Soccer Association (WUSA) debuted shortly after that event. The league had major investors from the television industry, ensuring that the games would be broadcast and that they should get national attention. Unfortunately, sponsors did not support the effort, meaning the league was losing tens of millions of dollars a year even after the players took pay cuts. After the third season, the league suspended operations and would not return (Longman, 2003). In 2009, Women's Professional Soccer (WPS) hoped to pick up where WUSA left off, but that would not be the case. After three seasons that included multiple teams folding, missed payments to the players, and fighting among team ownership, the league called it quits in 2012 (Oshan, 2012).

Hoping to learn from the mistakes of previous professional leagues, the National Women's Soccer League (NWSL) was formed shortly after the demise of WPS and debuted in 2013. As a change, the new league would be operated by the United States Soccer Federation and players would be paid by their home country's federation (Bell, 2013). The goal was to create a league that could be sustainable while also giving opportunities to women's soccer players to turn their passion into a career. Ten years after the league debuted, that early plan was paying off. The 2022 season saw television viewership, sponsor revenue, and in-game attendance all on the rise (Goff, 2022). However, that growth was not without struggles along the way. As the 2019 season began, the league did not have a national television deal and sponsorships were hard to come by (Associated Press, 2019). It was the national team's performance in the World Cup a few months later that helped save the day. Shortly after the American team won the 2019 championship, ESPN noted the popularity and high television viewership of the sport and agreed to show the 14 NWSL games remaining in the season, including several playoff match-ups and the league championship game (Bupp, 2019).

# Sponsorships

ESPN was not the only surprising addition to the NWSL family following the 2019 World Cup. Amid the Americans' locker room celebration, the team shunned the traditional bottles of champagne and instead were drinking bottles of Budweiser. That appeared to be foreshadowing, as the beer company announced shortly after the event concluded that they had entered into a multiyear sponsorship deal with the NWSL (Linehan, 2019a). Not only that, but Budweiser also then created the "Future Official" campaign to advertise not to consumers but to other companies, encouraging them to step up and sponsor the league as well (Dosh, 2019). Budweiser would later admit that they did not expect to make their money back on the sponsorships, but instead implied that supporting the league simply felt like the right thing to do (Linehan, 2019b).

## The Fight for Equal Pay

The United States women's soccer team had won multiple world championships and was widely regarded as the best team on the planet. The American men's team had nowhere near the past success of the women's team but was ahead in one major aspect: pay. The players on the men's team received higher game bonuses and more money when playing in the World Cup, no matter what the result. In addition, the men received more money for daily expenses and when appearing for a sponsor (Das, 2016; 2019). In 2016, five players on the women's team filed a federal complaint with the Equal Employment Opportunity Commission, accusing U.S. Soccer of wage discrimination (Das, 2016). After three years of that complaint not getting the attention the players thought it deserved, 28 members of the team then filed a gender discrimination lawsuit against the soccer organization (Das, 2019).

An unexpected ally stepped up when the men's team agreed to share some of its World Cup money with the women's team. That opened the door for a potential agreement. In February 2022, U.S. Soccer and the women's team agreed to a settlement that guaranteed equal pay for the women's team when compared to the men's. In addition to equal pay moving forward, the U.S. Soccer Federation agreed to pay $24 million in back pay, which, while not explicitly stated, implied that money should have been equal for the previous years (Das, 2022).

For decades, women in almost all industries have made less money than men have, often while doing the same jobs (Barroso & Brown, 2021). The U.S. team's victories on the field have made them legendary, but their achievement of equal pay will likely have more societal impact than any goal they will ever score. A member of the collective bargaining team for the women's players association said afterward that, while this benefited the current players, it was perhaps just as important for the next generation: "I feel a lot of pride that there are going to be girls who are going to grow up and see what we've accomplished and recognize their value instead of having to fight to see it themselves" (Das, 2022, para. 21).

## The Legacy of Title IX

Title IX gave millions of girls opportunities that previously did not exist. When looking at the United States women's soccer team, it is impossible to ignore the direct impact that legislation had. Twenty-seven years after it was passed in 1972, the 1999 World Cup team changed the narrative surrounding women's sports in the United States. The players on that team had grown up with Title IX, having opportunities to participate that previously did not exist. Twenty years later, the 2019 team had watched the '99ers and had the knowledge that anything was possible for a woman athlete. Perhaps the United States soccer team would never have become what it ultimately did without the passing of Title IX.

## Summary

The United States women's soccer team has grown from an afterthought to one of the most popular and successful teams in American sports history. After being basically ignored in the first years of its existence, the team went on to win multiple World Cups, cementing its place among the best in the world. However, the team's lasting legacy might be off the field. While most women's sports are ignored by the media, this club is on national television, is treated like real athletes, and has sponsorships from some of the biggest companies in the world. Its battle for equal pay demonstrated the societal impact of the women beyond just their ability to play the game. In addition, the team touches on important topics such as nationalism, LGBTQ+ issues, and representation of strong women. With the passing of equal pay agreements, future members of the team will be assured that the legacy of the team should live on for decades to come.

## REVIEW QUESTIONS

1. How did Title IX affect the rise of the U.S. women's soccer team?
2. How did the 1996 Olympics lead to the 1999 World Cup being held in large stadiums?
3. How did the 1999 World Cup demonstrate that this team addressed many topics beyond just their play on the field?
4. How did the U.S. women's soccer team fight for equal pay?

# 20

# Women in the Sports Media

## CHAPTER OBJECTIVES

After completing the chapter, the reader should be able to do the following:

- Recognize the pioneering women in the sports media
- Understand the past issues surrounding women in the locker room
- Identify obstacles that women in the sports media must overcome
- Discuss what women can do to continue to break through in the sports media

In the late 1980s and early 1990s, NBC had the broadcast rights to some of the most popular sporting events. Major football, baseball, and basketball games were all on the network, as was the Olympics. Fans tuned in by the millions to watch, and greeting them on television before and after almost every game was Gayle Gardner. She hosted an update segment 45 weekends a year that gave the latest sports news and scores. With that position, she became one of the first women to appear weekly on a major television network, and for a generation of sports fans she was the voice of televised sports.

However, even while Gardner was at the peak of her popularity and visibility, there were behind-the-scenes forces keeping her down. For six weeks in 1990, her bosses elected to keep her off the air; her contract was unsettled, and she faced (later unfounded) rumors that she was difficult to work with. For Gardner and other women in the sports media, the battle was familiar, and it is one that has continued to exist in the decades since. While she would later work out a deal with

NBC, executives admitted she was still paid less than her male counterparts, and Gardner herself said that sports media was "still a boys' club and always will be" (Jenkins, 1991; Knight-Ridder News Service, 1993, para. 9). For decades, women faced obstacles that men in journalism did not, such as a lack of access to locker rooms. However, access has changed and women are starting to get prominent roles in sports media, and it is some of the pioneers in the field, like Gardner, who deserve much of the credit.

## Pioneers

It is difficult to identify who exactly was the first woman in the sports media, as there was not a monumental moment that is recognized as when a woman broke an employment barrier. While not confirmed to be the sole answer to the trivia question, many point to "Middy" Morgan as perhaps the first ever woman sports journalist; in the 1870s, she was covering horse racing for *The*

*New York Times* (Ross, 1936). However, it is safe to say that, whether it was Morgan or someone else, the early women in the profession certainly did not have it easy. Women have long struggled to find acceptance in many fields that were long dominated by men, and sports journalism was no exception. Without a singular pioneer to focus on, it is important to recognize some of the women who help set a path for the ones who came after them.

## Jeannie Morris

Sportswriter Jeannie Morris has a lot of "firsts" to her credit. She was the first woman to write a sports column for a major American newspaper, although the *Chicago American* billed her as Mrs. Johnny Morris instead of Jeannie. Not having her first name appear in the byline was just one of her problems, as demonstrated when she was later sent to report on a Bears-Vikings game in Minnesota. At the time, women were not allowed in the press box, so Morris had to sit outside, on top of the media area, in the middle of a blizzard. After a successful sportswriting career she moved to broadcasting, where in 1975 she became the first woman to cover a Super Bowl live on television. For one last "first," she later became the first woman to win a Ring Lardner Award for excellence in sports journalism, one of the most prestigious awards in the sports media (Kogan, 2020; NPR, 2020).

## Phyllis George

In the 1970s, CBS executives elected to shake up the network's NFL pregame show and brought in three new hosts. Two were traditional sports media hires, with longtime sportscaster Brent Musburger and former player Irv Cross joining the program. However, it was the third hire that was revolutionary at the time. Former Miss America Phyllis George was hired as a reporter, instantly making her the most prominent woman in sports broadcasting. Her hire was questioned by some, but almost instantly she became an important part of the show thanks to her revealing interviews with some of the biggest names in football (Sandomir, 2020). With those three as the hosts, and the addition of Jimmy "the Greek" Snyder the following season, the *NFL Today* began a run of being the most-watched NFL pregame show for 18 consecutive seasons (Bleier, 2021). Perhaps even more important to George's legacy was that she was breaking ground simply by being there. As was noted in her 2020 obituary in *The New York Times*, George gave hope to women in the industry who had not had it before:

*She was unquestionably a pioneer. To many young women who hoped to have careers in sportscasting, seeing her sharing the studio desk with Mr. Musburger, Mr. Cross and Mr. Snyder and discussing the day's games was inspiring. (Sandomir, 2020, para. 7)*

## Lesley Visser

In 1974, Boston College student Lesley Visser was awarded a Carnegie Foundation grant, an award that was given to 20 women who wanted to begin careers in professions that were 95 percent male. Visser wanted to be a sportswriter and, thanks to the opportunity provided by the grant, she joined the sports department at *The Boston Globe*. Visser proved herself immediately, and soon after she became the first woman to be an NFL beat writer when she was given the task of covering the New England Patriots.

Visser's success at *The Boston Globe* opened the door for her to work part-time as a broadcaster at CBS Sports, a move she made full-time in 1987. While at CBS, she covered the NBA, MLB, college basketball, and college football. She would later move to ABC Sports and then back to CBS, covering more major events at both networks. In fact, Visser is the only sportscaster—male or female—to have worked on a television network broadcast of the Super Bowl, Olympics, World Series, NBA Finals, horse racing's Triple Crown, and the men's Final Four basketball tournament. She would later become the first woman inducted into the Pro Football Hall of Fame for her work as a journalist (Deitsch, 2022; Sports Broadcasting Hall of Fame, n.d.).

## Pam Oliver

After working as a news reporter at several local television stations throughout the United States, and then transitioning to sports, reporter Pam Oliver started at ESPN in 1993. However, it was the move to Fox Sports two years later that made her a familiar face to fans of the NFL for decades. She could often be seen on the sidelines giving updates during some of the biggest football games each week. For Fox, she covered numerous Super Bowls, was part of the top broadcasting team, and was the lead features reporter for the pregame show on that channel. Thanks to her over 25 years at the network, and her reputation as one of the best in the business, Oliver became the longest-tenured sideline reporter in the NFL, having been on the field during live broadcasts for over 500 games (Fox Sports, n.d.).

Michael Zagaris/San Francisco 49ers/Getty Images

**Pam Oliver is the longest-tenured sideline reporter in the NFL.**

# Locker Room Access

For decades, sports locker rooms were only accessible to sports journalists who were men. In fact, women reporters were told very explicitly they were not welcome there, as it was written directly on press credentials that women and children were not allowed in the locker room. Leagues, teams, and some players were supposedly worried about women being there while the male athletes were in various stages of undress after finishing a game. Due to those concerns, and likely some chauvinistic mentalities, the women reporting on the games were forced to wait until players and coaches came out of the locker room to get their interviews. This would put them behind schedule when it came to deadline and also meant that many of the players' immediate thoughts afterward had already been provided to the male reporters.

# The 1977 World Series

While some sports, notably professional hockey's NHL, had relaxed their policies on women in the locker room by the mid-1970s, that was not the case elsewhere. Major League Baseball still banned women from entering, and the 1977 World Series would become a major turning point in the fight for access. The Dodgers and the Yankees, two of the most popular teams in the league,

were set to face off. Before the series began, league officials reaffirmed their stance that women would not be allowed in the locker room, stating that they were concerned about how the players' wives and children would react to a woman being there (Stern & Sundberg, 2013).

Following the Yankees' series-clinching win in Game 6, media members—all men—filed into the winning locker room to get interviews with the triumphant champions. The women reporters, including *Sports Illustrated*'s Melissa Ludtke, stood outside the locker room for an hour and 45 minutes waiting for the players, including World Series MVP Reggie Jackson, to come out to talk with them. When Jackson finally did emerge from the locker room, he did not give an interview to Ludtke, stating that he was too tired (Stern & Sundberg, 2013).

# The Lawsuit

Less than a year later, Ludtke, with the support of her editors at *Sports Illustrated*, filed a federal lawsuit against the commissioner of Major League Baseball, stating that her constitutional rights to equal access were being violated by not allowing her into the locker room. At just 26 years old, Ludtke was taking on one of the biggest sports entities in the world—and she won. The 1978 ruling determined that her Fourteenth Amendment rights were violated because the no-women policy was preventing her from doing her job equal to other

Focus On Sport/Getty Images

**Reggie Jackson of the New York Yankees is interviewed by Bob Uecker in the locker room after the Yankees won the 1977 World Series.**

reporters. Because the ruling was given in a New York court, Ludtke and other women with media credentials could now have access to the locker room of the New York Yankees. The rest of the American League soon followed, but several National League teams held out for several more seasons before the new MLB commissioner mandated equal access for all reporters. It took a few more years, and a few more lawsuits, before women were allowed in every sports locker room (Stern & Sundberg, 2013).

## Lisa Olson

It was hoped that the issues involving women in the locker room were now settled, but new problems quickly arose. Every reporter now had access, but not everyone was happy about it; there were still some athletes, coaches, and fans who did not want them there. Fans wrote angry letters, and some coaches still kicked the women out (even though they were not supposed to), but it was an incident in 1990 that brought renewed frustration regarding the plight of women who were simply trying to do their jobs as sportswriters.

Lisa Olson, a writer for the *Boston Herald*, was in the New England Patriots' locker room following practice when she was harassed by several players. Three of the Patriots yelled obscene statements, while one, Zeke Mowatt, approached her without any clothes on and

made crude gestures towards her. Olson went public with what happened to her, and the NFL, following pressure from other women sports journalists, investigated the incident. Olson's account was proven true, and the players were all fined thousands of dollars, as was the Patriots organization (George, 1990).

However, for Olson, the incident did not end there. Instead of being disappointed in his players for how they acted, the owner of the Patriots implied that Olson was to blame for what happened and called her "a classic bitch" (Whitaker, 1990). Some of the worst vitriol aimed at Olson came from the Patriots fans. She was booed by the crowd at a Patriots game, received 100 obscene phone calls and 250 pieces of hate mail from New England supporters, her car tires were slashed, and her apartment was broken into (Ricchiardi, 2005; Whitaker, 1990). The harassment was too much, and Olson took a job in Australia writing for the *Sydney Daily Telegraph Mirror* (Ricchiardi, 2005).

## Unwanted Criticism

While issues in the locker room have dissipated over the years, new obstacles have been revealed to women in the sports media. Perhaps most prominently is the criticism many face while simply trying to do their jobs. There are more women in the sports media than ever before, but for some, the idea of a woman talking about sports is still unwanted. In some cases, the language used goes beyond simple criticism and becomes sexist and cruel. Those negative comments traditionally come from three main groups: men in the sports media, athletes, and fans.

## Men in the Sports Media

While not a member of the sports media himself, former CBS News commentator Andy Rooney said, "The only thing that really bugs me about television's coverage is those damn women they have down on the sidelines who don't know what the hell they're talking about" (ESPN News Services, 2002, para. 2). While the then-83-year-old was likely out of touch with modern television broadcasts, he still was a popular figure and his comments have been copied by others since, with a recurring theme from these men that, in their opinion, women do not belong on a sports broadcast. In 2013, Damon Bruce said on his San Francisco radio show that not only should women not be there, but that they were ruining his enjoyment of the game:

> I enjoy many of the women's contributions to the sports—well that's a lie [laughing]. I can't even pretend that's true. There are very few—a small handful—of women who are any good at this at all. That's the truth. The amount of women talking in sports to the amount of women who have something to say is one of the most disproportionate ratios I've ever seen in my life. But here's a message for all of them . . . All of this, all of this world of sports, especially the sport of football, has a setting. It's set to men. (Barmann, 2013, para. 6)

Sadly, Bruce was not alone in making sexist comments. Atlanta radio host Mike Bell was suspended by his station after he insulted the qualifications of ESPN's Jessica Mendoza during her appearance on the network's American League Wild Card baseball game (SI Wire, 2015). A Chicago radio host was fired after he tweeted a question to his followers asking if broadcaster Maria Taylor's outfit on *Monday Night Football* was more appropriate for that job or for an adult video awards ceremony (Heim, 2020).

## Comments from Athletes

An important part of any sports journalist's job is to interact with athletes. While the vast majority of athlete-journalist interactions are positive, there are instances in which male athletes have not acted appropriately around female journalists. Two such incidents involved NFL quarterbacks—one long retired and one at the height of his popularity.

In 2003, the New York Jets were honoring some of their greatest players in team history during a *Monday Night Football* broadcast on ESPN. During the second quarter, sideline reporter Suzy Kolber was interviewing Joe Namath, the quarterback of the 1969 Super Bowl champion Jets team and one of the players being honored. As Kolber asked him about watching the current New York team struggle, Namath leaned in and said, "I want to kiss you . . . I couldn't care less about the team struggling" (Griffith, 2003, para. 8). Namath would later admit he was intoxicated at the time and used the incident as the catalyst to clean up his life (Cimini, 2019). However, Kolber had to live with the unfortunate comments, despite her being an innocent bystander. She did not speak publicly about the incident for nearly a decade, but during that time it became a moment that would live on through Internet lore, including through a sports comedy website that named itself "Kissing Suzy Kolber" (Yoder, 2012). Kolber did not ask to be a part of this unfortunate incident, but Namath gave her no choice.

In 2017, Cam Newton was two seasons removed from being named the NFL's Most Valuable Player and was the starting quarterback for the Carolina Panthers. During a press conference, Jordan Rodrigue, the Panthers beat reporter for the team's hometown newspaper *The Charlotte Observer*, asked Newton about the route running of one of the team's receivers. After she finished her question, Newton said, "It's funny to hear a female talk about routes" (Hoffman, 2017, para. 3). The NFL and the Pro Football Writers of America both criticized Newton, and yogurt company Dannon ended its sponsorship agreement with the quarterback the next day. The NFL hoped to assure other women in the sports media that this was an isolated incident, releasing a statement that read: "The comments are just plain wrong and disrespectful to the exceptional female reporters and all journalists who cover our league. They do not reflect the thinking of the league" (Hoffman, 2017, para. 9).

The common thread for both incidents involving Kolber and Rodrigue is that the women were simply attempting to do their jobs. Both were asking relevant football-related questions to the athletes they were interviewing and instead found themselves in the middle of a controversy of which they did not ask to be a part. They were singled out because of their sex—Namath would likely not tell a male sideline reporter he wanted to kiss him, and Newton had not previously questioned the football knowledge of any male journalists.

## Fans on Social Media

While unwanted comments from male journalists and athletes can lead to unfortunate situations for women in the sports media, there is nothing that compares to the vitriol that exists on social media from many fans. Women in sports journalism often face vulgar and offensive comments from fans sending messages from anonymous social media accounts. A look through the replies of a social media post from a female sports journalist reveals the numerous awful comments with which these women must deal. Sideline reporter Laura Okmin said that one of the main issues with social media is that, while women knew these comments existed, they used to be able to ignore them. Now these comments are delivered directly to a journalist's phone:

> *For so many of us who have been doing this for 30 years, it was perceived voices in our heads. Now these women are legitimately getting on their phone and hearing these voices in real time. They're reading people telling them about their hair, and their face, and their body. And that absolutely kills me that these young women have to deal with that. (Hull, 2022, p. 203)*

Perhaps most disturbing is the fact that oftentimes these hateful words directed at the women have nothing to do with sports. Journalist Julie DiCaro said the social media messages are not about simply disagreeing with the reporter:

> *(The social media posts) are calculated to destroy, demean, and denigrate the women they target in a public forum. It's not enough for such fragile men to simply tell a woman she's wrong, or even that she's stupid. These comments attempt to cut much deeper, striking women at what misogynists see as their most valuable characteristics: appearance, sexual purity, sweetness and submissiveness. (DiCaro, 2015)*

DiCaro and fellow Chicago sports journalist Sarah Spain joined forces in 2016 to create a video in which unsuspecting men read some of the Twitter messages that have been sent to them. The 4-minute, 15-second piece starts with a few humorous messages, but takes a dramatic turn about halfway through, when the tweets become more vulgar. The men can barely say the words as they read messages wishing bodily harm and even death upon DiCaro and Spain (Just Not Sports, 2016). It became clear following the publication of the video that this was not an isolated incident impacting just those two. Other women in sports journalism retweeted and posted the video, commenting about how they faced similar messages every day (Mettler, 2016).

Sarah Spain and Julie DiCaro raised awareness of the harassment women who work in sports media face.

Charley Gallay/Getty Images for Alliance for Women in Media

# Unique Job Challenges for Women

Sports journalism is very different from most traditional jobs. For one, it is anything but a 9 a.m. to 5 p.m., Monday through Friday profession. Most sporting events take place at night, with the biggest games often occurring on the weekends. Therefore, it is not unusual for a sportswriter or broadcaster to work from 2:30 p.m. to 11:30 p.m., with two days off during the week (Wednesday and Thursday, for example). With social media, journalists are expected to give updates on breaking news the instant it happens, even if they are technically "off the clock" (see chapter 6 for more). While the job is different from most other professions, there are even more unique challenges for women in the field. Issues involving motherhood, ageism, physical appearance, and sexism in hiring are topics that women sports journalists face that men do not. Sportswriter Karen Crouse said that, when it came to several of the female-specific issues, "I could tell a male sportswriter (about issues that affect her) and he would look at me like I'm from Mars because these experiences are uniquely ours in this business" (Ricchiardi, 2005, para. 58).

## Motherhood

There may be no more gender unique issue for women than the prospect of motherhood. The hours and demands of a sports journalist are challenging enough without having to request weeks off to have a baby and then take care of that infant while also attempting to cover the next big sporting event. Some sports broadcasters have associated pregnancy and their job in the sports media with phrases such as "obstacle," "risk," "fear," "sacrifice," "vulnerable," and "uphill battle" (Jessop, 2020). For those reasons, it is not surprising that some women in the industry cite family issues as the most significant reason for why they might leave the field, as many believed that a career in sports journalism meant they would not be able to start their own family (Hardin & Shain, 2005; Hardin & Whiteside, 2009).

In a 2022 study that focused specifically on motherhood and sports broadcasters at local television stations, more than 50 percent of those surveyed either agreed or strongly agreed with the statement "I have put off starting or adding to my family due to worries about my job." Responses included: "I am concerned whether or not it is plausible to have a family and work in this field,"

"I am going to get out of the business in order to hopefully one day have a family of my own," and "I would not want to be pregnant in this environment." More than half reported that they felt they would be treated differently on the job if they were pregnant, with one local sports broadcaster writing: "The thought of being scrutinized in the public eye for growing a pregnant belly and then being expected to snap back to the same size is another aspect I would be anxious about" (Hull et al., 2022).

In a blog several years after the birth of her son, ESPN sideline reporter Kris Budden revealed that she hid her pregnancy from viewers, athletes, and her bosses for as long as she could. She wrote:

> It's no secret that there aren't many women in sports in their 40s. Maybe I thought that becoming a mom would put me "over the hill" in the TV age . . . that it meant I reached the peak of my career and everything after that was downhill. (Budden, 2017, para. 5)

For her, it was not as much about how being pregnant might slow her down, it was instead another issue: how being a mom might make her look "old."

## Ageism

As discussed in this chapter, Fox Sports' Pam Oliver is one of the longest-tenured sideline reporters at the network. However, her time there almost ended abruptly. Just before the start of the 2014 season, Fox announced that not only was Oliver being demoted from the top broadcast team, but that she would no longer be on the sidelines at all. While that decision would eventually be revisited, and Oliver remained with Fox several additional seasons, many questioned if her age had something to do with the decision. As one reporter commented after the decision to demote Oliver, "Oliver turned 53 in March, and women in their 50s on sports television have long been an endangered species" (Deitsch, 2014, para. 15). This is an issue that is unique to women, as there are men in broadcasting who held prominent positions well into their 70s and 80s. For example, when Amazon started exclusively showing NFL games on Thursday nights in 2022, the streaming platform hired 77-year-old Al Michaels as its main announcer. In addition, he was given a three-year contract, meaning he could still be working there when he turns 80 (McGregor, 2022). One would be hard-pressed to find a woman in sports broadcasting still on the job in her 80s.

## Judged on Appearance

Part of the issue with ageism for women in broadcasting is that they are often judged on their appearance more than men seem to be. In 2010, ESPN's Tony Kornheiser took time out of his radio show to openly criticize the outfit of *SportsCenter* host Hannah Storm:

> *Hannah Storm in a horrifying, horrifying outfit today. She's got on red go-go boots and a Catholic school plaid skirt . . . way too short for somebody in her 40s or maybe early 50s by now. She's got on her typically very, very tight shirt. She looks like she has sausage casing wrapping around her upper body. (James, 2010, para. 5)*

While Kornheiser was suspended for his comments, it demonstrated the no-win situation that faces many women in sports broadcasting, who are often judged by their looks first and knowledge and ability second. ESPN's Sarah Spain said, "Either you're too beautiful and you don't know what you're talking about, or you're too ugly and I don't want to watch you" (Markham, 2013, para. 20). Erin Andrews, a reporter for Fox Sports, also noted the discrepancy:

> *I always bring up the fact that people are so worried about what I'm doing or that I care about the way I look . . . [but] we have some of the best-looking guys at Fox. They are wearing gorgeous suits. They have a hair and makeup team there powdering them. They work out all the time. [They're] beautiful men wearing beautiful clothes, and no one says anything about that. That's the only time I kind of get salty about it, because I'm like, how am I any different from these guys? (Buxton, 2016, para. 4)*

Even in local television, the emphasis on looks persists. One research study surmised that those hiring for sports positions "seemed to believe that viewers would accept a female sportscaster if she was a 'beauty queen.' As a result, some news directors prioritized looks over sports knowledge" (Sheffer & Schultz, 2007, p. 92).

## Sexism in Hiring

Women face significant roadblocks to simply gaining jobs in the sports media. The Institute for Diversity and Ethics in Sport looked at over 100 newspapers and websites in 2021 and gave those sports media outlets a grade of "F" for their gender hiring. Over 80 percent of sports editors, over 85 percent of sports writers, and over 82 percent of sports columnists throughout the country were men (Lapchick, 2021). Those women who do secure employment are often faced with the implication of tokenism. This creates an overwhelming pressure to perform well, which leads to burnout and often an early departure from the industry (Hardin & Whiteside, 2009).

## Future of Women in the Sports Media

While there are certainly many obstacles that women in the sports media face, there have been many accomplishments that signal the tide may be turning. Linda Cohn is the longest-tenured anchor on ESPN's flagship program *SportsCenter*, having hosted over 5,000 of the episodes in the network's history (Hall, 2018). CBS Sports debuted a sports talk show that featured all-female talent, a first in the history of sports on television (Fleming, 2014). Before Amazon started broadcasting a weekly NFL game and only had the rights to a select few games, they tabbed Hannah Storm and Andrea Kremer as their announcers, making them the first broadcast team made up of only women to call an NFL game (Feldman, 2018). At one point, *The Washington Post*'s primary beat writers covering the District of Columbia's four major men's professional teams were all women (WashPostPR, 2017). In 2018, an article on *The Verge* proclaimed, "The person running your favorite football team's Twitter is probably a woman," and noted that nearly half of NFL social media accounts were overseen by a woman (de la Cretaz, 2018).

## Summary

Women in the sports media have never had it easy. For years they were banned from locker rooms and media rooms, treated poorly by a variety of different stakeholders, and fought through obstacles that were unique to them. However, while those challenges will continue to exist, it is important to remember those who paved the way for those in the industry. From Lesley Visser being the first NFL beat writer to Pam Oliver giving the latest updates on the sidelines at games, women today have more role models than ever when it comes to a career in sports. It remains a "boys club" in many aspects, but seeing a woman host the Super Bowl coverage (Maria Taylor), anchor *SportsCenter* more times than any other (Linda Cohn), or cover professional sports for a newspaper or website (many examples) demonstrates that perhaps some of those previous limitations are starting to diminish. Despite the obstacles that existed for years, women can, and will, be successful in the sports media for decades to come.

## REVIEW QUESTIONS

1. What were some of the early obstacles facing women in the sports media?

2. Why was locker room access considered an important issue for women in the sports media?

3. Why are unwanted comments from athletes especially challenging for women in the sports media?

4. What are some unique job challenges that face women in the sports media industry?

# 21

# Media Coverage of LGBTQ+ in Sports

## CHAPTER OBJECTIVES

After completing the chapter, the reader should be able to do the following:

- Identify key figures in LGBTQ+ sports history
- Understand why Jason Collins' announcement was groundbreaking
- Discuss the media's impact on LGBTQ+ athletes
- Examine the current issues involved with transgender athletes

For decades, the idea of an openly gay player in professional team sports seemed to be something that was purely fantasy. In fact, for many years, the only example of this happening was in a fictional Broadway play. *Take Me Out* told the story of a professional baseball player announcing that he was gay, with several of his teammates struggling with this announcement. The play won numerous awards during its initial run in 2003, but the storylines in the performance were not being repeated in the real world (Towers, 2022).

Instead, gay athletes were electing to wait until after their retirement to reveal their sexuality. Many were citing previous negative comments from potential teammates and sports leaders as a reason why, for their own protection, it was better to keep the fact that they were a member of the **LGBTQ+** (which stands for Lesbian, Gay, Bisexual, Transgender, Queer, and others) community a secret. That would change in 2013 when basketball player Jason Collins announced that he was gay, setting the stage for him to become the first openly gay player in one of the major professional team sports

in the United States. Others would soon follow, but not always with the help of the media.

## LGBTQ+ In Society

While this chapter focuses on sports, the increased acceptance of the LGBTQ+ athletic community can be seen in the parallel changing of attitudes in society as a whole. In the early 1960s, same-sex relationships were illegal in every state in the United States, but starting with Illinois in 1961, some states began changing those laws. It was not until a Supreme Court decision in 2003 that same-sex relationships were decriminalized nationally by the federal government (Davidson, 2022). In 2015 a Supreme Court decision made same-sex marriages legal in every state (Liptak, 2015).

These anti-LGBTQ+ laws being repealed were also a reflection on the changing attitudes of the American public. By 2013, more than 90 percent of American LGTBQ+ adults said that they believed society had become more accepting of them in the previous ten years

(Pew Research Center, 2013). In addition, acceptance had reached many different avenues of American life, with members of the LGTBQ+ community in elected office, the entertainment industry, and activism leadership positions (Asmelash, 2023). However, the sporting world was not as quick to accept LGBTQ+ athletes.

# LGBTQ+ Sports Pioneers

Whenever there is something that is considered "new" or "different" in the sports world, the first people to fall into that category are considered pioneers. Whether it is on the field or off, these athletes often have to overcome barriers that others do not have to face. For decades, there was not an openly gay player in most professional sports; the people discussed in this section helped pave the way for today's gay athletes.

## David Kopay

When discussing LGBTQ+ pioneers in in sports, the conversation often begins with David Kopay. Kopay was a running back in the NFL from 1964 to 1972, splitting time among five different teams. Three years after his retirement, there was an article in the *Washington Star* in which an unnamed football player spoke about how difficult it was to be a homosexual in sports. The newspaper was bombarded with mail from readers who doubted the validity of the article, claiming that there was no way a gay person would be in the NFL. Kopay suspected he knew who the player was but did not want to expose his former teammate. Instead, Kopay himself reached out to the article's writer, wanting to tell his story. Shortly after, the newspaper published a piece in which Kopay became one of the first openly gay players, although retired, in professional sports (Buzinski, 2011).

## Glenn Burke

While Kopay hid his sexuality from most of those around him in the league, baseball player Glenn Burke did not. Burke told his Los Angeles Dodgers teammates, management, and beat writers that he was gay. However, the news did not travel beyond that circle; the media refused to write about it in the newspaper or discuss it on television. Therefore, while it was well known in the locker room, it remained a secret to the public outside of baseball.

The Dodgers were not supportive of his sexuality, as evidenced by the fact that the team's executives offered him $75,000 to marry a woman. He would refuse that offer, and the team traded him to the Oakland Athletics, a move several teammates believed happened because management knew Burke was gay. With the Athletics, his manager, Billy Martin, used homophobic slurs when introducing Burke to teammates, and within a year Burke retired from baseball at just 27 years old (Barra, 2013). He would come out to the public after his retirement in 1982, saying: "It's harder to be a gay in sports than anywhere else, except maybe president. Baseball is probably the hardest sport of all" (Smith, 1982, p. 63).

## Billie Jean King

Billie Jean King was at the top of her game in the world of tennis in the 1970s and had crushed Bobby Riggs in the "Battle of the Sexes" in 1973 (see chapter 18 for more on that historic event). She had won 12 Grand Slam singles championships, was ranked no. 1 in the world, and would later be inducted into the International Tennis Hall of Fame. However, at the height of her success, King was also keeping a closely guarded secret that she was gay, and despite being married to her husband, she was in a relationship with a woman. King worried that publicly revealing her sexuality would hurt her career off the court, so it remained something, much to the detriment of her mental health, that she kept private. Her secret would become public knowledge in 1981 when the woman she had formerly been in a relationship with filed a lawsuit against King looking for half of her financial winnings in the time they were together. King was right that coming out would hurt her career, as she lost hundreds of thousands of dollars in endorsement deals after she was outed by her ex (Newsham, 2021).

While King would retire from tennis a few years after the revelations, her legacy has far surpassed anything she could have ever accomplished on the court. She has long been a pioneer in the push for gender equality in athletics, often cited as an inspirational figure for women in sports. The home of the U.S. Open tennis tournament in New York was renamed the USTA Billie Jean King National Tennis Center in 2006 as a way to honor her contributions to the sport, making it one of the few stadiums in the country that is named after a woman (Sandomir, 2006). In 2009, U.S. president Barack Obama awarded her the Presidential Medal of Freedom, one of the highest honors an American citizen can receive. Amazingly, she would also be awarded France's equivalent of that prize from French president Emmanuel Macron in 2022, as he cited her work in

Focus on Sport/Getty Images

**Billie Jean King speaks with reporters in 1973.**

bringing LGBTQ+ issues to the forefront in that country (Baseline Staff, 2022).

## Billy Bean

Baseball player Billy Bean also waited until after his retirement from the league to reveal that he was gay. An outfielder for several different teams in the late 1980s and early 1990s, Bean made his announcement in 1999, and would later write a book detailing his experiences in the professional ranks. Bean has become a key member of Major League Baseball's outreach and inclusion policies since his retirement. In 2014, he was named MLB's first Ambassador for Inclusion, a role designed to support the LGBTQ+ community in baseball (Footer, 2014). When announcing the position, MLB commissioner Bud Selig cited Bean and Glenn Burke's struggles while playing as a reason the position was needed: "I wish that our game had someone in place to whom Billy and Glenn could have turned when they played; a friend, listener, a source of support" (Footer, 2014, para. 7).

## Caitlyn Jenner

In 1976, U.S. athlete Bruce Jenner won the gold medal in decathlon at the Summer Olympics, breaking the world record in the process. Jenner appeared on the cover of cereal boxes, acted in movies, and became one of the most popular athletes in the United States. How-

ever, Jenner, one of the most dominant male athletes in history, would make an announcement in 2015 that shocked many: Jenner came out as a transgender woman and asked to be known as Caitlyn.

In a nationally televised interview on ABC, Jenner explained her decision, detailed how she had been taking hormones since the 1980s, and used the "she" pronoun when discussing Caitlyn (ABC News, 2015). For many viewers, this interview was likely the first nationally televised conversation in which they were hearing about these topics. Jenner proudly proclaimed, "I am a woman" (1:38) and immediately became perhaps the most famous transgender person in the world. She would later receive ESPN's Arthur Ashe Courage Award; however, as discussed in chapter 17 of this book, that honor did not come without controversy (Moyer, 2015).

## Post-Retirement Announcements

While the number of professional athletes revealing they were gay was rising, they seemingly all had one thing in common: They were all making the announcements after their playing careers were over. No active players were coming out, as instead it was former athletes who had already stepped away from the games, the locker rooms, and their teammates. Nearly all explicitly stated that their sexuality had not suddenly changed following retirement, but that they instead felt the need to hide this during their careers. When one sees the comments of teammates and fellow players when they were asked about the possibility of having a gay teammate, it should be no surprise why so many elected to keep their sexuality a secret:

- **Basketball player Tim Hardaway:** "First of all, I wouldn't want him on my team. Second of all, if he was on my team, I would really distance myself from him because I don't think that's right and I don't think he should be in the locker room when we're in the locker room."

- **Football player Jeremy Shockey:** "They're going to be in the shower with us and stuff, so I don't think that's gonna work. That's not gonna work, you know?"

- **Basketball player Shavlik Randolph:** "As long as you don't bring your gayness on me, I'm fine. As far as business-wise, I'm sure I could play with him. But I think it would create a little awkwardness in the locker room."

Seeing and hearing the reactions from teammates about even the possibility of having a gay teammate would likely be enough to give players pause about coming forward with their sexuality. The locker room, often considered a sanctuary and safe place for players, would suddenly be anything but. For basketball player John Amaechi, it was not necessarily the reaction of his fellow players that he was worried about, but instead the owner of his team:

> I played for a team in Utah for example where our owner ran into our locker room when the film "Brokeback Mountain" came out and screamed at everybody that he wasn't going to let that film play on his cinemas, and he happened to own most of the cinemas in Salt Lake City. That's a not too subtle way of letting everybody know where he stands on the position of homosexuality, and it's not the kind of thing that inspires you to then stand up and say, "Yes, I'm gay." I absolutely was convinced that at that point I would've lost my job. (Fedor, 2011, para. 7)

Watching his owner's reaction to *Brokeback Mountain*, a movie about a romantic relationship between two male cowboys, was enough for Amaechi to keep to himself and not reveal that he was gay until he retired. The last line about him realizing that he would likely lose his job with the team is eye opening. Players considering coming out not only had to think about the reaction of teammates, but also now had to worry about their income.

# Jason Collins

With the background of the unspoken, and sometimes openly spoken, discrimination that would likely face gay athletes, it is perhaps not a surprise that for decades there was not an active publicly gay player in the four major professional team sports in the United States. However, in 2013 that was about to change. In April of that year, the NBA's Jason Collins became a pioneer in the history of LGBTQ+ athletes in sports.

## *Sports Illustrated* Story

Pictured on the cover of *Sports Illustrated*, with a caption that read "The Gay Athlete," Collins broke barriers. The first-person article started with a straightforward admission: "I'm a 34-year-old NBA center. I'm black. And I'm gay" (Collins, 2013, para. 1). In the article, Collins recounted the decisions he made throughout his life regarding his sexuality, including feeling the need to hide it, living in fear, and finally recognizing that it was a secret he could no longer keep. However, Collins still had fears about how his declaration would be received among others in the NBA:

> I've been asked how other players will respond to my announcement. The simple answer is, I have no idea. I'm a pragmatist. I hope for the best, but plan for the worst. The biggest concern seems to be that gay players will behave unprofessionally in the locker room. Believe me, I've taken plenty of showers in 12 seasons. My behavior wasn't an issue before, and it won't be one now. My conduct won't change. I still abide by the adage, "What happens in the locker room stays in the locker room." I'm still a model of discretion. (Collins, 2013, para. 28)

*Sports Illustrated*'s website had the most unique visitors in its history on the day Collins' article was posted (Laird, 2013). He would soon learn that, while there would be some critics, the overall response from the public and fellow NBA players was overwhelmingly positive.

## Reaction

U.S. president Barack Obama spoke with Collins on the phone the day the article was published and would later say how proud he was that a barrier had been broken (Associate Press, 2013a), while Martina Navratilova, John Amaechi, and Kobe Bryant were among the athletes who sent public messages of support to Collins

Garrett W. Ellwood/NBAE via Getty Images

**Jason Collins plays for the Brooklyn Nets in a game against the Denver Nuggets in February 2014.**

(Associated Press, 2013b). One ESPN basketball analyst said that he was relieved that the well-spoken, funny, and widely respected Collins was the pioneer, calling him, "the perfect ambassador for gay rights in professional team sports" (Elhassan, 2013, para. 3). However, not everyone at ESPN shared the same feelings. On the network the evening the article was published online, NBA reporter Chris Broussard said, "I don't agree with homosexuality. I think it's a sin" (Mitchell, 2013, para. 1).

## Collins' NBA Career Following the Announcement

At the time of his announcement, Collins' contract was about to expire, meaning he would soon be without a team. He had made it clear that he hoped to continue playing, which led some to wonder which, if any, NBA teams would be willing to sign him (Beck & Branch, 2013). Collins was nearing the end of his career, his production was dropping likely due to his age, and some teams might have viewed his admission as a possible distraction in the locker room. When the next season started, Collins was still without a team. In fact, it was not until over 50 games into the 82-game NBA season that the Brooklyn Nets signed him to a 10-day contract. After suiting up and playing against the Los Angeles Lakers,

Collins officially became the first publicly gay athlete to play in a game in one of the four major professional team sports in the United States. Collins' no. 98 jersey, worn in honor of Matthew Shepard, a gay teenager killed in a hate crime in 1998, became the top seller on the NBA online store (Keh, 2014). The Nets would sign Collins to another 10-day contract before ultimately agreeing to keep him on the roster for the remainder of the 2013-2014 season (Harper, 2014). At the conclusion of the season, Collins announced his retirement from the league (Collins, 2014).

## Michael Sam

In the weeks before the 2014 NFL Draft, University of Missouri football player Michael Sam announced that he was gay. Sam, one of the top defensive players in the country, was set to become the first openly gay player in the NFL. However, following his announcement and some poor workouts with teams, the defensive lineman fell from a projected early- to mid-round pick to the seventh and final round of the draft. Despite a strong performance in the preseason, Sam was cut by the St. Louis Rams and never appeared in a regular-season game. Chapter 22 has more information about Michael Sam, his coming-out announcement, and how the perception of his sexuality may have affected his professional career.

## Carl Nassib

It was seven years later when the Las Vegas Raiders' Carl Nassib did what Sam was not able to do and became the first openly gay player to play in a regular-season NFL game. Nassib, who had already been in the league for five years, made the announcement rather quietly. Instead of major press conferences, magazine cover articles, or coordinated releases among some of the biggest media outlets in the world, Nassib simply shot a "selfie" Instagram video in his backyard to deliver the news. There was not an accompanying dramatic speech. Instead, it would have been difficult for him to be more nonchalant: "What's up people? I'm Carl Nassib. I'm at my house in West Chester, Pennsylvania. I just wanted to take a quick moment to say that I'm gay" (Nassib, 2021).

Later in the video, Nassib announced that he was going to donate $100,000 to The Trevor Project, an organization dedicated to suicide prevention for LGTBQ+ youth. Traffic on the organization's website went up 350 percent in the days following Nassib's Instagram post and the NFL matched his donation with $100,000 of its own (Chadiha, 2021). Teammates, coaches, and opponents were vocal in their support of Nassib, perhaps signaling a change in how these announcements would be perceived in the world of sports (Lutz, 2021).

## Gender Differences

While Collins', Sam's, and Nassib's announcements about their sexuality made headlines, that is often not the case when the subject is a woman. Some of that may be due to public assumptions. Patrick Burke, the founder of an advocacy group for LGBTQ+ athletes, said, "In sports right now, there are two different stereotypes—that there are no gay male athletes, and every female is a lesbian" (Borden, 2013, para. 16). A few months before Jason Collins made his historic declaration, women's basketball player Brittney Griner announced that she was gay. Griner had been one of the most dominant college players in recent memory and was about to be the top overall pick in the upcoming WNBA draft. While Collins would be on the cover of

*Sports Illustrated,* get phone calls from the president, and receive praise from his fellow players, Griner's revelation was met with near silence. Many suspected that the reasoning was simply because she was a woman. Women's sports have often battled the perception that every athlete who plays is a lesbian, so when one announces that she is, the revelation is not considered something out of the norm, which results in lesser attention and media coverage (de la Cretaz, 2022).

## Troubling Media Coverage

As the Jason Collins story demonstrated, the media has an interest in stories involving LGBTQ+ athletes. Collins was provided with the opportunity to do a first-person narrative that would appear on the cover of the most prominent sports magazine in the United States. He would later be interviewed on various television networks, and his first game back in the NBA was played in front of a large contingent of journalists. However, just because the media *wants* to cover these stories does not mean that they always do it correctly. Instead, journalists have been at the center of some of the more unfortunate moments in LGBTQ+ sports history.

## Martina Navratilova

In 1981, Martina Navratilova was one of the best tennis players in the world, having already won several major tournaments. She gave an interview with a reporter from New York's *Daily News* newspaper in which she discussed her romantic relationship with another woman. However, at the time of the interview, one of the tennis tour's major sponsors, the cosmetics company Avon, was threatening to pull their money from the tour after it was revealed that Billie Jean King had an affair with a woman. Navratilova, fearful that her admission might be the final straw for Avon, asked the author not to publish the story. However, the newspaper's leadership would not grant her request (Tignor, 2013). Against her wishes, the *Daily News* published the article on July 30, 1981, stating that Navratilova was bisexual, had been in relationships with women, and was worried that her public admission would hurt women's tennis (Goldstein, 1981). What was not stated in the article was how the newspaper had printed the information even after she had asked them not to. As Navratilova predicted, Avon did leave the tour, taking their $16 million commitment

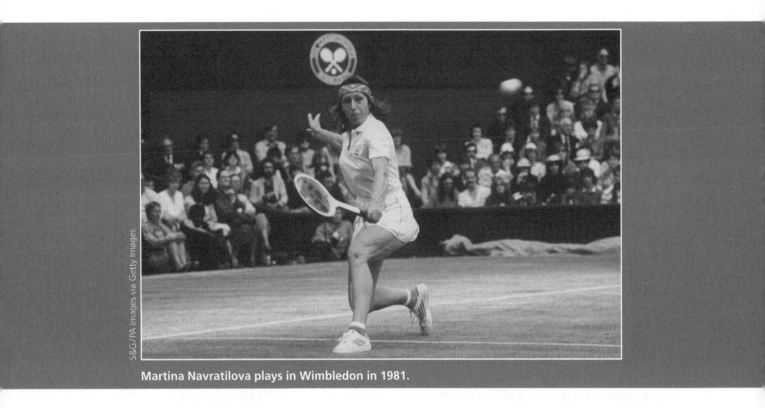

**Martina Navratilova plays in Wimbledon in 1981.**

with them (Tignor, 2013). For the tennis star, her opportunity to reveal her sexuality on her own terms was taken from her by the newspaper whose reasoning was that they did not want to see it published in another media outlet first.

## Dr. V

In 2014, *Grantland*, a sub-site of ESPN.com, published an article titled "Dr. V's Magical Putter." The story started as a tale of a new golf putter, one that online reviews said was going to revolutionize the industry. However, as the article progressed, the narrative became less about the putter itself and more about its inventor, Dr. Essay Anne Vanderbilt, also known as Dr. V. The author of the *Grantland* piece, Caleb Hannan, recounted the challenges he had trying to get an interview with Dr. V, her insistence that the story be about the putter and not her, and his attempts to verify her background. It was in those background checks in which the story would take a turn. Hannan discovered through his research that some of the personal information Dr. V had provided was not entirely accurate. Her career path had not gone like she stated, she had lived in different locations than she had claimed, and, in a question that would frame the direction of the rest of the piece,

Hannan wrote that he asked an interview subject, "Are you trying to tell me that Essay Anne Vanderbilt was once a man?" (Hannan, 2014 para. 48). The story of Dr. V then became solely focused on Hannan's attempts to get the real story about Dr. V's past, all while she continued to insist that he not publish the story. The piece ended with the tragic revelation that, with the knowledge that the article was likely moving forward despite her objections, Dr. V had committed suicide (Hannan, 2014).

While some initially praised the article based on its storytelling and plot twists, the public narrative surrounding the piece soon changed. Many questioned how *Grantland* could publish an article that outed a transgender woman, a decision that seemingly directly led to her suicide. Bill Simmons, the editor in chief of *Grantland*, would later write that the biggest mistake they made was not having anyone familiar with the transgender community read the article before it was published (Simmons, 2014). Christina Kahrl, a baseball writer who is transgender, wrote that Hannan's article, "figures to be a permanent exhibit of what not to do, and how not to treat a fellow human being" (Kahrl, 2014, para. 1). Kahrl added that the author was right to question Dr. V's history regarding her professional experience but should not have discussed her gender identity if that was something she did not want in the article (Kahrl, 2014). Despite objections, the article has remained online through *Grantland*'s website, with Simmons saying that keeping the story on the page will hopefully result in people learning from the many mistakes they made (Simmons, 2014).

## *The Daily Beast* at the Olympics

In 2016, Nico Hines, a reporter for the website *The Daily Beast*, wrote an article titled "I got three Grindr dates in an hour in the Olympic Village." Hines, while covering the Olympics, signed up for dating apps on his phone, including Grindr, a service aimed at LGBTQ+ members. Hines, who is not gay, recounted how he matched with several men on Grindr and revealed enough personal information in the story to make those athletes easily identifiable. However, many of those he matched with were not openly gay, and several lived in countries in which being gay was considered a crime. Therefore, Hines had put some of them in very serious personal danger. The backlash was fierce to the article, forcing *The Daily Beast* to first remove the identifying information and issue an apology (Maltais, 2016). However, that did not stop the criticism, and the website's editors would eventually pull the article from the website entirely (The Daily Beast, 2017).

*The Daily Beast* had not done enough research to recognize the damage they would cause by publishing this story. The author outed athletes and possibly caused damage to their lives based on the politics their home countries. Even in the United States at the time, many states had laws that could allow companies to fire employees simply for being gay (Maltais, 2016). This article was yet another example of the mainstream media not knowing the possible implications of publishing a story that would have a direct impact on the LGBTQ+ members involved in that story.

## Transgender Athletes

In 1976, tennis player Renée Richards became one of the early pioneers among transgender athletes. Richards, a transgender woman, played in several professional women's tennis tournaments, but not without controversy. She had to file lawsuits just to have the opportunity to play, journalists' stories questioned her right to be there, and several of her opponents withdrew before she would play a single match (Tignor, 2021).

While there have been some success stories, including Chris Mosier becoming the first trans athlete to earn a spot on Team USA (Zeigler, 2015), the road has not become easier for transgender athletes in the years since Richards made headlines. In 2022, University of Pennsylvania swimmer Lia Thomas became the first transgender athlete to win an NCAA Division I national championship. However, the criticism that followed that win would threaten to overshadow her victory. Thomas, who swam on the men's team for three seasons before joining the women's team, was accused by some of ruining the sport of women's swimming because she had "an unfair advantage" over the competition (Barnes, 2022; Powell, 2022). When several states in the United States introduced bills designed to limit or even ban transgender athletes from competing in sports, Thomas was often cited as the reason that women's sports needed "protection" (Chen, 2022).

## Summary

For decades, gay athletes had come to the conclusion that revealing their sexuality during their playing days would be a mistake. Instead, they would wait until after retirement to announce that they were gay. In major team sports, Jason Collins was the first to break the barrier, and his first-person essay in *Sports Illustrated* is considered a pioneering moment for LGBTQ+ athletes in sports. While there remain gender differences in the perceptions of the audience when these announcements are made, they are also becoming more commonplace. When the NFL's Carl Nassib revealed he was gay in an Instagram video, he said, "I hope that one day videos like this, and the coming out process, are just not necessary" (Nassib, 2021, :27), implying that he hoped it would become more commonplace and less something that was considered unique. However, media coverage of these announcements and the LGBTQ+ sports community remains somewhat challenging. The media seemingly wants to cover these stories, but they do not always do it correctly.

### KEY TERM

**LGBTQ+**—An acronym that stands for Lesbian, Gay, Bisexual, Transgender, Queer, and others.

## REVIEW QUESTIONS

1. Why did many athletes wait until after their retirement to announce that they were gay?
2. Why was Caitlyn Jenner's interview on ABC considered groundbreaking television?
3. What are some of the gender differences with how the media discusses LGBTQ+ issues in sports?
4. Why might the media have difficulties in accurately and fairly reporting stories that involve LGBTQ+ in sports?

# 22

# Michael Sam

## CHAPTER OBJECTIVES

After completing the chapter, the reader should be able to do the following:

- Understand the history of Michael Sam in terms of LGBTQ+ athletes in sports
- Identify the media's role in Sam's announcement
- Analyze how Sam's sexuality might have influenced his NFL career
- Compare the public and NFL reaction to Sam to the reaction to Carl Nassib

In the weeks before the 2014 NFL Draft, *Outsports* cofounder Cyd Zeigler recalled getting a text that read "The eagle has landed" (Zeigler, 2014a, para. 2). The implication of that message was that a player in the NFL was about to publicly announce that he was gay. That player would later be revealed to be University of Missouri defensive star Michael Sam. The plan was coming into motion in the background: Sam would make his groundbreaking announcement, become a high draft pick, make a team out of training camp, and then begin his historic NFL career. However, in the weeks and months following, only the announcement happened. Instead, after Sam revealed his secret to the world—a "secret" that was anything but to many in the media—and then plummeted in the draft, was released before the season started, and ultimately never played a snap in a regular-season game.

While chapter 21 of this book recounts the struggles that many LGBTQ+ athletes face in professional sports, Sam's case is worth examining further. In the "macho" world of professional football, having an openly gay player in the NFL was seen as a potentially historic moment. However, Sam's NFL career ended up grounded before it could ever take off. Was it for football reasons or for sexuality reasons? While no one may ever know for sure, Sam's story demonstrates that, while making it to the NFL is incredibly difficult, having to overcome prejudices and perceptions along the way can make it even more challenging.

## The College Football Star

Sam was one of the top defensive players in college football during his time at the University of Missouri. In his senior year, Sam led the Southeastern Conference (SEC) in sacks and was named the SEC co-defensive player of the year. In addition, Sam was selected as a first team All-American by several different organizations and was a finalist for national defensive player of the year awards (ABC 17 News Team, 2013). Based on his statistics and well-deserved honors in his senior year, many expected Sam to be at worst a mid-round pick in the 2014 NFL Draft. However, Sam was about to become one of the most famous players available in the draft, and it had almost nothing to do with his football ability.

## Telling His Teammates

Before Sam's senior year at Missouri, he informed his teammates during a team bonding exercise that he was gay. As part of the activity, players were supposed to reveal something that no one knows about them, and Sam took that moment to tell his secret to his teammates and coaches. He said that while their reaction was over-whelmingly positive and supportive, most kept the news to themselves and did not publicly reveal his sexuality (Connelly, 2014). Despite that, rumors had already been posted on online message boards about his sexuality, so throughout the 2013 season, perhaps to avoid questions that he might not have been ready to answer, Sam spoke to reporters after only one game, essentially creating his own media blackout (Staples, 2014). However, after the football season was over, Sam decided that he was ready to go public, and the media would play a key role in his announcement.

## The Announcement

In January 2014, while preparing to enter the NFL, Sam was taking meetings with several different player agents with the goal of picking one that would help with his announcement (Zeigler, 2014a). If everything went perfectly, Sam would be on track to be the first openly gay active player in the NFL, so his news was going to be historic. His publicity team determined that the announcement would be released on multiple outlets at the same time—*The New York Times*, ESPN, and *Outsports*, which is a website dedicated to coverage of LGBTQ+ athletes. The timing was set as well, with Sam coming forward just after the NFL Scouting Combine, a yearly showcase for players hoping to get drafted (Zeigler, 2014a). However, as the famous proverb states, "The best laid plans of mice and men often go awry," and it soon became very clear that the carefully crafted plan from Sam and his publicity team was going to change.

## The Not-So-Secret Secret

Those close to Sam soon found out that his secret was anything but. *Outsports'* Zeigler was given access to Sam and his advisers during this time and wrote a recap of what was happening behind the scenes in the time before Sam's coming-out announcement. In his story, Zeigler revealed that many more people knew about Sam's sexuality than anyone had suspected:

> *Even as the plan was being formulated, it was like outrunning an avalanche. Every day it became more apparent that too many people knew what was coming. While [Jason] Collins had kept his coming out a secret held among just a few trusted confidants, Sam's sexual orientation would soon become the worst-kept secret in the sports media. (Zeigler, 2014a, para. 33)*

According to Zeigler, it was clear that the local media in Missouri, as well as those at Fox Sports and the NFL, were all aware that Sam was gay. In addition, NFL teams were not directly asking him about it, but Sam said several asked questions that implied curiosity about his sexuality during their interviews with him at the Senior Bowl, a postseason showcase for the best college football seniors (Zeigler, 2014a). At the University of Missouri's college newspaper, a sports reporter estimated that half the staff, including every editor, was aware of Sam being gay (Garcia, 2019). With so many apparently already knowing, it was decided that the timing of the announcement was going to have to be moved up so that Sam would be able to tell his story on his own terms. However, even that new schedule was not going to be soon enough. Just before the revised date, media outlets from all over the world were reaching out to Sam, looking to land an interview with him, presumably to ask about his sexuality. The eye-opening moment occurred when a writer from *Sports Illustrated* reached out and said he knew everything that was coming and wanted to be the first one to report it. After talking with Sam's advisers, that writer agreed not to run the story, but it was clear they could not wait any longer. One day earlier than expected, Michael Sam was going to make his historic announcement (Zeigler, 2014a).

Just after 8 p.m. ET on Sunday, February 9, 2014, *The New York Times* and ESPN published stories on their respective websites that contained interviews with Sam in which he announced he was gay (Branch, 2014; Connelly, 2014). Zeigler's behind-the-scenes article on *Outsports* was posted at the same time, completing the three-pronged revelation that Sam and his advisers had planned (Zeigler, 2014a). In all three stories, it was emphasized that Sam wanted to be the first to tell the world about his sexuality, instead of having a journalist report the story without Sam's involvement. By moving

Michael Sam is congratulated by teammates after sacking the quarterback in a September 2012 game against Arizona State.

the timing of the story up, Sam was able to, as he said, "own my truth" (Branch, 2014, para. 8).

## Public Reaction

The public reaction to Sam's announcement was one of acceptance. Politicians, NFL players, and football legends all expressed their support (Good, 2014), and the NFL released a statement that read: "We admire Michael Sam's honesty and courage. Michael is a football player. Any player with ability and determination can succeed in the N.F.L. We look forward to welcoming and supporting Michael Sam in 2014" (Branch, 2014, para. 11). Additionally, Jason Collins, the first male professional athlete to come out in U.S. team sports, tweeted his support for Sam (Collins, 2014). While there was certainly some negative reaction, even Sam himself was seemingly overwhelmed by the positive. A few hours after the articles were posted, Sam wrote on Twitter, "I want to thank everybody for their support and encouragement, especially @espn, @nytimes and @nfl. I am proud to tell my story to the world!" (Sam, 2014).

## Sam's Football Future

With Sam's announcement now public, he was on track to be the first openly gay active player in the NFL. However, while the public reaction was overwhelmingly supportive, there were concerns about how the various teams in the league would react to the news. Sam, who was once considered a potential third-round pick in the NFL, was now being seen in a different light by talent evaluators. An article on *Sports Illustrated*'s website painted a bleak picture for Sam's future in professional football; the authors interviewed eight NFL coaches and executives, and all eight believed Sam's announcement would cause him to drop to a later round than projected (Thamel & Evans, 2014). Even worse for Sam, one general manager told a reporter that he did not believe Sam would be drafted at all following his announcement (King, 2014). The implication was clear: By announcing he was gay, Sam had become a less appealing player to teams in the NFL.

## Pre-Draft Attention

While Sam's NFL future was possibly in danger due to external factors, the defensive star still had opportunities to turn the attention back to his playing ability. Sam's initial plan was to make his announcement after the NFL Scouting Combine, but after moving the date up, that event would prove to be his first major showcase in front of scouts and coaches. Unfortunately for Sam, his performance there did not lead to a desired result. His 40-yard dash time was slower than expected, he struggled in several drills, and his number of reps at the bench press was among the lowest. The concern on the field surrounding Sam appeared to be that, while he excelled in college, he might struggle finding a position in the NFL due to his size and speed (Samuel, 2014).

What was clear was that Sam had gone from just another potential mid-round pick to the most scrutinized and examined player in the draft. On the NFL Network, analysts spent nearly as much time dissecting Sam's workout as they did Jadeveon Clowney, the player who would ultimately be selected with the first overall pick (Levy, 2014). Numerous media outlets published articles focused solely on Sam and his performance at the Combine, with titles such as "Michael Sam disappoints in the 40" and "Michael Sam: Combine results and instant reaction" (Conway, 2014; Smith, 2014). On NFL.com, there were articles in which team owners and general managers were asked if they would take Sam in the draft (Patra, 2014). One reporter critical of the focus wrote, "If Sam's just a late-round pick, why not treat him like one?" (Levy, 2014, para. 29).

## Draft Day

On the day of the draft, those who suggested that Sam's draft slot would fall below expectations were proven correct. Whether it was his announcement that he was gay or his struggles in the workouts beforehand that affected his standing, the projected third-round pick ended up having to wait much longer than expected. It was not until the seventh and final round, pick 249 out of 256, that Sam heard his name called. The St. Louis Rams made the selection, with their head coach saying that it was not a ceremonial or sentimental choice, but that his team was now better with Sam on it (Silver, 2014).

Since 1980, the NFL Draft has aired on ESPN. What was once a way for the network to simply try to establish itself as a viable sports channel, the draft had evolved into one of its biggest viewership draws of the year. In addition to the top picks that are invited to New York City to meet the league's commissioner during the big day, ESPN places video cameras in the homes of players who are not at the ceremony but are still expected to be highly drafted. This allows the network to get video of the player and his family and friends reacting to the news. Despite Sam likely not being a high pick, ESPN had elected to put a camera with him since his selection was going to be a historic one.

Shortly after he was chosen by the Rams, ESPN showed video that had been recorded minutes earlier of Sam receiving the phone call informing him that he was about to be selected. The video shows Sam overcome with emotion as he begins openly crying. In recounting their call later, the Rams' coach would say that Sam was "so emotional that he couldn't speak" (Silver, 2014, para. 9). After hanging up with the coach, the video showed Sam hugging and repeatedly kissing his boyfriend (ABC News, 2014). This is a moment that has happened on these home draft cameras for years—a player is drafted and shares a moment with his significant other. However, for the first time in NFL Draft history, the person on the receiving end of that affection was a man.

After the moment was broadcast, the reaction was strong on social media, with some of it negative. Former NFL player Derrick Ward tweeted "I'm sorry but for that Michael Sam is no bueno for doing that on national tv" and "Man U got little kids lookin at the draft. I can't believe ESPN even allowed that to happen" (Ward, 2014a; 2014b). Perhaps due to the pockets of online negativity, many came to Sam's defense. ESPN's Stuart Scott tweeted "Don't like?..that's a 'you' problem" (Yan & Alsup, 2014, para. 23).

## Media Attention

Just as he was before the draft, Sam was the focus of many media stories afterward during his time with the St. Louis Rams. His preseason games resulted in full articles that were not about the game or the result, only about Sam's performance (Pelissero, 2014). Others reported how, during the preseason, Sam's jersey was one of the best-selling on NFLShop.com (Wagoner, 2014). Seemingly every move Sam made, and every comment by a teammate or coach about him, became a major story.

ESPN's Josina Anderson was one of those reporters looking to get the latest information on the rookie. During training camp, Anderson did a report in which she discussed Sam's transition to the NFL, how he was fitting in with his teammates, and, inexplicably, Sam's showering habits in the locker room. Live on ESPN, Anderson said she had talked to one unnamed Rams teammate who said he believed Sam was waiting before showering to not make others uncomfortable, and then directly quoted another player who said that he had not taken a shower at the same time as Sam and that there could be many reasons why the rookie was not showering with his teammates (Thomas, 2014). Reaction to the report was almost universally negative, with the editor of *Outsports* calling it "pathetic" (Zeigler, 2014b, para. 3). Rams head coach Jeff Fisher said, "I'm extremely disappointed. I think it's unethical. I think it's very,

Michael Buckner / Getty Images For ESPYS

**Michael Sam accepts the Arthur Ashe Award for Courage at the 2014 ESPYs.**

very unprofessional" (Thomas, 2014, para. 2; 3). ESPN would later issue an apology, writing, "ESPN regrets the matter in which we presented our report. Clearly yesterday we collectively failed to meet the standards we have set in reporting on LGBT-related topics in sports" (Krulewitz, 2014).

## Professional Football Career

Sam would fall short of his goal of being the first openly gay player to participate in a regular-season NFL game. At the end of the 2014 preseason, Sam was one of the final players released by the Rams. The Rams head coach said the decision was one that was made purely for football reasons and not because of Sam's sexuality. He added, "I was pulling for Mike. I really was" (Wagoner, 2014, para. 9). With Sam no longer under contract with the Rams, the Dallas Cowboys signed him to their team's practice squad, but after seven weeks in which he was not promoted to the active roster, the Cowboys released him as well (Eatman, 2014). One reporter would write that a general manager told him, "Teams want to sign Michael Sam but fear the media attention" (Freeman, 2014, para. 10).

Sam would not get another call from an NFL team, so he turned to other leagues in an attempt to con-

tinue his football career. In 2015, he signed a two-year contract with the Montreal Alouettes of the Canadian Football League (CFL) but ended up playing only one game before leaving the organization (Associated Press, 2015). Following his departure from the Alouettes, Sam announced that he was taking a break from football to focus on his mental health (Loumena, 2015). However, much like many athletes, his retirement from the game was not permanent, and he returned as a coach in the European League of Football. Sam was an assistant coach for the Barcelona Dragons in 2022 when one of that team's players announced his retirement. With an opening on the team, Sam moved from the coaching box to the playing field and suited up for the Dragons in a regular-season game, getting his football career back on track (Young, 2022).

## Michael Sam's Legacy

Since Sam did not ultimately become the first active openly gay player in an NFL regular-season game, some might wonder what his legacy is in the world of sports. On one hand, his impact becomes clear when talking to those who came out after him. Journalists have noted that Sam's announcement had a positive impact on young LGBTQ+ athletes who went public with their sexuality after him (Garcia, 2019). However, others might look at how Sam's career seemingly fizzled after his announcement and rightly wonder if his sexuality caused NFL teams to avoid him. Another journalist speculated that any gay football players kept their sexuality a secret after seeing how Sam's career may have been affected (Florio, 2021).

When the Las Vegas Raiders' Carl Nassib announced he was gay in 2021, he avoided many of the struggles that Sam had faced trying to enter the league. At the time of his announcement, Nassib had already been drafted, been a professional for several seasons, and established himself as a solid NFL player. He did not have to go above and beyond like Sam did because Nassib's play in the league had already demonstrated that he could be a contributing member of a football team. In fact, Nassib's announcement, as discussed in chapter 21, was met with some indifference and was treated as not necessarily a big deal. Perhaps that is Sam's ultimate, if not unfortunate, legacy. He faced criticisms that possibly contributed to his being driven from the league following his announcement, but that perhaps allowed future players such as Nassib to not have to face those comments. In turn, future LGBTQ+ athletes may see the reaction to Nassib and realize that a coming-out announcement might not cause the uproar it once did—which ultimately might be thanks to Sam.

# Summary

When ESPN, *The New York Times*, and *Outsports* published Michael Sam's story about his sexuality, he went from a relatively unknown potential NFL draft pick to possibly the most famous selection of all time. Suddenly, Sam was the focus of the draft—both by the media and by the teams. Once considered a mid-round pick, the added attention seemingly had a negative effect on his status, and Sam ended up being one of the final picks in the draft. While with the Rams, Sam's showering habits were scrutinized by the media and, despite his coach's public support, he did not make the team. Ultimately, his NFL career ended before he played in a regular-season game. Sam's story is one that leaves observers with possibly unanswerable questions: Was his career cut short due to his playing ability or because of the perceived impact his sexuality would have on the team?

## REVIEW QUESTIONS

1. Why was Michael Sam's "secret" about his sexuality not necessarily a secret to most?
2. Why did Michael Sam move up the date of his announcement that revealed he was gay?
3. How did Michael Sam's announcement about being gay possibly affect his draft status?
4. How did the media's focus on Michael Sam possibly affect his NFL career?

# PART
# IV
# CRISIS COMMUNICATION

It is an undeniable fact that people sometimes make mistakes. Those mistakes can be an accident, or they can be done with intent. Part IV of this book addresses how people can bounce back after their personal reputation has been harmed. Appropriately enough, this part starts with a description of crisis communication (chapter 23), which explains how people and organizations can defend themselves during a threat to their reputation.

From there, Part IV contains five case studies of people and organizations who endured some type of crisis and how they responded to that incident. Chapter 24 looks at Tiger Woods, who had one of the most meteoric rises in sports history, only to see his reputation suffer following off-course incidents that raised questions about his character. Like Woods, Lance Armstrong's wounds were self-inflicted: The seven-time Tour de France champion was found to have cheated during all his victories (chapter 25). Armstrong went from an American hero to a disgraced competitor in the eyes of many.

When LeBron James announced he was "taking my talents to South Beach" live on ESPN, both the basketball superstar and the television network found themselves in a storm of negative publicity (chapter 26). Both were accused of "selling out," and it took each many years to recover from the public perception of *The Decision*. The media endured a similar crisis following the sudden passing of Kobe Bryant (chapter 27). In the rush to get information out to the public, many journalists made factual errors about who had died in the helicopter crash. Several media outlets faced public outrage at what they reported, when they reported it, and what the families knew before details were made public.

Chapter 28 demonstrates what can happen when the media is on their game, as traditional journalists and YouTube content creators helped to uncover one of the biggest cheating scandals in baseball history. However, as the Houston Astros sign-stealing scandal became known, it also led to one of the worst responses to a crisis in sports history.

*THEORETICAL FOUNDATION*

# Crisis Communication

## CHAPTER OBJECTIVES

After completing the chapter, the reader should be able to do the following:

- Understand what constitutes a crisis
- Identify the key elements involved in crisis communication
- Discuss past instances of how crisis communication has been used in sports
- Debate the successes and failures of previous responses to crisis in sports

Following the 2008 Olympics, Michael Phelps, fresh off winning a record eight gold medals, might have been one of the most famous athletes in the world. With that fame came money, and the swimmer was hired by several companies to endorse and advertise their products. However, it almost all came to an end the following year when a British tabloid newspaper published a photograph of Phelps smoking marijuana from a bong pipe at a college party in South Carolina. The Olympic hero was suspended by USA Swimming and lost a major sponsorship with Kellogg's (Macur, 2009).

In an era when many athletes might have said the photo was altered, the picture was taken out of context, or simply stayed quiet until the controversy died down, Phelps did the opposite. He admitted the photo was of him, apologized, and promised it would not happen again (Crouse, 2009). In one of the lowest moments of his life, Phelps responded by taking full responsibility for the incident. Based on the fallout, it appeared that his efforts to repair his image were a success. His other

sponsors stuck with him, USA Swimming said they supported him, and the media seemingly dismissed what happened. One group of researchers said that Phelps' strategy should be used in the future by all those facing a crisis that is undeniable (Walsh & McAllister-Spooner, 2011). Phelps and his advisers successfully used crisis communication to repair his image, get him back in the pool, and redeem him in the eyes of the public.

## Crisis Communication Defined

Author and professor Alan Jay Zaremba stated that there are three recurring characteristics of a crisis:

- They are atypical events that might be predictable but are not expected when they occur.
- They can be damaging to an organization or individuals within an organization.

- They compel organizations to communicate with audiences to limit the damage that may be caused by the crisis (Zaremba, 2010).

It is that last characteristic that encapsulates the idea of **crisis communication**. During a crisis situation, the individual or organization being affected will often want to communicate with various members of the public in an attempt to reduce the effects of the crisis. They will first need to identify who should receive information about the incident. In some cases, it could be the general public, while in other situations, the information may be of interest to only those who work at the organization, so the communications will be internally focused. Crisis communication professionals will also create the content of the message that will be released, determine through what channels it will be released, and respond to any feedback that arises from that communication (Zaremba, 2010). While there are many subsets to crisis communication, two that are often used by those impacted are reputation management and image repair.

## Reputation Management

**Reputation management** is the practice of attempting to influence how the public evaluates an organization or individual (Fombrun, 1996; Smith, 2013). A company or person's reputation exists prior to any crisis. For example, most people already have an established opinion of Walmart. However, if a crisis event occurred that involved the company, that reputation could be made better or worse based on the events causing the crisis and Walmart's response to it.

In sports, NFL television viewership was considerably lower in 2016 when compared to previous seasons. Blame was placed on incidents that hurt the league's reputation, such as concussion issues and national anthem protests (Perloff, 2016). This demonstrates the importance of the crisis communication during an incident that affects a reputation. The NFL earns billions of dollars from television networks with the promise of high viewership. If the number of people watching the games begins to drop, the league may not be viewed as positively by the various media companies. Therefore, the league must do whatever it can to improve its reputation and regain those viewers who might have left.

## Image Repair Theory

**Image repair theory** (IRT) states that when a person's image is threatened, the person uses various strategies in order to repair it. IRT explains how people and organizations attempt to repair the public's opinion of that entity following a crisis. There are five categories in which image repair strategies fall:

- *Denial:* Denying that it occurred or shifting the blame to others
- *Evading responsibility:* Making excuses or suggesting the action was justified
- *Reducing offensiveness:* Attempting to reduce the negativity that is felt by the audience
- *Corrective action:* Attempting to correct the problem by either returning to the previous state or making changes to ensure it will not happen again
- *Mortification:* Admitting responsibility and asking for forgiveness (Benoit, 1995)

## History of Crisis Communication

There is not an accepted answer to the question "when did crisis communication begin?" In a book about the subject, authors noted that there are two incidents, despite being several decades apart, that are often cited as the beginnings of modern crisis management and communications. The first occurred in 1906 when a train fell off a bridge, causing the deaths of 53 people aboard. The railroad company released a statement about the incident to journalists, and it was printed in *The New York Times*. The second often-cited event occurred in 1982 when seven people were killed after taking Tylenol that contained cyanide. The company that manufactures Tylenol quickly responded by issuing warnings to hospitals and instituting a nationwide recall of all its products (Frandsen & Johansen, 2020). In both cases, the companies involved made public decisions to address the crisis and attempt to fix the damage that had been done.

## Crisis Communication in Sports

Crisis communication is not limited to the business world, as sports teams and athletes often find themselves having to explain situations that tarnish their image or put them in an awkward position. Examples include:

- Football player Richie Incognito was accused of bullying a teammate in 2013. In an effort to protect his image, Incognito used Twitter to attack his accusers and a television interview to shift the blame to others (Schmittel & Hull, 2015).

- In 2019, Houston Rockets general manager Daryl Morey tweeted support for Hong Kong, which upset leaders in China. For the NBA, this was a crisis, as the league has valuable business relationships with the Chinese government. The NBA commissioner issued a statement saying that Morey's words did not represent the league's opinion (NBAPR, 2019).

- In 2012, the NHL locked out its players following a labor disagreement, leading to a cancellation of more than a third of the season. The two sides had alternative ways of dealing with the crisis of games being canceled; the league remained silent, while the players kept fans regularly informed in an effort to gain support (Red Banyan, 2014).

The next five chapters of this book will discuss in depth cases that involve crisis communication in sports. Those chapters include Tiger Woods attempting to repair his image following a sex scandal (chapter 24), Lance Armstrong defending himself from doping allegations (chapter 25), LeBron James facing blowback after announcing his free agent decision (chapter 26), journalists atoning for mistakes in the coverage of the death of Kobe Bryant (chapter 27), and the Houston

Astros' response to cheating allegations (chapter 28). As a preview of how crisis communication is used in sports, a brief exploration into two situations will conclude this chapter: Ryan Lochte at the 2016 Olympics and racism charges at ESPN.

# Ryan Lochte at the 2016 Olympics

When naming some of the greatest swimmers in Olympic history, Ryan Lochte's name should be near the top of the list. Following the 2016 games, only Michael Phelps had won more overall medals than Lochte in the long history of Americans at the Games (Glock, 2017). His success in the pool might have only been matched by the fun he had out of it, as was chronicled in his short-lived reality television show, *What Would Ryan Lochte Do?* (Yahr, 2016). However, Lochte's partying persona was no laughing matter after a night out with teammates at the 2016 Olympics. Soon after, the swimmer found himself cast as the villain in a major international incident.

## Background of the Case

After completing his final race of the 2016 Olympics in Brazil, Lochte claimed that he and three of his teammates were out in Rio when they were robbed at gunpoint. In an interview relaying what happened, Lochte said, "The guy pulled out his gun, he cocked it, put it to

Ryan Lochte (left) and Michael Phelps (right) celebrate after winning gold medals in the Rio 2016 Olympics.

Donald Miralle / Sports Illustrated via Getty Images

my forehead and said get down" (Today, 2016, 2:46). However, within days, Lochte's harrowing tale proved to be fiction. A surveillance video instead showed the swimmers breaking into a locked bathroom at a gas station, with the owner later stating that the group vandalized his building (Wright, 2016). Days after the video went public, Lochte posted an apology on Instagram. He then appeared on both NBC and Brazil's TV Globo admitting he made the entire incident up, saying that the gun being held to his head "didn't happen" (NBC Sports Group, 2016, para. 9). Following the revelation of the truth, sponsors dropped him, he was suspended by USA Swimming, and it was estimated that Lochte cost himself at least $5 million in future income due to the damage to his image (Drehs, 2016; Perez, 2016; Rishe, 2016).

## Lochte's Crisis Communication

In order to help repair his image during the crisis, Lochte used both television interviews and social media to reach out to the public. In five television interviews, Lochte primarily used the strategy of *mortification*, in which one admits responsibility and asks for forgiveness (Hull & Boling, 2018). In an interview with TV Globo, Lochte said, "I'm embarrassed. I'm embarrassed for myself, for my family, and for my country" (Daily Mail, 2018, 4:07). Lochte left no room for interpretation or waffling, as he fully admitted that he had made the entire story up.

On social media, Lochte primarily used the strategy of **bolstering**, which is an aspect of reducing offensiveness and is defined as the process of attempting to remind the audience about the good the person has done in the past. On Twitter and Instagram, Lochte posted about his athletic accomplishments, family, charitable work, and behind-the-scenes life as a soon-to-be dad and also a contestant on the popular television show *Dancing with the Stars*. All these posts were designed to remind his followers about the good he had done previously or what he was doing to change moving forward (Hull & Boling, 2018).

Lochte's image repair strategies during his crisis were ultimately a success. While nearly all of his sponsors left him shortly after he admitted fabricating the story about the robbery, Lochte would eventually bounce back. He picked up several new endorsements in the months following, including several that played to the scandal's lasting impact. A company that manufactures cough drops hired Lochte to be the face of their "in the season of forgiveness" campaign, a reference to both the forgiving nature of the drops on a sore throat and Lochte's quest for forgiveness (Birkner, 2016; Johnson

& Saliba, 2016). Perhaps further proving the success of his crisis communication, an article appeared in *ESPN The Magazine* about a year later with the title, "Do you really still hate Ryan Lochte?" (Glock, 2017).

# Racism Charges at ESPN

As was discussed in chapter 15, there is a lack of racial diversity among sports journalists, with more than 80 percent in the industry being White (McCreary, 2018). However, the Institute for Diversity and Ethics in Sports reported in 2018 that one of the few media organizations with a good history in diversity was ESPN. The network was cited as being an industry leader in the hiring of minority editors, writers, and columnists for ESPN.com (Lapchick, 2018). However, some behind-the-scenes employees at ESPN television claimed that racism was still prevalent. In an article in *The New York Times*, more than two dozen current and former ESPN employees said the company "did not provide meaningful career paths for Black employees" (Draper, 2020, para. 12). While those issues simmered with the behind-the-scenes workers, it was an incident involving one of the most prominent on-air personalities at the network that created a crisis situation at the network.

## Background of the Case

In 2020, ESPN announced that Maria Taylor would be the host of the network's coverage of the NBA Finals. Fellow ESPN reporter Rachel Nichols, who is White, complained to a friend in a phone call that Taylor only got the job because she is Black. In that call, Nichols said:

> If you need to give her [Taylor] more things to do because you are feeling pressure about your crappy longtime record on diversity—which, by the way, I know personally from the female side of it—like, go for it. Just find it somewhere else. (Draper, 2021, para. 5)

What Nichols did not know was that the camera on her laptop was active and her phone conversation was being recorded on a video server back at ESPN. Someone at the network watched the recording, made a copy of it on a cellphone, and then shared it with others. While the incident was apparently handled internally for nearly a year, it became a national story when *The New York Times* published all the details in a tell-all piece in 2021 (Draper, 2021). Suddenly, both Nichols and ESPN were in the spotlight for the race-based comments and the network's response.

## Crisis Communication of Those Involved

The day after the article was published in *The New York Times*, Nichols began the basketball show she hosted by reading a prepared statement:

> *The first thing they teach you in journalism school is, "Don't be the story." And I don't plan to break that rule today or distract from a fantastic Finals. But I also don't want to let this moment pass without saying how much I respect, how much I value our colleagues here at ESPN. How deeply, deeply sorry I am for disappointing those I hurt, particularly Maria Taylor. And how grateful I am to be a part of this outstanding team. (Mangan, 2021)*

Nichols's statement falls under the concept of mortification within image restoration theory, as it is a straightforward apology. She did not deny anything, did not pass the blame onto anyone else, and did not attempt to minimize the impact of what she said.

ESPN elected not to issue any public statements about the article, but instead used the strategy of corrective actions in an effort to repair the network's image. ESPN elected to remove Nichols as the sideline reporter for the championship series, announcing in a statement: "We believe this is the best decision for all concerned in order to keep the focus on the NBA Finals" (The Athletic Staff, 2021, para. 2). The corrective action taken by the network was simply to remove Nichols from the situation. She was able to remain the host of her daily NBA show *The Jump*, but Taylor hosted the NBA Finals, appearing on the pregame and halftime shows during the series.

While the reassignment of Nichols provided a short-term corrective action, there were still bigger changes to come. The day after the NBA Finals ended, ESPN announced that Taylor was leaving the network after the two sides could not agree on a contract extension (ESPN Press Room, 2021). She would not be the only one to depart, as, despite having a year left on her contract, Nichols would not appear on the channel again after ESPN canceled her show *The Jump* (Ourand, 2021). The network's response to the crisis, once it could not agree to a contract with Taylor, revealed that the best course of action was perhaps to start from scratch and erase any lingering memories of the conflict (Hull & Walker, 2023). An entirely different NBA pregame and halftime broadcast team was selected, and Nichols' old show, *The Jump*, was replaced with a new basketball-centric program in the same time slot (Marchand, 2021). As for Nichols herself, her image repair strategies appeared to be successful, as she was not out of work long, signing a deal with Showtime Sports to be a part of the basketball coverage at that network shortly after her ESPN contract expired (Draper, 2022).

# Summary

A crisis can be damaging to an organization or individuals within that group. In order to mitigate the effects of that crisis, organizations communicate details to the audience, a process known as crisis communication. These efforts are designed to improve the affected party's reputation in the public's eye. In the world of sports, crises often occur outside of the action in the games, such as players making errors in judgment in their personal lives or something happening that negatively affects an organization. Ryan Lochte lied about being robbed and had to find a way to repair his image after losing lucrative endorsement contracts. ESPN faced a crisis when recorded comments of one of its employees created a question about race representation at the network. Ultimately, these incidents, and others like them, demonstrate the need for crisis communication when a company or individual is going through a situation that can potentially damage a reputation or image.

## KEY TERMS

**bolstering**—An aspect of reducing offensiveness that is defined as the process of attempting to remind the audience about the good the person has done in the past.

**crisis communication**—During a crisis situation, the individual or organization being affected will often want to communicate with various members of the public in an attempt to reduce the effects of the crisis.

**image repair theory**—Explains how people and organizations attempt to repair the public's opinion of that entity following a crisis.

**mortification**—In terms of crisis communication, mortification is admitting responsibility and asking for forgiveness.

**reputation management**—The practice of attempting to influence how the public evaluates an organization or individual.

## REVIEW QUESTIONS

1. Why is crisis communication an important part of a reaction to a crisis event?
2. What are the five categories of image repair theory?
3. How did Ryan Lochte's crisis communication help repair his image after the 2016 Olympics?
4. Crises happen in sports, but they rarely involve the games themselves. Why might this be?

*CASE STUDY*

# Tiger Woods

## CHAPTER OBJECTIVES

After completing the chapter, the reader should be able to do the following:

- Analyze the early career path of Tiger Woods
- Identify why Woods had a strained relationship with the media
- Recognize how Woods attempted to "control the narrative" throughout his career
- Debate how companies involved in athlete sponsorship should react if their athlete is involved in a scandal
- Identify the impact the Internet had on Woods' career

In 2019, as Tiger Woods was lining up the tournament-winning putt on the 18th hole to win The Masters, CBS golf announcer Jim Nantz said, "Many doubted we'd ever see it . . ." Woods then rolled in the short putt and Nantz concluded his thought with: ". . . the return to glory" (The Masters, 2019, :00). The crowd roared in the background as the cameras followed the champion off the green and into the arms of his young son, with the two celebrating together in their matching red shirts—a Woods final-round staple throughout his career.

However, to say that the newly crowned champion had a "return to glory" might actually be too simplistic of a description of what had just happened. Decades earlier, Woods was on track to become the greatest golfer of all time, but a scandal in his personal life suddenly put the popular golfer in an unflattering light. His career was marred by off-the-course struggles both of his own doing

and from injuries that were out of his control. Woods' career was a roller coaster of very high highs and very low lows, and it all started at a very young age.

## Early Life and Amateur Career

Eldrick Woods was born in 1975, but was soon better known by the name Tiger, a nickname given to him in honor of one of his father's friends. His father claimed that at just six months old, Tiger was hitting golf balls and was well on his way to a historic golf career (de Jonge, 1995). At just three years old, Woods participated in a putting contest on *The Mike Douglas Show* against Bob Hope, one of the most recognizable celebrities of the time (Dethier, 2020). Soon after, he was winning world titles at age 8 and became a three-time winner of both the United States Junior Amateur Championship and the United States Amateur Championship. Along the way, Woods accepted a scholarship to Stanford University, where he, perhaps not surprisingly, won the NCAA individual golf championship (Dostaler, 2019).

# Woods Turns Professional

After two years of college, Woods had accomplished almost everything possible as an amateur, so he announced he was leaving Stanford to turn professional and join the PGA Tour. One could safely assume that the potential money that could be made was a factor in his decision, as the talented golfer could not accept any prize money if he wanted to keep his amateur status. Instead, Woods was about to cash in on his seemingly endless potential. Before taking his first shot as a professional, Woods signed a five-year, $40 million endorsement deal with Nike and an agreement estimated to be around $1 million a year for three years with Titleist (The New York Times, 1996).

## "I am Tiger Woods"

With a $40 million investment, Nike wasted little time in promoting the newest centerpiece of their golf apparel line. Just days after signing the deal, a television commercial titled "Hello, world" debuted, listing Woods' impressive list of accomplishments on the screen over video of him throughout the years (Wertheim, 2003).

While his talent on the course was obvious, and perhaps did not need an introduction, Nike was also focusing on Woods' unique background. Since nearly the beginning of the sport, the majority of golfers have been White, but Woods would later describe himself as "Cablinasian," his own term to describe his mixed heritage of Caucasian, Black, Indian, and Asian (Associated Press, 1997b). To address that, Nike created a second ad campaign in which boys and girls from diverse backgrounds were shown playing golf and saying, "I am Tiger Woods" (Wertheim, 2003). The implication was that the makeup of golf was about to change, and that Woods was going to make it accessible for everyone, not just the traditional White male player. A member of Nike's golf division said about Woods at the time, "He's going to bring minorities to the game and youth to the game," noting that African Americans comprised just 3.6 percent of golfers at the time of Woods' debut (Glassman, 1996, para. 25).

# Immediate Success

Within two months of his professional debut, Woods proved that he was worth the early hype by winning his first tournament. Two weeks later, amazingly, he won again. In just three months on the PGA Tour, Woods was named the organization's Rookie of the Year, while *Sports Illustrated* (*SI*) honored him with its "Sportsman of the Year" award. In the accompanying *SI* article, the author wondered if Woods would be able to live up to his promise and survive the rigors of being a highly sought-after athlete, or if the media and public's needs would ultimately claim another victim (Smith, 1996).

# The *GQ* Interview

Between the Nike hype and Woods quickly backing it up with his play on the course, the rookie had almost instantly become one of the most in-demand athletes in all of sports. When *GQ*, a monthly men's magazine, landed an exclusive all-access interview with Woods, it was recognized as one of the first behind-the-scenes profiles of the future star. However, what fans got in the piece was unexpected. Instead of the buttoned-up, straitlaced player who was seen on the course, Woods demonstrated a more juvenile side. The piece recounted how Woods told off-color and offensive jokes and used racist language (Pierce, 1997).

The response to the piece was one of shock and disappointment. Some called for Woods to apologize for the jokes he told in the article. Instead of being the future of golf who could do no wrong, Woods was suddenly facing criticism that he had not seen before (Anderson, 1997a). He went on the defensive, blaming the author for the depiction:

> It's no secret that I'm 21 years old and that I'm naïve about the motives of certain ambitious writers. The article proves that, and I don't see any reason for anyone to pay $3 to find that out." (Associated Press, 1997a, para. 5)

While the article could have been just a small speed bump in the long career of Woods that was about to come, it ultimately had very long-term implications. That *GQ* interview is cited as the end of Woods' relationship with the media (Bissinger, 2010). He, and perhaps his advisers, felt burned by the piece and the associated blowback, and made a concerted effort to no longer grant interviews with media members that would be about topics beyond his play on the course. Knowing that he was always going to be the center of attention, Woods retreated from the spotlight if the focus was not about his career. Instead, his interviews and press availabilities became generic "golf talk" that gave little insight into the man. One writer said:

> Tiger learned very well to talk forever and say nothing... An emotional response to a flawless round was "I had a pretty good day." He never got rude or rattled. He never got irritated with a stupid question, in large part because he knew the camera was always on him. (Bissinger, 2010, para. 17)

More than 25 years later, that interview with *GQ* was still seen as perhaps the only honest and open conversation he ever had with a journalist.

## An Immediate Rise to Stardom

While Woods' relationship with the media changed following that article, it did not seem to have any impact on his athletic career. Less than a year after his debut, Woods won The Masters, which is widely regarded as the most prestigious golf tournament in the world. Not only did he win the championship, but he did so by 12 shots, which is an unheard-of amount in most golf tournaments, let alone in what is considered one of the more challenging courses on the tour (Anderson 1997b). By

June of 1997, Woods was ranked no. 1 in the world, and in 2001, he completed the "Tiger Slam," the name given to his accomplishment of being the champion of all four major golf tournaments at the same time (Scheibe, 2020; Smits, 2011).

Woods was at the top of the tour's leaderboard and also at the top of the "most popular" list among golf fans. That fact could clearly be seen in television viewership in what would be known as "The Tiger Effect." The former president of CBS Sports, a network that broadcast many PGA events, once estimated that when Woods was playing in a tournament, the viewership ratings would be 30 to 35 percent higher than events in which he did not play (Golden, 2014).

## Personal Life

While his play on the course was seemingly without peer, winning eight major championships before his 27th birthday, Woods' personal life was coming into shape as well (Infoplease, 2022). In October 2004, Woods married Elin Nordegren at a ceremony in Barbados (Harrison, 2004). The pair would have two children, a daughter born in 2007 and a son born in 2009 (Associated Press, 2009). For Woods, his life appeared to be at its apex, with a successful career on the course and a stable family situation at home. However, that fairy tale story was about to change dramatically.

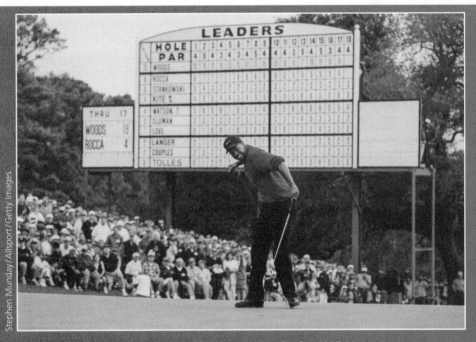

Stephen Munday / Allsport / Getty Images

**Tiger Woods celebrates after sinking a putt to win the 1997 Masters.**

## Off-Course Trouble Begins

Tiger Woods was seemingly unbeatable on the course, and what were once curious whispers soon became an open discussion that he could be on his way to becoming perhaps the greatest golfer of all time. Jack Nicklaus had won the most major golf tournaments in history with 18, and Woods was on a pace to not only break that record but shatter it (Gaines, 2013). While Woods was focused on the course, it was a story about his personal life that was about to derail the champion.

## *National Enquirer* Story

On November 25, 2009, the *National Enquirer* published a story that stated Tiger Woods was having an affair with a New York City nightclub hostess. The newspaper had tracked the woman in question to a hotel in Australia, the same hotel that Woods was staying at as he was playing in a tournament. When confronted, she denied the affair, but the newspaper printed the story anyway, believing that she was being less than truthful (Melchior, 2009).

While the story was on the front page of the magazine, it did not gain much attention beyond that. That is likely because of who produced the content. The *National Enquirer* is considered a **tabloid** in the world of journalism, meaning that they tend to produce content that tends more toward the sensational. In addition, the magazine's reputation was already low even when compared to other tabloid outlets, due to its lack of basic editing and reporting standards (Farhi, 2010). Therefore, the story went largely unnoticed by the public.

## Thanksgiving Night in 2009

Two days after the *Enquirer* story, on Thanksgiving night, Woods' life and career would change forever. At around 2:30 in the morning, Woods crashed his SUV into a fire hydrant and tree outside of his house in Florida. This did make major headlines, with several media outlets providing the details of the accident, including how his wife, Elin, used a golf club to smash the back window of the vehicle to help him escape the wreckage (ESPN.com, 2009a).

However, as more details were revealed in the immediate aftermath, some began to question the story. TMZ, another tabloid news outlet, reported that Elin had confronted Woods about the alleged affair on the night of the accident. The two had argued and Woods was trying to leave the house when Elin chased him outside.

It was then, TMZ reported, that Elin broke out the back window of the SUV with the golf club, causing Woods to become distracted and crash the vehicle (TMZ, 2009). Two days after the crash, Woods issued a statement about the accident on his website TigerWoods.com. He wrote that he had some cuts, bruises, and was "pretty sore." In addition, and perhaps surprisingly, Woods also indirectly addressed the *National Enquirer* article and the rumors that were starting to emerge. He wrote: "Although I understand there is curiosity, the many false, unfounded and malicious rumors that are currently circulating about my family and me are irresponsible" (Woods, 2009a, para. 3).

## *US Weekly*

Those rumors did not slow down, and the interest in Woods' personal life was about to hit a fever pitch. *US Weekly* published their own front-page article with "YES, HE CHEATED" in large, bold yellow letters on the cover. The magazine included an interview with a different woman who claimed to be Woods' mistress, and she told all the salacious details of their relationship (US Weekly, 2009).

While *US Weekly* is also a tabloid publication, often reporting on the personal lives of celebrities, the growing public interest meant that this article received much more attention than the one that was published days earlier in the *National Enquirer*. Even ESPN referenced it on its website, providing the details of what was in the piece (ESPN.com, 2009b). While the *National Enquirer*, TMZ, and *US Weekly* may not have been considered reputable news sources by some, their stories were starting to become a key part of the reporting of the developing scandal.

## Controlling the Narrative

Dating back to the aftermath of his interview with *GQ* more than a decade earlier, Woods had held the media at a distance. However, at this time, his personal life was of more interest than his golfing career, and journalists, if given the opportunity, would likely ask Woods questions that he probably would not want to answer. Therefore, instead of granting interviews to the media, Woods elected to control the narrative himself, and only addressed topics that he wanted discussed. As will be summarized later in this chapter, Woods was one of the first athletes to recognize how he could use the Internet to his advantage.

## Website Statements

The day after the *US Weekly* article was published, another statement appeared on TigerWoods.com. In the piece, which contained a "by Tiger Woods" byline, the first direct acknowledgment of the articles, and the truth that was likely in them, was addressed. He wrote: "I have let my family down and I regret those transgressions with all my heart" (Woods, 2009b, para. 1). However, in addition to his admission and an apology, Woods also turned the tables on the media, seemingly blaming them for how the events in the last few weeks had transpired and the impact their articles were having on his family:

> Although I am a well-known person and have made my career as a professional athlete, I have been dismayed to realize the full extent of what tabloid scrutiny really means. For the last week, my family and I have been hounded to expose intimate details of our personal lives. The stories in particular that physical violence played any role in the car accident were utterly false and malicious. Elin has always done more to support our family and shown more grace than anyone could possibly expect. But no matter how intense curiosity about public figures can be, there is an important and deep principle at stake which is the right to some simple, human measure of privacy. (Woods, 2009b, para. 2, 3)

One week later, in another first-person, "by Tiger Woods" piece on his website, Woods announced that he was taking a hiatus from golf to work on his family issues. In addition, he acknowledged how he was "deeply aware of the disappointment and hurt my infidelity has caused to so many people, most of all my wife and children." This was a telling sentence, as it was the first time he had used the word *infidelity*, which gave truth to the rumors that had been surrounding his personal life (Woods, 2009b, para. 1).

Woods had used his website to reveal exactly what he wanted to say to his fans. He could include certain details while excluding others. By not facing questions from the media, Woods did not have to answer unwanted questions. This plan allowed him to partially control the narrative surrounding these early stories.

## More Stories Emerge

Woods might not have been granting interviews with journalists, but that was not stopping them from reporting on his story. As the details were emerging, the *New York Post*, another tabloid journalism outlet, put Woods on its cover 20 days in a row (Ashford, 2009). The *National Enquirer* reported having the first photos of the golfer since the accident and published grainy images of Woods walking outside of an addiction facility. The magazine would accompany those photos with a report that Woods was there to treat a sex addiction (Post Staff Report, 2010). Since Woods was not speaking directly with the media, and he remained one of the most talked-about athletes due to his personal life, these outlets had to do reporting on their own about the latest in his life.

## "Press Conference"

By mid-February of 2010, Woods had released several written statements on his website, but had not spoken publicly about what had transpired in the previous few months. Therefore, it was major news when it was announced that he would make a public statement on February 19 in which he would address the events in his life. Many in the media hoped that this would be an opportunity to set the record straight about what had happened, what was happening now, and where Woods would go from here.

However, this was not the typical press conference. In fact, it was not really a press conference at all. The people in attendance were mostly friends and family, the few journalists allowed in the room were not allowed to ask a question, and Woods read a statement for nearly 15 minutes before departing. In the statement he apologized, acknowledged his infidelity, admitted he had begun counseling, and said he planned to return to golf at some point in the near future (Araton, 2010).

With no questions allowed, Woods was able to script every aspect of his first statement in months. He and his public relations team decided who could attend, what would be said, and how long it would last. However, the response to this session was anything but positive. While three media members were allowed inside, another 300 were in the building but banished to separate rooms to watch it on television. The Golf Writers Association of America called it a "staged event" and passed on the offer to let three more writers attend in person (Araton, 2010). Other reactions to the speech were that his words were insincere, he was unnecessarily overly critical of the media, he came across as awkward, and that he did not say enough (Hudson, 2010).

Tiger Woods reads a statement in a February 2010 press conference.

## Dueling Interviews

Less than a month later, Woods was ready to return to the golf course and play his first competitive rounds in months. That return would happen at The Masters, meaning that not only was he back, but he was going to play at the biggest tournament and the site of some of his most memorable wins. Knowing that he would likely not be able to avoid the media's questions once he arrived at the tournament, Woods agreed to do two separate interviews before the event began. He granted ESPN and The Golf Channel five minutes each to ask him questions in a one-on-one setting, with seemingly nothing out of bounds. In the ESPN version, reporter Tom Rinaldi asked Woods about some of the more challenging moments during his time away from the game:

> **Rinaldi:** *In the last four months, Tiger, what's been the low point?*
> **Woods:** *I've had a lot of low points. Just when I didn't think it could get any lower, it got lower.*
> **Rinaldi:** *An example?*
> **Woods:** *When I was in treatment, out of treatment, before I went in, there were so many different low points. People I had to talk and face like my wife, like my mom.*
> **Rinaldi:** *What was that moment like, either one?*

> **Woods:** *They both have been brutal. They've both been very tough. Because I hurt them the most. Those are the two people in my life who I'm closest to and to say the things that I've done, truthfully to them, is . . . honestly . . . was . . . very painful. (ESPN .com, 2010, para. 32-37)*

While Woods may not have been able to control the questions being asked, he did decide who could get the time with him. It is certainly not a coincidence that the tabloid journalism outlets who first reported many of the details of his infidelity were not invited to be a part of the interview sessions. Instead, two sports-related media companies were given the exclusive access, perhaps with the hope that they would only briefly ask about the adultery and instead focus more on his golfing comeback.

## Sponsor Debate

Woods' fall from grace had implications beyond just his own personal life and playing career. At the time of the Thanksgiving night crash, Woods was one of the highest paid athletes based on endorsements (Shambora, 2009). However, those companies now had to decide if they wanted to move forward with an admitted adulterer as one of their spokespersons. The decision as to what to do with Woods was not universal. Accenture, AT&T, Gatorade, and Gillette all dropped their endorsement deals with the golfer within a month of the scandal being made public (Skidmore, 2010). Conversely, Electronic Arts, the makers of the wildly popular *Tiger Woods PGA Tour* video game series, elected to continue their arrangement with Woods, partially because they had the next version of the game nearly ready to release to the public (Robertson, 2010). While those companies all had deals with Woods, none was bigger than his endorsement contract with Nike. At the time, it was believed that the two had extended their initial agreement twice more, most likely with a deal worth between $20 million and $40 million a year (Harig, 2013). At least publicly, Nike never wavered in their support of Woods, and remained committed to the endorsement deal the two had signed a few years earlier (Augusta Chronicle, 2010).

## Return to the Course

Woods' 2010 return to The Masters might have looked different as far as fewer sponsors advertising on his golf bag, but his play on the course looked remarkably similar. Despite turning his life upside down in the previous months due to his off-course actions, he ended up finishing in fourth place in a field filled with the world's best (Rhoden, 2010). By March 2013, Woods game was seemingly back to where it was years earlier, and after winning a tournament in Orlando, Woods had once again become the top-ranked player in the world (Associated Press, 2013a).

Nike, which had stuck by Woods' side during the scandal, marked his return to the top spot with a print ad that proclaimed, "Winning takes care of everything." While Nike was looking to celebrate Woods' accomplishment, the advertisement seemed inappropriate to some. The implication that winning could make fans forget the adultery and mistakes that Woods had made was not received positively. Critics said the ad sent the wrong message, but also admitted, "the reality is what he said is true" (Associated Press, 2013b, para. 14; Boren, 2013).

Around that same time, Woods, who had divorced Elin in 2010, announced that he was in a romantic relationship with Olympic skier Lindsey Vonn (Zinser, 2010). Further demonstrating Woods' desire to release information to the public on his terms, the two jointly announced they were dating on their respective Facebook pages (BBC, 2013). The relationship's end was also revealed on Facebook, with the two each announcing

in 2015 that they had mutually agreed to end their partnership (Chiari, 2015).

## 2017-2021 Roller Coaster

While the scandals involving his extramarital affairs might have become a thing of the past as Woods' career continued to move forward, his life became anything but stable. The primary focus of his career had become his battles with injury. Starting in 2013, Woods began suffering from severe back pain, an ailment that is not uncommon for golfers because of their swings. Once in 2014 and twice in 2015, Woods underwent back surgery. That was followed in 2017 by a more significant lower back fusion surgery (Hall, 2022).

## 2017 Arrest

On Memorial Day of 2017, Woods was arrested for driving under the influence (DUI) near his home in Florida. He was found unconscious parked on the side of the road and would later plead guilty to the charges. Woods, perhaps not surprisingly, released a statement instead of granting interviews, and said that he took full responsibility for the arrest and that the situation was caused by a reaction to medicine (Associated Press, 2017).

Between his injuries and the arrest, some journalists began to wonder if fans would ever see the "Old Tiger" ever again, or if the rest of his playing time would be a sad conclusion to his once outstanding career. However, when reflecting on the previous decade and all that Woods had put himself through with personal issues and injury, *The New York Times* framed the question differently: "Tiger Woods's return would be good for golf. But what about for him?" (Crouse, 2017).

## 2018-2019 Golf Success

Those who counted out Woods were proven wrong a year later, when he took first place at the Tour Championship event, his first victory in five years (Porter, 2018). As Woods marched to his first victory in more than five years, fans were glued to their televisions watching every stroke. Viewership ratings for the tournament were up 206 percent from the previous year when Woods did not participate, demonstrating that "The Tiger Effect" was still alive and well in televised golf (Berhow, 2018).

Woods followed that victory up with a win at the 2019 Masters, the first time he had won the event since 2005 (Crouse, 2019). It was not just Woods benefiting from his return to glory. During his Masters win, he had used the Bridgestone Tour B XS golf ball as part of a new endorsement deal. In the aftermath of his victory, Bridgestone saw a 209 percent increase in engagement on Twitter, a 400 percent increase on Facebook, and a more than 200 percent increase in website traffic. In addition, and perhaps most importantly to Bridgestone, there was a tremendous increase in sales of that ball in the ensuing months. Similar sales increases were seen from the companies that made Woods' clubs (Taylor Made), the shirt he wore during the final round (Nike), and that sold tickets for the next tournament in which he was scheduled to play (VanHaaren, 2018).

## 2021 Car Accident

In February 2021, Woods was involved in a single-car accident in California when he was speeding, lost control of his vehicle, and went off the road (Draper, 2021). His Twitter account, @TigerWoods, released a statement that was not from Woods, but instead from the chief medical officer of the hospital that treated Woods. In the quote, the doctor explained that a procedure was completed on Woods' right leg. The statement then concluded with unsourced information that he was awake and recovering (Woods, 2021a).

In the following months, Woods demonstrated that perhaps his old habits were hard to break, as he released his own updates on his condition through his social media accounts. A picture on his Instagram page showed Woods in a walking boot and on crutches in April, while the first video of him swinging a golf club since the accident was posted to his Twitter account in November with the words "Making progress" as the accompanying text (Woods, 2021b, 2021c).

## Tiger Woods: Internet Superstar

Woods' career first hit the world stage in the mid- to late 1990s, and the timing of his rise coincides almost perfectly with the era when the Internet was starting to become more accessible to all. Therefore, one could argue that Woods was perhaps the first sports superstar of the Internet era. Due to that timing, he is also one of the most widely talked-about athletes in history. He has been at the top of the end-of-the-year "most searched" lists on Internet search engines multiple times, demon-strating that fans were constantly looking for the latest information on his career and life (Cradock, 2021; Gaines, 2011).

His rise during the growth of the Internet also gave him the ability to connect with the audience in a different manner from those who had come before him. As will be discussed in chapter 30, athletes have realized that they can use the Internet to speak directly to fans without needing to conduct an interview with journalists who then relay the quotes to the public. While this is common practice now, Woods is perhaps the first athlete to figure out, and take advantage of, the Internet's ability to exclude the traditional media from story dissemination. When the extramarital affairs became public, Woods made statements on his website. Those were later replaced with social media posts that would show up directly on his followers' feeds. Woods not only became an Internet superstar, but also someone who was one of the first to use the various platforms to deliver his own message.

## Summary

As of this writing, it appears as if Tiger Woods will fall short of passing Jack Nicklaus' record 18 major tournament wins. However, he might still end up as the most memorable golfer of all time. Starting from his historic Nike ad campaigns that welcomed him to the tour and focused on how he would open golf up to all races and genders, Woods began a meteoric rise to the top of his sport. However, off-course personal issues would put him in the spotlight for an entirely different reason.

As the world wondered about Woods' personal life, he turned to the Internet to keep the public informed about his latest developments. Woods avoided journalists' questions by releasing statements on his website and conducting a "press conference" before agreeing to two interviews with carefully selected media outlets. It was a trend that would continue throughout his career, even as his athletic and personal lives went through more ups and downs. Ultimately, while Woods will be remembered as an outstanding golfer, his ability and desire to "control the narrative" surrounding his career and life is one that has had a lasting impact on all of sport. Athletes now routinely follow Woods' playbook and release information themselves instead of relying on journalists to do it for them.

## KEY TERM

**tabloid**—A journalism outlet that produces content that tends more toward the sensational.

## REVIEW QUESTIONS

1. In addition to his golfing prowess, what made Tiger Woods an appealing athlete for Nike to partner with in a record endorsement deal?

2. Why was the first article about Woods' extramarital affairs in the *National Enquirer* not taken seriously?

3. Why might Woods have released several statements on his website instead of speaking directly to the media in the early days of his scandal?

4. How did the Internet contribute to the star power of Tiger Woods?

# Lance Armstrong

## CHAPTER OBJECTIVES

After completing the chapter, the reader should be able to do the following:

- Understand what made Lance Armstrong a hero to many
- Evaluate how sponsors must determine when to stick with an athlete and when to move on
- Examine the media's role in a story when the story may be "too good to be true"
- Determine if Armstrong's image repair strategies were successful

The question "Who is Lance Armstrong?" is one that has many answers. One could label him a survivor, a champion, a philanthropist, a liar, or a cheater—and despite those very different descriptors, all would be correct. For the purposes of this chapter, the label of "media sensation" might be the most appropriate. Being one of the biggest sports stars in the United States was a result of the media's infatuation with his story, but that story may have kept them from digging deeper into cheating allegations against Armstrong. This raises questions about the **impartiality** of journalists and how Armstrong, who once used the media to advance his legacy, is attempting to use it to repair his tarnished image.

## Armstrong's Rise to Fame

Armstrong's rise from a relatively unknown athlete to one of the biggest stars in the world is certainly unpredictable. However, his was a story that inspired many Americans. It was ultimately a tale of overcoming disease, getting fired from a job, and then rising up to become the most successful person in his profession. It was a story that even a Hollywood producer might consider too over the top if it were pitched to a movie studio, but it was true—and many Americans could not get enough of it.

## Early Racing Career

Armstrong's sporting youth was spent running, swimming, and cycling, so it should not be a surprise that his first professional athletic accomplishments came in the triathlon, a sport that combines those three disciplines. Before he had even turned 20 years old, Armstrong was a two-time national champion in the sprint triathlon (Sortal, 1989). However, his focus would turn solely to cycling and soon after he was winning international competitions and ranked in the top ten in the world (Glier, 1996).

## Cancer Diagnosis

However, in October of 1996, at just 25 years old, Armstrong was diagnosed with testicular cancer. The cancer had spread to his brain, his lungs, and his abdomen, and the outlook was not promising. His doctor at the time stated that he believed not only was Armstrong's racing career over, but that the cyclist had almost no hope of living. However, after surgeries to remove tumors, 12 weeks of chemotherapy, and a mixture of cancer-fighting drugs, Armstrong, less than one year after the initial diagnosis, was declared cancer-free (Keown, 2012).

## Return to Racing

While Armstrong never doubted that he would return to the bike and competitive racing, others were not as sure. His racing team certainly had no expectations, and they fired Armstrong shortly after he was released from treatment (Associated Press, 1997). Looking for a new sponsor, the American lined up a less lucrative deal to be a part of the United States Postal Service team (Ellison, 1999).

It did not take long for Armstrong to show that he was still someone to watch out for on the cycling circuit. In 1998, he won the Tour of Luxembourg, his first international competition in the two years since his initial cancer diagnosis. After several more impressive finishes, the major victory was right around the corner. In 1999, Armstrong won the Tour de France, widely considered the biggest and most prestigious bicycle race in the world (Cohen, 2020). While winning the race is remarkable, doing so after being diagnosed with cancer, and being just the second American ever to win, made it even more amazing. However, that 1999 victory was just the beginning.

## The Best Ever*

Before Armstrong, five riders had tied for the most wins ever with five Tour de France victories, and only one of those had won it five years in a row. Those records were about to be crushed. After winning the race in 1999, Armstrong proceeded to win the next six in a row, making him the first ever seven-time winner of the Tour de France (Cohen, 2020). However, as the asterisk in the heading of this section indicates, these impressive wins were about to come under heavy scrutiny. Before the day of reckoning came, Armstrong was about to become bigger than just a sports star.

## An American Hero

It is not an exaggeration to state that during the time of his Tour de France wins, Armstrong was considered by many to be an American hero. He was the best at his sport, representing his country, and helping to raise millions of dollars for charity. Even his sponsor, the United States Postal Service, was about as American as any athlete sponsor could be. One could certainly point to the media attention he was receiving as a key factor in his public image. His story was a true rags-to-riches tale, and journalists helped Armstrong cultivate that story with the constant attention that he was getting.

## Award-Winning Cyclist

Armstrong's ever-expanding trophy case did not stop with just the Tour de France victories. Numerous media outlets and athletic organizations awarded the cyclist with their top honors. These include

- Associated Press (AP) Male Athlete of the Year
- United States Olympic Committee SportsMan of the Year
- *Sports Illustrated* Sportsman of the Year
- ESPN's ESPY Award for Best Male Athlete
- Vélo d'Or: Awarded to the best bicycle racer of the year by *Vélo* magazine

At the time, one would be hard-pressed to find anyone who would have argued with giving him those awards. In fact, Armstrong even won some of them several times, including AP Male Athlete of the Year four years in a row (2002-2005) and the Vélo d'Or a record five times (1999, 2000, 2001, 2003, 2004).

## Philanthropist

While there was no debating that Armstrong was one of the best athletes in the world, many would argue that his work off the bike was just as impressive. Following his cancer diagnosis, Armstrong established the Lance Armstrong Foundation. The organization focused on cancer survivorship, using the term "Livestrong" as a way to motivate those with cancer to continue fighting the disease. Perhaps most prominently, in 2004 the organization began selling yellow silicone gel bracelets with the word *LIVESTRONG* engraved on them as a way for people to show support for those with cancer. The wristbands became a must-have fashion accessory and a

Lance Armstrong celebrates as he wins stage 17 of the Tour de France in 2004.

symbol of strength for those affected by the disease. An incredible 80 million of the bracelets were sold, and the foundation raised over $500 million for cancer research and services (English, 2012). It was Armstrong who was front and center of those fund-raising efforts, acting as the face of the organization while also donating $6.5 million of his own money to the cause (Pearson, 2012).

## Media Sensation

As is commonly the case, as Armstrong's popularity grew among the public, many different organizations were trying to latch onto his rising star. He wrote two books that appeared on *The New York Times* bestseller list, hosted the NBC comedy show *Saturday Night Live*, and hosted ESPN's ESPY Awards telecast in 2006. Magazines from *Sports Illustrated* to *Men's Health* to *Esquire* all put him on the cover with the hope that his star power would help sell more issues. Media companies were hoping that fans who loved Armstrong—and there were a lot of them—would watch, read, or buy anything to which he was attached.

Armstrong was in heavy demand from companies as a product endorser as well. He had deals with various racing-related companies, including bike manufacturer Trek and sunglasses maker Oakley. Anheuser-Busch paid Armstrong to be a spokesman for its Michelob Ultra low-calorie beer, and his biggest and most lucrative partner-

ship was with Nike. The athletic apparel company made products that centered on both the racer himself and his Livestrong brand. There were Livestrong shirts and shoes for sale on the Nike website and in stores, and estimates are that the company paid Armstrong about $40 million throughout the approximately 16 years they had a deal. The partnership was so strong that the employee gym at Nike's Oregon headquarters was named the Lance Armstrong Fitness Center (Rovell, 2012).

## Cheating Allegations

While Armstrong was running away with Tour de France wins, there were some in the sport who began implying that he was not winning legally. A 2004 French-language book, *L.A. Confidential: Lance Armstrong's Secrets*, was one of the first publications to explicitly state that Armstrong's wins were not legitimate. The authors, Pierre Ballester and David Walsh, gathered evidence from a former masseuse for Armstrong's riding team who stated that part of her job was disposing of syringes and giving Armstrong makeup to conceal needle marks on his arms (Ballester & Walsh, 2004).

Around the time of the book's publication, a French newspaper reported that several of Armstrong's urine samples from his 1999 victory had later tested positive for the blood booster EPO (Macur, 2012). EPO, the abbreviation for erythropoietin, is a hormone that stimulates red blood cell production. If a lab-produced EPO hormone is injected, the extra blood cells should lead to an increased blood oxygen capacity, which allows athletes to work harder and longer before they become exhausted (Honan, 2011). This, if used in an endurance event such as the Tour de France, would give the injected rider an unfair advantage over his competition.

## Armstrong's Denials

Amid the accusations of drug use and doping, Armstrong maintained his innocence. Following the publication of *L.A. Confidential*, Armstrong sued one of the authors and the publishers of the book for **libel**, which is the publication of a knowingly false statement in order to damage someone's reputation (ESPN.com news services, 2004). When he was not battling his opponents in the courtroom, he was repeating explicit denials to the media. Some of his most forceful comments were later collected for an article in *The Guardian* (McMillan, 2013):

- *July 1999:* "I can emphatically say I am not on drugs."
- *December 2000:* "We are completely innocent."
- *January 2004:* "I do not take performance-enhancing drugs."
- *August 2005:* "I have never doped. I can say it again, but I've said it for seven years."
- *November 2005:* "How many times do I have to say it? . . . Well, it can't be any clearer than 'I've never taken drugs.'"
- *July 2010:* "As long as I live, I will deny it."

## Sponsorship Loyalty

While Armstrong was defending himself against cheating allegations, he had a loyal partner that stood by his side. At the time, Nike was making millions of dollars off Armstrong merchandise while also donating millions back to his Livestrong charitable efforts. So when the cyclist wanted to continue to show how strongly he denied the doping allegations, Nike gave him a national platform. In a 30-second television advertisement that features video of him training, submitting to a blood test to check for doping, and riding his bike at night in a heavy rainstorm, Armstrong's voice can be heard saying, "Everybody wants to know what I'm on. What am I on? I'm on my bike, busting my ass six hours a day. What are you on?" as a Nike logo appears on the screen (Sports

iTeam Blog, 2012, para. 2). The message was clear: Armstrong had become the best in the world simply through hard work and Nike was proud to support him.

## Short-Lived Retirement

Following his seventh consecutive Tour de France win in 2005, Armstrong announced his retirement from professional cycling. He stated that he wished to spend more time with his family and focus more on his charitable work. However, as is sometimes the case with world-class athletes, that retirement did not stick. He announced his return in 2008, which led to a third-place finish in 2009's Tour de France and a 23rd-place finish in 2010's edition. A few months later, Armstrong announced that he was retiring for good (Macur, 2011). While the low finish might have been a factor in his second retirement announcement, the whispers surrounding his possible cheating were getting louder. It was only a matter of time before Armstrong's cycling career, image, and life were about to be changed forever.

# Busted

In 2012, the United States Anti-Doping Agency (USADA) released the results of their investigation into Armstrong and proclaimed that he had been engaged in "the most sophisticated, professionalized, and successful doping program that sport has ever seen" (Peralta, 2012, para. 3). The evidence presented made it abundantly clear that Armstrong had cheated on the way to his many victories. After years of proclaiming his innocence, the now-tarnished hero was at a crossroads: He could either continue to fight these charges or admit defeat and come clean on what was really going on during his racing career.

## The Findings

In October of 2012, USADA published a 200-page report that contained witness testimony, financial records, lab results, and scientific evidence that all pointed to the fact that Armstrong was doping. An accompanying website included affidavits, photos, email exchanges, videos, and even excerpts from Armstrong's own books that proved his guilt and established that he had close relationships with those who were accused of helping him cheat. Additionally, USADA investigators retested old blood samples of Armstrong and interviewed former teammates who, while under oath, had no choice but to tell the truth about what was really going on during his victories. It was not that Armstrong was necessarily passing multiple drug tests, but that he was instead simply passing on taking them. The report details how he and his teammates would go out of their way to avoid drug testers by hiding when the testers would come to their houses or dropping out of races when testers showed up at the team's hotel (USADA, n.d.).

Even before the findings were made public, USADA had already decided on Armstrong's future. Months before the official release, the organization banned Armstrong from competitive cycling, coaching, or any other official role with an Olympic sport for the rest of his life. In addition, every single one of his results was voided dating back to 1998. Therefore, Armstrong is no longer considered a seven-time winner of the Tour de France (Macur, 2012). Visitors to the Tour de France website will see that there is no listed winner of the races in the years that Armstrong "won" (History, n.d.).

## An Admission of Guilt

Following his initial banishment from the sport, Armstrong remained adamant that he had not cheated. He fought back against the USADA, saying that the case against him was "an unconstitutional witch hunt" and that "there is zero physical evidence to support [the chief executive of USADA's] outlandish and heinous claims" (Macur, 2012, para. 3; para. 11). However, following the release of USADA's detailed report, it become more

challenging for Armstrong to continue with his denials. Less than three months after the report went public, *The New York Times* reported that the disgraced star was considering publicly admitting that he had used performance-enhancing drugs and engaged in blood doping during his career (Macur, 2013a).

An interview with Armstrong in which he admits his guilt would be one in which any sports journalist would want to participate. The confession would be big news throughout the world, so both American and international media members would be lining up to be the one to ask the tough questions. Therefore, Armstrong himself had a great deal of power regarding how he wanted this admission to go. He could choose to do a press conference with many journalists or a one-on-one interview with a hand-picked interviewer. In January 2013, it was announced that Armstrong would do a "no-holds-barred" interview with Oprah Winfrey (Almasy, 2013). Winfrey, while perhaps one of the most famous interviewers of all time thanks to her daytime talk show that aired for 25 years, was not a sports journalist, so Armstrong's choice of her was somewhat surprising.

However, before the interview, he said to the Associated Press, "I told her to go wherever she wants and I'll answer the questions directly, honestly, and candidly" (Vertuno, 2013, para. 7). The interview was recorded near Armstrong's home in Austin, Texas, and aired over two nights on the Oprah Winfrey Network. The first

George Burns/Oprah Winfrey Network via Getty Images

Lance Armstrong speaks with Oprah Winfrey during a January 2013 interview.

episode begins with Winfrey telling Armstrong that she is going to ask him straightforward "yes or no" questions.

- **Winfrey:** Did you ever take banned substances to enhance your cycling performance?
- **Armstrong:** Yes.
- **Winfrey:** Yes or no, was one of those banned substances EPO?
- **Armstrong:** Yes.
- **Winfrey:** Did you ever blood dope or use blood transfusions to enhance your cycling performance?
- **Armstrong:** Yes.
- **Winfrey:** Did you ever use any other banned substances, like testosterone, cortisone, or human growth hormone?
- **Armstrong:** Yes.
- **Winfrey:** Yes or no, in all seven of your Tour de France victories, did you ever take banned substances or blood dope?
- **Armstrong:** Yes. (OWN, 2013, :55)

It is that last question and answer that was perhaps most damning to Armstrong's legacy. The admission that he had used banned substances for *all seven* of his Tour de France victories had now officially made him a cheater on the biggest stage. His victories, which had inspired millions, were all now tainted.

## History Revisited

With the publication of USADA's report and Armstrong's admission of his guilt, many began to reassess their association with the now-tarnished cyclist. His five Vélo d'Or awards, given to the best bicycle racer of the year, were rescinded, and he was forced to return the bronze medal he won in the 2000 Summer Olympics (Nevres, 2019; Reuters staff, 2013). A few months after the report, the Lance Armstrong Foundation changed its name to the Livestrong Foundation and Armstrong stepped down as the organization's chairman (MacLaggan, 2012).

The most financially damaging loss for Armstrong was from the exodus of his sponsors. Many companies had paid the then-champion an estimated total of between $15 million and $18 million dollars a year to endorse their various products, but after he was banned from racing and his reputation had taken a major hit, Nike, Anheuser-Busch, RadioShack, Trek, and Oakley all dropped Armstrong from their payrolls (Blodget,

2012). Even his most loyal fans were finding themselves conflicted, as the millions who bought yellow Livestrong bracelets were forced to consider whether they should continue to wear them (English, 2012).

## The Years Since

Despite his inability to race professionally, Armstrong was still in high demand. His victories had captivated the nation, and his fall from grace was considered just as newsworthy. Documentaries, books, and narrative films based on Armstrong's story were all released. One documentary, *The Armstrong Lie*, was originally supposed to be the behind-the-scenes story of his comeback attempt, but the focus shifted when the truth was revealed (Travers, 2013).

Armstrong, long known for his competitive nature, found himself battling opponents not on his bike, but in the courtroom. An insurance company sued Armstrong to recoup the bonus money they had paid him following his Tour de France wins, and a newspaper sought to recover the money they had paid Armstrong after losing a libel suit. Both of those lawsuits were settled out of court, but Armstrong's biggest legal rival was still waiting. The U.S. government had joined a fraud lawsuit against Armstrong, saying that he owed $100 million dollars to American taxpayers for doping while riding as a member of the U.S. Postal Service team. The Department of Justice stated that Armstrong's denial that he used performance-enhancing drugs meant he was committing fraud against the federal government that had paid over $30 million in endorsement money to his team. Just before the case was set to go to trial, Armstrong settled with the government, agreeing to pay $5 million (Hsu, 2018).

With his lawsuits settled, Armstrong quietly put himself back in the cycling world's spotlight. Unable to compete himself, he instead created a podcast titled *THEMOVE*, a show focused on the Tour de France, and NBC hired Armstrong to be an analyst for its coverage of the 2019 race. While he was not back on the bike, he was involved in it, and there was mixed reaction to his return. Some questioned the idea of having an admitted cheater report on the very race he cheated in, but others welcomed back his expertise and candor regarding the action (Malach, 2019). In a column about *THEMOVE* podcast, one British journalist wrote: "Described in some quarters as this Tour's guilty pleasure, one question above all others has been prompted by the success of [*THEMOVE*]: is it finally OK to like Armstrong again?" (Glendenning, 2017, para. 3).

## Image Repair

The question of being able to like Armstrong again ties into his attempt to repair his now-tarnished image. Armstrong's public persona took a major hit following the USADA's report, as he was now considered by millions to be both a liar and a cheat. One public relations expert said Armstrong's reputation was "in crisis" because "most people don't trust what comes out of his mouth" (Vertuno, 2013, para. 11). His first attempt at repairing his image was his long-awaited interview with Oprah Winfrey. However, the public sympathy never materialized. One article summed up the interview as "a smart PR move that turned out badly" because, while Armstrong did admit his wrongdoings, he appeared to lack any sort of remorse when giving his answers (Brock, 2013). A writer from *The New York Times* ended her analysis of the interview by pointing out that Armstrong avoided the two words that might have helped repair his image more than anything:

> *Throughout Winfrey's interview, Armstrong failed to do the one thing many people had been waiting for: he failed to apologize directly to all the people who believed in him, all the cancer survivors and cycling fans who thought his fairy-tale story was true.*
>
> *Not once did he look into the camera and say, without qualification, "I'm sorry." (Macur, 2013, para. 29-30)*

## The Media's Role in This Story

The accusations about Armstrong's cheating were prevalent for years, but the media, especially in the United States, seemed to turn a blind eye. While this case study focuses on the highs and lows of Armstrong's career, it is impossible to ignore the media's role in this story. For many journalists, his battle against cancer made the cyclist almost impossible to criticize. Famed sports columnist Rick Reilly wrote, "Doesn't Armstrong deserve the benefit of the doubt? A man who's worked tirelessly for and inspired people you know, people in your life, people who don't even know yet that they will need him for inspiration?" (Reilly, 2010, para. 34). In another column titled "Did Lance Armstrong cheat? I don't care," ESPN.com's LZ Granderson wrote, "I am having a hard time getting worked up enough to vilify a man whose foundation has raised nearly $400 million to fight cancer" (Granderson, 2011, para. 5).

However, for perhaps Armstrong's biggest media critic, his diagnosis was irrelevant to the doping. David Walsh, coauthor of *L.A. Confidential*, one of the first books questioning Armstrong's feats, felt that other journalists were ignoring what he believed was the obvious truth. Walsh labeled many media members as "fans with typewriters," implying that they were more excited to cheer for Armstrong than they were to do the investigative portion of their job as journalists. Walsh was not blind to the reason:

> *It felt like the cancer was a big factor from day one. A lot of people didn't think it was appropriate to ask what were very necessary questions. I think part of the reason they didn't want to ask those questions was because the guy had come back from cancer. For me, that was irrelevant. I just didn't think that should stop us from asking questions. (Pugh, 2012, para. 25-26)*

The Armstrong story should force news consumers to rethink how the media reports on certain stories that might sound too good to be true. Is it possible to be a reporter without being a fan? Additionally, can the media tell an amazing, inspiring story while still keeping an open mind about the fact that they may need to be critical of the subject of those stories? In the case of Armstrong, the answer to both of those questions at the time was "no."

Based on the Armstrong story, here are some tips for investigative sports journalists when looking into major stories:

- "Question everything."
- "Conduct as many interviews as possible."
- "Don't accept something as a fact until you can confirm it."
- "If something sounds too good to be true, it might be."

## Epilogue: Armstrong Wasn't Alone

While Armstrong was certainly the main focus of the doping scandals in professional cycling, he was far from the only one guilty of not following the rules. In fact, in his interview with Oprah Winfrey in 2013, Armstrong indicated as much:

- **Winfrey:** In your opinion, was it humanly possible to win the Tour de France without doping? Seven times in a row?

- **Armstrong:** Not in my opinion. (OWN, 2013, 1:36)

Essentially, Armstrong is saying that he could not have won without doping because almost everyone else was doing it too. Years later, it appears that might be true. In the seven years in which Armstrong "won" the Tour de France, 87 percent of the top-10 finishers were later either confirmed to have been doping or were heavily suspected of doing so (Gaines, 2015). It should be noted that all seven of Armstrong's wins that were vacated have not been retroactively awarded to the second- or third-place rider. Instead, the director of the Tour de France has simply said that no one won the event those years. The editor of the cycling magazine *Vélo* summarized it best: "What good does it serve anyone to take the victory away from somebody who doped and give it to someone else who doped? This decision makes a statement that this was a dark period. They're saying, 'We don't want to award it to anybody'" (Schrotenboer, 2012, para. 8).

# Summary

For about a 10-year period, Lance Armstrong was an inspiration to millions—including many media members. Stories flowed about his recovery from cancer to become the greatest cycling champion of all time. While some international journalists questioned the legitimacy of his victories, Armstrong's denials and the American media's apparent desire to not investigate those claims helped him keep his title as a hero. However, once the USADA presented their evidence, everyone involved could no longer ignore the obvious: Armstrong had cheated.

After years of going on the offensive with forceful denials that he was using performance-enhancing drugs, Armstrong suddenly found himself on the defensive. A tell-all interview with Oprah Winfrey did little to temper the frustrations many had with him, major companies were dropping him as an endorser, and others—including the U.S. government—were taking him to court. Ultimately, many wonder if it should have gotten to that point in the first place. Why was Armstrong allowed to get away with lying for all those years? Therefore, the story of Lance Armstrong's rise to fame is perhaps one that is more about the media and less about him. The saga shows what happens when journalists become complicit partners in an inspirational story that they helped create. Instead of investigating and looking for the truth, the media allowed Armstrong to continue as a hero without any questions, despite the rumors and whispers that were surrounding him. In the end, the media likely did a major disservice to their audience and perhaps Armstrong himself.

## KEY TERMS

**impartiality**—Treating everyone equally and not showing favoritism.

**libel**—The publication of a knowingly false statement in order to damage someone's reputation.

## REVIEW QUESTIONS

1. What are some of the reasons why Lance Armstrong was such a popular figure as he was winning Tour de France titles?
2. Why was the American media seemingly not willing to listen to or investigate the cheating allegations against Armstrong?
3. Why might Armstrong have chosen Oprah Winfrey to conduct the interview in which he admitted guilt?
4. How has Armstrong attempted to make a public comeback in the years since he was found guilty of cheating?

CASE STUDY

# LeBron James and *The Decision*

## CHAPTER OBJECTIVES

After completing the chapter, the reader should be able to do the following:

- Understand the history behind *The Decision*
- Identify why LeBron James faced criticism
- Identify why ESPN faced criticism
- Examine the legacy of *The Decision* more than a decade later

In 2010, LeBron James made a decision that hundreds of NBA players had made before him when he left his present team to sign elsewhere as a free agent. However, his signing was unlike any before. On the basketball side, his move from Cleveland to Miami caused a shift of power in the NBA, starting the era of the "super teams." Despite that, it was the way in which James made the move that perhaps created the biggest outcry. With millions of people watching live on ESPN during a show titled *The Decision*, James stunned fans by announcing his future in this made-for-TV event, a shift away from a time when sports journalists or the teams themselves were the ones who revealed the news. Within days of the program, both James and ESPN found themselves in the crosshairs of public criticism. However, years later, one could argue that *The Decision*, while widely panned at the time, has gone on to become one of the most influential moments in the history of the sports media and **athlete empowerment**.

## Before *The Decision*

There was seemingly little debate that James always had the potential to be one of the greatest players in NBA history. Before *The Decision*, before his NBA championships, before his multiple Most Valuable Player awards, and before becoming one of the top scorers in league history, there was already an expectation of greatness for the young star. In fact, those predictions of future stardom came very early, as James was being touted as "The Chosen One" on the cover of *Sports Illustrated* during his junior year of high school (Wahl, 2002).

## Best High School Player

James was born and raised in Akron, Ohio, a city about 40 miles south of Cleveland. When he reached the high school ranks, the hype around his potential basketball career was at astronomical levels. One longtime NBA observer said, "He's the best high school player I've ever seen" (Jones, 2014, para. 15), while a former NBA coach commented, "There are only four or five players in the NBA that I wouldn't trade to get LeBron right now" (Wahl, 2002, p. 64).

While it would seem almost impossible to back up those lofty predictions, his play on the court was doing just that. James was named Ohio's "Mr. Basketball" three years in a row, was the back-to-back winner of the USA Today Male Basketball Player of the Year award, and led his high school to three Ohio state championships in his four seasons. Even ESPN took notice: For the first time ever, they showed high school basketball games on their network, broadcasting James' team taking on—and defeating—the top-ranked high school team in the country (Bilas, 2002). Just as Kobe Bryant did seven seasons before him (see chapter 27 for more on Bryant's decision), James declared for the NBA Draft directly out of high school.

## #1 Overall Pick

The NBA determines what team will get the top pick in its draft through a lottery system in which the worse a team's record is, the better chance they have of winning the rights for the no. 1 overall pick. Before the 2003 draft, the Denver Nuggets and James' hometown Cleveland Cavaliers had identical 22.5 percent chances of getting the top pick, thanks to their matching records (the worst in the league) the year before. The night of the draft, the Cavaliers' Ping-Pong balls came up first, and within a half hour of the lottery ending, the team informed James they would be selecting him with that no. 1 pick (Windhorst, 2013).

## Early Career Success

Before James had even played a single minute in the NBA, he signed a seven-year endorsement deal with Nike (Windhorst, 2013). Between that agreement, the other endorsement deals that soon followed, his selection as the top pick in the draft, and proclamations that he was the best high school player ever, the expectations surrounding the rookie were astronomical. However, it did not take long for fans and the rest of the league to realize that the publicity was well deserved.

From 2003 to 2010, James led the Cavaliers back from last place to the playoffs and championship contention. He won the Rookie of Year in 2004, two MVP awards, and led the team to the NBA Finals in 2007. However,

that Finals trip ended in a four-game sweep by San Antonio, continuing the city of Cleveland's championship drought since 1964. Despite that loss, James' individual future was bright. However, his future with the team was murky. Following the 2010 season, James' contract with the Cavaliers would end, and at just 25 years old, he was about to become perhaps the most sought-after free agent in league history.

## *The Decision* Background

A player signing a free agent contract with a new team was nothing unique, as it had been happening for decades in professional sports. Traditionally, a player would sign with a team and either the team would make an announcement, or a journalist would be the first to report it. However, as would soon be revealed, the superstar was about to announce his future in a way that had never been done before.

## A Mailbag Beginning

In 2009, Bill Simmons was a columnist at ESPN.com, and one of his most popular features was a semi-regular mailbag column in which he would answer reader questions. It was never a very serious endeavor, as a mailbag in August of that year practically ignored sports and instead addressed movies, alcoholic drinks, women shaving their legs, and the question of who is the creepiest person alive (Simmons, 2009). Therefore, it is probably not a surprise that in a mailbag a few months later, "Drew from Columbus, Ohio" pitched Simmons his idea for an unusual television show:

> **Drew:** *What if LeBron announces he will pick his 2010-11 team live on ABC on a certain date for a show called "LeBron's Choice?" What type of crazy ratings would that get?*
>
> **Simmons:** *If LeBron were smart, he would market the event through his company, sell the rights to a network and reveal his choice on that show . . . He could even make it pay-per-view . . . I'm pretty sure they'll pony up for $44.99 for "Decision 2010: LeBron's Verdict." (Van Natta Jr., 2020, para. 2-3)*

Simmons not only responded positively to Drew's idea in the column, but he then tried to make the show actually happen. Years later, Simmons would reveal that he pitched the concept of a live free agency reveal show to both James' associates and ESPN during NBA All-Star Weekend in February 2010. According to Simmons,

James' agent and adviser loved the idea, but ESPN was seemingly not as interested. That changed a few months later when reporter Jim Gray said he pitched the same idea to James' inner circle, who then decided to gauge the interest of ESPN's head of content, John Skipper (Van Natta, 2020). The network was ready to listen this time.

## The Agreement

James' associates wanted the proposed show to air on ESPN, but had a few conditions they wanted the network to sign off on:

- ESPN would have to donate one hour of prime-time programming for the airing show for free.
- ESPN would give up all the advertising rights and revenue, with the understanding that James' team would donate all proceeds to charity.
- ESPN would produce the entire show and pay for all the production costs.
- Despite not being an ESPN employee, Jim Gray would host the show.

Skipper agreed to all four requests, seeing the value of having the program on his channel, while also recognizing the charitable aspect of the show. Just before the ten-year anniversary of *The Decision* airing on ESPN, Skipper recalled his mindset at the time:

*I think I decided pretty quickly I was OK donating the hour. I thought this would get enough attention and it would be worthwhile for viewers. I didn't mind losing the ad time. Part of this would be a charitable contribution. . . . At the end of the day, the rationale was it's what we had to do to get the show. And I felt that getting the show, having LeBron announce on our air, the rating we would get, the attention we would get would be good for our business. (Chiang, 2020, para. 13)*

With that, the agreement was made. James would make his free agency announcement on ESPN in a one-hour program titled *The Decision*, while the Boys & Girls Clubs of America would be the charitable beneficiary of all the advertising revenue. However, despite the deal, the program almost didn't make it to air.

Larry Busacca/Getty Images for Estabrook Group

*The Decision.*

## Second Thoughts?

As the live broadcast of *The Decision* approached, James' agent and another close adviser to the NBA superstar began to have second thoughts about the show. Questions started to arise about how the program might backfire on James, especially if he decided to leave Cleveland and announce that he was playing elsewhere (Van Natta Jr., 2020). Then-NBA commissioner David Stern was also strongly against the show, even going as far as calling Skipper and demanding that the network back out. Some have even reported that James himself was having doubts about *The Decision* just hours before it was to begin. One reporter stated that a source close to James told him that he believed that on the day of the broadcast, the free agent was about to cancel the show (Fedor, 2020). However, despite the hesitation and the pleas from the league commissioner, the program went on as scheduled.

## *The Decision*

At 9 p.m. ET on July 8, 2010, *The Decision* began on ESPN. Airing live from the Boys & Girls Club in Greenwich, Connecticut, James and Gray sat in chairs in the middle of a basketball court surrounded by children from the club. While the announcement could have been over quickly with one "What team are you playing for next season?" question, Gray and James milked the drama for all it was worth. It took Gray 18 questions, including "Are you still a nail biter?," before getting to the one everyone was waiting for. At 9:28 p.m., *The Decision* had a decision:

> **Gray:** *The answer to the question everybody wants to know: LeBron, what's your decision?*
> **James:** *This fall, man this is very tough, this fall I'm going to take my talents to South Beach and join the Miami Heat.*
> **Gray:** *Miami Heat? That was the conclusion you woke up with this morning?*
> **James:** *That was the conclusion I woke up with this morning.* (ESPN, 2018, 5:03)

The Heat would make it official the next day, announcing James' six-year, $110.1 million deal. Joining James in Miami would be Dwyane Wade and Chris Bosh, two All-Stars themselves, giving the Heat three of the best players in the league. The contract had an opt-out for James after four seasons, meaning he could end the deal early and become a free agent again in the summer of 2014 (ESPN.com, 2010). However, that mattered little at the time. James had rocked the NBA with his announcement and the reaction to both the player himself and ESPN was overwhelmingly negative.

## Criticism of James

The worries that James' opting to leave the Cavaliers might lead to a blowback from the public proved to be accurate. However, the amount of negativity took James and his associates by surprise (Chiang, 2020). In the days, months, and even years following *The Decision*, James became a villain to many for his role in the program. For some, James leaving his hometown team in Cleveland for the glitz and glamour of Miami was enough for them to turn on James. Even the phrasing of how he made it public—"I'm taking my talents to South Beach"—caused many to be disgusted. The outrage in Cleveland was to be expected, but it went beyond just Ohio. An ESPN.com poll found that 60 percent of sports fans surveyed believed James had "permanently damaged" his image (Ohlmeyer, 2010). Another survey revealed that 39 percent of the American public viewed him in a negative light following the show. Just a few months earlier, before *The Decision*, that number was at just 22 percent (Rovell, 2010).

Also, as stated previously, this had never been done before when it came to free agent decisions, so that might have played a role in the backlash as well. Instead of a team announcing the signing or a journalist reporting the news, James announcing his decision himself on national television was seen by some—especially by journalists—as a selfish act. One reporter wrote, "You can't spell James without 'me,' and it's more difficult to defend James for this arrogant exercise than it is to defend him in the pick and roll" (Thomaselli, 2010, para. 21). In a retrospective article that was published eight years later, *The Ringer*'s Bryan Curtis wrote, "Sportswriters were OK with a player taking his talents elsewhere, but they weren't OK with the method he used to take them" (Curtis, 2018, para. 10).

The criticism was so over-the-top in some cases, that there was discussion if it was about more than just basketball. James' business manager argued that the pushback was rooted in racism (Stanley, 2010). This was a Black basketball player, telling his White team owner and a mostly White audience about his future on his own terms, a move that was then roundly criticized by White sports journalists. Even James himself wondered about the motivation behind some of the hate. In an interview with CNN, he was asked if he believed race played a role in the criticism he was receiving, and said, "I think so, at times. There's always a race factor" (Tanneeru & King, 2010, para. 7).

## Criticism of ESPN

While James was the subject of scorn from many, he was hardly the only target. ESPN's involvement in the show painted them as an accomplice in the entire ordeal. For many in the media, the network had crossed a journalistic line by essentially becoming business partners with an athlete whom they were supposed to be covering impartially. Even in the days before the program aired, ESPN was facing criticism, including the claim that "ESPN executives have clearly made the determination that relationships and ratings are more important than journalistic integrity" (Buckley, 2010, para. 14).

Those early comments about ESPN's involvement would look tame when compared to the outrage in the days following *The Decision*. ESPN's ombudsman, a position NPR described as one that "investigates complaints and concerns about matters of accuracy, fairness, balance and good taste" (Dvorkin, 2006, para. 4), relayed some of the main criticisms facing the network in a column on ESPN.com a few weeks after the show:

- *The Baltimore Sun*: "ESPN led the way Thursday night in some of the most debased sports coverage I can remember seeing."
- *The Washington Post*: "The most troubling aspect of the whole ill-conceived mess was ESPN's willingness to hand over an hour of prime-time television to an egomaniacal athlete the network should be covering as a news story. Does this not-so-subtle form of checkbook journalism pass the smell test anywhere else but in Bristol, Conn.?"
- *Los Angeles Daily News*: "The truth is, how does anyone believe anything else ESPN reports about James from this point forward?"
- *Sports Illustrated*: "The Decision is the worst thing ESPN has ever put its name to." (Ohlmeyer, 2010)

The main issue that many journalists had with the program was the idea that ESPN "paid" for news. The idea of paying for interviews goes against almost every journalistic standard because it can cause the audience to question the validity of those speaking: Are they saying this because they truly feel this way or because they are being getting money to talk? ESPN would likely counter that they did not directly pay James, but

instead helped create a scenario that resulted in a large donation to charity. However, no matter where the money was ultimately going, ESPN traded primetime airtime and the associated advertising revenue—about $6 million—to James for the story. At no point during the broadcast did the network remind viewers of the financial arrangement with James, that James oversaw the selling of the advertisements, or that Jim Gray was selected by James' advisers to do the interview. Instead, the program ran on ESPN with no indication that James himself was essentially running the show. ESPN's director of news said his department had nothing to do with *The Decision* and was adamant afterward that he was not pleased with how it had transpired:

> The problem here was that the decision directly involved the presentation of news and ultimately had a damaging impact on our reputation as journalists. You can't justify paying for news. There are no excuses here. The hope is that we learned something from this, that we won't repeat the error, and that we can restore any lost confidence in our ability to objectively report and present the news. (Ohlmeyer, 2010, para. 56-57)

However, while ESPN was being widely criticized for its role in *The Decision*, it is fair to ask if any media outlets might have done things differently. While every journalist wants to believe their company would "do the right thing" and not give James a free platform to make his announcement, that might not necessarily be the case. *The Decision* had millions talking about and watching ESPN, and created added exposure for the network. A writer for the *Boston Herald* summed it up when addressing the criticism ESPN was facing from journalists upset at the partnership—his newspaper probably would have done the same thing:

> One nagging question remains: Would any of these media outlets, given the opportunity to be the exclusive soap box for such an announcement, say no? If LeBron's people dialed up the Herald and offered to make his announcement via a live chat with [Boston Herald reporter] Dan Duggan on bostonherald.com, the answer would be, "What time?" (Buckley, 2010, para. 15-16)

## Successes

While there was plenty of criticism to go around following the airing of *The Decision*, there were some successes to take away from the experience. Perhaps the biggest winner in the show (besides the Miami Heat) were the charities benefiting from the program. James elected to donate the advertising proceeds to the Boys & Girls Clubs of America. Sponsors such as Microsoft, University of Phoenix, State Farm, VitaminWater, and McDonald's all paid large sums to be a part of the program through commercials. In total, the show reportedly raised $6 million in advertising revenue, with about $2.5 million going to the Boys & Girls Clubs of America, and the remaining amount spread out among other organizations (Thomaselli, 2010).

Before the event, ESPN's head of content, John Skipper, agreed to put the show on his network because he believed the number of viewers would be high. His prediction was proven correct. An average of 9.9 million people in the United States watched the show, with an estimated 13.1 million watching when James said he was taking his talents to South Beach. Perhaps not surprisingly, the television markets with the three most viewers were Cleveland-Akron, Ohio; Columbus, Ohio; and Miami, Florida (NielsenWire, 2010). A more detailed breakdown of Cleveland's viewership found that one out of every four homes in the city tuned in to watch James say that he was leaving them. The network earned tremendous viewership numbers but suffered through intense criticisms that stained the company for years following the airing of the broadcast. An Associated Press story called it ESPN's "deal with the devil" (Bauder, 2010, para. 1).

## Another Decision

James' time with the Heat was an undeniable success. The team won two championships in the four years he was there, and James himself won the MVP award twice and was named *Sports Illustrated*'s Sportsman of the Year. However, even as James was cementing his legacy as one of the greatest basketball players of all time, *The Decision* was still a key part of his history. During the 2011 season, James began to express some regrets about the way he announced his move to Miami. In an interview with ESPN, James said:

> If I could look back on it, I would probably change a lot of it. The fact of having a whole TV special, and

Angelo Merendino/Corbis via Getty Images

LeBron James reacts to a standing ovation at a 2014 community celebration in Ohio welcoming him home.

*people getting the opportunity to watch me make a decision on where I wanted to play, I probably would change that. Because I can now look and see if the shoe was on the other foot and I was a fan, and I was very passionate about one player, and he decided to leave, I would be upset too about the way he handled it. (Munzenrieder, 2011, para. 3)*

Following his fourth year with the Heat, James elected to use the opt-out in his contract, which allowed him to become a free agent again. Once again, one of the best players in the NBA was back on the market. This time, there would be no television show, but the sports media would still be prominently involved.

On July 11, 2014, *Sports Illustrated* (*SI*) posted a first-person article on its website from James titled "I'm Coming Home," in which he announced his intention to re-sign with his hometown Cleveland Cavaliers. In the article, James again expressed regrets about the manner in which he left Cleveland the first time, explained why going to Miami was the best move for him personally and professionally at the time, and stated how his ultimate goal was to bring a championship to the city of Cleveland (James, 2014).

While James is listed as the author of the article, there is an additional credit that states "as told to Lee Jenkins" (James, 2014). Jenkins, an *SI* writer, had initially proposed the idea to James' team about the first-person essay being a way in which he could reveal his free agency destination. The day before the article posted, James agreed to work with *SI*, and conducted a series of interviews with Jenkins. The author then transcribed those comments, rewrote them into an article, and released it to the public. In order to keep James' decision a secret right up until the website published his story, only six people at *SI* saw the story before it went live (Petchesky & McKenna, 2014). An editor at Time, Inc., which owned *SI* at the time, said the article caused the biggest rise in readership on the SI.com website in over a decade (Trachtenberg, 2014).

ESPN was widely criticized for giving up its airtime to James so that he could make his announcement on *The Decision*. However, four years later, *SI* faced no such criticism despite doing nearly the exact same thing—giving up space in its magazine for James' first-person article. In fact, *SI*'s Jenkins was widely praised for his role in landing such a big "scoop." Jim Gray, the host of *The Decision* who was also widely panned for his role in the show, found himself confused at the differing reactions: "[They] thought because *Sports Illustrated* did it somehow that was better? Really? . . . I didn't write the answers for LeBron. I asked him questions. . . . You saw the hypocrisy right there" (Curtis, 2016, para. 43). Perhaps it was not the platform change that caused the differing reaction, but instead the destination. For *The Decision*, James turned his back on Cleveland, but for *SI*'s version, James was the hero for returning to his home state of Ohio.

# Yet Another Decision

When James returned to Cleveland, he did so with a goal of winning an NBA championship. In his second season, he did just that, as the Cavaliers upset the heavily favored Golden State Warriors, bringing the city its first championship in any sport since 1964. Following the NBA Finals, James was set to become a free agent again. However, this time there was very little drama because he was expected to remain with the team. Instead, once again, it was his method of making the announcement that was unique.

In a video posted to the website *Uninterrupted*, James announced, "Anytime I have got anything new or exclusive, I'm bringing it to y'all first, so I just want to let y'all know I'm re-signing back with the Cleveland Cavaliers" (Uninterrupted, 2016, :08). James made his first two free agency announcements through sports media superpowers ESPN and *Sports Illustrated*. Many wondered what made him choose a relatively unknown website for his latest career declaration. However, a deeper dive revealed the obvious answer: *Uninterrupted* was founded and partially owned by LeBron James himself. The company describes itself as "an athlete empowerment brand" that has a goal of letting athletes speak out on a variety of topics beyond sports directly to the public through videos, without needing the traditional media's involvement (Uninterrupted, n.d.). As a way to kick-start his own company, James provided an instant boost in traffic by making the biggest announcement of the NBA's offseason on his own website.

# Yes, Another Decision

In 2018, after four seasons in Cleveland, James was, once again, set to become a free agent. The rumors were floating that the hometown hero was once again going to bolt from Cavaliers, as many speculated that his two homes in Los Angeles would make the L.A. Lakers a prime destination (Youngmisuk, 2018). However, there was also the history of *The Decision*. James spurning Cleveland and leaving for Miami made him a villain in Ohio, so there was some consideration if he would stay with the team to avoid the criticism. From a media standpoint, knowing how poorly his previous departure on live television was received, how James would make his free agency destination known this time was of great interest.

On July 1, 2018, Klutch Sports, the sports agency that represents James, sent a tweet that read: "LeBron James, four time NBA MVP, three time NBA finals MVP, fourteen time NBA All Star, and two time Olympic gold medalist has agreed to a four year, $154 million contract with the Los Angeles Lakers" (Klutch Sports Group, 2018). That was the entire announcement. There were no quotes from James himself, no videos, no traditional media involvement. With that tweet, James had once again left Cleveland.

However, this time, the response was much different when compared to after *The Decision*. Perhaps it was because James had helped to deliver a championship to the city, but the journalists who had vilified the star years earlier were now wishing him the best. *The Cleveland Plain-Dealer* newspaper had a headline of "Promise Kept," with an accompanying photo of James holding the NBA Finals MVP trophy after winning the 2016 title. Other articles titled "Best wishes and Godspeed to the greatest Cavalier" and "LeBron held up his end, now has earned right to finish career in L.A." appeared in the newspaper that same day (Rosenthal, 2018).

## The Legacy of *The Decision*

While *The Decision* was widely panned at the time, it is impossible to ignore the legacy of the program over a decade later. Many will cite that program as the beginning of the "player empowerment" era in the NBA. For years, players were at the mercy of NBA owners and media members, with little opportunity to control the narrative surrounding them. In a one-hour television special, James changed that forever. He decided that he wanted to leave his hometown and join two of his close friends to form a modern-day "super team" in Miami, and he wanted to deliver the news on his own terms. While the show certainly had its flaws, it is impossible to not see the fingerprints of *The Decision* on the modern NBA.

One only has to look to fellow basketball star Kevin Durant's move to the Golden State Warriors in 2016. Durant, one of the best players in the NBA at the time, joined the best team in the league (although one that had just lost the NBA Finals to James' Cavaliers) and made the announcement in a first-person essay on *The Player's Tribune* website (Durant, 2016). It was a move straight from James' playbook—joining a "super team" and making the free agent announcement himself. Two years after that, Paul George partnered with ESPN to create a three-part video special about his NBA free agency, a move that was met with little criticism of George or ESPN (Curtis, 2018).

*The Decision* also revealed a change in how players interact with the media. Previously, if a player wanted to get information to the public, they would need to contact a journalist and hope they would write a story about it. Now the media is on the sidelines, watching these players make announcements, both big and small, from their individual social media accounts. For journalists, this rise in power of team and player media should be concerning (see chapter 30 for more information about team and player media).

## Summary

As expected, LeBron James' free agency in the summer of 2010 turned into one of the biggest stories in NBA history. However, thanks to *The Decision*, the conversation was not solely about where he ended up. At the time, James was widely vilified for being a part of the show, and ESPN received similar criticism for giving up airtime in exchange for the announcement. James would later say he wished he had done the show differently, and when future free agent decisions arose, he instead revealed his destinations in a magazine, on a website, and on social media. Over a decade later, the show remains an important moment in sports and media history, as it led to the beginning of the athlete empowerment era and also led to more media organizations partnering with athletes. James signing with the Heat changed the NBA, but the long-term impact of *The Decision* went well beyond his years in Miami.

## KEY TERM

**athlete empowerment**—A term used to describe athletes making their own decisions and not relying on others to tell their story.

## REVIEW QUESTIONS

1. What were the stipulations that ESPN agreed to with LeBron James before airing *The Decision*?

2. What were some of the criticisms of LeBron James in the immediate aftermath of *The Decision*?

3. What were some of the criticisms of ESPN in the immediate aftermath of *The Decision*?

4. After the initial free agency announcement on ESPN, how did James announce his future free agent destinations?

*CASE STUDY*

# Death of Kobe Bryant

## CHAPTER OBJECTIVES

After completing the chapter, the reader should be able to do the following:

- Evaluate the media's coverage in the initial hours following the helicopter crash involving Kobe Bryant
- Identify how media retractions can damage a journalistic reputation
- Discuss the media's struggle with the complicated legacy of Kobe Bryant
- Recognize how challenging reporting on breaking news can be for journalists

*This chapter contains information about a sexual assault which may be upsetting to some readers.*

While this chapter focuses on Kobe Bryant, it also demonstrates the challenges faced by journalists when reporting on news that is rapidly changing. Bryant was, and continues to be even after his death, one of the most popular basketball players among both diehard and casual fans. He won championships and individual awards and retired as one of the top scorers in league history. Following his retirement, Bryant further embraced his role as a father to four girls while also planning for a life beyond the game. His sudden death in a helicopter crash in 2020 drew global attention, so the media was scrambling to uncover the details of what happened, figure out how to address an incident in his past, and balance between getting it right and being the first to report information. However, in their quest to be first, many media members made mistakes, emphasizing the issues involved with reporters in breaking news situations.

## Kobe Bryant History

In 1978, Kobe Bryant was born in Philadelphia, Pennsylvania, to Pam Bryant and former NBA player Joe "Jellybean" Bryant. His father played professionally in Italy, so Kobe spent many of his younger years overseas before the family moved back to the United States when he was 13. Soon after that return, Bryant quickly became one of the country's top high school basketball players, earning scholarship offers from some of the best college programs.

At the time, National Basketball Association (NBA) rules allowed players who were high school graduates to declare for the NBA Draft and go directly from high school to the NBA.[1] Very few took advantage of the rule, as the prospect of going from high school games to professional ones was seen as an overwhelming challenge

---

[1]This rule has since been changed. As of the publishing of this textbook, NBA rules state that players must be at least 19 years old and that at least one season has passed since their high school graduation before they are eligible for the NBA Draft.

for most. However, in 1996, Bryant became the sixth player in league history to announce he was going to forego college and head to the NBA straight out of high school. The Charlotte Hornets selected the 17-year-old with the 13th overall pick before trading his draft rights to the Los Angeles Lakers (Curwen & Wharton, 2020; Stein, 2020).

## Early Career

Bryant's career with the Lakers got off to a modest start, as he mainly came off the bench during his first two seasons. However, he quickly became a fan favorite. Despite starting just one game in his second season, the fans voted him to be a starter in the All-Star Game. Things started to look up during his third season, as Bryant started every game for Los Angeles, averaging nearly 20 points per game. The next three seasons were marked by incredible team success, as the Lakers, led by Bryant and Shaquille O'Neal, won three straight NBA Championships in the 1999-2000, 2000-2001, and 2001-2002 seasons (Curwen & Wharton, 2020; Stein, 2020).

## Off the Court

While Bryant's career on the court was on the rise, he was seemingly just as successful off it. Before he played a single game in the NBA, Adidas signed him to a multimillion-dollar contract to wear the company's sneakers during games. Bryant also inked deals with both McDonald's and Nintendo, making him one of the highest-paid athletes in the NBA in terms of endorsement dollars (Sexton, 2011). In addition, he was starting a family. In 1999, Bryant met and began dating Vanessa Laine. The two became engaged six months later and were married in April 2001. By January 2020, Kobe and Vanessa had four daughters: Natalia, Gianna (Gigi), Bianka, and Capri.

## Sexual Assault Case

In 2003, Bryant was arrested in Eagle, Colorado, and charged with one count of felony sexual assault. The charge was a result of an incident in which a woman accused Bryant of raping her at a Colorado hotel in which she worked. The basketball star admitted that he had a sexual encounter with the woman, but claimed it was consensual. Bryant, who was one of the most popular players in the NBA at the time, saw his reputation take a major hit (Henson, 2020). Several endorsement deals were canceled and Nike, which had just signed him away from Adidas months earlier, held off on releasing a Bryant-branded sneaker (Badenhausen, 2004).

A little more than a year later, the assault case was dropped by prosecutors after the hotel employee refused to testify at the trial. Following the dismissal of the case, Bryant made a public statement in which he apologized to the woman, her family, and his own family. He said, "I want to apologize to her for my behavior that night and for the consequences she has suffered in the past year," and "I now understand that she did not consent to this encounter" (Associated Press, 2004, para. 1, 2). The woman would later file a civil lawsuit against Bryant that was settled out of court (Henson, 2005).

## Late Career

Despite his arrest, Bryant's basketball career was far from over. He remained with the Lakers, changing his jersey number from 8 to 24, and his basketball career continued an upward trajectory. Bryant was named the NBA's Most Valuable Player (MVP) in 2008, won two more NBA championships, and won two Olympic gold medals with Team USA. In his final NBA game, Bryant scored 60 points, finishing his career as one of the greatest players in NBA history with a resumé that very few will ever match (Stein, 2020).

## Post-Career Enterprises

There are any number of stories of former professional athletes who struggled stepping away from the game and into retirement. Players find themselves with financial problems, emotional issues, or legal run-ins. Bryant, however, seemed to have his post-playing career on the right track. In 2018, he won an Academy Award for Best Animated Short Film for his movie *Dear Basketball* (ESPN News Services, 2018), while a series of children's books he helped to create, *The Wizenard Series*, reached the top spot on *The New York Times* best-seller list (Amato, 2020). In addition, before retiring, Bryant became an early investor in the sports drink company BodyArmor. He owned more than 10 percent of that brand, and was reportedly also looking for new businesses to invest in once his basketball career was over (Badenhausen, 2014).

Harry How/Getty Images

**Kobe Bryant walks to center court during his jersey retirement ceremony in 2017.**

# January 26, 2020

On the morning of January 26, 2020, the Los Angeles 9-1-1 center began receiving calls informing them that there had been an aircraft crash in Calabasas, California (Associated Press, 2021). Less than an hour later, the Los Angeles County Sheriff's Department published a tweet that confirmed that it was a helicopter that had gone down in the mountainous area (LA County Sheriffs, 2020). Months later, it would be revealed that heavy fog had played a role in the crash, as the pilot struggled to navigate in the low visibility (Toropin et al., 2020). However, at the time, the Sheriff's Department was still working to determine what happened and attempting to reach the wreckage site to see if there were any survivors. As the deputies were still at the scene assessing the damage, a tweet from the celebrity gossip website TMZ delivered the startling news: "BREAKING: Kobe Bryant Has Died In A Helicopter Crash" (TMZ, 2020).

## Initial Reporting

Shortly after the initial report from TMZ, other news outlets began publishing their own updates on the situation. However, the early hours of the reporting after that first tweet could best be summarized by the word *confusion*, as while almost everyone agreed that Kobe Bryant was riding in the helicopter, there was a great deal of disagreement as to who else had died in the crash (Loveless, 2020; Tracy, 2020).

On ABC News, reporter Matt Gutman stated that Kobe and all four of his children were killed in the crash, while competitor NBC News reported that five people had been killed (Loveless, 2020; NBC News, 2020; Tracy, 2020). There was widespread speculation on social media that Rick Fox, a former teammate of Bryant's on the Lakers, was also killed in the crash, but a television host put a stop to that rumor by stating he had just texted with Fox, who confirmed that he was very much alive (Greenberg, 2020). Even the United States president, Donald Trump, tweeted about the crash, writing that Bryant and three others had been killed (Tracy, 2020). An ABC News reporter tweeted that the news outlet had now confirmed that none of Bryant's four daughters were on board, while less than one minute later, TMZ tweeted that one daughter had died in the crash (Franco, 2020; TMZ Sports, 2020). Those reports, along with others, led to a great deal of confusion as seemingly everyone had different information. Less than 90 minutes after TMZ sent the original tweet revealing that Kobe Bryant had died in a helicopter crash, the following updates were on social media:

- Five people are dead
- All four daughters are dead
- Five people on board

- Former teammate Rick Fox was also on board
- Former teammate Rick Fox was not on board
- None of Bryant's daughters were on board
- One of Bryant's daughters was on board
- Bryant and three others killed
- Bryant, his daughter, and another player and their parent were aboard

It is hard to ignore the fact that some of these reports contradict each other. As one Twitter user pointed out: "Kobe, Rick Fox, a pilot, and 4 daughters doesn't equal 5 people. Someone information is wrong" (Ibrahimovic, 2020). It would ultimately turn out that many of these initial reports were wrong.

## The Facts Come Out

While there was much early speculation about who was on the helicopter, it was not until later in the day that the entire list of those on the trip was released. Ultimately, there were nine people who died on board the flight that was traveling to a girls' basketball game. Those nine were

- Kobe Bryant, 41 years old,
- Gianna (Gigi) Bryant, 13 years old,
- Sarah Chester, 45 years old,
- Payton Chester, 13 years old,
- Keri Altobelli, 46 years old,
- John Altobelli, 56 years old,
- Alyssa Altobelli, 14 years old,
- Christina Mauser, 38 years old, and
- Ara Zobayan, 50 years old.

There had been rampant speculation in the short time following the crash that the entire Bryant family was on board, but Kobe and Gigi were the only members of the family that perished in the crash. Payton was the daughter of Sarah Chester, Alyssa was the daughter of Keri and John Altobelli, and both were basketball teammates of Gigi's. Christina Mauser was an assistant coach on the girls' team and Ara Zobayan was the pilot of the helicopter (Times Staff, 2020).

## Retractions from the Media

Once the official record of who was on board the helicopter was released, many media members had to make retractions based on their previous reporting. Perhaps most prominently, ABC News's Matt Gutman, the

reporter who stated that all four of the Bryant daughters were on board the helicopter, issued an apology and correction to his story both on television and on social media, writing on Twitter: "I apologize to Kobe's family, friends and our viewers" (Gutman, 2020). One sportscaster pointed out the various incorrect reports on his Twitter account, comparing the mistakes from ABC, Fox, and TMZ. He wrote, "I hope some people lose their jobs today for rushing reports" (Doughty, 2020). While Gutman was not fired for his error, ABC News did suspend him for an undisclosed amount of time, a decision he seemed to agree with: "We are in the business of holding people accountable, and I hold myself accountable for a terrible mistake, which I deeply regret" (Battaglio, 2020, para. 6).

## Police Procedure

It is difficult to determine how so many media outlets made mistakes in their reporting in the first minutes following the helicopter crash, but it is possible that several issues could have been avoided had they followed the typical protocol when reporting on deaths. Traditionally, law enforcement does not release the names of those who have died in accidents until the families of those affected have been notified. The reasoning behind this practice is that law enforcement would rather be the people delivering this horrible news in a face-to-face scenario as opposed to having someone find out a loved one had died by watching the news. The news media usually also follows this protocol, and they typically refrain from announcing deaths until the police have given them an indication that the family had been notified. For example, the *Los Angeles Times* acknowledged the helicopter crash in early tweets, but did not confirm that Byrant was on board, citing the fact that the victims had not been publicly identified (Tracy, 2020).

However, there is ample evidence that TMZ reported the news before the families had been notified. Vanessa, Kobe's wife, would later say that a family assistant was the one who told her that there had been a crash involving the helicopter. As Vanessa was trying to call Kobe to see if he was okay, her phone began receiving notifications that her husband had died in the crash (Abrams & Draper, 2021). This much is clear: The news was not first given to the families by the Los Angeles County Sheriff's Department. In a press conference shortly after the crash, the sheriff confirmed that there were nine people on board the helicopter but would not identify them. He said:

*There is wide speculation of who the identities are, however, it would be wildly inappropriate right now to identify anyone by name until the coroner has made the identification through their very deliberate process and they've made the notification to the next of kin. It would be extremely disrespectful to understand that your loved one was perished, and you learned about it from TMZ. (WTHR.com staff, 2020, para. 6)*

Another member of Sheriff's Department would later tweet, "I understand getting the scoop but please allow us time to make personal notifications to their loved ones. It's very cold to hear of the loss via media Breaks my heart" (Murakami, 2020).

## TMZ

While TMZ was the first to report the news of Bryant's death, it came with public criticism beyond even the comments from the authorities. However, before addressing that blowback, it is important to understand the history of the outlet and where it stands in the world of media and journalism. TMZ started as an entertainment news website in 2005, with a television show (*TMZ on TV*) following in 2007. The initial focus of both TMZ.com and *TMZ on TV* was celebrity gossip and paparazzi-style photos. A reliance on these types of stories put TMZ in the category of a tabloid journalism outlet, which is a label given to media companies that focus on sensational and outlandish stories that have little impact on society as a whole. Therefore, TMZ is not considered a "serious" journalism outlet and has been long criticized for the type of stories they report, how they get those stories, and the lack of sensitivity they often display when reporting on celebrity deaths. Despite that negative reputation, it is impossible to ignore that the website and television show are both incredibly popular with millions of devoted readers and watchers. Additionally, TMZ has gotten its share of "scoops" before other, more reputable news outlets, including most famously when it was the first to announce that legendary singer Michael Jackson had died (Darcy, 2020).

However, TMZ's rush to be the primary source in the Bryant story may have come at a price to its already tarnished reputation. After the Sheriff's Department indicated that they had not been able to contact Bryant's family before TMZ announced his death, the reporting practices of the website were heavily criticized. Actress Ellen Pompeo asked her followers on social media to sign a petition to get the television show canceled (D'Zurilla,

2020), while others focused on TMZ's practice of paying for stories, something that is frowned upon by most traditional newsrooms (Darcy, 2020). TMZ founder Harvey Levin was quick to defend the reporting of his team, insisting that before they published the tweet, his staff had talked to people close to Bryant's family and were assured that Vanessa was already aware that Kobe and Gigi had died. However, it was not just the Bryant family on board the helicopter that day. When pressed in a radio interview about the ethics of publishing the news before the other families of those in the helicopter could be notified, Levin seemed to admit fault by saying, "that is a fair point" (Ritschel, 2020).

# Additional Media Coverage

While the story of the helicopter crash was understandably major news on the day of the accident, the story did not quickly fade from the public interest. With Bryant's status as one of the most famous athletes in the modern era, news outlets continued to do follow-up reports in the days and months after the crash. As the stories moved beyond the crash itself, how to discuss aspects of Bryant's non-basketball life were met with an intense debate. While he was praised for his role as a father, his past transgressions were impossible for many to ignore.

## Bryant's Past

Bryant will almost certainly be remembered as one of the greatest basketball players of all time. He finished as one of the NBA's top scorers, won numerous championships, and was destined to be a member of the Basketball Hall of Fame. However, in the days following his death, some outwardly wondered if the sexual assault charge against Bryant should be listed as a part of his legacy. As one writer from *The Washington Post* commented, "Should it be ignored, as many fans would have preferred? Or clearly acknowledged? Was this 'not the right moment'? Or was it the only moment there is—when a superstar's career and life were being assessed?" (Sullivan, 2020, para. 16). As several noted afterward, Bryant left behind a complicated legacy. A *New York Daily News* columnist wrote a remembrance that was filled with on-court accolades and praise for his post-basketball life, but also: "The worst moment of his public life did not define the rest of his life. But it also cannot be ignored" (Lupica, 2020, para. 5). Similarly, sportswriter Christine Brennan tweeted: "Kobe Bryant's career was majestic, his loss immeasurable. And yes, the very serious allegation of sexual assault in 2003 is part of his story" (Brennan, 2020). Responses to that tweet were divided, with some agreeing that it needed to be mentioned, while others questioned if immediately after Bryant's death was the proper time to bring up the incidents from his past.

Shortly after the helicopter crash, Felicia Sonmez, a reporter from *The Washington Post*, tweeted a link to a 2016 story that had many of the details about the sexual assault allegations from 2003. The backlash came fast, and Sonmez later posted a screenshot of her email inbox that contained angry messages from Bryant supporters. However, by the end of the day, it was more than just random Twitter users who were upset with the reporter's tweets. The paper's executive editor sent an email to Sonmez, in which he wrote, "A real lack of judgement to tweet this. Please stop. You're hurting this institution by doing this" (Abrams, 2020, para. 4). Later that night, Sonmez was suspended by the newspaper, a decision that was widely panned by her coworkers (Abrams, 2020). Ultimately, it was not her tweet linking to the news story that got her suspended, but instead the screenshot of her email inbox that displayed names and email addresses of

those who had contacted her. Leaders from *The Washington Post* said that screenshot was a violation of the newspaper's social media policy (Keys, 2020).

The death of Kobe Bryant was not the first time, nor will it be the last, in which the media struggled with telling the full life story of someone who had just passed away. While Bryant was unquestionably an outstanding basketball player, the allegations of sexual assault were a part of his past. Diehard Bryant fans almost certainly did not want to read about his previous arrest in the early moments following his death, but media members cannot simply ignore the past. In instances like this one, it may be a situation in which it is difficult to please everyone in the audience.

## #GirlDad

While the media and the public debated how to properly address (or not) the sexual assault charge, a different aspect of Bryant's life was almost universally praised. It all seemingly started during a segment on ESPN's *SportsCenter*, in which anchor Elle Duncan shared her own personal story about the basketball legend. In a

Kobe Bryant attends a Lakers game with his daughter Gianna Bryant in November of 2019.

commentary that was approximately 90 seconds long, Duncan told the story of the one time she met Bryant. She was pregnant at the time and, according to her story, Bryant excitedly asked her if she was having a girl or a boy. When the journalist responded that it was going to be a girl, Bryant responded that "girls are the best" and "I would have five more girls if I could. I'm a girl dad" (ESPN, 2020, :28; :58). As her commentary on *SportsCenter* continued, Duncan began to tear up, before ending with, "I suppose the only small source of comfort for me is knowing that he died doing what he loved the most: Being a dad; being a girl dad" (ESPN, 2020, 1:23).

Duncan's story, while focused on Bryant, soon became something bigger. The segment became the start of the "Girl Dad" movement, as fathers of girls began posting photos and stories on social media with the hashtag #GirlDad (Kimble, 2020). A Twitter spokesman said the hashtag had been used almost 200,000 times in the first few days after the crash, with famous athletes, musicians, actors, and regular, everyday dads chiming in (Respers France & Kaur, 2020). Bryant's widow, Vanessa, even used the phrase "girl dad" in her eulogy (Kimble, 2020).

While there are only a select handful of people who will ever play professional basketball, and an even smaller number who played the game at Bryant's level, there are millions of people who are a #GirlDad. This trait of Bryant's was one of the few elements of his life in which many could relate to a superstar on the same level. That might be why Duncan's commentary became a viral sensation. For many, it was not Bryant the basketball superstar who had passed away, but a dad of four girls—something that many could identify with.

## In the Months Afterward

Shortly after the crash, a disturbing story emerged in which a Los Angeles County sheriff's deputy was accused of showing off gruesome photos from the site where the helicopter went down. According to the *Los Angeles Times*, the deputy was in a bar three days after the crash and began showing the bartender photos of the dead bodies and the crash wreckage (Tchekmedyian & Pringle, 2020). It was later revealed that a Los Angeles County fire captain also showed the photos to others at a fire department function. Following the public release of this information, the Bryant, Chester, Mauser, and Altobelli families all sued Los Angeles County for invasion of privacy and negligence. Both the Mauser and Altobelli

families reached a financial settlement before going to trial, but Vanessa Bryant, Kobe's widow and Gianna's mother, and Chris Chester, whose wife and daughter were on board the helicopter, refused to settle (Winton, 2022). The jury sided with Bryant and Chester, and the two families each received multimillion-dollar awards as part of their courtroom victory (Cowan & Jolly, 2022).

Additional lawsuits against the company that owned the helicopter, the company that operated the helicopter, and the estate of the pilot of the helicopter were also filed. In those cases, Bryant was joined by three other families that lost family members in the crash. Those lawsuits were settled out of court for an undisclosed amount before going to trial (Schrotenboer, 2021).

While the crash brought an early end to Bryant's life, his legacy on and off the basketball court remains strong. As stated previously in this chapter, Bryant had begun planning for his future while wrapping up his basketball career. One of those early financial decisions he made was to invest $6 million for a 10 percent ownership stake in the BodyArmor sports drink company. Less than a year after his death, Coca-Cola, which already owned 15 percent of the company, paid $5.6 billion to purchase the remaining 85 percent of the beverage brand, including Bryant's portion. That purchase meant that Bryant's estate would make $400 million on the sale. As a nod to the basketball legend's impact on the business, a press release announcing the sale was sent at 8:24 a.m.—a combination of the two jersey numbers Bryant wore for the Lakers, 8 and 24 (Brooks, 2021).

Perhaps nothing illustrated Bryant's impact on current basketball players more than a look at their feet. Even after his retirement, Bryant was still a paid endorser of Nike, and his sneakers were still some of the most popular on the court and in fashion. Of the more than 300 players who participated in the NBA's "Covid bubble" games in Orlando in the months following Bryant's death, nearly a third wore a Bryant signature shoe (Windhorst, 2021). However, his deal with Nike expired about a year after the helicopter crash, and Vanessa, upset with how the company was distributing the sneaker, elected not to renew it (DePaula, 2021). With no new signature sneakers being produced, NBA players began hoarding the pairs they could find so they could wear them in games. Some players estimated they were spending over $10,000 buying Bryant-model sneakers on the secondary market so they would not run out (Windhorst, 2021). However, those fears were short lived, as in March 2022, nearly a year after the deal had expired, Vanessa and Nike announced a new long-term contract (DePaula, 2022). The fact that Nike still saw value in partnering with Bryant's estate and quickly rereleased previous versions of his signature shoe demonstrates the impact he had even years after his retirement and death.

# Breaking News

While this chapter focuses on the events of January 26, 2020, it also demonstrates how reporting on **breaking news**, or news that is currently happening or updating in real time, can be a challenge for reporters. Many journalists will readily admit that reporting breaking news is one of the most challenging aspects of the job because updates are happening quickly, it can be difficult to get authorities to confirm information because they are also busy dealing with the situation, and there is a rush to get the latest information out to the public. The rise in the use of news station websites and social media has also influenced how updates from breaking news events are delivered. Previously, journalists needed to have details ready by the time the newspaper went to print or when the evening newscast was set to air. Usually, those deadlines were at the very end of the day, so in the case of the helicopter crash, reporters would have had the entire afternoon and the majority of the evening to gather information, confirm the identities of those on board, and write a complete story of the day. Instead, in the era of websites and social media, the media is expected to send updates immediately. The public is scrolling social media feeds during breaking news, looking for up-to-the-second information on the latest details. This may explain how so many mistakes happened during the initial reporting. These journalists had to rely on information that they may not have been able to confirm, but they needed to get it out quickly out of a fear that a competitor might beat them to the story.

In some cases, breaking news can catch a news outlet unprepared, which can lead to unforgivable mistakes. It should be noted that most news outlets have obituary videos or stories already created for famous people so that material can be disseminated very quickly without needing to start from a blank slate. For example, it is safe to assume that *The New York Times* has obituaries already written for the living United States presidents. However, Bryant was in his early 40s when he was suddenly killed, so many news outlets were likely scrambling to create

obituaries to honor his legacy. One such place, Britain's BBC television network, put together a video tribute about Kobe and Gianna. However, as the narrator of the piece recited Kobe's long list of career accomplishments, video of Los Angeles Laker LeBron James was shown on the screen. For nearly 15 seconds, it was clear that the BBC had confused the two players for each other. The BBC was quick to apologize both online and on air, but the damage was done, with many expressing extreme unhappiness about the mix-up (Hassan, 2020). For news outlets such as ABC News and the BBC, having to follow up initial reports with apologies created a situation that could lead to a lack of confidence in the news station among viewers who might have been watching at the time.

# Summary

In a recap of the media's mistakes in the first hours after the helicopter crash, a reporter from Northwest Public Broadcasting cited words from CBS News' Scott Pelley: "If you're first, no one will remember. If you're wrong, no one will ever forget" (Loveless, 2020, para. 31). The death of Kobe Bryant was a loss for basketball fans, as one of the greatest players in NBA history was killed much too young. At the same time, the Sunday morning crash will also be remembered as one of the lowest days in journalism history. With the exception of the knowledge that Kobe was on board, seemingly every follow-up story had some sort of factual error. Once they did have the information straight, the media still struggled with how, or even if, to address Bryant's sexual assault charge from his past.

The major takeaway from this incident for news consumers is to rethink how they follow reports during breaking news situations. The public should consider where they are getting the information from and how many media outlets are reporting this same information. If it is a single unsubstantiated report, then they should approach it with skepticism. Additionally, it is important to recognize that, during breaking news, initial reports are not necessarily the final reports. There are many aspects to the story that can change as more details are released.

## KEY TERMS

**breaking news**—News that is currently happening or updating in real time.

## REVIEW QUESTIONS

1. How had Kobe Bryant prepared for his career after basketball?
2. What were some of the issues surrounding TMZ's reporting of Bryant's death?
3. Why did media outlets struggle summarizing Bryant's life shortly after his passing?
4. What are some of the challenges with reporting breaking news?

# 28

# Houston Astros Cheating Scandal

## CHAPTER OBJECTIVES

After completing the chapter, the reader should be able to do the following:

- Understand the history of the Houston Astros
- Examine the team's response to the comments from Brandon Taubman
- Analyze how the nontraditional media helped to report on a major sports story
- Evaluate the team's response to the sign-stealing scandal

Chapter 5 discussed *Sports Illustrated* and the history behind the cover jinx. As a reminder, it had been demonstrated that if a team or player were featured on the cover, then bad luck would soon follow. In 2014, *SI* put that theory to the test by declaring on the cover of a June issue that the Houston Astros, the undisputed worst team in baseball at the time, would be the World Series champions in 2017 (Reiter, 2014). Amazingly, that prophecy came true, as the Astros went from worst to first and did win that title. The magazine put the Astros back on the cover shortly after the championship-clinching game with "It happened!" written in large font (Kolur, 2017).

However, a few seasons later, that win would be questioned by many. A news report on a sports website and a follow-up investigation from independent fans found that the Astros were not following the rules. Several months later, the Astros' response to this story left many just as angry about that as the actual cheating allegations. The team's crisis communication strategy during this time is cited by many as what *not* to do.

## History of the Houston Astros

Before getting into the scandal and the ensuing fallout that is the focus of this chapter, a brief history of the Houston Astros will help demonstrate the ups and (mostly) downs of this franchise. Despite being in the league for over 60 years, the team and its fans have had little to cheer about, as they found themselves toward the bottom of the standings with a subpar record for decades. However, after a stretch in which the team was historically bad, they turned things around and became champions . . . even though that title might not have been completely on the up-and-up.

## Expansion in 1962

Major League Baseball (MLB) expanded to Houston in 1962 with the addition of the Houston Colt .45s. The owners had held a "name the team" contest and the person who suggested Colt .45s said the name "fit the frontier image of Texas and that the famous gun played an important role in the history of the American West" (Fink, 2017, para. 3). Not only was the team named after a gun, but the logo and uniforms featured a smoking pistol below the word *Colt*. In today's game, an image of a just-fired gun on a professional sports jersey would likely never be approved by the league. In fact, when the Astros were celebrating the 50th anniversary of the franchise in 2012 and wanted to wear replicas of the original jerseys, MLB initially did not allow the gun to be a part of the design. However, after thousands of fans complained about the altered logo, MLB ultimately relented, and the jerseys with the pistol were worn twice in the 2012 season (McTaggart, 2012).

Rich Pilling/MLB Photos via Getty Images

**J.R. Richard (left) and Nolan Ryan (right) of the Houston Astros pose before a game in 1980.**

## Name Change

The Colt .45s name was short-lived. Three years after their inaugural season the team moved into the Astrodome, the world's first domed sports stadium. Along with the move, and with a nod to Houston being the primary home of the U.S. space agency NASA, the name was changed to the Houston Astros (short for astronauts) (McTaggart, 2021). The owner at the time also wanted to show how modern the team and city were becoming. He said, "The name and insignia will help dispel the image of Texas as a land of cowboys and Indians, and it behooves every citizen in this area to call attention to the 20th century aspects of Texas and Houston" (McTaggart, 2021, para. 4). Also contributing to the name change was the fact that Colt Firearms Company wanted a cut of the Colt .45s team revenue and the owner was looking for a way to avoid making those payments (McTaggart, 2021).

## Struggles on the Field

With a few exceptions, the Astros' on-field history was fairly forgettable. From 1962 to 1996, the team reached the playoffs just three times and did not reach a World Series until 2005, a series they lost in four straight games. With little winning to celebrate, the team was perhaps best known not for their playing, but for their uniforms. In 1975, the Astros introduced the "rainbow" jerseys that featured red, orange, and yellow horizontal stripes from the chest to the waist, a large blue star, and the player's number on the pants. One author wrote that the players looked like "large orange popsicles" in the jerseys, while the players themselves initially wondered if the jerseys were part of a joke (Hulsey, n.d., para. 19). They are almost certainly the most polarizing in sports history, having been named both one of the "Most Stylish" and "Ugliest" uniforms of all time (Kitchen, 2013; SI Staff, 2014).

While the team was not very good for a long period, they were historically bad in the early 2010s. The Astros were, record-wise, the worst team in baseball in 2011, 2012, and 2013. Perhaps making things even worse for the team was the fact that it appeared as if the fans had lost interest. The team's combined attendance total from the 2012 and 2013 season was slightly more than they had reached in 2007 alone (Reiter, 2014). Not only were fans not watching at the ballpark, but they also weren't tuning in on television, either. In an early-season game in 2014, the Astros played the Los Angeles Angels in a game that registered a 0.0 television rating in Houston.

That meant that none of the almost 600 televisions that were being monitored for viewership in the city were watching the game (Tayler, 2014). It is safe to say that at least one of the 500,000 households in the entire city of Houston tuned in, but that 0.0 rating demonstrated that the actual number of viewers was not very high.

## World Series Champions

While one might assume that no team wants to be the worst in baseball, there are certain advantages to being bad. In fact, being bad was essentially the Astros' strategy. Management had decided that they would take advantage of baseball's draft rules and, instead of being "good," or even "so-so," they would actively try to be the worst team for a few seasons (Reiter, 2014). Since the Astros were so bad, they were given higher picks in the MLB Entry Draft, which meant they had first shot at selecting some of the best high school and college players available. The team picked first overall in 2012, 2013, and 2014, and then had both the second and fifth selections in 2015. They would also have high picks in all the remaining rounds of the draft. While not all the players selected turned out to be major league superstars, those drafts helped stockpile the team with young talent that would soon turn the team into winners (Young, 2017). Following a surprising first-place finish in its division in 2015, the Astros' plan fully came together in 2017 as the team won its first World Series in franchise history (Witz, 2017).

## Roberto Osuna

While the major scandal was still a few months away, an incident involving a member of the Astros front office would be a strong hint of how the team would respond to criticism. In 2018, relief pitcher Roberto Osuna was playing for the Toronto Blue Jays when he was arrested for domestic assault (Cwik, 2018). As a result, MLB suspended him for 75 games for violating the league's domestic violence policy (Baer, 2018). Around the same time, the Astros determined that they needed help in their bullpen and elected to trade for Osuna, despite the player being suspended for his indefensible actions. Fans and the media condemned the move. One prominent baseball reporter wrote that, "In trading for Roberto Osuna, the Houston Astros show they have no conscience" (Passan, 2018, para. 1), while Astros fans took to social media to express their disappointment that the team had acquired someone accused of domestic

assault (Psihogios, 2018). In a press conference following the move, the Astros' general manager said the team had a zero-tolerance policy regarding domestic violence, but that also Osuna deserved a second chance (Passan, 2018).

The following season, with Osuna leading the American League in saves, the Astros headed back to the World Series. In the locker room celebration following their American League Championship win, *Sports Illustrated's* Stephanie Apstein reported that Astros assistant general manager Brandon Taubman was heard yelling, "Thank God we got Osuna! I'm so f—— glad we got Osuna!" in front of three female reporters, one of whom was wearing a domestic violence awareness bracelet (Apstein, 2019). Other media outlets quickly confirmed the story, but the Astros went on the defensive. The team released a statement saying the report was "misleading and completely irresponsible" and accused *Sports Illustrated* of fabricating the story (Folkenflik, 2019, para. 21).

However, less than 24 hours later, the Astros slightly changed their tune. In a new statement, Taubman admitted he said the words, but said they were about Osuna's play and had nothing to do with the player's past transgressions. The team's owner, Jim Crane, wrote that the "Astros continue to be committed to using our voice to create awareness and support on the issue of domestic violence" (Rupar, 2019, para. 13). Baseball journalists were disappointed that the Astros did not retract their statement about Epstein's story being misleading and fabricated (Olney, 2019). Further reporting not only confirmed that Taubman had made the outburst, but that he did appear to be directly responding to the presence of the reporter who was wearing the domestic violence bracelet in the locker room when saying how happy he was that the team acquired Osuna (Folkenflik, 2019).

The story came to a head two days later when the Astros put out a final statement on the matter, with this one having an entirely different message from the previous two. The team stated that after several conversations with members of the media and Astros employees, they had determined that Taubman's comments were intentionally directed toward the reporters. The team stated, "We were wrong" and apologized to the *Sports Illustrated* reporter whom they accused of fabricating the story and "to all individuals who witnessed the incident or were offended by the inappropriate comment" (Doolittle, 2019, para. 4). The statement ended with the announcement that Taubman had been fired by the club.

The Osuna/Taubman incident illustrated the Astros' poor response to an incident involving their club. When the story was first reported, the team immediately bashed the journalist and implied that the story was fiction. The next day, the team hedged slightly, with Taubman saying that his comments were misinterpreted. Finally, the team collected all the facts and admitted that its initial statement was wrong, the reporter was right, and Taubman was gone. The Astros had attempted to defend their own employee using an "us versus them" strategy. That mentality, which led to an embarrassing retraction from the team, would surface again just a few months later.

# The Scandal

At the same time as the Taubman story was being reported and debated, the Astros were in the midst of a World Series in which they were the heavy favorites. The team refused to label the incident a distraction (Hoffman, 2019), but they shockingly lost the championship series to the underdog Washington Nationals. Just over a month later, as the offseason was starting to ramp up, the team was back in the headlines as part of one of the biggest scandals in MLB in decades.

## Signs and Sign Stealing

Before recapping the story that broke the scandal, it is necessary to provide some background information for those who may not follow baseball closely. Before every baseball is thrown to the batter, the catcher relays what type of pitch he wants the pitcher to throw by putting down hand signals between his legs. These are known as "signs." If the catcher wants a fastball, he will usually put down one finger. The pitcher knows this means "fastball" and can either take that suggestion or shake his head and the catcher will provide another option.

During the game, the pitcher and the catcher are usually the only two players on the field who know the pitch that is about to be thrown. This is important because if the batter knew the pitch, he would have a better chance of getting a hit. For example, if the batter is aware that a fastball is coming, he would be ready to swing earlier than if he knew a slower pitch was coming. Since the beginning of baseball, teams have tried to decode their opponents' signals to get an advantage. Players would watch the opposing coaches to see if any sort of hand motion meant that a specific pitch or play was about to happen. This method of simply using one's own eyes to attempt to crack the opponent's signs is not illegal, but

MLB has specific rules that state teams cannot use any sort of *electronic equipment* during games for the purpose of stealing signs or giving their players an advantage (Corcoran, 2018).

## The Initial Story

In November 2019, the website *The Athletic* published a story that claimed the Astros used illegal electronic means to steals signs in 2017. The journalists reported that the team had a video camera in the outfield at their home stadium that was focused on the opposing team's catcher behind home plate who was giving the signs to the pitcher. That video was connected to a television monitor that was located in a hallway directly behind the Astros' dugout. Team employees would watch the catcher's signs through a hidden camera on the monitor, see what pitch the pitcher would throw, and then use that information to decode the signs (Rosenthal & Drellich, 2019). By the letter of the law in MLB, this meant that the Astros had cheated the year they won the World Series because they used electronics during the game in an attempt to gain an unfair advantage.

Once the signs were successfully figured out, the team employees watching on the monitor would signal to the batter what pitch was coming. Despite the high-tech operation, the signal itself was about as low-tech as possible—they simply banged on a trash can. Loud bangs as the pitcher was about to throw meant that an offspeed pitch was coming. With these signals, the batter was better prepared for what the pitcher was going to do. The article stated that not every player on the team used it, but that some preferred to hit at home because of the benefit of the trash can (Rosenthal & Drellich, 2019). However, whether it was one player, a few players, or the entire team, the damage was done. The article had labeled the Astros a team of cheaters, and it was about to get a lot worse.

## Nontraditional Media

The initial article on the Astros sign stealing methods was published on *The Athletic* and written by two prominent baseball writers, Ken Rosenthal and Even Drellich. Both have MLB press credentials, which means they can go to the ballparks with media access to interview players, have access to coaches and front office members, and sit in the press box during games. Those with those credentials and working for a major media outlet are considered part of the **traditional media**. For decades, these traditional media journalists consisted of those who worked for newspapers, television news broadcasts, and radio news broadcasts.

Some prominent sports websites, such as *The Athletic*, would be also considered traditional media because they operate similar to newspapers, despite not having an actual physical printed edition. However, many sports websites would likely fall under the category of **nontraditional media**. These are organizations or individuals who are not credentialed for games, have no access to the players, and give updates on the team from their own homes. In many cases, these websites are run by fans who are simply looking for a way to write about their favorite team.

While *The Athletic* gets the credit for being the first to report the Astros' story, it was members of the nontraditional media that quickly provided the evidence to back up the article (Lee, 2020). Perhaps no one did that better than Jimmy O'Brien, a diehard baseball fan who ran Twitter and YouTube accounts under the name "Jomboy." In the initial article, the reporters referenced a specific game between the Astros and the Chicago White Sox in which the White Sox pitcher appeared to notice the banging that was coming before he threw certain pitches. O'Brien found that game online, edited various plays from the game together, and added his own commentary before posting the video to Twitter. Over five million people have watched the clip where O'Brien essentially proves that the banging was happening before offspeed pitches. After showing one at-bat where the banging is clearly heard, he says, "That sequence is so upsetting. There is no way that's not done without technology" (Jomboy, 2019, 1:00). O'Brien then published several more videos of himself breaking down additional games to demonstrate that this was not an isolated incident (Lee, 2020). Marcus Stroman, at the time a pitcher for the Toronto Blue Jays, retweeted a Jomboy video that showed him being the victim of the trash can banging, with "this is crazy" as the caption (Stroman, 2019).

O'Brien became an online detective, and his was one of the most sought-after accounts in the wake of the cheating scandal revelation, but he was also quick to point out that he had other Internet sleuths on his side. While the journalists from *The Athletic* spent months conducting interviews, doing research, having editors review the story, and double-checking each element before publication (Rosenthal, 2023), O'Brien said "I crowdsource this s—" (Lee, 2020, para. 11). On his pod-cast the day after his videos were posted, O'Brien said that followers of his account kept emailing him different video clips throughout the day (Jomboy Media, 2019).

While the Jomboy account might have gotten the most publicity, it was far from the only amateur detective to provide evidence of cheating. A 17-year-old high school student who ran a New York Yankees fan Twitter account posted a screenshot from the 2017 World Series documentary that clearly shows a monitor and a trash can right behind the Astros' dugout (Lee, 2020). An Astros fan listened to 8,274 pitches that were thrown during the 2017 season and provided examples of a banging sound on nearly 14 percent of those pitches. He posted all his information, with video proof, on a website he created at SignStealingScandal.com (Barron, 2020).

While a traditional media outlet broke the story, it was fans on the Internet who were gathering and providing the proof afterward. As O'Brien said, "I didn't break the news. I helped accelerate it" (Lee, 2020, para. 10). This reporting of this scandal demonstrated that while major media outlets are still the driving force when it comes to uncovering major stories, someone does not necessarily need to work for one of those outlets to have an impact. It was not ESPN or *Sports Illustrated* reporters who ended up earning millions of views and social media clicks by providing additional information to go along with the initial story. Instead, it was fans running their own social media and websites who provided the video proof following the initial story.

## Punishment and Responses

In January 2020, Major League Baseball, after conducting dozens of interviews, reviewing team documents, and examining game video, confirmed that the Astros had illegally used a video camera system to steal signs in both 2017 and 2018. The team was fined $5 million, lost first- and second-round draft picks in both 2020 and 2021, and the team's general manager and manager were both suspended for a full season. The Astros took that final punishment a step further and fired them both the same day that MLB released its findings (Wagner, 2020). In a controversial decision, the MLB commissioner granted all the players immunity in exchange for the truth about what had happened; therefore, none of the players were punished for their roles in the scandal (Waldstein, 2020a). While MLB did admit the illegal sign stealing happened, it refused to say if the garbage can banging actually influenced any games. Without proof of the games being influenced, the league elected not to vacate the Astros' 2017 World Series championship (Wagner, 2020).

## Press Conference

Before the 2020 season, the Astros held a press conference at their spring training facility in order to address the sign-stealing scandal. First to speak was Jim Crane, the team's owner, who said that he did not feel that the sign stealing affected the games. Less than a minute later, he was asked by a reporter to verify that was what he said, and the owner immediately contradicted himself with his response: "I didn't say it didn't impact the game" (Draper, 2020, para. 3). The owner repeatedly blamed the then-manager and general manager—two people who were no longer with the organization—while saying that the players did not deserve any of the criticism for what happened. He also released himself of any blame, saying "I don't think I should be held accountable" (Daniels, 2020, para. 8). As for the players, two of the team's best, José Altuve and Alex Bregman, each gave statements that lasted less than two minutes and then left before answering questions from the gathered media. Bregman said his piece in a robotic-sounding, monotone voice, while Altuve said that the team was now focused on winning another championship. When the locker room was opened afterward for the media to ask questions, their teammates did not fare much better, with some saying that they did not feel they needed to apologize to opposing players (Draper, 2020).

## Crisis Communications

From when the initial story from *The Athletic* was published, the Astros had four months to prepare for

Alex Bregman (left) and José Altuve (right) of the Houston Astros look on as owner Jim Crane reads a prepared statement at a February 2020 press conference addressing the cheating scandal.

Michael Reaves/Getty Images

this press conference, and by nearly every account, the team's response was a swing and a miss. Reporters labeled the press conference "embarrassing," "tone deaf," "an absolute disaster," and "a joke" (Reed, 2020). One wrote:

> The Astros have had an entire offseason to figure out a way to mollify the public, even if they weren't actually sorry, and the woeful display Crane put on didn't even manage to drag them back to the bare minimum standard of perfunctory insincerity. (Baumann, 2020, para. 15)

It was not just sports reporters who were shocked at how poorly the team was prepared for the press conference, as public relations professionals were also stunned at the Astros' response. When discussing the team's owner, one expert said, "I want to see someone who is truly contrite and is really fired up about fixing this, about winning back trust. And what I saw was a guy reading with all the emotion of a dial tone" (Baccellieri, 2020, para. 4). Another expert said that the team was ignoring the basic tenets of crisis management by not accepting responsibility or expressing remorse (Daniels, 2020). For those involved in crisis communication, the Astros had done the exact opposite of the recommended plan.

## Public Response

While the media and public relations experts were shocked at the Astros' lack of contrition regarding the scandal and fallout, fans from other teams were ready to let the players know how they felt. Houston had quickly become one of the most hated teams in baseball and the players were loudly booed throughout spring training and were expected to face a similar wrath in the regular season. The Astros were even booed at their own stadium during a spring training game (NBC Sports Washington, 2020).

However, just as it looked as if the hate the team would face in stadiums from the fans would be a yearlong issue, the coronavirus pandemic changed everything. As a precautionary measure to stop the spread of the virus, MLB started the 2020 season without fans in the stadiums. Instead of hearing tens of thousands of fans hurling insults at them at every road game, the Astros were instead met with silence. One fan said, "How many different ways can they get away with what happened? They don't even have to face the wrath of the fans" (Waldstein, 2020b, para. 4). Instead, fans hired a plane to fly over the stadium with a "Houston Asterisks" banner, set up Twitter accounts dedicated to the "Astros Shame Tour," and simply stood outside empty stadiums to boo (Waldstein, 2020b). While fans were livid about the Astros' scandal, they would have to wait almost an entire season before being able to let the team know in person how they felt.

# Summary

The case study involving the Houston Astros and sign stealing is one that touches on several different topics that have been discussed in this book. For the journalism side, the story demonstrated that, while the traditional media did the initial work to get the story reported, it was nontraditional media members who provided the video evidence. This illustrates that people no longer have to work for large legacy-media outlets in order to make an impact on the world of sports. With the Internet's ability to spread a story globally, it is the content in the story itself that often becomes more important than who reports it.

For public relations practitioners, the Astros' initial press conference four months after the story was first reported was an example of how not to handle a crisis. The team showed little remorse, refused to take responsibility, and left many fans and media members perhaps angrier than they were before. Teams involved in future scandals will likely use the Astros' example as a guide for what methods are unsuccessful when trying to earn back the public's trust.

## KEY TERMS

**nontraditional media**—Media organizations or individuals who are not credentialed for games, not associated with a newspaper, television or radio station, and often give updates on the team from their own homes.

**traditional media**—Media outlets that usually consist of newspapers, television broadcasts, and radio broadcasts with journalists who have access to games, locker rooms, and other restricted press areas.

## REVIEW QUESTIONS

1. How did the Houston Astros' response to the *Sports Illustrated* article regarding Roberto Osuna and Brandon Taubman evolve in the several days following the publication of the story?

2. What is the difference between the traditional media and the nontraditional media?

3. Why was "Jomboy" an important part of the Houston Astros sign-stealing story?

4. Why was the Astros' crisis communication strategy considered a failure?

# PART

# V

# EMERGING TRENDS IN SPORTS, MEDIA, AND SOCIETY

It is difficult to know exactly what the future holds for sports and the sports media. For example, ESPN wisely invested heavily in its sports app for smartphones, but incorrectly assumed that 3D televisions would be widely adopted. However, as of the publication of this book, there are a few emerging trends that appear to have staying power and are likely to be an important part of the sports world for decades to come.

Before discussing specific trends, Part V begins with a breakdown of the two-step flow concept (chapter 29). This theory relates how information flows from one person to the next, but the emerging trend here is how social media and the Internet has changed this flow. People used to only be able to communicate with those close to them, but the Internet has expanded conversations globally, allowing those who might not have had an influence to now be opinion leaders.

Fans used to rely on journalists working at newspapers and television stations to get the latest sports news, but now they can hear directly from the teams and players themselves (chapter 30). This rise in team and player media gives the audience a direct connection to the athletes, which might be a troubling sign for journalists. Many reporters are still dealing with the lasting impacts of media restrictions enacted during the rise of the COVID-19 virus (chapter 31), so the media is struggling to find its place in the current reporting world.

Two formerly taboo subjects in sports bookend the final three chapters, with deep dives on athletes and mental health (chapter 32) and sports betting (chapter 34). For decades, athletes were encouraged to fight through any mental challenges they might have, while American sports fans could only bet on sports in a select few places. However, now athletes are dropping out of major competitions to focus on their mental health, and placing a bet on a sporting event can be done right from one's smartphone. Chapter 33 acknowledges one of the fastest-growing areas in sports: competitive video gaming.

29

*THEORETICAL FOUNDATION*

# Two-Step Flow and Weak Ties

## CHAPTER OBJECTIVES

After completing this chapter, the reader should be able to do the following:

- Understand the concept of two-step flow
- Identify how two-step flow has evolved in the era of social media
- Evaluate the importance of weak ties in communication
- Summarize an example of two-step flow and weak ties in the world of sports

The clock is winding down at a junior high school basketball game in Louisiana. Karen Smith's dad is recording the action on his cell phone as his pint-sized daughter heaves the ball from half-court as the final buzzer sounds . . . and it's good! The crowd goes wild, and Karen's dad has the whole thing on video. He quickly uploads the final shot to one of his social media accounts with the caption, "Check it out! Karen won the game!"

Karen's aunt in San Diego sees the video and shares it with her followers, which then causes it to be seen by the aunt's friend in New York. That friend then shares it to his followers, one of whom works for ESPN. That person passes it along to his bosses, and within minutes the sports network reaches out to Karen's dad to see if they can show the video on *SportsCenter*. That initial

post of the buzzer-beating shot has gone national, and ESPN's broadcaster says, "This might be the best junior high basketball highlight ever!" to the millions of viewers of watching.

This might seem like a far-fetched scenario, but ESPN shows amazing plays from all sorts of different locations regularly, and the scenario from the previous paragraphs is exactly how it might play out. For the purposes of this chapter, it also demonstrates the concept of the strength of weak ties, as the video went national thanks to people who had no immediate connection to Karen after the first few shares on social media. Weak ties, along with the two-step flow, are two important concepts when it comes to explaining the transfer of information and the forming of opinions.

223

# Two-Step Flow of Communication

For decades, researchers have been attempting to figure out how people get their information and how they form opinions regarding what they have learned. As newspapers, radios, and televisions became more prominent, many assumed that it was the mass media that played a major role in this process. In order to study this further, professor Paul Lazarsfeld conducted a study in which he examined how people in Ohio were determining who to vote for during the 1940 presidential election in the United States. Four years later, he expanded his research to include the entire United States, and, based on the results of those two studies, he came to a surprising conclusion (Baran & Davis, 2011).

Lazarsfeld found that the mass media had very little influence on how people chose to vote. Instead, it was the sharing of information between friends and family that played the most prominent role in determining which candidate would be selected by individual voters on Election Day. Therefore, it was **interpersonal communication**, defined as direct interactions between two people, that was the major factor.

So, who were these people who held a great deal of influence on their friends and family? Lazarsfeld and his graduate student Elihu Katz determined that influencers would get their information from the mass media and then pass along their own interpretations of the news to others (Katz & Lazarsfeld, 1955). They gave those sharing the information the title of **opinion leaders**, and the people receiving the information were labeled **opinion followers**. Therefore, information flowed in two steps: from the media to the opinion leaders and then from the opinion leaders to the opinion followers. That led to the naming of this phenomenon as the **two-step flow of information**. Figure 29.1 visualizes how the theory works.

# Two-Step Flow in the Social Media Era

Two-step flow was a concept that was developed before the era of social media, so it is worth revisiting the theory to see if it is still valid now that new means of communication have been developed. In that regard, many scholars have stated that the two-step flow is in fact still relevant in modern times, but that the players in the model have changed. In fact, the two-step flow might be more relevant than ever as opinion leaders now have access to more than just those in their immediate physical area.

Previously, opinion leaders were almost exclusively friends or family who were in close physical contact with opinion followers. However, opinion leaders can now be almost anyone with a social media account and a message to share, as previous limitations of location are gone because social media connects users from all over the world. Therefore, an opinion leader's social circle can grow tremendously because their location is no longer an important part of the conversation. For example, a fan of the Dallas Cowboys does not necessarily have to live in Dallas to have an online voice about the team.

In addition, the media previously functioned as gatekeepers with the power to decide what information reached the public (see chapter 1 for more information on gatekeeping). However, with social media, a single user can have a message reach a global audience without the traditional media's help. Opinion leaders can now be

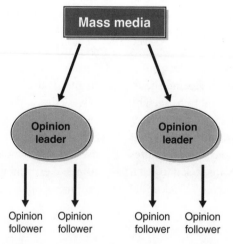

**FIGURE 29.1**   Two-step flow of information.

anyone with a large social media following. This can often be seen in the rise of "social media influencers." These users often have hundreds of thousands, if not millions, of followers and can decide new trends, what stories are important, and to what people should be paying attention.

However, the assumption that one must have a large following to be influential is not necessarily accurate. Instead, the **Million Follower Fallacy** has demonstrated that follower count is practically meaningless when it comes to determining influence. Specifically for Twitter, researchers found that the number of retweets of a message was driven by content of the tweet, not the identity of the sender (Cha et al., 2010). This further demonstrates how nearly anyone can become an opinion leader in the era of social media. A video does not need to be initially posted on a social media account with millions of followers in order for it to be seen by millions. Instead, as demonstrated by the example at the beginning of this chapter, a random fan with ten followers can capture an amazing video on his cell phone, post it to his account, and after several retweets, that video has gone global. This can be attributed to the **strength of weak ties.**

## Strength of Weak Ties

As would be expected, people often form tightly knit groups that are made up of friends and family. However, those groups can be somewhat limiting because there is a greater than 50 percent chance that any two people within that group already know each other (Christakis & Fowler, 2009). With common connections, it becomes difficult to bring new ideas into the group because everyone knows the same people and is experiencing the same events. Since the connection is so close, these relationships among those in a friend and family group became known as "strong ties" (Granovetter, 1973).

Therefore, more casual friendships or acquaintances were known as "weak ties." For many years, those researching the two-step flow of information often ignored these weak ties because it was assumed that they had no effect on how people received their news. Researchers assumed that only those who had a close connection could be influential. However, in an unexpected turn of events, Granovetter (1973) established that it was actually the weaker connections that are more effective than the stronger ones in the dissemination of information. He determined that weak ties act as a connector between different groups, and therefore are crucial in introducing new information (Granovetter, 1973). For example, because everyone in the same in-group is hearing the same opinions, it is nearly impossible for the group to consider new ideas. However, if an outsider can introduce a different concept to just one member, then that person can pass it along to their in-group, thus bringing in a new opinion.

The importance of weak ties was first realized before the development of the Internet. However, thanks to social media the concept of weak ties might be even more important than ever. Face-to-face conversations among in-groups still have to occur between people within the same physical area, but the Internet has allowed people to be exposed to opinions throughout the world simply through their social media feeds. Opinion leaders now have the opportunity to reach an audience that may not have been previously available to them.

## Two-Step Flow and Weak Ties Example

In 2013, leadership at the University of North Carolina Wilmington (UNCW) recommended that both the men's and women's swimming and diving teams be eliminated to save money in the athletic department. However, before the official cuts were to occur, members of both teams mobilized on social media, created a plan to save their team, and began contacting anyone and everyone who might be able to help them keep the team afloat. Ultimately, their efforts were successful: They garnered 14,000 signatures of support on an online platform, and the university's chancellor elected to save the teams from elimination. The process the athletes used is an example of the strength of weak ties in relation to the two-step flow.

During the two-week period in which the teams were facing elimination, the Twitter activity of the members of the swimming and diving teams was analyzed. With none of the team members having more than a few hundred followers at the time, their strategy was to engage with those who had bigger followings in the hope that those people could draw more attention to the online petition. The athletes did this through engaging with the Twitter accounts of entertainment celebrities, sports stars, and swimming legends. Of the more than 1,750 tweets sent by the team in those two weeks, almost 10 percent were messages in which they were reaching out directly to those who they believed could help their cause. Amazingly, it worked, as several did retweet the link to the online petition—including Lance Armstrong (more on him in chapter 25), who retweeted the petition to his more than three million followers (Hull, 2014).

UNCWSports.com

**The David B. Allen Natatorium on the campus of UNC Wilmington.**

While the UNCW swimmers and divers might not have been aware they were proving the effectiveness of weak ties and the evolution of the two-step flow, it is evident in the results that they did exactly that. The team realized early that social media was going to be most effective in trying to save their program. One member of the team said, "Social media was a priority. In today's world, you can spread news like wildfire online. We knew it would be the fastest and easiest way to get the word out" (Hull, 2014, p. 543). In the flow of information, the athletes had become the opinion leaders by promoting their story without needing the traditional media of newspapers and television broadcasts. Another swimmer said that by taking control of the narrative themselves, they were able to mobilize the support of the public quicker: "I think if this had happened 15 years ago it would have taken over a month to get to the level [of support] we did in just a week or so. I am so thankful we had social media" (Hull, 2014, p. 544).

The strength of weak ties can be demonstrated by the fact that none of the members of the team had more than 300 followers on Twitter and, since they are all on the same team, many of those followers were probably the same people (strong ties). Therefore, to get more support, the team members reached outside their network of followers to engage others (weak ties). However, as noted in the Million Follower Fallacy, it is the content of the tweet that is most important when attempting to get information to spread. Therefore, the UNCW team members had to be very strategic when crafting their messages. They focused on their sport getting cut and asking for help from Olympic swimmers and others who have a passion for the sport.

By focusing on famous swimmers, many of whom retweeted them, the team was able to expand their audience from their several hundred followers to tens of thousands of Twitter users. Olympian Ryan Lochte sent the petition to his one million followers in a tweet that was then retweeted by another 250 people. The UNCW team members did not know Lochte personally, and likely did not know all the 250 people who retweeted it, so it was the weak ties made through Lochte that proved to be invaluable. The possible cut of the teams made headlines in Wilmington, North Carolina, but was certainly not front-page news in the rest of the country. However, thanks to those weak ties, the story was now everywhere online, as followers of some of the most famous swimmers in the world, no matter where they lived, were learning about this situation. Less than two weeks after the online petition was posted, it had been viewed in 911 cities, 38 countries, and 17 different languages (Quigley, 2013). Shortly after, the UNCW chancellor announced that the programs would not be eliminated.

# Summary

For decades, the two-step flow of information was regarded as one of the primary explainers as to how people formed their opinions regarding important issues. Opinion leaders would get information from the mass media and share their feelings on those topics with opinion followers. Those connections were often dictated by physical location, as people could only primarily have conversations with those in the same area. However, social media allowed people to send a message that could go global, and suddenly anyone could become an opinion leader. The passing of information and opinions was also once thought to be done mostly through those with a personal connection. Instead, research has determined that those who are not part of a person's immediate circle are actually more likely to be able to introduce new ideas to a group. As social media has become a bigger part of how the world communicates, some of the ideas behind the two-step flow and weak ties have changed, but both remain important theories in how people form opinions.

## KEY TERMS

**interpersonal communication**—Direct interactions between two people.

**opinion followers**—People who form opinions based on information that was given to them by the opinion leaders.

**opinion leaders**—Those who get their information from the mass media and then pass that information along to opinion followers.

**strength of weak ties**—A communication theory that states that people not in an immediate friend/family group are more influential than those who are when it comes to introducing new ideas to a group.

**Million Follower Fallacy**—Demonstrated that social media follower count is practically meaningless when it comes to determining influence.

**two-step flow of information**—The process by which information flows from the media to the opinion leaders and then from the opinion leaders to the opinion followers.

## REVIEW QUESTIONS

1. What is the difference between opinion leaders and opinion followers?
2. How has the two-step flow evolved with the creation of social media?
3. What did the Million Follower Fallacy demonstrate?
4. How are weak ties important in the flow of information?

# 30

# Team and Player Media

## CHAPTER OBJECTIVES

After completing the chapter, the reader should be able to do the following:

- Understand the power the traditional media had for many years
- Define *team media* and *player media*
- Recognize some of the key moments in the development of team and player media
- Identify the appeal of team and player media for the teams and players

In late 2021, before playing their inaugural season, the NWSL's San Diego Wave FC traded for U.S. national team star Alex Morgan in a deal with the Orlando Pride. As expected, the trade of one of the biggest soccer stars in the country was of a great interest to national sports outlets such as *The Athletic* and local newspapers such as *The San Diego Union-Tribune* (Linehan, 2021; Zeigler, 2021). However, as the deal was coming together, no journalist had interviews with Morgan or anyone else associated with the Wave FC or the Pride regarding the trade.

Instead, a story posted on SanDiegoWaveFC.com—the team's official website—had quotes from Morgan, a behind-the-scenes video of her wearing a San Diego Wave FC T-shirt was posted on the Wave FC's Twitter account, and Morgan posted an image in which she thanked Orlando's fans, her former teammates, and others involved with the Pride organization on her own Twitter account (Morgan, 2021; San Diego Wave FC, 2021a, 2021b). Any number of national or local media members would have welcomed the opportunity to get those

quotes, the video, or an interview with Morgan about her time in Orlando. However, the fact that the team and the player were releasing that information directly to the fans, without needing the traditional media, helps demonstrate the rise of team and player media.

## The Traditional Media

Before discussing this new way in which fans are getting information directly from the teams and players, it is worth examining how news was delivered before this trend. For many years, fans would get the latest updates from what many call "traditional media." Traditional media members were journalists who worked for newspapers, radio, and television news outlets. In the era before the Internet, if a fan did not watch a game live, they had to read about it in the newspaper, listen to a recap on the radio, or watch the highlights on television. This led to a situation in which a select few people controlled how the public learned about what was happening in the world of sports. In addition, that meant that the recap a fan was getting was the recap as seen through the eyes of the reporter. As discussed in chapter 1, this plays into the concept of the gatekeeper, in which the media has the power to decide what information reaches the public and what aspects of that story will be reported.

Teams wanting to alert their fans about specific information were essentially at the mercy of the traditional media. The team's public relations official might want fans to know about an upcoming promotion or an active roster change, but if the journalist does not think that is worth relaying to the audience, then the team is essentially out of luck. For players, the traditional media formed a similar boundary between themselves and the fans. If a tennis player wanted to inform fans of a tournament she was playing in, she would need the journalists to let the public know. The two could conduct an interview, but there would be no guarantee that the reporter would include the quotes that the tennis player was hoping for. In fact, that reporter might not even ask a question about the tennis tournament, and instead focus the entire interview on a completely different topic. These journalists in the traditional media held an incredible amount of power when it came to what news and information would and would not reach the public.

## The Impact of the Internet

The influence of the traditional media took a small step back with the development of the Internet and easily creatable websites. While newspapers and television stations produced their own web addresses that allowed them to relay information to the audience outside of their traditional means, the opportunity was also there for fans to do the same. Anyone could sign up to create a free website through a variety of different web hosting communities. On those pages, fans could write their own content for an online audience. People no longer needed to work at a major media outlet to have a voice regarding their favorite team. For example, a fan living in Boston could write a news blog about the New York Mets despite living hundreds of miles from the team and not actually attending games. A writer for a Kansas City Chiefs blog living in New York "would sit on his computer in Brooklyn watching live streams of Chiefs press conferences" before writing his story (Massie, 2015, para. 11). These fan-driven websites demonstrated that non-journalists could report on the team without needing press credentials from major newspapers to do it.

It was not just fans creating their own website; teams were developing Internet homes, too. It might seem somewhat silly now, but a team having its own website was a fairly novel concept when the Internet was first reaching the mainstream. Though teams were making these websites, there was not much to them. A 1996 capture of the NFL's Atlanta Falcons website (atlantafalcons.com) showed basic graphics, lots of text, and a few subsections that included merchandise sales, the schedule, and the roster. The "news wire" section was simply a listing of press releases that had been sent to media members.

## Team Media Begins

Those early websites were the beginning of what ultimately became team media. Through those pages, teams could communicate directly with the audience without needing the traditional media to serve as the gatekeeper. While that 1996 version of the Atlanta Falcons page might look crude when compared to today's polished websites, a fan could go directly to the team's site and see rosters, news, and transcribed interviews with players. In the past, a fan would need to pick up a newspaper to get that information.

Therefore, **team media** can be best summarized as teams reporting on themselves. This could be simple information that is easily accessible (such as a list of coaches) to something that only the team can provide (such as a video from inside the locker room immediately after the game). Team media can consist of social media posts, behind-the-scenes videos, interviews with players, and basically anything else involving the team that the team itself is producing and distributing to the public.

## Bengals Hire Hobson

One of the first teams to recognize the potential of team media was the NFL's Cincinnati Bengals. In 1999, the Bengals hired Geoff Hobson, a sports reporter at *The Cincinnati Enquirer*, to write for the team's website at Bengals.com. Instead of working for the traditional media, Hobson was now a Bengals team employee. Despite that arrangement, the team said that he would be an independent reporter and write stories about the team from a neutral vantage point for the website.

However, his hiring came at a very curious time. The Bengals were in the process of trying to get the city of Cincinnati to help fund a new stadium for the team. One of the biggest critics of that plan was Hobson, and he routinely wrote about it while at *The Cincinnati Enquirer*. Once he shifted to Bengals.com, he stopped writing articles criticizing the stadium. He would say at the time that he "doesn't have time to write about the stadium issue" (Trumpbour, 2006).

## Conflict of Interest?

Hobson's hire put a spotlight on perhaps the biggest concern regarding the rise of team media, which is the appearance of a conflict of interest. Journalists have long been taught to be impartial observers of the action and report just the facts about the games and events. However, team media employees are in a unique situation. Many might rightly ask: If a journalist is covering a team while working for and getting paid by that team, then how can they be impartial?

While team media journalists might push back at the idea that they are simply painting the team in a positive light, it is sometimes hard to ignore the differences. For example, in 2021, the Los Angeles Rams beat the New York Giants 38–11, and someone reading the game recaps from Giants.com and the *New York Post* might wonder if the reporters were at the same game. From Giants.com:

> The Giants spent most of Sunday afternoon looking for points, yards, and big plays. When they came up short partly because so many of their important offensive players were missing, the Giants refused to look for excuses. (Eisen, 2021, para 1)

The story does admit that the team lost, but places some of the blame on the fact that some key players did not play. The Giants.com reporter also stated that the team refused to make any excuses, a sign of a team that was continuing to fight despite their five losses in six games. Fans reading this article might come away feeling better about the Giants and its performance even after the loss. However, that story was certainly very different from what was in *The New York Post*:

> Memories of better times are all the Giants have now. The present is disgraceful. There are no signs the future will be any better. (Schwartz, 2021, para. 2)

Certainly, the sportswriter from *The New York Post* did not leave fans with an encouraging feeling, calling the team disgraceful and implying the Giants will struggle for many years to come. While it might have been overly harsh, that reporter is supposed to give an impartial view of the action. The truth regarding the game might lie somewhere in between those two stories.

With this example, it becomes apparent why team media sources would want to release their own recap of games and not rely on the traditional media to be the sole information provider. Teams can "spin" any result to look better than it might actually be. For example, on social media, a team account would likely send fewer posts when the team is losing as a way to somewhat ignore the action on the field. The conflict of interest lies in teams wanting to keep fans informed, but also wanting those fans to leave with a positive opinion of their team.

## Filling a Need

It is hard to ignore the positive spin that is often a part of team media, but in some cases, the team is simply trying to fill a need. In 2009, the Los Angeles Kings hockey team found themselves getting less coverage in local newspapers due to budget cuts in those newsrooms. Writers were no longer being sent on the road with the team, and the Kings recognized that this was leading to a lack of stories. In order to fill the void, the Kings hired their own reporter to work for their website. The team signed a journalist from the *Los Angeles Daily News* to travel with the team, go to every practice and game, and write stories and commentaries for Kings.NHL.com. At the time, a Kings spokesman said the move was not about creating positive coverage of the team, it was simply about getting any coverage at all: "We have a passionate fan base who want instant information about our team, but there's been declining news coverage of us" (Pérez-Peña, 2009, para. 3).

## Team Media in College

The concept of team media is not exclusive to the professional ranks, as amateur, college, and even high school teams are now producing their own content to be disseminated to the public. Some of it might be as simple as a Twitter account for a high school that updates scores of the games in progress. Others could be more complex, creating graphics, videos, and photos that give news on all aspects of the team from both behind the scenes and during the games. Similar to the Los Angeles Kings, many college programs are starting to use team media as a way to make up for the coverage they might not be getting from the local and national media. While a major college football and basketball team might have reporters at every game, some of the traditionally less popular sports might not have any journalists show up. Through team media, the schools themselves can spotlight all the sports beyond just the major draws.

In 2017, the University of South Carolina Gamecocks took this a step further by rebranding their media relations department to the "Athletics Communication and Public Relations" department. While that might not seem like a major change, it was the description of the new title that was a nod to the rising influence of team media. Steve Fink, the head of that department, was quoted in the press release as saying: "While a fundamental part of our responsibility remains committed to assisting the media in providing coverage of the institution, its athletics programs, administrators, coaches and student-athletes, we no longer rely solely on the messages carried by external media sources" (GamecockCentral, 2017, para. 4). This demonstrates that, on nearly every level, fans can get the latest information on their team directly from the team itself, a dramatic shift from the years in which the traditional media was the gatekeeper of information.

# Player Media

Similar to how teams are connecting directly with fans, the players themselves have been able to do the same. Using social media, players can have their own news and updates show up directly on the feeds of fans' accounts. This has created the idea of **player media** where players are, just like teams, bypassing the traditional media and creating their own content directly for fans. Players are creating personal updates through social media, athlete-run websites, and podcasts. While that is appealing for the players, it has created a situation where the traditional media can find itself on the outside looking in when it comes to interviewing athletes.

## Social Media

As discussed in chapter 6, social media has given athletes a platform to communicate with an audience about a variety of topics. For example, a golfer used Twitter to discuss his sponsorship renewal, a baseball player revealed his free agency decision on YouTube, and a basketball player announced his retirement in an Instagram post (Spieth, 2022; Bauer, 2021; Parsons, 2022). Previously, these athletes' announcements would have been revealed in the media after an interview with a

Pittsburgh Steelers running back Le'Veon Bell updates his social media status after a game against the Green Bay Packers in 2017.

Shelley Lipton/Icon Sportswire via Getty Images

journalist, and while that was a successful method, it also led to some possible holes in the delivery of the announcement: Fans would have to be watching a news broadcast or reading the newspaper on the exact right day to see the information, and players who are not superstars might not get the attention they believe the announcement deserves. Through social media, an athlete can make the announcement to a group of people who have already expressed an interest in the athlete by following their account, and that athlete can say exactly what they want for as long as they want, without any of the time or space limitations that exist in a newspaper or television broadcast.

With social media, athletes can be their own media outlet, reporting news about themselves through newly created self-promotion accounts. Basketball's Kevin Durant and his agent created *The Boardroom*, a sports news website designed with a goal of covering the business side of sports. Around the same time this venture was getting started, Durant was a free agent and was looking to sign with a new team. Once he had decided on the Brooklyn Nets, his agent suggested that Durant break the news on his new venture:

> I said to Kevin, "Listen, I know you want to be low profile about it, but let's just control the narrative. There's no reason for you to have to worry about anyone taking it out of context, and we're trying to build a business. You should do what I think is best for you, and I think that we should try to have this as a real launch pad to 'The Boardroom' as a brand." (Moran, 2020, para. 11)

The move to announce Durant's free agency destination on The Boardroom's Instagram account turned out to be a smart one. Before his post, the account had fewer than 30,000 followers, but by that evening, it had over 200,000 followers (Moran, 2020). Fans looking for the latest developments on Durant's destination did not need to watch the traditional media but could instead get the details from the social media accounts of the company owned by the player himself.

# The Players' Tribune

In 2014, recently retired baseball player Derek Jeter announced that he was cofounding a website that would give athletes a chance to tell stories from their own perspective. *The Players' Tribune* was designed to have articles written directly by the athletes, instead of a reporter taking a few select quotes and creating a story around that. These articles would be fully the words of the athletes, even with their names listed in the byline as the authors.

In one of the website's early prominent stories, the Boston Red Sox's David Ortiz used the platform to angrily push back against allegations that he was a steroid user. In the article, he discussed, often with colorful language, baseball's testing policies, how one reporter used to harass him about steroids, and how, despite never testing positive for a banned substance, he was often considered a cheater by many fans (Ortiz, 2015). The story was one that any traditional media outlet would have loved to have had and, in fact, one did. *The Boston Globe* had gotten many of the same quotes from Ortiz weeks earlier but was waiting to publish the story until opening day of the baseball season. Not printing it immediately caused the sports editor of *The Boston Globe* to have concerns that another media outlet might have it first, and while he was right, he had not considered this newly formed website: "I worried about ESPN or Yahoo or The Boston Herald somehow doing a similar story. But I didn't think about The Players' Tribune" (Sandomir, 2015, para. 7).

## Big Stories

While the Ortiz story in 2015 was one of the first to draw attention to this new website, a first-person article posted a few months later brought *The Players' Tribune* into the mainstream. Basketball superstar Kobe Bryant, one of the most recognizable and popular athletes in the world, announced on the website that he was going to retire at the end of the season. His "Dear Basketball" article was essentially a love letter to the sport, in which he wrote about all it had done for him, but how it was time to say goodbye (Bryant, 2015). Bryant's retirement was, understandably, one of the biggest stories in the sports world, and it was *The Players' Tribune* that had it. In fact, the story garnered so much attention that it ended up crashing the website (Mandell, 2015).

Before playing for the Brooklyn Nets, Kevin Durant was previously a free agent in 2016, and certainly every media outlet wanted to be the first to report where Durant was heading. Instead, it was Durant himself in a first-person article on *The Players' Tribune* that revealed he would be signing with the Golden State Warriors (Durant, 2016). Once again, *The Players' Tribune* had the scoop, but it was still not entirely prepared. Just as with Bryant's announcement, the website crashed almost immediately after Durant's story went live (Greenberg, 2016).

### Sensitive Topics

While the website has given athletes a platform to discuss key moments in their career, it has also provided an opportunity to some to speak out about issues that previously were not discussed in sports. One of the early articles was a piece from former NBA player Larry Sanders about how his struggles with his mental health contributed to his decision to step away from the game (Sanders, 2015). In 2018, basketball All-Star and NBA champion Kevin Love explained that he had been suffering from panic attacks, making him the first prominent player to reveal his mental health battles (Love, 2018). Due to his superstar status, Love's article in *The Players' Tribune* was considered one of the first to bring mental health conversations regarding athletes to the forefront. While chapter 32 has more about the rise in awareness of mental health among athletes, those articles speak

to the trust that athletes had with *The Players' Tribune*. Instead of speaking with a journalist and hoping that person will tell the story how the athlete wants, the athlete can control the narrative himself or herself by writing these first-person articles directly from their own vantage point.

## Podcasts

Podcasts allow fans to hear interviews and conversations between some of their favorite athletes. Current and former sports stars have created podcasts in which they recap games, discuss behind-the-scenes events, and debate sports news. In 2017, two players on the Cleveland Cavaliers started the podcast *Road Trippin'* in which they simply interviewed their teammates throughout the season (Hsu, 2021). It is a format that has been repeated by many others, as players interview each other, getting answers that only teammates and others in the league might be able to get. Of course, interviewing players

Draymond Green interviews Trae Young for a live edition of The Draymond Green Show presented at the Uninterrupted Festival in July 2023.

was a key part of the job for the traditional media, so these podcasts were becoming yet another way in which journalists could feel their jobs being threatened.

During the 2022 NBA Finals, the Golden State Warriors' Draymond Green took the concept of the podcasting athlete to an entirely new level. After every game, Green, who was playing in the games himself, would retreat to his hotel room and break down the game. He discussed what worked, what did not, and gave in-depth descriptions of some of the biggest plays of the game. Some traditional members openly wondered if Green was more concerned with his podcast than he was with the games, especially after a subpar performance in Game 3 (Gordon, 2022). However, for diehard fans who might be tired of watching traditional NBA analysts on ESPN or other networks, the opportunity to hear directly from one of the players in the game, immediately after the game, is something that is hard to ignore.

## The Appeal of Team and Player Media

Player and team media is appealing for a variety of reasons for those involved, but the ability to avoid the traditional media might be the biggest draw. If players and teams want to communicate directly with their fans, they no longer need journalists to act as the middleman and relay whatever information needs to be passed along. For some of the athletes, a theme of *trust*, or a lack of it, seems to be a key reason why they want to try to ignore journalists. Former NFL cornerback DeAngelo Hall was an early adopter of Twitter because, in his words, "If you have something posted on your Twitter site, that's exactly what you have to say. It hasn't been doctored up by a writer or any of the media" (Yahoo! Sports, 2009, para. 12). When promoting why athletes should want to be a part of *The Players' Tribune*, Derek Jeter said, "It's a trusted place, a place where they can speak freely and not have to worry about how their words are twisted and turned" (Feinberg, 2015, para. 5).

## Concerns for Traditional Media

For traditional media, this rise in teams and players delivering their own news should be especially concerning. When LeBron James announced he was signing with the Los Angeles Lakers in 2018, the deal was revealed through his own agency on Twitter (Youngmisuk, 2018). James' fan base got the information from James himself, and can now follow the Lakers' website, Lakers' social media accounts, and James' social media for the latest information on the player and the team. With all those options available, a fan might not feel the need to read the *Los Angeles Times* or ESPN. One of the primary reasons for reading journalists is to get the latest news, and now team and athletes are able to fulfill that purpose themselves.

With this shift, some traditional media entities have developed a "if you can't beat them, join them" mentality. As NBA star Paul George was entering his own free agency, he wanted to document his plan for his fans. A three-part first-person documentary about his quest aired on ESPN during its popular *SportsCenter* program (Hall, 2018). This was essentially free advertising for George and it was ESPN that was giving him the platform. Instead of competing against the player to deliver this news, the sports television network partnered with him to become an ally in the player media movement.

## Summary

Sports journalists will likely forever have a gatekeeping role in the process of getting information from the source to the audience. However, the creation of team and player media has somewhat limited that power when it comes to certain stories. Teams and players can deliver stories, quotes, and information direct to the audience, without needing a journalist to act as the middleman. For teams, this creates a situation in which every story they want out to the public can be published on their website, while negative stories, such as those about a painful loss, can be "spun" to look less damaging. For athletes, they can tell their story exactly how they want it to be told, as many have a strong distrust of the media. Team and player media should be seen as a threat to traditional media members, because if fans can get information and news directly from the teams and players themselves, then many fans might be asking why they need the traditional media.

### KEY TERMS

**player media**—Players bypassing the traditional media and creating their own content directly for fans.

**team media**—Teams reporting on themselves.

## REVIEW QUESTIONS

1. Why was the traditional media especially influential before the Internet was created?
2. What is team media and how is it different from traditional media?
3. Why might team media be considered a conflict of interest?
4. Why is *The Players' Tribune* an example of player media?

# 31

# Lasting Impact of COVID-19

## CHAPTER OBJECTIVES

After completing the chapter, the reader should be able to do the following:

- Understand the history of COVID-19 and sports
- Identify how the shutdown affected sports journalists
- Evaluate the sports media's response to having a lack of games to report on
- Understand the long-term effects that COVID-19 changes had on the sports media

An entire book could be written about the impact COVID-19 had on sports in 2020 and beyond. High school athletes lost entire seasons and college athletes had championships canceled. Millions of dollars of ticket revenue were lost due to fans being banned from arenas. Some athletes publicly debated and even refused to get the COVID-19 vaccine, while the long-term effect of the disease on athletes who contracted it may not be known for decades. The issues stemming from the pandemic involving fans, teams, and the athletes are numerous.

However, for the purpose of this book, the focus will be on how the pandemic affected the sports media. Fans rely on journalists to provide the latest updates on their favorite teams and players, but once the games shut down, there were no updates to provide. Outlets such as ESPN had to get creative to fill airtime by showing old games, documentaries, and baseball from the other side of the world. As months passed without any action, some sports journalists found themselves out of a job. When the events finally did return, those who were lucky

enough to still be employed were now a part of a much different sports media landscape.

## What Is COVID-19?

According to the Centers for Disease Control and Prevention (CDC), the coronavirus disease 2019, commonly referred to as COVID-19, is a disease caused by a novel virus named SARS-CoV-2. It was first discovered in December 2019 in China and quickly spread throughout the world. Those who are infected might feel like they have a cold, the flu, or pneumonia. The CDC states that while most people have mild symptoms, more than a million people died in the United States from the disease (CDC, 2021).

## How Did We Get Here?

On February 2, 2020, the Kansas City Chiefs won the Super Bowl in front of 62,417 fans in Miami, Florida (Wilner, 2020). At the time, COVID-19 was almost exclusively in China, as the first case outside that country had just been discovered a few days earlier (World Health Organization, 2020). While the world's attention was very slowly turning toward this emerging threat, the sports community was still weeks away from it being a major concern. However, once it started to affect the United States, the changes happened dramatically fast, and no sport was spared from the impact.

## The Early Days

On February 23, the Italian government banned public events in northern Italy, including two matches in the soccer league Serie A, after the virus had started to spread to that area (Reuters Staff, 2020). In the beginning of March, the NBA recommended to its players that they stop signing autographs and high-fiving fans, while some MLB teams started handing out pre-autographed baseballs to fans, instead of having the player sign in front of a crowd (Lacques, 2021; Reynolds, 2020). While American leagues were making minor concessions, the differences in how the COVID-19 situation was being addressed in the rest of the world were stark. On March 8, an Italian soccer game became the first sporting event outside of China to be played without any fans in attendance, while on the same night in Los Angeles, the Lakers and Clippers played in front of a sold-out arena filled with 19,068 fans (Associated Press, 2020; Dampf, 2020).

## Locker Room Access

While games in the United States were progressing normally, leagues were about to make a major change behind the scenes. On March 9, the NBA, NHL, MLB, and MLS all closed media access to the locker room. Officials from each league stated that the move was not made to ban reporters, but instead to ensure the safety of the players and the team staff members (Bieler & Bogage, 2020). While reporters acknowledged the purpose and reasoning behind the new policy, it also created concerns. For decades, sports journalists have been able to enter the locker room after the game and at other designated times as a way to speak directly to the players for their stories. This locker room access provides reporters a chance to get to know the players, create sources, and develop story ideas that can be published in the future.

Dan Shaughnessy, a longtime journalist with *The Boston Globe*, authored a column that afternoon titled, "Don't use coronavirus to close locker rooms to media forever." In the piece, he wrote: "Fans hungry for information about their teams would do well to understand what is lost when you take sports reporters out of the locker room," and recounted several examples of stories and quotes he got from players in the locker room that he believed he would not have gotten had the interviews taken place in a more formal setting (Shaughnessy, 2020, para. 21). The fear among these writers was that once locker room access was taken away due to COVID-19, it might never return.

One sportswriter did not see the big deal. Grant Wahl, a soccer writer, tweeted, "I don't think we ever need to be in a locker room. Doing mixed-zone postgame interviews with the USWNT outside their locker room has never been a problem" (Wahl, 2020). Wahl was referring to the United States Women's National Team in soccer, where, as a man, he was not allowed in the locker room to interview the players, so those athletes were brought out to a different area where he could interview them. However, he was in the minority, as the Associated Press Sports Editors organization and six other sportswriter groups issued a joint statement requesting that locker room access was not "unnecessarily limited in either the short or long term" (Glasspiegel, 2020, para. 2).

## Player Reactions

In early March, before the pandemic became a global issue, the prospect of playing games without fans was not one about which the players were overly excited. When asked about it, NBA star LeBron James said, "Play games without the fans? No, that's impossible. I ain't playing . . . If I show up to an arena and there are no fans there, I ain't playing" (Nair, 2020, para. 4, 5). However, just four days later, as the headlines surrounding COVID-19 became more dire and it became clear that something was going to have to change, James' opinion sounded much different: "If they feel like it's best for the safety of the players, the safety of the franchise, the safety of the league to mandate that, then we all listen to it" (Youngmisuk, 2020, para. 5).

With COVID-19 very quickly becoming the biggest story in the world, it was nearly impossible for sports journalists to ignore the virus and the impact it might have on the games and events. Instead of being solely asked about upcoming opponents, the questions now included topics such as social distancing and what the players were doing to avoid getting the disease. While many expressed concerns, some were still defiant. Utah

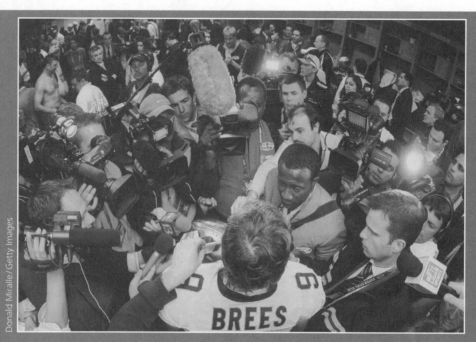

Donald Miralle/Getty Images

**Before COVID, athletes and media members frequently shared very close quarters.**

Jazz player Rudy Gobert ended a press conference with the gathered media by jokingly touching every microphone and audio recorder in front of him (Quinn, 2020). The journalists in attendance chuckled in amusement at the stunt, but it was anything but a laughing matter just two days later.

# March 11, 2020

While COVID-19 was on the minds of many in early March, it was still seen as a distant threat that was affecting the rest of the world more than the United States. Concerns were starting to be raised, but with the exception of a professional tennis tournament in California, the games were going on as scheduled. The first impact on a major team sports event happened on March 10, when the Ivy League canceled its men's and women's basketball tournaments, a move was called a "horrible, horrible, horrible decision" in the immediate aftermath on Twitter by a player on the Harvard men's team (Aiken, 2020; Gleeson & Myerberg, 2020).

The next day, March 11, would later be referred to as "the day that changed everything" (ESPN.com, 2021). Just before 2 p.m. ET, the mayor of San Francisco banned events in which there would be more than 1,000 people in attendance, so the NBA's Golden State Warriors, whose arena is in that city, announced they would play the next game without any fans (Lacques, 2021). Later

that day, the NCAA president announced that the upcoming men's and women's basketball tournaments would be played with only essential staff and a limited number of family members in attendance (NCAA, 2020). While those decisions made headlines, it was an NBA game in Oklahoma City that was about to turn the sports world upside down.

## Jazz versus Thunder

On the night of March 11, the Oklahoma City Thunder were set to host the Utah Jazz. The players warmed up and the starting lineups were introduced, but just seconds before the opening tipoff was set to take place, the referees huddled with the coaches and officials from each team. Minutes later, both squads, without explanation to anyone outside of the teams, went back to the locker room. Thirty minutes later, the public address announcer in the arena told fans that the game was postponed and that everyone should head home.

Less than an hour later, multiple media outlets were reporting that the game's postponement was due to a player on the Jazz testing positive for COVID-19. That player was Rudy Gobert, the same player who playfully touched the microphones and audio recorders of all the journalists in attendance at his press conference just a few days earlier. Within minutes of journalists reporting the news of Gobert's positive test result, the NBA suspended its season indefinitely. Every in-progress game was completed, but players on the New Orleans Pelicans and Sacramento Kings made the decision not to start their game after the postponement announcement (ESPN.com, 2021; Lacques, 2021). The NBA was the first major sports league to make schedule-altering decisions regarding coronavirus, but by the end of the day, it was clear that they would not be the last.

## The Next Day

By the morning of March 12, one can safely assume that discussions about the status of seasons were happening at nearly every level of sports, from youth events all the way up the professionals. However, major changes did not happen immediately. In the Big East men's basketball conference tournament, St. John's and Creighton tipped off and played the first half of their game before officials decided to cancel the rest of the tournament. Soon after, the postponements and cancelations came fast, including:

- The Big Ten, ACC, Big 12, SEC, and Pac-12 all canceling their basketball tournaments.
- MLB stopping spring training and postponing the start of the regular season.
- NHL suspending its regular season indefinitely.
- The NCAA canceling both the men's and women's basketball tournaments and all other championships in the winter and spring seasons.
- The PGA Tour suspending The Players Championship after the first round concluded and canceling the next four tournaments on the schedule.
- MLS postponing all its matches for the next 30 days. (Holmer, 2021; Keh, 2020)

## More Suspensions and Cancelations

In the ensuing days, many more leagues throughout the world either canceled or postponed seasons, events, and any other type of gathering. By March 23, ESPN had compiled a list of hundreds of sports that had been affected by the disease—everything from the Archery World Cup in Guatemala City to the Asian Canoe Slalom Championships in Thailand to the World Team Table Tennis Championships in South Korea (ESPN News Services, 2020). Other major events canceled, postponed, or altered included

- The Masters golf tournament,
- NASCAR races,
- the Wimbledon tennis tournament,
- the Little League World Series,
- the NFL Draft,
- horse racing's Triple Crown,
- the start of the WNBA season,
- high school sports,
- the Boston Marathon, and
- the Tour de France. (Los Angeles Times, 2020)

While all those events are certainly important to fans of each sport and the sports world as a whole, the biggest postponement was perhaps the decision regarding the 2020 Olympics in Tokyo. Every four years, the Summer Olympics brings together athletes, coaches, and spectators from all over the world to one location to face off in a variety of events. It is considered by many to be the premier sporting event in the world, and one for which the host countries spend years preparing. However, as the pandemic started to spread, it was becoming clear that the 2020 Olympics were not going to happen as scheduled. In late March, the International Olympic Committee announced that the 2020 games would now take place in 2021, a decision that an economist estimated would cost the Tokyo Olympic organizers as much at $5.75 billion (Wharton, 2020).

# No Live Sports and the Sports Media

The COVID-19 pandemic affected millions of people, and likely no one is going to feel any extra sympathy for sports journalists during this time, but the fact remains that sports media members suddenly found their entire profession in a state of uncertainty. The primary job of sports reporters and broadcasters is to cover games and events—and almost overnight there were no games on the schedule.

In the early days of the pandemic, some journalists did "what COVID-19 means for teams and athletes" stories (Owen, 2020), but there are only so many times that can be told. Broadcasters dove into the archives to replace canceled live games, with CBS Sports airing classic NCAA men's basketball games, MLB Network replaying great opening days of the past, and ESPN showing old professional wrestling events (Cafardo, 2020; Kelly & Casella, 2020; Shapiro, 2020). Journalists who were scheduled to cover events such as the NCAA basketball tournaments suddenly had no place go. One broadcaster wrote, "I went from having plans to be out of town for most of the months of March and April to suddenly begin in quasi-quarantine" (Hull & Romney, 2020, p. 499).

## Changing Job Descriptions

Sports journalists found themselves not only unable to go to games, but, just like millions of other people throughout the world, also working from home. ESPN reporters were giving updates from their living rooms, with iPads taking the place of studio cameras and, in the case of baseball reporter Jeff Passan, his son's LEGO collection directly next to his home studio (Martin, 2020). Atlanta sportscaster Kelly Price was provided lights, tripods, microphones, and a phone to turn her home office into a home television studio. In addition, almost all interviews were done over video conferencing, a process full of mixed feelings from many journalists, as some did not mind, and others missed the personal contact that was now gone without face-to-face interviews (Hull & Romney, 2020).

While working from home was part of the job, it was the job itself that was changing for many sports journalists. In a research study that took place in the first weeks following the immediate shutdown, the majority of sports broadcasters surveyed said they were being assigned news stories in addition to their sports reporting responsibilities. A few said they were not doing sports at all and were now exclusively news reporters (Hull & Romney, 2020).

## Virtual Sports

While jobs were changing and past games were being shown to fill time, there were still large gaps in the programming schedule for both sports leagues and the networks that traditionally carry the games. Some outlets turned to video games as a way to fill that void. Shortly after its season was suspended, NASCAR created the eNASCAR iRacing Pro Invitational Series. Several people affiliated with the sport, including some of the drivers themselves, competed in full-length races on virtual racetracks through the video game *iRacing*. Fox Sports, which was set to broadcast the actual races before the season was shut down, showed these virtual races instead, even bringing in their regular announcers to describe the action. The races were a huge hit, as over a million fans tuned in to a race in Texas, making it the most watched video game competition in television history (Weaver, 2020).

NASCAR via Getty Images

**Daniel Suarez races in the eNASCAR iRacing Pro Invitational Series in March 2020.**

## The Last Dance

ESPN devotes 24 hours a day, seven days a week, 365 days a year to sports coverage. When the sports schedule is packed, it is a channel that fans can turn on in the morning and leave on all day and never miss a beat. However, during the sports shutdowns caused by COVID-19, the games were not being played, the commentators had nothing to debate, and shows like *SportsCenter* had a limited number of stories that could be featured. The network that spends nearly every second of every day talking about sports had no sports to discuss.

In 2018, ESPN and Netflix had announced they were partnering to create a 10-part documentary about the history of Michael Jordan and the Chicago Bulls. The series, called *The Last Dance*, was set to debut in June 2020. The documentary would feature interviews with Jordan, his teammates and coaches, his rivals, media members, and even former U.S. president Barack Obama (Chavez, 2019; Christie, 2018). However, in the middle of March, with the world essentially shut down and sports fans craving any type of new content, the June premiere date was no longer going to cut it. Instead of waiting, the network announced that *The Last Dance* would debut in April, with two episodes airing each Sunday night for five weeks (Lopez, 2020).

The decision to move up the premiere date turned out to be a wise one for a number of reasons for ESPN. Perhaps most importantly, the network was able to satisfy its audience by giving them something they were craving: new sports content to watch when there was none to be had. This decision was rewarded through viewership, as an average of 5.6 million people watched each episode live, and another 12.8 million watched through either time-shifted or on-demand viewing, making it the most-watched documentary content in the network's history.

However, the boost was not just big for the show itself. The editions of *SportsCenter* that aired immediately following the episodes had some of the highest viewership numbers of the year, a podcast devoted to the show was the most downloaded ESPN podcast, and Facebook pre- and post-shows brought in millions of viewers (Volner, 2020). In addition, other shows on ESPN now had content to discuss. With no games to argue about, programs such as the debate show *First Take* now focused on *The Last Dance*. For example, one segment was devoted to debating if the documentary put more pressure on LeBron James to be successful (ESPN, 2020). Not only did *The Last Dance* give ESPN

ten one-hour shows, but it also provided additional opportunities for debate, analysis, and conversation that otherwise was not occurring due to the sports shutdown.

## Korean Baseball Organization

The Korean Baseball Organization (KBO) was one of the first leagues in the world to resume games. The South Korean league started its 2020 season without fans in attendance and with a surprising new media partner. ESPN, still searching for content to fill its airwaves, agreed to a deal to show six KBO games a week starting with the league's opening day on May 5. ESPN had become the league's exclusive English-language network and its baseball announcers called the action from their homes, with the games airing on ESPN, ESPN2, and the ESPN app. However, a fan had to be pretty dedicated to watch the live broadcasts, as the weekday games started at 5:30 a.m. ET, Saturdays at 4 a.m. ET, and Sundays at 1 a.m. ET (Martin, 2020). Those fans watched though, as the Opening Day broadcast of the NC Dinos taking on the Samsung Lions averaged 173,000 viewers on ESPN (Sports TV Ratings, 2020).

## The NFL Draft

One of the most prominent non-game events on the NFL calendar each year is the league's draft. In 2020, the draft was supposed to take place in Las Vegas, Nevada, with thousands of players, team officials, and fans in attendance. The pandemic changed those plans, and the league turned the draft into a virtual event where general managers made their player selections from home and NFL commissioner Roger Goodell announced the picks from his basement in New York (Seifert, 2020). While the logistics behind the online draft caused some concern among NFL team officials, it also created a unique opportunity for the television broadcast.

ESPN and the NFL Network traditionally produce their own draft coverage, but in 2020, they elected to combine forces and produce a show that would air simultaneously on both networks. Some announcers participated from ESPN's headquarters in Connecticut, while others reported remotely from their homes (Associated Press, 2020). In addition, cameras were in the homes of many of the top picks, adding up to a total of over 600 video feeds from homes across the United States (NFL Communications, 2020). On the night of the draft, any technology concerns were immediately squashed as the coverage went off without a hitch. In his review of the draft's coverage, *Sports Illustrated*'s media analyst wrote that it "couldn't have gone any smoother" (Traina, 2020, para. 1). Just as was the case with *The Last Dance*, people were desperate for sports content, and the 2020 NFL Draft became the most watched ever. More than 55 million viewers tuned in during the three-day event, up 16 percent from the previous year, with an estimated 8.4 million people watching all three days (NFL Communications, 2020).

## Are Sports Journalists Needed?

While fans were watching sports documentaries and the NFL Draft, they still were not able to watch live sports based in the United States. Leagues were remaining on the sidelines, and that meant it had been months since many sports journalists had reported on the teams and leagues they were tasked to cover. It perhaps came as no surprise that management at many media outlets were seemingly asking, "if there are no sports, what do I need sports journalists for?" Between April and June, the website *The Athletic* laid off 8 percent of its staff, the owners of *Sports Illustrated* instituted staff-wide pay cuts,

and the sports website *SB Nation* furloughed dozens of its workers (Draper, 2020).

For game broadcasters involved in live sports productions, the shutdown did not just mean they simply did not have to go to work—it meant they were likely not getting paid. Many of the announcers and crew members do not have a yearly salary but are instead paid by the game. One broadcaster said he had 75 games on his schedule that were canceled between March and June, estimating that a third of his yearly income was wiped out. Another play-by-play announcer said that without the steady stream of income he received from doing games, he had to start taking money from his retirement account to help pay his bills (Dellenger, 2020). Sports media members had spent decades covering every home run, touchdown, goal, and race. However, with no sports to discuss, the games suddenly took on a newfound sense of personal importance. As one baseball writer said, "my livelihood is predicated on baseball existing" (Curtis, 2020, para. 3).

## The Games Return

In July 2020, after months of inactivity, the games began to return. The MLB, NBA, WNBA, and NHL all set restart dates for that month. The leagues approached

LeBron James speaks remotely to the media after practice as part of the NBA Restart 2020.

Andrew D. Bernstein/NBAE via Getty Images

the renewal of the seasons differently, with the NHL skipping directly to the playoffs while the NBA elected to play a few regular-season games first (Mather, 2020). What was universal throughout was the fact that each league was taking precautions in an attempt to protect the players and the fans from exposure to COVID-19. For example, MLB players were tested for COVID-19 every day, those not playing were forced to wear masks in the dugout, and every ball that was touched by multiple players was immediately replaced (Wagner, 2020). The MLB teams would play their shortened season their home stadiums—except for the Toronto Blue Jays, who were forced to temporarily relocate because of Canadian travel restrictions—but several other leagues created a new "home away from home" scenario to keep players in and COVID-19 out.

## "The Bubble"

As a way to keep players safe, several leagues created central locations that would host all the games. These became known as "bubbles" because once the teams were in, they could not leave, and new people could not enter. For example, the NBA created its bubble at Walt Disney World's Wide World of Sports complex in Orlando, Florida. The players, coaches, and essential team personnel were isolated and quarantined at Disney hotels, with games taking place at arenas on the complex's campus with no fans present. Perhaps surprising to many, the plan actually worked, as each week the NBA proudly announced that all the players on location in Orlando had tested negative for COVID-19 (Anderson, 2020).

However, it was not just the players who were quarantined in the bubble, as media members found themselves under the same restrictions. Once they entered the bubble to cover the games, they were not able to leave. Journalists had temperature checkpoints to pass, had to wear masks whenever in public, and were given sensors to place around their necks that set off an alarm if they were within six feet of another person (Anderson, 2020). In addition to the journalists covering the games, ESPN and TNT broadcasted each matchup on television. Over 200 ESPN employees spent more than three months on Disney property, essentially creating a small city on the grounds of the Wide World of Sports (DelGallo, 2020).

## Limited Media Access

While the players were back, many journalists were still kept at a distance from the action. Locker room access was eliminated months earlier and remained that way even when the games resumed. In-person interviews were replaced by virtual interviews that traditionally took place on the conferencing platform Zoom. Without open access to the locker room, journalists were now at the mercy of team officials when it came to who they would be able to speak to after games. Officials would decide the one or two players that would be put on the Zoom call and that would be the extent of the interviews. In addition, the virtual format made it difficult for reporters to make a personal connection with the players, which many believed limited the quality of the stories. One newspaper columnist said, "I miss digging out stories that happen organically from having casual one-on-one conversations with athletes or coaches in the locker room about their sport or their personal lives" (Jones, 2021, para. 13).

## Remote Broadcasts

For play-by-play announcers, not being able to be in the locker room was the least of their concerns—some of them were not even allowed in the building. These announcers, who call the action during games, were instead describing the scene from a studio or even from their own homes. MLB's opening day game took place in Washington, DC, but that's not where Fox's crew was: Play-by-play announcer Joe Buck was in Denver, analyst John Smoltz was in New Jersey, and the game's broadcast producer was in Los Angeles (Timanus, 2020). TNT announcer Kevin Harlan's daughter posted a video of her dad announcing an NBA preseason game from his basement with the comment "having him upstairs for dinner then go downstairs for tip off was a new one!" (Dekker, 2020).

While these broadcasts were deemed necessary due to COVID-19 protocols, they were not without problems. Announcers who were forced to watch the games on television would occasionally get confused by what was happening, as the cameras were not always able to quickly pick up the action. Baseball announcers commented how remote broadcast forced them to have to wait to see what the result of the play was before describing it out of fear of making a mistake. In addition, technical difficulties caused players to be misidentified, audio problems, and loss of video during the game (Strauss, 2022).

## The Ensuing Years

The sports world slowly returned to what somewhat resembled a pre-pandemic normalcy, with sold-out stadiums, the removal of mask and social distancing policies, and leagues playing full seasons with no threat of cancelations. However, the games returning did not mean everything was back to normal for sports journalists. It was over two years before the NBA and NFL allowed journalists back in the locker room (Bucholtz, 2022). As the 2022 MLB season began, some teams elected to keep doing remote broadcasts as a way to save money (Strauss, 2022). NBC spends billions of dollars for the rights to broadcast the Olympics, but in both 2021 and 2022, the network elected to have their announcers call the action from Connecticut instead of on location in Japan and China (Reedy, 2022). For the sports media, many of the changes that occurred due to COVID-19 may ultimately not be temporary, affecting how they do their job and how fans get updates about their favorite teams, sports, and players.

## Summary

COVID-19 changed the lives of people throughout the world. Based on that, it might seem trivial to discuss the disease in the context of sports and the sports media. However, it is impossible to ignore the role sports played in the pandemic. In a podcast about the day the NBA shut down, sportswriter Sara Todd said

*In a really short amount of time, we went from knowing nothing and taking almost zero precaution to really starting to address this. And so, it feels like Rudy Gobert testing positive and leading to the NBA shutting down potentially saved thousands of lives. (Henderson, 2020, 1:01:37)*

On the day Gobert tested positive for COVID-19, it was sports journalists who were the first to report the story. As the pandemic continued, they informed sports fans about season shutdowns, the latest player news, and the eventual return of the games. Along the way, these journalists had to get creative in their reporting, found their jobs in jeopardy, and realized the return to action was not a return to pre-pandemic player-access levels. The long-term effects of the COVID-19 sports shutdown may be felt for journalists for years to come.

When the Tokyo Olympics took place in 2021, not all aspects of sports broadcasting were back to normal.

## REVIEW QUESTIONS

1. Why were reporters initially concerned about losing access to locker rooms during the early days of COVID-19?

2. How did sports journalists adapt when leagues began postponing games due to COVID-19?

3. Why was *The Last Dance* an important part of ESPN's programming during COVID-19?

4. Why might having announcers not at the games live describing the action be an issue?

# 32

# Mental Health

*This chapter contains discussion regarding depression and suicide that may be upsetting to some readers.*

In Game 7 of the 2010 NBA Finals, the Los Angeles Lakers' Ron Artest hit a three-pointer with just over a minute left to clinch the game and help win his team the title. In the live postgame interview on national television, with confetti streaming down around him and a brand new "NBA Champions" hat on his head, Artest acknowledged his friends and family before thanking a surprising connection:

> *My psychiatrist. She really helped me relax a lot. Thank you so much. It's so difficult to play, there is so much commotion going on in the playoffs and she helped me relax. I thank you so much. (NBA, 2010, :22)*

For some of those watching, it might have seemed like just another off-the-wall comment from a player who was known to have a rather unique personality. However, for others, Artest's admission that he went to a psychiatrist was reassuring. Fellow NBA player Roy Hibbert would later say, "I felt that when he did that, it kind of opened the doors to make it somewhat OK. I think it was great that he actually did that" (Holmes, 2015, para. 2). Mental health awareness was not a topic that was openly discussed in the sports world, so Artest's declaration was one of the first instances in which it went mainstream. While sports was not fully ready for acceptance, the mental health discussion was about to begin.

## What Is Mental Health?

Before discussing the rise of the awareness of mental health in sports, it is first important to define the term. However, that is not as easy as it may sound. An examination of media coverage of mental health and mental illness found that there was not an agreed-upon definition for those topics (Klin & Lemish, 2008). Without one accepted answer for "What is mental health?," it can be difficult to understand what the topic consists of exactly.

The World Health Organization (WHO), an agency of the United Nations aimed at promoting health, says that proper mental health enables people to cope with the stresses of life and that "people with mental health conditions are more likely to experience lower levels of mental well-being" (WHO, 2022b, para. 3). The WHO estimates that 5 percent of adults throughout the world suffer from depression, which is one of the more prominent examples of a mental health disorder (WHO, 2022a). Specifically in the United States, the National Institute of Mental Health estimated that in 2022 nearly one in five Americans lived with a mental illness (NIH, 2022).

## Media Coverage of Mental Health

One of the major obstacles surrounding the public perception of mental health was that media coverage had often represented the topic in a negative light. Mental

Al Tielemans/Sports Illustrated via Getty Images

**Kerri Strug grimaces in pain after landing her vault on an injured ankle in the 1996 Olympics.**

illness was associated by journalists with topics relating to violence, creating a stereotype among the audience that all people suffering from a mental illness must be dangerous (Dietrich et al., 2006; McGinty et al., 2016; Whitley & Wang, 2017). For example, a research study revealed that those who got information about mental health from the electronic media had a lower tolerance and opinion of people with mental illness than those without (Granello et al., 1999). While that study was not primarily focused on sports, the results are applicable to athletics. If the public is less likely to accept someone with anxiety or depression, that would likely not change just because that person is a star athlete.

## The Stigma of Mental Health in Sports

For many years, and for reasons beyond just media perception, athletes were seemingly discouraged from discussing their mental health. Sports are traditionally considered avenues for those who are physically and mentally tough, and who fight through setbacks in order to reach the desired goal. In 1996, gymnast Kerri Strug completed a vault with an injured leg to help the American squad win the team gold medal. Strug, limping and having to be carried off the mat by her coach, was labeled a hero, while one journalist compared her toughness to a soldier going into battle in a war movie (Vecsey, 1996). To many, athletes such as Strug are supposed to be willing to go through anything no matter what the pain, so concerns about mental health have been perceived negatively and taken to imply that one was weak and not able to compete on the biggest stage (Longman, 2021).

Additionally, mental ailments can be harder than a physical injury to diagnose. For example, an X-ray can show that a bone is broken, but there is no test that can determine if a player's anxiety is causing problems for them. This can lead to criticism from coaches and fans who are not understanding why an athlete cannot compete at their best when they appear to have nothing physically wrong. Instead of facing that backlash, athletes would traditionally instead keep their mental health concerns to themselves and try to ignore the problems.

However, ignoring or avoiding mental health concerns can create additional problems. Elite athletes are more vulnerable to mental illness than the general population, and there is a greater risk of bouts of depression among men in sports (Doherty et al., 2016; Souter et al., 2018). One expert who works with athletes said, "The idea that an athlete—or anyone trying to perform at their peak—need not pay attention to their mental health is negligent" (Gavin, 2021, para. 22). As a younger generation of athletes emerges, one that has grown up in a society in which more attention has been placed on mental health, those previous taboos are starting to be ignored.

# Prominent Athletes and Mental Health

The rise of mental health awareness in sports can be traced directly to the athletes themselves. These concerns have likely existed for years, but players were often encouraged to ignore those feelings and instead focus on the games and events (Longman, 2021). Eventually, it took several athletes speaking up to bring the issue of mental health awareness out of the shadows of a private struggle and into the public eye. Those athletes include

- Royce White,
- DeMar DeRozan,
- Kevin Love,
- Naomi Osaka,
- Simone Biles, and
- Michael Phelps.

## Royce White

One of the first prominent athletes to draw attention to mental health was basketball player Royce White. White was a standout at Iowa State University, and was open with the media and the public about his generalized anxiety disorder. In 2012, due to his intense fear of flying, White was given permission to travel to Iowa State road games through alternative means. When his team played Louisville, instead of being on the hour-long flight with teammates, his grandfather drove him 600 miles from Iowa to the arena in Kentucky (Jacobs, 2012). Despite the obstacles created by the anxiety, White became one of the best college players in the country and appeared to be on his way to a career in the NBA. However, that was when his mental health became a bigger part of his story.

Before the 2012 NBA draft, White was labeled the "mystery pick" and the "most perplexing prospect," not because of his play, but because of his anxiety (Torre, 2012, para. 1). The Houston Rockets elected to take a chance on White's talent and drafted him 16th overall, but the honeymoon was brief. White would soon inform the Rockets that he wished to travel to some games by bus instead of by plane, and he refused to join the team until they agreed to his wishes (Medcalf, 2012). While the team stated they would "continue to support him now and going forward" (Wrenn, 2012, para. 16), the two sides could not come to an agreement, and the team suspended White (Zillgitt, 2013). The Rockets would eventually trade White before he played a single minute for the club. He would end up on the Sacramento Kings, where he played in just three games before ending his NBA career.

White did play several seasons overseas, but his NBA career was cut short presumably not because of his playing ability, but his mental health and anxiety. In later interviews, he would state that the Rockets organization was used to dealing with broken bones, but was seemingly unsure of how to treat a mental issue. He said, "There's a disconnect between health and mental health. I said, 'This is my anxiety disorder and you're not respecting it the same as a physical health condition'" (Zillgitt, 2013, para. 22). After his NBA career ended in 2014, White continued to push the league to create a mental health policy, something that he believed would have helped him during his disputes with the Rockets (Devine, 2018). The issue did not appear to be a priority for the league during White's time there, but several years later, two high-profile admissions changed the perception regarding mental health in sports.

## DeMar DeRozan

On February 17, 2018, the Toronto Raptors' DeMar DeRozan sent a simple, six-word tweet that read: "This depression get the best of me . . ." (DeRozan, 2018). DeRozan would later tell a reporter that he was in his hotel room in Los Angeles during All-Star Weekend and that he was "going through [stuff]" and it was "a real, emotional moment for me" (Lee, 2022, para. 11). At the time, he hoped that his admission of his struggles would help others who were going through similar issues (Smith, 2018).

Unlike when White had difficulties getting the Rockets and the NBA to agree on how to handle his mental health concerns, his Raptors teammate Fred VanVleet noted how the NBA and the National Basketball Players Association (NBPA) began taking mental health more seriously almost immediately after DeRozan's tweet:

*He changed a billion-dollar business. He changed it pretty much single-handedly [by] speaking out. And then obviously a lot of guys felt more comfortable, and that's what it's about. So, for him to do that was huge and we won't know the impact, we'll never know the impact, but we just know that it's a great impact that he had on the league and on guys, on players, coaching staff, whoever—that this is DeMar DeRozan and he goes through [expletive] like everybody else. (Sportsnet Staff, 2020, para. 4)*

## Kevin Love

One month after that late-night tweet, another prominent NBA player would follow DeRozan's lead by publicly admitting that he too was struggling with mental health issues. In a first-person article published on the website *The Players' Tribune*, Kevin Love detailed his issues with panic attacks, specifically recounting an incident during a game against the Atlanta Hawks in 2017:

*After halftime, it all hit the fan. Coach Lue called a timeout in the third quarter. When I got to the bench, I felt my heart racing faster than usual. Then I was having trouble catching my breath. It's hard to describe, but everything was spinning, like my brain was trying to climb out of my head. The air felt thick and heavy. My mouth was like chalk. I remember our assistant coach yelling something about a defensive set. I nodded, but I didn't hear much of what he said. By that point, I was freaking out. When I got up to walk out of the huddle, I knew I couldn't reenter the game—like, literally couldn't do it physically. (Love, 2018, para. 11)*

Love, considered a basketball superstar by many, was suddenly one of the most in-demand players in the league, and it had nothing to do with his play. His admission made front-page news, and the article became more than just a personal story—it was a call to action to raise awareness about mental health struggles. His thesis of the article, "Everyone is going through something that we can't see," was meant to speak to more than just athletes. He finished the article by reminding his readers that if they were having a difficult time, they should seek help as he did (Love, 2018).

While Love's admission might have been surprising to many, the response demonstrated that he had made the right decision by going public. He received thousands of positive emails, had team and league officials thanking him for openly discussing mental health, and teammate LeBron James told him, "Today you helped a lot of people" (Stevens, 2018, para. 11). Even with the multitude of honors and accolades that came from his basketball career, Love would say that writing that article was the biggest and most important thing he had done in his career (Stevens, 2018).

LeBron James and Kevin Love greet each other after an October 2021 game.

Adam Pantozzi/NBAE via Getty Images

## Naomi Osaka

In 2021, Naomi Osaka was one of the most successful tennis players both on and off the court. She had won the United States Open in 2018 and 2020, helping her become the highest-paid female athlete in the world. As the 2021 French Open approached, Osaka announced that she would not participate in post-match news conferences with journalists because she said that the negative questions about how she was playing were affecting her mental health. After winning her first-round match, she did just as she promised and skipped the mandatory media session, resulting in a $15,000 fine from French Open officials (Futterman, 2021).

There would be no second-round press conference for her to avoid. Osaka withdrew from the tournament the next day because, in her words, she did not want to be a distraction during the tournament. In an Instagram post, the tennis star stated that she had suffered through long bouts of depression and that speaking to journalists brings her a great deal of anxiety (Osaka, 2021a). While many of her fellow tennis players did not openly criticize her boycott of the press, her competitors did say that they would not have made the same decision. Many cited the importance of the media in helping to grow and publicize the game, and that not speaking to them could ultimately hurt tennis as a whole (Clarey, 2021).

However, in the months following, the voices supporting Osaka began to grow louder. Fellow tennis player Nick Kyrgios called her inspirational, while Serena Williams acknowledged that she had been in similar situations (Henry, 2021; Jacobs, 2022). Osaka acknowledged that her admission demonstrated that she was not the only one who was having difficulties. In a first-person article in *Time* magazine, she wrote:

> It has become apparent to me that literally everyone either suffers from issues related to their mental health or knows someone who does. The number of messages I received from such a vast cross section of people confirms that. I think we can almost universally agree that each of us is a human being and subject to feelings and emotions. (Osaka, 2021b, para. 4)

When she traveled to the Olympics a few months later, Osaka said she was overwhelmed by the support she received from her fellow athletes, perhaps further demonstrating that she was correct in her assessment that many other athletes suffer in silence. Upon reflection during that time, it was perhaps most disappointing that, even as mental health awareness had been rising in sports, Osaka still felt the pressure that athletes had been facing for decades: "I kind of felt ashamed in that moment because as an athlete you're kind of told to be strong and push through everything" (GMA, 2022, 2:13).

## Simone Biles

As the Summer Olympics approached in 2021, *The New York Times* published an article titled "Simone Biles and the Weight of Perfection." The piece discussed not only her place as perhaps the greatest gymnast of all time, but also the struggles she was having with her mental health. Biles described falling into a deep depression and how therapy helped her cope with those feelings (Macur, 2021a). The article was supposed to serve as a preview for what many predicted would be many more gold medal–winning performances in the following week. Instead, the title referencing "the weight of perfection" turned out to be predictive in a different way.

Biles withdrew from the team competition following the first day of the event after she performed a vault that was not up to her usual standards. USA Gymnastics said her departure was due to a "medical issue," but a different narrative would soon emerge (Macur, 2021b). Biles would admit that she did not feel her best physically, but also that she was not mentally prepared to continue. She discussed having "the weight of the world" on her shoulders and that she wanted to protect both her mind and her body (Crouse, 2021).

For many, it was the timing of Biles' announcement that was the most shocking. Athletes work practically their entire lives to have a shot at the Olympics, often ignoring both physical and mental pain in order to get there. However, Biles went in the opposite direction by stating that her mental health was more important to her than a shot at winning another gold medal. While some critics questioned her decision, other Olympians called her an inspiration (Branch, 2022; Crouse, 2021). At the Winter Olympics the next year, several athletes said that Biles verbalized what many of them had been feeling for years, which gave them the strength to speak about their personal situations. Several posted on social media about their fears, spoke about mental health in press conferences, and relayed how they were now speaking to psychologists (Branch, 2022).

In a demonstration of how the conversation regarding mental health had evolved, Biles was not shy about openly discussing her struggles in the public. However, just a few years earlier, another Olympic great suffered in silence, worried about what an admission of his mental anguish might mean for his career.

## Michael Phelps

No Olympian has ever won more gold medals (23) or total medals (28) than American swimmer Michael Phelps. However, as he was becoming the most decorated athlete in Olympic history, he was privately struggling with suicidal thoughts and depression. Just before what would be his final Olympics in 2016, Phelps admitted all in an interview with NBC Sports, showcasing a side of his life of which the public was unaware (McCarthy, 2016). The swimmer who appeared to have everything come easy when he was in the pool was having mental health challenges out of the water. He would later admit that he felt depressed after every Olympics he competed in—all five of them over a 16-year period—and had contemplated suicide following an arrest for driving under the influence in 2014 (Capatides, 2018).

Phelps was once singularly focused on being the fastest swimmer in the world, but in retirement, his attention instead turned toward mental health awareness in sports. He created a documentary titled *Weight of Gold* that examined the mental health issues facing Olympians, while his charitable foundation focused on mental health in children (Gregory, 2021; Scutti, 2018). His willingness to speak about his own experiences has made him an expert of sorts that the media seeks out for interviews when athletes such as Osaka and Biles make their public declarations.

In the years since his admission, numerous people have told Phelps that his decision to go public with his story likely saved lives by letting people know they were not the only ones suffering. The Olympic great says those stories are worth more than any of his accomplishments in the pool: "Those moments and those feelings and those emotions for me are light years better than ever winning an Olympic gold medal. You have the chance to save a life, and that's way more powerful" (CBS News, 2018, para. 7).

## The Trouble With Social Media

As was discussed in chapter 6, social media has become an important part of how athletes can communicate directly with fans. However, a 2022 report in *The Wall Street Journal* also demonstrated the impact the social networks can have on athletes' mental health. While sports stars such as Biles have used social media to reveal their struggles with the pressures involved with the events, the platforms can also create problems when they are filled with negative comments from other users regarding an athletic performance. Biles said she avoids Twitter for that exact reason, but others find it hard to log off when companies are expecting their athletes to create sponsored posts for extra income (Wells & Radnofsky, 2022). This trend of mental stress caused by social media is not exclusive to sports, as researchers have found that social media use increased anxiety and depression among college students (Walsh, 2022).

## Resources for Athletes

A positive of athletes speaking out about mental health has been that not only is the topic more widely accepted, but that leagues and organizations have begun putting resources toward helping players with mental health symptoms. Shortly after DeMar DeRozan and Kevin Love went public with their mental health concerns, the NBPA hired its first director of mental health and wellness (Associated Press, 2018). Many MLB teams have started focusing on more than just on-field coaching and have hired mental skills coaches to work with the players at all levels of their organizations (Bandujo, 2021). In the NFL, a Comprehensive Mental Health and Wellness Committee was formed as a partnership between the league and its players. The formation of that committee resulted in a league-wide rise of players meeting with a behavioral health team clinician (Clemmons, 2021). On the college level, the NCAA started a mental health summit event, created interactive modules for coaches, athletes, and administrators, and organized a mental health advisory group to better help student-athletes (Henry, 2022).

While the resources have improved, those involved in making those changes say the biggest difference has been the willingness of the players to embrace the opportunities. In an article in *The New York Times*, NFL player Solomon Thomas recalled a teammate in 2016 pointing out the team's therapist in the lunchroom and saying to Thomas, "We can't go over there. Otherwise, we look like we're crazy" (Clemmons, 2021, para. 1). Instead, superstar athletes such as DeRozan, Love, Osaka, Biles, and Phelps are not only publicly declaring their struggles with mental health, but also advocating for people to seek help if they too are having problems. In 2010, Ron Artest appeared to be an anomaly when he thanked his therapist after making a three-pointer in the NBA Finals, but as the years have progressed, he has become far from the only athlete to admit to getting help with mental health.

## Summary

Mental health has gone from taboo subject in sports to front-page news thanks to several prominent athletes speaking out on the topic. For years, athletes were encouraged to push through the pain and told that mental issues were a sign of weakness. Media coverage did not help change that narrative, as mental health problems were often associated with violence. However, when athletes such as Kevin Love, Naomi Osaka, and Simone Biles spoke about their battles with the mental side of the game, the conversation soon evolved. All three were open about how their mental health was influencing their performance, with Osaka and Biles both withdrawing from competitions to focus on these concerns. Media coverage would soon begin to change, as the athletes were lauded as heroes instead of criticized as they might have been in the past. Other athletes would acknowledge their own battles, citing the public declarations of those stars as giving them the confidence to come forward. In addition, leagues and organizations began offering more resources for athletes in an effort to focus on mental health just as they do for physical ailments.

## REVIEW QUESTIONS

1. Why has mental health long been a taboo subject in sports?

2. How was the response to DeMar DeRozan expressing his mental health concerns different from the response to Royce White?

3. Why was the reaction to Naomi Osaka dropping out of the French Open due to mental health concerns somewhat polarizing at first?

4. Why is social media considered a place that can be difficult for athletes' mental well-being?

# 33

# Esports

It is the final lap of the biggest race of the season, and the two leaders are bumper to bumper. The drivers maneuver through the turns, each trying to pass the other as the finish line approaches. The second-place vehicle is about to make the big move, eyeing the checkered flag, but just as he hits the gas, he runs over . . . a banana peel?!?! The go-kart spins out and the driver, a gigantic angry gorilla named Donkey Kong, gesticulates wildly in defeat as he watches the winning driver, an Italian plumber named Mario, cross the finish line to win the Mushroom Cup.

This is not the scene from the latest NASCAR or Formula One race, but instead one that happens in living rooms all over the world thanks to Nintendo's *Mario Kart* video game series. What might seem like fun and games among family and friends has become a multibillion-dollar industry. As of March 2022, there had been over 166 million copies of *Mario Kart* sold since the game's inception in 1992 (White, 2022). However, these video game battles are not just happening among families: Competitive video gaming is broadcast live to millions of viewers throughout the world watch-

ing on the Internet. The gamers themselves have become international superstars and the prize money rivals that of some of the most prominent sporting events in the world. Even major media outlets have started to take notice of esports.

## Who Plays Video Games?

Before getting into the details of competitive video gaming, it is important to understand the societal impact of the industry. A 2021 study found that about 227 million people play video games in the United States, which is more than two-thirds of the country's population. Additionally, it is not just a hobby for kids; the Entertainment Software Association reported that 80 percent of those players are over the age of 18, with the average age of a gamer being 31 years old. Across all ages and players, 55 percent of gamers are men and 45 percent are women (Entertainment Software Association, 2021).

Video games are not just entertainment; they are also major income drivers for the companies that produce them. In 2019, the movie *Avengers: Endgame* debuted as the highly anticipated next chapter in the Marvel Cinematic Universe. The movie broke several box office records, including becoming the first film ever to make over $1 billion in ticket sales when it reached that number on its fifth day in the theaters. However, it was not the first entertainment product to reach a billion dollars in sales. Instead, it was a video game—*Grand Theft Auto V*—that first did it the year prior. Not only did that game reach a billion dollars in sales, it did it quicker than *Avengers: Endgame*, hitting the magic number in only three days (Ashaari, 2019). By 2022, the game had sold over 170 million copies and earned over $6 billion for the company that produces it (Strickland, 2022).

## What Is Esports?

**Esports**, a shortened version of *electronic sports*, is the name given to competitive video game playing. These competitions can be between teams, one-on-one, or in a round-robin format where the highest score wins. These gaming events have been happening since the creation of early arcade games, either formally or informally. Arcades would organize events to reward the highest score on a machine, or groups of friends could decide the best player among themselves.

## Early Days of Esports

The *Guinness Book of World Records* states that the first esports competition took place in 1972 at Stanford University. At the time, a popular game among computer programmers was *Spacewar!*, a game that pitted two players against each other, with each controlling a rocket with the goal of shooting down their opponent. In order to determine who was the best at the game, players descended onto Stanford's campus for the Intergalactic Spacewar Olympics. While winners of some of the modern major video game competitions can earn thousands of dollars, the prize for what is recognized as the first esports event was fairly modest: a year's subscription to *Rolling Stone* magazine (Guinness Book of World Records, n.d.).

While video games were growing in popularity, people had to leave their house and go to an arcade in order to play. Those hooked on the games were going in droves to play the latest machines. In 1980, the arcade game *Pac-Man* made over $1 billion—which is even more impressive when considering that, with a cost of one quarter to play, it made that amount 25 cents at a time (Goodall, 2020).

The release of **home consoles**, or video game systems that connected directly to televisions, continued to fuel the explosive growth of video games. The Atari 2600 was one of the first home consoles, but it suffered from slow sales early in its existence. That all changed with the release of *Space Invaders*, a game in which players control a shooter on the bottom of the screen and try to destroy the aliens that are descending from the top of the screen. The game might look fairly crude by today's standards, but it was revolutionary at the time, selling over two million copies in its first year and making the Atari a must-have item for those interested in home gaming (Hutcheon, 1983). With the release of *Space Invaders* on a home console, people now had the opportunity to play one of their favorite arcade games without leaving their house. While the *Spacewar!* competition is recognized as the first esports event, there were only 24 people that participated. When the Space Invaders Tournament took place less than a decade later in 1980, more than 10,000 gamers signed up to see who was the best in the world (Larch, 2022).

When everyone is in the same location, it is easy to know who has the high scores. For example, determining who was the best *Space Invaders* player at the arcade simply meant seeing who had the most points on the machine at the end of the tournament. However, when everyone was not in one location, it was nearly impossible to figure out who was best because individual machines were not connected to any sort of central record-keeping service. Therefore, each machine had its own high score, but no way of knowing where that score stood in relation to the rest of the machines scattered throughout the globe. In order to recognize the "best of the best," an arcade owner named Walter Day created the "Twin Galaxies National Scoreboard." Gamers could send in videos of their high score, and he would keep track of who had the most points or quickest times. Day's leaderboards became the official scoreboard of the early days of esports, as competitors from all over the country could see the updated records in video game magazines (Wright, 2018).

### *Starcade*

Esports battles went national in 1982 when cable television network WTBS debuted *Starcade*, a video game competition show. The contestants, ranging in age from 5 to 65, would answer video game trivia questions

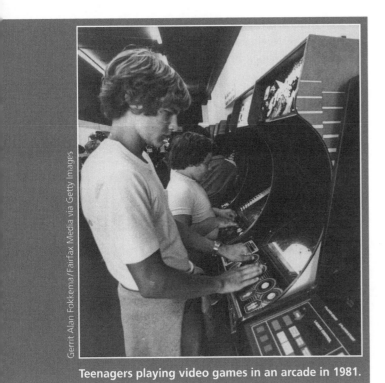

Teenagers playing video games in an arcade in 1981.

and then play arcade games with the goal of getting a higher score than their opponent. While the game show had competitive gaming, it was also essentially a 30-minute advertisement for games themselves, as many of them were set to debut shortly in local arcades (Starcade, n.d.). The show itself only lasted a few seasons, but the fact that competitive video gaming was getting national exposure was something unique for the time. These joystick battles were out of the dimly lit arcades and instead on the bright lights of television.

## Nintendo Entertainment System

While *Starcade* was bringing esports to a national audience in the early 1980s, it did not start a trend of televised video game competitions. Instead, those TV sets were being used to *play* the latest and greatest games through the use of a few cables that plugged into the back of the television. What started with the Atari 2600 years earlier would evolve in the late 1980s, when video gaming changed forever with the introduction of the Nintendo Entertainment System (NES). The NES brought, for that time, cutting-edge graphics and fun gameplay that captivated millions. Mario, Zelda, Little Mac, and others became household names, and Ninten-

do's video game library meant people were spending less time at the arcade to get their gaming fix.

To capitalize on the popularity, Nintendo created their own esports competition, the Nintendo World Championships, in 1990. The event toured 29 cities in the United States, each crowning a local winner, before culminating with the finals in Los Angeles, California (Cifaldi, 2016). Video game competitions were starting to pop up more often, but the games being played at those events were starting to change. Events in which players scored the highest single-game score were being replaced with games that involved head-to-head match-ups such as the aforementioned *Mario Kart* for the new Super Nintendo Entertainment System (SNES) and the arcade game *Street Fighter II*.

## Online Gaming

Another big change to esports came in the 1980s and 1990s thanks to the emergence of online gaming. With the Internet, gamers could be in different physical locations and still compete against each other. For example, the game *Netrek*, which is considered the first online sports game, allowed 16 players from different parts of the world to all play against each other in their attempt to capture planets in a virtual galaxy (Kelly, 1993). In the first major online esports tournament, over 2,000 gamers battled it out on the Internet in the first-person shooter *Quake* (Phillips, 2020).

## Twitch

The Internet changed not only how esports were played, but also how they were watched. Broadcasting video game competitions on television did not initially catch on in the United States, but that was not the case in South Korea. A few television channels in that country broadcast esports 24 hours a day, and South Korea is often considered one of the first places that brought competitive video gaming to the masses (Korea.net, 2012). The South Korean audience demonstrated that there was an interest in watching esports, but it did not truly take off in the United States until the development of Twitch in 2011.

Twitch is a **live-streaming** platform in which people can broadcast videos to an online audience. The early days of the service had a variety of channels, but it became clear that esports was overwhelmingly the most popular destination for those who were watching. Research demonstrated that tens of millions of people would spend hours watching others play video games, and approximately two years after its launch, Twitch had 35 million unique visitors a month (Lawler, 2013). With those impressive numbers, the service caught the eye of some of the biggest companies in tech, and in 2014 Amazon purchased Twitch for $1.1 billion (Wingfield, 2014). As of this writing, the popularity of Twitch has not slowed since the sale. The service averages 35 million daily viewers, there are 2.5 million are watching at any moment, and 1.3 trillion minutes of video were streamed in 2022 (Twitch Advertising, n.d.).

## Gaming Celebrities

With millions of people watching for trillions of minutes, it should not come as a surprise that some of the streamers have gone from anonymous video game players to gaming celebrities. One of the most recognizable is Richard Tyler Blevins, better known to his fans by his online nickname, Ninja. He rose to fame playing the game *Fortnite* on his Twitch stream, and not only was he good at the game, but he was also entertaining to those who watched. With each win and each new viewer, his celebrity rose beyond just the gaming community. Young gamers tuned in to his live broadcasts in record numbers, culminating with his stream in which he played *Fortnite* with hip-hop music artist Drake. That session in 2018 was watched by 630,000 viewers, making it the most-watched stream in the platform's history. While Ninja has not revealed the exact amount, gaming experts estimate that he makes over $500,000 a month from streaming—and that does not include his sponsorship money from companies such as Red Bull (Teng, 2018).

## Pro Athletes on Twitch

While some video gamers have become celebrities, some celebrities—especially athletes—are turning to video games as a new way in which they can engage with their fans. NFL wide receiver JuJu Smith-Schuster was on the cover of *Sports Illustrated* in 2019, but instead of playing football, he was wearing a video gaming headset and had an Xbox controller in his hands. In the accompanying article, Smith-Schuster was seemingly just as proud of his *Fortnite* skills as he was his ability on the football field (McKnight, 2019).

Perhaps one reason that streaming video games is a popular activity for professional athletes is that they often have a great deal of downtime. The players go to practices and games, but the rest of their schedule can often be wide open. Therefore, some athletes will sit in their hotel rooms and play video games to pass the time. With the development of Twitch, those players can now have an audience. In 2020, fans watching NBA star Devin Booker streaming his game of *Call of Duty* were there as Booker found out, at the same time everyone else did, that the NBA was suspending its season due to the coronavirus pandemic. Fans watched and listened as Booker, with a shocked look on his face, heard the details of the shutdown, all while continuing to play the game (Gilbert, 2020).

## Team Competitions

The development of multiplayer games created a new batch of competitions in which teams, not individuals, became the focus. Just like professional athletes, these teams spend hours practicing together before the big competitions, with one *League of Legends* team leader estimating that they work at it anywhere from 10 to 12 hours a day. Some of the players will also live together so they can have more time practicing their strategy with their teammates (Kim, 2017). One *League of Legends* gamer recounted his team's daily routine during training:

- 8:00 a.m.—Wake up
- 8:30 a.m.-10:30 a.m.—Gym, shower, breakfast
- 10:30 a.m.-11:30 a.m.—Video review
- Noon-3:00 p.m.—Team practice no. 1
- 3:00 p.m.-4:00 p.m.—Break
- 4:00 p.m.-7:00 p.m.—Team practice no. 2
- 7:00 p.m.-8:00 p.m.—Dinner
- 8:00 p.m.-midnight—Solo practice (NIB, 2017)

Those are long days, but all that work is worth it if they can become one of the best teams in the world. The top gamers receive salaries from the team organizers and can also earn a part of a multimillion-dollar prize if they win the *League of Legends* championship (Wutz, 2021).

## Traditional Sports Teams and Leagues

It is not only gaming teams, but also traditional sports teams that are getting into the virtual action. One of the most successful sports video game franchises is the basketball game *NBA 2K*. Seeing the growing popularity of both the video game and competitive gaming, the NBA partnered with the game's creators to develop the NBA 2K eLeague in 2017. Everything about the eLeague was

Robert "Blaber" Huang of Cloud9 competes at the League of Legends World Championship 2023.

nearly identical to the actual NBA: Five or six gamers would play on a team together and face off with other teams in a regular season, all with the goal of making the playoffs and winning the league championship. Just like how NBA teams will draft the best college players after the season to improve their teams, there is even a draft of new gamers to join the virtual teams after the season is over (NBA Communications, 2017). As of 2023, there were 25 teams in the league, with 22 of them directly affiliated with NBA teams. For example, the Hornets Venom GT organization is partnered with the NBA's Charlotte Hornets.

As discussed in chapter 31, many professional sports organizations turned to esports as a way to keep fans and players engaged during the early days of the coronavirus pandemic. NASCAR created the eNASCAR iRacing Pro Invitational Series shortly after its racing season was suspended in 2020. Drivers competed online in video game racing, running some of the same tracks that were now closed due to the pandemic. Fox Sports, looking to fill the void left by the actual races being postponed, broadcasted several of the virtual races on Fox and the cable channel FS1. Over a million fans tuned in for each of the first two weeks, making it the most watched esports television broadcast in history (Washington, 2020). Around the same time, Major League Baseball players who were in the midst of their own postponed season participated in a tournament playing a popular baseball video game, *MLB The Show 20*. Thirty players controlled their own teams, playing against each other online with fans watching on Twitch and the MLB Network (Cohen, 2020; Toribio, 2020).

## College Programs

Colleges and competitive video gaming have gone together since the early days of esports, from the first competition at Stanford to students simply battling it out in their dorms. The popularity led to an increase in club teams, but it was not until 2014 when Robert Morris University (RMU) created a varsity esports team that offered potential students scholarships for the purpose of playing and competing in *League of Legends* events (Reames, 2018). Once RMU started their program, others soon followed, and there are now more than 200 varsity programs in competitive video gaming throughout the United States, with an estimated $15 million in scholarships awarded (ADU, 2021). This boom in programs has led to the creation of the National Association of Collegiate Esports (NACE), which is essentially the video game equivalent to the NCAA. It organizes events in a variety of different video games.

Some estimate that this increased interest in esports at colleges can be attributed to the desire to improve enrollment. Higher education institutions are attempting to figure out how to offer programs that are of interest to potential students for recruitment, and esports has fit that description. Knowing that millions of teenagers play video games, it seems only natural that these colleges and universities are creating programs that are specifically targeting that age group (ADU, 2021).

# Bringing Esports to the Masses

The growing popularity of esports can be attributed to a number of factors that have already been discussed in this chapter, but the simple availability of the competitions and the gamers themselves might be one of the biggest reasons. Esports broadcasts resemble major sporting events shown on television with multiple cameras, exciting graphics, and announcers describing the action. Much like a play-by-play announcer describes the action of a football game, a **shoutcaster** describes what is happening during an esports competition. The shoutcaster is often accompanied by an expert who can dive into the strategy being implemented by the teams. This allows diehard fans to get the level of analysis they expect from a high-level event, while also giving explanations to fans who might still be learning.

To talk among themselves, gamers turned to the popular app Discord. The social media and messaging platform allows people to connect in chat rooms that are designed for specific topics. Discord became especially popular among those playing video games, as they used the service to discuss game strategy, highlights, and their successes. Organizers of the app estimate that they have more than 150 million active users each month (Browning, 2021). In addition, some of the more popular gaming celebrities have their own Discord pages, giving them the opportunity to interact with their audience. This is similar to the live chat features that are often seen on Twitch live streams, in which gamers can answer questions and interact with their audience. While the games themselves are often the draw, the technological advances surrounding esports have certainly aided in the growth of the phenomenon. Fans have access to the games through broadcasts, access to each other through Discord, and access to their favorite gamers through live streams.

# Media Coverage

With millions of viewers and players, video games have become a topic that the media cannot ignore. There is an audience for video game news and esports results, and journalists who might not be associated with video games have started to take notice. In fact, two of the biggest media outlets who were the first to embrace video game news were a sports media powerhouse and one of the most revered newspapers in America.

## ESPN

ESPN dipped its toes into esports with the broadcast of *Madden Nation* in 2005. The part video game competition, part reality television show followed a group of gamers playing *Madden NFL*, a popular football video game. The players traveled around the country on a bus together, playing the game and having their lives recorded by the cameras stationed inside the bus and at the gaming events. At stops in each city, the lowest-ranked player would face off with a new opponent for the opportunity to either stay on the bus or get replaced. At the end of the tour, the two remaining gamers faced off for the opportunity to become that season's champion (Robinson, 2005). For ESPN, which was the home of some of the biggest sporting events in the world, the show was an opportunity to reach a new audience of video game fans.

In January 2016, ESPN officials announced they were going to provide daily, in-depth coverage of esports. The network created a video game section of its website, hired writers devoted strictly to esports, and broadcast video game tournaments and leagues on television. The network's goal was to become the main destination for those looking for the latest competitive video gaming news (Smith, 2021). In 2018, ESPN put Ninja on the cover of *ESPN The Magazine,* a space normally devoted to the most prominent athletes in the world (Teng, 2018). Not everyone on the network was on board, as ESPN radio host Colin Cowherd said, "If I am ever forced to cover guys playing video games, I will retire" (Shea, 2015, para. 2). While the coverage was successful, winning multiple awards for its reporting, ESPN elected to stop its daily coverage of esports following massive layoffs at the network in 2020 (Smith, 2021).

## *The Washington Post*

*The Washington Post* will likely always be associated with its reporting on one of the most important stories in American history: the bugging of the Democratic Party headquarters at the Watergate Hotel in Washington, DC, which ultimately led to the resignation of President Richard Nixon. However, in 2019, the newspaper known for winning Pulitzer Prizes and watching over government officials somewhat surprisingly started a section devoted to video games and esports. It was a sign that even the biggest of newspapers could no longer ignore this growing industry. The section, known as *Launcher*, was aimed at both diehard gamers and those who might not know much about esports (Hume, 2019). The development came almost accidentally, as a journalist wrote an article for the newspaper's website in 2017 about a controversial aspect of a *Star Wars* video game. The article became one of the most read on *The Washington Post* website, signifying that there was a demand for such content (McCarthy, 2019). However, much like ESPN's coverage, *Launcher* was ended by the newspaper following layoffs in 2023 (Hume, 2023).

## Is Esports a Sport?

Before concluding this chapter, it is worth asking the question that many may already be thinking: Is competitive video game playing really a sport? The answer to that might depend on who is asked. Before ESPN became heavily involved in esports, the president of the network said about video gaming: "It's not a sport—it's a competition. Chess is a competition. Checkers is a competition. Mostly, I'm interested in doing real sports" (Chmielewski, 2014, para. 2). Most definitions of the word *sport* include some sort of reference to physical activity, so one can rightly ask how one is active when playing video games usually involves sitting in a chair and barely moving for hours at a time. However, when compared to team sports, there is a great deal of overlap. Esports players spend hours practicing, must mesh successfully with teammates, and need excellent hand-eye coordination to be successful. There are certainly arguments to be made on both sides of the debate.

One of the biggest sports organizations in the world might be the group that settles the question of esports categorization. The International Olympic Committee (IOC) stated that esports could be considered a sport based on the amount of training and preparation needed to be successful, and that it was considering if video games could be part of future Olympics (Grohmann, 2017). In 2021, the IOC created the Olympic Virtual Series to take place immediately before the Tokyo Summer Olympics. The competition featured video game events in auto racing, baseball, cycling, rowing, and sailing. The program was seen as a test case of sorts

as the IOC continued to consider officially adding esports to the Olympics (Bieler, 2021).

While there is debate over the sporting qualification of competitive video gaming, the winners of esports competitions are often paid like "real" athletes—and sometimes even better. In 2019, the winner of the Fortnite World Cup earned more money ($3 million) than Tiger Woods won that same year for being the champion of The Masters golf tournament ($2.07 million) (Holt, 2019). The prize money at the *Dota 2* world championship in 2021 was $47.2 million, just a million less than the $48.2 million offered at the tennis tournament Wimbledon (Rivera, 2021; Wutz, 2021). While esports may or may not be a sport, it certainly could be a lucrative career for those who are good enough to be among the best in the world.

## Summary

While some might discount esports' place in the world of sports, the metrics demonstrate its societal importance. There are millions who watch and play, there are billions of dollars involved, and it is cross-cultural because people can play others from all over the world. What started as small, single-player events in arcades have become global thanks to Internet connectivity. Now tournaments can have matchups featuring anyone from anywhere, and millions can watch along on platforms such as Twitch. Some esports events are broadcast with the same qualities as the biggest sporting events in the world. Professional esports athletes are recruited to the best teams and given salaries, homes, and unlimited practice time to become the best at their chosen game. The rise of esports has even caught the attention of officials at the International Olympic Committee, as that organization is considering adding video gaming to the Games' roster of events. Whether it is actually a sport might be irrelevant, as it is something that has captured the attention of millions.

## KEY TERMS

**esports**—Competitive video gaming.
**live-streaming**—The ability to watch or broadcast videos in real time over the Internet.
**home consoles**—Video game systems that connect directly to televisions.
**shoutcasting**—Announcing the action at an esports event for a broadcast.

## REVIEW QUESTIONS

1. Why did the development of home consoles increase interest in video games?
2. What is Twitch and why is it an important player in the growth of competitive video gaming?
3. How have traditional sports and esports come together?
4. Why have traditional media outlets begun to embrace esports as an event worth covering?

# Sports Betting

## CHAPTER OBJECTIVES

After completing the chapter, the reader should be able to do the following:

- Identify some of the key moments in sports betting history
- Understand why professional sports leagues changed their opinion on sports betting
- Recognize why sports betting is important to sports media entities
- Examine the dangers of sports betting for gamblers

For many, the best part of the NCAA men's and women's basketball tournaments happens before the first game is even played. Once the field is announced on the Sunday night before the tournament begins, millions of fans fill out a bracket, picking winners of every game. For example, in 2023, over 20 million people filled out a free men's bracket at ESPN.com, and that is just one of many websites that have a tournament selection game (Ota, 2023). However, after making their selections, many fans will also wager a few dollars in a betting pool. The American Gaming Association estimates that more than $2 billion is wagered each year on March Madness pools (Arag, n.d.). While it might seem like harmless fun, these pools were, for many years, technically illegal in nearly every state.

Betting on sports was long considered a taboo subject. Players were not allowed to do it, and leagues feared the impact of betting on their games, but many fans were placing illegal wagers. However, the tone, and the laws, regarding sports betting shifted in the mid-2010s. While sports betting is becoming more accepted throughout the United States, the journey to that point was anything but smooth.

## Betting on Horse Racing and Boxing

While the majority of this chapter will focus on sports betting in a more modern context, it should be noted that gambling on the results of a sporting event is not a new concept. Much of the early interest in both horse racing and boxing was driven by the opportunity to bet on those sports. In the late 1800s horse racing became perhaps the most popular spectator sport in the United States, with more than 300 horse racing tracks being built in the country. Those tracks were as much about betting on the races as they were places to watch a sport (Editors Team, 2023). As the country wrestled with the legality of sports betting, even banning the practice in the early 1900s, a baseball team's involvement in a gambling scheme led to one of the first major scandals in sports.

## The "Black Sox" and Rule 21(d)

In 1919, a group of gamblers paid players on the Chicago White Sox several thousand dollars each in exchange for them not playing their best in the World Series. The White Sox's starting pitcher hit a batter with a pitch early in the first game, signifying that the "fix was in" and that the team would lose. That pitcher then made several uncharacteristic mistakes in the 9–1 loss, raising the suspicions of many in attendance. Knowing the White Sox would likely lose, the gamblers bet heavily on the opposing Cincinnati Reds.

After the 1920 season, with rumors that gamblers were influencing even more games, a grand jury began to investigate the sport of baseball. Shortly thereafter, a member of the White Sox testified and admitted to everything that he and several of his teammates had done. All eight players on the White Sox, now labeled the "Black Sox" due to the black eye they gave the sport, were banned from baseball for life (Andrews, 2014). League officials gave a strong punishment to the players to demonstrate that gambling would not be tolerated and that the games would be legitimate.

To further display the league's strong opposition to what happened with the White Sox, Rule 21(d) was passed and has been posted in every MLB locker room since 1927 (Wulf, 2019). The rule is explicit:

> *Any player, umpire, or Club or League official or employee, who shall bet any sum whatsoever upon any baseball game in connection with which the bettor has a duty to perform, shall be declared permanently ineligible. (MLB, n.d., para. 5)*

By posting the rule in every stadium, there should be no debate or question among those involved in the game. Betting on games in which the player is involved is a direct violation of this rule and will result in a ban from the sport.

## Paul Hornung and Alex Karras

In 1961, Paul Hornung was named the MVP of the NFL, but was temporarily out of the league just two seasons later. The running back and another player, Alex Karras, were suspended indefinitely by the league's commissioner for betting on NFL games. Hornung bet as much as $500 per game, while Karras' wagers ranged from $50 to $100. At the time, the commissioner said that gambling was the only way that the league's popularity could be affected negatively, so his indefinite ban for the players was appropriate. However, "indefinitely" became just one season, as Hornung and Karras were two of the most popular players in the league; the commissioner reversed his decision in 1964. The stain of the gambling accusations did not affect the two players' careers, as both were eventually inducted into the Pro Football Hall of Fame (Gardner, 2022).

## "Jimmy the Greek"

From 1976 to 1987, fans watching the NFL pregame show on CBS got a preview of the day's games, the latest injury updates, and, informally, gambling advice. Jimmy Snyder, better known as "Jimmy the Greek," would appear on the show to predict the results of that day's games. However, Snyder, who was a prominent Las Vegas bookmaker, drew the attention of more than just the casual fan. Sports betting was illegal in most of the United States and was not a topic the NFL wanted to be associated with, so Snyder had to couch his gambling advice in indirect language. He would not only pick the winners, but also give his predicted final score. By giving the score, gamblers would know that if the Giants were favored by 7, and Snyder picked them to win by 10, then they should bet on the Giants to cover the spread (Podolsky, 2021). While not directly stated, it was one of the first public acknowledgments of betting on a nationally televised sporting event.

## Pete Rose

While the Black Sox, Hornung, and Karras were notable incidents of players betting on sports, there is no more famous case than that of baseball player Pete Rose. Rose was a 17-time All-Star, a three-time World Series champion, and the Most Valuable Player of the 1973 season. In addition, he has the most hits in Major League Baseball history, making him, without question, one of the greatest players in the history of the sport. However, instead of enjoying his retirement as a member of the Hall of Fame, Rose has been banned from the sport and has left a permanent black mark on the league.

### The Investigation

In 1989, while acting as the manager of the Cincinnati Reds, Rose admitted to MLB officials that he had placed bets on a variety of sports but was adamant that baseball was not one of them. Approximately a month later, *Sports Illustrated* published an article that alleged Rose had, in fact, bet on baseball (Neff, 1989). With this new information, MLB hired a lawyer, John Dowd, to investigate what was and was not true about Rose's betting habits. The 225-page "Dowd Report" revealed that not only was Rose betting on baseball games, but he had placed many wagers on the Cincinnati Reds, the team he was manager of at the time (The Dowd Report, 1989).

## The Punishment

By betting on the Reds while he was managing the team, Rose had violated Rule 21(d). MLB officials permanently placed Rose on the ineligible list, meaning he could no longer be a manager or work with Major League Baseball or any of its teams, and he would be barred from election into the Baseball Hall of Fame

Chuck Solomon /Sports Illustrated /Getty Images

**Pete Rose hits during batting practice in 1985.**

(Chass, 1989). This meant that one of the greatest hitters in baseball history was now no longer welcome in the sport that had made him famous. Rose would attempt several times to be reinstated, but each time was rebuffed by the league's commissioner.

## The Denials and the Admission

Rose continued to deny ever betting on baseball, and it was his belief that he should have never been banned in the first place. After being voted onto the MLB All-Century Team in 1999 by the fans, Rose was given a chance to come clean about his betting past. Instead, live on NBC, he said, "I'm not going to admit to something that didn't happen" (Price, 2015, para. 22).

In 2004, Rose did finally come clean in his autobiography and stated that he had bet on baseball, but that he only did so as a manager and not a player, and never bet against his own team. He hoped his admission would help his case for reinstatement and possibly improve his image (Curry, 2004). Instead, the book might have done more harm than good, as many of Rose's most loyal supporters who had believed his denials were blindsided by his admission.

## Bets as a Player

Even after the printing of his book, Rose denied that he placed any bets while he was an active player. He told a New York radio host, "Never bet as a player: That's a fact" (Weinbaum & Quinn, 2015, para. 18). However, a report from ESPN in 2015 proved that was yet another lie. The investigative program *Outside the Lines* acquired copies of pages from a notebook that detailed the history of Rose's gambling during the 1986 season. Rose, who was a player on the Reds at the time, bet on baseball on at least 30 different days over a 5-month period, including 21 days in which he bet on his own team (Weinbaum & Quinn, 2015). If Rose had any hope of being reinstated from baseball, it appeared that those chances were over. In the history of betting on sports, there may be no former athlete who signified the dangers of gambling more than Pete Rose. He remains one of the greatest to ever play, but his place in baseball history was tarnished forever by his decision to bet on the games in which he was a participant.

# Federal Law

For decades, sports leagues made it explicitly clear that they wanted no formal association with gambling or sports betting. While leagues would be naive to not recognize the positive impact gambling has on the popularity of sports, they worried about what sports betting could do to a locker room. Leagues needed to only look at the Black Sox to see what could happen if gamblers could influence the results. Therefore, it was not surprising that professional leagues had no interest in looser gambling laws.

Instead, stricter laws were placed on the books. The Professional and Amateur Sports Protection Act of 1992 made it illegal for states to allow sports betting. At U.S. Senate Judiciary Committee hearings before the law was passed, NBA commissioner David Stern was one of those who spoke in support of the law, demonstrating his league's fear of betting. Delaware, Montana, and Oregon's sports lotteries, as well as Nevada's sportsbooks, were exempt from the law because those states had existing sports betting laws. However, this law meant that people living in any of the other states could not bet on sports. Of course, that was not *exactly* true. *The New York Times* estimated in 2018 that there were $150 billion in illegal wagers made every year in the United States through offshore wagering or bookies (Liptak & Draper, 2018). Despite that, it was somewhat of a challenge to make a bet on a game, as a gambler would need to know someone who could help them place a bet. Ultimately, even with the passage of the Professional and Amateur Sports Protection Act, those fears of corruption were realized in the NBA in 2007. However, it was not a player that was influencing the final scores.

# Tim Donaghy

In 2007, it was revealed that NBA referee Tim Donaghy had been involved in a sports betting scheme. The plan started with Donaghy giving insider information to a bettor based on what he knew about the referees in a game. For example, Donaghy would later recount how he knew that specific referees did not like certain coaches, so the calls would likely favor the other team. While the people betting on the games were making money, winning more than 70 percent of the games at one point, the plan soon threatened to bring down the entire NBA. Instead of solely giving information about other games, Donaghy began providing insider tips about games he was refereeing.

The gamblers involved had someone on the inside, as a referee has an enormous influence on how a game is played. For example, in baseball, a strike zone could be altered when a certain team is up; a soccer referee could call offside and negate a goal; and a football referee could call holding on more plays for one team than the other. Specifically in basketball, more fouls could go against a star player or a specific team, impacting that team's ability to play their best lineup. An ESPN review of all Donaghy's games found that in 23 of 30 games, Donaghy's foul calls favored the team on which he and his betting partners had wagered. ESPN calculated that the odds of that happening randomly were 6,155 to 1 (Eden, 2020).

Much like the Black Sox scandal of nearly 100 years earlier, Donaghy's involvement with bettors could give the impression that the games being played were not legitimate. This not only caught the attention of the NBA, but also the FBI, because taking money to influence games is against the law. After an investigation conducted by both the league and the government, it was determined that Donaghy was the only referee involved in the scandal. Donaghy pleaded guilty to two felony charges based on his role in the betting scheme and was sentenced to 15 months in prison (Schmidt, 2008).

# If You Can't Beat 'Em . . .

Despite the very public and potentially league-destroying moves by Donaghy, several leagues were starting to rethink their stances toward sports betting. Perhaps surprisingly, less than a decade after the referee scandal, it was the NBA that had become the most vocal proponent of legal betting. The league's commissioner, Adam Silver, wrote an op-ed in *The New York Times* in 2014 titled "Legalize and Regulate Sports Betting." Silver wrote that gambling on sports had become a part of American society and that the previous laws banning it in most states were now outdated. While the commissioner was adamant that sports betting should be legal, he was also conscious of the impact betting might have on his sport:

> *Let me be clear: Any new approach must ensure the integrity of the game. One of my most important responsibilities as commissioner of the N.B.A. is to protect the integrity of professional basketball and preserve public confidence in the league and our sport. I oppose any course of action that would compromise these objectives.*

*But I believe that sports betting should be brought out of the underground and into the sunlight where it can be appropriately monitored and regulated. (Silver, 2014, para. 10-11)*

# Leagues Embrace Las Vegas

Due to its strong connection to gambling and sports betting, professional sports leagues had long shunned the state of Nevada and, specifically, the city of Las Vegas. The Las Vegas Strip is home to around 30 casinos and most have a spacious sportsbook in which fans can bet on nearly every game in every sport. That opportunity for easy access to betting had long kept leagues away, but the NBA held the 2007 All-Star Game in Las Vegas, perhaps as a way to test the city's viability for a permanent team. It did not go well. More than 400 people were arrested, police and casinos were not ready for the number of people that showed up for the game, and the mayor of the city called it "a disastrous weekend" (Gordon, 2020, para. 3).

While that weekend might have slowed the momentum for professional sports in Las Vegas, it did not permanently stop it. In 2016, the NHL awarded an expansion team to the city, and the Vegas Golden Knights took to the ice the next year in an arena located just steps from the Strip. The team was an instant success both on the ice—making the Stanley Cup Final in its first season—and in the casinos. One sportsbook operator estimated that 27 percent of all bets placed on hockey in the team's inaugural season were on Golden Knights games. Those bets consisted of both fans betting on Vegas and also fans of visiting teams who came to Las Vegas to see their team play and bet on their team to win (Everson, 2018).

Following the Golden Knights' arrival, the floodgates were open for professional sports in Las Vegas. The WNBA soon announced that the franchise in San Antonio was moving to Nevada (to become the Las Vegas Aces), and the NFL approved the Oakland Raiders'

Jeff Bottari/NHLI via Getty Images

The Vegas Golden Knights pose for a team photo as their Stanley Cup Championship banner is raised in 2023.

move to a new stadium there as well (Associated Press, 2017; Belson & Mather, 2017). Not only did Las Vegas become the home of the Raiders, but the NFL also placed other flagship league events there. The 2022 NFL Draft took place just off the Las Vegas Strip, and the city was awarded the 2024 Super Bowl, to take place in the Raiders' stadium (Gordon, 2022).

## The Law Changes

Even before the Raiders moved to Las Vegas, the tone around sports betting in the United States was already beginning to change. Some states were recognizing that they could potentially be losing out on millions of dollars by not having the opportunity to offer sports betting to their residents. Leading the way was New Jersey, as officials in that state believed the government was losing out on $600 million per year by not having sports gambling. In a state that was already struggling economically, that lost revenue was too much to ignore. After a vote demonstrated that its residents were in favor of legalized gambling, the state of New Jersey attempted to overturn the Professional and Amateur Sports Protection Act of 1992 (Robbins, 2014).

New Jersey's efforts went to the courts, and eventually *Murphy vs. The NCAA* (Murphy was Philip Murphy, the governor of New Jersey) went all the way to the U.S. Supreme Court. In 2018, the majority of the Supreme Court justices ruled that the 1992 law was unconstitutional (Liptak & Draper, 2018), and the issue of sports betting was now up to each individual state to decide. Less than a month after the Supreme Court's decision, Delaware's governor placed the inaugural wager in his state, the first legal sports bet outside of Nevada in the United States (Salam, 2018). Other quickly followed, and by the end of 2022, there were around 30 states that had legal sports betting. However, not every state was on board. For example, in Texas, one of the most populated states in the country, bills that would have legalized betting did not even get out of legislative committees in 2021 (Houston, 2022). Despite the nationwide opportunity to start legal sports betting, it was becoming clear that it was anything but a unanimous decision to adopt new laws.

## Changing Betting Methods

For years, sports betting on individual games was limited to two primary bets:

- Who will win the game?
- Will Team X win or lose by a certain number of points? That point number is known as the spread. For example, the Wildcats are playing the Sharks and the Wildcats are a 7-point favorite. If a bettor picks the Wildcats, they would need the Wildcats to win by more than 7 to win the bet. However, if the bettor picks the Sharks, then the Sharks could lose by less than 7, or win the game outright, for that bettor to win. If the Wildcats win by 7, then the game is a "push," and everyone would get their money back.

In addition, longer bets could be made before a season begins such as:

- Who will win the championship?
- Will a team win more or fewer games than a predetermined number set by the sportsbook?
- Who will win various individual awards, such as most valuable player?

During major events, there are usually some "wacky" bets that can be made beyond the usual fare. For example, the Super Bowl is famous for these bets, including wagering on how long the national anthem will last, picking the winner of the coin toss (a literal flip of a coin), and guessing the color of the Gatorade that will be poured over the winning coach.

Another major change to sports betting is that smartphone betting apps have allowed fans to wager on games (in states where it is legal) without needing to physically go to a sportsbook or casino. Fans can download one of the many betting sites onto their phones and have an entire sportsbook at their fingertips. This has also created a new way to bet, with a method called "microbetting." These are wagers that are made during the game and can be made repeatedly throughout. Examples include:

- Will Team X come back to win this game?
- Will the kicker make or miss this field goal?
- How many free throws will Player X make during this trip to the line?

With smartphones, people can make these bets quickly and in real time. If a bettor was at a sportsbook, they would need to walk up to a betting window and hope the bet could be manually entered in time. However, with the smartphone app, these bets can be made with just a push of a few buttons and, more importantly to the sportsbooks, can be made tens of times throughout a game.

# The Media and Sports Betting

As would be expected, many of the companies already associated with betting and gambling were quick to embrace newfound opportunities. Casino companies MGM and Caesar's developed betting apps, while daily sports wagering sites DraftKings and Fan Duel expanded their portfolios to offer betting, especially "microbetting," on their apps. While gambling websites were becoming successful on their own, they also began working with media partners. The logic appeared to be that, by partnering with known media brands, these gambling companies could add credibility to their own company while also gaining exclusive access to a loyal group of followers.

## Media Partnerships

For several years, *Barstool Sports*, a popular sports blog, was partially owned by Penn Entertainment, a company that primarily dealt with casinos. In August 2022, as more states were adopting legalized gambling, Penn agreed to purchase the entirety of *Barstool* for $325 million (Perez, 2022). As part of its partial ownership, the company had already started the Barstool Sportsbook, a sports betting app. Not only did *Barstool* employees encourage their loyal followers to use their app, but they livestreamed their popular writers and podcasters watching sports and discussing their bets. For Penn, this was an opportunity to launch a sports betting app with a company that already had a loyal following, giving it millions of potential customers at launch. Even more appealing was the fact that more than half of *Barstool*'s audience is under 30 years old (McCarthy, 2021), a demographic that is among the most interested in sports betting.

While *Barstool Sports* is one of the most popular sports media destinations for the younger generation, it still stands far behind ESPN in the overall sports landscape. Therefore, when Penn Entertainment had an opportunity to switch its partnership from *Barstool* to ESPN in 2023, it jumped at the chance. In August of that year, ESPN and Penn announced a 10-year deal to create an online sports betting destination called ESPN Bet. Penn agreed to run the sportsbook and paid ESPN $1.5 billion for the use of the ESPN brand, access to ESPN's on-air personalities, and the ability to use ESPN's promotional tools. In addition, almost one year after paying hundreds of millions of dollars for control of *Barstool*, Penn sold the website back to its founder, Dave Portnoy, for just $1.

While *Barstool* gave Penn instant credibility in the sports betting space, the company should have the opportunity to reach an even bigger and more affluent audience through the ESPN partnership (Browning,

A Barstool Sportsbook inside the Hollywood Casino Morgantown in Pennsylvania.

2023). As one gambling insider pointed out, Penn's partnership with *Barstool* did give them access to a younger generation, but that group traditionally has a lower net worth, meaning they would not be able to bet as much money (Rovell, 2023). As a result of the deal, the Barstool Sportsbook app and website would become ESPN Bet, but a partnership with a sports media empire is not a guarantee for success. Less than a month before the announcement of ESPN and Penn's partnership, Fox Bet, the sports betting outlet run by Fox broadcasting, announced it was closing after failing to gain enough customers (Feuer & Sayre, 2023).

## Betting on TV

When "Jimmy the Greek" was giving score predictions on the CBS NFL pregame show, he was not explicitly discussing betting, but was instead hinting at the gambling lines. After sports betting became legal in the majority of U.S. states, it was nearly impossible to watch a game on television or listen to a sports podcast without seeing or hearing a gambling advertisement. During the 2021 World Series, Fox Sports openly promoted its sports betting contest "Fox Bet Super 6" with a "chance to win Papi's money," a reference to studio analyst David "Big Papi" Ortiz. The graphic on the screen relayed that, by downloading the app, fans had a "free chance to win $25,000." During the game, the betting references continued. When the Houston Astros' José Altuve hit a home run in Game 4, announcer Joe Buck reminded fans that had they wagered $10 at the beginning of the game that Altuve would homer they would now have $45. While Buck was speaking, a graphic was shown with the Fox Bet Sportsbook logo on it (Stephen's Baseball Archives, 2022).

In 2019, ESPN debuted *ESPN Daily Wager*, its first show dedicated to sports betting. The hosts discuss the games, the betting lines, and possible bets, and then pick "winners." Other networks have followed suit, with Fox creating *Fox Bet Live* and the Major League Baseball Network debuting *The Bettor's Eye*. While these networks might be attempting to address the betting interests of their audience, there may also be selfish motivations as well. If fans become more interested in games due to gambling, they may watch more games on television. For example, a regular-season matchup between two relatively unknown schools in college basketball might not be appointment viewing for many. However, if fans have wagered on that game, it might suddenly be a game they cannot miss. This increased viewership would be a benefit to the networks, so it should come as no surprise that outlets such as ESPN have embraced sports betting.

## Conflict of Interest?

With gambling companies getting involved with sports media entities, it raises questions about possible conflicts of interest and the effect that journalists can have on the betting lines. This concern was brought to the forefront during the 2023 NBA Draft when *The Athletic* basketball insider Shams Charania sent a social media message that Scoot Henderson, who was expected to be picked third, was actually "gaining momentum" as the possible no. 2 pick in the draft. Charania, who is known for his breaking news scoops and having information before most other NBA reporters, caused the betting odds for Henderson to be chosen second to shift dramatically on the gambling website FanDuel thanks to his tweet. However, as *The Washington Post* later pointed out, there was "another twist" to Charania's news: In addition to working for *The Athletic*, he is also a paid contributor to FanDuel (Strauss, 2023, para. 4). Essentially, FanDuel had created betting lines and a FanDuel employee had influenced them, which brought in new bets for the company. The situation made many in journalism and sports betting uncomfortable, and they questioned how Charania could be employed by the two companies at the same time. Both *The Athletic* and FanDuel said they had no issues with the arrangement, but many pointed out that this could create a major problem in the future should a journalist want to take advantage of their influence, and further demonstrated the blurring of the lines between sports media and gambling (Strauss, 2023).

## League Partnerships

For decades, professional sports leagues actively fought against legalized sports gambling. Commissioners warned of the dangers of more betting opportunities for those involved in the games, citing Pete Rose and Tim Donaghy as examples of what could go wrong. As league officials changed their stances and betting became legal in the majority of the country, these sports leagues soon found new ways to make money through sports betting. Much like many media properties, the leagues entered into partnerships and advertising deals with some of the biggest betting companies. DraftKings and BetMGM agreed to be the co-executive betting partners of Major

League Baseball, while the National Football League reached deals with BetMGM and a variety of other companies to be "approved sportsbook operators" for the NFL season (Legal Sports Report, n.d.). In 2019, MLB and MGM resorts reached a partnership that was reportedly worth $80 million to the league (Wulf, 2019).

In addition, fans watching games on television or sitting on the stands could hardly miss the many sports betting advertisements that are plastered throughout stadiums. At Fenway Park, home of the Boston Red Sox, a DraftKings sign stood above the iconic "Green Monster" leftfield wall, while the Washington Capitals debuted a Caesar's Sportsbook patch on their jerseys. Not only can fans see advertisements for gambling when at games, but in some locations, they can actually bet there. In 2021, the sports arena in Washington, DC, opened a sportsbook right inside the concourse. Fans can leave their seat at a Wizards (NBA) or Capitals (NHL) game and walk directly into the in-arena sportsbook to bet. When asked if he would do anything differently, the owner of the teams and the arena said his only regret was that the sportsbook was not bigger (Kilgore, 2021).

However, these gambling partnerships are not only about money. One reason that leagues wanted to legalize gambling in more locations was to take the betting out of shady back rooms and instead into more tightly regulated environments. In March 2022, NFL wide receiver Calvin Ridley was suspended indefinitely after it was revealed he had gambled on NFL games. Unlike Pete Rose and the Black Sox, Ridley was injured at the time and did not bet on games in which he was playing. However, as is the case in nearly every sport, simply betting on games, playing in them or not, is considered a serious offense. The NFL commissioner wrote to Ridley: "Your actions put the integrity of the game at risk, threatened to damage public confidence in professional football, and potentially undermined the reputations of your fellow players throughout the NFL" (Patra, 2022, para. 4).

What made the case even more remarkable was how the NFL found out about Ridley's betting: The sportsbook operator told them. Ridley had to enter his Social Security number to start gambling on a betting app, and once he was in the system, his bets were flagged and the information was sent directly to the NFL (D'Andrea, 2022). By legalizing sports betting, and making it heavily regulated, professional sports had accomplished its goal. It was very clear that players could not bet on games without the league finding out.

# Gambling Addiction

Shortly after his suspension was announced, Calvin Ridley sent a tweet that read, "I bet 1500 total I don't have a gambling problem" (Ridley, 2022). While Ridley was adamant that he did not have an addiction to sports betting, it is perhaps the biggest concern regarding the loosening of the laws. About 2 percent of the United States population, about 6.6 million people, suffers from gambling addiction. Shortly after sports betting became legal in Connecticut, calls to that state's Problem Gambling Hotline quadrupled. Several gamblers cited the ease of being able to place a bet as one of the main factors in this increase. A recovering gambling addict told *The New York Times*, "You can do it 24/7 from right on your phone" (Fazio, 2021, para. 18), referencing the "always on" nature of betting and the emphasis on in-game "microbets."

Even more troubling for some is that the group that is more vulnerable to gambling addiction is those in their late teens and early 20s. One group estimated that 6 percent of college students have a serious gambling problem, with concerns that those issues could lead to psychological difficulties or unmanageable debt (Fazio, 2021). That addiction can then create lifelong problems for those who develop a gambling addiction in their early professional years.

# Summary

In less than 25 years, sports betting went from a taboo subject in sports to a topic that was nearly impossible to ignore. Between the Black Sox, Pete Rose, and Tim Donaghy, sports betting was something that teams, leagues, and players were not even considering discussing because it was deemed more harmful than good. However, once states began realizing that they were losing out on millions of dollars, and leagues determined that regulated sports betting might be beneficial when it comes to monitoring potential athlete betting, their stances began to change. After the repeal of a 1992 federal law, sports betting became an industry worth tens of billions of dollars a year, with leagues and media outlets seeing some of that windfall after becoming partners with some of the biggest gaming companies. However, there are many concerns about the long-term impact that sports betting could be creating, including an increase in gambling addiction.

## REVIEW QUESTIONS

1. Why is the "Black Sox" scandal still on the minds of baseball executives more than 100 years after it happened?

2. Why was "Jimmy the Greek" appearing on CBS's NFL pregame show a monumental moment for sports betting?

3. Why did many of the professional leagues change their minds regarding sports betting and move to have it legalized after decades of opposing it?

4. What are some of the concerns with the increase in sports betting opportunities?

# REFERENCES

## Chapter 1

Badii, N., & Ward, W.J. (1980). The nature of news in four dimensions. *Journalism Quarterly, 57*(2), 243-248.

Berkowitz, D., Allen, C., & Beeson, D. (1996). Exploring newsroom views about consultants in local TV: The effects of work roles and socialization. *Journal of Broadcasting & Electronic Media, 40*(4), 447-459.

Groshek, J., & Tandoc, E. (2017). The affordance effect: Gatekeeping and (non) reciprocal journalism on Twitter. *Computers in Human Behavior, 66*, 201-210.

Jackson, W. (2021, December 14). Steph Curry breaks Ray Allen's record, becomes all-time three-point leader. *SI.com*. www.si.com/nba/2021/12/15/steph-curry-breaks-ray-allens-record-becomes-all-time-leader-three-pointers

Lapchick, R.E. (2020). The 2021 sports media racial and gender report card: Associated Press sports editors (APSE). *The Institute for Diversity and Ethics in Sport*. www.tidesport.org/_files/ugd/138a69_e1e67c118b784f4caba00a4536699300.pdf

Lapchick, R. (2021). The 2021 sports media racial and gender report card: Associated Press Sports Editors (APSE). *The Institute for Diversity and Ethics in Sport. The Institute for Diversity and Ethics in Sport*. www.tidesport.org/_files/ugd/138a69_e1e67c118b784f4caba00a4536699300.pdf

Lewin, K. (1947). Frontiers in group dynamics II. Channels of group life: Social planning and human action. *Human Relations, 1*, 143-153.

Shoemaker, P.J., & Vos, T.P. (2009). *Gatekeeping theory*. Routledge.

Snider, P.B. (1967). "Mr. Gates revisited": A 1966 version of the 1949 case study. *Journalism Quarterly, 44*(3), 419-427.

Stempel, G.H. III. (1962). Content patterns of small and metropolitan dailies. *Journalism Quarterly, 39*(1), 88-91.

White, D.M. (1950). The "gate keeper": A case study in the selection of news. *Journalism Quarterly, 27*, 383-390.

## Chapter 2

Anderson, D. (1975, October 2). Title retained after ugly end to the "Thrilla in Manila." *The New York Times*. www.nytimes.com/2016/06/11/sports/title-retained-after-ugly-end-to-the-thrilla-in-manila.html

Baseball Reference. (n.d.). Marty Barrett. www.baseball-reference.com/players/b/barrema02.shtml

Berkow, I. (2000, January 2). The eloquent words of legendary writers. *The New York Times*. https://archive.nytimes.com/www.nytimes.com/library/sports/backtalk/010200century-writers.html

Betts, J.R. (1952). *Organized sport in industrialized America*. Columbia University Press.

Blood, R. (2000, September 7) Weblogs: A history and perspective. Retrieved from www.rebeccablood.net/essays/weblog_history.html

Bryant, J., & Holt, A.M. (2009). A historical overview of sports and media in the United States. In *Handbook of sports and media* (pp. 22-45). Routledge.

Caldwell, D. (2014, September 30). When Fordham introduced football to television. *The Wall Street Journal*. www.wsj.com/articles/when-fordham-introduced-football-to-television-1412123075

Campbell, R., Martin, C.R., & Fabos, B. (2019). *Media & culture*. Bedford/St. Martin's.

Catsis, J.R. (1996). *Sports broadcasting*. Nelson-Hall Publishers.

Columbia Athletics. (2009, May 17). Columbia vs. Princeton: First televised sporting event marks 70th anniversary. https://gocolumbialions.com/news/2009/5/17/3738874

Covil, E.C. (n.d.). Radio and its impact on the sports world. *American Sportscasters Online*. www.americansportscastersonline.com/radiohistory.html

Cramer, M. (2016, September 12). As TV and football celebrate 65 years of marriage, the relationship grows deeper. *The Dallas Morning News*. www.dallasnews.com/opinion/commentary/2016/09/12/as-tv-and-football-celebrate-65-years-of-marriage-the-relationship-grows-deeper/

de Zúñiga, H.G., Lewis, S.C., Willard, A., Valenzuela, S., Lee, J.K., & Baresch, B. (2011). Blogging as a journalistic practice: A model linking perception, motivation, and behavior. *Journalism, 12*(5), 586-606.

Fitzpatrick, F. (2016, February 4). First televised NFL game: An Eagles defeat. *The Philadelphia Inquirer*. www.inquirer.com/philly/sports/eagles/20160205_Eagles_lost_first_televised_NFL_game.html

Gisondi, J. (2018). *Field guide to covering sports*. Thousand Oaks, CA: CQ Press.

Given, K. (2016, February 20). Nazis pioneered broadcasting . . . and made Jesse Owens a star. *WBUR*. www.wbur.org/onlyagame/2016/02/20/jesse-owens-olympics-germans-nazi-radio

Halberstam, D.J. (2019, September 29). Born 80 years ago, college football on TV was limited by the NCAA's grip until stopped by the Supreme Court. *Sports Broadcast Journal*. www.sportsbroadcastjournal.com/born-80-years-ago-college-football-on-tv-was-limited-by-the-ncaas-grip-until-the-supreme-court-said-let-go/

Henry Chadwick. (n.d.). National Baseball Hall of Fame. https://baseballhall.org/hall-of-famers/chadwick-henry

History.com Editors (2020, August 25). First televised Major League Baseball Game. *History*. www.history.com/this-day-in-history/first-televised-major-league-baseball-game

Hu, J. (2001, October 30). Baseball officials plan live video streaming. *CNET*. https://archive.is/20120711061344/http://news.com.com/2100-1023-275123.html

KDKA. (2010, April 1). *KDKA firsts*. https://pittsburgh.cbslocal.com/2010/04/01/kdka-firsts/

Kissel, K.P. (1992, November 10). HBO started 20 years ago in Wilkes-Barre. https://apnews.com/article/7234e60624a3ac1b2c33c4fb690dc235

Koplovitz, K. (2015, September 30). How Muhammad Ali, Joe Frazier and satellites changed TV history. *Media Village*. www.mediavillage.com/article/how-muhammed-ali-joe-frazier-and-satellites-changed-the-course-of-television-history/

Koppett, L. (1999, Spring). Baker Field: Birthplace of sports television. *Columbia College*. www.college.columbia.edu/cct_archive/spr99/34a.html

Leddy, C. (2015, September 28). The fight that helped cable take flight. *Multichannel News*. www.nexttv.com/news/fight-helped-cable-take-flight-394103

Leverette, M., Ott, B.L, & Buckley, C.L. (2008). *It's not TV. Watching HBO in the post-television era*. Routledge.

Litsky, F. (2003, May 11). Sam Lacy, 99, sportswriter who fought against racism. *The New York Times*. www.nytimes.com/2003/05/11/obituaries/sam-lacy-99-sportswriter-who-fought-against-racism.html

Madden, B. (2007, June 17). The true story of the midnight massacre. *New York Daily News*. www.nydailynews.com/sports/baseball/mets/midnight-massacre-article-1.224970

McChesney, R.W. (1989). Media made sport: A history of sports coverage in the United States. In L. Wenner (Ed.), *Media, sports, & society* (pp. 49-69). Sage Publications.

McCurdy, B. (n.d.). Graham McNamee: The inventor of play-by-play. *American Sportscasters Online*. www.americansportscastersonline.com/mcnameearticle.html

McGowen, R. (1939, August 26). First day for the small screen. *The New York Times*. https://archive.nytimes.com/www.nytimes.com/packages/html/sports/year_in_sports/08.26.html

NBC Sports Group. (2022, February 9). Super Bowl LVI on NBC, Peacock & Telemundo: "By the numbers." https://nbcsportsgrouppressbox.com/2022/02/09/super-bowl-lvi-on-nbc-peacock-telemundo-by-the-numbers/

NCAA. (2020). *College football history: Notable firsts and milestones*. www.ncaa.com/news/ncaa/article/2020-01-31/college-football-history-notable-firsts-and-milestones

Nufer, D. (1991, August 26). Present at the re-creation. *Sports Illustrated*. https://vault.si.com/vault/1991/08/26/present-at-the-re-creation-bob-robertson-broadcasts-baseball-games-the-old-fashioned-way-making-it-up-as-he-goes-along

Olympics. (n.d.). Berlin 1936 medal table. https://olympics.com/en/olympic-games/berlin-1936/medals

Pro Football Hall of Fame. (n.d.). Ebbets Field hosts football history. www.profootballhof.com/football-history/the-1930s-and-the-first-televised-game/

Reedy, J. (2022, February 11). Super Bowl 56: A viewer's guide to get you through Sunday. *Associated Press*. https://apnews.com/article/super-bowl-56-guide-a5505caf4e359dcbefa2fcf1d1e8b23f

Rice, G. (1924, October 18). The four horsemen. *New York Herald Tribune*. https://archives.nd.edu/research/texts/rice.htm

Romano, F.V. (2017). *The golden age of boxing on radio and television: A blow-by-blow history from 1921 to 1964*. Carrel Books.

Schneider, J. (2019, March 4). Graham McNamee: Radio's first superstar announcer. *Radio World*. www.radioworld.com/columns-and-views/roots-of-radio/graham-mcnamee-radios-first-superstar-announcer

Smith, R.A. (2001). *Play-by-play: Radio, television, and big-time college sport*. Johns Hopkins University Press.

This Is Where You Find Baseball. (2022, December 2). *Red Sox vs Tigers (8-10-1986)* [Video]. YouTube. www.youtube.com/watch?v=Aphc0xOsqRI

Vascellaro, C. (2013, April 22). How Sam Lacy helped integrate Major League Baseball. *The Baltimore Sun*. www.baltimoresun.com/opinion/op-ed/bs-ed-sam-lacy-20130422-story.html

Washburn, P.S., & Lamb, C. (2020). *Sports journalism*. University of Nebraska Press.

# Chapter 3

AdPerfect. (n.d.). The evolution of classifieds. www.adperfect.com/the-evolution-of-classifieds

Alfano, P. (1983, May 24). TV sports; ESPN struggling, but making an impact. *The New York Times*. www.nytimes.com/1983/05/24/sports/tv-sports-espn-struggling-but-making-an-impact.html

Andreeva, N., & Johnson, T. (2019, December 27). Cable ratings 2019: Fox News tops total viewers, ESPN wins 18-49 demo as entertainment networks slide. *Deadline*. https://deadline.com/2019/12/cable-ratings-2019-list-fox-news-total-viewers-espn-18-49-demo-1202817561/

Bachman, R. (2012, November 21). ESPN strikes deal for college football playoff. *The Wall Street Journal*. www.wsj.com/articles/SB10001424127887324851704578133223970790516

Battaglio, S. (2022, October 18). Amazon's Prime Video gets exclusive rights to NFL "Black Friday" game in 2023. *Los Angeles Times*. www.latimes.com/entertainment-arts/business/story/2022-10-18/prime-video-gets-exclusive-rights-to-first-nfl-black-friday-game-starting-in-2023

Belson, K., & Draper, K. (2021, March 18). N.F.L. signs media deals worth over $100 billion. *The New York Times*. www.nytimes.com/2021/03/18/sports/football/nfl-tv-contracts.html Bennett, D. (2011, May 24). The revolutionary strategy that made ESPN an $8 billion company. *Business Insider*. www.businessinsider.com/espn-an-8-billion-company-2011-5

Brown, T. (2019, September 5). How to watch ESPN Plus on your TV: What is it, what does it cost and what does it include? *The Oregonian*. www.oregonlive.com/sports/2019/09/how-to-watch-espn-plus-on-your-tv-what-is-it-what-does-it-cost-and-what-does-it-include.html

Casey, J. (2022, August). Nielsen's industry-leading U.S. national TV panel reaches over 42,000 households, comprised of 101,000 directly measured viewers. *Nielsen*. www.nielsen.com/news-center/2022/nielsens-industry-leading-u-s-national-tv-panel-reaches-over-42000-household/

Castillo, J., & Shaikin, B. (2020, April 1). Dodgers TV blackout is over; Spectrum deal puts SportsNet LA on DirecTV, AT&T TV. *Los Angeles Times*. www.latimes.com/sports/dodgers/story/2020 -04-01/spectrum-deal-puts-sportsnet-la-on-att-platforms-dodgers -games-can-be-viewed

Crupi, A. (2022, November 30). Disney to spend $44.9 billion on sports rights through 2027. *Sportico*www.sportico.com/feature /disney-to-invest-44-9-billion-on-sports-rights-through-2027 -1234697032/

The Daily Upside. (2021, August 26). NFL broadcasters await early returns on $105-billion investment. *The Motley Fool*. www.nasdaq .com/articles/nfl-broadcasters-await-early-returns-on-$105-billion -investment-2021-08-27

Darwish, M. (2020, November 22). Matt Roush & "CBS This Morn- ing" remember who shot J.R. on "Dallas" 40 years later (VIDEO). *TV Insider*. www.tvinsider.com/957647/who-shot-jr-dallas-larry -hagman-matt-roush-cbs-this-morning/

Diaz, S. (2007, August 31). On the internet, a tangled web of classified ads. *The Washington Post*. www.washingtonpost.com/wp -dyn/content/article/2007/08/30/AR2007083002046.html?hpid =sec-tech

FCC. (2011, June 9). Newspapers. *Information Needs of Communities*. https://transition.fcc.gov/osp/inc-report/INoC-1-Newspapers.pdf

Fischer, S. (2022, November 8). Disney misses on revenue and earnings but tops subscriber predictions. *Axios*. www.axios.com /2022/11/08/disney-earnings-november-2022-misses

Fletcher, B. (2022, October 27). Comcast loses 561k cable subs, Peacock grows to 15m. *Fierce Video*. www.fiercevideo.com/video /comcast-loses-561k-cable-subs-peacock-grows-15m

Hull, K. (2022). *Sports Broadcasting*. Human Kinetics.

Miller, B. (1979, August 31). From the archives: With the launch of ESPN, "Television goes (even more) sports crazy." *CT Insider*. www .ctinsider.com/connecticutmagazine/article/From-the-archives -With-the-launch-of-ESPN-17046515.php

Mullin, B. (2022, December 18). Want to understand television's trou- bles? Look at AMC. *The New York Times*. www.nytimes.com/2022 /12/18/business/media/amc-networks-streaming-cable.html

Nielsen. (n.d.) TV ratings. www.nielsen.com/us/en/solutions /measurement/television/

Pew Research Center. (2021, June 29). Newspapers fact sheet. www .pewresearch.org/journalism/fact-sheet/newspapers/

Pierson, D. (1987, March 16). NFL finally opens the door to cable. *Chicago Tribune*. www.chicagotribune.com/news/ct-xpm-1987-03 -16-8701210017-story.html

Rowan, D., & Hurst, M. (2022, February). Super Bowl LVI draws more than 101 million TV viewers. *Nielsen*. www.nielsen.com /news-center/2022/super-bowl-lvi-draws-more-than-101-million -tv-viewers/

Rueter, J. (2022, November 16). MLS, Apple announce details of new deal: What to make of pricing, later kickoff times. *The Athletic*. https://theathletic.com/3904200/2022/11/16/mls-apple-tv-details/

Shaikin, B. (2022, April 13). Q&A: What's the deal behind Apple TV's deal to broadcast baseball games? We asked MLB. *Los Ange- les Times*. www.latimes.com/sports/story/2022-04-13/mlb-tv -streaming-apple-tv-deal-games

Simonetti, I. (2022, June 29). Over 360 newspapers have closed since just before the start of the pandemic. *The New York Times*. www.nytimes.com/2022/06/29/business/media/local-newspapers -pandemic.html

Smith, G., Ingold, D., & Pogkas, D. (2022, October 17). Sports TV rights are costlier than ever—but they're cable's last lifeline. *Bloomberg*. www.bloomberg.com/graphics/2022-sports-tv-rights -us-nfl-nba-mlb-espn-nbc-fox/

Strauss, B. (2020, May 14). Amid layoffs and furloughs, sportswriters wonder what will be left of a storied profession. *The Washington Post*. www.washingtonpost.com/sports/2020/05/14/amid-layoffs -furloughs-sportswriters-wonder-what-will-be-left-once-storied -profession/

SVG Staff. (2022, April 7). Peacock gets into MLB streaming with 18 exclusive games; NBC Sports to produce Sunday morning schedule. *Sports Video Group*. www.sportsvideo.org/2022/04/07/peacock -gets-into-mlb-streaming-with-18-exclusive-games-nbc-sports-to -produce-sunday-morning-schedule/

Tracy, M. (2020, August 5). Digital revenue exceeds print for 1st time for New York Times company. *The New York Times*. www.nytimes .com/2020/08/05/business/media/nyt-earnings-q2.html

Zinser, L. (2008, November 18). ESPN outbids Fox Sports and wins B.C.S. rights. *The New York Times*. www.nytimes.com/2008/11/19 /sports/ncaafootball/19bcs.html

# Chapter 4

Adams, V. (1964, January 26). TV notes: Olympics and secret agents. *The New York Times*. https://timesmachine.nytimes.com /timesmachine/1964/01/26/97164850.html?pageNumber=363

Allen, K. (2015, February 21). FTW: 6 myths about the Miracle on Ice. *Coloradoan*. www.coloradoan.com/story/sports/2015/02 /21/miracle-ice/23742039/

Ansari, A. (2022, March 9). Why Tokyo 2020 will be the biggest: The complete list of sports and medals on offer. *Olympics.com*. https://olympics.com/en/featured-news/how-many-games-sports -tokyo-2020-olympics

Battaglio, S. (2022, February 23). Despite historic ratings low for the 2022 Winter Games, NBCUniversal remains bullish on Olympics. *Los Angeles Times*. www.latimes.com/entertainment-arts/business /story/2022-02-23/tv-audience-for-nbcs-olympics-coverage-hits -a-record-low

Billings, A.C., Angelini, J.R., & MacArthur, P.J. (2018). *Olympic television: Broadcasting the biggest show on earth*. Routledge.

Billings, A.C., Angelini, J.R., & MacArthur, P.J. (2021, August 9). Women dominate NBC Tokyo Olympic primetime coverage by record margin. *Five Ring TV*. https://fiveringtv.com/2021/08/09 /women-dominate-nbc-tokyo-olympic-primetime-coverage-by -record-margin/

Billings, A.C., Angelini, J.R., & MacArthur, P.J. (2022, February 21). Women's sports dominate NBC's primetime Olympic broadcast in historic fashion. *Five Ring TV*. https://fiveringtv.com/2022/02 /21/womens-sports-dominate-nbcs-primetime-beijing-olympic -broadcast-in-historic-fashion/

Billings, A.C., Angelini, J.R., & Wu, D. (2011). Nationalistic notions of the superpowers: Comparative analyses of the American and Chinese telecasts in the 2008 Beijing Olympiad. *Journal of Broadcasting & Electronic Media, 55*(2), 251-266.

Chad, N., & Reid, T. (1989, March 7). With its era of dominance past, ABC now looks to regroup. *The Washington Post.* www.washingtonpost.com/archive/sports/1989/03/07/with-its-era-of-dominance-past-abc-now-looks-to-regroup/f4153c49-2e19-43ef-a157-080587a1e22c/

Crouse, L. (2008, August 15). In pool or out, Olympic star stands apart. *The New York Times.* www.nytimes.com/2008/08/16/sports/olympics/16phelps.html

de Moraes, L. (2019, May 21). "Big Bang Theory" series so-long crowd grows to 23.4M in live+3. *Deadline.* deadline.com/2019/05/big-bang-theory-series-live-plus-three-day-viewing-23-44-million-viewers-tv-ratings-1202619990/

Dempsey, J. (1996, December 3). CBS, TNT team for games. *Variety.* https://variety.com/1996/scene/vpage/cbs-tnt-team-for-games-1117466417/

Ellerbee, B. (n.d.). 1960, CBS at Squaw Valley Olympics. *Eyes of a Generation.* https://eyesofageneration.com/the-start-of-something-big-instant-replay-in-1960-cbs-paid-50000-for-the/

ESPN [@espn]. (2021, July 29). A golden moment for Suni Lee. She wins gold in the all-around [Tweet]. Twitter. https://twitter.com/espn/status/1420731888268988423

Gaines, C. (2017, March 7). Cable and satellite TV customers pay more than $9.00 per month for ESPN networks whether they watch them or not. *Business Insider.* www.businessinsider.com/cable-satellite-tv-sub-fees-espn-networks-2017-3

Given, K. (2016, February 20). Nazis pioneered broadcasting . . . and made Jesse Owens a star. *WBUR.* www.wbur.org/onlyagame/2016/02/20/jesse-owens-olympics-germans-nazi-radio

Goldberg, J. (1999, December 3). SI awards: Ali the century's greatest. Retrieved from www.courant.com/news/connecticut/hc-xpm-1999-12-03-9912030176-story.html

The Guardian. (1896, February 5). The revival of the Olympic Games. https://uploads.guim.co.uk/2021/04/06/5_February_1896.jpg

The Herald. (1896, April 9). The Olympic Games. https://chroniclingamerica.loc.gov/lccn/sn85042461/1896-04-10/ed-1/seq-1/

History.com Editors. (2022, January 2010). The Olympic Games. *History.com.* https://www.history.com/topics/sports/olympic-games

Isidore, C. (2014, May 7). NBC nails Olympics rights through 2032. *CNN.* https://money.cnn.com/2014/05/07/news/companies/nbc-olympics/index.html?iid=EL

Larossa, M. (2016). Broadcasting the Olympic Games: The media and the Olympic Games—Historical Overview. *The Olympic Museum.* https://stillmed.olympic.org/media/Document%20Library/Museum/Visit/TOM-Schools/Teaching-Resources/Broadcasting-the-Olympic-Games/FicheInfo_DiffusionJO_historique_ENG.pdf

Lindsey, R. (1979, September 27). ABC-TV pays record 225 million for '84 Olympics. *The New York Times.* www.nytimes.com/1979/09/27/archives/abctv-pays-record-225-million-for-84-olympics-rise-in-advertising.html

Maraniss, A. (2018, October 15). The Mexico City Olympics protest and the media. *AndScape.* https://andscape.com/features/mexico-city-olympics-protest-media-john-carlos-tommie-smith/

McKay, J. (2002, December 13). The end of innocence. *ESPN.com.* www.espn.com/abcsports/columns/mckay_jim/2002/0904/1427112.html#

McNear, C. (2016, August 4). NBC's one-hour Olympics tape delay is absurd. *The Ringer.* www.theringer.com/2016/8/4/16036352/nbcs-olympics-tape-delay-is-absurd-81efc2dd349

Mifflin, L. (1984, July 30). Biggest TV production ever: 180 hours. *The New York Times.* www.nytimes.com/1984/07/30/sports/biggest-tv-production-ever-180-hours.html

Mulligan, T.S. (1992, July 25). Barcelona '92 Olympics: TripleCast sales remain woefully short of projections. *Los Angeles Times.* www.latimes.com/archives/la-xpm-1992-07-25-sp-3983-story.html

NBC New York. (2008, July 8). NBC announces 3,600 hours of Beijing Olympic games coverage. www.nbcnewyork.com/local/nbc_announces_3_600_hours_of_beijing_olympic_games_coverage/1615913/

NBC Sports Group Press Box. (2021, June 7). NBCUniversal to present unprecedented 7,000 hours of programming for Tokyo Olympics this summer. https://nbcsportsgrouppressbox.com/2021/06/07/nbcuniversal-to-present-unprecedented-7000-hours-of-programming-for-tokyo-olympics-this-summer

The New York Times. (1936, August 5). Olympics in Television. https://timesmachine.nytimes.com/timesmachine/1936/08/06/87970559.html?pageNumber=24

Nidetz, S. (1994, February 25). Kerrigan-Harding TV ratings 6th all-time. *Chicago Tribune.* www.chicagotribune.com/news/ct-xpm-1994-02-25-9402250278-story.html

The Olympic Museum. (n.d.). Live! Broadcasting the Olympic Games. *Google Arts & Culture.* https://artsandculture.google.com/story/live-broadcasting-the-olympic-games-the-olympic-museum/PQWBLZwQTYN6Jg?hl=en

Olympics.com. (n.d.). Paris 1924: The Olympic Games come of age. https://olympics.com/en/news/paris-1924-the-olympic-games-come-of-age

Reedy, J. (2020, February 21). Miracle on Ice shows how much Olympics on TV have changed. https://apnews.com/6167daf10b894dc016008ac3ed488b0b

Reedy, J. (2022, February 8). Several factors contribute to NBC's lower Olympic ratings. *AP News.* https://apnews.com/article/winter-olympics-nbc-low-ratings-02ad7acdf1104dd475e16ef4c4be10d6

Rosenberg, J. (2018, November 1). History of the 1920 Olympics in Antwerp, Belgium. *ThoughtCo.* www.thoughtco.com/1920-olympics-in-antwerp-1779595

Sandomir, R. (1992, June 29). Olympics; Triplecast: An Olympian blunder or innovation? *The New York Times.* www.nytimes.com/1992/06/29/sports/olympics-triplecast-an-olympian-blunder-or-innovation.html

Sandomir, R. (2000, February 22). TV Sports; "Miracle on Ice' of 1980 looks different today. *The New York Times.* www.nytimes.com/2000/02/22/sports/tv-sports-miracle-on-ice-of-1980-looks-different-today.html

Sandomir, R. (2010, February 19). Learning to live with tape delay. *The New York Times*. www.nytimes.com/2010/02/20/sports/olympics/20sandomir.html

Sandomir, R. (2012, June 27). NBC goes digital for Olympics, but tape will still roll in prime time. *The New York Times*. www.nytimes.com/2012/06/28/sports/olympics/nbc-will-show-every-olympic-event-live-online.html

Sandomir, R. (2016, August 17). Little is medal-worthy about NBC's coverage of foreign athletes. *The New York Times*. www.nytimes.com/2016/08/18/sports/olympics/nbc-television-coverage-of-foreign-athletes-united-states.html

Shedden, D. (2015, April 6). Today in media history: In 1896 reporters described the first modern Olympics. *Poynter*. www.poynter.org/reporting-editing/2015/today-in-media-history-in-1896-reporters-described-the-first-modern-olympics/

Socolow, M.J. (2022, February 21). The real viewership story of the Beijing Olympics. *Slate*. https://slate.com/culture/2022/02/winter-olympics-tv-ratings-youtube-social-media-viewership-huge.html

Strecker, E. (2012, July 31). Olympics: Missy Franklin victory spoiled by NBC. *Entertainment Weekly*. https://ew.com/article/2012/07/31/nbc-missy-franklin-olympic-coverage/

Tannenwald, J. (2016, July 11). NBC won't broadcast Rio Olympics opening ceremony live. *The Philadelphia Inquirer*. www.inquirer.com/philly/sports/olympics/NBC_wont_broadcast_Rio_Olympics_opening_ceremonies_live.html

Vaccaro, M. (2015, February 21). "Do you believe in miracles?": The 8 best sports calls ever. *New York Post*. https://nypost.com/2015/02/21/do-you-believe-in-miracles-the-8-best-sports-calls-ever/

Wertheim, L.J. (2021). *Glory days: The summer of 1984 and the 90 days that changed sports and culture forever*. Mariner Books

# Chapter 5

Affinito, K. (2000, November 14). Sports Illustrated for Women increases circulation rate base and frequency. *Time Warner*. https://web.archive.org/web/20180329054002/http://www.timewarner.com/newsroom/press-releases/2000/11/14/sports-illustrated-for-women-increases-circulation-rate-base-and

Associated Press. (2002, April 6). CNN/SI off the air May 15. https://apnews.com/article/55c451e110beccbe7b77979a6eedc4d6

Bevis, C. (n.d.). Sports Illustrated. *Encyclopedia.com*. https://www.encyclopedia.com/media/encyclopedias-almanacs-transcripts-and-maps/sports-illustrated

Bredholt, R. (2012, July 25). Most-read magazines in American change little from last year. *Cision*. https://www.cision.com/2012/07/most-read-magazines-in-america-change-little-from-last-year/

Bulls Insider. (2020, May 13). Steve Wulf talks Michael Jordan's *Sports Illustrated* ban, baseball days. www.nbcsports.com/chicago/bulls/steve-wulf-talks-michael-jordans-sports-illustrated-ban-baseball-days

Chavez, C. (2017, December 1). *Sports Illustrated*'s Sports Person of the Year: By the numbers. *SI.com*. www.si.com/sportsperson/2017/12/01/sportsperson-of-the-year-numbers-notes

CNBC (2010, January 27). The business behind the SI swimsuit issue. www.cnbc.com/2010/01/27/The-Business-Behind-the-SI-Swimsuit-Issue.html

Cohen, K. (2021, August 5). Opinion | The Sports Illustrated swimsuit issue's models are diverse. Their poses are not. *The Washington Post*. www.washingtonpost.com/opinions/2021/08/05/sports-illustrated-swimsuit-issues-models-are-diverse-their-poses-are-not/

Curtis, B. (2010, February 9). The Sports Illustrated swimsuit issue. *Slate*. https://slate.com/news-and-politics/2010/02/the-sports-illustrated-swimsuit-issue-an-intellectual-history.html

Davis, L.R. (1997). *The swimsuit issue and sport. Hegemonic masculinity in* Sports Illustrated. State University of New York Press.

Deford, F. (1989, February 7). How it all began. *Sports Illustrated*, 38-45.

Edmonds, R. (2018, January 9). *Sports Illustrated* is now reduced to a biweekly publication. *Poynter*. www.poynter.org/business-work/2018/sports-illustrated-is-now-reduced-to-a-biweekly-publication/

Fleder, R. (2005). *Sports Illustrated 50: The anniversary book*. Sports Illustrated Books.

Grant, K. (2017, August 2). Time Inc extends successful Sports Illustrated swimsuit brand, plans to represent models. *The Street*. www.thestreet.com/investing/stocks/time-inc-extends-successful-sports-illustrated-swimsuit-brand-plans-to-represent-models-14253643

Holland, G. (1955, January 3). 1954 & its sportsman: Roger Bannister. *Sports Illustrated*, 6-16.

Isidore, C. (2005, February 16). Bikini empire. *CNN Money*. https://money.cnn.com/2005/02/15/news/fortune500/swimsuit/

Kelly, K.J. (2008, November 22). Adios, Time's SI Latino. *New York Post*. https://nypost.com/2008/11/22/adios-times-si-latino/

Kelly, K.J. (2011, February 11). *Sports Illustrated* suits up for subscription app. *New York Post*. https://nypost.com/2011/02/11/sports-illustrated-suits-up-for-subscription-app/

Kelly, K.J. (2019 June 17). *Sports Illustrated*'s media ops are getting a new operator. *New York Post*. https://nypost.com/2019/06/17/sports-illustrateds-media-operations-just-got-sold-again/

Lee, D. (2020, November 30). 2021 media kit. *Sports Illustrated*. https://images.saymedia-content.com/.image/cs_srgb/MTc3MTkyNzg3MTY5NTE5MzUz/2021_si_media-kit_maven_113020.pdf

Liebeskind, K. (2005, February 25). *Sports Illustrated* introduces Spanish-language edition. *Portada*. www.portada-online.com/hispanic-media/hispanic-newspapers/sports-illustrated-introduces-spanish-language-edition/

Lippe-McGraw, J. (2022, March 31). Kathy Ireland reveals how SI swimsuit transformed her career. *Sports Illustrated Swimsuit*. https://swimsuit.si.com/swimnews/kathy-ireland-reveals-si-swimsuit-transformed-career

Lombardi, M. (2019, August 6). Sports Illustrated unveils college football preview issue with 4 star quarterbacks getting the covers. *The Spun*. https://thespun.com/college-football/sports-illustrated-college-football-preview-issue-2019-covers

LoRé, M. (2022, May 25). Sports Illustrated "is on fire right now." *Forbes*. www.forbes.com/sites/michaellore/2022/05/25/sports-illustrated-is-on-fire-right-now/?sh=7029f66d3111

MacCambridge, M. (1997). *The franchise*. Hyperion.

MacCambridge, M. (2018, April 11). "Who can explain the athletic heart?" *The Ringer*. www.theringer.com/2018/4/11/17220176/sports-illustrated-future-meredith-sale-history

Madden, L. (2013, February 8). Kate Upton on the cover of Sports Illustrated swimsuit issue for the second consecutive year. *Forbes*. www.forbes.com/sites/lancemadden/2013/02/08/kate-upton-on-the-cover-of-sports-illustrated-swimsuit-issue-for-second-consecutive-year/?sh=5f6337fe667b

Marchand, A. (2010, May 5). Derek, SI Jinx could be coming for you. *ESPN*. www.espn.com/blog/new-york/yankees/post/_/id/1882/derek-si-jinx-could-be-coming-for-you

McCarthy, M. (2021, February 1). Inside *Sports Illustrated*'s paywall plan for "premium" content. *Front Office Sports*. https://frontofficesports.com/si-metered-paywall-ryan-hunt-sports-illustrated-feb-2/

McManus, M. (1976). The Cover Story. In C. Krucoff (Ed.), *Magazine publishing management: A practical guide to modern magazine publishing* (p. 195). Folio Magazine Publishing.

Media Life. (2002, October 17). *Sports Illustrated* Women gets ax. https://web.archive.org/web/20021020110353/http://www.medialifemagazine.com/news2002/oct02/oct15/4_thurs/news1thursday.html

Parco, N. (2016, March 23). Curse them: A look at the victims of the *Sports Illustrated* cover jinx. *New York Daily News*. www.nydailynews.com/sports/victims-sports-illustrated-cover-jinx-article-1.2574796

Posnanski, J. (2017). SI prediction gave Cleveland false hope in '87. *MLB.com*. www.mlb.com/news/sports-illustrated-gave-87-indians-false-hope-c215708352

Price, S.L. (2015, December 14). Serena Williams is Sports *Illustrated*'s 2015 Sportsperson of the Year. *SI.com*. www.si.com/sportsperson/2015/12/14/serena-williams-si-sportsperson-year

Roberts, D. (2019, November 13). Exclusive: Sports Illustrated will reduce print output to monthly. *Yahoo!*. www.yahoo.com/now/exclusive-sports-illustrated-will-reduce-print-output-to-monthly-214408997.html

SI Kids Media Kit. (2021). https://images.saymedia-content.com/.image/cs_srgb/MTc3MTkyODY2NjI2NDEzNzI5/si-kids---2021-media-kit_maven_112020.pdf

Silber, T. (2018, May 29). Big ideas for a magazine newsstand industry in distress. *Forbes*. www.forbes.com/sites/tonysilber/2018/05/29/big-ideas-for-a-magazine-newsstand-industry-in-distress/?sh=7327d90d5930

Smith, F. (1964, January 20). Swimsuits that are made to get wet. *Sports Illustrated*, 30-35.

Smith, T. (2002, January 21). That old black magic. *Sports Illustrated*, 50-61.

Spector, D. (2013, February 12). The *Sports Illustrated* swimsuit issue: A $1 billion empire. *Yahoo Finance*. https://finance.yahoo.com/news/sports-illustrated-swimsuit-issue-1-161000843.html

Spiker, T. (2003). Cover coverage: How US magazine covers captured the emotions of the September 11 attacks—and how editors and art directors decided on those themes. *Journal of Magazine and New Media Research*, 5(2), 1-18.

Stelter, B., & Gold, H. (2018, March 21). Meredith is putting *Sports Illustrated* and *Time* magazines on the block. *CNN*. https://money.cnn.com/2018/03/21/media/meredith-time-fortune-magazine-for-sale/index.html

Trebay, G. (2019, May 8). At 45, Tyra Banks is back on the cover of Sports Illustrated. *The New York Times*. www.nytimes.com/2019/05/08/style/tyra-banks-sports-illustrated-swimsuit-issue.html

Wagner, L. (2017, September 29). What will *SI* do with Peter King's The MMQB? *Deadspin*. https://deadspin.com/what-will-si-do-with-peter-kings-mmqb-1818552646

Wells, R. (1955, December 12). Badgered dog. *Sports Illustrated*, 36-40.

Wulf, S. (1989, November 15). Puppies, poison ivy and a dashing duke. *Sports Illustrated*, 8-18.

# Chapter 6

Associated Press. (2010, October 11). Agent scandal costs UNC three players. *ESPN*. www.espn.com/college-football/news/story?id=5673405

Barbour, B. (2015, May 29). Marvin Austin's "Club LIV" tweet was five years ago today. *Tar Heel Blog*. www.tarheelblog.com/2015/5/29/8686135/marvin-austins-club-liv-tweet-was-five-years-ago-today

Barshop, S. (2017, August 27). J.J. Watt tells Houston to stay safe; Glover Quinn concerned for family. *ESPN*. www.espn.com/nfl/story/_/id/20479424/houston-texans-jj-watts-sends-message-support-harvey-flood-victims

Beard, A. (2012, March 12). NCAA hits UNC football with 1-year postseason ban. *USA Today*. http://usatoday30.usatoday.com/sports/college/football/2012-03-12-4195768565_x.htm

Brassil, G.R. (2021, May 29). Sedona Prince has a message for you. *The New York Times*. www.nytimes.com/2021/05/29/sports/ncaabasketball/sedona-prince-ncaa-basketball-video.html

Bryant, H. (2011, May 12). Not for sale: Mendenhall's voice. *ESPN*. www.espn.com/espn/commentary/news/story?page=bryant/110511

Dittmore, S.W. (n.d.). Making the message count: Rebranding the media relations department. *ADU*. https://athleticdirectoru.com/articles/making-the-message-count/

ESPN.com News Services. (2011, May 3). Rashard Mendenhall doesn't hold back. *ESPN*. www.espn.com/nfl/news/story?id=6471433

ESPN.com News Services. (2012, October 5). Cardale Jones: Classes pointless. *ESPN*. www.espn.com/college-football/story/_/id/8466428/ohio-state-buckeyes-cardale-jones-tweets-classes-pointless

Fry, J. (2012, July 6). ESPN faces challenges in Twitter era. *ESPN*. www.espn.com/blog/poynterreview/post/_/id/373/espn-faces-challenges-in-twitter-era

Gregory, S. (2009, June 5). Twitter craze is rapidly changing the face of sports. *Sports Illustrated*. www.si.com/more-sports/2009/06/05/twitter-sports

Heifetz, D. (2018, May 27). How LeBron turned his Instagram feed into a page for social activism. *The Ringer*. www.theringer.com/nba/2018/5/27/17396446/lebron-james-instagram-social-activism-playoffs

Hennig-Thurau, T., Malthouse, E.C., Friege, C., Gensler, S., Lobschat, L., Rangaswamy, A., and Skiera, B. (2010). The impact of new media on customer relationships. *Journal of Service Research, 13*(3), 311-330.

Hull, K. (2014). A hole in one (hundred forty characters): A case study examining PGA tour golfers' Twitter use during The Masters. *International Journal of Sport Communication, 7*(2), 245-260.

Hull, K. (2016). "I love Twitter": A case study exploring local sports broadcasters' impressions of Twitter. *International Journal of Sport Communication, 9*(4), 519-533.

Hull, K., & Abeza, G. (2021). Introduction to Social Media in Sport. *World Scientific Book Chapters*, 1-28.

Hull, K., & Lewis, N.P. (2014). Why Twitter displaces broadcast sports media: A model. *International Journal of Sport Communication, 7*(1), 16-33.

Kim, J.K., and Hull, K. (2017). How fans are engaging with baseball teams demonstrating multiple objectives on Instagram. *Sport, Business and Management, 7*(2), 216-232.

McCarthy, M. (2019). NBA and Twitter team up to bring "virtual sports bar" to life. *Front Office Sports.* https://frntofficesport.com/nba-twitter-finals/

McCoy, K. (2022, February 11). What a $6.5 million Super Bowl ad can buy in digital media. *Digiday.* https://digiday.com/marketing/what-a-6-5-million-super-bowl-ad-can-buy-in-digital-media/

NCAA. (2012, March 12). University of North Carolina, Chapel Hill public infractions report. https://web3.ncaa.org/lsdbi/search/miCaseView/report?id=102358

Pegoraro, A. (2010). Look who's talking—athletes on Twitter: A case study. *International Journal of Sport Communication, 3*(4), 501-514.

Robertson, M. (2018, February 16). Athletes' social snaps go behind-the-scenes at 2018 Olympic Games. *SF Gate.* www.sfgate.com/olympics/slideshow/Athletes-social-snaps-go-behind-the-scenes-at-178522.php

Sehl, K. (2019, October 29). 12 tips for creating engaging visual content on social media. *Hootsuite.* https://blog.hootsuite.com/epic-guide-creating-social-media-visuals/

SI Wire. (2017, May 7). Cardale Jones pokes fun at school tweet with funny cap at Ohio State graduation. *Sports Illustrated.* www.si.com/college/2017/05/07/cardale-jones-graduation-cap-ohio-state-tweet

Witz, B. (2022, March 15). Her video spurred changes in women's basketball. Did they go far enough? *The New York Times.* www.nytimes.com/2022/03/15/sports/ncaabasketball/womens-march-madness-sedona-prince.html

Zilles, C. (2022, January 17). How social media is changing the sports viewing experience. *Social Media HQ.* https://socialmediahq.com/how-social-media-is-changing-the-sports-viewing-experience/

# Chapter 7

AL.com. (2009, December 29). Tim Tebow's eye black Bible verses: A guide. www.al.com/press-register-sports/2009/12/tim_tebows_eye_black_bible_ver.html

Baran, S.J., & Davis, D.K. (2012). *Mass communication theory* (6th ed.). Wadsworth.

Burke, T. (2013, June 11). ESPN mentioned Tim Tebow 137 times in 120 minutes. *Deadspin.* https://deadspin.com/espn-mentioned-tim-tebow-137-times-in-120-minutes-512618294

Butterworth, M. (2013, June 1). The limits of the passion of, and for, Tim Tebow. *National Communication Association.* www.natcom.org/communication-currents/limits-passion-and-tim-tebow

Cespedes Family. (2015, February 15). A decade of Sunday night baseball: Is it really always Red Sox/Yankees? *Baseball Essential.* www.baseballessential.com/news/2015/02/16/a-decade-of-espn-sunday-night-baseball-is-it-really-always-red-soxyankees/

Cohen, B.C. (1963). *The press, the public, and foreign policy.* Princeton University Press.

Dirocco, M. (2008). Tim Tebow: Swamp king. *Men's Journal.*

Duffy, T. (2013, August 31). Tebow mania: The rise of sports' first social media superstar. *The Big Lead.* www.thebiglead.com/posts/tebow-mania-the-rise-of-sports-first-social-media-superstar-01dxkh3aedqm

Frenette, G. (2009, November 25). UF's Tim Tebow stayed true to beliefs. *The Florida Times-Union.* www.jacksonville.com/story/sports/college/uf-gators/2009/11/26/uf-s-tim-tebow-stayed-true-to-beliefs/15965292007/

Gaines, C. (2012, December 11). Too much Tebow? ESPN realizes there is such a thing. *Business Insider.* www.businessinsider.com/too-much-tebow-espn-realizes-there-is-such-a-thing-2012-12

Iyengar, S., Peters, M.D., & Kinder, D.R. (1982). Experimental demonstrations of the "not-so-minimal" consequences of television news programs. *American political science review, 76*(4), 848-858.

Kahn, Y. (2021, May 13). The Tim Tebow backlash isn't really about Tim Tebow. *First and Pen.* https://firstandpen.com/the-tim-tebow-backlash-isnt-really-about-tim-tebow/

Koblin, J. (2012a, August 14). SportsCenter spends the day celebrating Tim Tebow's birthday. *Deadspin.* https://deadspin.com/sportscenter-spends-the-day-celebrating-tim-tebows-birt-5934761

Koblin, J. (2012b, October 3). "You can't talk enough Tebow": ESPN's instructions to on-air talent. *Deadspin.* https://deadspin.com/you-cant-talk-enough-tebow-espns-instructions-to-on-5948667

Lippmann, W. (1922). *Public opinion.* The Free Press.

MacKay, J. (2013). *Tim Tebow.* Gale.

McCombs, M.E., & Shaw, D.L. (1972). The agenda-setting function of mass media. *Public Opinion Quarterly, 36*(2), 176-187.

Paulsen. (2010, January). BCS National Championship Game numbers. *Sports Media Watch.* www.sportsmediawatch.com/2010/01/bcs-national-championship-game-numbers/

Paulsen. (2010, April). NFL Draft most-viewed ever on ESPN. *Sports Media Watch.* www.sportsmediawatch.com/2010/04/nfl-draft-most-viewed-ever-on-espn/

Powell, B. (2008, July 22). Tim Tebow says no to Playboy. *Awful Announcing.* https://awfulannouncing.com/2008-articles/tim-tebow-says-no-to-playboy.html

Reimer, A. (2016, February 24). A recent poll proves there can never be enough Tim Tebow coverage. *Forbes.* www.forbes.com/sites/alexreimer/2016/02/24/tim-tebow-popularity-is-still-high/?sh=6b1779ed4112

Rivals.com. (2016, September 8). *Tim Tebow.* https://n.rivals.com/content/prospects/2006/tim-tebow-236

Tenety, E. (2012, January 9). Tim Tebow's 316 yards inspire "John 3:16" searches. *My Black Lab.* https://bayintegratedmarketing

.wordpress.com/2012/01/09/tim-tebows-316-yards-inspire-john-316-searches/

Whitley, D. (2018, September 27). Ten years later, Tim Tebow's speech echoes on. *Orlando Sentinel*. www.orlandosentinel.com/opinion/os-ae-tebow-speech-david-whitley-0927-story.html

# Chapter 8

Billings, A.C., Angelini, J.R., & MacArthur, P.J. (2018). *Olympic television: Broadcasting the biggest show on earth*. Routledge.

Casey, C. (2016, January 14). NFL: 10 most watched Monday Night Football games of all time. *Sportscasting*. www.sportscasting.com/the-10-highest-rated-monday-night-nfl-games-of-all-time/

Chase, C. (2015, December 8). The real story of Howard Cosell, John Lennon and the shocking "MNF" announcement. *For the Win*. https://ftw.usatoday.com/2015/12/howard-cosell-john-lennon-monday-night-football-video

Cosell, H. (1973). *Cosell*. Playboy Press.

ESPN Press Room. (2011, April 21). 50th anniversary of Wide World of Sports celebrated. https://espnpressroom.com/us/press-releases/2011/04/50th-anniversary-of-wide-world-of-sports-celebrated/

Florio, M. (2015, December 2). 30 years ago tonight, Monday Night Football had its highest rating ever. *Pro Football Talk*. https://profootballtalk.nbcsports.com/2015/12/02/30-years-ago-tonight-monday-night-football-had-its-highest-rating-ever/

Maraniss, A. (2018, October 15). The Mexico City Olympics protest and the media. *AndScape*. https://andscape.com/features/mexico-city-olympics-protest-media-john-carlos-tommie-smith/

McChesney, R.W. (1989). Media made sport: A history of sports coverage in the United States. In L. Wenner (Ed.), *Media, sports, & society* (pp. 49-69). Sage Publications.

Paley Center for Media. (n.d.). ABC's Wide World of Sports {Thrilla in Manilla; Hockey} (TV). https://www.paleycenter.org/collection/item/?q=head&p=46&item=T78:0606

Ross, C. (n.d.). Evel Knievel and Wide World of Sports: A winning combination. *ESPN*. www.espn.com/abcsports/wwos/e_knievel.html

Rushin, S. (1994). Roone Arledge. *Sports Illustrated*. 54-55.

Sandomir, R. (2005, April 19). Monday nights are changing; N.F.L. off ABC. *The New York Times*. www.nytimes.com/2005/04/19/sports/football/monday-nights-are-changing-nfl-off-abc.html

Sandomir, R. (2006, August 11). ABC Sports is dead at 45; Stand by for ESPN. *The New York Times*. www.nytimes.com/2006/08/11/sports/othersports/11sandomir.html

Sandomir, R. (2016, June 4). Muhammad Ali and Howard Cosell: Foils and friends bound by mutual respect. *The New York Times*. www.nytimes.com/2016/06/05/sports/muhammad-ali-and-howard-cosell-foils-and-friends-bound-by-mutual-respect.html

Shapiro, L. (1995, April 24). Howard Cosell dies at 77. *The Washington Post*. www.washingtonpost.com/wp-srv/sports/longterm/memories/1995/95pass12.htm

Smith, G. (1994). Forty for the ages. *Sports Illustrated*. 46-47.

Sun, R. (2018, January 9). How the real battle of the sexes match broke TV records and inspired Trump. *The Hollywood Reporter*. www.hollywoodreporter.com/news/general-news/how-real-battle-sexes-match-broke-tv-records-inspired-trump-1071798/

*The New York Times*. (1968, April 21). N.F.L. doubles its Monday night TV. https://timesmachine.nytimes.com/timesmachine/1968/04/21/91226531.html?pageNumber=346

Thomas, R.M. (1995, April 25). The man in the yellow blazer. *The New York Times*. http://archive.nytimes.com/www.nytimes.com/packages/html/sports/year_in_sports/04.25.html

TLPFAS. (2010, December 3). *John Lennon shot 12-8-80 Howard Cosell tells the world twice John Lennon was dead*. [Video]. YouTube. www.youtube.com/watch?v=n73GFvAyIjs

Vaccaro, M. (2015, February 21). "Do you believe in miracles?": The 8 best sports calls ever. https://nypost.com/2015/02/21/do-you-believe-in-miracles-the-8-best-sports-calls-ever/

Vogan, T. (2018). *ABC Sports: The rise and fall of network sports television*. University of California Press.

Washburn, P.S., & Lamb, C. (2020). *Sports journalism*. University of Nebraska Press.

Wertheim, L.J. (2021). *Glory Days: The summer of 1984 and the 90 days that changed sports and culture forever*. Mariner Books

# Chapter 9

Adler, K. (2021, January 22). ESPN digital in 2020: ESPN Digital in 2020: 34 straight months at no. 1, ESPN app grows leadership position by. *ESPN Press Room*. https://espnpressroom.com/us/press-releases/2021/01/espn-digital-in-2020-34-straight-months-at-no-1-espn-app-grows-leadership-position-by-42-percent-espn-tops-11-5-million-subscribers-social-climbs-to-no-1-for-best-year-on-record/

Belson, K. (2006, September 29). Mobile ESPN to end service aimed at sports customers. *The New York Times*. www.nytimes.com/2006/09/29/technology/29phone.html

Brady, J. (2018, January 18). ESPN's evolution: Snapchat, esports and attribution guidelines. *ESPN*. www.espn.com/blog/ombudsman/post/_/id/912/espns-evolution-snapchat-esports-and-attribution-guidelines

Brown, T. (2019, September 5). How to watch ESPN Plus on your TV: What is it, what does it cost and what does it include? *The Oregonian*. www.oregonlive.com/sports/2019/09/how-to-watch-espn-plus-on-your-tv-what-is-it-what-does-it-cost-and-what-does-it-include.html

CCTA. (n.d.). History of Cable. https://calcable.org/learn/history-of-cable/

Chad, N. (1987, October 18). To TV sports fans, ESPN grows from novelty to necessity. *The Washington Post*. www.washingtonpost.com/archive/sports/1987/10/18/to-tv-sports-fans-espn-grows-from-novelty-to-necessity/497e6ee0-dc18-42f0-b868-e72e3567d739/

City News Service. (2022, May 3). NFL Draft is TV viewers' no. 1 pick. *Los Angeles Times*. www.latimes.com/entertainment-arts/tv/story/2022-05-03/tv-ratings-story-for-the-week-of-april-25-may-1-wed-may-4-2022

Cotey, J.C. (2005, August 24). ESPNU to add to college saturation. *Tampa Bay Times*. www.tampabay.com/archive/2005/02/25/espnu-to-add-to-college-saturation/

Couch, T. (2017, February 9). #TBT: ESPN sails into new territory with America's Cup. *ESPN Front Row*. www.espnfrontrow.com/2017/02/tbt-espn-sails-new-territory-americas-cup/

Cozart, L. (2014, April 3). #TBT: ESPN.com through the years. *ESPN Front Row*. www.espnfrontrow.com/2014/04/tbt-espn-com/

Derscheid, J. (2020, May 22). "... it's critical to share your experiences and let them know there's no direct path to your goal." *ESPN Front Row*. www.espnfrontrow.com/2020/05/its-critical-to-share-your-experiences-and-let-them-know-theres-no-direct-path-to-your-goal/

Crupi, A. (2020, November 5). ESPN eliminates 500 positions as Disney budgets for a multi-billion-dollar rights spree. *Yahoo! Finance*. finance.yahoo.com/news/espn-eliminates-500-positions-disney-140346813.html

Dixon, E. (2022, August 11). ESPN+ reaches 22.8m subs as Disney posts US$5.1bn streaming revenue for Q3. *SportsPro Media*. www.sportspromedia.com/news/disney-espn-plus-streaming-dtc-subscribers-q3-2022-earnings-revenue/?zephr_sso_ott=uaMXfT

Draper, K. (2018, April 12). ESPN tries to get with a mobile, app-driven world. *The New York Times*. www.nytimes.com/2018/04/12/sports/espn-app.html

Eaton-Robb, P. (2008, December 26). Chris Berman is ESPN's face. *Seattle Times*. www.seattletimes.com/sports/other-sports/chris-berman-is-espns-face/

Ebiz. (n.d.). Top 15 most popular sports websites. www.ebizmba.com/articles/sports-websites

Ellenport, C. (2020, April 22). A bold new network, a preposterous idea: How the NFL Draft came to TV. *Sports Illustrated*. www.si.com/nfl/2020/04/22/how-espn-televised-nfl-draft-for-the-first-time

ESPN Front Row. (2018, December 18). *First SportsCenter 1979*. [Video]. Vimeo. https://vimeo.com/307153790

ESPN Press Room. (n.d.). ESPN, Inc. fact sheet. https://espnpressroom.com/us/espn-inc-fact-sheet/

Fabrikant, G. (1987, June 9). It's first and goal for ESPN. *The New York Times*. www.nytimes.com/1987/06/09/business/it-s-first-and-goal-for-espn.html

Fang, K. (2015, December 28). In its first five years, Longhorn Network isn't the success that ESPN had hoped for. *Awful Announcing*. https://awfulannouncing.com/2015/in-its-first-five-years-longhorn-network-isnt-the-success-that-espn-had-hoped-for.html

Frager, R. (1993, October 1). Whether you get it or not, ESPN2 has no tried or true. *The Baltimore Sun*. www.baltimoresun.com/1993/10/01/whether-you-get-it-or-not-espn2-has-no-tie-to-the-tried-and-true/

Freeman, M. (2001). *ESPN: The uncensored history*. Rowman & Littlefield.

Front Row Staff. (2019a, September 4). ESPN at 40: Chapter 1 of 4. *ESPN Front Row*. www.espnfrontrow.com/2019/09/espn-at-40-chapter-1-of-4/

Front Row Staff. (2019b, September 5). ESPN at 40: Chapter 2 of 4. *ESPN Front Row*. www.espnfrontrow.com/2019/09/espn-at-40-chapter-2-of-4/

Gordon, A. (2015, April 29). The embarrassing failure that made ESPN a mobile juggernaut. *Vice*. www.vice.com/en/article/53vvg3/the-embarrassing-failure-that-made-espn-a-mobile-juggernaut

Hall, A. (2016, January 28). #LCo5KSC: ESPN's Linda Cohn to anchor record 5,000th SportsCenter. *ESPN Press Room*. https://espnpressroom.com/us/press-releases/2016/01/lco5ksc-espns-linda-cohn-to-anchor-record-5000th-sportscenter/

Hall, A. (2022, August 2). Linda Cohn celebrates 30 years at ESPN with new, multiyear contract. *ESPN Press Room*. https://espnpressroom.com/us/press-releases/2022/08/linda-cohn-celebrates-30-years-at-espn-with-new-multiyear-contract/

Hofmeister, S. (1997, September 4). ESPN agrees to buy cable TV's Classic Sports Network. *Los Angeles Times*. www.latimes.com/archives/la-xpm-1997-sep-04-fi-28622-story.html

IGN Staff. (1999, November 4). Konami, Disney and ESPN bond. *IGN*. www.ign.com/articles/1999/11/05/konami-disney-and-espn-bond

Kohler, J. (2013, March 19). Michael Roarty dies at 84; marketer helped build Anheuser-Bush brand. *Los Angeles Times*. www.latimes.com/local/obituaries/la-xpm-2013-mar-19-la-me-michael-roarty-20130319-story.html

Koo, B. (2020, April 28). Are cable and satellite companies really aiming for rebates from ESPN and other sports networks? *Awful Announcing*. https://awfulannouncing.com/espn/are-cable-and-satellite-companies-really-aiming-for-billion-dollar-rebates-from-espn-and-other-sports-networks.html

Leitch, W. (2007, February 1). The last days of ESPN2. *Deadspin*. https://deadspin.com/the-last-days-of-espn2-233272

Malinowski, T. (2019, September 7). The Bourbons, the Schlitz and the missing tapes—the story of ESPN's first broadcast. *ESPN*. www.espn.com/espn/story/_/id/27530046/the-bourbons-schlitz-missing-tapes-story-espn-first-ever-broadcast

McAtee, R. (2018, April 2). What ESPN's new streaming service doesn't have and what it needs. *The Ringer*. www.theringer.com/sports/2018/4/2/17190026/espn-plus-streaming-service-april-12

Mehler, M., & Paikert, C. (2018, February 7). The game that started the madness: Magic vs. Bird in 1979 Michigan State-Indiana State final. *Sports Illustrated*. www.si.com/college/2018/02/07/magic-johnson-larry-bird-michigan-state-indiana-state-1979-excerpt

Melvin, P. (2018, September 20). ESPN+ hits one million paid subscribers in just over five months. *ESPN Press Room*. https://espnpressroom.com/us/press-releases/2018/09/espn-hits-one-million-paid-subscribers-in-just-over-five-months/

Miller, J.A., & Shales, T. (2011). *Those guys have all the fun*. Little, Brown and Company.

Morton, J. (2019, August 18). Five years on, student-athletes made SEC Network a success. *Tuscaloosa News*. https://www.tuscaloosanews.com/news/20190818/five-years-on-student-athletes-made-sec-network-success

Mulligan, T.S. (1997, November 20). Expansion team. *Los Angeles Times*. www.latimes.com/archives/la-xpm-1997-nov-20-fi-55695-story.html

Panitz, B. (2023, October 24). ESPN becomes most-followed brand on TikTok. *ESPN Press Room*. https://espnpressroom.com/us/press-releases/2023/10/espn-becomes-most-followed-brand-on-tiktok/

Pierson, D. (1987, March 16). NFL finally opens the door to cable. *Chicago Tribune.* www.chicagotribune.com/news/ct-xpm-1987-03 -16-8701210017-story.html

Rosenthal, P. (2019, September 8). How ESPN—now 40 years old— changed the sports world from your growing cable bill and round-the-clock programming to the glut of bowl games. *Chicago Tribune.* www .chicagotribune.com/sports/breaking/ct-cb-espn-40th-anniversary -changed-sports-20190906-ogxokpxedjgwdekdlmgudb6myq-story .html

Sandomir, R. (1996, November 1). Plays of the day, all day, every day. *The New York Times.* www.nytimes.com/1996/11/01/sports /plays-of-the-day-all-day-every-day.html

Sandomir, R. (2013, May 2). SEC will start TV network in 2014. *The New York Times.* www.nytimes.com/2013/05/03/sports /ncaafootball/sec-will-have-own-tv-network-starting-in-2014.html

Sandomir, R. (2015, January 4). Stuart Scott, ESPN's voice of exuberance, dies at 49. *The New York Times.* www.nytimes.com/2015 /01/05/sports/stuart-scott-espn-sportscaster-is-dead-at-49.html

Soltys, M. (2022, July 26). ESPN earns 25 million TikTok followers. *ESPN Front Row.* www.espnfrontrow.com/2022/07/espn-earns-25 -million-tiktok-followers/

Strauss, B. (2019, April 30). ESPN the Magazine is closing down. *The Washington Post.* www.washingtonpost.com/sports/2019/04 /30/espn-magazine-is-closing-down/

Vogan, T. (2015). *ESPN: The making of a sports media empire.* University of Illinois Press.

Yoder, M. (2015, October 27). ESPN has to make up over $3 billion in lost revenue and increased fees. *Awful Announcing.* https:// awfulannouncing.com/2015/espn-make-3-billion-lost-revenue -increased-fees.html

# Chapter 10

Associated Press. (1986, August 4). New Fox network signs up 79 TV stations across U.S. *The New York Times.* www.nytimes.com/1986/08 /04/arts/new-fox-network-signs-up-79-tv-stations-across-us.html

Baysinger, T. (2013, March 7). Fox isn't shy about challenging ESPN. *Broadcasting+Cable.* www.nexttv.com/blog/fox-isnt-shy-about -challenging-espn-119233

Carter, B. (1994, May 24). Fox will sign up 12 new stations; takes 8 from CBS. *The New York Times.* www.nytimes.com/1994/05/24/us /fox-will-sign-up-12-new-stations-takes-8-from-cbs.html

Curtis, B. (2018, December 13). The great NFL heist: How Fox paid for and changed football forever. *The Ringer.* www.theringer.com /nfl/2018/12/13/18137938/nfl-fox-deal-rupert-murdoch-1993 -john-madden-terry-bradshaw-howie-long-jimmy-johnson-cbs-nbc

ESPN. (2002). Worst sports innovations. www.espn.com/page2/s /list/readers/innovations/worst.html

Fang, K. (2017, July 10). The Fox Sports 1/FS1 timeline reveals a network that showed no patience. *Awful Announcing.* https:// awfulannouncing.com/fox/the-fox-sports-1fs1-timeline.html

Goodman-Hughley, E.N. (2020, January 30). Super Bowl halftime show never the same after Jennifer Lopez and "In Living Color." *ESPN.* www.espn.com/espn/story/_/id/28592073/super-bowl -half-show-never-same-jennifer-lopez-living-color

Hale, M. (2012, April 20). Fox network at 25: Blazing trails and burning bridges. *The New York Times.* www.nytimes.com/2012 /04/21/arts/television/the-fox-network-celebrates-its-25th -anniversary.html

In Living Color. (n.d.). https://www.emmys.com/shows/living -color

Jackson, D. (1997, January 29). Fox scores Super Bowl victory. *The Washington Post.* www.washingtonpost.com/archive/lifestyle/1997 /01/29/fox-scores-super-bowl-victory/6faa176b-8ce3-4607-a59f -ed8ed23b6711/

Kogan, J., Wolodarsky, W. (Writer), & Moore, R. (1992, January 23). Lisa the Greek (Season 3, Episode 14) [TV series episode]. In J.L. Brooks, M. Groening, A. Jean, M. Reiss, S. Simon (Executive Producers), *The Simpsons.* Gracie Films; Twentieth Century Fox Film Productions.

Lippman, J. (1990, September 7). Fox network gets cable affiliates deal with TCI. *Los Angeles Times.* www.latimes.com/archives/la-xpm -1990-09-07-fi-566-story.html

McCarthy, M. (2022, December 21). World Cup final gives Fox Sports a viewership record. *Front Office Sports.* https://frontofficesports .com/world-cup-final-gives-fox-sports-a-viewership-record/

Morgan, E. (2021, April 15). On this day: "In Living Color" premieres on TV in 1990. *Outsider.* https://outsider.com/entertainment/on -this-day-in-living-color-premieres-tv-1990/

Mulvihill, M. [@mulvihill79]. (2023, January 6). *Total minutes of live sports event viewing in 2022:* [Tweet]. Twitter. https://twitter .com/mulvihill79/status/1611412156020555776

NFL. (n.d.). In Living Color halftime show. www.nfl.com/100 /originals/100-greatest/game-changers-73

O'Connor, J.J. (1990, May 29). Review/Television; Bringing a Black sensibility to comedy in a series. *The New York Times.* www.nytimes .com/1990/05/29/arts/review-television-bringing-a-black-sensibility -to-comedy-in-a-series.html

Presspass. (n.d.). *Fox Sports.* www.foxsports.com/presspass/

Reedy, J. (2019, May 1). Fox Sports 1 showing patience, growth with studio lineup. *Associated Press.* www.yahoo.com/entertainment/fox -sports-1-showing-patience-growth-studio-lineup-190811913.html

Sandomir, R. (1994, September 10). HOCKEY; Fox outbids CBS for N.H.L. games. *The New York Times.* www.nytimes.com/1994/09 /10/sports/hockey-fox-outbids-cbs-for-nhl-games.html

Sandomir, R. (2000, September 27). BASEBALL; NBC ends bid, so Fox will get contract. *The New York Times.* www.nytimes .com/2000/09/27/sports/baseball-nbc-ends-bid-so-fox-will-get -contract.html

Sandomir, R. (2014, June 12). The innovation that grew and grew. *The New York Times.* www.nytimes.com/2014/06/13/sports/the -tv-score-box-that-grew-and-grew.html

SBJ. (2017, January 23). One glowing moment. *Sports Business Journal.* www.sportsbusinessjournal.com/Journal/Issues/2017/01 /23/NHL-at-100/Glowing-puck.aspx

Williams, D. (2013, January 31). When Up With People dominated halftime. *ESPN.* www.espn.com/blog/playbook/fandom/post/_/id /17649/when-up-with-people-dominated-halftime

Wulf, S. (1993, December 27). Out Foxed. *Sports Illustrated.* https:// vault.si.com/vault/1993/12/27/out-foxed-rupert-murdochs

-upstart-network-snatched-the-nfl-from-cbs-in-a-coup-that-will-change-the-face-of-televised-sports

Wyshynski, G. (2017, October 19). Seriously, the time is right to bring in the FoxTrax glow puck 2.0. *ESPN.* www.espn.com/nhl/story/_/id/21080555/nhl-bring-back-infamous-glow-puck

# Chapter 11

Associated Press. (2013, August 23). ESPN drops out of PBS project on NFL head injuries. *ESPN.com.* www.espn.com/espn/wire?section=nfl&id=9594860

Belson, K. (2015, September 1). Sony altered "Concussion" film to prevent N.F.L. protests, emails show. *The New York Times.* www.nytimes.com/2015/09/02/sports/football/makers-of-sonys-concussion-film-tried-to-avoid-angering-nfl-emails-show.html

Centers for Disease Control and Prevention. (2019, February 12). What is a concussion. https://www.cdc.gov/headsup/basics/concussion_whatis.html

Deitsch, R. (2013, August 25). Did the NFL put pressure on ESPN to divorce Frontline? *SI.com.* https://web.archive.org/web/20130830112859/http://sportsillustrated.cnn.com/nfl/news/20130825/media-circus-espn-nfl-frontline/index.html

Ezell, L. (2013, October 8). Timeline: The NFL's concussion crisis. *PBS.org.* www.pbs.org/wgbh/pages/frontline/sports/league-of-denial/timeline-the-nfls-concussion-crisis/

Fainaru-Wada, M., & Fainaru, S. (2013, October 2). Chat: Mark Fainaru-Wada, Steve Fainaru. *ESPN.com.* http://web.archive.org/web/20191101022228/http://www.espn.com/sportsnation/chat/_/id/49069/league-of-denial-authors

Fainaru-Wada, M., & Fainaru, S. (2013). *League of denial.* Three Rivers Press.

Farber, M. (1994, December 19). The worst case. *Sports Illustrated.* 38-46.

Flint, J. (2013, August 23). ESPN cutting ties to "League of Denial" will boost awareness for show. *Chicago Tribune.* www.chicagotribune.com/sports/la-et-ct-espn-frontline-nfl-20130823-story.html

Hebert-Farrell, D., & Scott, D. (2012, November 16). Frontline & ESPN's "Outside the Lines" team up to examine NFL concussions. *PBS.org.* www.pbs.org/wgbh/pages/frontline/sports/concussion-watch/frontline-espns-outside-the-lines-team-up-to-examine-nfl-concussions/

Humphrey, M. (2013, October 8). What is the NFL fan to do after Frontline's "League of Denial?". *Forbes.* www.forbes.com/sites/michaelhumphrey/2013/10/08/what-is-the-nfl-fan-to-do-after-frontlines-league-of-denial/?sh=398f2fb5c65e

Kaplan, D. (2013, December 16). "League of Denial" sales lag, despite publicity. *Sports Business Journal.* www.sportsbusinessjournal.com/Journal/Issues/2013/12/16/Leagues-and-Governing-Bodies/Denial.aspx

Kirk, M. (Director). (2013). *League of denial: The NFL's concussion crisis* [Documentary]. Frontline.

Landesman, P. (Director). (2015). *Concussion.* [Film]. Columbia Pictures.

Lelinwalla, M. (2015, October 5). Interview: "League of Denial" authors Mark Fainaru-Wada and Steve Fainaru talk concussion crisis in NFL. *TechTimes.* www.techtimes.com/articles/90580/20151005/interview-league-denial-authors-mark-fainaru-wada-steve-talk-concussion.htm

Lipsyte, R. (2013, August 25). Was ESPN sloppy, naive or compromised? *ESPN.com.* www.espn.com/blog/ombudsman/post/_/id/96/was-espn-sloppy-naive-or-compromised

Miller, J.A., & Belson, K. (2013, August 23). N.F.L. pressure said to lead ESPN to quit film project. *The New York Times.* www.nytimes.com/2013/08/24/sports/football/nfl-pressure-said-to-prompt-espn-to-quit-film-project.html

Moughty, S. (2013, August 22). A note from Frontline: ESPN and "League of Denial." *PBS.org.* www.pbs.org/wgbh/frontline/article/a-note-from-frontline-espn-and-league-of-denial/

Pen America. (2014, April 16). 2014 PEN/ESPN Award for Literary Sports Writing. https://pen.org/2014-penespn-award-for-literary-sports-writing/

Richwine, L., & Baker, L.B. (2013, August 23). ESPN denies it quit head injuries documentary over NFL ties. *Reuters.* www.reuters.com/article/us-espn-nfl/espn-denies-it-quit-head-injuries-documentary-over-nfl-ties-idINBRE97M0WO20130823

Sandomir, R. (2005, February 5). PRO FOOTBALL; citing N.F.L., ESPN cancels "Playmakers." *The New York Times.* www.nytimes.com/2004/02/05/sports/pro-football-citing-nfl-espn-cancels-playmakers.html

Sandomir, R. (2013, October 9). Partly by shunning documentary, ESPN lifts it. *The New York Times.* www.nytimes.com/2013/10/10/sports/football/by-shunning-concussion-documentary-espn-gives-it-a-lift.html

Schwarz, A. (2009a, September 29). Dementia risk seen in players in N.F.L. study. *The New York Times.* www.nytimes.com/2009/09/30/sports/football/30dementia.html

Schwarz, A. (2009b, December 20). N.F.L. acknowledges long-term concussion effect. *The New York Times.* www.nytimes.com/2009/12/21/sports/football/21concussions.html

Scott, D. (2012, November 16). Front & center: Outside the Lines and Frontline partner to investigate NFL concussions. *ESPN Front Row.* www.espnfrontrow.com/2012/11/front-center-outside-the-lines-and-frontline-partner-to-investigate-nfl-concussions/

Scott, D. (2013, October 2). Fainaru brothers at ESPN today to discuss forthcoming book, League of Denial: The NFL, Concussions and the Battle for Truth. *ESPN Front Row.* www.espnfrontrow.com/2013/10/fainaru-brothers-at-espn-today-to-discuss-forthcoming-book-league-of-denial-the-nfl-concussions-and-the-battle-for-truth/

Sherman, E. (2013, August 26). ESPN fallout to Frontline pullout: Not even own staffers are buying "branding" story. *Sherman Report.* www.shermanreport.com/espn-fallout-to-frontline-pullout-not-even-own-staffers-are-buying-branding-story/

Shpigel, B. (2021, December 16). What to know about C.T.E. in football. *The New York Times.* www.nytimes.com/article/cte-definition-nfl.html

Taddonio, P. (2014, April 2). Frontline wins Peabody Award for "League of Denial." PBS.org. www.pbs.org/wgbh/frontline/article/frontline-wins-peabody-award-for-league-of-denial/

Waldron, T. (2013, August 26). ESPN quit PBS concussion partnership over "sensational," "over the top" documentary trailer. *Think Progress.* https://archive.thinkprogress.org/espn-quit-pbs-concussion

-partnership-over-sensational-over-the-top-documentary-trailer-21deddaa5986/

Zirin, D. (2013, August 26). ESPN journalists speak out on concussion documentary. *The Nation*. www.thenation.com/article/archive/espn-journalists-speak-out-concussion-documentary/

# Chapter 12

Auerbach, N. (2022, August 18). Big Ten announces TV rights deals totaling over $8 billion with Fox, CBS and NBC. *The Athletic*. https://theathletic.com/3518414/2022/08/18/big-ten-tv-deal-details-rights/

Bradley, J.E. (2009, October 19). The place to be. *Sports Illustrated*. https://vault.si.com/vault/2009/10/19/the-place-to-be

Bucholtz, A. (2022, July 2). FBS AD says Fox and ESPN are "quietly" driving realignment by relaying valuations: "We're not picking random schools." *Awful Announcing*. https://awfulannouncing.com/ncaa/fbs-ad-fox-espn-realignment-valuations.html

Crawford, B. (2019, May 14). Report: FOX moves top college football game to noon slot. *247 Sports*. https://247sports.com/Article/College-football-2019-schedule-Big-Ten-Big-12-FOX-media-rights-132020272/

Draper, K., & Blinder, A. (2020, December 10). SEC reaches $3 billion deal with Disney, drawing CBS ties toward an end. *The New York Times*. www.nytimes.com/2020/12/10/sports/ncaafootball/sec-disney-deal.html

Duffey, K. (2014). Former Pac-12 coach takes shot at Texas A&M, SEC. *Saturday Down South*. www.saturdaydownsouth.com/tamu-football/former-pac-12-coach-takes-shot-texas-sec/

Dunnavant, K. (2004). *The 50 year seduction*. Thomas Dunne Books.

Goodbread, C. (2014, October 20). Bo Pelini questions ESPN, SEC relationship. *NFL.com*. www.nfl.com/news/bo-pelini-questions-espn-sec-relationship-0ap3000000414414

Gulick, B. [@brendangulick22] (2022, September 3). Rece Davis just told the crowd "if you think some television contract is gonna keep us from coming to the banks of the Olentangy, HELL NO!" Great atmosphere here this morning on set from @CollegeGameDay. [Video attached] [Tweet]. Twitter. https://twitter.com/brendangulick22/status/1566049071621701633

Koo, B. (2019, November 27). Fox is making progress competing with ESPN by presenting itself as an alternative to perceived SEC favoritism. *Awful Announcing*. https://awfulannouncing.com/ncaa/fox-is-making-progress-competing-with-espn-alternative-sec-favoritism.html

McVeigh, G. (2022, December 7). The 10 most-watched college football games of the 2022 season. *On3*. www.on3.com/news/most-watched-games-2022-season-college-football-fox-cbs/

Miller, J.A., Eder, S., & Sandomir, R. (2013, August 24). College football's most dominant player? It's ESPN. *The New York Times*. www.nytimes.com/2013/08/25/sports/ncaafootball/college-footballs-most-dominant-player-its-espn.html

Myers, J. (2022, December 13). Heisman Trophy winners, runners-up since 1935. *NCAA.com*. www.ncaa.com/news/football/article/2022-12-10/heisman-trophy-winners-and-runners-each-year-1935

NCAA. (n.d.). Championship history. www.ncaa.com/history/football/fbs

Ourand, J. (2019, December 20). SEC football leaving CBS after 2023, likely for ESPN/ABC. *Sports Business Journal*. www.sportsbusinessjournal.com/SB-Blogs/Breaking-News/2019/12/SEC.aspx

Ourand, J., & Smith, M. (2016, April 19). Sources: Fox, Big Ten closing in on media rights agreement. *Sports Business Journal*. www.sportsbusinessjournal.com/Daily/Closing-Bell/2016/04/19/Big-Ten.aspx

Parks, J. (2022, August 14). College football rankings: How the AP Top 25 poll works. *SI.com*. www.si.com/fannation/college/cfb-hq/ncaa-football-rankings/college-football-rankings-ap-top-25-poll-explained-how-it-works

Russo, R.D. (2014, October 21). As SEC dominates ranking, calls of #SECBias rise. *ESPN*. www.espn.com/espn/wire?section=ncf&id=11740771

Sandomir, R. (1994, February 12). FOOTBALL; CBS gets football, college variety. *The New York Times*. www.nytimes.com/1994/02/12/sports/football-cbs-gets-football-college-variety.html

Sandomir, R. (2006, June 22). Big Ten Network is set up with Fox. *The New York Times*. www.nytimes.com/2006/06/22/sports/ncaafootball/22tv.html

Sandomir, R. (2013, May 2). SEC will start TV network in 2014. *The New York Times*. www.nytimes.com/2013/05/03/sports/ncaafootball/sec-will-have-own-tv-network-starting-in-2014.html

Schwartz, N. (2014, October 24). Chris Fowler blasts people who believe ESPN has an SEC bias. *USA Today*. https://ftw.usatoday.com/2014/10/chris-fowler-espn-sec-bias

SEC Staff. (2022). SEC leads nation for 16th consecutive year in NFL draft. *SEC Sports*. www.secsports.com/article/33821910/sec-leads-nation-16th-consecutive-year-nfl-draft

Shea, A. (2022, August 10). The Big Ten didn't learn ANYTHING from the NHL's mistake. *Barrett Media*. https://barrettsportsmedia.com/2022/08/10/the-big-ten-didnt-learn-anything-from-the-nhls-mistake/

Shepkowski, N. (2021, December 14). 12 most-watched college football games of 2021. *USA Today*. https://fightingirishwire.usatoday.com/lists/college-football-tv-viewers-alabama-notre-dame-michigan-msu-ohio-state-cfp-georgia-dawgs-tide-auburn/

Sherman, R. (2014, October 25). Brent Musburger on alleged SEC bias: "Deal with it. They're the best." *SB Nation*. www.sbnation.com/lookit/2014/10/25/7071597/brent-musburger-on-medias-sec-bias-deal-with-it-theyre-the-best

Siegal, R.M. (2013, May 2). The Southeastern Conference and ESPN announce new TV network and digital platform. *ESPN Press Room*. https://espnpressroom.com/us/press-releases/2013/05/the-southeastern-conference-and-espn-announce-new-tv-network-and-digital-platform/

Speak. (2021, December 30). *Joel Klatt previews CFB playoff, Harbaugh's success at Michigan, SEC bias real?* [Video]. YouTube. www.youtube.com/watch?v=ItJjIEQr9SM

Sprung, S. (2018, November 15). AA Q&A: ESPN's Paul Finebaum talks his new expanded role at the network, the SEC and biases, and more. *Awful Announcing*. https://awfulannouncing.com/espn/aa-qa

-espns-paul-finebaum-talks-his-new-expanded-role-at-the-network
-the-sec-and-biases-and-more.html

Stone, C. (1995, August 5). Top of the heap: Want to win a national title? Don't play in the SEC, by far the toughest conference in the land. *Sports Illustrated*. https://vault.si.com/vault/1995/08/05/top-of-the-heap-want-to-win-a-national-title-dont-play-in-the-sec-by-far-the-toughest-conference-in-the-land

Taylor, P. (2006, October 16). Battle of the South. *Sports Illustrated*. https://vault.si.com/vault/2006/10/16/battle-of-the-south

Wittry, A. (2022, January 12). Track which conferences are winning the 2021-2022 bowl season. *NCAA.com*. www.ncaa.com/news/football/article/2022-01-10/2021-22-conference-bowl-records-scores-updates-through-college-football-playoff

# Chapter 13

Abrams, D., & Hogg, M.A. (2006). *Social identifications: A social psychology of intergroup relations and group processes*. Routledge.

Ashforth, B., & Mael, F. (1989). Social identity theory and the organization. *Academy of Management Review, 14*(1), 20-39.

Brown, N.A., Devlin, M.B., & Billings, A.C. (2013). Fan identification gone extreme: Sports communication variables between fans and sport in the Ultimate Fighting Championship. *International Journal of Sport Communication, 6*(1), 19-32.

Echevarria, R.G. (n.d.). Latin Americans in Major League Baseball through the first years of the 21st century. *Britannica*. www.britannica.com/topic/Latin-Americans-in-Major-League-Baseball-910675

Fiol, C.M. (2002). Capitalizing on paradox: The role of language in transforming organizational identities. *Organization Science, 13*(6), 653-666

Hull, K., Kim, J.K., & Stilwell, M. (2019). Fotos de Béisbol: An Examination of the Spanish-language Instagram Accounts of Major League Baseball Teams. *Howard Journal of Communications, 30*(3), 249-264

Jenkins, R. (2014). *Social identity* (4th ed.). New York: Routledge.

Korzenny, F., & Korzenny, B. A. (2005). *Hispanic marketing: A cultural perspective*. Routledge.

Kulik, B. (2009). Beisbol SBN: 2009 MLB season. *Slide Player*. slideplayer.com/slide/4865560/

Lapchick, R. (2016, April 20). The 2016 racial and gender report card: Major League Baseball. www.tidesport.org/_files/ugd/7d86e5_f1f1ed90bffe4044a335f170871a4989.pdf

Lopez, M.H. (2013, October 22). Hispanic identity. *Pew Research*. www.pewhispanic.org/2013/10/22/3-hispanic-identity/

Madsen, W. (1964). *The Mexican-American of South Texas*. New York: Holt, Rinehart & Winston.

Newman, M. (2015, March 3). Latino push helps At Bat app top North American charts. *MLB.com*. m.mlb.com/news/article/111004492/mlb-teams-up-with-latinworks-as-part-of-diversity-effort/

Padilla, A., Carlos, M., & Keefe, S. (1976). Mental health service utilization by Mexican American. In M.R. Miranda (Ed.), *Psychotherapy with the Spanish-Speaking: Issues in research* (pp. 9-20). Los Angeles: Spanish-Speaking Mental Health Research University Center.

Santiago-Rivera, A.L., Arrendondo, P., & Gallardo-Cooper, M. (2002). *Counseling Latinos and la familia*. Thousand Oaks, CA: Sage Publications.

Singh, N., Baack, D. W., Pereira, A., & Baack, D. (2008). Culturally customizing websites for US Hispanic online consumers. *Journal of Advertising Research, 48*(2), 224-234.

Skogrand, L., Hatch, D., & Sing, A. (2005). Understanding Latino families, implications for family education. Utah State University. http://extension.usu.edu/files/publications/publication/FR_Family_2005-02.pdf

Swan, S., & Wyer, R.S. (1997). Gender stereotypes and social identity: How being in the minority affects judgements of self and others. *Personal and Social Psychology Bulletin, 23*(12), 1265-1276.

Tajfel, H. (1978). *Differentiation between social groups: Studies in the social psychology of intergroup relations*. London: Academic Press.

Tajfel, H., & Turner, J.C. (1985). The social identity theory of intergroup behavior. In S. Worchel & L.W. Austin (Eds.), *Psychology of intergroup relations* (pp. 7-24). Chicago: Nelson-Hall.

Underwood, R., Bond, E., & Baer, R. (2001). Building service brands via social identity: Lessons from the sports marketplace. *Journal of Marketing Theory and Practice, 9*(1), 1-13.

Wang, Z., Walther, J.B., & Hancock, J.T. (2009). Social identification and interpersonal communication in computer-mediated communication: What you do versus who you are in virtual groups. *Human Communication Research, 35*(1), 59-85.

Wann, D.L., & Branscombe, N.R. (1990). Die-hard and fair-weather fans: Effects of identification on BIRGing and CORFing tendencies. *Journal of Sport and Social issues, 14*(2), 103-117.

Wann, D.L., & Branscombe, N.R. (1993). Sports fans: Measuring degree of identification with their team. *International Journal of Sport Psychology, (24)*1, 1-17.

Zhang, D., Lowry, P.B., Zhou, L., & Fu, X. (2007). The impact of individualism—collectivism, social presence, and group diversity on group decision making under majority influence. *Journal of Management Information Systems, 23*(4), 53-80.

# Chapter 14

Baran, S.J., & Davis, D.K. (2012). *Mass communication theory* (6th ed.). Wadsworth.

Clavio, G., & Eagleman, A.N. (2011). Gender and sexually suggestive images in sports blogs. *Journal of Sport Management, 25*(4), 295-304.

Cranmer, G.A., Brann, M., & Bowman, N.D. (2014). Male athletes, female aesthetics: The continued ambivalence toward female athletes in ESPN's The Body Issue. *International Journal of Sport Communication, 7*(2), 145-165.

Eastman, S.T., & Billings, A.C. (1999). Gender parity in the Olympics: Hyping women athletes, favoring men athletes. *Journal of Sport and Social Issues, 23*(2), 140-170.

Entman, R.M. (1993). Framing: Towards clarification of a fractured paradigm. *Journal of Communication, 43*(4), 51-58.

Godoy-Pressland, A., & Griggs, G. (2014). The photographic representation of female athletes in the British print media during the London 2012 Olympic Games. *Sport in Society, 17*(6), 808-823.

Goffman, E. (1974). *Frame analysis: An essay on the organization of experience*. Harvard University Press.

Hardin, M., Lynn, S., Walsdorf, K., & Hardin, B. (2002). The framing of sexual difference in SI for Kids editorial photos. *Mass Communication & Society, 5*(3), 341-359.

Hull, K., Smith, L.R., & Schmittel, A. (2015). Form or function? An examination of ESPN magazine's "Body Issue." *Visual Communication Quarterly, 22*(2), 106-117.

Kian, E.M., Bernstein, A., & McGuire, J.S. (2013). A major boost for gender equality or more of the same? The television coverage of female athletes at the 2012 London Olympic Games. *The Journal of Popular Television, 1*(1), 143-149.

Martin, A., & McDonald, M.G. (2012). Covering women's sport? An analysis of *Sports Illustrated* covers from 1987-2009 and ESPN The Magazine covers from 1998-2009. *Graduate Journal of Sport, Exercise & Physical Education Research, 1*, 81-97.

Tankard Jr., J.W. (2001). The empirical approach to the study of media framing. In *Framing public life* (pp. 111-121). Routledge.

Weber, J.D., & Carini, R.M. (2013). Where are the female athletes in *Sports Illustrated*? A content analysis of covers (2000–2011). *International Review for the Sociology of Sport, 48*(2), 196-203.

# Chapter 15

Anderson, D. (1991, October 13). Sport of the times; the Braves' tomahawk phenomenon. *The New York Times*. www.nytimes.com/1991/10/13/sports/sports-of-the-times-the-braves-tomahawk-phenomenon.html

APA. (n.d.) Race and ethnicity. www.apa.org/topics/race-ethnicity

Arth, Z.W., & Billings, A.C. (2019). Touching racialized bases: Ethnicity in Major League Baseball broadcasts at the local and national levels. *Howard Journal of Communications, 30*(3), 230-248.

Azzi, A. (2021, March 3). Before her first meet in a year, Simone Manuel reflects on how her own story is told. *NBC Sports*. https://onherturf.nbcsports.com/2021/03/03/swimmer-simone-manuel-2021-tyr-pro-san-antonio/

Barnes, K. (2022, June 22). Jonquel Jones and the untold story of the WNBA's reigning MVP. *ESPN*. www.espn.com/wnba/story/_/id/34109460/jonquel-jones-untold-story-wnba-reigning-mvp

Barry, D. (2016, May 21). A heated linguistic debate: What makes "redskin" a slur? *The New York Times*. www.nytimes.com/2016/05/22/sports/football/redskins-poll-prompts-a-linguistic-debate.html

Bell, M. (2021, July 23). New for '22: Meet the Cleveland Guardians. *MLB.com*. www.mlb.com/guardians/news/cleveland-indians-change-name-to-guardians

Berkow, I. (1988, February 1). Redskins rout Broncos, 42–10, in Super Bowl. *The New York Times*. www.nytimes.com/1988/02/01/sports/redskins-rout-broncos-42-10-in-super-bowl.html

Billings, A.C. (2004). Depicting the quarterback in black and white: A content analysis of college and professional football broadcast commentary. *Howard Journal of Communications, 15*(4), 201-210.

Billings, A.C., & Black, J.E. (2018). *Mascot Nation: The controversy over Native American representations in sports*. University of Illinois Press.

Borzi, P. (2016, March 1). The Sioux nickname is gone, but North Dakota hockey fans haven't moved on. *The New York Times*. www.nytimes.com/2016/03/03/sports/hockey/with-sioux-nickname-gone-north-dakota-hockey-fans-are-fighting-change.html

Brady, E. (2013, May 9). Daniel Snyder says Redskins will never change name. *USA Today*. www.usatoday.com/story/sports/nfl/redskins/2013/05/09/washington-redskins-daniel-snyder/2148127/

Carter, B. (2007, April 10). Radio host is suspended over racial remarks. *The New York Times*. www.nytimes.com/2007/04/10/business/media/10imus.html

Carter, B., & Steinberg, J. (2007, April 12). CBS drops Imus radio show over racial remark. *The New York Times*. www.nytimes.com/2007/04/12/business/media/12cnd-imus.html

Carter, B., & Story, L. (2007, April 12). NBC News drops Imus show over racial remark. *The New York Times*. www.nytimes.com/2007/04/12/business/media/12dismiss.html

Commanders. (n.d.). The 1930s. www.commanders.com/team/history/1930-by-the-decade

Commanders. (2020, July 13). Statement from the Washington Football Team. www.commanders.com/news/washington-redskins-retiring-name-logo-following-review

Cranmer, G.A., Bowman, N.D., Chory, R.M., & Weber, K.D. (2014). Race as an antecedent condition in the framing of Heisman finalists. *Howard Journal of Communications, 25*(2), 171-191.

Curtis, B. (2020, July 1). The future of the Black play-by-play announcer. *The Ringer*. www.theringer.com/sports/2020/7/1/21309644/black-play-by-play-announcers-minor-league-baseball

Draper, K. (2020, July 13). ESPN employees say racism endures behind the camera. *The New York Times*. www.nytimes.com/2020/07/13/sports/espn-racism-black-employees.html

Eastman, T., & Billings, A.C. (2001). Biased voices of sports: Racial and gender stereotyping in college basketball announcing. *Howard Journal of Communications, 12*(4), 183-201.

Entman, R.M. (1993). Framing: Towards clarification of a fractured paradigm. *Journal of Communication, 43*(4), 51-58.

ESPN.com. (2016, May 13). Carlos Gomez feels insulted by newspaper's use of quote. www.espn.com/mlb/story/_/id/15528312/carlos-gomez-houston-astros-discusses-feeling-disrespected-newspaper-column

Gandhi, L. (2013, September 9). Are you ready for some controversy? The history of "redskin." *NPR*. www.npr.org/sections/codeswitch/2013/09/09/220654611/are-you-ready-for-some-controversy-the-history-of-redskin

Gibbs, L. (2016, August 12). After historic swimming gold, Simone Manuel addresses police brutality and racism. *Think Progress*. https://archive.thinkprogress.org/simone-manuel-first-black-woman-olympic-swimming-5d811405c438/

Hull, K., Walker, D., Romney, M., & Pellizzaro, K. (2022). "Through our prism": Black television sports journalists' work experiences and interactions with Black athletes. *Journalism Practice*, 1-18.

Jennings, C. (2022, May 20). Rafael Devers growing more comfortable with second language, and with leadership role for Red Sox. *The Athletic*. https://theathletic.com/3323744/2022/05/20/rafael-devers-red-sox-leadership/

Lapchick, R.E. (2020). The 2021 sports media racial and gender report card: Associated Press Sports Editors (APSE). *The Institute for Diversity and Ethics in Sport*. www.tidesport.org/_files/ugd/138a69 _e1e67c118b784f4caba00a4536699300.pdf

Lapchick, R.E. (2022). The 2022 racial and gender report card: Major League Baseball. *The Institute for Diversity and Ethics in Sport*. www.tidesport.org/_files/ugd/403016_5c311ff6920442b780924 552fd8fdc88.pdf

Lewis, M., Bell, T.R., Billings, A.C., & Brown, K.A. (2019). White sportscasters, Black athletes: Race and ESPN's coverage of college football's National Signing Day. *Howard Journal of Communications*, *31*(4), 1-14.

*Los Angeles Times*. (1910, July 6). The fight and its consequences. www.usprisonculture.com/blog/wp-content/uploads/2012/10 /wordtoblackman.pdf

Madden, M. (2012, October 18). Hail to the pigskins. *Washington City Paper*. https://washingtoncitypaper.com/article/457165/hail -to-the-pigskins/

McCarthy, D., & Jones, R.L. (1997). Speed, aggression, strength, and tactical naivete: The portrayal of the Black soccer player on television. *Journal of Sport and Social Issues*, *21*(4), 348-362.

McCartney, R. (2014, May 28). 1933 news articles refutes cherished tale that Redskins were named to honor Indian coach. *The Washington Post*. www.washingtonpost.com/local/1933-news-article-refutes -cherished-tale-that-redskins-were-named-to-honor-indian-coach /2014/05/28/19ad32e8-e698-11e3-afc6-a1dd9407abcf_story.html

McDonald, S. (2020, July 2). Nike pulls Redskins online merchandise, hours after FedEx demands a name change. *Newsweek*. www .newsweek.com/nike-pulls-redskins-merchandise-online-store-after -fedex-demands-name-change-1515210

NCAI. (n.d.). Ending the era of harmful "Indian" mascots. www .ncai.org/proudtobe

Neuman, S. (2020, July 2). Washington NFL team's sponsor FedEx formally asks for team name change. *NPR*. www.npr.org/sections /live-updates-protests-for-racial-justice/2020/07/02/886984796 /washington-nfl-teams-sponsor-fedex-formally-asks-for-team -name-change

New York Times. (1994, June 9). Call St. John's the Red Storm. www.nytimes.com/1994/06/09/sports/call-st-john-s-the-red -storm.html

NFL.com. (2020, July 3). Washington Redskins to undergo thorough review of team's name. www.nfl.com/news/washington-redskins-to -undergo-thorough-review-of-team-s-name

Plotz. D. (2013, August 8). The Washington _____. *Slate*. https://slate.com/culture/2013/08/washington-redskins-nickname -why-slate-will-stop-referring-to-the-nfl-team-as-the-redskins.html

Pollin, T. (2013, June 6). Dropping back in NFL history: Lone Star and the Redskins. *Football Nation*. https://web.archive.org/web /20140116230440/http://www.footballnation.com/content /dropping-back-nfl-history-lone-star-and-the-redskins/22983/2/

Prince, R. (2016, May 14). Houston paper sorry after quoting broken English. *Journal-isms*. www.journal-isms.com/2016/05/houston -paper-sorry-in-quoting-broken-english/

Rainville, R.E., & McCormick, E. (1977). Extent of covert racial prejudice in pro football announcers' speech. *Journalism Quarterly*, *54*(1), 20-26.

Schmidt, A., & Coe, K. (2014). Old and new forms of racial bias in mediated sports commentary: The case of the National Football League draft. *Journal of Broadcasting & Electronic Media*, *58*(4), 655-670.

Shapira, I. (2016, May 19). A brief history of the word "redskin" and how it became a source of controversy. *The Washington Post*. www.washingtonpost.com/local/a-brief-history-of-the-word -redskin-and-how-it-became-a-source-of-controversy/2016/05/19 /062cd618-187f-11e6-9e16-2e5a123aac62_story.html

Shin, A. (2014, August 22). Washington Post editorial board stops using the word "Redskins." *The Washington Post*. www .washingtonpost.com/local/washington-post-editorial-board-stops -using-the-word-redskins/2014/08/22/39864ae0-2a0a-11e4-8593 -da634b334390_story.html

SI Staff. (n.d.). July 28, 1969, table of contents. *SI Vault*. https://vault .si.com/vault/1969/07/28/42953-toc

Silverman, M. (2020, December 10). "Actually pathetic." Black journalists are severely underrepresented in the Boston media landscape. *The Boston Globe*. www.bostonglobe.com/2020/12/10 /sports/boston-sports-media-diversity-survey/

Smith, B.T. (2016, May 4). Carlos Gomez knows he's a disappointment to Astros fans. *Houston Chronicle*. www.houstonchronicle.com /sports/columnists/smith/article/Carlos-Gomez-knows-he-s-a -disappointment-to-7394244.php

Solomon, G. (1988, January 17). "Jimmy the Greek" fired by CBS for his remarks. *The Washington Post*. www.washingtonpost.com /archive/politics/1988/01/17/jimmy-the-greek-fired-by-cbs-for -his-remarks/27536e46-3031-40c2-bb2b-f912ec518f80

Steinberg, D. (2014, June 3). The great Redskins name debate of . . . 1972? *The Washington Post*. www.washingtonpost.com/news/dc -sports-bog/wp/2014/06/03/the-great-redskins-name-debate-of -1972/?arc404=true

Sterling, W. (2021, July 11). Star UConn guard Paige Bueckers uses ESPYs speech to honor Black women. *CNN*. www.cnn.com/2021 /07/11/us/paige-bueckers-espys-speech/index.html

Strauss, R. (2007, April 11). Rutgers women send Imus an angry message. *The New York Times*. www.nytimes.com/2007/04/11 /sports/ncaabasketball/11rutgers.html

Wagner, L. (2017, September 29). What will *SI* do with Peter King's The MMQB? *Deadspin*. https://deadspin.com/what-will-si-do-with -peter-kings-mmqb-1818552646

Waldstein, D. (2018, January 29). Cleveland Indians will abandon Chief Wahoo logo next year. *The New York Times*. www.nytimes .com/2018/01/29/sports/baseball/cleveland-indians-chief-wahoo -logo.html

Waldstein, D., & Schmidt, M.S. (2020, December 13). Cleveland's baseball team will drop its Indians team name. *The New York Times*. www.nytimes.com/2020/12/13/sports/baseball/cleveland-indians -baseball-name-change.html

Washburn, P.S., & Lamb, C. (2020). *Sports journalism*. University of Nebraska Press.

Washington, J. [@jessewashington]. (2016, August 11). *At Olympic press conference for only black woman to win individual swimming medal, I'm the only black journalist* [Video attached] [Tweet]. Twitter. https://twitter.com/jessewashington/status /763943451628965890

Whiteside, E. (2022, August 31). Serena Williams forced sports journalists to get out of the "toy box"—and cover tennis as more than a game. *The Conversation*. https://theconversation.com/serena-williams-forced-sports-journalists-to-get-out-of-the-toy-box-and-cover-tennis-as-more-than-a-game-189024

Whitten, P. (2017, February 1). Black history month: African-American swimmers—why the disparity? *USA Swimming*. www.usaswimming.org/news/2017/02/01/african-american-swimmers-why-the-disparity

# Chapter 16

Abrams, J., & Weiner, N. (2020, October 16). How the most socially progressive pro league got that way. *The New York Times*. www.nytimes.com/2020/10/16/sports/basketball/wnba-loeffler-protest-kneeling.html

Acho, E. (2020, August 23). National anthem protests pt.1 w/ Roger Goodell | Uncomfortable conversations with a Black man Ep 8 [Video]. YouTube. www.youtube.com/watch?v=ljgkEcc4B1k

Associated Press. (2011, April 29). Persistence pays off: Niners trade up to land QB Kaepernick. *NFL.com*. www.nfl.com/news/persistence-pays-off-niners-trade-up-to-land-qb-kaepernick-09000d5d81f94e09

Associated Press. (2013, February 4). Ravens overcome power outage, survive rally to win Super Bowl. *ESPN*. www.espn.com/nfl/recap?gameId=330203025

Bieler, D., Maske, M., & Boren, C. (2017, September 26). "Trump can't divide this": Cowboys, along with owner Jerry Jones, kneel before anthem in Arizona. *The Washington Post*. www.washingtonpost.com/news/early-lead/wp/2017/09/25/cowboys-players-take-a-knee-with-owner-jerry-jones-before-standing-for-anthem/

Boren, C. (2016, September 7). Roger Goodell on Colin Kaepernick: "We believe very strongly in patriotism in the NFL." *The Washington Post*. www.washingtonpost.com/news/early-lead/wp/2016/09/07/roger-goodell-on-colin-kaepernick-we-believe-very-strongly-in-patriotism-in-the-nfl/

Boren, C. (2017a, September 24). NFL Week 3: Raiders sit as a team while Redskins link arms; Steelers, Titans, Seahawks skip anthem. *The Washington Post*. www.washingtonpost.com/news/sports/wp/2017/09/24/nfl-week-3-president-trump-urges-boycott-over-player-protests-injury-updates-scores-fantasy-football-tips/

Boren, C. (2017b, July 31). Ravens owner admits that Colin Kaepernick's protest is a factor in whether to sign him. *The Washington Post*. www.washingtonpost.com/news/early-lead/wp/2017/07/31/ravens-owner-admits-that-colin-kaepernicks-protest-is-a-factor-in-whether-to-sign-him/

Boren, C. (2020, August 26). A timeline of Colin Kaepernick's protests against police brutality, four years after they began. *The Washington Post*. www.washingtonpost.com/sports/2020/06/01/colin-kaepernick-kneeling-history/

Brady, E. (2021, February 10). Why is the national anthem played before American sporting events? And when did it start? *USA Today*. www.usatoday.com/story/sports/2021/02/10/national-anthem-sports-why-played-mark-cuban-colin-kaepernick/6702871002/

Branch, J. (2017, September 7). The awakening of Colin Kaepernick. *The New York Times*. www.nytimes.com/2017/09/07/sports/colin-kaepernick-nfl-protests.html

Chan, J.L. [@jenniferleechan]. (2016, August 26). *This team formation for the National Anthem is not Jeff Fisher approved. #HardKnocks* [image attached] [Tweet]. Twitter. https://twitter.com/jenniferleechan/status/769354272735531009

Creswell, J., Draper, K., & Maheshwari, S. (2018, September 26). Nike nearly dropped Colin Kaepernick before embracing him. *The New York Times*. www.nytimes.com/2018/09/26/sports/nike-colin-kaepernick.html

Cyphers, L., & Trex, E. (2020, September 10). From the archives: History of the national anthem in sports. *ESPN*. www.espn.com/espn/story/_/id/6957582/from-archives-history-national-anthem-sports

Diamos, J. (1996, March 14). PRO BASKETBALL; Abdul-Rauf vows not to back down from N.B.A. *The New York Times*. www.nytimes.com/1996/03/14/sports/pro-basketball-abdul-rauf-vows-not-to-back-down-from-nba.html

Doehler, S. (2023). Taking the star-spangled knee: The media framing of Colin Kaepernick. *Sport in Society*, *26*(1), 45-66.

Douglas, W. (2020, August 1). Dumba kneels during anthem, speaks out against racism at qualifiers. *NHL.com*. www.nhl.com/news/wild-defenseman-matt-dumba-kneels-during-national-anthem/c-317771894

Draper, K., & Belson, K. (2018, September 3). Colin Kaepernick's Nike campaign keeps N.F.L. anthem kneeling in spotlight. *The New York Times*. www.nytimes.com/2018/09/03/sports/kaepernick-nike.html

ESPN.com staff. (2017, September 25). Transcript: Steelers' Alejandro Villanueva explains anthem "ordeal." *ESPN*. www.espn.com/blog/pittsburgh-steelers/post/_/id/25288/full-transcript-alejandro-villanueva-on-steelers-pregame-ordeal

Fainaru-Wada, M. (2017, February 14). The revival of Mahmoud Abdul-Rauf. *ESPN*. www.espn.com/espn/otl/story/_/id/18686629/before-colin-kaepernick-protested-national-anthem-nba-star-mahmoud-abdul-rauf-did-same-own-way

Florio, M. (2016, August 27). Kaepernick sits during national anthem. *Pro Football Talk*. https://profootballtalk.nbcsports.com/2016/08/27/kaepernick-sits-during-national-anthem/

Garafolo, M. [@MikeGarafolo]. (2016, August 27). *He's actually done it all preseason. No one noticed. First time in uniform was last night.* [Tweet] Twitter. https://twitter.com/MikeGarafolo/status/769498231243993088

Goldman, T. (2018, September 6). How sports met "The Star-Spangled Banner." *NPR*. www.npr.org/2018/09/06/644991357/how-sports-met-the-star-spangled-banner

Gottlieb, J., & Maske, M. (2017, September 23). Roger Goodell responds to Trump's call to "fire" NFL players protesting during the national anthem. *The Washington Post*. www.washingtonpost.com/news/early-lead/wp/2017/09/22/donald-trump-profanely-implores-nfl-owners-to-fire-players-protesting-national-anthem/

Graber, S.M., Figueroa, E.J., & Vasudevan, K. (2020). Oh, say, can you kneel: A critical discourse analysis of newspaper coverage of Colin Kaepernick's racial protest. *Howard Journal of Communications*, *31*(5), 464-480.

Jones, M. (2018, April 26). Steelers' Alejandro Villanueva donates royalty check earned from newfound popularity to AFC North cities. *USA Today*. www.usatoday.com/story/sports/nfl/steelers/2018/04/26/steelers-alejandro-villanueva-donates-royalty-check-afc-north-cities-anthem-protests/554640002/

Jones, M. (2019, November 21). Legalese, mistrust and late negotiating: How Colin Kaepernick and the NFL broke apart on workout. *USA Today*. www.usatoday.com/story/sports/nfl/2019/11/21/colin-kaepernick-nfl-workout-waiver-teams-quarterback/4259272002/

Klemko, R. (2012, November 28). It's official: Kaepernick named starter. *USA Today*. www.usatoday.com/story/sports/nfl/2012/11/28/kaepernick-named-starter-by-niners/1732503/

Martin, J., Asmelash, L., Kim, A., & Close, D. (2020, August 28). Athletes across US sports take a stand, as games are called off in solidarity with Bucks' boycott. *CNN*. www.cnn.com/2020/08/26/sport/milwaukee-bucks-boycott-playoff-game/index.html

Maske, M. (2019a, February 15). Colin Kaepernick, Eric Reid settle collusion grievances against NFL and teams. *The Washington Post*. www.washingtonpost.com/sports/2019/02/15/colin-kaepernick-eric-reid-settle-collusion-grievances-against-nfl-teams/

Maske, M. (2019b, November 16). Colin Kaepernick throws for NFL scouts, says he has "been ready for three years." *The Washington Post*. www.washingtonpost.com/sports/2019/11/16/colin-kaepernick-workout/

Morales, C. (2021, November 16). What we know about the shooting of Jacob Blake. *The New York Times*. www.nytimes.com/article/jacob-blake-shooting-kenosha.html

Murungi, M. (2020, November 20). Players have been kneeling for months. Now what? *The New York Times*. www.nytimes.com/2020/11/20/sports/mls-playoffs-bpcmls.html

O'Neal, L. (2016, September 1). Kaepernick saga raises questions about the media. *Andscape*. https://andscape.com/features/kaepernick-saga-raises-questions-about-the-media-diversity/

Perez, A.J. (2017, September 25). Alejandro Villanueva's Steelers merchandise becomes No. 1 seller in 24-hour span. *USA Today*. www.usatoday.com/story/sports/nfl/steelers/2017/09/25/alejandro-villanueva-steelers-merchandise-becomes-top-seller-nfl-anthem/700601001/

Peter, J. (2016, September 1). Colin Kaepernick: I'm not anti-American, will donate $1 million. *USA Today*. www.usatoday.com/story/sports/nfl/49ers/2016/09/01/colin-kaepernick-national-anthem-protest-police-socks/89743344/

Schefter, A. (2019, November 12). NFL invites teams to Colin Kaepernick workout Saturday. *ESPN*. www.espn.com/nfl/story/_/id/28067012/nfl-invites-teams-colin-kaepernick-workout-saturday

Smith, S.A. [@stephenasmith]. (2019, November 16). *He doesn't want to play.* [Video attached] [Tweet]. Twitter. https://twitter.com/stephenasmith/status/1195866091068764160

Wagner, J. (2020, July 23). On Opening Day, a rarity for M.L.B.: Support for Black Lives Matter. *The New York Times*. www.nytimes.com/2020/07/23/sports/baseball/mlb-black-lives-matter.html

Warren, J. (2016, September 2). Media's own lack of diversity may be one legacy of the Colin Kaepernick controversy. *Poynter*. www.poynter.org/newsletters/2016/medias-own-lack-of-diversity-may-be-one-legacy-of-the-colin-kaepernick-controversy/

Washington, J. (2016, September 1). Still no anthem, still no regrets for Mahmoud Abdul-Rauf. *Andscape*. https://andscape.com/features/abdul-rauf-doesnt-regret-sitting-out-national-anthem/

Wesseling, C. (2015, November 2). Niners bench Colin Kaepernick; Blaine Gabbert to start. *NFL.com*. www.nfl.com/news/niners-bench-colin-kaepernick-blaine-gabbert-to-start-0ap3000000572076

Wyche, S. (2016, August 27). Colin Kaepernick explains why he sat during national anthem. *NFL.com*. https://web.archive.org/web/20200731220137/https://www.nfl.com/news/colin-kaepernick-explains-why-he-sat-during-national-anthem-0ap3000000691077

Yoder, M. (2017, September 28). Fox making surprising decision to not show national anthem at NFL games this week? *Awful Announcing*. https://awfulannouncing.com/nfl/fox-making-surprising-decision-not-show-national-anthem-nfl-games-week.html

# Chapter 17

Battaglio, S. (2019, May 20). ESPN president Jimmy Pitaro is fighting the cord-cutting wave. *Los Angeles Times*. www.latimes.com/business/hollywood/la-fi-ct-pitaro-espn-disney-20190520-story.html

Battaglio, S. (2023, August 15). "SportsCenter" anchor Sage Steele exits ESPN after settlement. *Los Angeles Times*. www.latimes.com/entertainment-arts/business/story/2023-08-15/sportscenter-anchor-sage-steele-exits-espn-after-settlement

Bedard, G.A. [@GregABedard] (2017, January 29). *Go nuts banning muslims from countries that haven't harmed us . . . as soon as you end the 33,000 annual gun deaths in* [Tweet]. Twitter. https://twitter.com/gregabedard/status/825569409502674944

Bogage, J. (2018, September 14). Jemele Hill makes her departure from ESPN official. *The Washington Post*. www.washingtonpost.com/sports/2018/09/14/outspoken-trump-critic-jemele-hill-confirms-her-departure-espn/

Bonesteel, M. (2017, October 21). ESPN's Jemele Hill: "I deserved that suspension." *The Washington Post*. www.washingtonpost.com/news/early-lead/wp/2017/10/21/espns-jemele-hill-i-deserved-that-suspension/

Bontemps, T., & Andrews, M. (2020, August 26). Three game 5s set for Wednesday postponed after Bucks' decision to not take floor. *ESPN*. www.espn.com/nba/story/_/id/29747523/three-game-5s-set-wednesday-postponed-bucks-decision-boycott

Brady, J. (2016, November 8). Inside and out, ESPN dealing with changing political dynamics. *ESPN*. www.espn.com/blog/ombudsman/post/_/id/767/inside-and-out-espn-dealing-with-changing-political-dynamics

Brunt, C. (2020, December 30). Athletes act: Stars rise up against racial injustice in 2020. *Associated Press*. https://apnews.com/article/breonna-taylor-election-2020-nfl-race-and-ethnicity-nba-192cec690b8e54d0c2464e17bd836437

Crawford, K. (2017, February 5). Jemele Hill, Michael Smith bring unique style brand to "SportsCenter." *Detroit Free Press*. www.freep.com/story/sports/2017/02/05/espn-jemele-hill-michael-smith-sportscenter/97517714/

Chang, R. (2021, June 3). How Billie Jean King led the equal pay for play battle. *History*. www.history.com/news/billie-jean-king-equal-pay-for-play

Curtis, B. (2017, February 16). Sportswriting has become a liberal profession—here's how it happened. *The Ringer*. www.theringer.com/2017/2/16/16042460/how-sportswriting-became-a-liberal-profession-dc7123a5caba

Draper, K. (2017, September 13). Comments by Jemele Hill of ESPN a "fireable offense," White House says. *The New York Times*. www.nytimes.com/2017/09/13/sports/jemele-hill-espn-white-house.html

Draper, K., & Belson, K. (2017, October 9). Jemele Hill suspended by ESPN after response to Jerry Jones. *The New York Times*. www.nytimes.com/2017/10/09/sports/football/jemele-hill-suspended-espn.html

ESPN. (2017, November). Social Media. www.espnfrontrow.com/wp-content/uploads/2017/11/NOV-2-RECEIVED-UPDATED-SOCIAL-MEDIA-GUIDELINES-10.221.pdf

ESPN.com News Services. (2012, March 23). Heat don hoodies after teen's death. *ESPN*. www.espn.com/nba/truehoop/miamiheat/story/_/id/7728618/miami-heat-don-hoodies-response-death-teen-trayvon-martin

ESPN.com News Services. (2015, July 15). Caitlyn Jenner vows to "reshape the landscape" in ESPYS speech. *ESPN*. www.espn.com/espys/2015/story/_/id/13264599/caitlyn-jenner-accepts-arthur-ashe-courage-award-espys-ashe2015

Flynn, K. (2020, September 1). ESPN and competitors ditch their "stick to sports" mantra. Politics is now fair game. *CNN*. www.cnn.com/2020/09/01/media/politics-in-sports-media/index.html

Granderson, L.Z. (2012, August 13). The political Michael Jordan. *ESPN*. www.espn.com/nba/story/_/id/8264956/michael-jordan-obama-fundraiser-22-years-harvey-gantt

Hess, C. (2021, July 14). Nearly 50 years ago, Kareem Abdul-Jabbar called for an end to institutional racism in Milwaukee. Little has changed. *WPR*. www.wpr.org/nearly-50-years-ago-kareem-abdul-jabbar-called-end-institutional-racism-milwaukee-little-has-changed

King, J.C. (2017, February 14). Should athletes stick to sports? *The New York Times*. www.nytimes.com/2017/02/14/magazine/should-athletes-stick-to-sports.html

Manzullo, B. (2017, September 13). ESPN: "Inappropriate" for Jemele Hill to call Donald Trump a white supremacist. *Detroit Free Press*. www.freep.com/story/sports/2017/09/13/jemele-hill-tweets-donald-trump-white-supremacist/661002001/

Maraniss, A. (2018, October 15). The Mexico City Olympics protest and the media. *AndScape*. https://andscape.com/features/mexico-city-olympics-protest-media-john-carlos-tommie-smith/

Martin, J., Asmelash, L., & Close, D. (2020, August 28). These teams and athletes refused to play in protest of the Jacob Blake shooting. *CNN*. www.cnn.com/2020/08/27/us/nba-mlb-wnba-strike-sports/index.html

Moyer, J.M. (2015, July 16). Why some critics don't think Caitlyn Jenner deserved the Arthur Ashe Courage Award. *The Washington Post*. www.washingtonpost.com/news/morning-mix/wp/2015/07/16/why-some-critics-dont-think-caitlyn-jenner-deserved-the-arthur-ashe-courage-award/

Mudrick, M., Sauder, M.H., & Davies, M. (2019). When Athletes don't "stick to sports": The relationship between athlete political activism and sport consumer behavior. *Journal of Sport Behavior*, 42(2).

New York Times. (2017, October 13). The *Times* issues social media guidelines for the newsroom. *The New York Times*. www.nytimes.com/2017/10/13/reader-center/social-media-guidelines.html

Phillips, C.J. (2018, August 21). New ESPN president Jimmy Pitaro should know sports and political commentary have a long and vital history together. *New York Daily News*. www.nydailynews.com/sports/football/ny-sports-phillips-espn-20180820-story.html

Putterman, A. (2017a, July 11). Caitlyn Jenner at the ESPYS: The night the right wing turned on ESPN. *Awful Announcing*. https://awfulannouncing.com/espn/caitlyn-jenner-at-the-espys-the-night-the-right-wing-turned-on-espn.html

Putterman, A. (2017b, October 9). Jemele Hill suspension draws (mostly angry) reaction from sports media, beyond. *Awful Announcing*. https://awfulannouncing.com/espn/jemele-hill-suspension-draws-mostly-angry-reaction-sports-media-beyond.html

Redford, P. (2017, February 2). Gregg Popovich gave an insightful monologue on white privilege and black history month. *Deadspin*. https://deadspin.com/gregg-popovich-had-an-insightful-monologue-on-white-pri-1791945369

Rhoden, W.C. (2013, June 20). In Ali's voice from the past, a stand for the ages. *The New York Times*. www.nytimes.com/2013/06/21/sports/in-alis-voice-from-the-past-a-stand-for-the-ages.html

Sanchez, R. (2014, December 12). Rich & poor, black & white: Many in US unified in anger at Eric Garner case. *CNN*. www.cnn.com/2014/12/11/us/police-slayings-reaction-roundup

Sandomir, R. (2016, June 4). Muhammad Ali and Howard Cosell: Foils and friends bound by mutual respect. *The New York Times*. www.nytimes.com/2016/06/05/sports/muhammad-ali-and-howard-cosell-foils-and-friends-bound-by-mutual-respect.html

SI Wire. (2016, September 26). Which sports figures are supporting Hillary Clinton, Donald Trump or Gary Johnson. www.si.com/more-sports/2016/09/26/athlete-presidential-endorsements-donald-trump-hillary-clinton-gary-johnson

Simmons, B. (2017, October 13). ESPN can't stick to sports. But can it stick by its talent? *The Ringer*. www.theringer.com/bill-simmons/2017/10/13/16469520/espn-jemele-hill-suspension-week-6-nfl-picks

Sports Business Journal. (2019, July 25). ESPN data: Majority of viewers want politics out of sports. www.sportsbusinessjournal.com/Daily/Issues/2019/07/25/Media/ESPN.aspx

Stelter, B. (2017, September 15). ESPN chief Skipper to staff: "ESPN is not a political organization." *CNN*. https://money.cnn.com/2017/09/15/media/john-skipper-espn-staff-memo/index.html

Strauss, B. (2017, September 29). "This is bad for America, but great for us." *Politico Magazine*. www.politico.com/magazine/story/2017/09/29/clay-travis-alt-right-espn-conservative-liberal-215658/

Washington, J. (2020, May 4). We finally have answers about Michael Jordan and "Republicans buy sneakers, too." *Andscape*. https://andscape.com/features/we-finally-have-answers-about-michael-jordan-and-republicans-buy-sneakers-too/

Westfall, S.S. (2014, December 18). President Obama: More sports stars should speak out on social issues. *People*. https://people.com/celebrity/president-obama-more-sports-stars-should-speak-out-on-social-issues/

# Chapter 18

Associated Press. (2007, July 17). Eleven years later, the WNBA arrives. *Herald-Tribune*. www.heraldtribune.com/story/news/2007/07/17/eleven-years-later-the-wnba-arrives/28559909007/

Baldwin, M. (2005, June 1). Winning combination: college softball has become a big winner for ESPN. *The Oklahoman*. www.oklahoman.com/story/news/2005/06/01/winning-combinationbrcollege-softball-has-become-a-big-winner-for-espn/61940260007/

Balasaygun, K. (2022, October 15). In the college sports pay era, female athletes are emerging as big economic winners. *CNBC*. www.cnbc.com/2022/10/15/that-nike-bronny-james-nil-deal-was-a-big-deal-for-women-too.html

Barnes, K. (2019, August 8). NBA 2K20 game to feature all 12 WNBA teams. *ESPN*. www.espn.com/wnba/story/_/id/27344188/nba-2k20-game-feature-all-12-wnba-teams

Bazelon, E. (2012, August 9). That *New York Times* piece on Lolo Jones got a lot right about women in sports. *Slate*. https://slate.com/culture/2012/08/lolo-jones-new-york-times-jere-longman-s-attack-on-the-american-hurdler-got-a-lot-right-about-women-in-sports.html

Billings, A., & Angelini, J. (2019). Equity achieved? A longitudinal examination of biological sex representation in the NBC Olympic telecast (2000–2018). *Communication & Sport, 7*(5), 551-564.

Billings, A.C., Angelini, J.R., & MacArthur, P.J. (2021, August 9). Women dominate NBC Tokyo Olympic primetime coverage by record margin. *Five Ring TV*. https://fiveringtv.com/2021/08/09/women-dominate-nbc-tokyo-olympic-primetime-coverage-by-record-margin/

Billings, A.C., Angelini, J.R., & MacArthur, P.J. (2022, February 21). Women's sports dominate NBC's primetime Olympic broadcast in historic fashion. *Five Ring TV*. https://fiveringtv.com/2022/02/21/womens-sports-dominate-nbcs-primetime-beijing-olympic-broadcast-in-historic-fashion/

Billings, A.C., & Young, B.D. (2015). Comparing flagship news programs: Women's sport coverage in ESPN's SportsCenter and FOX Sports 1's FOX Sports Live. *Electronic News, 9*(1), 3-16.

Brennan, C. (2021, July 7). Women's College World Series tops College World Series in viewership. *Just Women's Sports*. https://justwomenssports.com/reads/womens-college-world-series-tops-college-world-series-in-viewership/

Brisbane, A.S. (2012, August 9). Lolo Jones article is too harsh. *The New York Times*. https://archive.nytimes.com/publiceditor.blogs.nytimes.com/2012/08/09/lolo-jones-article-is-too-harsh/

Brooks, A. (2022, April 5). 2022 NCAA Division I women's basketball championship is most-watched season finale in nearly two decades—4.85 million viewers on ESPN networks. *ESPN Press Room*. https://espnpressroom.com/us/press-releases/2022/04/2022-ncaa-division-i-womens-basketball-championship-is-most-watched-season-finale-in-nearly-two-decades-4-85-million-viewers-on-espn-networks/

Clarke, L. (2022, January 10). NCAA men's and women's Final Fours get new Twitter handles, logos. *The Washington Post*. www.washingtonpost.com/sports/2022/01/10/ncaa-final-four-men-women-logos/

Cooky, C., Council, L.D., Mears, M.A., & Messner, M.A. (2021). One and done: The long eclipse of women's televised sports, 1989–2019. *Communication & Sport, 9*(3), 347-371.

Cooky, C., Messner, M.A., & Hextrum, R.H. (2013). Women play sport, but not on TV: A longitudinal study of televised news media. *Communication & Sport, 1*(3), 203-230.

Dachman, J. (2022, March 18). March Madness 2022: ESPN's NCAA women's hoops tourney production is bigger than ever as ratings skyrocket. *SVG News*. www.sportsvideo.org/2022/03/18/march-madness-2022-espns-ncaa-womens-hoops-tourney-production-is-bigger-than-ever-as-ratings-skyrocket/

Deford, F. (2010, May 19). Roller derby has its booms and busts; currently on upswing. *Sports Illustrated*. www.si.com/more-sports/2010/05/19/roller-derbyrevival

Donnelly, P., & Donnelly, M. (2013, March 4). The London 2012 Olympics—a gender equality audit. *Play the Game*. www.playthegame.org/news/the-london-2012-olympics-a-gender-equality-audit/

Dool, G. (2018, July 10). Maya Moore is SLAM's first female cover star in 20 years. *Folio*. https://web.archive.org/web/20200919122334/https://www.foliomag.com/maya-moore-slams-first-female-cover-star-20-years/

Drucker, J. (2021, May 13). TBT: The Mother's Day Massacre—Bobby Riggs over Margaret Court. *Tennis.com*. https://www.tennis.com/news/articles/tbt-the-mother-s-day-massacre-bobby-riggs-over-margaret-court

Duncan, M.C., Messner, M., & Williams, L. (1991). Coverage of women's sports in four daily newspapers. *LA84 Foundation*. https://la84.org/coverage-of-womens-sports-in-four-daily-newspapers/

Dutch, T. (2022, March 17). Nike develops athlete think tank to increase access for girls in sport. *Self*. www.self.com/story/nike-think-tank-launch

Elchlepp, K. (2023, February 8). ESPN swings for the fences with regular season softball schedule featuring nearly 3,000 matchups. *ESPN Press Room*. https://espnpressroom.com/us/press-releases/2023/02/espn-swings-for-the-fences-with-regular-season-softball-schedule-featuring-nearly-3000-matchups/

Fagan, K. (2013, August 27). Sex sells? Trend may be changing. *ESPN*. www.espn.com/espnw/nine-for-ix/story/_/id/9604247/sex-sells-trend-changing-espnw

Fagan, K. [@katefagan3]. (2015, June 23). Also, comparing TV ratings of men's & women's sports is like comparing speed of two cars, but on one you left flat tires & never filled tank [Tweet]. Twitter. https://mobile.twitter.com/katefagan3/status/613320502250115072

Fastis, S. (1996, October 30). WNBA to begin play in 1997 with eight teams in NBA cities. *The Wall Street Journal*. www.wsj.com/articles/SB846731775511850500

Gavilanes, G. (2016, March 14). WNBA star Elena Delle Donne: "I can't wait for the day people want to talk about your skills and not your looks." *People*. https://people.com/sports/elena-delle-donne-talks-sexism-in-basketball/

Geurin, A.N. (2017). Elite female athletes' perceptions of new media use relating to their careers: A qualitative analysis. *Journal of Sport Management, 31*(4), 345-359.

Greenspan, J. (2013, September 20). "Battle of the Sexes": When Billie beat Bobby. *History*. www.history.com/news/billie-jean-king-wins-the-battle-of-the-sexes-40-years-ago

Hull, K. (2017). An examination of women's sports coverage on the Twitter accounts of local television sports broadcasters. *Communication & Sport, 5*(4), 471-491.

Kirkpatrick, C. (1973, October 1). There she is, Ms. America. *Sports Illustrated*. https://vault.si.com/vault/1973/10/01/there-she-is-ms-america

Lefton, T. (2022, February 22). ESPN sells out women's NCAA Tournament ads. *Sports Business Journal*. www.sportsbusinessjournal.com/Daily/Morning-Buzz/2022/02/22/NCAA-women.aspx

Longman, J. (2012, August 4). For Lolo Jones, everything is image. *The New York Times*. www.nytimes.com/2012/08/05/sports/olympics/olympian-lolo-jones-draws-attention-to-beauty-not-achievement.html

Macht, D. (2012, August 8). Lolo Jones: Media "ripped me to shreds." *NBC Philadelphia*. www.nbcphiladelphia.com/news/sports/lolo-jones-media-ripped-me-to-shreds/1937072/

Martin, T.G., McNary, E., Suh, Y.I., & Gregg, E.A. (2018). A content analysis of pictorial content in entertainment and sports programming networks (ESPN): The magazine's body issue. *Journal of Physical Education and Sport Management, 9*(1), 1-9.

Megdal, H. (2022, June 15). Why Major League Soccer's TV deal matters for the WNBA—Washington Mystics talk big win—must-click women's basketball links. *The IX*. www.theixsports.com/features/why-major-league-soccers-tv-deal-matters-for-the-wnba-washington-mystics-talk-big-win-must-click-womens-basketball-links/

Mifflin, L. (1984a, August 4). Gymnastics; Gold to Retton in all-around. *The New York Times*. www.nytimes.com/1984/08/04/sports/gymnastics-gold-to-retton-in-all-around.html

Mifflin, L. (1984b, September 24). A lesson in gold-medal economics. *The New York Times*. www.nytimes.com/1984/09/24/sports/a-lesson-in-gold-medal-economics.html

Minsberg, T. (2021, July 22). When gender equality at the Olympics is not so equal. *The New York Times*. www.nytimes.com/2021/07/22/sports/olympics/olympics-athletes-gender.html

Morrison, S. (2014, February 19). Media is "failing women"—sports journalism particularly so. *Poynter*. www.poynter.org/reporting-editing/2014/media-is-failing-women-sports-journalism-particularly-so/

Myre, G. (2016, August 21). U.S. women are the biggest winners at the Rio Olympics. *NPR*. www.npr.org/sections/thetorch/2016/08/21/490818961/u-s-women-are-the-biggest-winners-in-rio-olympics

Ottaway, A. (2016, July 20). Why don't people watch women's sports. *The Nation*. www.thenation.com/article/archive/why-dont-people-watch-womens-sports/

Palmieri, J.E. (2022, January 31). Adidas continues to focus on attracting women to sports. *Yahoo! Sports*. https://sports.yahoo.com/adidas-continues-focus-attracting-women-185540500.html

Price, S.L. (2015, December 14). Serena Williams is *Sports Illustrated's* 2015 Sportsperson of the Year. *SI.com*. www.si.com/sportsperson/2015/12/14/serena-williams-si-sportsperson-year

Rajan, R. (2022, June 17). Viewership for 2022 NBA Finals on ABC finishes up 22 percent from last year. *ESPN Press Room*. https://espnpressroom.com/us/press-releases/2022/06/viewership-for-2022-nba-finals-on-abc-finishes-up-22-percent-from-last-year/

Rosenberg, A. (2012, August 6). The *New York Times* goes after hurdler Lolo Jones and gets Olympic sexism wrong. *Slate*. https://slate.com/culture/2012/08/lolo-jones-2012-olympics-the-new-york-times-goes-after-the-olympic-hurdler-and-gets-olympic-sexism-wrong.html

Rothman, L. (2017, June 23). How Title IX first changed the world of women's sports. *Time*. https://time.com/4822600/title-ix-womens-sports/

Schad, T. (2022, July 12). "Where the heck are the women?" Why women's sports could see financial boon in future TV deals. *USA Today*. www.usatoday.com/story/sports/2022/07/12/womens-sports-tv-financial-boon-coming/7810802001/

Shea, B. (2022a, April 6). Kansas-North Carolina averaged 18.1 million total viewers, most for NCAA title game in cable history. *The Athletic*. https://theathletic.com/4180448/2022/04/06/kansas-north-carolina-averaged-18-1-million-total-viewers-most-for-ncaa-title-game-in-cable-history/

Shea, B. (2022b, September 20). WNBA finals viewership dips but stays solid as NFL takes bite: Sports on TV. *The Athletic*. https://theathletic.com/3612516/2022/09/20/wnba-finals-ratings-nfl/

Stanford. (n.d.). The first game. https://125.stanford.edu/the-first-game/

Staurowsky, E.J., Flowers, C.L., Busuvis, E., Darvin, L., & Welch, N. (2022, May). 50 years of Title IX: We're Not Done Yet. *Women's Sports Foundation*. www.womenssportsfoundation.org/wp-content/uploads/2022/05/Title-IX-at-50-Report-FINALC-v2-.pdf

Streeter, K. (2022, November 8). New endorsements for college athletes resurface an old concern: Sex sells. *The New York Times*. www.nytimes.com/2022/11/08/sports/ncaabasketball/olivia-dunne-haley-jones-endorsements.html

TheOlympicsHistory. (2013, April 19). *Mary Lou Retton—1980's WHEATIES COMMERCIAL* [Video]. YouTube. www.youtube.com/watch?v=cztmXZR0sJ0

Thomas, K. (2010, October 15). ESPN slowly introducing online brand for women. *The New York Times*. www.nytimes.com/2010/10/16/sports/16espnw.html

Thomas, R.M. (1997, May 18). Joanie Weston, 62, a big star in the world of roller derbies. *The New York Times*. www.nytimes.com/1997/05/18/us/joanie-weston-62-a-big-star-in-the-world-of-roller-derbies.html

Tumin, R. (2022a, June 22). Title IX gave women greater access to education. Here's what it says and does. *The New York Times*. www.nytimes.com/2022/06/22/sports/what-is-title-ix.html

Tumin, R. (2022b, June 23). Fifty years on, Title IX's legacy includes its durability. *The New York Times*. www.nytimes.com/2022/06/23/sports/title-ix-anniversary.html

Tumin, R. (2023, April 3). N.C.A.A. women's tournament shatters ratings record in final. *The New York Times*. www.nytimes.com/2023/04/03/sports/ncaabasketball/lsu-iowa-womens-tournament-ratings-record.html

Uhlir, A. (1982, July 11). Political victim: The dream that was the A.I.A.W. *The New York Times*. www.nytimes.com/1982/07/11/sports/political-victim-the-dream-that-was-the-aiaw.html

VanTryon, M. (2022, January 5). The NCAA changed its Final Four logos. It's another step for women's basketball equality. *USA Today*. www.indystar.com/story/sports/college/2022/01/05/ncaa-changes-final-four-logos-social-media-handles-womens-equality-march-madness/9101782002/

Weber, J.D., & Carini, R.M. (2013). Where are the female athletes in Sports Illustrated? A content analysis of covers (2000–2011). *International Review for the Sociology of Sport, 48*(2), 196-203.

Witz, B. (2022, March 15). Her video spurred changes in women's basketball. Did they go far enough? *The New York Times*. www.nytimes.com/2022/03/15/sports/ncaabasketball/womens-march-madness-sedona-prince.html

WNBA. (2022, August 17). WNBA delivers most-watched regular season in 14 years and shatters fan engagement and on-court records. www.wnba.com/news/wnba-delivers-most-watched-regular-season-in-14-years-and-shatters-fan-engagement-and-on-court-records/

# Chapter 19

Allen, S. (2019, July 7). Trumps, Obamas, Clintons, congratulate USWNT after World Cup triumph. *The Washington Post*. https://www.washingtonpost.com/sports/2019/07/07/melania-trump-michelle-obama-congratulate-uswnt-world-cup-triumph/

Associated Press. (1995, June 16). SOCCER; Norway puts U.S. women on sideline. *The New York Times*. www.nytimes.com/1995/06/16/sports/soccer-norway-puts-us-women-on-sideline.html

Associated Press. (2015, July 6). Women's World Cup final seen by record 26.7 million in US. https://apnews.com/article/b3856beb3e0f47ca83173bc234109988

Associated Press. (2019, February 20). NWSL ends partnership with A+E Networks. https://apnews.com/article/e2f750bf30e7497ea63e87de8b4ee1cd

Banks, E. (2011, July 19). World Cup final sets two Twitter records. *CNN*. www.cnn.com/2011/TECH/social.media/07/18/world.cup.twitter.record.mashable/index.html

Barroso, A., & Brown, A. (2021, May 25). Gender pay gap in U.S. held steady in 2020. *Pew Research*. www.pewresearch.org/fact-tank/2021/05/25/gender-pay-gap-facts/

Bell, J. (2013, April 13). Another attempt at women's circuit, but with a twist. *The New York Times*. www.nytimes.com/2013/04/14/sports/soccer/national-womens-soccer-league-to-begin-play.html

Bonesteel, M. (2015, June 25). Seth Meyers, Amy Poehler ask SI writer who hates women's sports: "Really!?!" *The Washington Post*. www.washingtonpost.com/news/early-lead/wp/2015/06/25/seth-meyers-amy-poehler-ask-si-writer-who-hates-womens-sports-really/

Bupp, P. (2019, July 4). ESPN to show 14 NWSL games, including playoffs, for the rest of the 2019 season. *Awful Announcing*. https://awfulannouncing.com/espn/espn-to-show-14-nwsl-games-including-playoffs-for-the-rest-of-2019-season.html

Compton, J. (2019, July 5). Lesbian visibility at Women's World Cup has impact far off the field. *NBC News*. www.nbcnews.com/feature/nbc-out/lesbian-visibility-women-s-world-cup-has-impact-far-field-n1026741

Das, A. (2016, April 21). Pay disparity in U.S. Soccer? It's complicated. *The New York Times*. www.nytimes.com/2016/04/22/sports/soccer/usmnt-uswnt-soccer-equal-pay.html

Das, A. (2019, March 8). U.S. women's soccer team sues U.S. soccer for gender discrimination. *The New York Times*. www.nytimes.com/2019/03/08/sports/womens-soccer-team-lawsuit-gender-discrimination.html

Das, A. (2022, February 22). U.S. Soccer and women's players agree to settle equal pay lawsuit. *The New York Times*. www.nytimes.com/2022/02/22/sports/soccer/us-womens-soccer-equal-pay.html

Deitsch, R. (2019, June 10). Media circus: How Fox plans to cover the women's World Cup. *The Athletic*. https://theathletic.com/1018796/2019/06/10/media-circus-how-fox-plans-to-cover-the-womens-world-cup/

Dosh, K. (2019, October 24). Budweiser launches campaign to find new NWSL sponsors. *Forbes*. www.forbes.com/sites/kristidosh/2019/10/24/budweiser-launches-campaign-to-find-new-nwsl-sponsors/?sh=78d542bc650e

Fetters, A. (2019, July 12). What a time (for girls) to be alive. *The Atlantic*. www.theatlantic.com/family/archive/2019/07/us-national-womens-soccer-team-girls/593857/

FIFA. (1999, June 17). WWC99: Media accreditation approaches the 2,000 mark. https://web.archive.org/web/20190512062808/https://www.fifa.com/womensworldcup/news/wwc99-media-accreditation-approaches-the-000-mark-70854

FIFA. (2019, February 21). The 1999 gamble that paid off. www.fifa.com/tournaments/womens/womensworldcup/france2019/news/the-1999-gamble-that-paid-off

Goff, S. (2022, October 29). Ten years in, the growing NWSL is facing more scrutiny than ever. *The Washington Post*. www.washingtonpost.com/sports/2022/10/29/nwsl-title-game-attendance/

Goodman, J. (1999, July 20). U.S. women appear on Letterman. *Associated Press*. https://apnews.com/article/b4049c3614994a6fad645fc4f3511053

Hays, G. (2019, July 5). Morgan: Teacup critics part of "double standard." *ESPN*. www.espn.com/soccer/united-states/story/3893483/morgan----teacup-critics-part-of-double-standard

Hess, A.J. (2019, July 10). US viewership of the 2019 Women's World Cup final was 22% higher than the 2018 men's final. *CNBC*. www.cnbc.com/2019/07/10/us-viewership-of-the-womens-world-cup-final-was-higher-than-the-mens.html

Honan, K., & Christovich, A. (2019, July 10). New York celebrates World Cup-winning U.S. women's team. *The Wall Street Journal*. www.wsj.com/articles/new-york-celebrates-world-cup-winning-u-s-womens-team-11562792202

Jones, G.L. (1996, June 1). Women's soccer championship is coming to America in 1999. *The Washington Post*, 53.

Keh, A. (2015, June 24). Women's World Cup 2015: U.S. keeps winning as critics of its style keep grumbling. *The New York Times*. www.nytimes.com/2015/06/25/sports/soccer/womens-world-cup-2015-us-keeps-winning-as-critics-of-its-style-keep-grumbling.html?_r=0

Leyden, E. (Director). (2013). *The '99ers* [Film]. ESPN Films.

Linehan, M. (2019a, July 7). With new commercial and media deals, the NWSL is now slightly more poised to capitalize on World Cup bump. *The Athletic.* https://theathletic.com/1065982/2019/07/07/with-new-commercial-and-media-deals-the-nwsl-is-now-slightly-more-poised-to-capitalize-on-world-cup-bump/

Linehan, M. (2019b, July 29). In the glow of a World Cup win, the sponsorship landscape for U.S. women's soccer is more important than ever. *The Athletic.* https://theathletic.com/1104037/2019/07/29/in-the-glow-of-a-world-cup-win-the-sponsorship-landscape-for-u-s-womens-soccer-is-more-important-than-ever/

Linehan, M. (2021, July 15). Historic '96 Olympic women's soccer gold medal game finally getting aired in full, 25 years later. *The Athletic.* https://theathletic.com/2709408/2021/07/15/olympic-uswnt-gold-96-stream/

Lisi, C.A. (2010). The U.S. Women's Soccer team: An American success story. Scarecrow Press.

Longman, J. (1997, November 20). PLUS: SOCCER; Women's World Cup at Giants Stadium. *The New York Times.* www.nytimes.com/1997/11/20/sports/plus-soccer-women-s-world-cup-at-giants-stadium.html

Longman, J. (1999a, June 19). WOMEN'S WORLD CUP; All is ready, and the stands are full. *The New York Times.* www.nytimes.com/1999/06/19/sports/women-s-world-cup-all-is-ready-and-the-stands-are-full.html

Longman, J. (1999b, July 11). Refusing to wilt, U.S. wins soccer title. *The New York Times.* www.nytimes.com/1999/07/11/sports/refusing-to-wilt-us-wins-soccer-title.html

Longman, J. (2003, September 16). SOCCER; Women's soccer league folds on World Cup's eve. *The New York Times.* www.nytimes.com/2003/09/16/sports/soccer-women-s-soccer-league-folds-on-world-cup-s-eve.html

*New York Times.* (1999, July 12). WOMEN'S WORLD CUP; And strong TV ratings, too. www.nytimes.com/1999/07/12/sports/women-s-world-cup-and-strong-tv-ratings-too.html

Oshan, J. (2012, May 18). WPS "permanently suspends" operations, dissolves league. *SB Nation.* www.sbnation.com/soccer/2012/5/18/3028619/wps-permanently-suspends-operations-dissolves-league

Petri, A.E. (2022, June 27). Once an "easy way out" for equality, women's soccer is now a U.S. force. *The New York Times.* www.nytimes.com/2022/06/27/sports/soccer/title-ix-soccer.html

Quinn, D. (2016, September 13). Soccer star Abby Wambach reveals her pain growing up lesbian. *People.* https://people.com/celebrity/soccer-star-abby-wambach-on-pain-of-growing-up-lesbian/

Sandomir, R. (1996, August 5). Not all (women's) sports created equal on NBC. *The New York Times.* www.nytimes.com/1996/08/05/sports/not-all-women-s-sports-created-equal-on-nbc.html

S.A.S.H. (n.d.). USWNT results: 1990-1994. www.ussoccerhistory.org/usnt-results/uswnt-results/uswnt-results-1990-1994/

Schaerlaeckens, L. (2015, June 30). Buh-bye, "babe city": How sexist coverage of the U.S. women's soccer team is dying. *Vice.* www.vice.com/en/article/3d9gkk/buh-bye-babe-city-how-sexist-coverage-of-the-us-womens-soccer-team-is-dying

SI Staff. (2015, July 13). SI honors World Cup-winning U.S. women with a cover for each player. *Sports Illustrated.* www.si.com/soccer/2015/07/13/uswnt-sports-illustrated-cover-2015-world-cup

Tumin, R. (2022, June 22). Title IX gave women greater access to education. Here's what it says and does. *The New York Times.* www.nytimes.com/2022/06/22/sports/what-is-title-ix.html

USWNT. [@USWNT]. (2019, July 7). *Told ya.* [Tweet]. Twitter. https://twitter.com/uswnt/status/1147967201565167616

VanHaaren, T. (2019, July 3). Jersey sales soaring for USWNT, setting records. *ESPN.* www.espn.com/soccer/fifa-womens-world-cup/story/3892049/jersey-sales-soaring-for-uswntsetting-records

Vecsey, G. (1996, August 2). Women's soccer: 76,481 fans, 1 U.S. gold. *The New York Times.* www.nytimes.com/1996/08/02/sports/women-s-soccer-76481-fans-1-us-gold.html

Wahl, G. (2019, June 6). How the women's World Cup and USWNT were built from scratch. *Sports Illustrated.* www.si.com/soccer/2019/06/06/first-womens-world-cup-1991-uswnt-usa-sepp-blatter

Wrack, S. (2019, June 28). "You can't win without gay players," says USA's World Cup hero Megan Rapinoe. *The Guardian.* www.theguardian.com/football/2019/jun/28/cant-win-without-gays-usa-megan-rapinoe

# Chapter 20

Barmann, J. (2013, November 8). Bay area sportscaster Damon Bruce, of KNBR, goes on misogynistic rant. *SFIST.* https://sfist.com/2013/11/08/local_sportscaster_damon_bruce_of_k/

Bleier, E. (2021, October 20). Remembering "NFL Today" the groundbreaking show that made football America's pastime. *Inside Hook.* www.insidehook.com/article/sports/remembering-nfl-today-cbs

Budden, K. (2017, August 10). Why I hid my pregnancy on TV. *Touchdowns and Tantrums.* https://web.archive.org/web/20170815150943/http://touchdownsandtantrums.com/why-i-hid-my-pregnancy-on-tv/

Buxton, R. (2016, February 17). Erin Andrews on the problematic double-standard between male and female sportscasters. Huff Post. www.huffpost.com/entry/erin-andrews-female-sportscasters_n_56c4cacce4b0b40245c8bd7c"www.huffpost.com/entry/erin-andrews-female-sportscasters_n_56c4cacce4b0b40245c8bd7c

Cimini, R. (2019, May 7). Namath: Drinking kicked my butt for long time. *ESPN.* www.espn.com/nfl/story/_/id/26691377/namath-drinking-kicked-my-butt-long

Deitsch, R. (2014, July 14). Erin Andrews replaces Pam Oliver on Fox's No. 1 NFL team. *Sports Illustrated.* www.si.com/nfl/2014/07/14/pam-oliver-erin-andrews-fox

Deitsch, R. (2022, May 19). Lesley Visser on her trailblazing career, from John Madden to the fall of the Berlin Wall. *The Athletic.* https://theathletic.com/3320186/2022/05/19/lesley-visser-on-her-trailblazing-career-from-john-madden-to-the-fall-of-the-berlin-wall/

de la Cretaz, B. (2018, September 19). The person running your favorite team's Twitter is probably a woman. *The Verge.* www.theverge.com/2018/9/19/17852628/sports-social-media-women-twitter-nfl-nba-mlb

DiCaro, J. (2015, September 27). Threat. Vitriol. Hate. Ugly truth about women in sports and social media. *Sports Illustrated.* www.si.com/the-cauldron/2015/09/27/twitter-threats-vile-remarks-women-sports-journalists

ESPN News Services. (2002, October 10). Women sportscasters bristle at commentator's remarks. www.espn.com/nfl/news/2002/1010/1443917.html

Feldman, J. (2018, November 25). Hannah Storm and Andrea Kremer set the standard for new style of broadcasts. *SI.com*. www.si.com/media/2018/11/26/hannah-storm-andrea-kremer-all-female-duo-sportsperson-2018-moments

Fleming, K. (2014, December 26). Meet the women of TV's first all-female sports talk show. *New York Post*. https://nypost.com/2014/12/26/meet-the-women-of-tvs-first-all-female-sports-talk-show/

Fox Sports. (n.d.). Pam Oliver. www.foxsports.com/presspass/bios/on-air/pam-oliver/

George, T. (1990, November 28). Patriots and 3 players fined in Olson incident. *The New York Times*. www.nytimes.com/1990/11/28/sports/patriots-and-3-players-fined-in-olson-incident.html

Griffith, B. (2003, December 23). Namath incident not being kissed off. *The Boston Globe*. http://archive.boston.com/sports/other_sports/articles/2003/12/23/namath_incident_not_being_kissed_off/

Hall, A. (2018, July 19). Linda Cohn signs new ESPN deal; *SportsCenter* tenure continues, hockey profile increases. *ESPN Press Room*. https://espnpressroom.com/us/press-releases/2018/07/linda-cohn-signs-new-espn-deal-sportscenter-tenure-continues-hockey-profile-increases/

Hardin, M., & Shain, S. (2005). Strength in numbers? The experiences and attitudes of women in sports media careers. *Journalism & Mass Communication Quarterly*, 82(4), 804-819.

Hardin, M., & Whiteside, E. (2009). Token responses to gendered newsrooms: Factors in the career-related decisions of female newspaper sports journalists. *Journalism*, 10(5), 627-646.

Heim, M. (2020, September 15). Chicago radio host fired for tweet about Maria Taylor's outfit appropriate for "adult film awards." *AL.com*. www.al.com/sports/2020/09/chicago-radio-host-fired-for-tweet-about-maria-taylors-outfit-appropriate-for-adult-film-awards.html

Hoffman, B. (2017, October 4). Cam Newton draws rebuke for mocking female reporter. *The New York Times*. www.nytimes.com/2017/10/04/sports/football/cam-newton-reporter.html

Hull, K., Romney, M., Pellizzaro, K., & Walker, D. (2022). "It's impossible": Local sports broadcasters and the prospect of motherhood. *Journal of Sports Media*, 17(1), 69-89.

James, F. (2020, February 23). Tony Kornheiser suspended for dissing Hannah Storm's clothes. *NPR*. www.npr.org/sections/thetwo-way/2010/02/tony_kornheisers_hannah_storm.html

Jenkins, S. (1991, June 17). Who let them in? *Sports Illustrated*. https://vault.si.com/vault/1991/06/17/who-let-them-in-women-have-invaded-the-mens-club-of-tv-sportscasters-but-they-get-less-airtime-pay-and-prestige

Jessop, A. (2020, March 5). Regret or guilt: Female sports broadcasters on balancing careers and motherhood. *The Athletic*. https://theathletic.com/1637828/2020/03/05/regret-or-guilt-female-sports-broadcasters-on-balancing-careers-and-motherhood/

Just Not Sports. (2016, April 25). *#MoreThanMean—Women in sports "face" harassment* [Video]. YouTube. https://www.youtube.com/watch?v=9tU-D-m2JY8

Knight-Ridder News Service. (1993, November 19). Former NBC Sports anchor deals with weightier issues. *News & Record*. https://greensboro.com/former-nbc-sports-anchor-deals-with-weightier-issues/article_0a5013a6-31ea-5b79-a308-9d321c7e8eec.html

Kogan, R. (2020, December 14). Jeannie Morris, Chicago author and pioneering sports broadcaster, dead at 85. *Chicago Tribune*. www.chicagotribune.com/entertainment/tv/ct-ent-jeannie-morris-obit-20201214-sdwu633kejf3dmg3sjocioydsa-story.html

Lapchick, R. (2021). The 2021 sports media racial and gender report card: Associated Press Sports Editors (APSE). *TIDES*. www.tidesport.org/_files/ugd/138a69_e1e67c118b784f4caba00a4536699300.pdf

Markham, I. (2013, May 24). Sports journalism's beauty curse. *The Daily Beast*. https://web.archive.org/web/20130603202641/https://www.thedailybeast.com/witw/articles/2013/05/24/for-women-in-sports-media-beauty-still-the-strongest-currency.html

McGregor, G. (2022, September 15). Al Michaels salary breakdown: How much does Amazon NFL announcer make in 2022? *The Sporting News*. www.sportingnews.com/us/nfl/news/al-michaels-salary-amazon-nfl-2022/wvgdrf5aqwhv7tpab4nlufjr

Mettler, K. (2016, April 28). The disgustingly obscene "everyday" harassment of sports media women: A lesson for men. *The Washington Post*. www.washingtonpost.com/news/morning-mix/wp/2016/04/28/morethanmean-a-graphic-lesson-for-men-in-the-everyday-harassment-of-women-in-sports-media/

NPR. (2020, December 15). Jeannie Morris, pioneering sportscaster, dies at 85. www.npr.org/2020/12/15/946827221/jeannie-morris-pioneering-sportscaster-dies-at-85

Ricchiardi, S. (2005, December/January). Offensive interference. *AJR*. https://ajrarchive.org/article.asp?id=3788

Ross, I. (1936). Ladies of the press: The story of women in journalism by an insider. Harper.

Sandomir, R. (2020, May 16). Phyllis George, trailblazing sportscaster, is dead at 70. *The New York Times*. www.nytimes.com/2020/05/16/arts/television/phyllis-george-dead.html

Sheffer, M.L., & Schultz, B. (2007). Double standard: Why women have trouble getting jobs in local television. *Journal of Sports Media*, 2(1), 77-101.

SI Wire. (2015, October 7). Atlanta radio host suspended after insulting ESPN's Mendoza on Twitter. *Sports Illustrated*. www.si.com/mlb/2015/10/07/mike-bell-radio-host-insult-twitter-jessica-mendoza-espn

Sports Broadcasting Hall of Fame. (n.d.). Lesley Visser. www.sportsbroadcastinghalloffame.org/inductees/lesley-visser/

Stern, R., & Sundberg, A. (Directors). (2013). *Let them wear towels* [Film]. ESPN Films.

WashPostPR. (2017, March 6). Meet The Post's four female reporters covering D.C.'s sports teams. *The Washington Post*. www.washingtonpost.com/pr/wp/2017/03/06/meet-the-posts-four-female-reporters-covering-d-c-s-sports-teams/

Whitaker, L. (1990, October 15). Sport: Trouble in the locker room. *Time*. https://content.time.com/time/subscriber/article/0,33009,971392-1,00.html

Yoder, M. (2012, January 26). Suzy Kolber speaks about infamous Joe Namath interview for first time. *Awful Announcing*. https://awfulannouncing.com/2012-articles/suzy-kolber-speaks-about-infamous-joe-namath-interview-for-first-time.html

# Chapter 21

ABC News. (2015, April 25). *Bruce Jenner, in his own words | Interview with Diane Sawyer | 20/20 | ABC News* [Video]. You Tube. www.youtube.com/watch?v=JaqLG3myKUk

Asmelash, L. (2023, June 1). Celebrate Pride Month with these LGBTQ figures. *CNN.* www.cnn.com/2023/06/01/us/queer-figures-pride-history-cec/index.html

Associated Press. (2013, April 30). Obama says "couldn't be prouder" of Jason Collins. *Herald-Tribune.* www.heraldtribune.com/story/news/2013/04/30/obama-says-couldnt-be-prouder-of-jason-collins/29169357007/

Associated Press. (2013, April 29). Reaction to Jason Collins coming out as gay. ESPN. www.espn.com/espn/wire?section=nba&id=9224908

Barra, A. (2013, May 2). Actually, Jason Collins isn't the first openly gay man in a major pro sport. *The Atlantic.* www.theatlantic.com/entertainment/archive/2013/05/actually-jason-collins-isnt-the-first-openly-gay-man-in-a-major-pro-sport/275523/

Barnes, K. (2022, May 31). Former University of Pennsylvania swimmer Lia Thomas responds to critics: "Trans women competing in women's sports does not threaten women's sports." ESPN. www.espn.com/college-sports/story/_/id/34013007/trans-women-competing-women-sports-does-not-threaten-women-sports

Baseline Staff. (2022, June 3). Billie Jean King receives France's highest civilian honor—La Légion d'Honneur—from president Emmanuel Macron. *Baseline.* www.tennis.com/baseline/articles/billie-jean-king-receives-la-legion-d-honneur-emmanuel-macron-roland-garros

Beck, H., & Branch, J. (2013, April 29). With the words 'I'm gay,' and N.B.A. center breaks a barrier. *The New York Times.* https://www.nytimes.com/2013/04/30/sports/basketball/nba-center-jason-collins-comes-out-as-gay.html"www.nytimes.com/2013/04/30/sports/basketball/nba-center-jason-collins-comes-out-as-gay.html

Borden, S. (2013, April 18). Female star comes out as gay, and sports world shrugs. *The New York Times.* www.nytimes.com/2013/04/19/sports/ncaabasketball/brittney-griner-comes-out-and-sports-world-shrugs.html

Buzinski, J. (2011, October 4). Moment #1: Dave Kopay comes out as gay in newspaper interview. *Out Sports.* www.outsports.com/2011/10/4/4051948/moment-1-dave-kopay-comes-out-as-gay-in-newspaper-interview

Chadiha, J. (2021, December 21). NFL trailblazer Carl Nassib made enduring impact on nonprofit The Trevor Project. NFL.com. www.nfl.com/news/nfl-trailblazer-carl-nassib-made-enduring-impact-on-nonprofit-the-trevor-project

Chen, D.W. (2022, May 24). Transgender athletes face bans from girls' sports in 10 U.S. states. *The New York Times.* www.nytimes.com/article/transgender-athlete-ban.html

Collins, J. (2013, April 29). Why NBA center Jason Collins is coming out now. *Sports Illustrated.* www.si.com/more-sports/2013/04/29/jason-collins-gay-nba-player

Collins, J. (2014, November 19). Parting shot. Jason Collins announces NBA retirement in his own words. *Sports Illustrated.* www.si.com/nba/2014/11/19/jason-collins-retirement-nba

The Daily Beast. (2017, April 13). A note from the editors. www.thedailybeast.com/a-note-from-the-editors-1

Davidson, J.W. (2022, July 5). A brief history of the path to securing LGBTQ rights. *American Bar Association.* www.americanbar.org/groups/crsj/publications/human_rights_magazine_home/intersection-of-lgbtq-rights-and-religious-freedom/a-brief-history-of-the-path-to-securing-lgbtq-rights/

de la Cretaz, F. (2022, June 10). Behind the visible queerness in women's sports—and why it matters. *The Washington Post.* www.washingtonpost.com/lifestyle/2022/06/10/lesbian-culture-womens-sports/

Elhassan, A. (2013, April 29). NBA ready for an openly gay player? ESPN. www.espn.com/nba/story/_/page/5-on-5-130429-Collins/how-nba-react-jason-collins

Fedor, C. (2011, May 17). John Amaechi is still not convinced a player could come out while playing, cites Tony Dungy and former Jazz owner as reasons why. Sports Radio Interviews. https://web.archive.org/web/20110521010117/http://sportsradiointerviews.com/2011/05/17/gay-athletes-professional-athletes-coming-out-john-amaechi-rick-welts-nba/

Footer, A. (2014, July 15). MLB names Bean its first Ambassador for Inclusion. MLB.com. www.mlb.com/news/billy-bean-is-mlbs-first-ambassador-for-inclusion/c-84795004

Goldstein, S. (1981, July 20). Martina fears Avon's call if she talks. *Daily News.*

Hannan, C. (2014, January 15). Dr. V's magical putter. *Grantland.* http://grantland.com/features/a-mysterious-physicist-golf-club-dr-v/

Harper, Z. (2014, March 15). Brooklyn Nets sign Jason Collins for remainder of the season. *CBS Sports.* www.cbssports.com/nba/news/brooklyn-nets-sign-jason-collins-for-remainder-of-the-season/

Kahrl, C. (2014, January 20). What Grantland got wrong. *Grantland.* https://grantland.com/features/what-grantland-got-wrong/

Keh, A. (2014, March 2). Collins' Brooklyn debut recalls Robinson's in 1947. *The New York Times.* www.nytimes.com/2014/03/03/sports/basketball/jason-collins-brooklyn-debut-recalls-jackie-robinsons-in-1947.html

Laird, S. (2013, April 30). Jason Collins story gives "Sports Illustrated" record traffic day. *Mashable.* https://mashable.com/archive/jason-collins-sports-illustrated-traffic

Liptak, A. (2015, June 26). Supreme Court ruling makes same-sex marriage a right nationwide. *The New York Times.* www.nytimes.com/2015/06/27/us/supreme-court-same-sex-marriage.html

Lutz, T. (2021, June 22). "Proud of you": NFL players welcome Carl Nassib's decision to come out. *The Guardian.* www.theguardian.com/sport/2021/jun/22/carl-nassib-nfl-comes-out-as-gay-players-reaction-jj-watt-julian-edelman

Maltais, M. (2016, August 12). Bad form at the Olympics in Daily Beast's Grindr-baiting story. *Los Angeles Times.* https://www.latimes.com/local/education/la-fi-oly-daily-beast-grindr-lgbt-20160812-snap-story.html

Mitchell, H. (2013, April 30). Chris Broussard clarifies his ESPN remarks about Jason Collins. *Los Angeles Times.* www.latimes.com/sports/la-xpm-2013-apr-30-la-sp-sn-chris-broussard-jason-collins-20130430-story.html

Moyer, J.M. (2015, July 16). Why some critics don't think Caitlyn Jenner deserved the Arthur Ashe Courage Award. *The Washington Post.* www.washingtonpost.com/news/morning-mix/wp/2015/07/16/why-some-critics-dont-think-caitlyn-jenner-deserved-the-arthur-ashe-courage-award/

Nassib, C. [@carlnassib]. (2021, June 21). For more information on the life-saving work and resources of The Trevor Project click the link in my bio [Video]. Instagram. https://www.instagram.com/p/CQZXu_8nyy_/

Newsham, G. (2021, August 14). How Billie Jean King was outed by her secret lover, then shunned by the world. *New York Post.* https://nypost.com/2021/08/14/how-billie-jean-king-was-outed-by-her-secret-lover-then-shunned-by-the-world/

Pew Research Center. (2013, June 13). A survey of LGBT Americans. www.pewresearch.org/social-trends/2013/06/13/a-survey-of-lgbt-americans/

Powell, M. (2022, May 29). What Lia Thomas could mean for women's elite sports. *The New York Times.* www.nytimes.com/2022/05/29/us/lia-thomas-women-sports.html

Sandomir, R. (2006, August 3). Tennis center to be named for Billie Jean King. *The New York Times.* www.nytimes.com/2006/08/03/sports/tennis/03tennis.html

Simmons, B. (2014, January 20). The Dr. V story: A letter from the editor. *Grantland.* https://grantland.com/features/the-dr-v-story-a-letter-from-the-editor/

Smith, M.J. (1982, October). The double life of a gay Dodger. *Inside Sports.* 56-63.

Tignor, S. (2013, April 29). Martina's moment. *Tennis.* www.tennis.com/news/articles/martina-s-moment#.VCeN8PldUrU

Tignor, S. (2021, March 31). Decades later, Renée Richards breakthrough is as important as ever. *Tennis.* www.tennis.com/news/articles/decades-later-renee-richards-breakthrough-is-as-important-as-ever

Towers, A. (2022, April 4). Take Me Out review: A star-studded cast takes center stage on Broadway. *Entertainment Weekly.* https://ew.com/theater/take-me-out-broadway-review/

Zeigler, C. (2015, June 7). Trans endurance athlete Chris Mosier earns spot on Team USA. *OutSports.* www.outsports.com/2015/6/7/8743157/chris-mosier-trans-duathlon-team-usa

# Chapter 22

ABC 17. (2013, December 17). Michael Sam named consensus All-American. *ABC17News.* https://abc17news.com/news/2013/12/17/michael-sam-named-consensus-all-american/

ABC News. (2014, May 12). *Michael Sam celebrates emotional draft pick moment with boyfriend.* [Video]. YouTube. www.youtube.com/watch?v=FwVC5dw82Hk

Associated Press. (2015, September 26). Michael Sam "never" wanted to play for the Montreal Alouettes. *CBC.* www.cbc.ca/news/canada/montreal/michael-sam-nfl-montreal-alouettes-1.3245323

Branch, J. (2014, February 9). N.F.L. prospect Michael Sam proudly says what teammates knew: He's gay. *The New York Times.* www.nytimes.com/2014/02/10/sports/michael-sam-college-football-star-says-he-is-gay-ahead-of-nfl-draft.html?_r=0

Collins, J. [@jasoncollins98]. (2014, February 9). For the past 2 days I have met with @MikeSamFootball here in LA. He is a great young man who has shown tremendous courage and leadership. [Tweet]. Twitter. https://twitter.com/jasoncollins98/status/43271296484511744

Connelly, C. (2014, February 9). Mizzou's Michael Sam says he's gay. *ESPN.* www.espn.com/espn/otl/story/_/id/10429030/michael-sam-missouri-tigers-says-gay

Conway, T. (2014, February 24). Michael Sam: Combine results and instant reaction. *Bleacher Report.* https://bleacherreport.com/articles/1971528-michael-sam-combine-results-and-instant-reaction

Eatman, N. (2014, October 21). Cowboys waive Michael Sam from practice squad; Bishop among 2 added. *Dallas Cowboys.* www.dallascowboys.com/news/cowboys-waive-michael-sam-from-practice-squad-bishop-among-2-added-359861

Florio, M. (2021, June 22). Did Michael Sam get a fair chance in the NFL? *Pro Football Talk.* https://profootballtalk.nbcsports.com/2021/06/22/did-michael-sam-get-a-fair-chance-in-the-nfl/

Freeman, M. (2014, September 2). Michael Sam not being signed: On the media, excuse-making and homophobia. *Bleacher Report.* https://bleacherreport.com/articles/2183720-michael-sam-not-being-signed-on-the-media-excuse-making-and-homophobia

Garcia, M. (2019, March 25). Five years later, Michael Sam is doing just fine, thanks. *Out.* www.out.com/sports/2019/3/22/michael-sam-now-football

Good, D. (2014, February 10). Football reacts to Michael Sam coming out. *ABC News.* https://abcnews.go.com/Sports/football-reacts-michael-sam-coming/story?id=22437707

King, P. [@peter_king]. (2014, February 9). *One GM told me he doesn't think Sam will be drafted.* [Tweet]. Twitter. https://twitter.com/peter_king/status/432722481087279104

Krulewitz, J. (2014, August 27). On Tuesday's Michael Sam report: "ESPN regrets the manner in which we presented our report. Clearly yesterday we collectively failed to meet the standards we have set in reporting on LGBT-related topics in sports." *TwitLonger.* www.twitlonger.com/show/n_1s6b2uu

Levy, D. (2014, February 24). Jason Collins, Michael Sam and the media's role in the hype around gay players. *Bleacher Report.* https://bleacherreport.com/articles/1973194-jason-collins-michael-sam-media-making-the-moment-as-big-as-we-can

Loumena, D. (2015, August 14). Michael Sam leaves the Montreal Alouettes for personal reasons. *Los Angeles Times.* www.latimes.com/sports/sportsnow/la-sp-sn-michael-sam-leaves-alouettes-20150814-story.html

Patra, K. (2014, February 10). Michael Sam gets support from N.Y. Giants, Patriots. *NFL.com.* www.nfl.com/news/michael-sam-gets-support-from-n-y-giants-patriots-0ap2000000324767

Pelissero, T. (2014, August 8). Michael Sam confident after Rams debut, but scouts have doubts. *USA Today.* www.usatoday.com/story/sports/nfl/rams/2014/08/08/michael-sam-st-louis-rams-preseason-debut/13809111/

Sam, M. [@MichaelSam52]. (2014, February 9). I want to thank everybody for their support and encouragement, especially @espn, @nytimes and @nfl. I am proud to tell my story to the world! [Tweet]. https://twitter.com/MichaelSam52/status/432680996203270144

Samuel, E. (2014, February 25). Michael Sam unimpressive at NFL Scouting Combine, struggles in 40-yard dash and weight room. *Daily News.* www.nydailynews.com/sports/football/sam-fails-impress-field-combine-article-1.1700030

Silver, M. (2014, May 10). St. Louis Rams draft Michael Sam, make NFL history. *NFL.com.* www.nfl.com/news/st-louis-rams-draft-michael-sam-make-nfl-history-0ap2000000349452

Smith, M.D. (2014, February 24). Michael Sam disappoints in the 40. *Pro Football Talk.* https://profootballtalk.nbcsports.com/2014/02/24/michael-sam-disappoints-in-the-40/

Staples, A. (2014, February 9). Michael Sam's rise from unheralded recruit to unstoppable SEC force. *Sports Illustrated.* https://web.archive.org/web/20140212181053/http://sportsillustrated.cnn.com/college-football/news/20140209/michael-sam-missouri-unheralded-recruit-unstoppable-force/

Thamel, P., & Evans, T. (2014, February 9). How will news that Michael Sam is gay affect his draft stock. *Sports Illustrated.* https://web.archive.org/web/20140214101543/http://sportsillustrated.cnn.com/college-football/news/20140209/michael-sam-draft-stock/

Thomas, J. (2014, August 27). Fisher angry over ESPN report on Sam's "showering habits." *St. Louis Post-Dispatch.* www.stltoday.com/sports/football/professional/fisher-angry-over-espn-report-on-sam-s-showering-habits/article_d09bebec-44ff-5a3d-b5a3-89dc1b1d0abe.html

Wagoner, N. (2014, August 29). Michael Sam cut by Rams. *ESPN.* www.espn.com/nfl/story/_/id/11431047/michael-sam-cut-st-louis-rams

Ward, D. [@derrickward32]. (2014a, May 10). I'm sorry but that Michael Sam is no bueno for doing that on national tv. I'm fine with it being a new day in age but for him to do that on [Tweet]. Twitter https://twitter.com/derrickward32/status/465277780171554816

Ward, D. [@derrickward32]. (2014b, May 10). *Man U got little kids lookin at the draft. I can't believe ESPN even allowed that to happen.* [Tweet]. Twitter. https://twitter.com/derrickward32/status/465278424442212352

Yan, H., & Alsup, D. (2014, May 13). NFL Draft: Reactions heat up after Michael Sam kisses boyfriend on TV. *CNN.* www.cnn.com/2014/05/12/us/michael-sam-nfl-kiss-reaction

Young, R. (2022, June 1). Michael Sam reaches deal to join Barcelona Dragons after working as defensive line coach. *Yahoo! Sports.* https://sports.yahoo.com/michael-sam-reaches-deal-to-join-barcelona-dragons-after-working-as-defensive-line-coach-230937643.html

Zeigler, C. (2014a, February 9). "The eagle has landed." *Outsports.* https://www.outsports.com/2014/2/9/5396036/michael-sam-gay-football-player-missouri-nfl-draft

Zeigler, C. (2014b, August 26). Josina Anderson of ESPN feels the need to report on Michael Sam in the shower. *Outsports.* https://www.outsports.com/2014/8/26/6070681/josina-anderson-espn-michael-sam-shower

# Chapter 23

The Athletic Staff. (2021, July 6). ESPN removes Rachel Nichols from NBA Finals sideline coverage. *The Athletic.* https://theathletic.com/news/espn-removes-rachel-nichols-from-nba-finals-sideline-coverage/WY2dP9HujgA3/

Benoit, W.L. (1995). *Accounts, excuses, and apologies: A theory of image restoration strategies.* Albany: State University of New York Press.

Birkner, C. (2016, December 15). Ryan Lochte promotes "forgiving" throat drops in intentionally weird Pine Bros. ad. *Ad Week.* www.adweek.com/brand-marketing/ryan-lochte-promotes-forgiving-throat-drops-intentionally-weird-pine-bros-ad-175135/

Crouse, K. (2009, February 1). Phelps apologizes for marijuana pipe photo. *The New York Times.* www.nytimes.com/2009/02/02/sports/othersports/02phelps.html

Daily Mail. [DailyMail]. (2018, March 15). *Gold medalist Ryan Lochte to Brazil on national tv: I am sorry—Daily Mail* [Video]. YouTube. www.youtube.com/watch?v=qsjdaXZcmoM

Draper, K. (2020, July 13). ESPN employees say racism endures behind the camera. *The New York Times.* www.nytimes.com/2020/07/13/sports/espn-racism-black-employees.html

Draper, K. (2021, July 4). A disparaging video prompts explosive fallout within ESPN. *The New York Times.* www.nytimes.com/2021/07/04/sports/basketball/espn-rachel-nichols-maria-taylor.html

Draper, K. (2022, September 30). Rachel Nichols joins Showtime after contentious ESPN exit. *The New York Times.* www.nytimes.com/2022/09/30/sports/basketball/rachel-nichols-showtime-espn-maria-taylor.html

Drehs, W. (2016, September 8). Swimmer Ryan Lochte reportedly suspended 10 months. *ESPN.* www.espn.com/olympics/swimming/story/_/id/17493633/ryan-lochte-suspended-10-months-united-states-olympic-committee-usa-swimming

ESPN Press Room. (2021, July 21). Statements from ESPN and Maria Taylor. *ESPN Press Room.* https://espnpressroom.com/us/press-releases/2021/07/statements-from-espn-and-maria-taylor/

Fombrun, C.J. (1996) *Reputation: Realizing value from the corporate image.* Watertown, MA: Harvard Business School Press.

Frandsen, F., & Johansen, W. (2020). A brief history of crisis management and crisis communication: From organizational practice to academic discipline. In F. Frandsen & W. Johansen (Eds.), *Crisis communication* (pp. 17-58). De Gruyter.

Glock, A. (2017, June 6). Do you really still hate Ryan Lochte? *ESPN The Magazine.* www.espn.com/espn/feature/story/_/id/19506033/will-hate-ryan-lochte-end-story

Hull, K., & Boling, K.S. (2018). "I was very intoxicated": An examination of the image repair discourse of Ryan Lochte following the 2016 Olympics. In *Case studies in sport communication* (pp. 202-210). Routledge.

Hull, K. & Walker, D. (2023). Reputation management strategies at ESPN. In T.L. Rentner & D.P. Burns (Eds.), *Social issues in sports communication: You make the call* (pp. 97-107). Routledge.

Johnson, A., & Saliba, E. (2016, August 30). Ryan Lochte dives back in with alarming new endorsement deal. *NBC News.* www.nbcnews.com/news/us-news/ryan-lochte-dives-back-in-alarming-new-endorsement-deal-n640266

Lapchick, R. (2018, May 2). The 2018 Associated Press Sports Editors racial and gender report card. *ESPN.com.* www.espn.com/espn/story/_/id/23382605/espn-leads-way-hiring-practices-sports-media

Macur, J. (2009, February 6). Phelps is suspended and loses a key sponsor. *The New York Times.* www.nytimes.com/2009/02/06/sports/06iht-swim.1.19984715.html

Mangan, D. (2021, July 7). NBA reporter Rachel Nichols back on ESPN after one-day rest following Maria Taylor race furor. *CNBC*. www.cnbc.com/2021/07/07/nba-reporter-rachel-nichols-returns -to-espn-amid-maria-taylor-furor-.html

Marchand, A. (2021, October 5). Mike Greenberg, Stephen A. Smith are the winners in ESPN's drama-filled NBA shakeup. *New York Post*. https://nypost.com/2021/10/05/mike-greenberg-stephen-a-smith -get-what-they-want-in-espns-nba-shakeup/

McCreary, J. (2018, May 2). APNews: Study: Diversity remains in sports news departments Retrieved from https://apnews.com/a4 5d1d2abc7746aaa4dbeaa7f7987923/Study:-Diversity-remains-low -in-sports-news-departments

NBAPR. [@NBAPR]. (2019, October 6). *The following has been released by the NBA:* [Image attached] [Tweet]. Twitter. https:// twitter.com/NBAPR/status/1181007400729489409

NBC Sports Group (2016, August 20). Transcript—Matt Lauer exclusive interview with Ryan Lochte. *NBC Sports Group*. http:// nbcsportsgrouppressbox.com/2016/08/20/transcript-matt-lauer -exclusive-interview-with-ryan-lochte/

Ourand, J. (2021, August 25). ESPN takes Rachel Nichols off NBA programming. *Sports Business Journal*. www.sportsbusinessjournal .com/Daily/Closing-Bell/2021/08/25/Rachel-Nichols.aspx

Perez, A.J. (2016, August 22). Speedo, three other sponsors drop Ryan Lochte. *USA Today*. http://www.usatoday.com/story/sports /olympics/rio-2016/2016/08/22/speedo-ends-sponsorship-ryan -lochte/89099284/

Perloff, A. (2016, October 20). Power rankings: The reasons why NFL ratings are down. *SI.com*. www.si.com/nfl/2016/10/20/nfl -television-ratings-decline-causes

Red Banyan. (2014, April 10). NHL hockey lockout: A great PR case study on crisis communications. https://redbanyan.com/nhl -hockey-lockout-a-great-pr-case-study-on-crisis-communications/

Rishe, P. (2016, August 19). Ryan Lochte sinks future endorsement potential with actions worthy of an Olympic gold for stupidity. *Forbes*. www.forbes.com/sites/prishe/2016/08/19/ryan-lochte -sinks-future-endorsement-potential-with-actions-worthy-of-an -olympic-gold-for-stupidity/

Schmittel, A., & Hull, K. (2015). "Shit Got Cray Cray #MYBAD": An examination of the image-repair discourse of Richie Incognito during the Miami Dolphins' bullying scandal. *Journal of Sports Media*, 10(2), 115-137.

Smith, R.D. (2013) *Strategic planning for public relations* (4th ed.). Abington, UK: Routledge.

Today. [Today]. (2016, August 15). *Ryan Lochte talks to Billy Bush about being held up at gunpoint | Today* [Video]. YouTube. www .youtube.com/watch?v=IxrYj0yCyLE

Walsh, J., & McAllister-Spooner, S.M. (2011). Analysis of the image repair discourse in the Michael Phelps controversy. *Public Relations Review*, 37, 157-162.

Wright, B. (2016, August 18). Ryan Lochte robbery update: Video shows "US Swimmer" "fighting," "breaking down" Rio gas station restroom door. *International Business Times*. www.ibtimes.com/ryan -lochte-robbery-update-video-shows-us-swimmer-fighting-breaking -down-rio-gas-2403576

Yahr, E. (2016, August 19). Now you can watch Ryan Lochte's gloriously terrible reality show. *The Washington Post*. www.washingtonpost .com/news/arts-and-entertainment/wp/2016/08/19/now-you -can-watch-ryan-lochtes-gloriously-terrible-reality-show/

Zaremba, A.J. (2010). *Crisis communication: Theory and practice*. Routledge.

# Chapter 24

Anderson, D. (1997a, April 27). Tiger Woods also needs to apologize for distasteful jokes. *The New York Times*. www.nytimes.com/1997 /04/27/sports/tiger-woods-also-needs-to-apologize-for-distasteful -jokes.html

Anderson, D. (1997b, April 14). Tiger Woods, in a blaze, rewrites Masters' history. *The New York Times*. www.nytimes.com/1997/04 /14/sports/tiger-woods-in-a-blaze-rewrites-masters-history.html

Araton, H. (2010, February 19). Apologizing, Woods sets no return date for golf. *The New York Times*. www.nytimes.com/2010/02/20 /sports/golf/20woods.html

Ashford, M. (2009, December 30). Tiger Woods beat out 9/11 for most consecutive New York Post cover stories: 20 times in a row. *iMediaEthics*. www.imediaethics.org/tiger-woods-beats-out-911-for -most-consecutive-new-york-post-cover-stories-20-times-in-a-row/

Associated Press. (1997a, March 23). Joke may be on Woods, but he calls out GQ for shots at his dad. *Los Angeles Times*. www.latimes .com/archives/la-xpm-1997-03-23-sp-41342-story.html

Associated Press. (1997b, April 22). Tiger Woods describes himself as "Cablinasian." https://apnews.com/article/458b771085857928 1e0f1b73be0da618

Associated Press. (2009, February 9). Woods wife gives birth to son Charlie Axel. *Golf Channel*. www.golfchannel.com/article/associated -press/woods-wife-gives-birth-son-charlie-axel

Associated Press. (2013a, March 25). Tiger returns to No. 1, wins Bay Hill. *ESPN.com*. www.espn.com/golf/story/_/id/9096561 /tiger-woods-back-world-no-1-golf-wins-arnold-palmer-invitational

Associated Press. (2013b, March 26). Nike's Tiger Woods ad "Winning takes care of everything" causes firestorm on Twitter, Facebook, critics say it sends wrong message. *Daily News*. www.nydailynews .com/sports/more-sports/nike-tiger-ad-winning-takes-care-social -media-firestorm-article-1.1299825

Associated Press. (2017, August 16). Tiger Woods had 5 drugs in his system after arrest, police report says. *The New York Times*. www.nytimes.com/2017/08/16/sports/golf/tiger-woods-arrest -drugs.html

Augusta Chronicle. (2010, February 25). Nike remains "supportive" of Woods. www.augustachronicle.com/story/sports/college/golf /2010/02/26/nike-remains-supportive-woods/14612174007/

BBC. (2013, March 18). Tiger Woods and US skier Lindsey Vonn dating. www.bbc.com/news/world-us-canada-21839374

Berhow, J. (2018, September 24). Tiger Woods's Sunday triumph at Tour Championship was highest-rated PGA Tour telecast of 2018. *Golf*. https://golf.com/news/tournaments/tiger-woods-win-tour -championship-highest-tv-ratings-pga-tour-2018/

Bissinger, B. (2010, January 4). Tiger in the rough. *Vanity Fair*. www .vanityfair.com/culture/2010/02/tiger-woods-201002

Boren, C. (2013, March 27). Tiger Woods Nike ad causes a stir with "winning takes care of everything" message. *The Washington*

*Post.* www.washingtonpost.com/news/early-lead/wp/2013/03/27/tiger-woods-nike-ad-causes-a-stir-with-winning-takes-care-of-everything-message/

Chiari, M. (2015, May 3). Tiger Woods, Lindsey Vonn break up: Details, comments and reaction. *Bleacher Report.* https://bleacherreport.com/articles/2452602-tiger-woods-lindsey-vonn-break-up-details-comments-and-reaction

Cradock, M. (2021, December 10). Tiger Woods tops list of most googled athlete in the USA for 2021. *Golf Monthly.* www.golfmonthly.com/tour/tiger-woods-tops-list-of-most-googled-athlete-in-the-usa-for-2021

Crouse, K. (2017, September 28). Tiger Woods's return would be good for golf. But what about for him? *The New York Times.* www.nytimes.com/2017/09/28/sports/golf/tiger-woods-presidents-cup.html

Crouse, K. (2019, April 14). Tiger Woods, in a stirring return to the top, captures The Masters at 43. *The New York Times.* www.nytimes.com/2019/04/14/sports/tiger-woods-wins-masters.html

de Jonge, P. (1995, February 5). A zone of his own; Tiger Woods. *The New York Times Magazine.* www.nytimes.com/1995/02/05/magazine/a-zone-of-his-own-tiger-woods.html

Dethier, D. (2020, March 24). What Tiger Woods' first-ever tv appearance (at age 2!) taught us. *Golf.* https://golf.com/news/tiger-woods-youtube-project-first-tv-appearance/

Dostaler, S. (2019, April 14). Before they turned pro: Tiger Woods. *AmateurGolf.com.* www.amateurgolf.com/golf-tournament-news/18259/Before-they-turned-pro--Tiger-Woods

Draper, K. (2021, April 7). Tiger Woods was driving about 85 m.p.h. in a 45 m.p.h. zone when he crashed. *The New York Times.* www.nytimes.com/2021/04/07/sports/golf/tiger-woods-speeding-car-crash.html

ESPN.com. (2009a, November 27). Tiger Woods injured in crash. www.espn.com/golf/news/story?id=4693657

ESPN.com. (2009b, December 2). Woods: "I have let my family down." www.espn.com/golf/news/story?id=4705945

ESPN.com. (2010, March 21). Tiger Woods interview transcript. www.espn.com/golf/news/story?id=5015614

Farhi, P. (2010, Summer). Going respectable? The National Enquirer got high marks for its powerful, solidly reported exposes of the bad behavior of John Edwards and Tiger Woods. But much of the supermarket tabloid's day in and day out coverage falls far short of basic reporting and editing standards. *American Journal Review.* https://go.gale.com/ps/i.do?p=AONE&u=tel_oweb&id=GALE%7CA230256433&v=2.1&it=r

Gaines, C. (2011, November 30). Sharapova and Woods top Bing's list of most searched athletes of 2011. *Business Insider.* www.businessinsider.com/sharapova-tiger-woods-bing-most-searched-athletes-of-2011-2011-11

Gaines, C. (2013, August 9). CHART: Tiger Woods is still on pace to break Jack Nicklaus's record, but not for long. *Business Insider.* www.businessinsider.com/chart-tiger-woods-is-still-on-pace-to-break-jack-nicklauss-record-but-not-for-long-2013-8

Glassman, J.K. (1996, September 17). A dishonest ad campaign. *The Washington Post.* www.washingtonpost.com/archive/opinions/1996/09/17/a-dishonest-ad-campaign/f274223f-12bc-4caa-b70b-b6d0a384ee3c/

Golden, J. (2014, April 8). No Tiger Woods = Less money around the Masters. *CNBC.* www.cnbc.com/2014/04/08/absence-of-tiger-woods-at-masters-reaches-beyond-golf-greens.html

Hall, M. (2022, November 30). A history of Tiger Woods injuries. *Golf Monthly.* www.golfmonthly.com/features/the-game/tiger-woods-injuries-152945

Harig, B. (2013, June 3). Tiger Woods, Nike close to deal. *ESPN.com.* www.espn.com/golf/story/_/id/9336698/tiger-woods-close-signing-new-deal-remain-nike

Harrison, B. (2004, October 6). Tiger's love link—golf great takes bride in posh Barbados nuptials. *New York Post.* https://nypost.com/2004/10/06/tigers-love-link-golf-great-takes-bride-in-posh-barbados-nuptials/

Hudson, J. (2010, February 19). Tiger Woods teary apology: Live reactions. *The Atlantic.* www.theatlantic.com/culture/archive/2010/02/tiger-woods-s-teary-apology-live-reactions/346594/

Infoplease. (2022, April 8). Tiger Woods timeline. www.infoplease.com/tiger-woods-timeline

Melchior, B. (2009, November 25). Enquirer: Tiger cheating on his wife with "party girl." *Sports By Brooks.* https://web.archive.org/web/20091130002928/http://www.sportsbybrooks.com/enquirer-tiger-cheating-on-wife-with-party-girl-27124

New York Times. (1996, August 28). It's now confirmed, Tiger Woods is a pro. www.nytimes.com/1996/08/28/sports/it-s-now-confirmed-tiger-woods-is-a-pro.html

Pierce, C.P. (1997, March 31). Tiger Woods, the man. Amen. *GQ.* www.gq.com/story/tiger-woods-profile

Porter, K. (2018, September 23). 2018 Tour Championship leaderboard: Tiger Woods wins, thrilling golf world with first victory in five years. *CBS Sports.* www.cbssports.com/golf/news/2018-tour-championship-leaderboard-tiger-woods-wins-thrilling-golf-world-with-first-victory-in-five-years/

Post Staff Report. (2010, January 20). Photo shows Tiger Woods in Mississippi sex rehab center. *New York Post.* https://nypost.com/2010/01/20/photo-shows-tiger-woods-in-mississippi-sex-rehab-center/

Rhoden, W.C. (2010, April 11). A tie for fourth, quietly human. *The New York Times.* www.nytimes.com/2010/04/12/sports/golf/12rhoden.html

Robertson, J. (2010, January 6). Electronic Arts standing behind Tiger Woods. *NBC News.* www.nbcnews.com/id/wbna34729425

Scheibe, J. (2020, April 8). This day in sports: Tiger Woods wins a fourth consecutive major. www.latimes.com/sports/story/2020-04-08/this-day-in-sports-tiger-woods-wins-fourth-straight-major

Shambora, J. (2009, December 9). Tiger Woods' sponsorship deathwatch. *CNN.* https://money.cnn.com/2009/12/09/news/companies/tiger_woods_endorsements.fortune/

Skidmore, S. (2010, December 24). Tiger Woods loses Gillette endorsement. Will 2011 be a turning point? *Christian Science Monitor.* www.csmonitor.com/The-Culture/Latest-News-Wires/2010/1224/Tiger-Woods-loses-Gillette-endorsement.-Will-2011-be-a-turning-point

Smith, G. (1996, December 23). The chosen one. *Sports Illustrated.* https://vault.si.com/vault/1996/12/23/the-chosen-tiger-woods-was-raised-to-believe-that-his-destiny-is-not-only-to-be-the-greatest-golfer-ever-but-also-to-change-the-world-will-the-pressures-of-celebrity-grind-him-down-first

Smits, G. (2011, May 10). With Tiger Woods struggling, golfers on lookout for No. 1 ranking. *Florida Sun-Times*. www.jacksonville.com/story/sports/pga/2011/05/11/tiger-woods-struggling-golfers-lookout-no-1-ranking/15904383007/

The Masters. (2019, April 14). *Tiger Woods final putt and celebration at the 2019 Masters Tournament*. [Video]. YouTube. https://www.youtube.com/watch?v=pE-aOBGN8UM

TMZ. (2009, November 28). Tiger Woods injuries caused by wife, not SUV. www.tmz.com/2009/11/28/tiger-woods-elin-nordegren-fight-accident-suv-lacerations/

US Weekly. (2009, December 1). New woman claims affair with golfer Tiger Woods. www.usmagazine.com/celebrity-news/news/second-woman-claims-affair-with-tiger-woods-2009112/

VanHaaren, T. (2019, April 18). Golf balls, shirts and tickets: The financial impact of Tiger's win. *ESPN*. www.espn.com/golf/story/_/id/26552544/financial-impact-tiger-win

Wertheim, L.J. (2003, April 14). The ad that launched a thousand hits: Tiger Woods came under fire for failing to take a stand on Augusta National. After all, hadn't he volunteered for the job? *Sports Illustrated*. https://vault.si.com/vault/2003/04/14/the-ad-that-launched-a-thousand-hits-tiger-woods-came-under-fire-for-failing-to-take-a-stand-on-augusta-national-after-all-hadnt-he-volunteered-for-the-job

Woods, T. (2009a, November 29). Statement from Tiger Woods. *Tiger Woods.com*. http://web.tigerwoods.com/news/article/200911297726222/news/

Woods, T. (2009b, December 2). Tiger comments on current events. *TigerWoods.com*. https://web.archive.org/web/20091205082932/http://web.tigerwoods.com/news/article/200912027740572/news/

Woods, T. (2009c, December 11). Tiger Woods taking hiatus from golf. *TigerWoods.com*. https://web.archive.org/web/20100119055913/http://web.tigerwoods.com/news/article/200912117801012/news

Woods, T. [@TigerWoods]. (2021a, February 23). [Image attached] [Tweet]. Twitter. https://twitter.com/TigerWoods/status/1364447580520738820

Woods, T. [@tigerwoods] (2021b, April 23). *The course is coming along faster than I am. But it's nice to have a faithful rehab partner, man's best friend*. [Photograph]. Instagram. https://www.instagram.com/p/COBhSUNj95S/

Woods, T. [@TigerWoods]. (2021c, 2021, November 21). *Making progress* [Video attached] [Tweet]. Twitter. https://twitter.com/TigerWoods/status/1462448711682957322

Zinser, L. (2010, August 23). Woods divorce becomes final. *The New York Times*. www.nytimes.com/2010/08/24/sports/golf/24woods.html

# Chapter 25

Almasy, S. (2013, January 9). Oprah interview with Lance Armstrong airs January 17. *CNN*. www.cnn.com/2013/01/08/showbiz/lance-armstrong-oprah

Associated Press. (1997, October 10). Armstrong dropped by Cofidis. https://apnews.com/article/e3797dc34f9dbe7f8029feca81fbdbd1

Ballester, P., & Walsh, D. (2004). *L.A. Confidential: The secrets of Lance Armstrong*. La Martinière.

Blodget, H. (2012, October 18). RadioShack, Trek, Anheuser-Busch, and other sponsors dump Lance Armstrong. *Insider*. www.businessinsider.com/radioshack-nike-dump-lance-armstrong-2012-10

Brock, J. (2013, January 21). Lance Armstrong, Oprah Winfrey interviews: A smart PR move that turned out badly. *Mic*. www.mic.com/articles/23662/lance-armstrong-oprah-winfrey-interviews-a-smart-pr-move-that-turned-out-badly

Cohen, K. (2020, May 22). Timeline of Lance Armstrong's career successes, doping allegations and final collapse. *ESPN*. www.espn.com/olympics/cycling/story/_/id/29177227/line-lance-armstrong-career-successes-doping-allegations-final-collapse

Ellison, S. (1999, July 26). Lance Armstrong, an All-American boy, lifts sponsor with Tour de France win. *The Wall Street Journal*. www.wsj.com/articles/SB932935461305450219

English, B. (2012, November 13). For some, doping case hurts Livestrong image. *The Boston Globe*. www3.bostonglobe.com/lifestyle/style/2012/11/13/what-with-those-livestrong-bracelets/YbNPPFYAaaL4heUNMyQtaK/story.html?arc404=true

ESPN.com News Services. (2004, June 13). Book accuses Armstrong of using EPO. *ESPN*. www.espn.com/olympics/news/story?id=1821396

Gaines, C. (2015, January 2). Crazy stat shows just how common doping was in cycling when Lance Armstrong was winning the Tour de France. *Insider*. www.businessinsider.com/lance-armstrong-doping-tour-de-france-2015-1#

Glendenning, B. (2017, July 22). Whatever your opinions on Lance Armstrong, liking his podcast is not a sin. *The Guardian*. www.theguardian.com/sport/2017/jul/22/lance-armstrong-podcast-tour-de-france-cycling

Glier, R. (1996, May 13). Armstrong dominates to finish. *The Washington Post*. www.washingtonpost.com/archive/sports/1996/05/13/armstrong-dominates-to-finish/6790d2fd-9eac-4a5b-9966-359e7798a5e1/

Granderson. L. (2011, February 18). Did Lance Armstrong cheat? I don't care. *ESPN*. www.espn.com/espn/commentary/news/story?id=6135037

History. (n.d.). *Tour de France*. www.letour.fr/en/history

Honen, M. (2011). What is EPO? *Gizmodo*. https://gizmodo.com/what-is-epo-5803965

Hsu, S.S. (2018, April 19). Lance Armstrong settles $100 million U.S. Postal Service cycling fraud case for $5 million. *The Washington Post*. www.washingtonpost.com/local/public-safety/lance-armstrong-settles-100-million-us-government-doping-fraud-case-for-5-million/2018/04/19/effa18fe-4263-11e8-ad8f-27a8c409298b_story.html

Keown, T. (2012, July 10). Racing the demons. *ESPN*. www.espn.com/espn/story/_/page/Mag15Racingthedemons/cyclist-lance-armstrong-refuses-lose-cancer-espn-magazine-archive

MacLaggan, C. (2012, November 14). Exclusive: Livestrong cancer charity drops Lance Armstrong name from title. *Reuters*. www.reuters.com/article/us-cycling-armstrong-livestrong/exclusive-livestrong-cancer-charity-drops-lance-armstrong-name-from-title-idUSBRE8AE00020121115

Macur, J. (2011, February 16). Lance Armstrong retires from cycling. *The New York Times*. www.nytimes.com/2011/02/17/sports/17armstrong.html

Macur, J. (2012, August 23). Armstrong drops fight against doping charge. *The New York Times*. www.nytimes.com/2012/08/24/sports/cycling/lance-armstrong-ends-fight-against-doping-charges-losing-his-7-tour-de-france-titles.html

Macur, J. (2013a, January 4). In reversal, Armstrong is said to weigh admitting drug use. *The New York Times*. www.nytimes.com/2013/01/05/sports/cycling/lance-armstrong-said-to-weigh-admission-of-doping.html

Macur, J. (2013b, January 17). For Armstrong, a confession without explanation. *The New York Times*. www.nytimes.com/2013/01/18/sports/cycling/lance-armstrong-confesses-to-using-drugs-but-without-details.html?pagewanted=1&_r=1

Malach, P. (2019, July 11). Tour de France: Lance Armstrong's NBC presence spurs debate about his place in cycling. *Cycling News*. www.cyclingnews.com/news/tour-de-france-lance-armstrongs-nbc-presence-spurs-debate-about-his-place-in-cycling/

McMillan, S. (2013, January 18). Lance Armstrong's doping denials—in quotes. *The Guardian*. www.theguardian.com/sport/2013/jan/18/lance-armstrong-doping-denials-quotes

Nevres, M.Ö. (2019, December 20). Vélo d'Or winners (from 1992 to 2020, complete). *Cycling Passion*. https://cycling-passion.com/velo-d-or-winners/

OWN. [OWN]. (2013, January 17). *Lance Armstrong's confession | Oprah's Next Chapter | Oprah Winfrey Network* [Video]. YouTube. www.youtube.com/watch?v=N_0PSZ59Aws

Pearson, M. (2012, October 22). Doping scandal costs Armstrong sponsors, charity role. *CNN*. www.cnn.com/2012/10/17/us/lance-armstrong-doping/index.html

Peralta, E. (2012, October 10). Doping agency says 11 teammates testified against Lance Armstrong. *NPR*. www.npr.org/sections/thetwo-way/2012/10/10/162640916/doping-agency-says-11-teammates-testified-against-lance-armstrong

Pugh, A. (2012, October 11). David Walsh: "It was obvious to me that Lance Armstrong was doping." *PressGazette*. https://pressgazette.co.uk/david-walsh-it-was-obvious-me-lance-armstrong-was-doping/

Reilly, R. (2010, July 5). Armstrong keeps passing tests. *ESPN*. www.espn.com/espn/news/story?id=5355649

Reuters Staff. (2013, January 17). Armstrong stripped of 2000 bronze medal. *Reuters*. www.reuters.com/article/us-cycling-armstrong-olympics/armstrong-stripped-of-2000-bronze-medal-idUSBRE90G0MC20130117

Rovell, D. (2012, October 17). Nike drops Lance Armstrong. *ESPN*. www.espn.com/olympics/cycling/story/_/id/8514766/nike-terminates-contract-lance-armstrong

Schrotenboer, B. (2012, October 15). Tour de France sees no win in picking another loser. *USA Today*. www.usatoday.com/story/sports/cycling/2012/10/15/lance-armstrong-tour-de-france-doping/1635499/

Sortal, N. (1989, November 19). Armstrong "comes out" ahead of Pigg. *South Florida Sun Sentinel*. www.sun-sentinel.com/news/fl-xpm-1989-11-19-8902100812-story.html

Sports iTeam Blog. (2012, December 4). WATCH: Lance Armstrong gives anti-doping message in 2001 Nike commercial. *Daily News*. www.nydailynews.com/blogs/iteam/watch-lance-armstrong-anti-doping-message-2001-nike-commercial-blog-entry-1.1632330

Travers, P. (2013, November 7). The Armstrong Lie. *Rolling Stone*. www.rollingstone.com/tv-movies/tv-movie-reviews/the-armstrong-lie-107865/

USADA. (n.d.). U.S. Postal Service pro cycling team investigation. www.usada.org/athletes/results/u-s-postal-service-pro-cycling-team-investigation/

Vertuno, J. (2013, January 13). Lance Armstrong "to speak candidly" in Oprah interview. *Toronto Star*. www.thestar.com/sports/2013/01/13/lance_armstrong_to_speak_candidly_in_oprah_interview.html

# Chapter 26

Bauder, D. (2010, July 9). Was LeBron special ESPN's deal with devil? *Associated Press*. www.khou.com/article/entertainment/was-lebron-special-espns-deal-with-devil/285-342107065

Bilas, J. (2002, December 17). Did "LeBron Mania" go too far? *ESPN*. www.espn.com/columns/bilas_jay/1477784.html

Buckley, S. (2010, July 8). LeBron James' media sideshow like WrestleMania. *Boston Herald*. www.bostonherald.com/2010/07/08/lebron-james-media-sideshow-like-wrestlemania/

Chiang, A. (2020, June 24). ESPN docuseries reveals new details from LeBron James' "The Decision" 10 years later. *Miami Herald*. www.miamiherald.com/sports/nba/miami-heat/article243755147.html

Curtis, B. (2016, June 24). The Zelig of sports. *The Ringer*. www.theringer.com/2016/6/24/16043100/jim-gray-is-looking-for-his-next-exclusive-fc23ceb544e#.7nykbdsnd

Curtis, B. (2018, July 2). "The Decision" reloaded: How LeBron James's free-agency announcement changed the NBA. *The Ringer*. www.theringer.com/nba/2018/7/2/17524572/lebron-james-the-decision-miami-heat-2010

Durant, K. (2016, July 4). My next chapter. *The Player's Tribune*. www.theplayerstribune.com/articles/kevin-durant-nba-free-agency-announcement

Dvorkin, J.A. (2006, January 31). Does an ombudsman do any good? *NPR*. www.npr.org/sections/publiceditor/2006/01/31/5180984/does-an-ombudsman-do-any-good

ESPN. (2018, July 11). *[FULL] LeBron James' "The Decision" (7/8/2010) | ESPN Archives* [Video]. YouTube. https://www.youtube.com/watch?v=Afpgnb_9bA4

ESPN.com. (2010, July 9). Heat stars sign six-year deals. www.espn.com/nba/news/story?id=5368003

Fedor, C. (2020, June 24). LeBron James, "The Decision" and a decade of hindsight: ESPN docuseries reveals new details on LeBron's legacy-impacting night. *Cleveland.com*. www.cleveland.com/cavs/2020/06/lebron-james-the-decision-and-a-decade-of-hindsight-espn-docuseries-reveals-new-details-on-lebrons-legacy-impacting-night.html

James, L. (2014, July 11). LeBron: I'm coming back to Cleveland. *Sports Illustrated*. www.si.com/nba/2014/07/11/lebron-james-cleveland-cavaliers

Jones, R. (2014, December 30). Ohio player. *Slam*. www.slamonline .com/nba/ohio-player-lebron-james-first/

Klutch Sports Group. [@KlutchSports]. (2018, July 1). *LeBron James, four time NBA MVP, three time NBA finals MVP, fourteen time NBA All Star, and two time Olympic gold medalist has agreed to a four year, $154 million contract with the Los Angeles Lakers* [Tweet]. Twitter. https://twitter.com/KlutchSports/status/1013574315411849216

Munzenrieder, K. (2011, December 6). LeBron James finally admits "The Decision" TV show may have been a mistake. *Miami New Times*. www.miaminewtimes.com/news/lebron-james-finally-admits-the -decision-tv-show-may-have-been-a-mistake-6543442

NielsenWire. (2010, July 12). Nearly 10 million U.S. viewers watch LeBron's "Decision." https://web.archive.org/web /20120913144841/http://blog.nielsen.com/nielsenwire/media _entertainment/nearly-10-million-u-s-viewers-watch-lebrons -decision/

Ohlmeyer, D. (2010, July 21). The "Decision" dilemma. *ESPN*. https://www.espn.com/espn/columns/story?columnist=ohlmeyer _don&id=5397113

Petchesky, B., & McKenna, D. (2014, July 11). How Cleveland and *Sports Illustrated* won the LeBron James sweepstakes. *Deadspin*. https://deadspin.com/how-cleveland-and-sports-illustrated-won -the-lebron-jam-1603763328

Rosenthal, P. (2018, July 2). LeBron James got it right this time: He copied Michael Jordan. *Chicago Tribune*. www.chicagotribune.com /sports/bulls/ct-spt-lebron-james-michael-jordan-bulls-20180702 -story.html

Rovell, D. (2010, September 14). LeBron's Q score takes huge hit. *CNBC*. www.cnbc.com/id/39170785

Simmons, B. (2009, August 28). Summer of mailbag revisited. *ESPN*. www.espn.com/espn/page2/story?page=simmons/090827

Stanley, Z. (2010, September 30). LeBron James and Maverick Carter: Racism a factor in "the Decision." *Bleacher Report*. https:// bleacherreport.com/articles/477895-lebron-james-and-maverick -carter-racism-a-factor-in-the-decision

Tanneeru, M., & King, L. (2010, October 1). LeBron James, race and "The Decision." *CNN*. https://news.blogs.cnn.com/2010/10/01 /lebron-james-race-and-%E2%80%98the-decision%E2%80%99/

Thomaselli, R. (2010, July 12). How LeBron's entourage got his "Decision" on ESPN. *AdAge*. https://adage.com/article/news /lebron-s-entourage-decision-espn/144882

Trachtenberg, J.A. (2014, July 11). How SI.com got the big LeBron scoop and how its traffic soared. *The Wall Street Journal*. www.wsj .com/articles/BL-269B-1106

Uninterrupted (2016, August 11). *UNINTERRUPTED: LeBron James announces he will re-sign with Cleveland Cavaliers* [Video]. YouTube. www.youtube.com/watch?v=yfKzCPH1FGg

Uninterrupted. (n.d.). www.linkedin.com/company/uninterrupted/

Van Natta Jr., D. (2020, June 27). ESPN show confirms The Decision was fan's idea, not LeBron James'. *ESPN*. www.espn.com/nba/story /_/id/29375906/espn-show-confirms-decision-was-fan-idea-not -lebron-james

Wahl, G. (2002, February 18). Ahead of his class. *Sports Illustrated*. 62-67.

Windhorst, B. (2013, June 23). The chosen ones. *ESPN*. www.espn .com/nba/draft2013/story/_/page/2003-draft-history-1/an-oral -history-2003-lottery-draft

Youngmisuk, O. (2018, July 1). LeBron James agrees to four-year, $153.3 million deal with Lakers. *ESPN*. www.espn.com/nba/story /_/id/23967725/lebron-james-joining-los-angeles-lakers-4-year -1533-million-deal

# Chapter 27

Abrams, J., & Draper, K. (2021, October 23). Vanessa Bryant, in deposition, describes learning of deaths of Kobe and Gianna. *The New York Times*. www.nytimes.com/2021/10/23/sports/basketball /vanessa-bryant-helicopter-crash-lawsuit.html

Abrams, R. (2020, January 27). *Washington Post* suspends a reporter after her tweets on Kobe Bryant. *The New York Times*. www.nytimes .com/2020/01/27/business/media/kobe-bryant-washington-post -felicia-sonmez.html

Amato, N. (2020, April 1). Kobe Bryant's final project "The Wizenard Series: Season One" gets posthumous release. *Rolling Stone*. www.rollingstone.com/product-recommendations/books/kobe -bryant-book-wizenard-series-976780/

Associated Press. (2004, September 1). Text of Bryant statement. *The Baltimore Sun*. www.baltimoresun.com/bal-statement0901 -story.html

Associated Press. (2021, February 8). Timeline of chopper crash that killed Kobe Bryant, 8 others. *ABC News*. https://abcnews.go .com/Sports/wireStory/timeline-chopper-crash-killed-kobe-bryant -75753780

Badenhausen, K. (2004, September 3). Kobe Bryant's sponsorship will rebound. *Forbes*. www.forbes.com/2004/09/03/cz_kb _0903kobe.html?sh=5a21fc9e27c6

Badenhausen, K. (2014, May 24). Kobe Bryant invests millions in sports drink BodyArmor. *Forbes*. www.forbes.com/sites /kurtbadenhausen/2014/03/24/kobe-bryant-invests-millions-in -sports-drink-bodyarmor/?sh=2a10933312f6

Battaglio, S. (2020, January 29). ABC News suspends correspondent over erroneous report on Kobe Bryant crash. *Los Angeles Times*. www .latimes.com/entertainment-arts/business/story/2020-01-29/abc -news-has-suspended-correspondent-who-said-four-kobe-bryant -daughters-were-on-his-helicopter-matt-gutman

Brennan, C. [@cbrennansports]. (2020, January 27). *A father & daughter going to the girl's basketball game—such a beautiful slice of 21st century Americana—ends in unspeakable tragedy. Kobe Bryant's career was majestic, his loss immeasurable. And yes, the very serious allegation of sexual assault in 2003 is part of his story.* [Tweet]. Twitter. https://twitter.com/cbrennansports/status /1221770090531770371

Brooks, K.J. (2021, November 1). Kobe Bryant estate reportedly gains $400 million in BodyArmor sale. *CBS News*. www.cbsnews .com/news/kobe-bryant-coca-cola-bodyarmor-sale/

Cowan, J., & Jolly, V. (2022, August 24). Jury awards Vanessa Bryant $16 million in suit over Kobe Bryant crash photos. *The New York Times*. www.nytimes.com/2022/08/24/us/vanessa-bryant-verdict -crash-photos.html

Curwen, T., & Wharton, D. (2020, January 26). Kobe Bryant, from the start, was an athlete like no other. *Los Angeles Times*. www.latimes.com/sports/lakers/story/2020-01-26/lakers-kobe-bryant-obit

D'Zurilla, C. (2020, January 29). Ellen Pompeo accuses TMZ of abusive behavior after Kobe Bryant death coverage. *Los Angeles Times*. www.latimes.com/entertainment-arts/tv/story/2020-01-29/ellen-pompeo-tmz-kobe-bryant

Darcy, O. (2020, January 26). Police scold TMZ after outlet was first to report death of Kobe Bryant. *CNN*. www.cnn.com/2020/01/26/media/tmz-death-report-kobe-bryant/index.html

DePaula, N. (2021, April 19). Vanessa Bryant, Kobe Bryant estate elect not to renew partnership with Nike. *ESPN.com*. www.espn.com/nba/story/_/id/31293033/vanessa-bryant-kobe-bryant-estate-elect-not-renew-partnership-nike

DePaula, N. (2022, March 24). Kobe Bryant's estate reaches new long-term deal with Nike. *ESPN.com*. www.espn.com/nba/story/_/id/33588078/kobe-bryant-estate-reaches-new-long-term-deal-nike

Doughty, A. [@DougthyBetMGM]. (2020, January 26). *ABC: Kobe Bryant and 4 children killed. FOX: Kobe Bryant and 3 others killed. TMZ: Kobe Bryant survived by wife and 4 daughters. I hope some people lose their jobs today for rushing reports.* [Tweet]. Twitter. https://twitter.com/DoughtyBetMGM/status/1221530106579038208

ESPN. (2020, January 28). *Kobe Bryant loved being a "Girl Dad"—Elle Duncan | SportsCenter* [Video]. YouTube. www.youtube.com/watch?v=2GuASKiAqDc

ESPN News Services. (2018, March 4). Kobe Bryant's "Dear Basketball" wins Oscar for animated short. *ESPN*. www.espn.com/nba/story/_/id/22648342/kobe-bryant-dear-basketball-wins-oscar-best-animated-short

Franco, J. [@jennfranconews]. (2020, January 26). *#DEVELOPING: ABC News confirms Kobe Bryant's 4 daughters were not onboard the helicopter that crashed in California earlier today.* [Tweet]. Twitter. https://twitter.com/jennfranconews/status/1221534009995362304

Greenberg, J. [@JaredSGreenberg]. (2020, January 26). *I have personally communicated with Rick Fox via text since the news about Kobe dying came out PLEASE STOP spreading "news" unless you personally can confirm it!* [Tweet]. Twitter. https://twitter.com/JaredSGreenberg/status/1221532759480512514

Gutman, M. [@mattgutmanABC]. (2020, January 26). *Today I inaccurately reported it was believed that four of Kobe Bryant's children were on board that flight. That is incorrect. I apologize to Kobe's family, friends and our viewers.* [Tweet]. Twitter. https://twitter.com/mattgutmanABC/status/1221636913402007552

Hassan, J. (2020, January 27). BBC confuses LeBron James with Kobe Bryant in helicopter death coverage. *The Washington Post*. www.washingtonpost.com/world/2020/01/27/bbc-confuses-lebron-james-with-kobe-bryant-helicopter-death-coverage/

Henson, S. (2005, March 3). Bryant and his accuser settle civil assault case. *Los Angeles Times*. www.latimes.com/archives/la-xpm-2005-mar-03-sp-bryant3-story.html

Henson, S. (2020, January 26). What happened with Kobe Bryant's sexual assault case. *Los Angeles Times*. www.latimes.com/sports/story/2020-01-26/what-happened-kobe-bryant-sexual-assault-case

Ibrahimovic, N. [@Genesis_GGP]. (2020, January 26). *Kobe, Rick Fox, a pilot, and 4 daughters doesn't equal 5 people. Someone information is wrong.* [Tweet]. Twitter. https://twitter.com/Genesis_GGP/status/1221528799457828865

Keys, M. [@MatthewKeysLive]. (2020, January 27). *UPDATE: A person who works at the Washington Post says @feliciasonmez was NOT suspended for linking to the Daily Beast story on Twitter. Her suspension was related to a follow up tweet that contained a screen shot of her work email inbox, which revealed full names of emailers.* [Tweet]. Twitter. https://twitter.com/MatthewKeysLive/status/1221692681396473856

Kimble, L. (2020, February 26). Elle Duncan on why she shared that Kobe Bryant "girl dad" story—and the movement it started. People. people.com/sports/elle-duncan-on-why-she-shared-that-kobe-bryant-girl-dad-story-and-the-movement-it-started/

LA County Sheriffs. [@LASDHQ]. (2020, January 26). *#Update Downed aircraft is a helicopter. Flames extinguished. #Malibu deputies at crash site looking for survivors, 4200 blk Las Virgenes Rd #Calabasas #LASD.* [Tweet]. Twitter. https://twitter.com/LASDHQ/status/1221501617255505920

Loveless, M. (2020, January 26). Timeline of bad information in first wave of Kobe Bryant story. *Northwest Public Radio*. www.nwpb.org/2020/01/26/timeline-of-bad-information-in-first-wave-of-kobe-bryant-story/

Lupica, M. (2020, January 26). Kobe Bryant leaves behind one of sports' most complicated legacies. *New York Daily News*. www.nydailynews.com/sports/basketball/ny-kobe-bryant-dead-41-los-angeles-lakers-20200126-4ael3qq2oreo3b3njgamyscpna-story.html

Murakami, T. [@lasdmurakami]. (2020, January 26). *I am saddened that I was gathering facts as a media outlet reported the Kobe had passed. I understand getting the scoop but please allow us time to make personal notifications to their loved ones. It's very cold to hear of the loss via media Breaks my heart* [Tweet]. Twitter. https://twitter.com/lasdmurakami/status/1221578597032329216

NBC News. [@NBCNews]. *BREAKING: 5 people have been killed in a helicopter crash in Calabasas, California, LA Co. Sheriff's Dept. says.* [Tweet]. Twitter. https://twitter.com/NBCNews/status/1221518079290748928

Respers France, L., & Kaur, H. (2020, January 29). Kobe Bryant called himself a "girl dad." His words are inspiring proud fathers to celebrate their love for their daughters. *CNN*. www.cnn.com/2020/01/29/entertainment/kobe-bryant-gianna-girldad/index.html

Ritschel, C. (2020, January 29). TMZ claims "Kobe's people" said they could break death news after backlash intensifies. *Independent*. www.independent.co.uk/news/world/americas/kobe-bryant-death-tmz-police-crash-harvey-levin-ellen-pompeo-maria-shriver-a9308911.html

Schrotenboer, B. (2021, June 22). Vanessa Bryant settles wrongful death lawsuit vs. helicopter company, pilot's estate. *USA Today*. www.usatoday.com/story/sports/nba/2021/06/22/vanessa-bryant-settles-wrongful-death-lawsuit-over-kobe-crash/5315097001/

Sexton, J. (2011, September 22). Kobe Bryant's 5 most memorable endorsements. *Bleacher Report*. https://bleacherreport.com/articles/861724-kobe-bryants-5-most-memorable-endorsements

Stein, M. (2020, January 26). Kobe Bryant's brilliant and complicated legacy. *The New York Times*. www.nytimes.com/2020/01/26/sports/kobe-bryant-obituary.html

Sullivan, M. (2020, January 27). Media coverage of Kobe Bryant's death was a chaotic mess, but there were moments of grace. *The Washington Post*. www.washingtonpost.com/lifestyle/style/media-coverage-of-kobe-bryants-death-was-a-chaotic-mess-but-there-were-moments-of-grace/2020/01/27/d825ade4-4106-11ea-aa6a-083d01b3ed18_story.html

Tchekmedyian, A., & Pringle, P. (2020, March 3). A deputy allegedly showed off gruesome Kobe Bryant crash photos at bar. A cover-up scandal ensued. *Los Angeles Times*. www.latimes.com/california/story/2020-03-03/kobe-bryant-crash-photos-sheriffs-department-tried-to-keep-quiet

Times Staff. (2020, January 28). Mothers, fathers, daughters, coaches: Here are the 9 killed in the Kobe Bryant helicopter crash. *Los Angeles Times*. www.latimes.com/california/story/2020-01-27/kobe-bryant-helicopter-crash-victims

Toropin, K., Yan, H., & Andone, D. (2020, February 7). Here's what happened in the minutes before Kobe Bryant's helicopter crash. *CNN*. www.cnn.com/2020/01/28/us/kobe-bryant-crash-timeline/index.html

TMZ. [@TMZ]. (2020, January 26). *BREAKING: Kobe Bryant Has Died In A Helicopter Crash*. [Tweet]. Twitter. https://twitter.com/TMZ/status/1221516283671433216

TMZ Sports [@TMZ_Sports]. (2020, January 26). *#BREAKING: Kobe's daughter Gianna Maria was also on board the helicopter and died in the crash*. [Tweet]. Twitter. https://twitter.com/TMZ_Sports/status/1221534066022940673

Tracy, M. (2020, January 27). In haste to confirm Kobe Bryant news, news media stumbles. *The New York Times*. www.nytimes.com/2020/01/27/business/tmz-kobe.html

Windhorst, B. (2021, November 10). Why NBA players are hoarding Kobe Bryant's Nike sneaker line. *ESPN.com*. www.espn.com/nba/insider/insider/story/_/id/32585223/why-nba-players-hoarding-kobe-bryant-nike-sneaker-line

Winton, R. (2022, January 5). Judge rejects L.A. County's bid to dismiss Vanessa Bryant's lawsuit over crash photos. *Los Angeles Times*. www.latimes.com/california/story/2022-01-05/federal-judge-rejected-effort-by-la-county-to-dismiss-vanessa-bryants-lawsuit-over-crash-photos

WTHR.com staff. (2020, January 30). Petition calls to cancel TMZ following report of Kobe Bryant's death. *WTHR*. www.wthr.com/article/news/nation-world/petition-calls-cancel-tmz-following-report-kobe-bryants-death/531-f401de2b-2ca4-4c68-b788-b4aa2c56946e

# Chapter 28

Apstein, S. (2019, October 21). Astros staffer's outburst at female reporters illustrates MLB's forgive-and-forget attitude toward domestic violence. *SI.com*. www.si.com/mlb/2019/10/22/houston-astros-roberto-osuna-suspension

Baccellieri, E. (2020, February 13). Breaking down the Astros' latest public relations meltdown. *SI.com*. www.si.com/mlb/2020/02/13/houston-astros-public-relations-sign-stealing

Baer, J. (2018, June 22). Roberto Osuna suspended 75 games by MLB after assault investigation. *Yahoo! Sports*. https://sports.yahoo.com/roberto-osuna-suspended-75-games-mlb-assault-investigation-223721906.html

Barron, D. (2020, January 31). How one Astros fan charted 8,274 pitches and found 1,143 preceded by banging sounds. *Houston Chronicle*. www.houstonchronicle.com/sports/astros/article/Astros-chart-sign-scandal-cheating-pitch-fan-15020307.php

Baumann, M. (2020, February 13). The Astros' apology tour is off to a comically disastrous start. *The Ringer*. www.theringer.com/mlb/2020/2/13/21136476/jim-crane-houston-astros-sign-stealing-apology

Corcoran, C. (2018, October 18). "Everybody tries to cheat a little": The weird and wild history of MLB sign-stealing. *The Athletic*. https://theathletic.com/598405/2018/10/18/everybody-tries-to-cheat-a-little-the-weird-and-wild-history-of-mlb-sign-stealing/

Cwik, C. (2018, May 8). Blue Jays closer Roberto Osuna reportedly arrested for domestic assault. *Yahoo! Sports*. https://sports.yahoo.com/blue-jays-closer-roberto-osuna-reportedly-arrested-domestic-assault-174407648.html

Daniels, C. (2020, February 21). Crisis response strikeout: What are the Houston Astros thinking? *PR Week*. www.prweek.com/article/1674839/crisis-response-strikeout-houston-astros-thinking

Doolittle, B. (2019, October 24). Admitting "we were wrong," Astros fire assistant GM Brandon Taubman. *ESPN.com*. www.espn.com/mlb/story/_/id/27920694/admitting-were-wrong-astros-fire-assistant-gm-brandon-taubman

Draper, K. (2020, February 13). The Houston Astros comment on their cheating scandal: We're sorry. *The New York Times*. www.nytimes.com/2020/02/13/sports/baseball/astros-scandal-players.html

Fink, R. (2017, February 1). Houston Colt .45s. *Texas State Historical Association*. www.tshaonline.org/handbook/entries/houston-colt-45s

Folkenflik, D. (2019, October 22). Astros executive's rant at reporters draws firestorm on eve of series. *NPR*. www.npr.org/2019/10/22/772368868/astros-executives-rant-at-reporters-draws-firestorm-on-eve-of-series

Hoffman, B. (2019, October 24). Brandon Taubman, Astros executive, is fired over outburst. *The New York Times*. www.nytimes.com/2019/10/24/sports/baseball/brandon-taubman-fired-astros.html

Hulsey, B. (n.d.). The stars rise again. *Astros Daily*. https://astrosdaily.com/history/uniforms/

Jomboy [Jomboy_]. (2019, November 12). *Astros using cameras to steal signs, a breakdown*. [Video attached] [Tweet]. Twitter. https://twitter.com/Jomboy_/status/1194348775965437952

Jomboy Media. (2019, November 13). *Astros accused of cheating with a video camera | Talkin' Baseball* [Video]. YouTube. https://www.youtube.com/watch?v=FeWom6CRhME

Kitchen, M. (2013, August 7). The 17 most stylish sports uniforms of all time. *Esquire*. www.esquire.com/style/advice/g1537/best-sport-uniforms-2013/?slide=15

Kolur, N. (2017, November 6). Purchase Sports Illustrated's commemorative Astros covers, issues. *SI.com*. www.si.com/mlb/2017/11/06/sports-illustrated-houston-astros-world-series-commemorative-issue-cover

Lee, J. (2020, January 17). How the internet helped crack the Astros' sign-stealing case. *ESPN.com.* www.espn.com/mlb/story/_/id/28476354/how-internet-helped-crack-astros-sign-stealing-case

McTaggart, B. (2012, March 9). Astros to keep pistol on Colt .45s jersey. *MLB.com.* www.mlb.com/es/news/astros-to-keep-pistol-on-colt-45s-jersey/c-27141166

McTaggart, B. (2021, December 1). The history behind the Astros' team name. *MLB.com.* www.mlb.com/news/houston-astros-team-name-history

NBC Sports Washington. (2020, February 22). Astros booed, fans' signs taken, in Spring Training opener against Nationals. www.nbcsports.com/washington/nationals/astros-booed-fans-signs-taken-spring-training-opener-against-nationals

Olney, B [Buster_ESPN]. (2019, October 22). Until the Astros' FO acknowledges its statement last night was "misleading" and "completely irresponsible," it will have no credibility in this matter. You can't merely try to walk back that statement and attack on a reporter's credibility; you have to own the awful decision [Tweet]. Twitter. https://twitter.com/Buster_ESPN/status/1186731622202331136

Passan, J. (2018, July 31). In trading for Roberto Osuna, the Houston Astros show they have no conscience. *Yahoo! Sports.* www.yahoo.com/news/trading-roberto-osuna-houston-astros-show-no-conscience-134758777.html

Psihogios, S. (2018, July 31). Fans, players, media react to Roberto Osuna's controversial trade to Houston. *Yahoo! Sports.* ca.sports.yahoo.com/news/mlb-community-reacts-roberto-osunas-controversial-trade-houston-154530972.html

Reed, J. (2020, February 13). Sports world reacts to Astros' absurd, embarrassing press conference. *Sportsnaut.* https://sportsnaut.com/sports-world-reacts-to-astros-absurd-embarrassing-press-conference/

Reiter, B. (2014, June 30). Astro-matic baseball. *Sports Illustrated.* 30-38.

Rosenthal, K. (2023, February 21). Ken Rosenthal and Evan Drellich look back on Astros sign stealing scandal [Audio podcast episode]. In The Athletic Baseball Show. *The Athletic.* https://theathletic.com/podcast/243-the-athletic-baseball-show/?episode=412

Rosenthal, K., & Drellich, E. (2019, November 12). The Astros stole signs electronically in 2017—part of a much broader issue for Major League Baseball. *The Athletic.* https://theathletic.com/1363451/2019/11/12/the-astros-stole-signs-electronically-in-2017-part-of-a-much-broader-issue-for-major-league-baseball/

Rupar, A. (2019, October 24). The Houston Astros' self-created domestic violence controversy, explained. *Vox.* www.vox.com/2019/10/23/20928466/houston-astros-roberto-osuna-domestic-violence-sports-illustrated-controversy-explained

SI Staff. (2014, March 3). Ugliest uniforms in sports history. *SI.com.* www.si.com/extra-mustard/2014/03/03/ugliest-uniforms-sports-history#25

Stroman, M. [STR0]. 2019, November 14). *This is crazy.* [Tweet]. Twitter. https://twitter.com/STR0/status/1194978770719006721

Tayler, J. (2014, April 9). Houston Astros get 0.0 television rating for game against Los Angeles Angels. *SI.* www.si.com/mlb/2014/04/09/houston-astros-get-0-0-television-rating

Wagner, J. (2020, January 17). Astros manager and G.M. fired over cheating scandal. *The New York Times.* www.nytimes.com/2020/01/13/sports/baseball/astros-cheating.html

Waldstein, D. (2020a, February 22). He let the Astros players slide. Now he's paying for it. *The New York Times.* www.nytimes.com/2020/02/22/sports/baseball/rob-manfred-astros.html

Waldstein, D. (2020b, August 18). Even in a pandemic, everyone still hates the Astros. *The New York Times.* www.nytimes.com/2020/08/18/sports/baseball/houston-astros-joe-kelly-cheating.html

Witz, B. (2017, November 2). Astros outlast Dodgers to clinch first World Series title. *The New York Times.* www.nytimes.com/2017/11/02/sports/astros-world-series-champs.html

Young, M. (2017, October 24). What the 2014 Sports Illustrated cover got wrong about the Astros. *Houston Chronicle.* www.chron.com/sports/astros/article/What-2014-Sports-Illustrated-Astros-cover-wrong-12302188.php

# Chapter 29

Baran, S.J., & Davis, D.K. (2011). *Mass communication theory: Foundations, ferment, and future.* Wadsworth.

Cha, M., Haddadi, H., Benevenuto, F., & Gummadi, P.K. (2010). Measuring user influence in Twitter: The million follower fallacy. *ICWSM, 10,* 10-17.

Christakis, N.A., & Fowler, J.H. (2009). *Connected: The surprising power of our social networks and how they shape our lives.* Little, Brown.

Granovetter, M.S. (1973). The strength of weak ties. *American Journal of Sociology, 78*(6)1360-1380.

Hull, K. (2014). #Fight4UNCWSwimandDive: A case study of how college athletes used Twitter to help save their teams. *International Journal of Sport Communication, 7*(4), 533-552.

Katz, E., & Lazarsfeld, P.F. (1955). *Personal influence: The part played by people in the flow of mass communications.* Free Press.

Quigley, M. [thequiggles]. (2013, May 26). *Viewed in 911 cities, 38 countries and 17 languages. Sign our petition: change.org.* @SaveAquaHawks pic.twitter.com/u75N8tURM9 [tweet]. twitter.com/thequiggles/status/338671201813680129/photo/1

# Chapter 30

Bauer, T. (2021, February 5). *MY NEW HOME!!! | Trevor Bauer signs with Dodgers.* [Video]. YouTube. www.youtube.com/watch?v=KT7nUBwzOBM

Bryant, K. (2015, November 29). Dear basketball. *The Players' Tribune.* www.theplayerstribune.com/articles/dear-basketball

Durant, K. (2016, July 4). My next chapter. *The Players' Tribune.* www.theplayerstribune.com/articles/kevin-durant-nba-free-agency-announcement

Eisen, M. (2021, October 17). Second quarter costs Giants in 38–11 loss to Rams. *Giants.com.* www.giants.com/news/new-york-giants-vs-los-angeles-rams-recap-week-6-nfl-2021-daniel-jones

Feinberg, S. (2015, July 29). Derek Jeter, the aspiring media mogul (who dislikes media), reveals next big swing. *The Hollywood Reporter.*

www.hollywoodreporter.com/business/business-news/derek-jeter-aspiring-media-mogul-811572/

Gamecock Central. (2017, July 17). Release: Athletics media relations rebrands department. https://southcarolina.rivals.com/news/release-athletics-media-relations-rebrands-department

Gordon, J. (2022, July 6). The rise of the professional-athlete podcast. *The New York Times*. www.nytimes.com/2022/07/06/magazine/professional-athlete-podcast.html

Greenberg, N. (2016, July 4). Durant's decision to join Warriors sparks huge reaction, crashes Players' Tribune website. *The Washington Post*. www.washingtonpost.com/news/early-lead/wp/2016/07/04/durants-decision-to-join-warriors-sparks-huge-reaction-crashes-players-tribune-site/

Hall, A. (2018, June 25). Paul George's offseason to be featured in three-part *SportsCenter* series. *ESPN Press Room*. https://espnpressroom.com/us/press-releases/2018/06/paul-georges-offseason-to-be-featured-in-three-part-sportscenter-series/

Hsu, H. (2021, March 29). The rise of the athlete podcaster. *The New Yorker*. www.newyorker.com/magazine/2021/04/05/the-rise-of-the-athlete-podcaster

Kaplowitz, S. (2021, February 5). Trevor Bauer chooses LA Dodgers with new social media video. *ESPN El Paso*. https://krod.com/trevor-bauer-chooses-la-dodgers-with-new-social-media-video/

Linehan, M. (2021, December 6). San Diego Wave FC in final stages of acquiring Alex Morgan from Orlando Pride: Sources. *The Athletic*. https://theathletic.com/3687333/2021/12/06/san-diego-wave-fc-in-final-stages-of-acquiring-alex-morgan-from-orlando-pride-sources/

Love, K. (2018, March 6). Everyone is going through something. *The Players' Tribune*. www.theplayerstribune.com/articles/kevin-love-everyone-is-going-through-something

Mandell, N. (2015, November 29). Kobe Bryant's retirement announcement crashed the Players' Tribune website. *For the Win!* https://ftw.usatoday.com/2015/11/kobe-bryants-retirement-announcement-crashed-the-players-tribune-website

Massie, C. (2015, February 11). Covering teams in untraditional ways pays off. *Columbia Journalism Review*. https://archives.cjr.org/full_court_press/sports_team_blog_networks.php

Moran, E. (2020, October 2). Live . . . from Instagram. How athletes are breaking news on social media. *Front Office Sports*. https://frontofficesports.com/athletes-signings-social-media/

Morgan, A. [@alexmorgan13]. (2021, December 14). *Thank you, Orlando*. [Tweet]. Twitter. https://twitter.com/alexmorgan13/status/1470816046420566022

Ortiz, D. (2015, March 26). The Dirt. *The Players' Tribune*. www.theplayerstribune.com/articles/david-ortiz-on-the-record

Parsons, C. [@chandlerparsons]. (2022, January 18). *"Man, I don't even know where to begin . . . It's been a crazy last couple years and has put a lot* [Photograph]. Instagram. https://www.instagram.com/p/CY4LtAfFfJ/

Pérez-Peña, R. (2009, September 27). As coverage wanes, Los Angeles Kings hire own reporter. *The New York Times*. www.nytimes.com/2009/09/28/business/media/28kings.html

San Diego Wave FC. (2021a, December 13). San Diego Wave FC signs American soccer icon Alex Morgan ahead of inaugural season.

https://sandiegowavefc.com/san-diego-wave-fc-signs-american-soccer-icon-alex-morgan-ahead-of-inaugural-season/

San Diego Wave FC. [@sandiegowavefc]. (2021b, December 13). *2x World Cup Champion. Olympic Gold Medalist. NWSL Champion. 190 Caps. 115 International goals. Welcome to San Diego Wave FC, @alexmorgan13* [Tweet]. Twitter. https://twitter.com/sandiegowavefc/status/1470468782812450824

Sanders, L. (2015, February 26). Why I walked away from the NBA. *The Players' Tribune*. www.theplayerstribune.com/articles/larry-sanders-exclusive-interview

Sandomir, R. (2015, March 28). Athletes finding their voice in Derek Jeter's digital venture. *The New York Times*. www.nytimes.com/2015/03/29/sports/athletes-finding-their-voice-in-derek-jeters-digital-venture.html

Schwartz, P. (2021, October 17). Giants hit new low in disgraceful loss to Rams. *New York Post*. https://nypost.com/2021/10/17/giants-hit-new-low-in-disgraceful-loss-to-rams/

Spieth, J. [@JordanSpieth]. (2022, April 20.) *Excited to be part of the @UnderArmour family for 8 more years—I look forward to the next phase of* [Tweet]. Twitter. https://twitter.com/JordanSpieth/status/1516882056814505984

Trumpbour, R.C. (2006). *The new cathedrals: Politics and media in the history of stadium construction*. Syracuse University Press.

Yahoo! Sports. (2009, June 29). NFL players among sports' leaders on Twitter. https://news.yahoo.com/news/nfl-players-among-sports-leaders-164000818--nfl.html

Youngmisuk, O. (2018, July 1). LeBron James agrees to four-year, $153.3 million deal with Lakers. *ESPN*. www.espn.com/nba/story/_/id/23967725/lebron-james-joining-los-angeles-lakers-4-year-1533-million-deal

Zeigler, M. (2021, December 6). San Diego Wave reportedly close to acquiring Alex Morgan. *The San Diego Tribune*. www.sandiegouniontribune.com/sports/soccer/story/2021-12-06/san-diego-wave-reportedly-close-to-acquiring-alex-morgan

# Chapter 31

Aiken, B. [@BryceAiken]. (2020, March 10). *Horrible, horrible, horrible decision and total disregard for the players and teams that have put their hearts into this season*. [Tweet]. Twitter. https://twitter.com/BryceAiken/status/1237406417834979330

Anderson, S. (2020, September 30). What I learned inside the N.B.A. bubble. *The New York Times*. www.nytimes.com/2020/09/30/magazine/nba-bubble.html

Associated Press. (2020a, March 8). LeBron & Co. snap Clippers' streak at 6 with 112–103 victory. *ESPN*. www.espn.com/nba/recap/_/gameId/401161590

Associated Press. (2020b, April 13). ESPN, NFL Network to combo on NFL draft telecast. *ESPN*. www.espn.com/nfl/story/_/id/29029918/espn-nfl-network-combo-nfl-draft-telecast

Bieler, D., & Bogage, J. (2020, March 9). MLB, MLS, NBA and NHL to close locker rooms to reporters, citing coronavirus concerns. *The Washington Post*. www.washingtonpost.com/sports/2020/03/09/mlb-mls-nba-nhl-close-locker-rooms-reporters-citing-coronavirus-concerns/

Bucholtz, A. (2022, September 23). NBA locker rooms reopen to media for first time since 2020. *Awful Announcing*. https://awfulannouncing.com/nba/locker-rooms-nba-reopen-to-media-for-first-time-since-2020.html

Cafardo, B. (2020, March 20). ESPN to air encore presentations of WrestleMania. *ESPN Press Room*. https://espnpressroom.com/us/press-releases/2020/03/espn-to-air-encore-presentations-of-wrestlemania/

CDC. (2021, November 4). Basics of COVID-19. www.cdc.gov/coronavirus/2019-ncov/your-health/about-covid-19/basics-covid-19.html

Chavez, C. (2019, December 24). ESPN's latest trailer for "The Last Dance" features Michael Jordan, Bulls legends, President Obama. *SI.com*. www.si.com/nba/2019/12/24/espn-last-dance-documentary-trailer-michael-jordan-chicago-bulls-1997-1998

Christie, J.C. (2018, May 15). ESPN Films, Netflix announce multi-part documentary The Last Dance featuring Michael Jordan. *ESPN Press Room*. https://espnpressroom.com/us/press-releases/2018/05/espn-films-and-netflix-announce-multi-part-documentary-the-last-dance-featuring-michael-jordan/

Curtis, B. (2020, July 15). Sports are coming back. Is sports media coming back with it? *The Ringer*. www.theringer.com/sports/2020/7/15/21325404/sports-return-coronavirus-nba-mlb-nfl-journalism-media

Dampf, A. (2020, March 9). Sporting events in Italy to be halted because of virus. *Associated Press*. https://apnews.com/article/serie-a-tokyo-sports-general-japan-virus-outbreak-eadffad2de0652ee16e02e63ff90ba16

DelGallo, A. (2020, October 9). ESPN built a small city to broadcast games inside NBA bubble. *Orlando Sentinel*. www.orlandosentinel.com/sports/orlando-magic/os-sp-espn-nba-bubble-1009-20201009-uud5h24qefdtvp4gc6oubhd7ii-story.html

Dekker, O. H. [@OliviaDekker]. (2020, December 16). *This guy is impressive! 3rd game in 3 days on 3 networks, and the first broadcast from . . . the basement! Haha* [Tweet]. Twitter. https://twitter.com/OliviaDekker/status/1339086454903943168

Dellenger, R. (2020, June 26). "There's a lot of pain and uncertainty": The gloomy impact of the pandemic on sports broadcasting. *SI.com*. www.si.com/college/2020/06/26/sports-broadcasters-coronavirus-impact

Draper, K. (2020, June 5). The Athletic lays off 8 percent of staff. *The New York Times*. www.nytimes.com/2020/06/05/sports/the-athletic-layoffs.html

ESPN. (2020, May 18). *Did "The Last Dance" put more pressure on LeBron | First Take* [Video] YouTube. www.youtube.com/watch?v=17dxqjm3sB4

ESPN News Services. (2020, March 23). List of sporting events canceled because of the coronavirus. *ESPN.com*. www.espn.com/olympics/story/_/id/28824781/list-sporting-events-canceled-coronavirus

ESPN.com. (2021, March 11). Visual timeline of the day that changed everything: March 11. www.espn.com/espn/story/_/id/30546338/visual-line-day-changed-everything-march-11

Glasspiegel, R. (2020, March 9). Sportswriter groups petition against "unnecessarily" losing locker room access in coronavirus petition. *The Big Lead*. www.thebiglead.com/posts/coronavirus-apse-statement-locker-room-access-01e30x4cz8jh

Gleeson, S., & Myerberg, P. (2020, March 10). Ivy League cancels men's and women's basketball conference tournaments. *USA Today*. www.usatoday.com/story/sports/ncaab/2020/03/10/ivy-league-cancels-basketball-tournaments-amid-coronavirus-concerns/5010248002/

Henderson, J.L. (Senior Editorial Producer). (2021, March 11). March 11 2020 (Season 8, Episode 1). [Audio podcast episode]. In *ESPN 30 for 30*. ESPN.

Holmer, R. (2021, March 10). A timeline of the week the coronavirus halted the sports world. *NBC Sports*. www.nbcsports.com/washington/wizards/timeline-week-coronavirus-halted-sports-world-2020

Hull, K., & Romney, M. (2020). "It has changed completely": How local sports broadcasters adapted to no sports. *International Journal of Sports Communication, 13*(3), 494-504.

Jones, T. (2021, May 19). Opinion | Why sports reporting might never be the same after COVID-19. *Poynter*. www.poynter.org/newsletters/2021/covid-19-has-had-a-devastating-impact-on-sports-journalism/

Keh, A. (2020, March 12). Twenty-four hours when sports hit the halt button. *The New York Times*. www.nytimes.com/2020/03/12/sports/coronavirus-sports-canceled.html

Kelly, M., & Casella, P. (2020, March 26). 5 thrilling Opening Days on MLB Network today. *MLB.com*. www.mlb.com/news/opening-day-at-home-opening-day-classics

Lacques, G. (2021, March 11). From game on to lights out. *USA Today*. www.usatoday.com/in-depth/sports/2021/03/11/shutdown-anniversary-how-covid-19-silenced-sports-year-ago-today/6908986002/

Lopez, I. (2020, March 31). ESPN and Netflix set new April 19 premiere for highly anticipated documentary series "The Last Dance." *ESPN Press Room*. https://espnpressroom.com/us/press-releases/2020/03/espn-and-netflix-set-new-april-19-premiere-date-for-highly-anticipated-documentary-series-the-last-dance/

*Los Angeles Times*. (2020, March 30). How the coronavirus is affecting sports leagues and events. https://www.latimes.com/sports/story/2020-03-09/coronavirus-latest-news-sports-world

Martin, K.H. (2020, April 7). Home games: Jeff Passan, Tim Kurkjian report from their respective remote setups. *ESPN Front Row*. www.espnfrontrow.com/2020/04/home-games-jeff-passan-tim-kurkjian-report-from-their-respective-remote-setups/

Martin, K.H. (2020, May 4). ESPN reaches agreement with Eclat Media Group to exclusively televise six live KBO league games per week in U.S. starting with Opening Day on May 5. *ESPN Press Room*. https://espnpressroom.com/us/press-releases/2020/05/espn-reaches-agreement-with-eclat-media-group-to-exclusively-televise-six-live-kbo-league-games-per-week-in-u-s-starting-with-opening-day-on-may-5/

Mather, V. (2020, July 1). Welcome to a summer of sports, if all goes well. *The New York Times*. www.nytimes.com/2020/07/01/sports/july-seasons-restart-coronavirus.html

Nair, R. (2020, March 7). "I ain't playing" with no fans, says James. *Reuters*. www.reuters.com/article/us-health-coronavirus-nba/i-aint-playing-with-no-fans-says-james-idUSKBN20U0IQ

NCAA. (2020, March 11). NCAA President Mark Emmert's statement on limiting attendance at NCAA events. *NCAA.org*. www.ncaa.org/news/2020/3/11/ncaa-president-mark-emmert-s-statement-on-limiting-attendance-at-ncaa-events.aspx

NFL Communications (2020). 2020 NFL Draft most watched ever; sets new all-time highs for media consumption. https://nflcommunications.com/Pages/2020-NFL-DRAFT-MOST-WATCHED-EVER;-SETS-NEW-ALL-TIME-HIGHS-FOR-MEDIA-CONSUMPTION.aspx

Owen, R. (2020, March 18). TV Q&A: What happens to sports on local newscasts during COVID-19 pandemic? *Pittsburgh Post-Gazette*. www.post-gazette.com/ae/2020/03/18/TV-Q-A-What-happens-to-sports-on-local-newscasts-during-COVID-19-pandemic-PCNC-Discovery-Of-Witches/stories/202003180012

Quinn, S. (2020, March 12). Rudy Gobert touched every microphone at Jazz media availability Monday, now reportedly has coronavirus. *CBS Sports*. www.cbssports.com/nba/news/rudy-gobert-touched-every-microphone-at-jazz-media-availability-monday-now-reportedly-has-coronavirus/

Reedy, J. (2022, January 20). NBC won't send sports announcers to Beijing for Winter Olympics. *NBC Chicago*. www.nbcchicago.com/news/sports/beijing-winter-olympics/nbc-announcers-will-again-call-olympics-home-only-select-hosts-travel/2732178/

Reuters Staff. (2020, February 23). UPDATE 2-Soccer-Serie A matches among fixtures cancelled in Italy after coronavirus outbreak. *Reuters*. www.reuters.com/article/china-health-italy-soccer/update-2-soccer-serie-a-matches-among-fixtures-cancelled-in-italy-after-coronavirus-outbreak-idUSL5N2AN0AP

Reynolds, T. (2020, March 3). Coronavirus: NBA tells players to avoid high-fiving fans and autographing items. *Associate Press*. https://apnews.com/article/nba-miami-ap-top-news-sports-asia-virus-outbreak-d035c223cfaa84a38f799b92c80b3e17

Seifert, K. (2020, April 17). The 2020 NFL draft is going virtual: How it will work, and what you should know. *ESPN*. www.espn.com/nfl/draft2020/story/_/id/29026049/the-2020-nfl-draft-going-virtual-how-work-should-know

Shapiro, M. (2020, March 20). CBS Sports to air classic March Madness games after 2020 tournament cancellation. *SI.com*. www.si.com/college/2020/03/20/cbs-air-classic-march-madness-games

Shaughnessy, D. (2020, March 9). Don't use coronavirus to close locker rooms to media forever. *The Boston Globe*. www.bostonglobe.com/2020/03/09/sports/dont-use-coronavirus-close-locker-rooms-media-forever/

Sports TV Ratings. [@SportsTVRatings] (2020, May 7). *Wisdom of the crowds gets it right again! The initial Korean baseball game on ESPN (12:55AM start Monday night) averaged* [Tweet]. Twitter. https://twitter.com/SportsTVRatings/status/1258451089063624705

Strauss, B. (2022, April 23). Some MLB broadcasters still aren't back on the road. Viewers notice. *The Washington Post*. www.washingtonpost.com/sports/2022/04/23/masn-broadcasters-remote/

Timanus, E. (2020, July 24). Fox's Joe Buck never "more excited to go back to work" with baseball returning. *USA Today*. www.usatoday.com/story/sports/mlb/2020/07/24/yankees-nationals-game-step-toward-normalcy-fox-sports-joe-buck/5483902002/

Traina, J. (2020, April 24). Round 1 of the NFL Draft could not have gone better for ESPN: Trania Thoughts. *SI.com*. www.si.com/extra-mustard/2020/04/24/espn-nfl-draft-coverage-review

Volner, D. (2020, May 21). ESPN sees "The Last Dance" audience skyrocket with time-shifted/on-demand viewing; now averaging more than 12.8 million viewers per episode, up 128% from premieres. *ESPN Press Room*. https://espnpressroom.com/us/press-releases/2020/05/espn-sees-the-last-dance-audience-skyrocket-with-time-shifted-on-demand-viewing-now-averaging-more-than-12-8-million-viewers-per-episode-up-128-from-premieres/

Wagner, J. (2020, June 24). Baseball's new rules: No spitting, no arguing, and lots of testing. *The New York Times*. www.nytimes.com/2020/06/24/sports/baseball/mlb-coronavirus-rules.html

Wahl, G. [@GrantWahl]. (2020, March 7). *Many sports journalists will disagree, but I honestly don't think we ever need to be in a locker room. Doing* [Tweet]. Twitter. https://twitter.com/grantwahl/status/1236364288471601152

Weaver, M. (2020, April 3). Behind the scenes of iRacing on Fox. *Autoweek*. www.autoweek.com/racing/nascar/a32037977/behind-the-scenes-of-iracing-on-fox/

Wharton, D. (2020, March 24). Tokyo Olympics postponed because of the coronavirus outbreak. *Los Angeles Times*. www.latimes.com/sports/story/2020-03-24/tokyo-olympics-becomes-biggest-sporting-event-halted-by-coronavirus

Wilner, B. (2020, February 3). Super rally: Mahomes, Chiefs win NFL title with late surge. *Associated Press*. https://apnews.com/article/san-francisco-49ers-sports-general-super-bowl-football-ap-top-news-8f6178fbfa3844677b5fc374bc53b80f

World Health Organization. (2020, January 20). Novel Coronavirus (2019-nCov) situation report—1. https://www.who.int/docs/default-source/coronaviruse/situation-reports/20200121-sitrep-1-2019-ncov.pdf?sfvrsn=20a99c10_4

Youngmisuk, O. (2020, March 10). LeBron James says he'll listen if NBA bars fans over coronavirus. *ESPN*. www.espn.com/nba/story/_/id/28878573/lebron-james-says-listen-nba-bars-fans-coronavirus

# Chapter 32

Associated Press. (2018, May 31). NBA players union hires mental health director. *Los Angeles Times*. www.latimes.com/sports/nba/la-sp-nba-notes-20180531-story.html

Bandujo, K. (2021, April 8). Is aiding mental health the next frontier of MLB player development? *Baseball America*. www.baseballamerica.com/stories/is-aiding-mental-health-the-next-frontier-of-mlb-player-development/

Branch, J. (2022, February 8). How Olympians embraced mental health after Simone Biles showed the way. *The New York Times*. www.nytimes.com/2022/02/08/sports/olympics/olympics-mental-health-simone-biles.html

Capatides, C. (2018, April 17). Michael Phelps opens up about depression, says he thought about killing himself after Olympics. *CBS News*. www.cbsnews.com/news/michael-phelps-reveals-he-suffered-from-depression-thought-about-killing-himself-after-olympics/

CBS News. (2018, January 17). Michael Phelps: Helping others with depression "light years better" than Olympic gold. www.cbsnews

.com/news/michael-phelps-helping-others-with-depression-light-years-better-than-olympic-gold/

Clarey, C. (2021, May 28). At the French Open, Naomi Osaka seeks comfort on clay and no interviews. *The New York Times*. www.nytimes.com/2021/05/28/sports/tennis/french-open-2021-naomi-osaka.html

Clemmons, A.K. (2021, November 26). Pushed by the players, the N.F.L. works to embrace mental health. *The New York Times*. www.nytimes.com/2021/11/26/sports/football/nfl-mental-health.html

Crouse, L. (2021, July 27). Simone Biles just demonstrated a true champion mind-set. *The New York Times*. www.nytimes.com/2021/07/27/opinion/culture/simone-biles-just-demonstrated-a-true-champion-mind-set.html

DeRozan, D. [@demar_derozan] (2018, February 17). *This depression got the best of me . . .* [Tweet]. Twitter. https://twitter.com/demar_derozan/status/964818383303688197

Devine, D. (2018, March 20). Why Royce White is skeptical the NBA genuinely cares about players' mental health. *Yahoo! Sports*. https://sports.yahoo.com/royce-white-skeptical-nba-genuinely-cares-players-mental-health-155413843.html

Dietrich, S., Heider, D., Matschinger, H., & Angermeyer, M.C. (2006). Influence of newspaper reporting on adolescents' attitudes toward people with mental illness. *Social Psychiatry and Psychiatric Epidemiology, 41*, 318-322.

Doherty, S., Hennigan, B., & Campbell, M.J. (2016). The experience of depression during the careers of elite male athletes. *Frontiers in Psychology, 7*, 1-11.

Futterman, M. (2021, May 31). Naomi Osaka quits the French Open after news conference dispute. *The New York Times*. www.nytimes.com/2021/05/31/sports/tennis/naomi-osaka-quits-french-open-depression.html

Gavin, K. (2021, July 29). A game-changer for mental health: Sports icons open up. *Michigan Medicine*. www.michiganmedicine.org/health-lab/game-changer-mental-health-sports-icons-open

GMA. [@GMA]. (2022, December 6). .@naomiosaka *is such an inspiration. The four-time Grand Slam champion talks to @robinroberts about her new children's book, "The Way Champs Play," which is about empowering young people through sports.* [Video attached] [Tweet]. Twitter. https://twitter.com/GMA/status/1600123419625783299

Granello, D.H., Pauley, P.S., & Carmichael, A. (1999). Relationship of the media to attitudes toward people with mental illness. *The Journal of Humanistic Counseling, Education and Development, 38*(2), 98-110.

Gregory, S. (2021, June 2). "This will 100% save somebody's life." Athletes see a turning point for mental health after Naomi Osaka takes a stand at the French Open. *Time*. https://time.com/6053239/naomi-osaka-mental-health/

Henry, B. (2021, June 1). Serena Williams showed support to Naomi Osaka after she was criticized for not doing press at the French Open. *BuzzFeed.News*. www.buzzfeednews.com/article/benhenry/serena-williams-naomi-osaka-french-open-withdrawal

Henry, C. (2022, May 25). Social series highlights importance of mental health resources and education. *NCAA*. www.ncaa.org/news/2022/5/25/media-center-social-series-highlights-importance-of-mental-health-resources-and-education.aspx

Holmes, B. (2015, August 6). Q&A: Why Metta World Peace needed a sports psychologist. *ESPN*. www.espn.com/nba/story/_/id/13385190/why-metta-world-peace-needed-sports-psychologist

Jacobs, S. (2022, October 6). Nick Kyrgios a big fan of "inspirational" Naomi Osaka, saying "I love what she brings to the sport." *Tennis365*. www.tennis365.com/tennis-news/nick-kyrgios-big-fan-inspirational-naomi-osaka-amazing-athlete/

Jacobs, J. (2012, March 15). Iowa State's Royce White a complex, remarkable man. *Hartford Courant*. www.courant.com/sports/uconn-mens-basketball/hc-xpm-2012-03-15-hc-jacobs-uconn-iowa-state-0315-20120315-story.html

Klin, A., & Lemish, D. (2008). Mental disorders stigma in the media: Review of studies on production, content, and influences. *Journal of Health Communication, 13*, 434-449.

Lee, M. (2022, April 19). How the NBA got serious about mental health. *The Washington Post*. www.washingtonpost.com/sports/2022/04/19/nba-mental-health-demar-derozan/

Longman, J. (2021, July 28). Simone Biles rejects a long tradition of stoicism in sports. *The New York Times*. www.nytimes.com/2021/07/28/sports/olympics/simone-biles-mental-health.html

Love, K. (2018, March 6). Everyone is going through something. *The Players' Tribune*. www.theplayerstribune.com/articles/kevin-love-everyone-is-going-through-something

Macur, J. (2021a, July 24). Simone Biles and the weight of perfection. *The New York Times*. www.nytimes.com/2021/07/24/sports/olympics/simone-biles-gymnastics.html

Macur, J. (2021b, July 27). Simone Biles is out of the team final. *The New York Times*. www.nytimes.com/2021/07/27/sports/olympics/simone-biles-out.html

McCarthy, M. (2016, August 5). Michael Phelps admits he considered suicide amid post-retirement depression. *The Sporting News*. www.sportingnews.com/us/athletics/news/michael-phelps-bob-costas-rio-nbc-sports-olympics-london-rehab/1ozc0ksb05j9a1u31and8yeqjf

McGinty, E.E., Kennedy-Hendricks, A., Choksy, S., & Barry, C.L. (2016). Trends in news media coverage of mental illness in the United States: 1995-2014. *Health Affairs, 35*(6), 1121-1129.

Medcalf, M. (2012, October 3). Royce White wants to travel by bus. *ESPN*. www.espn.com/nba/story/_/id/8459655/royce-white-absent-houston-rockets-cites-mental-health

NBA. (2010, June 19). *Ron Artest post-game interview*. [Video]. YouTube www.youtube.com/watch?v=2hFWoycaXHg

NIH. (2022). Mental illness. www.nimh.nih.gov/health/statistics/mental-illness

Osaka, N. [@naomiosaka] (2021a, May 31). [Photograph]. Instagram www.instagram.com/p/CPi9kJHJfxO/

Osaka, N. (2021b, July 8). Naomi Osaka: "It's O.K. not to be O.K." *Time*. https://time.com/6077128/naomi-osaka-essay-tokyo-olympics/

Scutti, S. (2018, January 20). Michael Phelps: "I am extremely thankful that I did not take my life." *CNN*. www.cnn.com/2018/01/19/health/michael-phelps-depression/index.html

Smith, D. (2018, February 25). Raptors' DeRozan hopes honest talk on depression helps others. *Toronto Star*. www.thestar.com

/sports/raptors/2018/02/25/raptors-derozan-hopes-honest-talk-on-depression-helps-others.html

Sportsnet Staff. (2020, December 26). VanVleet: DeRozan changed NBA by "speaking out" about mental health. *Sportsnet*. www.sportsnet.ca/nba/article/vanvleet-derozan-changed-nba-speaking-mental-health/

Souter, G., Lewis, R., & Serrant, L. (2018). Men, mental health and elite sport: A narrative review. *Sports Medicine, 4*(57), 1-8.

Stevens, M. (2018, November 29). Kevin Love calls speaking out on mental health "the biggest thing" in his career. *The New York Times*. www.nytimes.com/2018/11/29/sports/kevin-love-mental-health-sports.html

Torre, P.S. (2012, July 2). The mystery pick is Royce White. *SI Vault*. https://vault.si.com/vault/2012/07/02/the-mystery-pick-is-royce-white

Vecsey, G. (1996, July 24). Sports of The Times; Strug took her chances for the gold. *The New York Times*. www.nytimes.com/1996/07/24/sports/sports-of-the-times-strug-took-her-chances-for-the-gold.html

Walsh, D. (2022, September 14). Study: Social media use linked to decline in mental health. *MIT Management*. https://mitsloan.mit.edu/ideas-made-to-matter/study-social-media-use-linked-to-decline-mental-health

Wells, G., & Radnofsky, L. (2022, February 27). Social media has become essential for athletes. It can also be miserable. *The Wall Street Journal*. www.wsj.com/articles/instagram-mikaela-shiffrin-simone-biles-geoff-kabush-11645979596

Whitley, R., & Wang, J. (2017b). Television coverage of mental illness in Canada: 2013-2015. *Social Psychiatry and Psychiatric Epidemiology, 52*, 241-244.

WHO. (2022a, July 8). Mental health. www.who.int/news-room/facts-in-pictures/detail/mental-health

WHO. (2022b, June 17). Mental health: strengthening our response. www.who.int/news-room/fact-sheets/detail/mental-health-strengthening-our-response

Wrenn, J.M. (2012, October 9). NBA rookie Royce White battles anxiety disorder and fear of flying. *CNN*. www.cnn.com/2012/10/09/living/royce-white-anxiety/index.html

Zillgitt, J. (2013, February 8). Royce White battles for mental health—his and others'. *USA Today*. www.usatoday.com/story/sports/nba/2013/02/08/royce-white-houston-rockets-anxiety-disorder/1890421/

# Chapter 33

ADU. (2021). The rise of collegiate Esports programs. https://athleticdirectoru.com/articles/the-rise-of-collegiate-esports-programs/

Ashaari, A. (2019, April 29). *Avengers Endgame* breaks all-time opening weekend box office record. *Kakuchopurei*. www.kakuchopurei.com/2019/04/avengers-endgame-breaks-all-time-opening-weekend-box-office-record/

Bieler, D. (2021, April 22). IOC announces inaugural slate of Olympic-licensed esports events. *The Washington Post*. www.washingtonpost.com/video-games/esports/2021/04/22/ioc-olympics-esports/

Browning, K. (2021, December 29). How Discord, born from an obscure game, became a social hub for young people. *The New York Times*. www.nytimes.com/2021/12/29/business/discord-server-social-media.html

Chmielewski, D. (2014, September 4). Sorry, Twitch: ESPN's Skipper says esports "not a sport." *Vox*. www.vox.com/2014/9/4/11630572/sorry-twitch-espns-skipper-says-esports-not-a-sport

Cifaldi, F. (2016, July 14). The story of the first Nintendo World Championships. *IGN*. www.ign.com/articles/2015/05/13/the-story-of-the-first-nintendo-world-championships

Cohen, A. (2020, April 13). "The Show" goes on with MLB Esports tournament. *Sports Techie*. www.sporttechie.com/mlb-esports-players-tournament-the-show/

Entertainment Software Association. (2021). 2021 essential facts about the video game industry. www.theesa.com/resource/2021-essential-facts-about-the-video-game-industry/

Gilbert, B. (2020, March 12). NBA player Devin Booker learned about the season's suspension due to the coronavirus pandemic while playing "Call of Duty" live on Twitch. *Business Insider*. www.businessinsider.com/nba-player-reacts-league-suspension-live-twitch-coronavirus-devin-booker-2020-3

Goodall, R. (2020, August 9). Concept to console: The history of Pac-Man. *The Boar*. https://theboar.org/2020/08/concept-to-console-the-history-of-pac-man/

Grohmann, K. (2017, October 28). E-sports just got closer to being part of the Olympics. *Reuters*. www.reuters.com/article/us-olympics-summit/olympics-e-sports-could-be-sports-activity-says-ioc-idUSKBN1CX0IR

Guinness Book of World Records. (n.d.). First esports event. www.guinnessworldrecords.com/world-records/648331-first-esports-event

Holt, K. (2019, July 29). Teen "Fortnight" champion won more than Tiger Woods at the Masters. *Engadget*. www.engadget.com/2019-07-29-fortnite-world-cup-bugha-prize-money-esports.html

Hume, M. (2019, October 15). Introducing Launcher, a new section covering video games and esports from The Washington Post. *The Washington Post*. www.washingtonpost.com/video-games/2019/10/15/introducing-launcher-new-section-covering-video-games-esports-washington-post/

Hume, M. (2023, March 31). What Launcher meant, and means, for games journalism. *The Washington Post*. www.washingtonpost.com/video-games/2023/03/31/launcher-mission-end/

Hutcheon, S. (1983, June 7). The video games boom has yet to come. *The Age*. https://news.google.com/newspapers?id=fC5VAAAAIBAJ&pg=4131,3188851

Kelly, K. (1993, June 1). The first online sports game. *Wired*. www.wired.com/1993/06/netrek/

Kim, M. (2017, February 16). Communal living is the secret sauce to esports success. *Inverse*. www.inverse.com/article/27923-esports-house-cloud9-tour

Korea.net. (2012, June 4). South Korea, the mecca of e-sports. https://web.archive.org/web/20140807025918/http://www.korea.net/NewsFocus/Sci-Tech/view?articleId=100629

Larch, F. (2022, August 19). History of eSports: How it all began. *ISPO*. www.ispo.com/en/markets/history-esports-how-it-all-began

Lawler, R. (2013, June 5). With 35m unique viewers a month, Twitch hires an in-house ad sales team to ramp up monetization. *Tech Crunch*. https://techcrunch.com/2013/06/05/twitch-in-house-sales-team/

McCarthy, M. (2019, October 11). Why The Washington Post chose to cover esports. *Front Office Sports*. https://frontofficesports.com/esports-washington-post/

McKnight, M. (2019, September 4). Much ado about JuJu. *Sports Illustrated*. www.si.com/nfl/2019/09/04/juju-smith-schuster-steelers-antonio-brown-social-media-youtube-popularity-fortnite

NBA Communications. (2017, February 9). NBA and Take-Two to launch "NBA 2K eLeague." https://pr.nba.com/nba-2k-eleague-launch/

NIB. (2017, February 20). Passing the Twitch test: How do professional gamers train? https://web.archive.org/web/20180409125839/https://www.nib.com.au/the-checkup/future-happenings/passing-the-twitch-test-how-do-professional-gamers-train

Phillips, L. (2020, April 1). The history of esports. *HotSpawn*. www.hotspawn.com/other/guides/the-history-of-esports

Reames, M. (2018, September 11). A history of esports in higher education. *HotSpawn*. www.hotspawn.com/dota2/news/a-history-of-esports-in-higher-education

Rivera, J. (2021, July 11). Wimbledon prize money: How much will the winners make in 2021? Purse, breakdown for field. *The Sporting News*. www.sportingnews.com/us/tennis/news/wimbledon-prize-money-2021-purse-breakdown/6zc30l4mxqbb17k4nqxn5r68n

Robinson, J. (2005, December 7). Madden Nation. *IGN*. www.ign.com/articles/2005/12/07/madden-nation

Shea, B. (2015, April 27). ESPN's Colin Cowherd says he would quit if forced to cover video games. *Game Informer*. www.gameinformer.com/b/news/archive/2015/04/27/espn-colin-cowherd-says-he-would-quit-if-forced-to-cover-video-games.aspx

Smith, N. (2021, February 16). The rise, fall and resonance of ESPN Esports. *The Washington Post*. www.washingtonpost.com/video-games/esports/2021/02/16/espn-esports/

Starcade. (n.d.). www.starcade.tv/starcade/games/index.html

Strickland, D. (2022, August 12). Grand Theft Auto earnings at $7.86 billion since GTA V launch. *TweakTown*. www.tweaktown.com/news/87904/grand-theft-auto-earnings-at-7-68-billion-since-gta-launch/index.html

Teng, E. (2018, September 18). Living the stream. *ESPN The Magazine*. www.espn.com/espn/feature/story/_/id/24710688/fortnite-legend-ninja-living-stream

Toribio, J. (2020, March 27). Game on! 4 MLBers play "MLB The Show" (8 ET). *MLB.com*. www.mlb.com/news/blake-snell-major-leaguers-to-play-mlb-the-show

Twitch Advertising. (n.d.). Audience. twitchadvertising.tv/audience/

Washington, D. (2020, March 31). Virtual racing entertaining NASCAR fans, drivers during COVID-19 pandemic. *Alabama Newscenter*. https://alabamanewscenter.com/2020/03/31/virtual-racing-entertaining-nascar-fans-drivers-during-covid-19-pandemic/

White, S. (2022, August 1). Super Mario Kart 30 years on—the most successful video game racing franchise ever. *Mirror*. www.mirror.co.uk/news/uk-news/super-mario-kart-30-years-27540319

Wingfield, N. (2014, August 25). What's Twitch? Gamers know, and Amazon is spending $1 billion on it. *The New York Times*. www.nytimes.com/2014/08/26/technology/amazon-nears-a-deal-for-twitch.html

Wutz, M. (2021). 7 biggest esports games by prize money in 2021. *For The Win*. https://ftw.usatoday.com/lists/esports-games-prize-money-2021

Wright, S.T. (2018, July 24). Twin Galaxies aims to be arbiter of not just high scores but competitive gaming. *Variety*. https://variety.com/2018/gaming/features/twin-galaxies-billy-mitchell-jace-hall-high-scores-1202883050/

# Chapter 34

Andrews, E. (2014, October 9). What was the 1919 "Black Sox" baseball scandal. *History*. www.history.com/news/black-sox-baseball-scandal-1919-world-series-chicago

Arag. (n.d.). Is participating in office pools a safe bet? www.araglegal.com/individuals/learning-center/topics/in-trouble-with-the-law/is-participating-in-office-pools-a-safe-bet

Associated Press. (2017, October 17). W.N.B.A. moves into Las Vegas, joining N.H.L. and N.F.L. *The New York Times*. www.nytimes.com/2017/10/17/sports/basketball/wnba-san-antonio-stars-las-vegas.html

Belson, K., & Mather, V. (2017, March 27). Raiders leaving Oakland again, this time for Las Vegas. *The New York Times*. www.nytimes.com/2017/03/27/sports/football/nfl-oakland-raiders-las-vegas.html

Browning, K. (2023, August 8). ESPN enters sports gambling in $2 billion deal with casino company. *The New York Times*. www.nytimes.com/2023/08/08/business/espn-penn-entertainment-gambling.html

Chass, M. (1989, August 24). Rose, in deal, is said to accept lifetime ban for betting on baseball. *The New York Times*. www.nytimes.com/1989/08/24/sports/rose-in-deal-is-said-to-accept-lifetime-ban-for-betting-on-reds.html

Curry, J. (2004. January 6). BASEBALL; Rose, in new book, admits betting on his team. *The New York Times*. www.nytimes.com/2004/01/06/sports/baseball-rose-in-new-book-admits-betting-on-his-team.html

D'Andrea, C. (2022, March 7). How Calvin Ridley got caught gambling on NFL games, explained. *USA Today*. https://ftw.usatoday.com/2022/03/calvin-ridley-nfl-suspension-explainer-atlanta-falcons

The Dowd Report. (1989, May 9). https://web.archive.org/web/20160625220526/http://www.thedowdreport.com/report.pdf

Eden, S. (2020, July 9). From the archives: How former ref Tim Donaghy conspired to fix NBA games. *ESPN*. www.espn.com/nba/story/_/id/25980368/how-former-ref-tim-donaghy-conspired-fix-nba-games

Editors Team. (2023, May 17). The history of sports betting in the USA. *Borgata Online*. https://sports.borgataonline.com/en/blog/history-of-sports-betting-in-the-usa/

Everson, P. (2018, February 24). Is gambling the Vegas Golden Knights' secret weapon? *America's Best Racing*. www.americasbestracing.net /gambling/2018-gambling-the-vegas-golden-knights-secret-weapon

Fazio, M. (2021, April 1). It's easy (and legal) to bet on sports. Do young adults know the risks? *The New York Times*. www.nytimes.com /2021/04/01/sports/sports-betting-addiction.html

Feuer, W., & Sayre, K. (2023, July 31). Fox to wind down sports-betting site Fox Bet. *The Wall Street Journal*. www.wsj.com/articles /fox-to-wind-down-sports-betting-site-fox-bet-f9fda8d2

Gardner, S. (2022, March 7). The NFL's complicated history with gambling, from Paul Hornung to Calvin Ridley. *USA Today*. www .usatoday.com/story/sports/nfl/2022/03/07/nfl-and-gambling -paul-hornung-sportsbooks-calvin-ridley/9417569002/

Gordon, S. (2020, May 5). NBA in Vegas: 2007 All-Star Game a "disastrous weekend." *Las Vegas Review-Journal*. www.reviewjournal .com/sports/basketball/nba-in-vegas-2007-all-star-game-a -disastrous-weekend-2021799/

Gordon, S. (2022, April 30). NFL draft primer for Super Bowl in Las Vegas. *Las Vegas Review-Journal*. www.reviewjournal.com/sports /nfl-draft/nfl-draft-primer-for-super-bowl-in-las-vegas-2569605/

Houston, M. (2022, October 28). Gov. Abbott open to expanding gambling options in Texas, spokesperson says. *KENS*. www.kens5 .com/article/news/local/abbott-gambling-laws-texas-lega-san -antonio/273-d3071fee-c812-4a86-819f-8f0652244e3d

Kilgore, A. (2021, May 26). Capital One Arena just knocked down the final wall between gambling and U.S. pro sports. *The Washington Post*. www.washingtonpost.com/sports/2021/05/26/capital-one -arena-sportsbook-william-hill/

Legal Sports Report. (n.d.). US sportsbook and casino team sponsorship tracker. www.legalsportsreport.com/sports-betting-deals/

Liptak, A., & Draper, K. (2018, May 14). Supreme Court ruling favors sports betting. *The New York Times*. www.nytimes.com /2018/05/14/us/politics/supreme-court-sports-betting-new -jersey.html

McCarthy, M. (2021, September 22). Fast-growing Barstool on pace to crack $200 million in revenue. *Front Office Sports*. https:// frontofficesports.com/barstool-sports-erika-nardini-growth/

MLB. (n.d.). Rule 21. http://content.mlb.com/documents/8/2/2 /296982822/Major_League_Rule_21.pdf

Neff, C. (1989, April 3). Rose's grim vigil. *Sports Illustrated*. https://vault.si.com/vault/1989/04/03/roses-grim-vigil-as -gambling-charges-and-the-media-engulfed-him-pete-rose-awaited -his-fate

Ota, K. (2023, March 16). ESPN tournament challenge sets new all-time record: 20 million brackets. *ESPN Press Room*. https://

espnpressroom.com/us/press-releases/2023/03/espn-tournament -challenge-sets-new-all-time-record-20-million-brackets/

Patra, K. (2022, March 7). Falcons WR Calvin Ridley suspended indefinitely through at least 2022 season for betting on NFL games. *NFL.com*. www.nfl.com/news/falcons-wr-calvin-ridley-suspended -indefinitely-through-2022-season-for-betting-

Perez, A.J. (2022, August 17). Penn to acquire rest of Barstool Sports. *Front Office Sports*. https://frontofficesports.com/penn-to-acquire -rest-of-barstool-sports/

Podolsky, R. (2021). *You are looking live*. Lyons Press.

Price, G. (2015, June 23). Pete Rose quotes: A look back at his gambling denials over the years. *International Business Times*. www .ibtimes.com/pete-rose-quotes-look-back-his-gambling-denials -over-years-1980008

Ridley, C. [@CalvinRidley1]. (2022, March 7). *I bet 1500 total I don't have a gambling problem* [Tweet]. Twitter. https://twitter.com /CalvinRidley1/status/1500939522632302594

Robbins, L. (2014, October 20). Sports betting in New Jersey is challenged. *The New York Times*. www.nytimes.com/2014/10/21 /nyregion/sports-betting-in-new-jersey-is-challenged.html

Rovell, D. (2023, August 9). Why Barstool Sportsbook failed. *Action Network*. www.actionnetwork.com/legal-online-sports-betting/why -barstool-sportsbook-failed

Salam, M. (2018, June 5). Delaware kicks off full-scale sports betting, a first outside of Nevada. *The New York Times*. www.nytimes.com /2018/06/05/sports/sports-betting-delaware.html

Schmidt, M.S. (2008, July 30). Former N.B.A. referee is sentenced. *The New York Times*. www.nytimes.com/2008/07/30/sports /basketball/30referee.html

Silver, A. (2014, November 13). Legalize and regulate sports betting. *The New York Times*. www.nytimes.com/2014/11/14/opinion/nba -commissioner-adam-silver-legalize-sports-betting.html

Steven's Baseball Archives. (2022, February 8). *Houston Astros at Atlanta Braves, 2021 World Series Game 4, October 30, 2021* [Video]. YouTube. www.youtube.com/watch?v=1kZ3hPAq_bw

Strauss, B. (2023, June 23). FanDuel makes betting lines. FanDuel's Shams Charania moves them. *The Washington Post*. www.washingtonpost .com/sports/2023/06/23/shams-charania-fanduel-draft/

Weinbaum, W., & Quinn, T.J. (2015, June 22). Entries into long-hidden notebook show Pete Rose bet on baseball as player. *ESPN*. www.espn.com/espn/otl/story/_/id/13114874/notebook -obtained-lines-shows-pete-rose-bet-baseball-player-1986

Wulf, S. (2019, October 9). Could the Black Sox scandal happen today? *ESPN*. www.espn.com/mlb/story/_/id/27798308/could -black-sox-scandal-happen-today

# INDEX

*Note:* The italicized *f* following page numbers refers to figures.

## A

ABC News  61, 65, 207, 208
ABC Sports
    ESPN sale  42, 65, 66, 72
    football coverage  93
    history  60-61, 65-66
    Olympics coverage  27-29, 32, 61-62
    programming  60-61, 62-65, 66
    soccer coverage  142
    *Wide World of Sports*  53, 61, 63-64
Abdul-Jabbar, Kareem  124
Abdul-Rauf, Mahmoud  116-117
academic fraud  48
activism and protest. *See* political issues; social issues
addiction, gambling  269
advertising. *See also* corporate sponsorships
    broadcasting rights and revenue  21-23, 200-201
    cable TV  68-69, 72
    classifieds  18, 19
    endorsements  120-121, 132-133, 134-135, 158, 173, 176, 180, 184-185, 186, 190, 191, 193, 197, 206, 211-212
    Internet/social media  18-19, 47, 50-51
    newspaper industry  18-19
    Olympics broadcasting  25, 29, 30, 32
    print media  18, 19, 36-37, 41
    radio media  11, 12
    SEC  93
    sports betting  268-269
    ticket sales vs.  12
African American athletes. *See also* specific athletes
    historic successes  10, 26, 106, 180
    limited media coverage  10, 106, 109-110

    political and social protest  27-28, 62, 115-122, 124
    racist media coverage  64, 106, 108
African American journalists
    demographics and diversity issues  106, 107, 117, 176-177
    race issues and commentary  117, 125-126, 176-177
    sports writing history  10
ageism  154, 155
agenda setting  53, 54-58. *See also* gatekeeping
    print media  55, 103-105
    SEC bias  90-95
    television  53, 57-58, 91
Ali, Muhammad  14, 63-64, 124
Altuve, José  219, 268
Amaechi, John  160
Amazon, streaming  23, 154, 155
American bias  30, 31
America's Cup (sailing)  67
Andrews, Erin  155
anxiety and depression  246, 248-251
appearance, physical
    focus on women  104, 134-135, 136, 143, 153, 155
    name, image, and likeness rules and deals  134-135, 138
Apple TV  23
AP polls, lists, and awards  91, 110, 189
arcade games  254
Arledge, Roone  61, 64-65
Armstrong, Lance  172, 188-195, 225
Artest, Ron  246, 251
athletes
    business of sports  17
    empowerment  196, 197, 199, 202, 203, 231-233
    Hispanic, and social identity  99-100

    injuries, illness, and accidents  82-89, 189, 194, 207-209, 247
    journalist relations  10, 38, 63-64, 117, 152-153, 180-181, 182-184, 186, 203, 219, 232, 233, 237, 243
    LGBTQ+ issues  157-164
    mental health  222, 246-252
    name, image, and likeness rules  134-135, 138
    sexism and sex crimes  150, 151, 152-153, 206, 209-210
    *SI* coverage  36, 38, 39, 40, 91
    social media pressures  134, 251
    social media use, and gatekeeping changes  4-5, 5*f*, 7, 15, 47-49, 51, 117, 137, 162, 182-183, 185, 186, 202-203, 222, 224-225, 228, 229, 231-234, 249-250
    "stick to sports" response  123-124, 128-129
*Athletic, The* (website)  217-218, 219, 242, 268
Atlanta Braves  110, 111
audience interest
    in-person attendance  11, 26, 47, 215, 261
    live events  12, 20-21
    major events  8, 20, 21, 27, 50-51, 142, 143, 201, 266
    media interactivity and  15, 47, 49-50, 51
    newsworthiness factor  4, 6, 34
    Olympics  26-27, 28, 29, 33-34, 62, 141-142
    radio  11, 12, 26
    sports betting effects  268
    in sports, generally  9, 11, 12, 18, 22, 37-38, 53, 60, 71-72, 134, 230, 241-242, 268
    *Sports Illustrated*  36-38, 39-40, 43

television's impact 53, 60, 61, 65
video games/esports 253-254,
   255-256, 257, 258-259
women's sports and coverage 134,
   137-138, 141-143, 144
Austin, Marvin 48

**B**

*Barstool Sports* (blog and app) 267-
   268
baseball. *See also* Major League Baseball (MLB)
cheating and betting 217-218,
   262-263
coverage: print 9, 10, 12, 36-37,
   39
coverage: radio 11, 12
coverage: television 12-13
Hispanic/Latino players and fans
   98-100, 110
Korean Baseball Organization 241
live streaming 15-16, 23, 98-99
national anthem 115
racial history 10, 108
statistics 9, 15
TV and cable broadcast revenue
   21
video games 257
basketball. *See also* National Basketball
   Association (NBA); NCAA
   basketball; Women's National
   Basketball League (WNBA)
coverage of women's 108-109,
   109-110, 134, 136-138
coverage: print 38
coverage: television/cable 21, 68,
   137-138, 197
video games 256-257
BBC 212
Bean, Billy 159
Bedard, Greg 125
Bell, Mike 152
Bennett, Martellus 123
Benoit, Andy 140
Berman, Chris 70
betting, sports 222, 261-269
biases, human
framing effects 102-105, 109, 117-
   118
group identity 97-98
opinion forming 223-224, 225

bias in media. *See also* gender issues
   and sexism
agenda setting 53, 54-58, 94, 103
framing 102, 103-105, 108, 109
gatekeeping power 4, 6-7, 34, 54,
   133, 228-229
national, at Olympics 12, 26, 30,
   31
objectivity expectations 103, 124,
   200, 229-230
SEC 53, 90-95
sports/athletes favored 31-32, 31*f*,
   34, 73, 194, 200
team media output 19, 51, 230
Big Ten football 92, 93, 94
Biles, Simone 250
Black Lives Matter movement 121-
   122, 124, 128-129
"Black Sox" scandal (1919) 262, 264
Blake, Jacob 121, 128-129
blogs 15, 229, 267-268
bolstering 176
Booker, Devin 256
boxing
coverage: print 8-9, 38, 108
coverage: radio 11, 12
coverage: TV and cable 14, 61,
   63-64
racist media coverage 108
sports betting 261
box scores (baseball) 9
Boys & Girls Clubs of America 198,
   199, 200-201
brain injuries 82-89
breaking news
journalistic responsibility 205,
   207-209, 212
newsworthiness 28, 62, 65, 212
Bregman, Alex 219
broadcasting. *See* broadcasting rights;
   live broadcasting; radio media;
   television media; specific networks
broadcasting rights
Olympics 26-27, 28-29, 32
profit sharing deals 136
TV, and costs 21, 22-23, 28-29, 32,
   53, 63, 65, 72, 78, 92-93, 136,
   138
Bruce, Damon 152
Bryant, Gianna 208, 209, 211

Bryant, Kobe
career success 197, 205-206, 209
death, and reporting of 172, 205,
   207-212
personal history 160, 209-211
retirement 232
Bryant, Vanessa 206, 208, 209, 211-
   212
Budden, Kris 154
Bueckers, Paige 109
Burke, Glenn 158, 159
business of sports media
broadcasting 18, 20-23, 28-29, 32,
   53, 60-61, 65-66, 77-78, 127
economic theory 17-18, 22, 47
Internet's effects 18-19, 47
newspapers model 18-19
periodicals sales 36-37, 39-40, 41

**C**

cable fees 20-21, 71-72, 74
cable television. *See* cable fees; cord
   cutting; ESPN; HBO; history
   of sports media; TBS; television
   media
cancer 189-190, 194
Carlos, John 27-28, 62, 124
casino gambling 265, 266, 267
catcher-pitcher signs 217, 218
CBS
college basketball coverage 137
football coverage 57, 76, 77-78, 91,
   92-94, 119, 149, 262
golf coverage 181
Olympics coverage 26-27, 29, 32
Chadwick, Henry 9
Charania, Shams 268
charity and philanthropy
athlete identities and causes 120,
   176, 188, 189-190, 191, 193,
   198, 251
social media use for 46, 47, 162
TV use for 198, 200-201
Chastain, Brandi 142
cheating
athlete behavior 48, 172, 175, 182-
   185, 188, 190-195
team scandals 172, 191-192, 214-
   220, 262, 264
Chicago White Sox 262, 264

children
    periodicals for 41, 104
    soccer players/fans 138, 140-141,
        143-144
    sports participation (Title IX)
        131, 140-141
    sports stars 179-180
chronic traumatic encephalopathy
    (CTE) 82-89
Cincinnati Bengals 229-230
Cincinnati Reds 262-263
classified ads 18, 19
Cleveland Cavaliers 196, 197-201,
    202-203, 233
Cleveland Indians 110-111, 113
CNN/SI 42
Cohn, Linda 70, 155
college sports
    academic fraud 48
    coverage: cable 14, 21, 72, 73,
        90-95, 137-138
    coverage: print 10, 39
    coverage: radio 11
    coverage: television 12-13, 57, 60,
        61, 68, 80, 92-95
    COVID-era play 238, 239
    gender inequality 47-48, 137-138
    live streaming 23, 138
    news gatekeeping and agenda set-
        ting 2, 3, 3f, 4-6, 5f, 56-57, 58,
        90-91
    social and team media 5, 47-48,
        137, 225-226, 230-231
    Title IX 131
    TV and cable broadcast revenue
        21, 57, 60, 91, 92-93, 138
    video games/esports 254, 257-258
Collins, Jason 157, 160-161, 162, 168
color photography 37
communications theory 103
    crisis communication 172, 173-
        174
    framing theory and effects 102-
        105, 109
    gatekeeping and agenda setting
        3-5, 54-55, 103, 228-229
    mass/traditional media 224, 228-
        229
    social media and change 5, 45-46,
        50, 51, 222, 223, 224-227
    two-step flow 222, 223-227
    visual communication 51

Concussion (movie) 85
concussions and CTE 82-89
cord cutting 22-23, 74
corporate accidents 174
corporate sponsorships. See also adver-
    tising
    ESPN history 68-69
    Native American team name issue
        113
    Nike/NFL 121
    social media 47
    sports betting 268-269
    women's soccer 145-146
Cosell, Howard 28, 62, 63-65, 124
Court, Margaret 131
COVID-19 pandemic 236-237
    athlete attitudes 237-239
    athlete impacts 236, 238-239, 243,
        244
    esports 240, 256, 257
    media impacts 128, 222, 236, 237-
        244
    sports play/cancellations 47, 121,
        211, 220, 236-244, 256
Crane, Jim 216, 219-220
crisis communication 172, 173-177,
    219-220
    Houston Astros 172, 214, 217-220
    Kobe Bryant 172, 205, 207-212
    Lance Armstrong 172, 188, 190-
        195
    LeBron James 172, 196, 197-203
    Tiger Woods 172, 179, 182-186
CTE (chronic traumatic encephalopa-
    thy) 82-89
Curry, Steph 4, 6
cycling 172, 188-189, 190-195

D
Daily Beast, The (website) 164
Decision, The (ESPN; 2010) 196, 197-
    202, 203
Delle Donne, Elena 136
DeRozan, DeMar 248-249, 251
Devers, Rafael 110
DiCaro, Julie 153
digital news and subscriptions 19,
    23, 73
DirecTV 22
Discord (app) 258
Donaghy, Tim 264
Drellich, Even 217-218

drug use
    athlete scandals 173, 185
    steroids and doping 172, 190-195,
        232
"Dr. V" 163-164
dual-revenue model 22
Duncan, Elle 210-211
Dunne, Olivia 135
Durant, Kevin 203, 232-233

E
Ebersol, Dick 29, 34
elections 123-124, 125, 224
eNASCAR iRacing Pro Invitational
    Series 240
endorsement advertising
    deals described 120-121, 132-133,
        134-135, 180, 186, 190, 191,
        197, 206, 211-212
    deals lost 158, 173, 176, 184-185,
        193, 206
    women 132-133, 134-135, 158
Entman, Robert 103
ESPN 67
    agenda setting 56, 57-58, 94
    awards 109-110, 124-125, 159,
        189, 190
    brand expansion 72-74, 92, 222,
        258
    broadcasting history 14, 16, 21-23,
        53, 67, 68-74, 79, 93-94
    competitors 42, 80
    COVID-era programming 239-
        242, 243
    Decision, The (2010) 196, 197-
        202, 203
    documentaries 53, 85-89, 234, 241
    esports coverage 258
    failures and challenges 73-74, 200
    gatekeeping power 5-6, 133
    journalism vs. profits 53, 74,
        86-88, 200
    LGBTQ+ sports coverage 161,
        163-164, 167, 169-170
    live sports investments 20, 21, 23,
        67, 72
    NFL partnership 53, 57-58, 65, 67,
        70-71, 72, 87-88, 94, 126, 169
    SEC bias 53, 90-95
    sports betting 267-268
    staff, race issues, and commentary
        107, 125-126, 127, 128-129,
        176-177

streaming 16, 23, 73, 74
subscription costs/revenue 22-23,
    71-72, 74
website and social media 14-15,
    73, 88, 121, 125-127, 136, 163-
    164, 182, 197
women's sports coverage 6, 133,
    134, 136, 137-138, 142, 145
esports 254, 259
    eNascar 240, 256
    history 254-255
    online and TV gaming 255-259
ethics issues. *See also* cheating; social
    issues
    academic fraud 48
    concussions and CTE, football
        82-89
    journalism's roles 55, 103-104,
        109, 112-113, 124, 172, 194,
        200, 205, 207-209, 212, 229-
        230, 268
    privacy 158, 211
    sports betting 261, 262-264, 268-
        269
    team decisions and culture 216-
        217, 218-220

**F**
Fainaru, Steve 83, 84, 88
Fainaru-Wada, Mark 83, 84, 88
family ties
    athlete pride 210-211
    Hispanic, and social identity 98,
        100
    police information protocol 208-
        209
    strength, and information flow
        224, 225
    women in journalism 154
fans. *See also* audience interest; teams
    baseball, and interest 12-13, 215-
        216, 220
    basketball, and *The Decision* 199-
        200
    blogs and websites 15, 229
    consumer behavior 22-23, 33-34,
        42-43, 47, 49, 50, 127
    COVID-era sports 236-237, 240,
        241, 242-243, 256, 257
    ESPN offerings 68, 69, 71-72, 127,
        241-242
    football, and head injury issue
        87-88

gatekeeping effects 2-3, 4-7, 5*f*,
    30-34, 36-37, 54, 224-225, 228-
    229
sexism of 153
social identity 98-100
social media use and engagement
    5, 7, 15, 45, 46-47, 49-50, 51,
    143, 153, 216, 218, 220, 224-
    225, 231-232
sports betting 222, 261-269
subscriptions 15-16, 22-23, 33,
    36-37, 38, 40-41, 73
television's impact 53, 60, 61
federal law
    gambling 264, 266
    gender discrimination 130-131,
        140-141, 146
    same-sex marriage 157
FIFA 141, 142
figure skating 29, 32
football. *See also* National Football
        League (NFL)
    agenda setting examples 55-58,
        90-95
    concussions and CTE 82-89
    coverage: print 10, 39, 149
    coverage: radio 12
    coverage: television/cable 8, 13,
        21, 60, 61, 65, 70-71, 72, 76-80,
        91-95, 149, 169, 241-242, 262
    live streaming 23
    SEC bias 53, 90-95
    TV and cable broadcast revenue
        18, 21, 53, 60, 65, 72, 78, 87-88,
        91, 92-93, 174
    viewership ratings 8, 20, 72, 78, 82,
        119, 174, 242
*Fortnite* (video game) 256
Foudy, Julie 143
Fox Broadcasting Company 76-77, 78
Fox, Rick 207-208
Fox Sports
    ageism and sexism 154, 155
    baseball coverage 80, 243, 268
    broadcasting history 53, 76-80
    football coverage 76, 77, 78, 79,
        91, 93, 94, 119, 149, 154
    hockey coverage 78, 79-80
    NASCAR 80, 257
    soccer coverage 143
    sports betting content 268
    women's sports coverage 133, 143

framing 102-103
    and objectivity 103-104, 109, 230
    sports and gender 104-105, 140,
        144
    sports and race 108, 109
    sports writing examples 102, 103,
        104-105, 108, 117-118
Frazier, Joe 14, 63-64
free agency decisions 118, 196-203,
    231, 232, 234
freedom of speech, and patriotism
    117-118
*Frontline* (TV program) 85, 86, 87,
    88

**G**
gambling 222, 261-269
Gantt, Harvey 123-124
Gardner, Gayle 148
gatekeeping 3-4. *See also* agenda set-
    ting; bias in media
    by athletes 180-181, 182-184,
        186, 196, 197-199, 202-203,
        233-234
    defined 2-3, 3*f*, 54
    evolution 4-5, 15, 203
    in media 2-7, 3*f*, 30, 54-55, 98,
        133, 228-229
    NBC Olympic coverage criticism
        30-34
    social media disruption 5, 50, 125,
        186, 212, 222, 224-225, 226,
        228-229, 234
gay athletes. *See* LGBTQ+ issues
gender issues and sexism. *See also*
        women's sports
    aesthetic/sexual focus on women
        39-41, 104, 134-136, 143, 153
    appearance judgment on women
        104, 134-135, 136, 143, 153,
        155
    equality promotion 63, 109-110,
        130-132, 140-141, 143-144,
        146, 158
    framing 104-105, 140, 144
    gatekeeping on 6
    inequality in coverage 55, 98, 104-
        105, 109-110, 130, 132-138,
        140, 141
    inequality in resources 47-48, 137,
        141, 146
    LGBTQ+ gender differences 162-
        164

gender issues and sexism. *See also*
    women's sports *(continued)*
    pay equity 141, 146
    sexist criticism and harassment
        151-154, 155, 216
    social media conversations 47-48,
        137, 140, 152, 153
    sports department hiring, staff, and
        access 133-134, 148, 149, 150-
        151, 154, 155
George, Paul 203, 234
George, Phyllis 149
Gobert, Rudy 237-238, 238-239, 244
Goffman, Erving 102
golf. *See also* Woods, Tiger
    COVID cancellations 239
    golfers' social media presence 47,
        183, 186
    tournament coverage and interest
        15, 179, 181, 184, 185-186
Gomez, Carlos 110
Goodell, Roger 118, 122, 126, 241
*GQ* (periodical) 180-181
Gray, Jim 198, 199, 200, 202
Green, Draymond 234
Griner, Brittney 162
group membership
    race and ethnicity 107
    social communication theory 224,
        225
    social identity theory 97-98
Gutman, Matt 207, 208
gymnasts 132, 135, 247, 250

**H**
Hall, DeAngelo 234
Hannan, Caleb 163
Hardaway, Tim 160
HBO 13-14, 68
head injuries 82-89
Hibbert, Roy 246
high school sports
    basketball stars 196-197, 205-206
    COVID cancellations 238
    football stars 56, 115
    Title IX and participation 131
Hill, David 78-79
Hill, Jemele 125-126, 127
Hines, Nico 164
Hispanic and Latino ethnicity
    baseball fans 98-99
    Hispanic and Latino athletes 99,
        100, 110

Hispanic social identity 98-100
history of sports media 8, 16
    cable 13-14, 21-22, 67-69
    esports 257-258
    Internet 14-16, 186, 222
    newsreels 10-11, 26
    Olympics 25-30, 130
    print 8-10, 12, 16, 26, 108, 148-
        149
    radio 11-12, 16, 26
    television 8, 12-13, 16, 26, 53,
        60-61
    traditional media 217-218, 228-
        229
    women's sports 55, 98, 130-134,
        138-139
Hitler, Adolf 12, 26
Hobson, Geoff 229-230
hockey. *See also* National Hockey
        League (NHL)
    coverage: cable 13
    coverage: TV, and innovations 78,
        79-80
    Olympics coverage 28, 32, 62
    print vs. team coverage 230
homophobia 157, 158, 159-160, 161,
        164, 168, 169-170
Hornung, Paul 262
horse racing 9, 261
Houston Astros
    history 214-217, 220
    sign-stealing scandal 172, 214,
        217-220
Hulu 23

**I**
image repair 174, 176, 177, 182-183,
        192-194
impartiality. *See* objectivity in jour-
        nalism
Imus, Don 108-109
Incognito, Richie 174-175
influencers (social media) 225-226
*In Living Color* (TV program) 77
Instagram 46, 47, 99-100, 162, 176,
        232, 249-250
instant replay 27
International Olympic Committee
        (IOC) 26, 27-28, 239, 259
international relations 175
Internet. *See also* social media; stream-
        ing media; websites

communication flow, and changes
        222, 223, 224-227
    online-first publishing 19, 42, 229
    online gaming 255-259
    print media/industries effects
        18-19, 42-43
    sports betting 222, 266-269
    sports media history 14-16, 186,
        222, 229-230
    unique offerings 14-15, 42, 43, 125
interpersonal communication 224
interviews
    athlete podcasts and sites 232-234
    locker rooms 148, 150-151, 237,
        243, 244
    PR/image repair 176, 184, 192-
        193, 194-195
    radio broadcasting: 10
    remote/video 240, 243
    sports writing and print 10, 110,
        150-151, 180-181, 192, 229,
        240
    television broadcasting 28, 62, 64,
        149, 192-193, 194-195, 198-
        201
IOC (International Olympic Commit-
        tee) 26, 27-28, 239, 259

**J**
Jackson, Keith 65
Jackson, Reggie 150
James, LeBron
    career success 196-197, 201, 202-
        203, 241
    COVID-era play 237
    free agent decisions 196-203, 234
    social causes and relationships 47,
        124, 198, 201, 249
Jenkins, Lee 202
Jenner, Caitlyn 124-125, 159
Jeter, Derek 232, 234
Johnson, Jack 108
Jones, Cardale 48, 49
Jones, Jerry 126
Jones, Lolo 135-136
Jordan, Michael 38, 123-124, 241
journalism. *See also* African American
        journalists; interviews; news-
        worthiness; nontraditional
        media; sportswriters
    agenda-setting in 54-56, 91, 103
    awards 85, 149, 153, 258-259

brain injury exposés 82-89
cable news 42
cable sports 53, 67, 69-70, 72, 73, 74, 86-88, 200
COVID-era roles and access 237-238, 239-240, 242, 243, 244
demographics and diversity 10, 41, 106, 107, 107f, 117, 143, 149, 154, 155, 176-177
ethics and objectivity 103-104, 112-113, 124, 172, 194, 200, 205, 207-209, 212, 229-230, 268
framing in 102-105, 108, 109, 117
gatekeeping history 2-3, 50, 228-229
gatekeeping theory and practice 3-7, 54-55, 133-134, 222
investigative 172, 182, 190-191, 194, 208-209, 217-218
newspaper industry 18-19
Olympics coverage 26, 27-28, 33, 61-62
polls and lists 91, 110
race, diversity, and opportunity 10, 106, 107, 117, 176-177
radio broadcasting styles 12
reporting protocol 208-209
social media transitions and policy 50, 51, 125, 126-127, 229
sports departments 9-10, 19, 61, 63-65, 133-134, 149, 154, 155, 212, 217-218, 240
tabloids 9, 182, 183, 184, 207-209
TV broadcasters and styles 61, 63-65, 70, 78, 243-244
TV news 207, 208, 212
women in sports media 143, 148-156, 216

**K**

Kaepernick, Colin 115-116, 117-118, 120-122, 124
Karras, Alex 262
Katz, Elihu 224
KDKA, Pittsburgh (radio) 11
King, Billie Jean 62-63, 124, 131-132, 158-159
King, Peter 42, 112-113
Knievel, Evel 63
Kolber, Suzy 152-153

Kopay, David 158
Korean Baseball Organization 241
Kornheiser, Tony 155
Kremer, Andrea 155

**L**

labor disputes 175
*L.A. Confidential Lance Armstrong's Secrets* (Ballester and Walsh) 190-191, 194
Lacy, Sam 9, 10, 11
language
    in framing 103, 108, 109
    non-native English-speaking athletes 110
    Spanish media 98-99, 110
Las Vegas, Nevada 265-266
Latino ethnicity. *See* Hispanic and Latino ethnicity
Lazarsfeld, Paul 224
*League of Denial* (documentary) 53, 82-89
*League of Legends* (video game) 256, 257
Lee, Suni 32, 33
legalization of gambling 264-269
Lennon, John 65
Lewin, Kurt 3
LGBTQ+ issues
    in society 157-158, 159-160
    sports media coverage 157-164, 166, 167-171
    sports pioneers 158-159, 166, 168
    U.S. Women's Soccer Team 144
libel suits 191, 193
live broadcasting
    business value 20-21, 29
    COVID cancellations 239-240, 242
    ESPN 20, 21, 23, 142
    Olympics 26-27, 28, 29, 32, 33
    radio, and styles 12, 26
    radio concerns and bans 12, 26
    vs. tape delay 32-33, 34
live streaming. *See* streaming media
Lochte, Ryan 175-176, 226
locker rooms
    COVID closures 237, 243
    homophobia issues 160, 169-170
    journalist access and interviews 148, 150-151, 237, 243, 244
Los Angeles Kings 230

Los Angeles Lakers 202-203, 206, 207-208, 234
Love, Kevin 233, 249, 251
Luce, Henry 36
Ludtke, Melissa 150-151

**M**

magazines. *See* print media; *Sports Illustrated*
Major League Baseball (MLB)
    COVID-era play 237, 239, 242-243, 244
    draft 216, 218
    on Fox Sports 80, 243, 268
    gay players and inclusion 158, 159
    Hispanic/Latino players and fans 98-100, 110
    live streaming 15-16, 23, 98-99
    major events coverage 12, 39, 217-218
    race barrier 10, 108
    social media use 46-47, 98-100
    social protest 121
    sports betting 262-263, 264, 268-269
    team names and mascots 110-111, 113
    team scandals 172, 214, 217-220
    TV and cable broadcast revenue 21, 72
    women journalists, treatment 150-151, 216
Major League Soccer (MLS)
    COVID cancellations 239
    on Fox Sports 80
    live streaming 23
    social protest 121
    TV and cable broadcast revenue 21, 72
Manuel, Simone 106
Manziel, Johnny 93
*Mario Kart* (video game) 254, 255
mascots 110-112, 113
McKay, Jim 28, 61, 62
McKee, Ann 84-85, 87
McNamee, Graham 12
media. *See* communications theory; nontraditional media; print media; radio media; social media; television media; traditional media
Mendenhall, Rashard 48-49

mental health 246-247
    athletes, and openness 222, 233,
        246-251
    media coverage 247, 250, 251
    stigma 247-248, 250
merchandising
    jerseys 120, 144, 161, 169
    Nike 121, 144, 186, 190, 191, 211-
        212
    sneakers 121, 124, 206, 211-212
    social media 46, 47, 50
Meredith, Don 65
Miami Heat 196, 199, 201-202, 203
Michaels, Al 28, 154
Mild Traumatic Brain Injury (MTBI)
    committee (NFL) 83, 84
military personnel 117-118, 119
MLB. *See* Major League Baseball
    (MLB)
MLS. *See* Major League Soccer (MLS)
Mobile ESPN 73-74, 222
*Monday Night Football* 61, 64-65, 87,
    126
Moore, Maya 136
Morey, Daryl 175
Morgan, Alex 144, 228
Morgan, "Middy" 148-149
Morris, Jeannie 149
Mosier, Chris 164
motherhood 154
movies
    athlete projects 206
    cable TV 13
    dramas 85
    exposé documentaries 82-89
    newsreels 10-11
multiplayer video games 256-258
Murdoch, Rupert 78, 79

**N**
Namath, Joe 152-153
name, image, and likeness rules 134-
    135, 138
NASCAR racing 80, 240, 257
Nassib, Carl 162, 171
national anthem, and protests 115,
    116-122, 124, 126, 174
National Baseball Hall of Fame 9, 10,
    263
National Basketball Association
    (NBA)
    COVID-era play 121, 237-238,
        238-239, 242-243, 244, 256

documentaries 234, 241
draft 197, 205-206, 268
esports (NBA 2K) 256-257
gay athletes 157, 160-161
James and *The Decision* 196-203
national anthem protests 116-117
player mental health 246, 248-249,
    251
player podcasts 233-234
social media use 46
social protests 121, 124, 128-129
sports betting 264-265, 268, 269
TV and cable broadcast revenue
    21
*National Enquirer* 182, 183
National Football Conference (NFC)
    78
National Football League (NFL)
    brain injury, and cognizance 82-89
    conferences 78
    COVID-era play and events 236-
        237, 241-242, 244
    draft 57-58, 71, 166-167, 168-169,
        171, 241-242, 266
    ESPN partnership 53, 57-58, 65,
        67, 70-71, 72, 87-88, 94, 126,
        169
    esports 258
    on Fox Sports 76, 77, 78, 79, 91,
        93, 94, 149, 154
    gay athletes 161-162, 166-171
    live streaming 23, 154, 155
    *Monday Night Football* 61, 64-65,
        87
    player mental health 251
    sexism and sexual harassment 151,
        152-153
    social protests and responses 115,
        116, 117-122, 124, 126, 174
    sports betting 262, 268, 269
    team names and mascots 111-113
    TV and cable broadcast revenue
        18, 21, 72, 87-88, 174
National Hockey League (NHL)
    COVID-era play 237, 239, 242-
        243
    on ESPN 79
    on Fox Sports 78-79, 80
    labor disputes 175
    print vs. team coverage 230
    social protest 121
    sports betting 265, 269

TV and cable broadcast revenue
    21
National Women's Soccer League
    (NWSL) 138, 145-146, 228
Native Americans
    athletes 110
    team name and mascot issues 110-
        113
Navratilova, Martina 160, 162-163
NBA. *See* National Basketball Associa-
    tion (NBA)
NBC
    baseball coverage 80
    football coverage 8, 20, 94
    gatekeeping criticisms 30-34
    network channels 29-30, 33-34
    Olympics coverage 25, 29-34, 31*f*,
        136, 141-142, 176, 244
    Peacock 23
    radio broadcasting 12
    television broadcasting 12-13, 68,
        148
NBC News 109, 207
NCAA basketball
    COVID-era play 47, 238, 239
    gender inequality 47-48, 137-138
    live and cable broadcasting 21, 68,
        73, 137-138
    media gatekeeping 5-6
    social media sharing 47-48, 137
    sports betting 261
NCAA soccer 141
Negandhi, Kevin 70
Netflix 241
Nevada sports teams 265-266
New Jersey state law 266
newspapers. *See* print media
newsreels 10-11, 26
newsworthiness
    breaking news 28, 62, 65, 205,
        209, 212
    factors 4, 6, 7
    highlights and "bests" 5, 14, 34, 42
Newton, Cam 152-153
*New York Times, The* (newspaper)
    media stories 19, 26, 31, 85, 87,
        117, 176-177
    social media policy 126-127
    sports stories 13, 26, 112, 135-136,
        192, 194
NFC (National Football Conference)
    78

NFL. *See* National Football League (NFL)

NHL. *See* National Hockey League (NHL)

Nichols, Rachel 176-177

Nielsen Media Research 20

Nike 120-121, 144, 180, 185, 190, 191, 197, 206, 211-212

Ninja (celebrity gamer) 256, 258

Nintendo 254, 255

nontraditional media 15, 217-218, 229, 232-234, 242

**O**

Obama, Barack 124, 144, 158, 160

objectivity in journalism
  bias examples 31, 194, 229-230
  expectations and ethics 103, 124, 200, 230, 268
  framing's effects 103-104, 109, 230

O'Brien, Jimmy 218

Okmin, Laura 153

Oliver, Pam 149, 154

Olson, Lisa 151

Olympic Games
  ABC coverage 27-29, 61-62
  athlete mental health 247, 250-251
  Berlin, 1936 12, 26
  Black athletes and coverage 26, 106
  cable and streaming coverage 29-30, 33-34
  gay athletes and media 164
  history 25-26, 130
  Lake Placid, 1980 28, 62
  Los Angeles, 1984 28, 62, 132
  Mexico City, 1968 27-28, 61-62, 124
  Munich, 1972 28, 61-62
  NBC coverage 25, 29-34, 136, 141-142, 176, 244
  print media coverage 26
  television history 12, 29-30, 61-62, 136, 141-142
  Tokyo, 2020/2021 239, 244

Omalu, Bennet 83-85

online gaming 255-259

opinion leaders and followers 224-225

Ortiz, David 232, 268

Osaka, Naomi 249-250

Osuna, Roberto 216-217

*Outsports* (website) 166, 167, 169

over-the-top media services. *See* streaming media

Owens, Jesse 26, 108

**P**

Paralympic Games 30

patriotism, and freedom of speech 117-118

pay equity 146

PBS 85-87, 88

performance-enhancing drugs 172, 190-195, 232

periodicals. *See* print media; *Sports Illustrated*

Phelps, Michael 173, 175, 250-251

philanthropy. *See* charity and philanthropy

Pitaro, Jimmy 127

pitcher-catcher signs 217, 218

play-by-play (broadcasting) 12, 26, 28, 243, 258

players. *See* athletes

*Players' Tribune, The* (website/platform) 232-233, 234, 249

*Playmakers* (TV program) 88

podcasts 86, 218, 233-234, 241, 267

police brutality and killings 121, 124, 128-129

police procedure and protocol 208-209, 211

political issues. *See also* social issues
  agenda setting 55
  athletes' statements 117-118, 123-124, 128
  information gathering 224
  Olympic stage 26, 27-28, 61-62, 124
  politicians, on social protests 118-119, 124
  "stick to sports" response 123-129

pregnancy 154

priming 55

Prince, Sedona 47-48, 137

print media
  African American press 10
  circulation and readership 18-19, 37, 38, 41-43
  early sports coverage 8-10, 12, 16, 26, 108, 148-149
  esports coverage 258-259

framing and agenda setting 55, 103-105

gatekeeping 2-4, 5, 6-7, 39, 133-134

newspaper business and losses 18-19

periodical business 37-38, 41-43

sports departments and policy 9, 19, 104, 110, 112-113, 126-127, 133-134, 149, 212, 217-218

technological innovations 9, 37, 42-43

Professional and Amateur Sports Protection Act (1992) 264, 266

protests and demonstrations. *See* political issues; social issues

public relations
  crisis response and communication 172, 173-177, 182-186, 188, 191-195, 216-220
  framing 102, 176, 230
  image repair and reputation management 174, 176, 177, 182-183, 192-194, 219-220
  social and team media 51, 183, 186, 229-234

**Q**

quarterbacks
  media bias 109
  media focus 39, 55-58, 91, 93
  sexism and harassment 152-153
  social protest stories 115-116, 117-122

**R**

race issues
  athlete activism and protests 27-28, 62, 115-122, 124, 126, 128-129
  athlete empowerment 199-200
  broadcasting incidents 64-65, 108-109
  gatekeeping on 6
  journalism segregation, diversity, and opportunity 10, 41, 106, 107, 117, 176-177
  at Olympic Games 26, 27-28, 62, 106, 124
  social identity and 98-100, 180
  sports media coverage of race 106-113, 117-118

radio media
  broadcasting styles and personalities 12, 26
  early sports coverage 11-12, 16, 26
Randolph, Shavlik 160
Rapinoe, Megan 144
Rasmussen, Bill and Scott 68
re-creation (broadcasting) 12
referees 264
regional coverage and focus
  bias of 54, 90-95
  ESPN history 68, 72, 90-91
  *Sports Illustrated* 39
religious messages 57
remote broadcasting 243-244
reputation management 174, 176, 182-183
Retton, Mary Lou 132
return on investment (ROI) 17-18
Rice, Grantland 9-10, 12, 108
Richards, Renée 164
Rickey, Branch 10
Ridley, Calvin 269
Riggs, Bobby 62-63, 131-132, 158
Rinaldi, Tom 184
*Road Trippin'* (podcast) 233-234
Robinson, Jackie 10, 108
Rodrigue, Jordan 152-153
role models 143-144
roller derby 130
Rooney, Andy 152
Rosenthal, Ken 217-218
Rose, Pete 262-263
Rozelle, Pete 65, 71

S

sales. *See* business of sports media; merchandising; ticket revenue
same-sex marriage 157
Sam, Michael 161-162, 166-171
Sanders, Larry 233
scandals. *See also* crisis communication
  athlete behavior 172, 173, 174-176, 179, 180, 182-186, 188, 190-195
  media outlets 176-177
  sports betting 262-263, 264, 269
  team cheating 172, 214-220, 262, 264
school funding, federal 130-131, 140
scoreboards 78-79

Scott, Stuart 70
Seaver, Tom 10
SEC (football)
  bias 53, 90-95
  cable broadcasting 72, 91-95
  network broadcasting 57, 91, 92
  star athletes 166
  success 94
Selig, Bud 159
sexism. *See* gender issues and sexism
sexual harassment and assault 151, 152-153, 206, 209-210, 216
Shaughnessy, Dan 237
Shockey, Jeremy 160
Silver, Adam 264-265
Simmons, Bill 126, 197-198
*Simpsons, The* (TV program) 76
Skipper, John 87, 127, 198, 199, 201
Smith, Michael 126
Smith-Schuster, JuJu 256
Smith, Stephen A. 121
Smith, Tommie 27-28, 62, 124
Snapchat 73
Snyder, Jimmy "the Greek" 108, 149, 262, 268
soccer. *See also* Major League Soccer (MLS)
  COVID cancellations 239
  girls', post-Title IX 138, 140-141, 143-144, 145, 146
  live streaming 23
  score displays 78-79
  team media 228
  TV and cable coverage 21, 80, 138, 140, 141-143, 145
  U.S. Women's Soccer Team 138, 140-146, 237
  World Cup 140, 141, 142-143, 144, 146
social distancing 237-238, 243-244
social identity
  in sports 98-100, 180
  theory 97-98
social issues 96. *See also* ethics issues; gender issues and sexism; LGBTQ+ issues; political issues; race issues
  athletes' activism and protest 27-28, 47-48, 62, 115-122, 124, 126, 128-129, 137, 158, 162
  gatekeeping of 6
  LGBTQ+ coverage 158-164

national movements 113, 117, 121-122, 124, 128-129
  reporter personalities and coverage 27-28, 62, 63, 117
social media 45-46
  athlete pressures 134, 251
  communication flow and changes 222, 223, 224-227
  erasing gatekeeping power 4-5, 7, 15, 46, 50, 125, 222, 224-225, 226, 228, 229, 231-234
  investigative journalism 172, 208, 218
  media criticism via 30, 47-48, 137, 140, 169
  policies 126-127, 210
  sexism and harassment 152, 153
  sports highlights sharing 34, 46, 73, 223
  sports media and 15, 45-51, 125-127, 137, 140, 162, 212, 234
  tabloid journalism 207-208
  unique offerings 15, 45-46, 49-50, 51, 125, 226
softball 138
Sonmez, Felicia 210
Spain, Sarah 153, 155
Spanish language
  MLB livestreaming 98-99
  native speakers and coverage 110
  uniforms 99
Spinks, Michael 38
sports betting 222, 261-269
*SportsCenter* (TV program)
  broadcasters 70, 125, 128, 155, 210-211
  gatekeeping power 5-6, 133
  history 14, 68, 69-70, 74
  *The Last Dance* 241
sports highlights
  gatekeeping 5-6
  programs 5-6, 42, 69
  social media sharing 34, 46, 73, 223
*Sports Illustrated* (periodical) 36
  awards 39, 136, 180, 189, 201
  brand extension 41-42, 43
  content and columnists 36-41, 42-43, 112-113, 160, 167, 202, 216, 242, 263
  cover and photography 36, 37, 38, 39, 42, 104-105, 133, 143, 160, 190, 214

history and readership 36-38, 41-43

lawsuits 150-151

SEC coverage 91

special issues 38-41, 43, 61

websites 42, 43, 112-113, 202, 242

women's sports coverage 39, 41, 131, 133, 136, 140, 143

sports media. *See* history of sports media; print media; radio media; social media; television media

sports teams. *See* team owners; teams

sportswriters 9, 104. *See also* journalism; print media

COVID-era roles and access 237-238, 239-240, 242, 243, 244

demographics 107, 117, 125, 149, 154, 155, 176

history 9-10, 108

newspaper industry woes 19

polls and lists 91, 110

*SI* history 36-37, 38, 42

social and political topic coverage 112-113, 117, 125-126

women 148-149, 150-151, 152-153, 154

stadiums 25, 113, 142, 229-230, 269

*Starcade* (video game) 254-255

state gambling laws 264, 266

statistics

baseball 9, 15

framing examples 102, 103

Internet sources 14-15, 42-43, 73-74, 229

scoreboards 78-79

women's sports coverage 133-134

Steele, Sage 128

Stern, David 199, 264

"stick to sports" messaging 123-129

Storm, Hannah 155

streaming media

broadcasting rights and revenue 21, 22-23

consumer behavior 20-21, 22-23, 33-34

ESPN 16, 23, 73, 138

NBC Olympic coverage 30, 33-34

sports media history 14, 15-16, 73

video gaming 255-256, 258

Strug, Kerri 247

Suarez, Daniel 240

subscription business model

cable 21-23

digital news 19, 23, 42

live streaming 15-16, 22-23, 33, 73

magazines 37, 38, 40-41, 42

newspapers 18-19

Super Bowl

advertising 50-51, 77

betting 266

broadcaster coverage 8, 149

champions' White House visits 123

halftime show 77

locations 236, 266

viewership and ratings 20, 21, 50, 78, 82

Supreme Court decisions 157, 266

swimming

athlete mental health 250-251

college programs support 225-226

Olympic athlete controversies 173, 175-176

Olympic coverage 31, 33, 106

transgender athletes 164

"swimsuit issue" *(SI)* 39-41, 43

**T**

tabloid journalism 9, 182, 183, 184, 207-209

tape-delay 32-33, 34

targeted advertising 50

Taubman, Brandon 216-217

Taylor, Maria 176-177

TBS 91

team owners

homophobia 160

radio concerns 12

scandal responses 216, 219-220

social protest reactions 113, 126

teams. *See also* free agency decisions; specific leagues

business of sports 17, 46-47

esports 256-258, 259

names/mascots 110-113, 215

scandals 172, 214, 217-220, 262, 264

season previews 39

social media, and gatekeeping changes 4-5, 5f, 7, 15, 46-47, 51, 222, 228, 229-231

social protest 118, 121-122, 124, 126

team media and PR 15, 19, 46-47, 51, 99-100, 155, 225-226, 228, 229-231, 233-234

Tebow, Tim 55-58

technological innovations 16

cable and satellite 13-14, 67-68

COVID-era broadcasting 240

DVRs 20-21

instant replay 27

Internet 14-16, 229

newsreels 10-11, 26

print media 9, 37

radio media 11, 12, 26

social media 5, 15, 45-46, 212, 226

sports betting 266-269

television 12-13, 26, 27, 53, 65, 78, 79-80

video games and esports 254-256, 258

television media. *See also* specific networks and channels

athlete-led events 196, 197-202, 203

broadcasting rights and revenue 18, 21-23, 26-27, 28-29, 32, 53, 65, 72, 78, 91, 92-93, 136, 138

broadcasting styles and personalities 12-13, 28, 61, 63-65, 78, 148

business of broadcasting 20-23, 53, 60-61, 76-78

cable sports 13-14, 42, 53, 67, 68-74, 137, 239-242, 243

early sports coverage 8, 12-13, 16, 26, 53, 60-61

financial bottom line 53, 119, 127

gatekeeping and agenda-setting 5-7, 53, 57-58, 133

obsolescence 15, 33-34

Olympics coverage 25, 26-34, 61-62, 136

precursors to 10-11, 12

viewership ratings 20-21, 28, 29, 65, 68, 80, 119, 134, 215-216, 242

tennis

"Battle of the Sexes" (1973) 62-63, 131-132, 158

coverage, gender and sexuality issues 158, 162-163

coverage, race issues 109

COVID-era play 238, 239

tennis *(continued)*
    player mental health 249-250
    stars 39, 109, 158-159, 162-163
    television coverage 61, 62-63
terrorism 28, 49, 62
Thomas, Lia 164
Thorpe, Jim 110
"Thrilla in Manila" (1975) 14, 63-64
ticket revenue 12, 17, 26
TikTok 47-48, 73
Time Inc. 36-37, 41, 42, 43
timeliness
    Internet benefits 14-15, 42-43, 50
    newsworthiness factor 4
Time Warner Cable 22
Title IX (1972)
    described 130-131
    girls' and women's soccer effects
        140-141, 146
TMZ 182, 207-209
TNT 29, 243
Tokyo Olympic Games (2021) 239,
    244
toughness expectations 247, 250, 251
Tour de France 189, 190-191, 192,
    193, 194-195, 239
traditional media 217-218, 228-229,
    234
transgender persons and athletes 159,
    163-164
Trump, Donald
    Kaepernick commentary 118-119
    opposition and protest 123, 125,
        126, 127
    Twitter use 144, 207
Twitch (gaming channel) 255-256,
    258
Twitter
    athletes' use 47-48, 144, 169, 174-
        175, 186, 202-203, 211, 218,
        225-226, 228, 231-232, 234,
        248-249
    fans' use 143, 153, 218, 220
    functionality 49-50, 127
    influencer power 225-226
    journalists' use 50, 121, 125-126,
        127, 140, 208, 209-210, 218,
        237
    politicians' use 144, 207
    sports teams' and leagues' use 46,
        144, 155, 225-226, 228

two-step flow concept (communica-
    tion) 222, 223-227

**U**
uniforms
    designs 215
    jersey sales 120, 144, 161, 169
    Spanish-language 99
*Uninterrupted* (website) 202
United States Anti-Doping Agency
    191-192, 193, 194
University of North Carolina Wilm-
    ington 225-226
U.S. Postal Service team (cycling)
    189, 191-192, 193
U.S. Soccer Federation 141, 142, 145,
    146
*US Weekly* (periodical) 182, 183
U.S. Women's Soccer Team 140
    history 141-146
    influence and impact 138, 143-
        144, 146
    interview access 237

**V**
vaccination 128, 236
Vanderbilt, Dr. Essay Anne 163
Vegas Golden Knights 265
videoconferencing 240, 243
video games 137, 185, 240, 253-259
video recording, baseball signs 217,
    218
video streaming. *See* streaming media
Villanueva, Alejandro 119-120
viral videos 223, 225
Visser, Lesley 149
visual communications 51

**W**
wage discrimination 141, 146
Wahl, Grant 237
Walt Disney Company 23, 65, 72,
    73-74, 88, 93
Wambach, Abby 143, 144
Washington, DC football teams 111-
    113
Washington, Jesse 106
*Washington Post, The* (newspaper)
    112, 155, 210, 258-259
Watt, J.J. 47
weak ties (social theory) 223, 225-
    226, 227

websites 14-15
    athletes' sites and uses 182-183,
        186, 202, 232-233, 234, 249
    ESPN 73, 88, 136
    fan blogs/sites 15, 229
    gambling 267
    gossip sites 182, 207-209
    LGBTQ+ coverage 164, 166, 167,
        168
    *SI* 42, 43, 112-113, 202, 242
    sports journalism and investiga-
        tions 217-218, 242
    teams' sites and uses 228, 229-230
Webster, Mike 83-85
*Weight of Gold* (documentary) 251
Weston, Joan 130
White, David Manning 3-4
White, Royce 248
Williams, Serena 39, 109, 136, 250
Winfrey, Oprah 192-193, 194-195
WNBA. *See* Women's National Basket-
    ball League (WNBA)
women in sports media
    history 148-156
    legal challenges 150-151
    pioneers 148-149
    unequal access and treatment 148,
        149, 150-151, 152-153, 216
    unequal ratios 133-134, 143, 148,
        149, 154, 155, 176
Women's College World Series (soft-
    ball) 138
Women's National Basketball League
    (WNBA) 136
    COVID-era play 242-243
    players 162
    social protests 121, 122
    television coverage/viewing 134,
        136-137
women's sports. *See also* gender issues
    and sexism; U.S. Women's
    Soccer Team; women in sports
    media
    equality and social issues 6, 63,
        104-105, 130-139, 146
    ESPN coverage 6, 134, 136, 137-
        138, 145
    facilities inequality 47-48, 137
    law 130-131, 140-141, 146
    media coverage 6, 63, 98, 104-105,
        130, 131-139, 140, 141-143,
        162

media gatekeeping and framing 6, 30, 32, 55, 98, 104-105, 109-110, 133-134, 140

Olympics participation and coverage 30, 32, 104, 132, 135-136, 142-143

*SI* coverage 39, 41, 104-105, 131, 136, 140, 143

social media sharing 47-48, 133

Women's United Soccer Association (WUSA) 145

Woods, Tiger
  career 179-182, 184, 185-186, 259
  scandals and communication 172, 179, 180-185

World Cup (soccer) 140, 141, 142-143, 144, 146

World Series (baseball) 39, 150-151, 214, 215, 216, 217-218, 262

writing structures 10

Wyche, Steve 117

**Y**

Young, Dick 9, 10

Courtesy of Michaela Baker Taylor

Kevin Hull, PhD, is an associate professor of journalism and the lead instructor of the sports media initiative at the University of South Carolina.

Before entering academia, Hull was a television sports broadcaster for an NBC affiliate in North Carolina for about seven years. In this role, he anchored and reported on local sports while also serving as photographer, editor, and producer for his own stories. His work has sent him to the Super Bowl, NCAA Tournaments, and many additional amateur and professional sporting events. Hull won several statewide awards for best sports feature from the Radio and Television News Directors Association of the Carolinas, and his department's sportscasts were the most watched in the market.

As a researcher, Hull focuses primarily on local sports broadcasters throughout the United States. He has studied the challenges new sports broadcasters face, the issues surrounding race and gender in the profession, and how universities are preparing students to enter the field of sportscasting. His published studies have discussed sports media education, how sportscasters are using social media, and sports media internships. His first textbook, *Sports Broadcasting*, was also published by Human Kinetics.